Synthesis Lectures on Human Language Technologies

Series Editor

Graeme Hirst, Department of Computer Science, University of Toronto, Toronto, Canada

The series publishes topics relating to natural language processing, computational linguistics, information retrieval, and spoken language understanding. Emphasis is on important new techniques, on new applications, and on topics that combine two or more HLT subfields.

Manfred Stede • Jodi Schneider •
Henning Wachsmuth

Argument Mining

Second Edition

Springer

Manfred Stede
Linguistics Department
Universität Potsdam
Potsdam, Brandenburg, Germany

Jodi Schneider
Information School
University of Wisconsin-Madison
Madison, WI, USA

Henning Wachsmuth
Institute of Artifical Intelligence
Leibniz University Hannover
Hannover, Germany

ISSN 1947-4040 ISSN 1947-4059 (electronic)
Synthesis Lectures on Human Language Technologies
ISBN 978-3-032-32290-6 ISBN 978-3-032-32291-3 (eBook)
https://doi.org/10.1007/978-3-032-32291-3

This work was supported by Universität Potsdam, University of Illinois Urbana-Champaign and University of Wisconsin–Madison and Leibniz University Hannover.

Originally published by Morgan & Claypool Publishers, 2018

This Springer imprint is published by the registered company Springer Nature Switzerland AG
The registered company address is: Gewerbestrasse 11, 6330 Cham, Switzerland

Preface

This is the second edition of a book that aims to give a comprehensive overview of natural language processing (NLP) research on argumentation. The first edition, titled *Argumentation Mining*, was published by Morgan & Claypool in December 2018, and Springer republished the ebook in June 2022 after acquiring Morgan & Claypool's catalog. Argumentation mining is the term originally used to refer to this research area. Subsequently, however, *argument mining* has become the more widely used term, hence we use it as the name of the second edition. Another related term, *computational argumentation*, is also used, particularly to emphasize that research in this area covers much more than just the mining of arguments, as this book will also show. We stick with argument mining since computational argumentation has so far seen the most attention in the more narrow context of formal argument analysis in artificial intelligence.

The first edition covered research largely up to 2017 only: just 14 of its 544 references were new (or in press) 2018 publications. When two authors of this book finished that manuscript in 2018, argument mining was still evolving as a new research area of NLP. Meanwhile, not only has the area experienced continuous growth, but it was also directly affected by the breakthroughs of NLP as a whole around the rise of pretrained language models (PLM) and large language models (LLMs) that have disruptively transformed the research landscape and its perception in the world. The time is thus ripe for an all new in-depth look at argument mining, and we are very happy on this occasion to have a third author on board who covered new directions of argument mining research that were dealt with only in cursory ways, if at all, in the first edition.

The second edition presents argument mining from its fundamentals up to the latest developments of 2025. We aim to give the reader a comprehensive (though not exhaustive) introduction to this exciting research area whose subject matter is so deeply rooted in the heart of human communication.

An Active Research Community In the seven years since the first edition was published, argument mining research has expanded dramatically and has become an established part of research in NLP, AI, and computational argumentation. The field has become much broader, with many more tasks and much more data fitting the realm of arguing. For the

NLP part of the community, a key event is the Workshop on Argument Mining,[1] held annually since 2014. NLP papers also regularly appear in the Association for Computational Linguistics's *CL conferences and journals, at the International Conference on Computational Linguistics (COLING), and at the Language Resources and Evaluation Conference (LREC). Key AI events run by the Association for the Advancement of Artificial Intelligence (AAAI) and the International Joint Conference on Artificial Intelligence (IJCAI), among others, publish work in argument mining and its applications. Dedicated argumentation conferences such as the International Conference on Computational Models of Argument (COMMA), Computational Models of Natural Argument (CMNA), and the European Conference on Argumentation (ECA) as well as journals such as *Argument & Computation* have also extended their spectrum to related NLP work.

A Growing Range of Applications Since the first edition, applications of argument mining have grown significantly as well. There is continued interest in debating technologies and argumentative chatbots. Some applications that the first edition briefly mentioned as emerging topics (e.g., argument search and rhetorical/argumentative writing support) have notably expanded, and new applications have emerged (e.g., fake news detection and deliberative democracy platforms). As a witness to growing interest, new workshops have been launched: The International Workshop on Argumentation and Applications (Arg& App) held its second event in 2025.[2] Meanwhile the second edition of the Workshop on Language-driven Deliberation Technology (DELITE)[3] is scheduled for 2026 at LREC. Practical applications were also highlighted at the International Conference on Recent Advances in Robust Argumentation Machines (RATIO) in 2024.[4]

Other Surveys Over the years, various shorter surveys have appeared, with Mochales Palau and Moens (2009) giving an early introduction, Peldszus and Stede (2013) emphasizing annotation, and Lippi and Torroni (2016) focusing on technical approaches. Wachsmuth et al. (2017c) give a unifying overview of argument quality assessment, Cabrio and Villata (2018) take a data perspective on argument mining, and Lawrence and Reed (2019) provide a general overview. Soon after our book's first edition was published, Janier and Saint-Dizier (2019) presented a book-length survey focusing on the linguistic side of arguing. Bridging to the social sciences, Vecchi et al. (2021) review argument mining efforts toward social good. Lauscher et al. (2022) discuss the role of knowledge in argument mining and Wang et al. (2023a) analyze the status quo of argument generation. Wachsmuth et al. (2024) revisit the state of the art in argument quality assessment, and Ruiz-Dolz et al. (2025) discuss computational argumentation as a whole from a human

[1] https://argmining-org.github.io/ (accessed January 18, 2026).

[2] https://argapp-workshop.github.io/ (accessed January 18, 2026).

[3] https://aclanthology.org/venues/delite/ (accessed January 18, 2026).

[4] https://link.springer.com/conference/ratio (accessed January 18, 2026).

argumentation perspective. The latest survey that we are aware of is a preprint (still undergoing revisions) on LLMs in argument mining (Li et al., 2025). In a way, the book at hand unifies the perspectives of all these surveys, while each of them may provide further insights.

From Edition 1 to Edition 2 Subsuming all central contents of the first edition, from basic argumentation concepts to pioneer work across the "core" tasks of argument mining and beyond, this second edition doubles the number of pages and grows the bibliography by 50% (875 references), providing increased depth and insights into many more tasks. It adds completely new chapters on perspective assessment, argument quality assessment, and argument reasoning, all of which span families of tasks that have emerged since the original book was conceived. Given the technological changes in NLP, we also completely rewrote our treatment of the common steps in argument mining, the overview of the main tasks and methods in argument generation, and our coverage of applications. Further, we provide an appendix of selected corpora that are available for argument mining along with an online overview on our corpus collection website http://purl.org/amresources. Importantly, this second edition is open access, free for anyone to read, thus making it substantially more accessible than the first edition has been.

Compared to the first edition, we aim to provide more guidance on selected methods for addressing all main argument mining tasks, while still giving an overview of the research area from its beginnings to its latest developments. We hope that, thereby, this book serves as a helpful introduction to new researchers in the realm of argument mining and that it deepens and completes the knowledge of those already working in the area for several years.

Thank you for reading.

Berlin, Germany Manfred Stede
Madison, WI, USA Jodi Schneider
Hannover, Germany Henning Wachsmuth
January 2026

Acknowledgments The completion of this book would not have been possible without the help of many different people in different stages of the writing process.

During the initial drafting of the contents of this book, we received various helpful inputs such as expert insights, literature pointers, and early feedback from the following people: Andrew Aberdein, Justin Eckstein, Kiel Gilleade, Kate Phillips, Ramon Ruiz-Dolz, Ekaterina Sviridova, Kit Terrey, Jan Albert van Laar, Jean Wagemans, and Dexter Williams. Dexter along with Shiwei Liu contributed to the corpus overview that we provide in the appendix.

Many thanks go to the two official reviewers of our complete book draft, Yufang Hou and the second anonymous reviewer. We are further thankful to a number of "internal" reviewers from our academic network whose feedback helped us optimizing individual chapters of this book: Khalid Al Khatib, Milad Alshomary, Puranjani Das, Yuanxi Fu, Halil Kilicoglu, Mengfei Lan, Timothy McPhillips, Ramon Ruiz-Dolz, Eva Maria Vecchi, Yilin Xia, Simon Wells, Heng Zheng, and Mark Matthias Zymla.

We are grateful to those providing favorable licensing policies, including the ACL Anthology for adoption of CC-BY licensing and the many STM Signatory Publishers for simplifying royalty-free reuse of scientific images. We thank the numerous individual authors and companies who either explicitly licensed their content or directly provided us permission. Kyung-Sun "Sunny" Kim provided invaluable help contacting one group of authors. Corinne McCumber provided exceptional and timely assistance in proofing the bibliography. Thanks also to Stephen Linhart for image formatting advice, and once again to Dexter Williams for handling many practical details of image reuse.

Personally, MS acknowledges support for the open access publication of the book by the German Research Foundation (DFG) within the project LARGA, project number 455911521, as part of the Priority Program *Robust Argumentation Machines (RATIO)* (SPP-1999).

JS acknowledges support from the University of Illinois Campus Research Board RB25118: Support for a Second Edition of the Argumentation Mining monograph. She was partially funded as the 2024 2025 Perrin Moorhead Grayson and Bruns Grayson Fellow at Harvard University's Radcliffe Institute for Advanced Study. She also benefited from discussions during the writing of this book at the Hybrid Argumentation and Responsible AI workshop held at the Leiden, Netherlands from March 31 to April 4, 2025. Her startup funds at the University of Wisconsin–Madison provided support for Dexter Williams' time. Some support for this research was provided by the Office of the Vice Chancellor for Research and Graduate Education at the University of Wisconsin–Madison with funding from the Wisconsin Alumni Research Foundation.

HW acknowledges support for the open publication of the book by the German Research Foundation (DFG) within the project OASiS, project number 455913891, as part of the Priority Program *Robust Argumentation Machines (RATIO)* (SPP-1999). Beyond that, he thanks Gabriela Molina León for accepting all the extra hours needed for this book along the way as well as for being open to discuss arbitrary details of the book whenever asked for.

Collectively, the three of us thank the anonymous participants in our 2023 "ArgMining Book 2.0 survey" for suggesting updates and helping us envision the target audience and the coverage they expected. We are very grateful to our students, colleagues, and collaborators for all the exchanges and discussions that established the ground for us to write this book. And last but not least, we thank Graeme Hirst for the initiative to start this second edition endeavor, for always fast responses to all our questions along the way, and for his patience in scheduling this project.

Competing Interests The authors have no competing interests to declare that are relevant to the content of this manuscript.

Contents

Introduction 1

Argument mining is inherently computational, building on various techniques from natural language processing (NLP) and different areas of artificial intelligence (AI). At its core, it deals with the development and evaluation of models and methods for the computational understanding and generation of human language, with the data underlying both of them, and with the applications that deploy them. However, argument mining is motivated in the treatment of *argumentation* specifically, a pervasive human activity in both spoken and written language that has been studied in linguistics as well as philosophy and other disciplines for millenia. Understanding the fundamental goals and ideas of argument mining hence also requires knowledge about the linguistic and argumentation-theoretic concepts it draws from.

In this first chapter, we therefore begin by studying one of the common definitions of *argument* and by explaining it point by point (Sect. 1.1). This is supplemented by outlining further central aspects of argumentation, such as the dimensions of *logos*, *ethos*, and *pathos*. We then move to the side of NLP, and characterize the research field of argument mining in Sect. 1.2, followed by an outline of motivations for studying the field in Sect. 1.3, and the intended audience of this book in Sect. 1.4. Finally, we explain the structure of the book in Sect. 1.5.

1.1 Arguments and Arguing

Starting from a compressed but insightful definition of argumentation, we give a first idea in this section of what humans and argumentation theory mean by arguing.

M. Stede et al., *Argument Mining*, Synthesis Lectures on Human Language Technologies, https://doi.org/10.1007/978-3-032-32291-3_1

1.1.1 A Definition

Argumentation (as an activity of human beings seeking to sort out their conflicting views) has been of interest to philosophers for a long time, with the best-known of the traditional work being that of Aristotle (ca. 350 B.C.E./ translated 2007). In his study *On Rhetoric*, he sought to develop a general theory of persuasion and applied it to three types of speeches: the deliberative speech, which advises on a course of future action; the judicial speech, which accuses or defends someone whose past activities are to be judged; and the epideictic speech, which praises or blames a person of public interest. As the concrete starting point for our introduction, however, we selected a definition proposed in much more recent work on argumentation theory by van Eemeren and Grootendorst (2004, p. 1):

> "Argumentation is a verbal, social, and rational activity aimed at convincing a reasonable critic of the acceptability of a standpoint by putting forward a constellation of propositions justifying or refuting the proposition expressed in the standpoint."

The main elegance of this definition is in its bringing together the range of crucial aspects in a rather compact form (a single sentence). Let us consider each aspect in a little more detail.

A Verbal Activity People can and do gesture and frown at each other, and occasionally this might be a way of resolving some disagreement. In our conception here, however, argumentation is an inherently linguistic activity—either in spoken or written mode. This is to be distinguished from, for instance, a fistfight, which can be a different means of sorting out a conflict.

A Social Activity *Social* emphasizes that argumentation is a matter of interaction among a number of people, with a minimum of two. Granted, many of us mull over a difficult decision for some time by mentally walking through the consequences of the alternatives, but genuine arguing requires a person to argue *with*. So, in some sense, we argue internally with ourselves when we seek to take a difficult decision.

A Rational Activity Obviously, we can perform verbal and social activities in very many ways. Among these, argumentation targets specifically the dimension of reason. When one person reminds the other "Be reasonable!", the point is to call for a style of dialogue that is not driven by emotional outbreak, power struggle, personal offense, etc., but by the sober exchange of—reasonable—arguments.

A Standpoint In argumentation, the heart of the matter is some issue on which people may have divergent views. Thus, the argument does not target an undisputed 'fact' but a 'standpoint' (or a 'stance'). Where there is no potential disagreement, there is no need to argue.

Convincing of Acceptability At the end of an argument, the parties involved may not necessarily be completely 'on the same page' about the standpoint. An argument usually does not prove beyond any doubt that one particular viewpoint is the single correct one. Instead, the party who initially was skeptical may now be somewhat more inclined to accept the view of the other party (if the argument was successful).

A Constellation of Propositions The shape of a justification might be quite simple, say, a single convincing sentence. But quite often it will be more complex and involve a web of interrelated points that the speaker carefully assembles in a non-arbitrary way; an example of such a constellation will be shown at the end of this section.

Justifying the Proposition of the Standpoint If the reader is more inclined to accept the particular standpoint after the argument is finished, that result is not just due to the speaker having pointed out that they are the boss, or some such; it is due to the speaker having successfully justified their view.[1]

A Reasonable Critic This phrase in fact combines two distinct aspects. *Reasonable* reinforces the point made earlier by the "rational activity": the argument is subject to scrutiny on the level of rational thought. But in addition, the presence of the external *critic* points to a social context in which the argumentation takes place. This can be common political discourse for which most people have the background, or it can be a much more specialized realm such as the scientific, medical, or legal realm. Whatever the context, it includes particular rules of conduct that have become convention, which the implicit judge of the argument watches over.

As an illustration for the theoretical considerations given so far, here is a short example from the Customer Debt Collection Practices (CDCP) corpus by Park and Cardie (2018), dealing with compensations for problems with air travel cancellations:

(1.1) [$400 is enough compensation,]$_1$ [as it can cover a one way fare across the US.]$_2$ [I checked in a passenger on a $98.00 fare from east coast to Las Vegas the other day.]$_3$

The controversial standpoint defended here is the sufficiency of the dollar amount of $400, captured in Proposition 1 in Ex. 1.1. The author justifies this standpoint with a small constellation of two propositions: Proposition 2 relates the amount to the ticket prices that are common in the U.S., and this general statement is in turn backed up in Proposition 3 with a concrete example from the author's experience.

[1] The proviso (given in the quotation from van Eemeren and Grootendorst) that the goal can also be to *refute* the proposition refers merely to the situation where said standpoint is about *not* believing something or doing something.

One question to ask at this point concerns the range of possible standpoints, or the range of 'things that we can argue for'. That range is naturally very wide, but broad classifications have been suggested, in addition to that by Aristotle mentioned above. For Eggs (2000), the three basic categories are:

- the *epistemic* argument: some proposition is true or false;
- the *ethical* (or *aesthetical*) argument: something is good or bad (or beautiful or ugly, or similar); and
- the *deontic* argument: some action should be done or not done.

Sometimes, the vocabulary used in an argument provides hints as to which category the standpoint belongs to—at least as long as the argument is not too indirect. For illustration, here is an example of an aesthetical argument, taken from a film review.[2] We marked some words indicating the realm of aesthetics in italics.

(1.2) Of all Greenaway's works [. . .], this is probably the British filmmaker's least effective. As with all of his films, the *choreography* of people and objects before the camera [. . .] is elaborate and *splendid*. The film also marks some of Greenaway's favorite thematic obsessions, including (in no particular order) *spiritual* and corporeal *rotting*, Sir Isaac Newton and arcane mullings on things historic, classical and numerical.
But Greenaway's *narrative* and his direction of actors—two elements which only recently has he concerned himself with—are without foundation. After the effects of the *visual* presentation have *worn off*, the film becomes rather *tiresome* to follow.

1.1.2 How Do We Argue?

Having described the static view of *what* constitutes argumentation, we now move to a more process-oriented perspective that is interested in *how* argumentation unfolds. We already emphasized that we are dealing with a social activity that involves a speaker and a hearer, where the latter can be a specific person, or alternatively a broader and possibly quite unspecific audience (as with the film review in *The Washington Post*). As argumentation may appear in both spoken and written form, the speaker may naturally also be a writer and the hearer a reader.[3]

[2] Desson Howe, *The Washington Post*. Review of 'The Belly of an Architect', June 29, 1990. http://www.washingtonpost.com/wp-srv/style/longterm/movies/videos/thebellyofanarchitectnrhowe_a0b289.htm (accessed January 15, 2026).

[3] Throughout the book, we sometimes use *speaker* and *hearer* as cover terms that should be taken to also subsume writers and readers; in other words, we generally do not distinguish between the different linguistic modes.

Let us start with the case where two (or more) people seek to resolve a disagreement. They engage in a debate and aim for reaching a conclusion that—at best—leaves everybody happy, or—at least—makes none of the participants too unhappy. This is a process that constitutes the heart of, for instance, political deliberation: making decisions after a careful and thorough weighing of the options and their potential consequences. Greek philosophy had a lot to say about the rules of conduct that enable successful deliberation; in more recent times, the German philosopher Habermas (1981) (among others) studied the role of rational activity in modern society and especially in communication. Within the field of argumentation theory, the pragma-dialectical school (van Eemeren and Grootendorst 2004) put forward a theory of what constitutes a 'critical discussion': what kind of behavior is expected of the participants, what protocol to use, and so on. Their work exemplifies foremost a *normative* approach to argumentation theory: It seeks to specify how things should be done, ideally. For the practical goals of argument mining, this may seem of a lesser relevance, but in fact, work in the pragma-dialectical school has also studied the linguistic aspects of the enterprise. For instance, van Eemeren et al. (2007) identified patterns of formulation that can typically occur at different stages of a critical discussion.

The normative perspective emphasizes the central role of rational thought in argumentation, as does the definition that we quoted in the beginning. Indeed, most arguments should ultimately reflect a pattern of sound reasoning, but still, in most real-world instances of argumentation, there are additional influences at work. For one thing, beyond claiming to demonstrate a sound inference, speakers may very well stress their own personal authority on the subject in order to reinforce the acceptability of their standpoint. They may point out that they have studied the matter for a long time, remind the hearer that they are formally in a teacher-student relationship, cite an external source that enjoys high public esteem, and much more. Obviously, such moves are independent of the underlying reasoning, but they can add 'weight' to the standpoint the speaker puts forward.

Furthermore, as we so far only hinted at, argumentation in most cases is a *process* that can stretch across multiple dialogue turns, or across a sequence of sentences. It brings together the "constellation of propositions", as the definition calls them, and importantly, speakers face the task of *organizing* that constellation in a linear linguistic contribution. Some portions of a complex argument may be closely related, others may be more distinct. Some points may be rated as more important or 'weighty' (by the speaker) than others. Therefore, the linearization of the argument's portions in a text should not be left to coincidence. On the contrary: being able to arrange one's argumentative speech in such a manner that it promises to be effective has for a long time been considered an art. The discipline in charge of this is *Rhetoric*, and it studies the relative merits of different strategies for communicating a standpoint. The psychological side of this task is *persuasion*: techniques for trying to make sure that the audience will respond to the speaker's message in the desired way. Persuasion is closely related to argumentation, but it clearly has other ingredients in addition.

In the terminology of Aristotle (ca. 350 B.C.E./ translated 2007), the three central factors determining the success of an argumentative exchange are labeled as follows.

- *Logos:* Speakers employ rules of sound reasoning:

  (1.3) That building needs to be demolished, because it is full of asbestos, which is known to be hazardous, and there is no way to stop its diffusion from the different parts of the building.

- *Ethos:* Speakers signal their authority or credibility (or that of their source):

  (1.4) That building needs to be demolished, because it is full of asbestos, as the report by the university engineers has shown.

- *Pathos:* Speakers seek to communicate their standpoint in a manner that seeks to evoke an emotional response:

  (1.5) That building needs to be demolished, because it is an irresponsible source of danger to the health and indeed the life of our children who spend so many hours in those poisonous rooms every day!

Of course, the three dimensions do not usually occur in isolation; most arguments will mix them with each other, to different degrees. But the logos dimension is arguably the most important one, and for argument mining often the most relevant. Notice that the definition we worked through at the beginning of the chapter also centered on logos ("a rational activity").

Both in dialogue and in monologue text, argumentation can become quite complex and give rise to intricate relationships among different linguistic units. As argument mining has so far focused mainly on written text (monologue, or social media interactions), we will in the following emphasize this perspective. In many argumentative texts, such as newspaper editorials or blog posts, the audience is not a clearly identified hearer but an unspecific set of readers. Still, the task for the speakers remains the same: they seek to influence the standpoint of the audience, and for doing that they need to anticipate the positions that the audience likely takes on the issue. In response to this *hearer model*, the speaker selects material to present in support of their view, and furthermore has the option to explicitly consider possible objections by the audience. Such counterconsiderations, as we will call them, represent the viewpoint not of the speaker but of the anticipated hearer—the 'opposing view'—and the speaker is advised to not only cite them but also refute them. Here is a (constructed) example, which has already been divided into its minimal units as a first step of analysis:

(1.6) [We really need to tear down that building.]$_0$ [Granted, it will be expensive,]$_1$ [but the degree of asbestos contamination is not tolerable anymore.]$_2$ [Also, it is one of the most ugly buildings in town!]$_3$

Argumentation structure is the term we will use for what was called a "constellation of propositions" in the definition given at the beginning of this chapter. Looking at Example 1.6, this structure consists of claims made by the speaker (here: unit 0), material they present in support of their claims (here: 3), as well as possible counterconsiderations (here: 1) and their refutations (here: 2). In a similar yet less explicit way, the author of Example 1.2 above first states the verdict (the director's least effective film), then presents a positive evaluation (nice choreography; an observation that is in opposition to the general verdict) before closing with an argument that supports the negative verdict, suitably initiated with the conjunction *but*.

Finally, to complicate matters, an argumentative text may of course also contain *non-argumentative* portions such as background information, whose identification is part of the overall task of argument mining.

1.2 Argument Mining in a Nutshell

For illustration, Fig. 1.1 gives a possible graph representation of the structure found in Example 1.6. It follows the notation proposed by Peldszus and Stede (2013), which is in turn based on that of Freeman (1991). Circular nodes denote statements representing the proponent's view, while the boxed node (Unit 1) indicates the voice of the opposing viewpoint. Unit 0 is the central claim of the text, on which Unit 1 places an *attack* of type *rebut*: It gives a reason why Unit 0 should not hold. The author proceeds with a counterargument (Unit 2), which is an *undercut* type of attack on the *rebut* relation, thus indicating that Unit 1 is not regarded as a good or sufficient argument against Unit 0. Finally, Unit 3 provides an argument directly in favor of Unit 0; this is commonly called the *support* relation.

We will look into such argument graphs in depth in Chap. 3 and the distinction between undercutting and rebutting is later taken up in Chap. 5. At this point, however, we regard a graph of this kind as one possible outcome of an argument mining process, and we will now use the example to briefly summarize the overall problem. In its full-fledged form, it can involve the following subtasks (not necessarily to be solved in this particular order).

1. Identify a text (or a portion of a text) as in principle of an argumentative kind (see Sect. 4.1). ⟶ This text is argumentative in its entirety.
2. Segment the text into *argumentative discourse units* (ADUs) (see Sect. 4.1.1). ⟶ The ADUs are Units 0, 1, 2, and 3.
3. Identify the central claim (see Sect. 4.2.1). ⟶ The central claim is Unit 0.

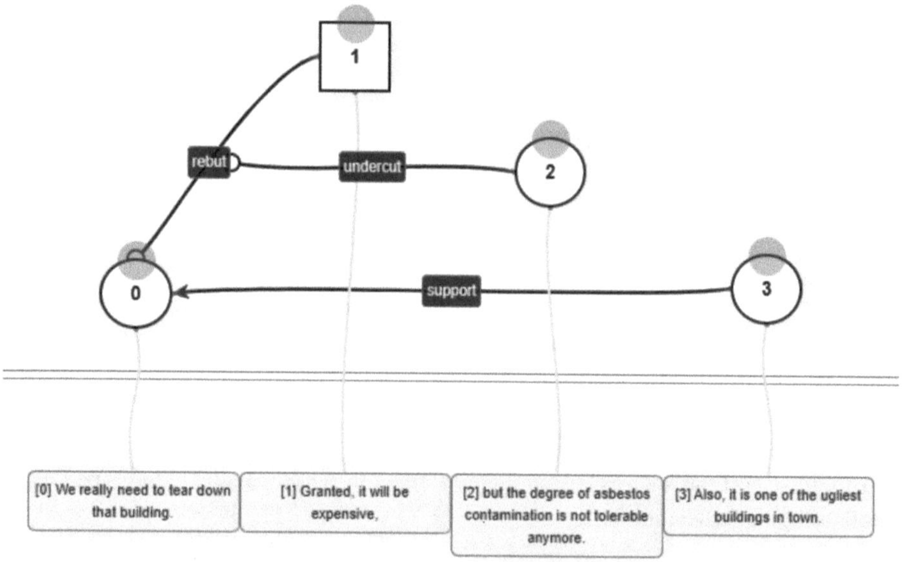

Fig. 1.1 Graph representation of argument structure for Example 1.6 with four units, 0–3, and three different types of relation: *rebut*, *undercut*, and *support*

4. Identify the role/function of ADUs (see Sects. 4.2.1 and 4.2.4). ⟶ Units 0, 2, and 3 represent the view of the proponent; Unit 1 represents the view of the opponent.
5. Identify relations between ADUs (see Chap. 5). ⟶ support (Unit 3, Unit 0); rebut (Unit 1, Unit 0); undercut (Unit 2, rebut (Unit 1, Unit 0))
6. Build the overall structural representation (see Sect. 5.3). ⟶ This yields the structure shown in the figure.
7. Identify the stance of the main claim (and hence that of the "proponent") (see Sect. 6.1). ⟶ Given the topic "Should the building be demolished?", the stance is *pro*.
8. Identify the perspective or framing that is employed for the premises (see Sects. 6.2 and 6.3). ⟶ Unit 1: economics; Unit 2: health; Unit 3: aesthetics.
9. Assess the quality of the argument (see Sect. 7.2). ⟶ For example, Unit 0 gets logically *sufficient* support from Unit 1–3, but Unit 3 may not be seen as phrased fully *appropriately*.
10. Reconstruct implicit reasoning (see Sect. 8.3). ⟶ For example, from Unit 2, it follows that the building poses a health hazard to inhabitants (and therefore, Unit 2 can undercut the rebut of Unit 0 by Unit 1).
11. Identify the argumentation scheme that describes the reasoning from premises to claim (see Sect. 8.1). ⟶ For example, Unit 2 (indirectly) supports Unit 0 via the scheme *argument from negative consequences*: if the building is not torn down, it will pose a health hazard to inhabitants.

12. Summarize the argument and rephrase it in a colloquial way (see Sect. 9.3). ⟶ "The speaker uses the asbestos problem and ugliness to call for demolition of the building, even if pricy."

Step 1 is of course unnecessary if the text genre under consideration is by definition argumentative. Otherwise, in a scenario where the type of text is not clearly known, an argumentativeness classification is needed. Step 2 can either be combined with some of the other tasks, or carried out as a separate procedure, which designates clauses, sentences, or sequences of them as ADUs of the argumentation structure. Steps 3–5 establish the information that is needed for building the graph in Step 6. Steps 7–11—which are mostly independent of each other—derive more fine-grained information that goes beyond the graph structure, such as the type of argument (from a range of predefined *scheme* classes) or various dimensions of argument quality: for example, is an argument logically cogent or rhetorically effective? Finally, Step 12 is a summarization task; other generation tasks may come up in situations where we aim for new arguments, rephrase given arguments, counter them, etc.

For many practical purposes, only some of these steps will be carried out in a real-world application of argument mining. Usually, the minimal core task is finding the claims and the premises. These 12 steps, however, serve as a preview for this book, with pointers to the sections where they will be covered in depth.

1.3 Why Study Argument Mining?

Traditionally, analyses of arguments relied on painstaking manual reconstruction and annotation. For example, manual analyses targeted checking the soundness of a given (line of) argument: *Fallacies* have been studied for millennia, with the goal to determine the conditions under which an argument that is typically fallacious may be reasonable after all. Purely-manual analysis, however, severely limits the scalability and speed of such investigations. Recently, first automatic methods have been proposed for fallacy detection, which we will discuss in Chap. 8.

When an argument is fully formalized and represented in logic, it can be treated as blobs, where only the overall structure is evaluated. For example, Fig. 1.1 can be viewed without attention to the meaning of text fragments, focusing just on the structure, wherein Unit 3 supports Unit 0; Unit 1 attacks Unit 0 and is in turn attacked by Unit 2. This can be interpreted as a bipolar argumentation framework, which we will introduce in Chap. 3. In this context, automatic reasoners can be used to determine whether an argument is *sound*. In the face of conflicting information, reasoners can also determine maximally consistent subsets. However, the application of such systems is naturally limited by the input available to them. Argument mining can fill this gap by finding suitable instances of real-life arguments in texts. We will discuss the connection between argumentation and reasoning in Chap. 8 and later give examples of reasoning tools in Chap. 10.

Global communication technologies, including social media, have raised interest in large-scale analysis of written conversations. Likewise, large corpora of open access scientific documents in some fields have enabled large-scale mining of knowledge. These efforts can be significantly enriched by argument mining, to truly support web-scale discourse and debate. One early success in this area was IBM Research's *Project Debater*, a dialogue system that could mine arguments and recompose them in argumentative speeches autonomously in order to have a debate with human beings (Slonim et al. 2021).

The rise of large language models (LLMs) has put NLP at the forefront of the current boom in AI. LLMs show human or near-human performance on many tasks, and they can impressively imitate many human communication processes, including argumentation. While the capabilities of LLMs to actually reason are a topic of ongoing debate (Shojaee et al. 2025), reasoning and argumentation are inherently connected. To what extent there can hence be a fruitful exchange between research on argument mining and on LLMs will be touched in different parts of this book.

Personal decision-making is another area that can benefit from argument mining. Chatbots and spoken dialogue systems are used increasingly widely, not least to argue for and against a given position. Argument mining technologies can help ensure that such systems argue reasonably, to better discern a user's arguments, and to respond to them intelligently using rational justification, inference, and referring to the user's values. Given the importance of arguments in human sensemaking and decision making, the ability to mine arguments from written texts can help: For example, an online discussion board could visually summarize the current state of a discussion, without constraining individual replies or needing a human analyst, showing each person's perspective and its relation to the overall discussion.

Automatically assessing the quality of arguments, once they are identified, has a lot of potential, too. Deliberations could be supported by marking the extent to which arguments (such as the asbestos discussion mentioned earlier in this chapter) are based on *logos, ethos* and *pathos*. Further, argument mining can be used to identify arguments in a written essay, to aid in essay scoring or to provide instantaneous feedback to learners. The Educational Testing Service in the US has investigated how argument mining can contribute to the evaluation of essays that students write for college admissions, or earlier in school (Ghosh and Klebanov 2024); we will come back to these topics throughout Chaps. 4 and 5, and in Chap. 10, we show various tools aiming to improve essay quality.

Finally, argument generation could play an important role in the rebuttal of fake news on social media, for example, by automatically giving counterconsiderations. Also, real-time argument summarization could be facilitated with argument mining, by enabling detailed arguments to be viewed at multiple levels of granularity: zooming out of the structure would show the main points in the argument, while zooming in would show the detail in each point. This would enable small groups to carefully check the validity of arguments. Chapter 9 will look into the main computational aspects of generating, rewriting, countering, and summarizing arguments.

1.4 Target Audience

We hope that this book attracts a broad audience interested in the computational treatment of human argumentation. The book is aimed primarily at graduate students and researchers in human language technologies. There is demand for synthesis of the latest research in argument mining for education, due to the growth in degree programs in NLP and related areas. AI and data science, the larger fields to which argument mining contributes, have seen a groundswell of interest from academia, industry, and the general public. High-paying industry research & development positions seek PhD-trained researchers. Undergraduate and professional master's training is also in demand.

The book is organized for use as the basis of a semester-long university course on argument mining. We envision one chapter per lecture. Yet chapters are extensive due to the rapid evolution of the field in the last decade. Hence a careful selection from each chapter may be needed for each lecture of such a course. Particularly, in the method-oriented parts of the book (Chaps. 4–9), we review various NLP approaches to the respective tasks; many of them in a concise summary only. However, we present selected approaches in detail, going in more depth through their main steps and giving insights into their experiments. These may be seen as candidates to focus on in the lectures. In all cases, we assume the reader to have a general background in NLP, being familiar with fundamental concepts and widely-used techniques. For an excellent and comprehensive introduction to the basics of NLP, we recommend the latest book version of Jurafsky and Martin (2026).

1.5 Overview of the Book

In Chap. 2, we approach the notion of argumentation from a linguistic perspective and discuss a range of phenomena that motivate distinctions between argumentative text and non-argumentative text. We also touch on a number of concepts that are closely related to argumentation, such as subjectivity, opinion, rhetoric, and framing. Chapter 3, in contrast, takes the viewpoint of argumentation theory and introduces several key aspects of argument reasoning, the formal representation of arguments, and several corpora that have been used in argument mining research.

With these preliminaries taken care of, we present the core tasks of argument mining in Chaps. 4 and 5; beginning with these chapters we presume a basic background in NLP techniques. First, Chap. 4 explains our approach to dividing argument mining into a number of relatively isolated subtasks, which reflects the practice of most current research. The chapter begins with the goals of segmenting argumentative text, including identifying text as argumentative, and covers identifying claims and premises, before surveying the methods used. Next, Chap. 5 considers the structure of arguments and how the different parts relate to one another, including distinguishing supports from attacks and building argument graphs.

With those core mining tasks covered, next, Chap. 6 considers NLP approaches to perspective assessment. Common tasks include recognizing stance, identifying topics and frames, and assessing bias, morals, and values. Chapter 7 considers how to assess the quality of the arguments found, such as their logical cogency and dialectical reasonableness. Chapter 8 considers how to classify the type of reasoning, detect flaws in reasoning, and reconstruct implicit parts of arguments. Chapter 9 discusses automatically producing argumentative text, rewriting and countering arguments, and summarizing individual arguments and debates, before Chap. 10 highlights applications for argumentation, including systems for debating, search, writing support, and argument analytics, among others, as well as argument mapping tools.

Finally, Chap. 11 provides a summary of the contents covered in this book, an outlook for future research and technologies, and ethical considerations.

Argumentative Language

2

In this chapter, we consider the linguistic side of argumentation: What does the language of arguing look like, and how does it differ from other ways of speaking or writing? The chapter thus is intended to serve primarily as background for readers who approach argument mining originally from a technical perspective but are also interested in the underlying linguistic phenomena and their terminology. We will also touch upon some NLP tasks that are related to argumentation, to build some bridges to areas the reader might be familiar with.

For a start, we consider the notion of *subjectivity* (Sect. 2.1), as argumentation is quite clearly an instance of subjective language use. Since a vast amount of NLP work on subjectivity centers specifically on *opinion*, and to a smaller extent on *stance*, we briefly explore their relationships to argumentation (Sect. 2.2). Then, we approach our topic from the perspective of *speech act theory*, which emphasizes the intentional side of producing language and suggests inventories of *illocutionary roles* that can be relevant for argument analysis (Sect. 2.3). Thereafter, we shift attention to the level of complete texts and turn to the idea of analyzing argumentation as one of five basic *discourse modes* that correlate with particular surface features of utterances or text (Sect. 2.4). The chapter closes with a look at *rhetoric*, that is, the art of crafting a text in such a way that it is most likely to have the intended effects on the readers; this includes a short introduction to the idea of framing and its connection to argumentation (Sect. 2.5).

2.1 Subjectivity: Private States and Verifiability

Linguistic utterances can occupy different positions in the space defined by the notions of *objectivity* and *subjectivity*. Consider these statements:

M. Stede et al., *Argument Mining*, Synthesis Lectures on Human Language Technologies, https://doi.org/10.1007/978-3-032-32291-3_2

(2.1) Buenos Aires is the capital of Argentina.
(2.2) Winston Churchill came to office in 1940.

Making a sound judgment on their truth requires some world knowledge, which in these cases is, for example, readily available on the smartphone. The sentences talk about reality and are prone to inter-subjective agreement; in the terminology of Park and Cardie (2014), they are *verifiable-public*, that is, anyone can verify or falsify them with the help of public information. For this reason they are not very typical matters of arguing, which in contrast would require uttering a *standpoint* (cf. Sect. 1.1)—and this is an inherently subjective move.

Subjectivity comes in many different forms, and perhaps the most simple form is a speaker reporting on their personal experiences. Park and Cardie (2014) call these *verifiable-private*: In principle they can be verified as long as trustworthy witnesses can be summoned. Two examples given by Park and Cardie are:

(2.3) My son has hypoglycemia.
(2.4) They flew me to NY in February.

Statements like these do not always give rise to interesting argumentation, either, and among the reasons for that are the private nature of the content and the described mode of verifiability. So let us move on to other kinds of subjective utterances:

(2.5) *Reveal an emotion:* Hooray!
(2.6) *Give an opinion:* That's a really bad wine.
(2.7) *Make a judgment:* You should not be given the prize.
(2.8) *Make a prognosis:* There will be snow tomorrow.
(2.9) *Give an estimate or speculation:* I guess that's a llama over there.

To characterize what these have in common, we follow Wiebe et al. (2005) in adopting the notion of *private state* from the English grammar of Quirk et al. (1985). The idea is: While a person's actions can be observed by the outside world, her current mental state (what does she think, how does she feel, etc.) is not open to that observation. It is entirely up to the speaker to decide whether and in what way to reveal a private state to their environment.[1]

Returning to the terminology of Park and Cardie (2014), Examples 2.5–2.7 are *unverifiable*: They cannot be proven or disproven with objective evidence. This is different for Examples 2.8 and 2.9 in the sense that evidence may in principle be obtained, by

[1] Of course, in a conversation, it is natural for interlocutors to hypothesize aspects of the other's private states, based on facial expression, prosody, etc.; but this is in turn a subjective assessment and thus quite different from ascertaining some item of inter-subjective truth.

waiting until the end of the next day, or by consulting an expert on the animal in question. Still, the set of Examples 2.5–2.9 differs in an important aspect from the two examples that we gave earlier: Upon hearing Examples 2.3 or 2.4, a listener may respond with "You are lying!" in case she has evidence to the contrary of the statements (and ascribes bad intention to the speaker). For Examples 2.5–2.9, however, this response would (under most circumstances) be highly unnatural, because revealing a private state cannot be construed as a lie. For Examples 2.6–2.9 it is perfectly alright to dispute the *content proposition* of the private state, that is, to disagree with the opinion, the judgment, the prognosis, and the speculation; but we cannot dispute the action of its revelation.

As their next step, Park and Cardie propose some constraints on how the different types of statements can be supported in argumentation: for unverifiable statements, speakers may give a *reason* ("I don't like this wine, because it has so much tannin"), while for verifiable-public statements they can provide *evidence*: "I tell you Winston Churchill came to office in 1940. I saw it on Wikipedia!" For verifiable private statements, as we pointed out, providing evidence can be more difficult and also less common, as they rarely give rise to persuasive argumentation. Park and Cardie state that they may be backed up with *optional evidence*.

Linking this to our core terminology, the scheme of Park and Cardie proposed three different types of claims, which are best supported by three different types of premises. In argument mining, automatically checking whether these claim and premise types match is one dimension of assessing argument quality, which will be our topic in Chap. 7.

2.2 Opinion, Stance, and Argument

Opinion mining and stance classification are well-established tasks in NLP and prominent cases of analyzing subjectivity (the latter task will also be detailed in Sect. 6.1). In this section, we therefore briefly discuss the relation of opinions and stance to argumentation.

2.2.1 Opinions

We saw a straightforward opinion in Example 2.6 above. In everyday language, the term *opinion* can cover a broad range of statements (many speakers would probably regard Examples 2.7–2.9 as opinions, too), but for NLP purposes it came to be restricted to positive or negative evaluations of, well, 'anything'. More formally, Liu (2015) defined an opinion as a tuple consisting of

- a *target*—the entity being evaluated: a product, a person, an institution, etc.;
- the *aspect* of the target that the evaluation pertains to (usually a part or an attribute);
- the expressed *sentiment* toward that target—on a discrete or continuous scale of negative, neutral or positive polarity;

- the *holder* of the opinion—often the speaker or author of the text;
- the *time* at which the opinion is known to hold.

A program performing opinion mining thus tries to locate the presence of an opinion in a document, and then to instantiate the tuple as far as possible. Sometimes the problem is reduced to finding merely the sentiment and the target, for example when opinions on commercial products are being collected; recently, however, aspect-based sentiment anaysis (Zhang et al. 2023a) has received a lot of attention, as it offers more useful information: In analyzing hotel reviews, for instance, one would like to distinguish judgments on location, price, personnel, food, and so on.

In language, evaluation is to a large extent encoded in words. Thus when opinion mining became popular in the mid-2000s, the task was tackled with lexicons that at first covered adjectives and later on also other categories (Taboada et al. 2011): "the wonderful wine / I like the wine / The wine runs down admirably / The wine is a bestseller." The lexicon developed by Taboada et al. contained around 5000 words along with a numerical score of their positive or negative so-called lexical *polarity*.

But not all opinions can be captured with such a generic lexicon. In *implicit* opinions, also called *polar facts*, the sentiment arises not from words that generally convey polarity but from factual statements that only imply an evaluation. These statements are domain-specific and rather difficult to detect automatically; two examples are:

(2.10) [camera review] The viewfinder is somewhat dark.
(2.11) [hotel review] The rooms turned out to be small.

The two attributes ("dark" and "small") are not in general negative, but when applied to the specific entities here ("viewinder" and "rooms"), they invite us to infer a disappointed attitude on the writer's side.

An opinion qualifies as a *standpoint* (in the sense of Sect. 1.1), and hence argument mining becomes a natural extension of opinion mining when speakers state their opinion and also provide one or more reasons for their evaluation. As this is a matter of 'like or dislike', the result is an *aesthetical* argument in the three-way classification given in Sect. 1.1. The opinion statement is the claim, and the reason serves as premise:

(2.12) I never enjoyed Wagner's operas. They are so enormously overloaded.

This easily extends to multiple reasons, and also to more complex structures where a reason can in turn be supported by other reasons. In Example 2.12, for instance, the speaker might continue with a statement providing evidence for the overloaded nature of a Wagner opera.

Rajendran et al. (2016) specifically address implicit opinions from the perspective of argumentation and propose a parallel to the task of reconstructing enthymemes, that is, arguments in which a premise or the conclusion are unstated and left for the hearer to construct. Given Examples 2.10 and 2.11 above, when the conclusion is a negative verdict by the reviewer, then an unstated major premise provides the link between the explicated minor premise and the conclusion:

(2.13) The viewfinder is somewhat dark (+ A dark camera viewfinder is considered bad).
→ I am not in favor of the camera.
(2.14) The rooms turned out to be small (+ A small hotel room is considered bad).
→ I am not in favor of the hotel.

Enthymeme reconstruction is a very difficult problem, but it has been addressed in argument mining to some extent in recent years, as we will discuss in Sect. 8.3.

2.2.2 Stance

The examples we just gave for deriving the like/dislike conclusion illustrate the task of stance detection. In the definition given by Schiller et al. (2021a), the goal is to predict one of the labels *pro, contra, neutral, unrelated* for a pair of two input texts: a description of an issue, and a statement by someone who provides their stance—i.e., the content of the label—on that issue. The issue description can be a noun phrase (as for the camera and the hotel above) or a full sentence or question, for example, "Should children be vaccinated against pertussis?" Similarly, the statement containing the stance can in principle range from a single sentence to a complex text (in many shared tasks, the statements are tweets or similar social media contributions). Accordingly, solving the problem can sometimes be achieved by plain sentiment recognition ("I have always been against that vaccination") yet in the general case can require complex inferencing from texts that implicitly convey the stance.

For opinion mining, we pointed out that argument mining is a natural extension if one is interested also in the reasons given for the opinion. Similarly, for stance detection one may want to know on what grounds the stance is inferred from a—possibly complex—text. If somewhere in the text the stance is communicated explicitly, this sentence forms the claim, and premises correspond to the reasons that the author provides in the rest of the text. Alternatively, the claim may be only implicit; in this case, finding the reasons (the arguments) is the key task. For example, Saha et al. (2024) propose an approach to constructing an 'explanation tree' for a stance that is extracted from a text.

Finally, notice that in contrast to opinion mining, where the sentiment can quite often be derived from the inherent polarity of words (and accounting for certain context effects like negation), there is no simple lexicon-based approach to stance detection. For one thing, there are only a few explicit stance markers (such as *to be in favor of, to advocate*) and they are not used very often. More importantly, the complexity of the contextual effects is much higher for deriving stance than for sentiment analysis. Consider these possible answers to the question "Should pertussis vaccination be mandatory for children?"[2]

(2.15) Children have a much better chance for a healthy life when they are vaccinated. (sentiment: pos; stance: yes)
(2.16) Luckily, pertussis is so rare today that we can safely ignore vaccination. (sentiment: pos; stance: no)
(2.17) Too many non-vaccinated children in our city have suffered badly from pertussis in the last decades. (sentiment: neg; stance: yes)
(2.18) These vaccines are very expensive and furthermore known for really bad side effects. (sentiment: neg; stance: no)

Bar-Haim et al. (2017a) provide an annotation scheme that takes the sentiment/stance dichotomy a step further, by including target-specific sentiment analysis. In their model, an argument concerns an overarching *topic*, which they formulate in the style of the British parliament; for example: "This house would abolish the monarchy." A *claim* is a statement that—possibly rather indirectly—takes a stance on this topic; for example, "hereditary succession is outdated" would convey a *pro* stance on the topic, i.e., on abolishing the monarchy. Computing this is not trivial, however; it requires detecting (i) a negative sentiment toward the target 'monarchy' in the topic; (ii) a negative sentiment toward the target 'hereditary succession' in the claim; and (iii) a consistency relation (as opposed to a contrast) between the two targets 'monarchy' and 'hereditary succession'. Thus the sentiment polarities on topic and claim targets interact with the consistency or contrast relation; examples for other combinations are provided in the paper by Bar-Haim et al. We will take a closer look at stance classification and its role in argument mining in Sect. 6.1.

2.3 Speech Acts and Arguments

We have introduced subjectivity in general, illustrated it with a number of subtypes, and looked at opinion and stance in some more detail. In this section, we will broaden the perspective from considering just the linguistic surface to also looking 'under the hood' of producing language: Telling an argument is an inherently *intentional*, goal-oriented activity—the speaker's aim is to influence the state of mind of the addressees or to change their behavior. This is, generally speaking, a matter of inflicting change on 'the world' by means of using language, which in linguistics is the realm of *speech act theory*:[3] It

[2] We assume a simple sentence-level sentiment analysis here; a more fine-grained target-sensitive sentiment can actually play a role in stance detection.

[3] For a slightly more elaborate, chapter-long introduction to the topic and a discussion of its contentious points, see Sadock (2005).

maintains that using language is a form of carrying out *actions*—comparable to switching on the light, cooking dinner, and so on—and therefore it has consequences; and these can to some extent be spelled out by a speech act analyst. In this view, an utterance made by a speaker, once completed, does not simply vanish but leaves its marks on the world (or at least on a small portion of it): The listener may have new information, or be doubtful of a previously assumed 'fact', or feel offended, etc. Then, as producing an argument (often) is supposed to persuade, there is a natural affinity between the realms of speech acts and argumentation.

2.3.1 Performative Verbs

The most profound 'changes to the world' are being induced by linguistic utterances that occur in situations such as the judge sentencing the defendant in court, an authority christening a ship, or the priest marrying a couple. Here, saying the sentence(s) will automatically affect the state of the world, in ways that can be described clearly in most cases.

Contexts like these were a central motivation for the work of Austin (1975), who is nowadays widely credited for the first systematic exposition of a theory of speech acts. Beyond the relatively dramatic examples just mentioned, Austin entertained—at least for some time—the hypothesis that a certain class of so-called *performative verbs* plays such a fundamental role in language that they can be used to paraphrase essentially any sentence in such a way that its function becomes transparent.[4]

(2.19) You shouldn't read that book. → I advise you not to read that book.
(2.20) What is your name? → I ask you to tell me your name.
(2.21) Yesterday I met a philosopher. → I assert that I met a philosopher yesterday.
(2.22) Max is the smartest kid in the world. → I claim that Max is the smartest kid in the world.
(2.23) It's about 15° out there.→ I estimate that it is about 15° out there.

The fact that people in daily life typically do *not* constantly use those extended versions contributes to ambiguity and sometimes to misunderstanding (but, arguably, makes communication much more interesting); recall our discussion of Examples 2.5–2.9 at the beginning of the chapter. This ambiguity in the roles that utterances can play also makes the task of argument mining difficult, because in some way or another, the status of individual

[4] In the examples, we use *to assert* for the act of providing information that under normal circumstances will not lead to controversy, whereas *to claim* pertains to a subjective standpoint in the sense of Sect. 1.1.

statements that take part in argumentation needs to be determined (and that would be much easier if those performative verbs were present).

The opposite of explicating a speech act with a performative verb is using language in such a way that it actually suggests a *different* speech act than the one the author intends to perform. The much-cited example "Can you pass the salt?" on the surface is a yes-no question but is interpreted by the hearer as a polite form of a request for action. Similar ambiguities occur frequently with declarative sentences that *prima facie* merely assert some information, yet are intended to convey an additional action. Examples 2.24 and 2.25 below are explicit apologies (with the first being more formal by using a performative verb), whereas in Examples 2.26 and 2.27 it is up to the hearer to read an apology into the utterance—this depends on the situational context, how familiar the interlocutors are, etc.

(2.24) I apologize for being late.
(2.25) Sorry I'm late.
(2.26) I'm a bit late, unfortunately.
(2.27) I'm afraid I didn't quite make it on time.

The phenomena of these so-called indirect speech acts have received much attention in linguistic pragmatics. The two main approaches to explaining them emphasize either a process of conventionalization over time, or the role of active inferencing on the hearer's side; see Sadock (2005).

2.3.2 Components of a Speech Act

As a prerequisite to disentangling the functioning of indirect speech acts, Austin (1975) (first edition 1962) proposed a tripartite structure of speech acts (which has subsequently been further developed by Searle 1969). The idea is that performing a speech act generally involves three sub-acts that occur (more or less) simultaneously.

- *Locutionary act:* producing the spoken or written *form* of the linguistic utterance. Example: Speaker says "For small children, pertussis can grow into a dangerous pneumonia."
- *Illocutionary act:* the *intention* or goal the speaker has in mind when performing the act.
  Example: Speaker intends hearer to believe the content of the statement, and to change their stance on pertussis vaccination to 'pro'.
- *Perlocutionary act:* the *effect* that the performance of the act has on the addressee. Example: Hearer is annoyed because speaker has already made this statement several times before.

One reason to distinguish illocution from perlocution is that an utterance may well have—from the speaker's perspective—unintended or even undesired effects, which in fact happens in our example above.

For argumentation, the perlocution is of obvious relevance, as it characterizes precisely that 'change of mind' on the addressee's side, which is the purpose of the speaker devising their argument. Research on *persuasion* seeks to measure the strength of such effects. For speech act theoreticians, however, the perlocution is a private state that is of limited interest; the heart of the matter is the perspective of the speaker and thus the illocutionary force of her utterance.

2.3.3 Categories of Illocutionary Acts

Austin's idea of collecting all the relevant verbs in a language in order to define the 'landscape' of speech acts is today generally regarded as a dead end for the advancement of speech act theory. Instead, a prominent task has been to come up with a classification (and definition) of generalized types of speech acts. A number of such typologies have been proposed, and a popular one is that by Searle (1976).

- *Representatives:* Speaker commits to the truth of an assertion.
- *Directives:* Speaker tries to make addressee perform some action.
- *Expressives:* Speaker expresses an emotional state.
- *Declaratives:* Speaker changes the state of the world by means of performing the utterance.
- *Commissives:* Speaker commits to doing some action in the future.

Within these broad classes, subtaxonomies may be postulated, and ultimately, specific speech acts may be defined. Searle (1969) proposed to construct systematic definitions by means of rules that characterize the propositional content of the utterance, the situational conditions that need to hold for the speech act to be performed successfully (*preparatory* rules), a *sincerity* rule committing the speaker to be sincere in expressing their psychological states, and an *essential* rule that describes the central pragmatic impact of the speech act in question. It is important to note that these rules (as opposed to, say, rules of grammar) are not about well-formedness—this is a notion that does not apply to speech acts. Instead, the key concept is that a speech act may be *felicitous*, to successfully serve its purpose. Infelicitous speech act attempts occur, for example, when somebody pronounces somebody else to be married but is in no legal position to do so; or when somebody promises an addressee to do him a favor yet does not really intend to do so (insincerity).

As an example of applying speech act analysis in argument mining, we mention the work of Reinig et al. (2024b), who use a taxonomy of 14 illocution types (shown in Fig. 2.1) to partially model the argumentation in parliamentary debate. They demonstrate

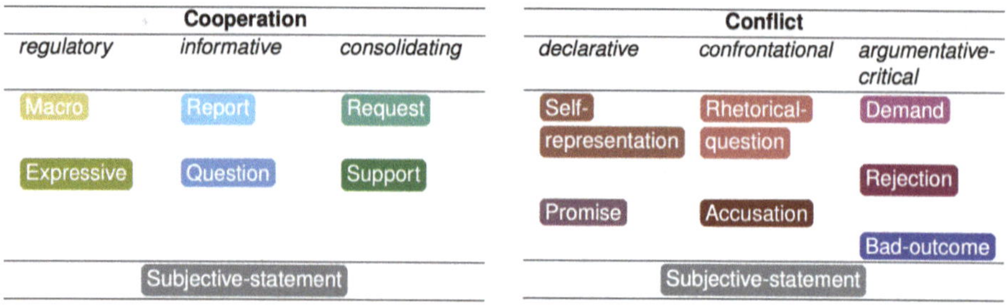

Fig. 2.1 Illocution types for analyzing parliamentary debate (Reinig et al. 2024b, p. 8289), used with permission

that the types can be classified automatically with promising results. When we relate the 14 types back to the five broad classes above, we find that the majority are subtypes of Searle's representatives, which is in line with many other empirically-grounded taxonomies that have been proposed. For practical application, the *representative* category is often of limited utility, because it covers a very wide range of actions.

2.4 Discourse Modes and the Argumentative Text

In Sect. 1.1.2, we mentioned a variety of text genres that are particularly relevant for argument mining. The idea of *genre* (a set of texts that fulfill a common purpose and have commonalities in terms of functional components and/or linguistic conventions) and its importance for many NLP tasks is widely acknowledged. In this section, however, we look at the related, lesser-known notion of *discourse mode*, and then specifically discuss some properties of argumentative language on the level of text.

2.4.1 Characterizing Discourse Modes

The genre is a property of a complete text document: it is a news editorial, a tweet, a student essay, a cooking recipe, and so forth. Genres can differ in terms of the text's purpose, customary text length, layout, sequencing of specific text portions, and other features. The notion of *discourse mode* (Smith 2003) is complementary to genre but need not necessarily apply to a text as a whole. It posits that there is only a small set of basic functions that a series of sentences, or a text passage, can fulfill.[5] These functions are to a good extent determined by the types of *discourse entities* (events, states, generalizations, abstractions) that are mentioned in the passage, and by the connections that are established between

[5] A very similar concept has been studied in German linguistics under the heading of *text type*, notably by Werlich (1975).

them. All these tend to correlate with certain surface-linguistic features, and one main theoretical goal for Smith therefore was to establish the discourse passage as a unit of analysis for linguistics. In Smith's approach, there are five classes:

- *Narrative:* Events and states are introduced, with events being temporally related. The semantic types of events (un-/boundedness) indicate the progression of narrative time. Temporal connectives and adverbials are frequent instruments of clause linkage.

  (2.28) The passengers landed in New York in the middle of the night and then moved on to Hoboken immediately.

- *Description:* Passages include states and ongoing or atelic[6] events. Text progression is driven by spatial rather than by temporal patterns; time is static. Locative phrases often appear in topic position.

  (2.29) Hundreds of people occupied the square. In front of them, the speaker was standing on a small podium.

- *Report:* Events, states, and sometimes general statives are introduced; they are not related to each other (as in narrative). Tensed verbs, modals, and temporal adverbs are frequent.

  (2.30) My sister visited the new exhibition yesterday.

- *Information:* Facts, propositions, and generalizing states are introduced, which need not be anchored in time and space. The text progresses through a 'metaphorical' space.

  (2.31) Krypton is one of the noble gases. It is one of the rarest elements on earth.

- *Argument:* Like information, this is an atemporal mode. States of affairs, facts, and propositions are introduced and related to each other, often contrastively.

  (2.32) The award was given to Paul, but he did not deserve it. His work is very shallow.

Even though the correlations between modes and linguistic features are obviously tendencies rather than strict rules, they can serve as useful indicators, and Smith's book

[6] A *telic* event is one that comprises both a preparation and a culmination phase, e.g., "traveling to London", "climbing the mountain". An atelic event is homogeneous in time: "being ill", "reading".

discusses them in much more detail. A computational approach to recognizing modes automatically was presented by Song et al. (2017).

Recall that the notion of discourse mode is meant to apply to passages of text, not necessarily to full documents. Many genres of text may very well contain stretches of different modes. A feature article in a newspaper or magazine, to give just one example, can switch from narrating personal experiences of the author to arguing in favor of a specific legislation that is currently under debate, and on to a description of a certain politician who would be particularly affected if that legislation were enacted. If such a text is the target of argument mining, the first step is to identify those passages that bear the argumentative discourse mode.

2.4.2 Linguistic Features of Argumentative Text

The argumentative text or portion of a text contains claims, premises related to claims (either in a support or attack relation), possibly interspersed with non-argumentative passages. Inspecting this from a linguistic perspective can be done in two ways: by checking for constellations of characteristic features of the surface language,[7] or by positing an intermediate level of linguistic analysis, and then relating this level to discourse modes, in particular to argumentation. We will briefly consider both ways.

Claims As we discussed earlier, there are many different types of claims, and accordingly it is not surprising that their linguistic variability is large. For evaluative judgments, we can expect words that are covered by sentiment lexicons; but for other types, the predictive value of linguistic signals is much lower. On the basis of a corpus study, Saint Dizier (2020) provided a list of markers that can occur in claims (but they do not have to); it includes

- specific performative verbs (cf. Sect. 2.3) such as *to claim, to recommend*;
- epistemic expressions such as *I think, it seems*;
- markers of levels of certainty, such as *I am certain, I feel, surely, probably*;
- modal verbs (e.g., *could, should*) and adverbs that express degrees of necessity or possibility (e.g., *necessarily, presumably*)

At least, claims have in common that they are subjective statements and thus at show tendencies to be marked as such, but of course there are other subjective statements that are not claims, so ambiguity still remains.

[7] Obviously, many of these features are specific to a language or a language family; for example, German is known to make heavy use of *particles*, whose relevance for argumentation has been studied by Hautli-Janisz and Butt (2016). Our exposition here, however, centers on English.

Premises In an 'ideal' argument, the subjective claim is supported by an objective statement (cf. our discussion of verifiability at the beginning of the chapter), but of course in reality authors may use almost any type of information and statement to back up a claim. When the realm of premises is broken down into systematic semantic subtypes (see below, and later Sect. 4.2.2), some of these types have affinities with linguistic signals—quoting a source often is done with a verb of communication; scientific or statistical evidence can contain numbers; and so on. But probably the most reliable marker of a premise is its position in the text, vis-a-vis the claim they are supporting or attacking.

Connections When the argumentative text contains not only one claim and one premise, but indeed a 'web' of claims, sub-claims, and premises in supporting or attacking role, all these units are very unlikely to appear next to each other without any explicit links.[8] The lexical items that are used for making such links (more or less) clear are called *connectives*: conjunctions (such as *and, but*) and certain adverbials (such as *therefore, because, although*). Very briefly, causal connectives can express a support relation between premise and claim; concessive connectives mark a counter-argument; and contrastive connectives indicate a switch from the *pro* to the *contra* side of the argument. For illustration, here is an artificial example with all argumentative links indicated by a connective:

(2.33) Many diseases have already have been wiped out by vaccines, **and so** we should make pertussis vaccination mandatory, **even though** it will be expensive. The health of the population is our most important goal, **after all**.

Often, connective use is optional, but especially the concessive and contrastive relations in argumentation usually need to be marked in some way, so that the flow of thought becomes understandable to the addressee. One study that considers how the linear order of different argumentative units affects the choice of connective (e.g.: [claim] *because* [premise] / [premise] *therefore* [claim]) is that of Eckle-Kohler et al. (2015) who found statistically-significant correlations between claim-premise constellations and connective use in German argumentative essays.

Of course, causal, concessive and contrastive relations are used in language not only in the presentation of arguments. A causal connection between two events, for instance, can appear in all five discourse modes presented above. Two usage cases of causal connectives that can be confused with argumentation are *Explanation* and *Justification*. Consider:

(2.34) Using airplanes is really a bad idea because they are among the worst air polluters we have ever created. (Argumentation/Persuasion)

[8] In NLP, these links are the subject of 'shallow discourse parsing' (Prasad et al. 2008) or rhetorical structure parsing (see Sect. 2.5.2 below).

(2.35) An airplane is able to take off because the shape of the wings produces an upward force when the air flows across them. (Explanation)

(2.36) I need to use airplanes a lot because my job requires me to be in different parts of the country every week. (Justification)

While in Example 2.34, a claim is supported by a premise, Examples 2.35 and 2.36 make use of the same *because*-construction but have different communicative effects. Example 2.35 is easily used in a context where the listener already believes that airplanes can take off—the speaker thus does not aim to convince the hearer of that fact. Instead, the new information for the hearer is (supposedly) in the second clause. This is the constellation of an *explanation*, where A is not a claim but an undisputed fact and B does not 'support' A but provides the reason why A holds. Example 2.36 can be regarded as a special case, where the explanation pertains to a personal decision. Hence, A does not necessarily have the status of an undisputed fact; the speaker has to consider that some hearers might not approve. This is the situation of *justification*: giving a reason for an attitude or an action that might be controversial—and if it is, then justification becomes a special case of argumentation.

Automatic classification of claims and premises based on linguistic features is tricky due to the optional status of the signals. However, it does work well on the level of text, because there is more material to compute statistics over. For example, the work by Petrenz and Webber (2011) and Krüger et al. (2017) addressed separating newspaper text into opinionated vs. non-opinionated sub-genres (essentially: editorials and letters to the editor vs. news). While this is not exactly the same as distinguishing argumentative and non-argumentative material, the task is quite similar. Krüger et al. measured the impact of a wide set of features and found that, amongst others, frequencies of certain connective groups, sentiment words and communication verbs are useful for making the distinction, but also some purely-syntactic features like verb tense.

The second approach to studying the language of the argumentative discourse mode is by establishing some systematic, intermediate layer of analysis and then correlating the resulting descriptions with modes. This route was taken for example by Becker et al. (2016). Following up on the huge body of linguistic research on aspectual verb classes, the authors focus on one crucial feature for separating discourse modes, viz. the *situation entity* (SE) types. They distinguish the following types:

- *State:* Armin has brown eyes.
- *Event:* Bonnie ate three tacos.
- *Report:* The agency said applications had increased.
- *Generic sentence:* Scientific papers make arguments.
- *Generalizing sentence:* Fei travels to India every year.
- *Fact:* Georg knows that Reza won the competition.
- *Proposition:* Georg thinks that Reza won the competition.
- *Resemblance:* Reza looks like he won the competition.

- *Question:* Why do you torment me so?
- *Imperative:* Listen to this.

These are general semantic categories that can be identified in any type of text, and the idea is that their frequency and combination varies between discourse modes. Becker et al. (2016) annotated these SE types in the texts of the argumentative microtext corpus of Peldszus and Stede (2016b) and by comparison to results from other genres they showed that the SE distribution can help distinguishing argumentative text passages from non-argumentative ones. Furthermore, Becker et al. demonstrated that the distribution of SE types correlates with the different types of argument component (premise/conclusion) and argumentative relations (support, attack). For example, they found that the vast majority of claims in the corpus are either *generic sentences* (e.g., "Alternative medical treatments should be subsidized in the same way as conventional treatments") or *states* (e.g., "These problems concern primarily the British and American intelligence services"); for premises, the spectrum is wider. At least in part, these and other findings can be expected to hold for other kinds of argumentative text as well.

2.5 Rhetoric and Framing

According to the *New Dictionary of the History of Ideas* (Carron 2005, p. 2122), "Rhetoric governs the effective use of verbal and nonverbal communication designed to influence an audience. (...) In its original and historical form, rhetoric is associated with the use of human discourse to persuade and can be defined as the art of speaking, of speaking well, or of speaking effectively with the aim of persuading." There clearly is a connection to argumentation here, and this relationship was studied intensively by Aristotle, whom we mentioned in the first chapter as the proponent of the three means of persuasion, logos, ethos, and pathos. In *On Rhetoric*, Aristotle remarks: "In making a speech, one must study three points: the means of producing persuasion, the style or language to be used, and the proper arrangement of the various parts." (Book III, Ch. 1) Along this line, in the following we first take a look at rhetorical effects of lexical and syntactic choices, and then turn to the role of linear order in presenting an argument effectively. Finally, we will discuss the notion of framing, a kind of rhetorical device that has gained some popularity in political discourse, and that cuts across the aforementioned two dimensions.

2.5.1 Rhetorical Choices in Phrasing

When a speaker wants a hearer to close the window, there are many possibilities to formulate the request and its argumentative support; here are just two of them:

(2.37) Close the window! It's cold.

(2.38) It is rather cold in here and I'm already not feeling so well. Would you be so kind to close the window for me?

In both cases, we have a directive speech act and a supporting argument, but stated very differently. Which one is more appropriate, and correspondingly, more effective, of course depends very much on context: Who is talking to whom under what circumstances. This may seem trivial, but the point is that a similar array of linguistic options for articulating a sentence is essentially always at the writer's disposal. We can choose rare and difficult words, or common and simple ones; we can speak or write in a long sequence of short sentences, or in a short sequence of complex, deeply structured sentences; and so forth. Fahnestock (2011) gives vivid examples of how small changes in word choice, sentence construction, and passage construction can produce different rhetorical effects. Similarly, the introduction by Kolln (2003) is also centered around the notion of linguistic choice and points to the different rhetorical effects of each choice, explaining the alternatives in terms of underlying grammatical concepts. To mention just one example, the author looks at the correlation between lexical and grammatical decisions and the resulting *intonation pattern* or *rhythm* of a sentence, which may very well influence the hearer's perception and can thus contribute to rhetorical effects.

One phenomenon that is often mentioned in connection with argumentation is that of *figures of speech*, also called *rhetorical figures*, which have been studied extensively in classical rhetoric. This, too, is a vast area, and we can only scratch the surface here. Two such examples are as follows.

- *Hyperbole:* "Phew, the distance from Newark to Manhattan is a hundred miles!"
  The statement is literally false, but the exaggeration is consciously used (and probably understood) to emphasize the speaker's point.
- *Tautology:* "That nice restaurant was really great."
  The two predications on the restaurant are barely distinguishable; yet the repetition can contribute to overall effect.

Mitrović et al. (2017) have extensively analyzed rhetorical figures and studied them as devices for producing effective arguments. Following up on their work, Lawrence et al. (2017b) tried to detect the presence of rhetorical figures in text automatically. They used the *Moral Maze* radio debate corpus (Lawrence et al. 2018) for their experiments. For actually computing correlations with argumentative moves, the number of instances of rhetorical figures found was too small, however. Also with an eye toward automation, Harris et al. (2018) proposed a new annotation scheme for rhetorical figures. They suggested focusing on computationally tractable figures such as antimetabole (reverse repetition of at least two words), which they map to several different rhetorical functions. With an eye on using rhetorical figures in argument synthesis, Al Khatib et al. (2020a) use a grammar rule approach to identify 26 syntactically-encoded rhetorical figures, and test it on examples taken from the rhetoric research literature.

2.5.2 Rhetorical Choices in Arranging Arguments

As with sentences, the structure of a text is not arbitrary, either. There are many factors influencing the choices of how to order sentences and link them together, with an important one being the genre of the text, which often suggests conventional linearizations. But usually, an author has considerable room left for making choices, which in turn can contribute to rhetorical effect. We look at two alternative ways of capturing this: a flat segmentation and labeling of a sequence of text spans, and the postulation of a hierarchical text structure.

The idea that a text can be analyzed as a sequence of genre-specific 'moves' goes back to Swales (1990), who suggested that a number of adjacent sentences constitute such a move, and that the text then be a contiguous sequence of moves. Among the genres studied was scientific writing, which (depending on the type of science) usually follows conventionalized patterns of 'when to say what' in a research paper (or in a grant proposal, a book, etc.). A computational implementation was later proposed by Teufel and Moens (2002), who coined the term *argumentative zoning* for this approach. Teufel and colleagues annotated passages of scientific papers for the roles they play as a part of the paper's overall contribution, and hence, zone labels include *aim* (research goal), *own* (description of author's work), *background* (generally accepted scientific background), *conclusion*, and several others. Having shown that substantial human annotator agreement can be achieved, the authors then trained automatic classifiers and demonstrated that the identification of zone labels can be automated with decent reliability.

In a similar vein, Yamada et al. (2017) studied legal arguments in Japanese court judgments, and ran a human agreement study on labeling units as *identifying* (setting a topic), *fact*, *background*, *conclusion*, and *framing* (argumentative material in support of the conclusion unit), and they obtained good annotator agreement ($\kappa = 0.7$).

A complementary, and genre-independent, perspective on text structure suggests that a text can be seen as a hierarchy of text spans that are (recursively) connected via so-called *coherence relations*. These relations state that a span can, for example, be followed by another one that *elaborates* on the former, as in this example, where the spans are marked with square brackets.

(2.39) *Elaboration:* [The new Smart Watch was introduced today.] [It costs $50 more than the old model.]

Recursion arises when these two segments in turn enter into a coherence relation, for example *Motivation*, which links a recommendation for the reader to the reason:

(2.40) *Motivation:* [[The new Smart Watch was introduced today.] [It costs $50 more than the old model.]] [You should really buy it.]

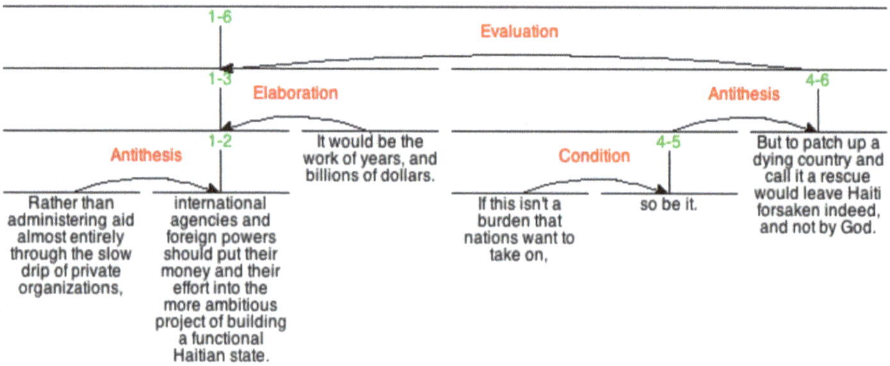

Fig. 2.2 Sample analysis of an argumentative text fragment according to the Rhetorical Structure Theory, taken from Stede (2011, p. 115), used with permission

Taking this idea to the level of the complete text, *Rhetorical Structure Theory* or RST (Mann and Thompson 1988) postulates that a well-formed tree structure can be built, which spans the text completely.[9] The authors postulate that some 25 different coherence relations are sufficient for analyzing most texts. A sample RST tree (for an excerpt of a text) is shown in Fig. 2.2. A well-known English RST corpus is the RST Discourse Treebank (Carlson et al. 2003), and it has led to a variety of parsers that try to build the tree structure for a text automatically (e.g., Koto et al. 2021). This in turn raises the question to what extent an RST tree for an argumentative text can be helpful for the task of parsing the graph structure of the argument. The relation between RST and argumentation was for the first time addressed by Azar (1999) and later by Villalba and Saint-Dizier (2012) and Green (2010); more recent work that exploits double-annotated corpora will be introduced later, in Sect. 5.3.2.

In general, automatic argument mining has not given too much attention to aspects of linear order yet, but there are some initial studies. Al Khatib et al. (2017) annotated arguments in a news editorial corpus for premise types, i.e., the kind of evidence that is supplied in a premise: anecdote, testimony, statistics, or other. They first looked at how these unit types are distributed across editorials, and then extracted characteristic sequencing patterns of premise types. Another study by Wachsmuth et al. (2018a) ran experiments with experts synthesizing short argumentative texts, with strategies that employ the logos/ethos/pathos dimensions in deciding the linear unfolding of the argument.

[9] RST is a theory of linguistic pragmatics; notice that for rhetoricians, the use of *rhetorical* in the name of RST is not uncontroversial, as there is certainly more to text-level rhetoric than what is captured by RST.

Adapted from **Alternet** (*Left*)

Employees-many of whom are undocumented immigrants from Mexico, Ecuador and elsewhere-toil seven days a week for less than minimum wage, with no overtime pay.

Adapted from **Breitbart** (*Right*)

Mass immigration has come at the expense of America's working and middle class, which suffered from poor job growth, stagnant wages, and increased public costs.

Fig. 2.3 Framing the migration issue in different ways (Roy and Goldwasser 2020, p. 7698), licensed under CC-BY 4.0 International

2.5.3 Framing

The notion of framing has been studied in a variety of scientific disciplines including psychology, linguistics, and various social sciences, and in recent years has also been increasingly visible in the public discourse. There is no generally agreed-upon definition, but a popular conception, which is often used also in the NLP community, regards framing as the choice of the perspective from which a particular situation is being portrayed. The developers of the Media Frames Corpus (Card et al. 2015), for example, postulate a taxonomy of 15 different perspectives (economic, morality, health and safety, etc.) and emphasize that an author who selects one of them for reporting an incident, does so in order to influence the audience's perception and their evaluation of the incident. The taxonomy is a proposal for a set of *generic* frames that would apply to a wide variety of topic domains; other framing research opts to define the perspectives specifically for a single target domain, in order to account for important differences that are relevant in that realm.

It should be noted, however, that framing goes beyond this choice of the perspective. Figure 2.3 shows an example from Roy and Goldwasser (2020), which demonstrates that two news sources can both adopt an *economics* frame for writing about migration, and yet arrive at very different political statements, which is to a large extent determined by the more fine-grained aspects of the economical consequences of migration, which an author can select or leave aside; this is the essence of the popular definition of framing that was proposed by Entman (1993).

Evidently, when framing is done intentionally to affect the opinion of an audience, it is closely related to argumentation and rhetoric. When producing a text, framing decisions occur at the pre-linguistic level of deciding 'what to say' (i.e., choosing the perspective and more specific aspects), at the level of phrasing sentences, and also at the level of text organization—some framing theoreticians have emphasized that the overall narrative that is presented in an opinionated text is also a result of framing decisions. We will discuss the argument mining perspective on framing in Sect. 6.2. A comprehensive overview of computational methods for framing analysis is provided by Mirzakhmedova et al. (2027).

2.6 Summary

In contrast to opinions, which in NLP have been studied heavily, arguments come in quite different shapes and are generally harder to detect automatically. Not surprisingly, the first phase of opinion mining research relied on lexicons, which in fact produced respectable results due to the prominent role of domain-independent 'opinionated' words. Unfortunately, there is no correspondingly-predictive role for 'arguing' words. Putting it more generally, while it is not impossible to provide lists of certain typical linguistic features of claims and premises (cf. Sect. 2.4.2), these are merely tendencies—their use is neither a necessary nor a sufficient condition for argumentation being present in an utterance.

Trivially, natural language is by nature *ambiguous*, and in the realm of subjective language—where arguments are definitely situated—this is considerably more acute than in 'objective descriptions' such as those in encyclopedias, Wikipedia, or news text. We have discussed the *performative verbs*, which in principle could be used by speakers to make their moves (the 'illocutions') explicit:

(2.41) I want to convince you that voting for party X is the right thing. Because: I assert that they have the best expertise in the field of economics.

But this is obviously too cumbersome; people simply do not talk this way. Instead, a wide range of quite different, more compact and—importantly—less transparent wordings is at their disposal to express a message like the voting recommendation above.

Therefore, in addition to inspecting individual sentences or clauses for their features, one can turn to the level of discourse (i.e., to the whole text or dialogue) and exploit the fact that there are some conventionalized patterns for arranging claims and their premises. Of course these are also only tendencies, but they can supplement the exploitation of clause-level signals. So far, discourse patterns have received much less attention than the clause features, but some connections between general text structure and the structure of argument have been investigated and exploited for argument mining, as we will explore in Sect. 5.3.2.

3 Representing Arguments

In this chapter we discuss representing arguments and give examples of how particular representations have been adopted in NLP research for argument mining. To mine arguments, we need some way to represent them. Those representations are given by argument models that describe the components of an argument, such as the 'standpoint' in our definition from Sect. 1.1.1, and relations between components such as 'support' and 'rebut' in our example from Fig. 1.1.

Numerous models have been proposed in the field of argumentation theory. There is no single best model: Approaches to argumentation depend on the type of text and the task. Argument models differ in how many components they distinguish, and how they connect these components. Various names are used: we will generally refer to the *standpoint* as a *claim*. Argumentation theory itself is interdisciplinary, and argument mining has been influenced by rhetoric, informal logic, and formal logic.

In the following, we first discuss argument components and structure (Sect. 3.1) and then take a look at the way in which argumentation extends classical inference with defeasible reasoning (Sect. 3.2), leading to patterns called *argumentation schemes* (Sect. 3.3). We survey other important argument models from argumentation theory, drawing on both informal models beyond argumentation schemes (Sect. 3.4) and common formal models (Sect. 3.5). We then review corpora, with a focus on influential corpora for argument mining and corpora using well-known argument models (Sect. 3.6). These and other selected corpora are summarized in Appendix A and a corpora website.[1]

[1] http://purl.org/amresources

M. Stede et al., *Argument Mining*, Synthesis Lectures on Human Language Technologies, https://doi.org/10.1007/978-3-032-32291-3_3

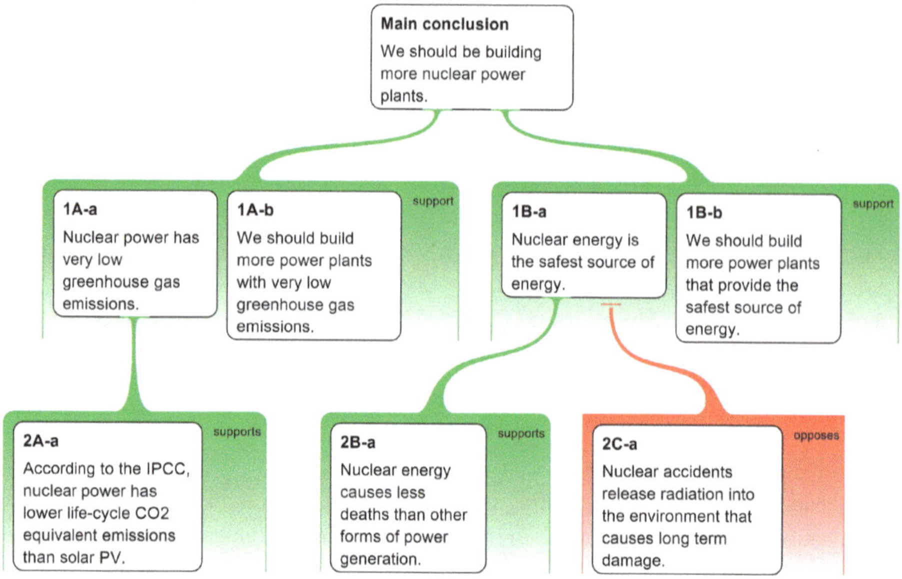

Fig. 3.1 A sample argument map with the main conclusion "We should be building more nuclear power plants." from Davies et al. (2019), used with permission

3.1 Argument Components and Structure

Main Components of Arguments Earlier we said that an argument consists of claims made by the speaker, along with material they present in support of their claim, as well as possible counterconsiderations, and their refutations. We can further define certain terminology used for argument structures. An argument structure is comprised of a constellation of propositions related to a *claim* (also called *standpoint* or *conclusion*), which is the proposition that the argument seeks to establish. Other propositions are used as *premises*, which are brought to bear, in *support* of the conclusion, and sometimes also to *attack* it. Any claim may play the role of final conclusion of some argument, and any conclusion can be made into a premise supporting further reasoning.

Diagramming Arguments into Argument Maps Diagramming can represent an argument's structure. We saw one argument map (or argument diagram) in Fig. 1.1 on p. 8; another is given in Fig. 3.1.

Typically, an argument map represents propositions with some geometric shape such as circles or rectangles. Often there is no visual distinction between the proposition's role in the argument, whether it serves as a top-level claim and final conclusion or an intermediate one. Text representing the proposition may appear directly in the diagram (as in Fig. 3.1) or may be referenced to a key (for instance Fig. 1.1 refers back to the text in Example 1.6). Support and attack relationships between the propositions are distinguished (with different

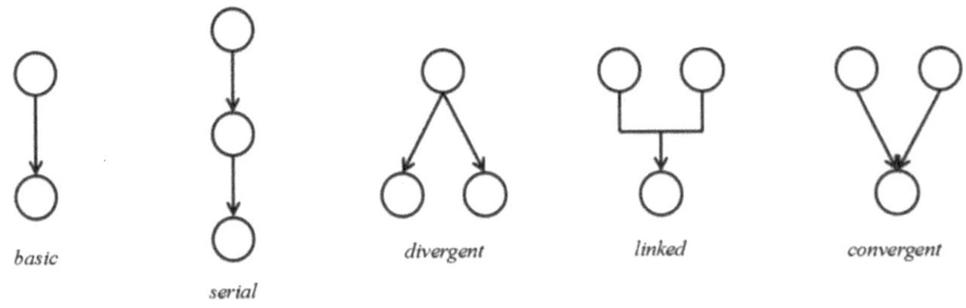

Fig. 3.2 Common basic argument structures from Pyon (2025), used with permission

line types, as in Fig. 1.1, or using colors, as in Fig. 3.1); sometimes only support or attack relationships are given.

Argument maps have been manually constructed for 150 years, particularly in philosophy, and came into legal argumentation in the early twentieth century (Walton 2005). They can show the big picture of a debate or controversy—which is sometimes quite big, such as Robert Horns' large-scale map of the artificial intelligence debate. Titled "Can Computers Think?", and exploring 50 years of philosophical argument, the map spreads over 7 poster-size pages and covers over 800 arguments presented by more than 300 people[2] (Horn 2003). Complex multi-part argument maps can be used to develop coherent public policy positions (Brun and Betz 2016); see for example "The Moral Controversy about Climate Engineering"[3] (Betz and Cacean 2011) and a book of multiple argument maps (Betz and Cacean 2012).

Determining the argument made by a given text can be complex. Interpretation decisions need to be made when mapping a typical text, based in part on how explicit and coherent the text is.

Basic, Serial, Divergent, Linked, Convergent The structure of arguments, including the relation of argument components to one another can also be considered, as shown in Fig. 3.2. Various proposals have been made. The essential distinction is whether there are multiple distinct premises that each stand alone to support a claim (convergent), whether two reasons together strengthen each other (linked), or whether a chain of reasoning is required where one premise supports an interim conclusion, which is the premise of the next argument (e.g. if p, then q, if q then r; serial), or where a single premise supports two or more conclusions (divergent). Some graphs and examples are shown compactly in Wei and Prakken (2012). Henkemans (2000) surveys historical approaches and enduring philosophical questions about distinguishing these structure types. Subtleties do arise; for instance,"[S]ome arguments contain assertions that have a bearing on conclusion support

[2] http://debategraph.org/Details.aspx?nid=75 (accessed January 15, 2026)

[3] http://www.argunet.org/2013/05/13/mapping-the-climate-engineering-controversy-a-case-of-argument-analysis-driven-policy-advice/ (accessed January 15, 2026)

but are not direct evidence for the conclusion," (Grennan 1997, pp. 71–72). This is an issue of relevance of conclusions, related to the knowledge of the hearer.

Objections, Counterarguments, and Counterconsiderations Argumentation theorists have spilled considerable ink cataloging the different ways of objecting to an argument. Critical questioning, making a procedural objection, and putting forth a new argument are examples.

A *counterargument* is an argument that attacks another argument. A counterargument may attack different parts of the given argument (one or more premises, the conclusion, and/or their inferential link) (Walton 2009). Some types of counterarguments have names. Pollock (1987, pages 40–41) distinguishes two types of counterarguments:[4] a *rebutter* gives a "reason for denying" the conclusion while an *undercutter* "attack[s] the connection between the reason[i.e., premise] and the conclusion rather than attacking the conclusion directly". In Sect. 9.2 we discuss counterargument generation.

Anticipated objections may be incorporated as *counterconsiderations* from the hearer's standpoint, as we discussed in Chap. 1 with Example 1.6 and Fig. 1.1. Argumentation theorists have experimentally studied how persuasive it can be to give counterconsiderations (Amjarso 2010). Counterconsiderations arise repeatedly in Sects. 4.2.4, 5.2.1, and 7.1.1 later.

Granularity Arguments are recursive, interlocking structures. The conclusion of one argument may be the premise of the next argument, building a more complex tree. Wyner et al. (2015, p. 51) distinguish between three different kinds of argument based on the features of this tree: an Argument (capital A) that cannot be subdivided into any other parts that are still arguments ("a one-step reason for a claim"); a Case, with only supporting evidence for a claim ("a chain of reasoning leading towards a claim"); and a Debate which has both supporting and conflicting evidence ("reasons for and against a claim (Debate)").

When we want to think about the internal structure of the argument, this distinction is helpful. The internal structure of an Argument of this sort is just made up of the components we discussed above. By contrast, a Case must have multiple inference steps, but without any attacks on the central claim. And the Debate can be broken into two Cases: one for the claim and one against it.

3.2 Extension of Classical Inference with Defeasible Reasoning

Argumentation extends classical inference, enabling tentative conclusions. By contrast, in classical logic, the conclusion is guaranteed to hold whenever the premises hold, using *classical inference rules*.

[4] More precisely, Pollock calls them 'rebutting defeaters' and 'undercutting defeaters'.

Defeasibility Argumentation is *defeasible*: it considers tentative conclusions, which can be revised when new information comes to light. That is, argumentation admits belief revision, is defeasible, and follows a *non-monotonic* logic. See Pollock (1987) for a classic treatment of defeasible reasoning, including distinguishing undercutting and rebutting (discussed above) and Koons (2025) for a recent survey on defeasibility.

Classical Inference Rules In classical logic, however, the conclusion is guaranteed to hold whenever the premises hold, using *classical inference rules*, such as syllogism, modus ponens, and modus tollens.

A *syllogism* derives a conclusion via inference from two premises which share a related term. For example:

(3.1) Socrates is a man; (*Minor premise*)
Every man is mortal; (*Major premise*)
Therefore, Socrates is mortal. (*Conclusion*)

A syllogism's premises are called minor and major. This distinction is based on which term they contain; the minor term is identified by the subject ('Socrates') of the conclusion while the major term is identified by the predicate ('mortal') of the conclusion. The rule *modus ponens* enables deriving the consequent, or right-hand side of a conditional:

(3.2) Given if p, then q.
Given p.
Therefore, q.

The rule *modus tollens* enables ruling out the antecedent, or left-hand side of a conditional:

(3.3) Given if p, then q.
Given not q.
Therefore, not p.

See Prior (2006) for further examples. In order to categorize reasoning patterns and fallacies, argumentation theory has collected its own schemes.

3.3 Argumentation Schemes

Argumentation schemes document common types of argumentation, and their inferential structures, which can be used to identify and evaluate real-world arguments.

An argumentation scheme expresses a defeasible inference rule for showing the acceptability of a standpoint. Various treatments of argumentation schemes, highlighting different aspects, have been given, with wide variation in the number of schemes. An authoritative overview of influential approaches can be found in Walton et al. (2018). Uses of argumentation schemes in artificial intelligence, including argument mining, are reviewed in Macagno (2021). An excellent review of argument models alongside corpora is given by Cardoso et al. (2023). Models are also discussed in other surveys of argument mining (Lytos et al. 2019). And Sviridova et al. (2026) include a thorough review of argument models in their survey on mining implicit argument structures. After introducing various argumentation schemes below, we discuss corpora using argumentation schemes later in this chapter in Sect. 3.6.8, and we return to annotation studies on argumentation schemes later in the book in Sect. 8.1.

3.3.1 Walton's Argumentation Schemes

Walton, Reed, and Macagno's Compendium of Schemes collects 60 schemes, along with critical questions that identify the potential points of weakness in an argument (Walton et al. 2008). One such scheme is *Position to Know*:

Major Premise: Source a is in a position to know about things in a certain subject domain S containing proposition A.
Minor Premise: a asserts that A (in Domain S) is true (false).
Conclusion: A is true (false).

They list three critical questions:

1. Is a in a position to know whether A is true (false)?
2. Is a an honest (trustworthy, reliable) source?
3. Did a assert that A is true (false)?

Critical questions point to potential weakness of a given scheme. Asking a critical question creates a burden of proof on the person advancing the argument.
Note here that the structure of different premises is sometimes distinguished, e.g. the minor premise "serves as independent evidence or support for the conclusion" whereas the major premise does not (Grennan 1997, p. 75).

We review several corpora based on Walton's argumentation schemes in Sect. 3.6.8; they were particularly influential in early argument mining research.

3.3.2 Argumentum Model of Topics

The Argumentum Model of Topics (AMT) (Rigotti and Greco Morasso 2010) draws on the dialectic study of argument patterns of *topoi* and *loci*, from ancient and medieval rhetoric

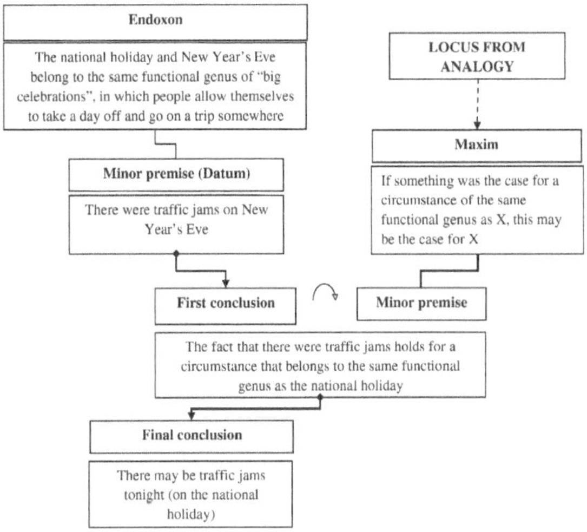

Fig. 3.3 An example argument using the Argumentum Model of Topics from Rigotti and Greco Morasso (2010, p. 499), used with permission

(see also Rapp 2023, Section 7). The name of a scheme, such as *cause-effect* or *analogy*, is only the first level: the procedural starting point. At the second level, certain inference patterns that the authors call 'maxims' are needed. In the third, each maxim activates a rule, such as modus ponens or modus tollens. An example maxim is the following (Rigotti and Greco Morasso 2010, p. 495):

1. If a certain goal is to be achieved, it is reasonable to activate a cause chain allowing to reach it
2. If no causal chain is available, the goal cannot be achieved
3. If a certain behavior is not oriented towards a goal (as it cannot be considered a proper human action), it cannot be endowed with any property typically congruous (Rigotti and Rocci 2001) with human action (responsibility, merit, guilt and so on).

Semantic analysis is used to fill the gap between the scheme type and the maxim. For instance, in the AMT analysis (Rigotti and Greco Morasso 2010) shown in Fig. 3.3, an assumption in the audience's common ground ('endoxon', following Aristotle) is made explicit, namely that the national holiday and New Year's Eve are comparable ("belong to the same functional genus"). Rigotti and Greco Morasso's AMT approach is more fine-grained than others, since a particular maxim must be specified and its applicability justified. A small amount of corpus annotation has experimented with AMT as we discuss in Sect. 3.6.8.

3.3.3 Pragma-Dialectic Argumentation Schemes and Beyond

Next we discuss pragma-dialectic argumentation schemes and work using and going beyond those schemes in order to operationalize argument categorization.

Pragma-Dialectic Argumentation Schemes The classical pragma-dialectic approach classifies schemes into three types: *sign* (reasoning from a sign based on what is generally the case), *comparison* (reasoning by similarity), and *cause* (reasoning using instrumentality) (Hitchcock and Wagemans 2011).

As a prototypical example of the second type, the 'argument from comparison' scheme compares two situations and uses their similarity as a justification. Analyzing "It's not at all necessarily to give James 10 dollars allowance, because his brother always got just 5 dollars a week." Hitchcock and Wagemans (2011, p. 187) write:

1 James (X) does not need 10 dollars a week (Y).
1.1 James' brother (Z) did not need 10 dollars a week (Y).
1.1′ James (X) is similar to James' brother with respect to the sum needed for their weekly allowance

along with three critical questions for the comparison scheme:

1. Are the things that are compared actually comparable?
2. Are there enough relevant similarities between the things that are compared?
3. Are there any relevant differences between the things that are compared?

The other two main pragma-dialectic schemes, sign and cause, have similar considerations; variants and subtypes of each of the three types are recognized.

Periodic Table of Arguments Wagemans's Periodic Table of Arguments (Wagemans 2016) builds on the subject-predicate structure of the pragma-dialectical schemes, the fact/value/policy typology of propositions (Ehninger and Brockriede 1963, p. 211), and the Aristotelian tradition of *topoi*. In continued development, Wagemans has updated the table visualization and classified additional schemes as shown in Fig. 3.4 (Wagemans 2025).[5]

Wagemans's Periodic Table of Arguments classifies argument schemes with three distinctions: form, substance, and lever. Form places the argument in a particular quarter (or quadrant) of Fig. 3.4: The top right is the α quadrant, moving counterclockwise to the β, γ, δ quadrants. Argument form describes the structural connection between the conclusion and premise.

Inside a given quadrant, grey boxes in the middle of Fig. 3.4 describe half-column groups of arguments sharing both form and substance. Argument substance indicates the content being related. Within the α and β quadrants, two letters are used, referring to the

[5] See also https://periodic-table-of-arguments.org (accessed January 13, 2026).

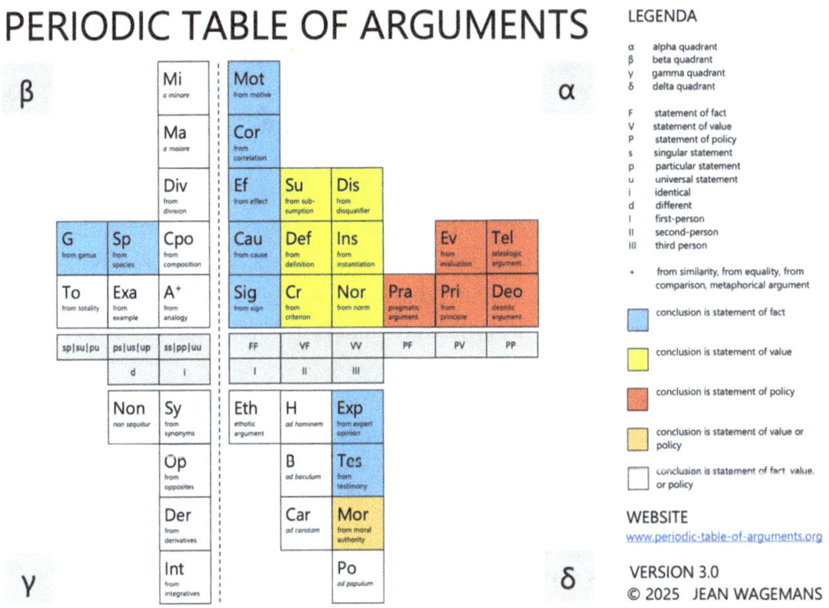

Fig. 3.4 Wagemans' Periodic Table of Arguments (2025 version 3.0) classifies argument schemes with three distinctions. First, form determines the quadrant. Then, substance narrows to a given half-column (group name in grey boxes). Finally, by also considering the lever, the precise argument type is classified with a specific name and symbol. Used with permission

conclusion (first letter) and the premise (second letter). In the α quadrant, letters refer to the basis of the propositions—fact (F) (empirically checkable statements of how things are), value (V) (judgements, evaluations, or appraisals), or policy (P) (what should be done). In the β quadrant, letters indicate the generalization level of the propositions—singular (s), particular (p), or universal (u). Describing γ and δ argument substance requires just a single letter. In the γ quadrant, the semantic relationship from the premise to the conclusion, is classified as identical (i) or different (d). The δ quadrant classifies how the speaker presented the argument: from the first (I), second (II), or third (III) person.

The argument lever indicates the reasoning pattern: why the premise makes the conclusion more acceptable. Given the form, substance, and lever, an argument type gets a name, abbreviation, and position.

For example, "That building really needs to be torn down (P) because that building is one of the most ugly buildings in town (V)" (extracted from Segments 0 and 3 of Example 1.6) can be classified as an α argument with the general form "a is X because a is Y" (see Wagemans 2025). It is a PV argument, with a policy (P) conclusion about an action we should take and value (V) premise given an evaluation. There are two possible types: principled argument (Pri) and argument from evaluation (Ev); the latter is more plausible.

In recent years, corpus annotation has operationalized the Periodic Table of Arguments as we discuss in Sect. 3.6.8.

3.4 Informal Argumentation beyond Argument Schemes

Bentahar et al. (2010) classify argumentation models into rhetorical models, dialogical models, and monological models. These types of models are complementary, each coming from different perspectives, as shown in Table 3.1. Monological models view arguments as tentative proofs, and link premises and claims to describe the microstructure: the internal inference structure of each argument. Rhetorical models view arguments based on an audience's perception, and link whole arguments in a rhetorical structure emphasizing the persuasion structure of arguments. Finally, dialogical models view arguments through the lens of defeasible reasoning and link whole arguments in a macrostructure: the dialogical structure.

Next we will cover some prototypical models exemplifying the monological, rhetorical, and dialogical perspectives. In particular, we discuss the Toulmin model, *The New Rhetoric*, and the Inference Anchoring Theory model, which respectively exemplify monological, rhetorical, and dialogical models as described by Bentahar et al. (2010, pp. 213–215). We also discuss the Issue-Based Information Systems (IBIS) model, which does not fit neatly into these three types.

3.4.1 Toulmin Model

One of the most influential models of argumentation, the Toulmin model, was first proposed by British philosopher Stephen Toulmin in 1958. This model takes a monological view of argumentation, focusing on the internal structure of an argument, which is viewed as a tentative proof. The Toulmin model has a detailed internal structure, as shown in Fig. 3.5. In the model, a claim is defeasibly supported by its grounds (also called the data), according to some warrant. If necessary, the warrant may be further supported by a backing. Qualifiers or rebuttals can also be diagrammed, but are not required.

In Fig. 3.5, the claim is "Anne now has red hair". Its grounds is "Anne is one of Jack's sisters". Its warrant is "Any sister of Jack's may be taken to have red hair", which has the backing, "All his sisters have previously been observed to have red hair." Its qualifier is "presumably". Its rebuttal is "unless Anne has dyed/ gone white/ lost her hair. . . ."

Table 3.1 Bentahar, Moulin, and Bélanger's taxonomy of argumentation models, adapted from (Bentahar et al. 2010, p. 215)

Model type	Argument evaluation is based on	What is linked	How they are linked	Structure
Monological	Tentative proofs	Premises, claims	Internal inference structure	Microstructure
Rhetorical	Audience's perception	Whole arguments	Persuasion structure	Rhetorical structure
Dialogical	Defeasible reasoning	Whole arguments	Dialogical structure	Macrostructure

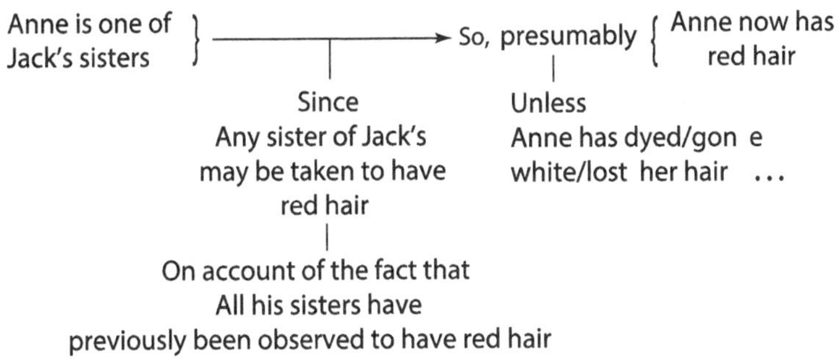

Fig. 3.5 Sample Toulmin diagram from Toulmin (2003), used with permission

The Toulmin model has been particularly widely used in argument mapping and education. Modified Toulmin models have been used in several corpora for argument mining, as we discuss in Sects. 3.6.3 and 3.6.6.

3.4.2 The New Rhetoric

Perelman and Olbrechts-Tyteca's 1969 book *The New Rhetoric: A Treatise on Argumentation* has been very influential. It takes persuasion and audience as central concerns: Argumentation, in their view, cannot be reduced to formal defeasible logic. Rather, arguments seek to persuade a given audience, or to convince the universal audience. Argumentation is thus persuasive act involving two or more interlocutors, and it is "relative to the audience to be influenced" (Perelman and Olbrechts-Tyteca 1969, p. 19). From this perspective, "The goal of all argumentation... is to create or increase the adherence of minds to the theses presented for their assent." (Perelman and Olbrechts-Tyteca 1969, p. 45). We can describe this as a rhetorical approach to argumentation.

3.4.3 Inference Anchoring Theory (IAT)

Inference Anchoring Theory (IAT) (Budzyńska and Reed 2011; Reed and Budzyńska 2011), models the connections between utterances in dialogue, and the locutions put forward by these utterances. IAT connects the dialogical process of argumentation (making an argument) with the monological argument (the reasons for a claim) produced (see Hitchcock 2007). To describe the argumentative connections, IAT proposes illocutionary schemes that describe how speech acts are performed in dialogue.

Example illocutionary schemes (see, e.g., Reed 2011) connect locutions to the logical arguments that they put forward, as shown in Fig. 3.6. Their main elements are transitions between statements, indicating the illocutionary force (e.g., asserting, challenging,

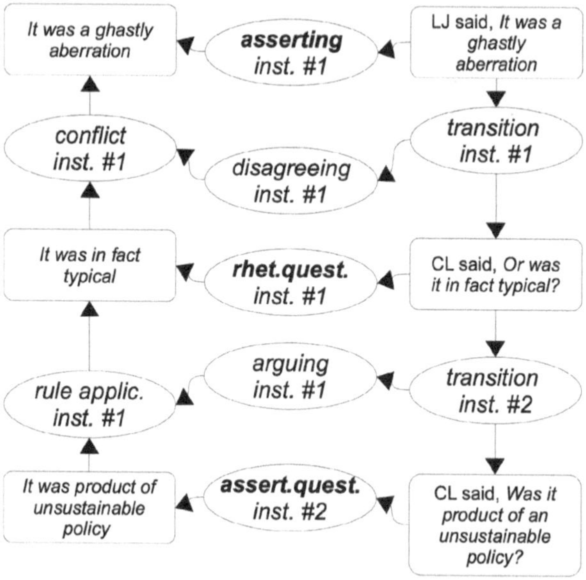

Fig. 3.6 Sample annotation for Inference Anchoring Theory based on Budzynska et al. (2014). Dialogue moves and the transitions between dialogue moves (on the right) are connected to their illocutionary force (in the middle). The propositional content of the dialogue, and inferences/conflicts between propositions, are represented on the left

questioning, arguing). IAT enables locutions in ordinary, everyday conversations to be translated into a dialogue game.

Locutions may contain propositions, but properties of locution events (such as when or where they are spoken or by whom) may be important, so locution events themselves can also be used in arguments (e.g., about the speaker's communicative ability or motivation or to establish that someone really said something). Thus, Reed and Budzyńska (2011) describe pragmatics as the connection between the locutions and the logical arguments put forward.

IAT was developed with argument mining in mind, and its annotation can rely on software tools OVA+/OVA3 (Janier et al. 2014).[6] IAT has been used in various corpora; one example, combining IAT with the Periodic Table of Arguments is discussed in Sect. 3.6.8.

3.4.4 IBIS Model

Not all models fit neatly into Bentahar's taxonomy. For instance, the IBIS model—Issue-Based Information Systems—was proposed in 1970 as a coordination and documentation

[6] https://ova.arg.tech (accessed January 15, 2026) and https://github.com/arg-tech/OVA3 (accessed January 15, 2026).

system for political decision-making such as in urban planning (Kunz and Rittel 1970). It is a process for turning an unstructured problem (a controversial topic in a particular context) into a decision. Parts of the controversial topic are framed as *issues*—questions that can be debated with *arguments* either pro or con. *Questions of fact* can reference external information.

IBIS has inspired numerous systems, including a computational argumentation formalism called the *Quantitative Argumentation Debate (QuAD) framework* (Baroni et al. 2015) which connects issues with questions, answers, pros, and cons.

3.5 Formal Models of Argumentation

Argumentation theory operates on a spectrum from formal to informal. We next describe models on the formal end of the spectrum, such as Dung's *argumentation frameworks*. These models enable computational evaluation in formal systems called *argument solvers*, which we return to in Sect. 10.1.3.

3.5.1 Dung's Argumentation Frameworks

Dung's influential 1995 paper (Dung 1995) models the attack structure between arguments. Dung is not concerned with the internal structure of the argument or with support relationships: this is a macroscopic view of argumentation in which constellations of arguments are evaluated based on defeasible reasoning.

An *argumentation framework* is a directed graph whose nodes represent arguments and whose edges represent relationships between arguments. More formally, Dung defines an argument framework as a pair $\langle S, attacks \rangle$ where S is a set of arguments and $attacks$ is a binary relationship on the arguments contained in $S \times S$. All arguments are considered to have the same strength and each attack is considered to be successful, unless it is in turn attacked. For instance, in Fig. 3.7, A attacks B and B attacks C. In this situation, it is not coherent to accept both B and either its attacker (A) or what it attacks (C). Figure 3.8 shows a more complex argument framework from Betz (2016).

Based on Dung's framework, *argument solvers* (Sect. 10.1.3) can compute the subsets (*extensions*) satisfying some property. Semantics (e.g. *credulous*, *skeptical*) are used to determine which coherent sets of arguments are jointly *acceptable* (Dung 1995). An argument a is *acceptable* with respect to the set that defends it. (A set S *defends* an

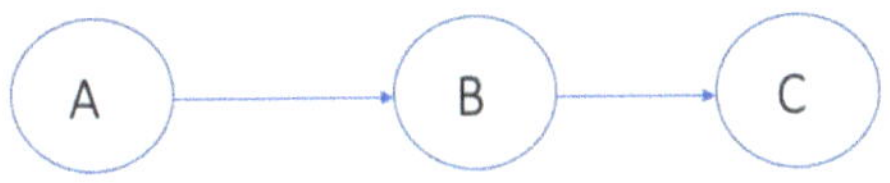

Fig. 3.7 In this example using Dung's argumentation framework, A attacks B and B attacks C. The admissible sets are: $\emptyset$, $\{A\}$, $\{B\}$, $\{C\}$, $\{A, C\}$

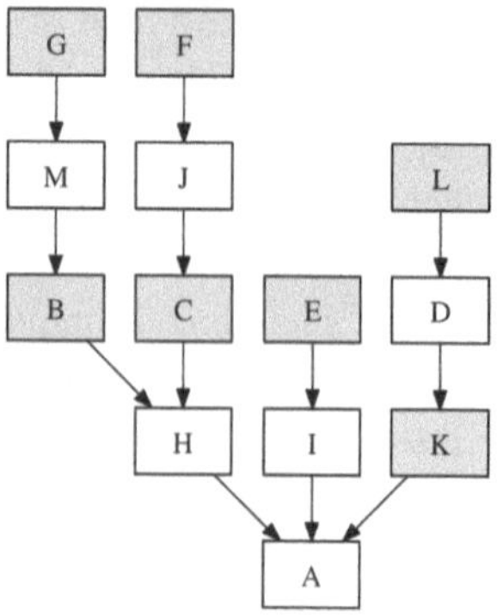

Fig. 3.8 Grey boxes indicate arguments that can belong to some *admissible* set in this labeling using Dung's argumentation framework. The argument A ("...Only nuclear power can supply our energy needs.") is attacked. Betz (2016) constructs this example to articulate a gap between formal acceptability and the evaluation of real-world controversies. Used with permission

argument a if for any argument b that attacks a, S contains an argument that attacks b.) Admissible sets must be conflict-free (no argument attacks another within the set) and consist of acceptable arguments with respect to the set.

3.5.2 Generalizations of Dung's Argumentation Framework

A number of approaches are modified from Dung's argumentation framework and used to evaluate the acceptability of manually and automatically mined arguments. Modifications may involve using probabilities or values to evaluate argument strength, or additional node types, or additional edge types (see e.g., the summary of Brewka et al. 2014 as well as sections of the *The Handbook of Formal Argumentation* Baroni et al. 2018 and Dov Gabbay et al. 2021). Structured argumentation approaches Besnard et al. (2014) may be built on various rule-based formalisms such as Assumption-Based Argumentation (ABA) (Toni 2014), Argumentation Service Platform with Integrated Components (ASPIC+) (Modgil and Prakken 2014), and Defeasible Logic Programming (DeLP) (García and Simari 2014). Below, as examples, we briefly discuss two approaches to structured argumentation.

Bipolar argumentation frameworks (Amgoud et al. 2008) allow two types of relationships, *support* as well as *attack*. They define different acceptability semantics, extending those of Dung.

Abstract dialectical frameworks Brewka and Woltran (2010) and Brewka et al. (2017) generalize Dung's argumentation framework by specifying an acceptance condition for each argument node. This enables abstract dialectic frameworks to express arbitrary relationships (rather than just attacks as in Dung's argumentation framework), and in particular positive and negative weights can be used, also encompassing bipolar argumentation.

3.6 Selected Corpora Influential for Argument Mining

This section selectively reviews corpora that have been particularly influential for argument mining and corpora using specific models. These and other selected corpora are summarized in Appendix A and our corpora website http://purl.org/amresources.

Several reviews focus on corpora: Cardoso et al. (2023) stress the argumentation-theoretic models discussed above. Lindahl and Borin (2024) compile agreement and machine learning results for numerous corpora, and Zhang et al.'s (2022a) review of legal argument mining provides a ready reference to legal corpora.

For general introductory material about corpora, (Jurafsky and Martin 2026, see Corpora in Chapter 2). Corpora typically measure inter-annotator agreement with Krippendorff's α, Cohen's κ, or Fleiss' κ; See Artstein and Poesio (2008).

3.6.1 Argument-Annotated Essays (AAE) Corpus, Version 2

The Argument-annotated Essays corpus (AAE)[7] annotation scheme indicates claims, premises, and support/attack relations as shown in Fig. 3.9. AAE has been widely used. It was previously known as the Persuasive Essays Corpus and has been abbreviated as AAE, PE, and PEC in the literature.

AAE version 2 (AAE2) (Stab and Gurevych 2017b) consists of 402 essays (7116 sentences) taken from the essayforum website.[8] AAE2's inter-annotator agreement was 0.81 for MajorClaim, 0.524 for Claim, and 0.824 for Premise in terms of Krippendorf's unitized α. Subsequently, additional layers of annotation have been added to AAE2 for several tasks (see Fig. 3.10).

To get at confirmation bias, also called myside bias, Stab and Gurevych (2016) distinguish AAE2 essays with at least one opposing argument, as opposed to only arguments supporting the author's viewpoint.[9] An inter-annotator agreement study (Krippendorff α

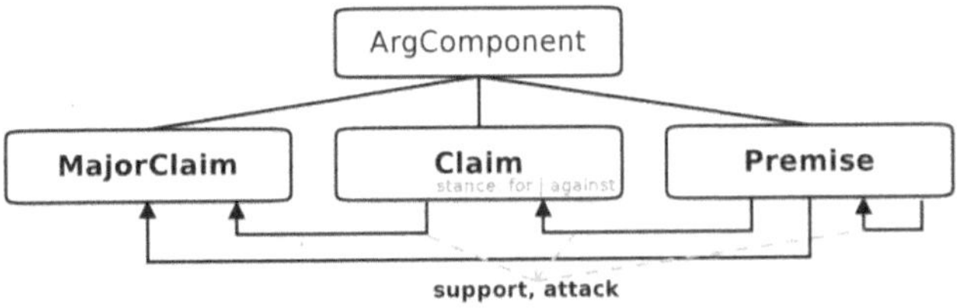

Fig. 3.9 The annotation scheme of AAE1 (Stab and Gurevych 2014a), also adopted for AAE2. Licensed under CC-BY 4.0 International

[7] https://tudatalib.ulb.tu-darmstadt.de/handle/tudatalib/2422 (accessed January 15, 2026).

[8] http://www.essayforum.com (accessed January 15, 2026).

[9] https://tudatalib.ulb.tu-darmstadt.de/handle/tudatalib/2429 (accessed January 15, 2026).

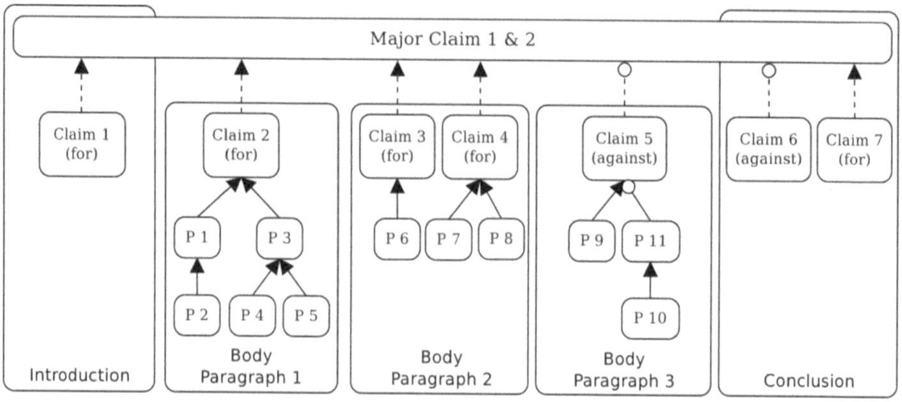

Fig. 3.10 An example essay annotation from AAE2, adapted from Stab and Gurevych (2017b).

0.787 on 80 essays) validates their approach of deriving myside bias from the existing argument structure annotations in AAE2.

Stab and Gurevych (2017a) annotated 1029 essay paragraphs as arguments to assess sufficiency—whether or not the "premises provide enough evidence for accepting or rejecting the claim" (Stab and Gurevych 2017a) (drawing on Johnson and Blair 2006). An inter-annotator agreement study on 433 arguments found Krippendorff α 0.7673. Sources of disagreement were long arguments with many premises; modal verbs (for instance, providing a single example is sufficient when asserting what "can" be); and undetermined qualifiers (e.g., "many").

Fine-grained claim and premise types were added to AAE2 by Schaefer et al. (2023).[10] Three claim types (policy, value, fact) were annotated with an overall Krippendorff's α of 0.52. Six premise types (testimony, statistics, hypothetical-instance, real example, common ground, other) were annotated with an overall α of 0.53).

Influenced by Wachsmuth et al. (2017c)'s analysis of argumentation quality assessment, Marro et al. (2022) annotated AAE2 for rhetorical strategy, cogency, and reasonableness.[11] The annotation of the 1908 arguments from AAE2's 402 essays with highest agreement was rhetorical strategy (ethos, logos, or pathos), with a Fleiss' κ of 0.85. For cogency and reasonableness, they drew on three five-point scales from Stapleton and Wu (2015)'s Analytic Scoring Rubric for Argumentative Writing, analyzing the data provided for a claim (interpreted as cogency); the counterargument data/supporting reasons for alternative points of view (which they refer to as 'Reasonableness Counterargument'); and the rebuttal data (which they refer to as 'Reasonableness Rebuttal'). Agreement for

[10] https://github.com/discourse-lab/arg-essays-semantic-types (accessed January 15, 2026).

[11] https://gitlab.com/santimarro/persuasive-essays-argument-quality-dataset (accessed January 15, 2026).

Topic: The sale of violent video games to minors should be banned		
S1	Violent video games can increase children's aggression	V
S2	Video game addiction is excessive or compulsive use of computer and video games that interferes with daily life	X
S3	Many TV programmers argue that their shows just mirror the violence that goes on in the real world	X
S4	Violent video games should not be sold to children	X
S5	Video game publishers unethically train children in the use of weapons	V

Fig. 3.11 Topic and associated claim candidates from (Levy et al. 2014, p. 1490) which was based on the original corpus (Aharoni et al. 2014).

Cogency was 0.68 Fleiss' κ (collapsing to a 3-point scale improved this to 0.86), 0.78 for Reasonableness Counterargument and 0.84 for Reasonableness Rebuttal. We will return to quality assessment in Chap. 7.

3.6.2 IBM Debater: Claims and Evidence Corpus

The IBM Debater - Claims and Evidence corpus[12] was constructed for Project Debater (see Sect. 1.3) and was previously known as the IBM argumentative structure dataset. The first version (Aharoni et al. 2014; Levy et al. 2014), focuses on claims and evidence manually extracted from Wikipedia on debate motions (topics) selected from the International Debate Education Association's (now defunct) *Debatabase*.

Topic-dependent claims are the basis of all versions; Fig. 3.11 shows example sentences regarded as topic-dependent claims ('V') or not ('X'). (Notice that, in other terminology, the 'topic' would itself qualify as a 'claim', as it could represent a thesis or demand.) Claims need not be complete sentences.

To construct the original corpus (Aharoni et al. 2014), five annotators independently identified supporting and contesting claims for each of 33 topics/debate motions from relevant Wikipedia articles (586 total). 1392 claims were validated from 321 Wikipedia articles. Evidence was sought for 350 of these claims relevant to 12 debates from 104 Wikipedia articles. Annotators examined the claim's source Wikipedia article to identify 1291 evidence statements (529 Anecdotal, 516 Expert, 431 Study, with categories allowed to overlap). Average κ was 0.39 in claim confirmation and 0.4 in evidence confirmation. The released version of the corpus (Rinott et al. 2015) expanded to claims extracted for 58 topics from 547 Wikipedia articles.

With an added stance classification layer, the corpus was re-released as the Claim Stance Dataset (Bar-Haim et al. 2017a). Five annotators annotated the 2394 claims from 55 topics as pro or con with respect to the topic. Manual annotation also separated 550

[12] https://research.ibm.com/haifa/dept/vst/debating_data.shtml (accessed January 15, 2026).

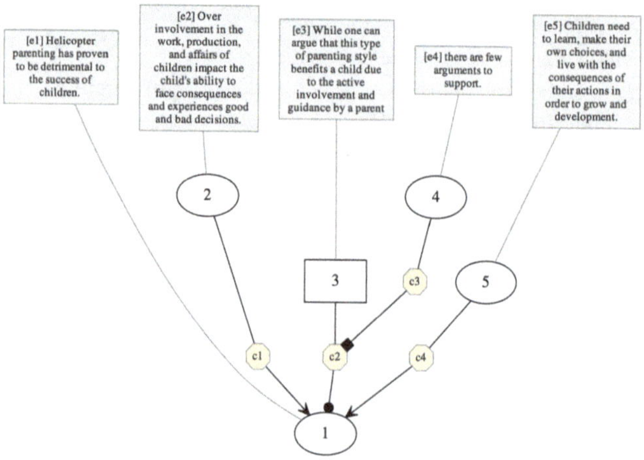

Fig. 3.12 Annotated text from Skeppstedt et al. (2018, p. 157). Relations may support (arrow head), rebut (circle head) or undercut (square head) the main claim 1, from the perspective of a proponent (numbers in ovals) or an opponent (numbers in rectangles). Licensed under CC-BY 4.0 International

claims into factual vs. non-factual claims; distinguished 1750 sentences as subjective vs. objective; and compiled lexicons for each evidence category.

3.6.3 Argumentative Microtext Corpus

The original Argumentative Microtext Corpus,[13] described in Peldszus and Stede (2016b), consists of 112 short argumentative texts written in German and professionally translated into English, which are annotated with complete argument structure trees. The structure, based on Freeman's (2011) modification of the Tolumin model, uses support and several different attack relations. Later, additional annotation layers were added: discourse structure (Stede et al. 2016), argumentation schemes based on Walton's (cf. Sect. 3.6.8) (Reisert et al. 2017) and the AMT (cf. Sect. 3.6.8) (Musi et al. 2018) schemes; we return to annotation studies on argumentation schemes in Sect. 8.1.1.

Subsequently, it was expanded with 205 crowdsourced texts collected in English (Skeppstedt et al. 2018);[14] after filtering, 171 were annotated into 932 argumentative units with support (convergent, example, linked support, restatement) and attack (rebut, undercut, linked attack). Figure 3.12 shows an example.

[13] Available at http://angcl.ling.uni-potsdam.de/resources/argmicro.html (accessed January 15, 2026). It has also been integrated into AIFdb. http://corpora.aifdb.org/Microtext (accessed January 15, 2026).

[14] Available from the same site as the original corpus.

[Calling a debtor at work is counter-intuitive; $]_a$ [if collectors are continuously calling someone at work, other employees may report it to the debtor's supervisor. $]_b$ [Most companies have established rules about receiving or making personal calls during working hours. $]_c$ [If a collector or creditor calls a debtor on his/her cell phone and is informed that the debtor is at work, the call should be terminated. $]_d$ [No calls to employers should be allowed, $]_e$ [as this jeopardizes the debtor's job. $]_f$

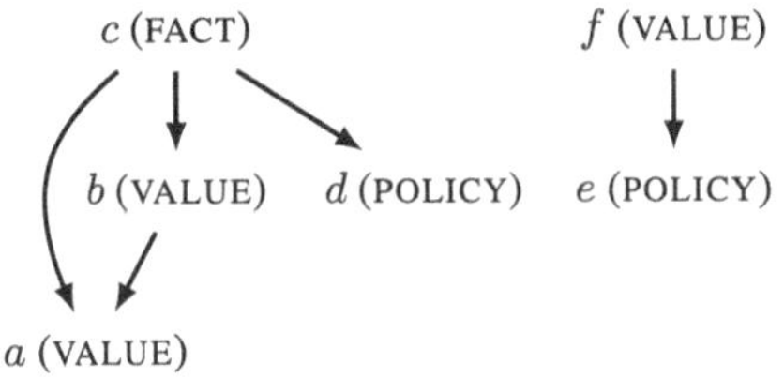

Fig. 3.13 Argumentation structure graph (Niculae et al. 2017, p. 985) from the Cornell eRulemaking Corpus (Park and Cardie 2018). Licensed under CC-BY 4.0 International

3.6.4 Cornell eRuleMaking Corpus

Park and Cardie (2018) released a corpus of user comments on government rule making.[15] Their annotation scheme uses specific argumentative role labels: *policy* and *value* for subjective judgments; *testimony* and *fact* for non-subjective personal experience and objective facts; and *reference* for URLs and citations. Relation types are *reason* and *evidence*. Two annotators agreed with Krippendorff's α of 0.648 for elementary units (sentences, argumentative clauses) and 0.441 for support relations.

Work using the corpus reported that 20% of the comments in the corpus give rise to non-tree representations, and that 28% of the comments are not annotated with any argumentative relations at all (Niculae et al. 2017). Figure 3.13 shows a sample text and annotation, where unit c supports three other units, and furthermore there is no single root (claim).[16]

3.6.5 Rutgers Language of Opposition Corpus

Ghosh et al. (2014) annotated blog comments on posts from technorati.com as shown in Fig. 3.14. Four technical topics were selected, represented by one original post and the

[15] Source website: http://regulationroom.org; the corpus is available at http://www.mathcs.richmond.edu/~jpark/data/jpark_lrec18.zip (accessed January 15, 2026).

[16] The support relation (c, a) results from automatically adding transitive closure over the links.

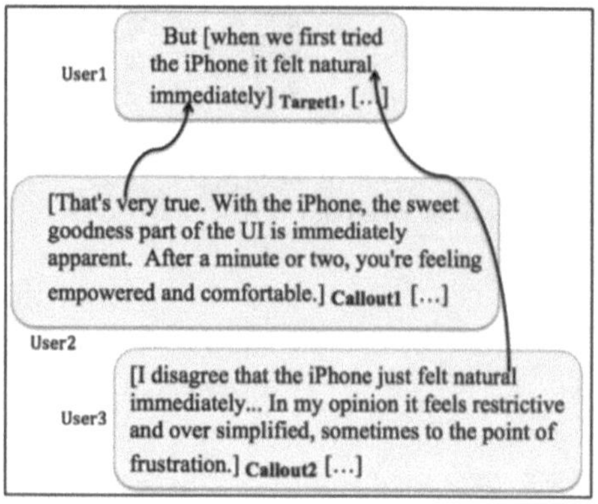

Fig. 3.14 Sample callout/target annotation (Ghosh et al. 2014, p. 39), used with permission

first 100 responding comments. The annotation of 'callout' (a dis/agreeing reaction of a user) and 'target' (the specific phrase that the callout responds to) is based on Pragmatic Argumentation Theory (van Eemeren et al. 1993). Wacholder et al. (2014) discusses the annotation process and the difficulty of interpreting inter-annotator agreement when the F_1 (ranging from 85.3 to 88.5) and Krippendorff's α (from 0.64 to 0.82) differed qualitatively, e.g., the topic with highest F_1 also had lowest Krippendorff's α. The corpus is available for research.[17]

3.6.6 The Web Discourse Corpus

The Web Discourse Corpus (Habernal and Gurevych 2017) modified the Toulmin model (Sect. 3.4.1) when annotating their corpus of user-generated web discourse. They kept the basic assumption of the Toulmin model that the argumentative role of a unit fully determines its position in the argument representation—and thus the scheme has no need to explicitly annotate any relations between units. In contrast to the microtext and persuasive essay schemes, it is hence not possible to build recursive structures (as needed for 'serial support' or complex counter-attack constellations). The annotation therefore is a flat labeling. An example is shown in Fig. 3.15.

However, Habernal and Gurevych did make a number of important modifications to the original Toulmin model. They removed the Qualifier and the Warrant, as these did not play a role in their corpus data. The notion of Backing was slightly redefined and now serves as 'additional evidence', which does not play the same role as a premise but still lends overall support to the argument. In order to account for counter-attacks, they introduce the unit type *Refutation*. And finally, to enable the annotation of texts where the claim is

[17] https://salts.rutgers.edu/identifying-the-language-of-opposition-in-online-interactions/ (accessed January 17, 2026).

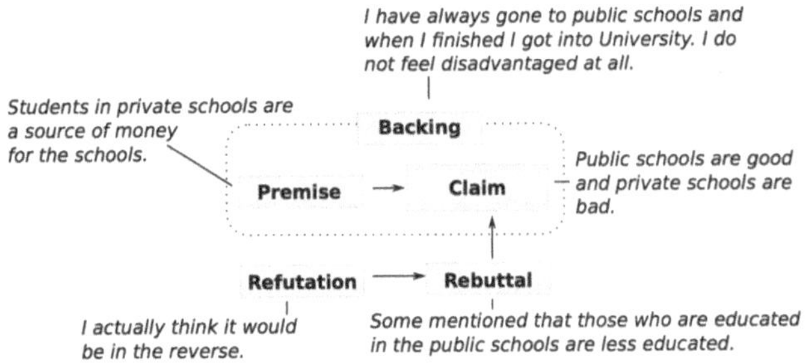

Fig. 3.15 Diagrammatic representation of an annotated argument in the Modified Toulmin Scheme, adapted from (Habernal and Gurevych 2017, p. 144). Copyright ©2017 Association for Computational Linguistics. All rights reserved

not explicit (which is often the case in their corpus), annotators were instructed to add an explicit statement of the author's stance, as inferred from the text.

Since the annotation process consists of breaking the text into units and labeling them, annotator agreement was evaluated in terms of Krippendorff's unitized α; an overall value of 0.48 was achieved. Habernal and Gurevych (2017) provide an in-depth analysis of the various types of disagreement that they found.

3.6.7 Webis-Editorial Corpus

The Webis Editorial corpus[18] (Al Khatib et al. 2016) annotated 300 editorials with argumentative discourse units and the evidence provided/role in the argument (e.g., Anecdote, Assumption, Common Ground, Statistics, Testimony). Editorials were published between December 2014 and January 2015 on three English-language online news sites, *Al Jazeera*, *Fox News*, and *The Guardian*. Agreement between three crowdsourced annotators was Fleiss κ 0.56. Final annotations used majority vote and post-processing to handle common errors; when all three annotators chose a different role, authors chose the final annotation.

3.6.8 Corpus Annotations following Argumentation Theory

Models from argumentation theory have been used in argument mining for corpus annotation; we highlight selected examples below. Many of these corpora are used for NLP tasks related to Argument Reasoning, as we discuss in Chap. 8.

[18] https://webis.de/data/webis-editorials-16.html (accessed January 15, 2026).

Corpus Annotation Using Walton's Argumentation Schemes Walton's argumentation schemes (Sect. 3.3.1) have been used to annotate various corpora, e.g., Green (2015), Song et al. (2014), Schneider et al. (2013b), Lindahl et al. (2019), Visser et al. (2019), Ruiz-Dolz et al. (2024), Reisert et al. (2017), Reed et al. (2008), and Mochales and Ieven (2009). We introduce some of these corpora below.

Starting with 60 Walton argumentation schemes (Walton et al. 2008, Chapter 9), Schneider et al. (2013b)) annotated 741 messages from 72 Wikipedia deletion discussions. In the first two rounds of annotation, one Ph.D. student identified the most prevalent schemes (14 Walton schemes with more than 2% occurrence) and added 3 non-argumentative categories to create an annotation manual. Then in the final two rounds of annotation, two students familiar with the corpus annotated, resulting in Cohen's κ of 0.48. The annotation was used to analyze differences in novice vs. expert Wikipedian arguments and to characterize argument acceptability.

Lindahl et al. (2019) asked Master's students in linguistics to annotate a corpus of 30 Swedish newspaper editorials without pre-segmenting. They started with the 30 most common schemes from Walton (2013) and ultimately found 22 Walton schemes.

Machine-human collaboration created the NLAS-multi corpus (Ruiz-Dolz et al. 2024) by prompting GPT-3.5-turbo to generate both pro and con arguments on 50 topics using 20 argumentation schemes, in both English and Spanish. The prompt used was: "Provide an <scheme> argument <stance> on the topic of <topic> following the argument pattern: <argument_description>." Human annotators with argumentation theory and linguistics expertise checked arguments for conformance; non-conformant arguments were removed with the prompt provided to (the economically more expensive variant) GPT-4 for a second round of checking. Inter-annotator agreement on a 10% subset was 0.65 Cohen's κ in English between four annotators and 0.22 Cohen's κ in Spanish between two annotators. According to the authors, the goal of the corpus is to enable the development of NLP methods that learn linguistic features from stereotyped patterns of argumentative reasoning.

Corpus Annotation Using the Argumentum Model of Topics AMT (Sect. 3.3.2) was used to annotate 30 persuasive essays (Musi et al. 2016) from AAE1 (see Sect. 3.6.1) and 40 microtexts (Musi et al. 2018) in the Argumentative Microtext Corpus (see Sect. 3.6.3). We return to this corpus in Chap. 8.

Corpus Annotation Using the Periodic Table of Arguments The periodic table of arguments has been used to annotate a corpus of transcripts of the first television debate between Clinton and Trump from the US 2016 election (US2016G1tvWAGEMANS)[19] (Visser et al. 2019). Take for example Clinton's statement

[19] Available at https://corpora.aifdb.org/US2016G1tvWAGEMANS(accessed January 15, 2026).

"And we finally need to pass a prohibition on anyone who's on the terrorist watch list from being able to buy a gun in our country. If you're too dangerous to fly, you are too dangerous to buy a gun." Annotators classified this as a 1st order predicate argument (sharing the subject "people on the terrorist watch list") defending a Policy proposal (should not be able to buy a gun) by using an analogy with a Value statement (too dangerous to fly) (Visser et al. 2019).

Corpus Annotation Based on Inference Anchoring Theory IAT (Sect. 3.4.3) has been widely used as a part of dialogue annotation, for example the 2016 US Presidential corpus (Visser et al. 2019) combined IAT for the dialogue structure with the Periodic Table of Arguments (Sect. 3.3.3) as a content classification. The IAT annotation is better described by Visser et al. (2020).

3.6.9 Other Corpora

Many other corpora relevant for argument mining could be highlighted, including for scientific peer reviews (Hua et al. 2019b), scientific argumentation (Lauscher et al. 2018b), legal argumentation (Poudyal et al. 2020), 50 years of US presidential campaign debates (Haddadan et al. 2019) to name a few. We give further details on some of these corpora later in the book, especially when we discuss automatically identifying argumentation schemes in Sect. 8.1. Selected corpora are summarized in Appendix A and a fuller collection of corpora are in the website http://purl.org/amresources.

3.7 Summary

This chapter gave an overview of representing arguments. First, from argumentation theory, we discussed argument components and structure (Sect. 3.1), defeasible reasoning (Sect. 3.2), and argumentation schemes that extend the idea of classical inference (Sect. 3.3). We surveyed important argument models exemplifying informal (Sect. 3.4) and formal (Sect. 3.5) approaches to argumentation. Throughout the book we will see further corpora developed for NLP research adopting these and other models; selected corpora are summarized in Appendix A and the website http://purl.org/amresources collects additional corpora relevant to argument mining. In this chapter we described selected corpora influential for argument mining (Sect. 3.6), highlighting the relationship to well-known argument models.

Argument Unit Identification

4

While the first three chapters gave relatively high-level overviews, we now turn to the computational side of argument mining (AM), where we assume readers to be equipped with a basic background in NLP techniques.

Unlike many of the standard tasks in NLP, the field of AM is not characterized as a single unified process, but as a constellation of a wide array of subtasks, which are of different prominence depending on the goals of the underlying target application. For the core tasks of argument *mining* (Chaps. 4 and 5), this diversity can to a large extent be explained with a split of the field into two directions (cf. Trautmann et al. 2020):

- *Document- or discourse-based AM* aims at uncovering the structure of an unfolding argument in a single text document, or in a (oral or social media) conversation.
- *Information-seeking AM* starts from a given topic or claim, and peruses huge collections of possibly heterogeneous documents (which need not be predominantly argumentative in nature) to detect self-contained argumentative statements that are relevant to the topic/claim.

The first direction was constitutive when AM became established as a field, while the second received traction predominantly by the IBM Debater project—the debating machine adopts a standpoint and sifts through its memory of text material to find arguments pro and contra the standpoint—and was henceforth adapted also by other research on argument retrieval.

Furthermore, even within these directions, there is a considerable variety in task definitions. For example, in order to obtain the gist of a social media conversation, it can be sufficient to extract claims and purported evidence material from each individual message of the thread. By contrast, for running a deep analysis of the argumentation strategies in the editorials from left-wing vs. right-wing newspapers, each text ideally should be mapped to

M. Stede et al., *Argument Mining*, Synthesis Lectures on Human Language Technologies, https://doi.org/10.1007/978-3-032-32291-3_4

a complete constellation of statements, their argumentative relationships, and the reasoning patterns underlying those relationships.

Due to such differing goals, a number of concrete AM tasks have been proposed over the years, and quite heterogeneous datasets have resulted as a consequence. In the literature, it has become commonplace to refer to the tasks with particular abbreviations, which are, however, not always used in the exact same way. In Chaps. 4 and 5 we will use the most common ones:

- *ACS: Argument Component Segmentation* distinguishes argumentative from non-argumentative text portions and demarcates individual argument components (ACs).
- *ACTC: Argument Component Type Classification* determines the types of given ACs, using a coarse-grained (e.g., claim, premise) or a more fine-grained (e.g., policy claim, fact claim, value claim) type inventory.
- *ARI: Argument Relation Identification* detects the presence of some (indetermined) argument relation between two ACs.
- *ARTC: Argument Relation Type Classification* determines the types of given relations (e.g., support, attack).

To illustrate, in the following example, adding the brackets and indices would be the result of the ACS step:

(4.1) If you wanna hear my view, I think that [the EU should allow rescue boats in the Mediterranean Sea.]$_A$ [Many innocent refugees will die if there are no rescue boats.]$_B$ [Nothing justifies to endanger the life of innocent people.]$_C$

Now the following information would be computed:

- *Coarse-grained ACTC:* $A \rightarrow$ claim; $B \rightarrow$ premise; $C \rightarrow$ premise
- *Fine-grained ACTC:* $A \rightarrow$ policy_claim; $B \rightarrow$ assumption_premise; $C \rightarrow$ common-ground_premise
- *ARI:* $R_1(B, A)$; $R_2(C, A)$
- *ARTC:* $R_1 \rightarrow$ support; $R_2 \rightarrow$ support

In this chapter, we address the ACS and ACTC tasks. Section 4.1 introduces the notion of argumentative units in text and shows computational approaches to their identification. In Sect. 4.2 we turn to the types and subtypes of argument components and to their automatic detection. Finally, Sect. 4.3 provides a bird's eye view of the methods that have been applied in argument mining (especially for ACTC) over the years, where a clear trend toward the integration of the sub-steps can be observed. Along the way, we will touch upon a range of other, more specific variants of AM tasks that researchers have addressed. The approaches to detecting argumentative *relations* between ACs will be discussed in the subsequent chapter.

4.1 Segmentation: Finding Boundaries of Argumentative Units

Segmenting a text into smaller units is relevant not only in argument mining, but also in discourse parsing or in other information extraction tasks. In AM, however, the specific challenge is to find units that have an appropriate form for making a contribution to an argument. Before we embark on this task, however, we take a quick look at the problem of identifying complete *texts* as argumentative.

Prelude: Distinguishing Argumentative from Non-Argumentative Texts The vast majority of work in argument mining research revolves around existing datasets and thus assumes that the text material under consideration for some AM task does indeed contain arguments. However, when arguments are being sought 'in the wild', which is the perspective of many practical applications, it can make sense to first check whether a given text is or is not argumentative. This is a classification problem that can target the *discourse mode* argumentative (see Sect. 2.4), or it can differentiate various *genres* from each other and thereby identify a genre that is likely to contain arguments. In a study investigating human agreement, Habernal and Gurevych (2017) asked three annotators to label 990 short documents (comments or forum posts from the web) as either *persuasive* or *non-persuasive*[1] with respect to the discussion topic and reached a Fleiss κ of 0.59. The authors inspected the cases of disagreement and noted a high dependency of decisions on annotators' familiarity with the topic, and on the context provided in the discussion website.

A similar type of documents that are small to begin with is Twitter/X posts—these are very often being classified as a whole, without any internal segmentation. For instance, Dusmanu et al. (2017) used a feature set including n-grams, Twitter-specific tokens like emoticons, dependency triples, and sentiment information for classifying complete tweets as argumentative or not, and they report an F_1-score of 0.78, obtained by a linear regression classifier.

For longer text, one line of research focused specifically on newspaper text and its division into non-argumentative material (reports, etc.) and potentially-argumentative parts (editorials, commentary, letters to the editor). Petrenz and Webber (2011) studied this task for the New York Times Annotated Corpus (NYTAC),[2] and found that models based on linguistic features outperformed bag-of-word models, which were more sensitive to shifts in topic than to shifts in text type. In the same spirit, Krüger et al. (2017) used texts with different topics, and they also varied the newspaper and the time of origin of the texts, by working with the Brown, NYTAC, and Wall Street Journal corpora. For distinguishing editorials and letters to the editor from news texts, they experimented with support

[1] This dichotomy is not identical, but close to the non-/argumentative distinction. Cf. footnote 14 in Habernal and Gurevych (2017, p. 140).

[2] https://catalog.ldc.upenn.edu/LDC95T21 (accessed January 15, 2026).

vector machines (SVMs, Joachims 2006) using a large linguistic feature set (including connectives, communication verbs, pronoun types, tense, and many others) and showed that it generally outperformed PoS and bag-of-lemma approaches. Alhindi et al. (2020) continued on this endeavour with experiments involving SVMs, BERT (Devlin et al. 2019) and recursive neural networks (RNNs), testing the robustness against changes in topic or publisher of the newspaper. In addition, they showed the utility of argumentative features (the presence of claims and premises, computed by a classifier trained on the dataset of Al Khatib et al. 2016) for the task, and thereby demonstrated the interdependence between the argument mining and the genre classification problems.

4.1.1 Argumentative Discourse Units (ADUs)

From EDUs to ADUs Once target texts are selected, one turns to finding the argumentative units therein. The notion of ADU is derived from that of the *Elementary Discourse Unit* (EDU), which is used in the field of *discourse parsing* and denotes the minimal linguistic unit that makes an independent contribution to the overall message of a text. In Example (4.2), the complex sentence consists of two EDUs that are semantically linked by the discourse relation *Concession*.

(4.2) [Lanzarote is one of my favorite islands,]$_{edu1}$ [even though the weather can be a little unpredictable even in summer.]$_{edu2}$

EDUs are defined structurally as syntactic *clauses* (loosely, a phrase with a verb), though not all types of clauses also form EDUs. The ADU, similarly, is the smallest linguistic unit that can make a complete independent contribution to an argument (Peldszus and Stede 2013). We can characterize it as:

> A span of text that plays a single role for the argument being analyzed, and is demarcated by neighboring text spans that play a separate argumentative role, or none at all.

This being a functional definition, there are in principle no clear structural constraints on what constitutes an ADU. Identifying ADUs can therefore be difficult, also for humans, as it is not always completely clear where in text an argument, or a part of it, starts and ends.

The relationship between EDUs as generic minimal units of discourse and ADUs as specific minimal units of argument is one of inclusion: ADUs may be larger than EDUs, or coincide with them; but they are never shorter. An empirical study by Saveleva et al. (2021a) started the AM process with a discourse parser that is trained to identify EDUs, and then found many cases where adjacent EDUs had to be fused to form an ADU. Here is one of their examples (Saveleva et al. 2021a, p. 47):

(4.3) [Congress have no power]$_{edu}$ [to pass a legislation]$_{edu}$ [forcing religious institutions about marriage.]$_{edu}$

→ [Congress have no power to pass a legislation forcing religious institutions about marriage.]$_{adu}$

The underlying problem of ADU identification is that a—possibly complex—argument originates in a speaker's mind, where cognitive processes involving different types of information map it to a linguistic form. The ADU then is merely a reflex of an underlying semantic representation or *proposition*.[3] Argument mining analyses these reflexes, and the majority of the practical research is indeed content with regarding an argument as a sequence of surface tokens. An exception is the work on Inference Anchoring Theory (see Sect. 3.4.3), where surface form and underlying proposition are distinguished in the modeling. Formally deriving propositions from textual ADUs, as objects that can enter into further computation, is not easy; Jo et al. (2019) describe in detail a method that involves reference resolution (e.g., for pronouns), the detection of reported speech, and other NLP tasks.

Key Statements So far, we defined ADUs as segments of a text that contribute to its argumentative structure in various ways, which later on get differentiated from one another. Research by Zelch et al. (2025a) proposes to single out one particular group of ADUs that collectively can be taken to represent the argumentative gist of the text; the authors call them *key statements*. Following the perspective of information-seeking IM, it is assumed that the overarching claim, for which the text provides a standpoint, is already given. Key statements are those ADUs that best represent the main arguments, similar to the notion of *central proposition* studied by Misra et al. (2015). In other words, ADUs that the author may use to in turn back up the key statements are disregarded in this analysis. Figure 4.1 shows an example. The text is from an online discussion on vegetarianism and shows the key statements underlined.

Zelch et al. (2025a) stress the high degree of subjectivity in exactly demarcating key statements. Therefore, they propose an elaborate evaluation methodology that (amongst other factors) allows for fuzzy boundaries; in the figure, the color coding indicates which material is regarded as optionally included in the key statements. Specifically, the authors posit that any segment (produced by human or automatic annotation) that (i) completely covers a single key statement and (ii) does not overlap with other key statements is regarded as a match. Technically, the authors experimented with various automatic segmentation methods and found that recent LLMs perform best, but the problem is overall quite difficult.

Generalizability As we have seen, the AC segmentation task has two different facets: (i) It distinguishes argumentative from non-argumentative portions in the text, and (ii) within

---

[3] Recall that at the very beginning of Chap. 1 we quoted from a definition of argument as a *constellation of propositions*.

Thanks for the timely response. To address my opponents argument, I want to emphasize that eating meat isn't necessary for maximum physical development. All of the vitamins, minerals etc. in meat can also be found in other foods. And does the taste of meat really outweigh the costs of killing? My conclusion: Vegetarianism is a good thing because it saves animals' lives, improves one's health and helps the environment. I didn't bring religion into this debate but almost all of the major religions (even the ones that allow meat eating) agree that vegetarianism is better than eating meat.

Fig. 4.1 Example of key statement annotation from Zelch et al. (2025a, p. 228). Key statements are underlined; their optional supplementary segments are colored. Licensed under CC-BY 4.0 International.

the argumentative portions, it separates different ACs from each other. Especially the first facet raises the question of how well models for making the binary distinction generalize from their training dataset to others, and how this is influenced by the genre and the domain (topic) of the texts. One genre-driven factor, for example, is the *density* of argumentative units: A short social media post may be completely argumentative, while in a news text whose main function is to report on certain events, there may be only a small proportion of ADUs.

A thorough study on the generalizability of models for separating argumentative and non-argumentative sentences was presented by Feger et al. (2025). They evaluated several implementations based on pretrained language models across 17 common AM datasets, focusing on the performance drops when they were tested on previously unseen data. These drops were substantial, and the authors attribute this to shortcut learning that attends to, amongst others, constellations of content words rather than to a more semantic notion of argumentativeness. This is a serious problem for practical applications of AM technology, and we will come back to generalizability at various points in this and the following chapter.

Argument Components In the AM literature, ADUs are often called *argument components* (ACs), and this shorthand already appeared at the beginning of the chapter in our enumeration of acronyms. *ADU* emphasizes the origin of the text span as a result of discourse analysis, while *AC* emphasizes its future role in the analysis of arguments. For the purposes of Chaps. 4 and 5, and in line with most of the research literature, we adopt this term and thus henceforth speak of ACs.

AC segmentation can be implemented as a distinct step as part of an AM pipeline, or it can be fused with the task of AC type identification (ACTC) where a *none* type is to be added to the inventory. In the remainder of this section, we focus on the first path, i.e., on a separate segmentation step; Sect. 4.2 will turn to the second path.

4.1.2 Segmentation Methods

Fundamentally, AC segmentation can be done in two different ways: (i) As a pipeline of a first, purely structure-based segmentation into (some specific type of) units, followed by a binary classification step on the units for AC detection; and (ii) as a stand-alone sequence labeling task that operates on the raw text. We will discuss them in turn.

Structural Pre-Segmentation The most straightforward implementation of this approach is making the simplifying assumption that ACs are by definition complete sentences. Then, a standard text tokenizer identifies sentence boundaries, and each sentence is subject to classification as non-/argumentative. In many research endeavors, this simplification has been applied over the years; one example is the work by Stab et al. (2018a), who start with documents that have been found as relevant for a given controversial issue (e.g., self-driving cars) and then classify sentences as containing a statement that is either in favor or against the issue. The practical advantage of the simplification is obvious: Sentence splitting is a standard NLP task that can be run with high accuracy for many languages.

(4.4) The ferry service should be discontinued, as it has produced huge deficits for most of the last ten years.

Example (4.4) demonstrates a potential drawback. For many purposes, it is not enough to discover that this sentence is argumentative; one wants to recognize that it contains two distinct ACs and therefore constitutes a complete argument with a claim about ferry service discontinuation and a premise about deficits. The magnitude of the problem of subsentential ACs differs between genres and corpora: In the widely-used AAE corpus of essays written by learners of English (Stab and Gurevych 2017b), only 8% of the sentences have more than one AC. In contrast, Hua et al. (2019b) report that 25% of the sentences in their corpus of scientific peer reviews contain more than one argumentatively-relevant proposition.

For this kind of situation, Mochales Palau and Moens (2009) in their early work on legal text applied ACTC to syntactic clauses rather than to full sentences. Similarly, Park and Cardie (2014) pre-segmented the sentences and, where necessary, also the clauses as potential ACs for their annotators. Habernal and Gurevych (2017) in their corpus of different kinds of web text had human annotators label by default complete sentences with AC types, but they were allowed to go to the subsentence level if a sentence is found to carry more than one AC. As a final example, for their corpus of US presidential debates, Haddadan et al. (2019) also performed the manual annotation generally on sentences, and on clauses where necessary; but for their automatic classification they remained on the sentence level throughout, taking the longest included AC span as the gold label for the sentence.

Recalling the affinities of discourse units and argumentative units (cf. the beginning of this section), it is not surprising that subsentential ACs usually correspond to clauses. Accordingly, for ACS on the subsentence level, syntactic parsing has sometimes been employed as a preparatory step. For example, Persing and Ng (2016) used manually-devised rules for filtering parse trees and obtaining argumentative units for analyzing student essays (the small version 1 of the AAE corpus by Stab and Gurevych (2014a)). They extracted AC candidates from a parse tree, and in their evaluation, they accounted for boundary mismatches with two separate measures: one for exact matching, and one for partial matching, where success is defined as 50% of the tokens being in agreement. They achieved 92.1% accuracy for partial match and 98.4% for exact match of candidates. Note that these can later still be found to be non-argumentative; i.e., in this first syntax-based step of their pipeline, Persing and Ng merely identify *potential* ACs.[4]

Sequence Labeling This second approach to segmentation directly confronts the fact that ACs can be shorter than a sentence or cover more than one single sentence, and do not necessarily correspond to well-defined linguistic units that a parser can identify.

A corpus that received a lot of attention for the ACS task (and also for others) is the second version of the above-mentioned AAE corpus, containing 402 texts written by adult learners of English (Stab and Gurevych 2017b). Annotators were asked to mark the text spans that express the proposition forming an AC and to leave out discourse markers that connect ACs (such as *because* or *even though*), cognitive predicates like *I think that* and other extraneous material. Inter-annotator agreement (IAA) was measured with Krippendorff's unitized alpha (α_U), which attends to the amount of overlap in a set of span annotations. With three annotators having labeled 80 essays, the authors report a joint α_U value of 0.77 for the three types of ACs that were used (which we will discuss in the next section). Here is a sample excerpt from an annotated essay (Stab and Gurevych 2017b, p. 629):

(4.5) To sum up, although [permitting cloning might bear some risks like misuse for military purposes]$_{Claim6}$, I strongly believe that [*this technology is beneficial to humanity*]$_{MajorClaim2}$. It is likely that [this technology bears some important cures which will significantly improve life conditions]$_{Claim7}$.

[4] This is in contrast to Lippi and Torroni (2016), who proposed syntactic patterns specifically for claim sentences; see Sect. 4.2.1.

Note that the non-annotated words in this example contain important clues for the roles of their neighboring ACs, regarding both their type and their entering relations to other ACs; we will return to the potential utility of these clues later.

Following earlier experiments with conditional random fields (CRFs) for argument mining by Goudas et al. (2014), Stab and Gurevych operationalized the problem as BIO tagging. The first phase of their approach to AM attended merely to the unlabeled segmentation (i.e., ACS) and thus in Example (4.5) it would merely insert the brackets. The CRF operated on manually-engineered features including the position of the token in the text, punctuation, part-of-speech, lowest common ancestor with surrounding tokens in the syntactic constituency tree, constituent types, lexical heads on the path to the root of the tree, and the conditional probability of the token following the preceding 1-, 2-, 3-grams. Using the full feature set proved to be most successful and led to a performance of $F_1 = 0.867$, which was almost on par with the human upper bound determined by the authors.

A subsequent thorough comparative study of the segmentation task was undertaken by Ajjour et al. (2017). The authors were interested in three research questions:

1. Which machine learning model performs best? ⟶ Comparison of a (single-token) SVM baseline, a CRF, and a Bi-LSTM-CRF
2. Which features are more or less predictive for the ACS task? ⟶ Comparison of a variant of Stab and Gurevych's features (e.g., adding embeddings for the Bi-LSTM)
3. How well do models perform in cross-domain tests? ⟶ Comparison of the AAE2 corpus by Stab and Gurevych (2017b), the news editorials corpus by Al Khatib et al. (2016), and the web discourse corpus by Habernal and Gurevych (2017)

The significant addition on the level of machine learning models thus is the Bi-LSTM-CRF, which captures not only the preceding tokens as context, but the entire text. In the experiments, it achieved the best results in most cases, regardless of the domain or the features. On the AAE2 corpus, the performance was almost two points better (macro-F_1 score; significant at $p < 0.001$) than that of Stab and Gurevych (2017b). In terms of features, for the in-domain analysis bag-of-words features turned out most helpful, whereas embeddings did generally not help. When training on one domain and testing on the other, structural features (whether the token is at beginning/middle/end of a sentence/clause/phrase) proved most robust. An important observation, however, was that the cross-domain scenario suffered from generally bad performance. We reproduce the results here in Fig. 4.2. The authors take this as an indication that the notion of AC is not quite the same across different corpora, and hence across different annotation guidelines. Evidence for this hypothesis is the high variance that Ajjour et al. found in the size of ACs, ranging from clause-like segments in the newspaper data to the frequent occurrence of multiple-sentence ACs in a Wikipedia dataset by Rinott et al. (2015)

Following the study by Ajjour et al., Bi-LSTMs remained popular in token-level ACS research for some years. Petasis (2019) discarded the manual feature engineering

Approach	Test on essays			Test on news editorials			Test on web discourse		
	Essays	News	Web	Essays	News	Web	Essays	News	Web
SVM	61.4	50.9	31.3	58.8	79.9	**22.6**	**39.1**	37.4	42.8
CRF	79.2	52.5	21.7	**69.8**	82.0	8.0	37.1	**37.6**	37.7
Bi-LSTM	**88.5**	**57.1**	**37.0**	60.7	**84.1**	20.9	20.9	36.6	**54.5**

Fig. 4.2 Performance results (macro-F_1 scores) of the three approaches (SVM, CRF, Bi-LSTM) for the ACS task across the test sets of three corpora by Ajjour et al. (2017), depending on the used training data (shown in the second header row). Adapted from Ajjour et al. (2017)

and experimented with different word embeddings and neural networks, finding that a Bi-LSTM-CRF with embeddings yields best performance. For the AAE2 corpus, he reported a macro-F_1 of 0.90, thus surpassing the previous results. Spliethöver et al. (2019) used the same corpus and tested the same embeddings as Petasis did (uncontextualized GloVe (Pennington et al. 2014), contextualized Flair (Akbik et al. 2018) and BERT). The architectures proposed in their paper build on Ajjour et al. (2017), omitting the second Bi-LSTM, and adding extra attention layers. The authors were especially interested in the effects of these and found that they actually do not increase performance. Also, in their experiments, the contextual embeddings did not have an advantage over GloVe.

Turning to a different corpus and slightly different task, Hua et al. (2019b) gathered 400 scientific reviews and labeled around 10,000 spans of argumentative propositions with the classes Evaluation, Request, Fact, Reference and Quote. Their first step was ACS, and they found that a Bi-LSTM-CRF beat both a plain CRF and the implementation of joint segmentation and type classification. Nonetheless, most ACS research in recent years moved to joint models, which we will discuss later in Sect. 4.3.

4.2 Argument Component Type Classification

In this section we address the ACTC task: Given a set of argumentative components (e.g., as a result of applying a segmentation step as discussed before, or because the unit is short per se, such as a tweet), determine their types. Sequencing ACS and ACTC amounts to the first two steps of the traditional argument mining pipeline, which was popular in the first years of argument mining research, though from the beginning there were also approaches that intertwined the two tasks.

As explained in the previous chapters, by far the most common approach to AC types, due to its general applicability, is the claim/premise model. In the first subsection, we discuss the identification of claims. This part will be structured according to the *text genres* that have been used, so that the sometimes huge differences between notions of 'claim' in the various datasets become apparent—which raises the important issue of model generalizability. Thereafter we give an overview of subtypes of claims that have been proposed and classified, and then summarize with a subsection on the variety of

{ [*SUPPORT*: The Court recalls that the rule of exhaustion of domestic remedies referred to in Article x of the Convention art. x obliges those seeking to bring their case against the State before an international judicial or arbitral organ to use first the remedies provided by the national legal system.
CONCLUSION: Consequently, States are dispensed from answering before an international body for their acts before they have had an opportunity to put matters right through their own legal systems.]

[*SUPPORT*: The Court considers that, even if it were accepted that the applicant made no complaint to the public prosecutor of ill-treatment in police custody, the injuries he had sustained must have been clearly visible during their meeting.
AGAINST: However, the prosecutor chose to make no enquiry as to the nature, extent and cause of these injuries, despite the fact that in Turkish law he was under a duty to investigate see paragraph above.
SUPPORT: It must be recalled that this omission on the part of the prosecutor took place after Mr Aksoy had been detained in police custody for at least fourteen days without access to legal or medical assistance or support.
SUPPORT: During this time he had sustained severe injuries requiring hospital treatment see paragraph above.
CONCLUSION: These circumstances alone would have given him cause to feel vulnerable, powerless and apprehensive of the representatives of the State.]

CONCLUSION: The Court therefore concludes that there existed special circumstances which absolved the applicant from his obligation to exhaust domestic remedies. }

Fig. 4.3 Text from an ECHR decision annotated with argument components and their types; from Mochales Palau and Moens (2009), used with permission

claims. Next, Sect. 4.2.4 turns to the identification of premises, followed again by a survey of subtypes that have been used.

4.2.1 Identifying Claims

The claim, undoubtedly, is at the heart of an argument—it states what the speaker or author wants us to believe, to accept, or to do. For some practical purposes, finding claims is in fact already sufficient as the granularity of analyzing argumentation (for example, when political party manifestos are to be analyzed for the goals of the party). In the following, we will illustrate different notions of claims that have been used, and annotated, in different types of text.

Legal Text The research that is often credited to be the first on argument mining, by Mochales Palau and Moens (2009), targeted decisions made by the European Court of Human Rights (ECHR). Arguments play a central role when the court justifies its ruling, as is illustrated by the example in Fig. 4.3.

The bracketing indicates the hierarchical structure: The first two paragraphs represent sub-arguments that both are given in support of the overall conclusion in the third paragraph. Thus, *conclusion* in their terminology corresponds to what we call a *claim*. For the central conclusions, the surface form "The court concludes that X" or some paraphrase can be regarded as typical; but notice that the interim conclusions can be descriptions of various kinds, in fairly general form.

Mochales Palau and Moens (2009) implemented a feature-based SVM model for classifying premises and conclusions, which takes as input sentences that have previously been predicted to be argumentative (cf. Sect. 4.1.2). The resulting F_1-scores for premise and conclusion are 0.68 and 0.74, respectively. Among their features are syntactic ones (subject type, main verb tense), domain-specific cues, token counts, position of sentence, and a contextual feature with the prediction for the previous and the following segment.

Following up on this work, Poudyal et al. (2020) released 42 ECHR decisions annotated with text spans containing premises, conclusions, and non-argumentative material, as well as the support relations between premises and conclusions. A BERT model reached an F_1-score of 0.77 for the non-/argumentative distinction and 0.86/0.63 for the subsequent premise/conclusion distinction.

Recently, Habernal et al. (2024) made a corpus of 373 richly-annotated ECHR decisions available, which do not use the coarse claim/premise scheme but distinguish 16 different types of argument, arranged in different groups, that provide a fine-grained account of arguing in this legal domain. For example, in the group *method of interpretation*, categories like *textual*, *historical*, or *systematic* represent established ways of legal reasoning.

Instructional Text Instructions, as they can be found in user manuals, often include advice and warnings; sometimes, these are backed up by an explanation designed to increase the reader's motivation to actually obey them. Here are two examples from Saint-Dizier (2012).

(4.6) Never put this cloth into the sun; otherwise it will shrink dramatically.
(4.7) It is essential that you switch off electricity before starting any operation. Electricity shocks are a major source of injuries and death.

As such, the structure and function correspond exactly to that of an argument, where the claim is of the specific type *instruction* to do or not do something. Based on a corpus study covering French and English text, Saint-Dizier concluded that such constructions have a highly regular linguistic form, making it relatively easy to identify them. In his approach, a set of manually-constructed rules serves to identify both the claim and the supporting statements. The rules exploit the linear order of the statements, and a set of common lexical patterns. These patterns may contain expressions on different levels of abstraction such as word form, word set, or part of speech. The rule language is processed by a dedicated text processing platform developed by the author, called <*TextCoop*>. Saint-Dizier reports recognition accuracies of 88%/91% (claim/support) for warnings and 79%/84% for advice.

Political Debate Haddadan et al. (2019) built a corpus of 39 transcripts of US presidential candidate debates, ranging from 1960 to 2016, and annotated spans that correspond to claims and premises. According to the authors, a claim may take the form of an advocated policy, a candidate's stance on a policy, an opinion on a particular issue, or their personal judgment. Here is an example, with the claim underlined and premises in italics (Haddadan et al. 2019, p. 4686):

(4.8) Kennedy-Nixon, October 13, 1960:
NIXON: Senator Kennedy's position and mine completely different on this. [<u>I favor the present depletion allowance</u>]. [*I favor it not because I want to make a lot of oil men rich*], but because [*I want to make America rich*]. Why do we have

> a depletion allowance? Because [*this is the stimulation, the incentive for companies to go out and explore for oil, to develop it*].

With these texts, differentiating between AC types is not easy. While distinguishing non-/argumentative lead to a κ of 0.57 among three annotators, for the claim/premise distinction it was only 0.40. The authors implemented SVM and feedforward neural network classification systems based on a rich set of linguistic features, which reached average F_1-scores of 0.64 and 0.65, while an LSTM with FastText embeddings (Grave et al. 2018) achieved a score of 0.67. Recently, Poiaganova and Stede (2025) arrived at slightly better results with a RoBERTa model (Liu et al. 2019b), and they also introduced a new corpus of political text (United Nations Security Council debates) and undertook cross-corpus classification experiments.

While Haddadan et al. worked with the claim/premise model, a similar corpus of presidential TV debates has been tackled by Visser et al. (2020) on the levels of Inference Anchoring Theory (IAT, cf. Chap. 3.4.3) and for one debate also annotated for argument schemes (cf. Sect. 8.1), where a three-layer framework provides a fine-grained account of the argumentative reasoning. Another IAT-annotated dataset is the large QT-30 dialogue corpus of British broadcast debates among politicians and members of the audience, introduced by Hautli-Janisz et al. (2022).

Company Earnings Conference Calls Following Alhamzeh et al. (2022), earnings conference calls are conversations between company executives and external financial analysist, where the executives first give a presentation on the company's performance, and then a Q&A session with the analysts forms the core of the event. Alhamzeh et al. focused on these sessions, and for 800 call transcripts they annotated the arguments in the answers given by the company executives, where they try to justify their opinions. Annotation uses the claim/premise model, and Fig. 4.4 shows an example.

Operator (Intro): From JPMorgan, Rod Hall.
Rod Hall (Question): Hi, guys. Thanks for taking my questions. I wanted to start off just going back to the 165 million subscriptions and ask Tim or Luca if you could comment on the unique number of users there. And I think you had made a comment, Tim, in your prepared remarks that the average revenue per user was up, or maybe that was you, Luca. But if you guys could just talk about any more color around that average revenue per user, it would be interesting to us. And then I have one follow-up to that. Thanks.
Luca Maestri (Answer): *Yes, I'll take it, Rod. We don't disclose into the number of subscriptions. Of course, we're just giving you the total count of subscriptions that are out there. Of course, there are several customers that subscribe to more than one of our services.*
[There is some level of overlap, but the total number of subscribers is very, very large, obviously less than 165 million]$\mathbf{P}_1$.
[But it's very good for us to see the breadth of subscriptions that we offer and that customers are interested in]$\mathbf{C}_1$. *It is very large.*[And if you remember, we quoted the same number a quarter ago and we talked about 150 million]$\mathbf{P}_2$
[So when you think about a sequential increase of 15 million subscriptions from the December quarter to the March quarter, it really gives you a sense for the momentum that we have on our content stores]$\mathbf{P}_3$.
[It's quite impressive to add 15 million subscriptions in 90 days.]$\mathbf{P}_4$. [.....]

Fig. 4.4 Annotated text from the FinArg corpus (Alhamzeh et al. 2022, p. 167). C_1=claim, P_n=premises. Licensed under CC-BY 4.0 International

The transcripts contain around 4500 claims and 4900 premises (as well as 4600 support and very few attack relations). Alhamzeh et al. (2022) fine-tuned DistilBERT (Sanh et al. 2019) on their data and obtained an F_1-score of 0.80 for the non-/argumentative distinction; results for ACTC are not provided.

Scientific Text A prominent corpus of scientific argumentation builds on the 'Dr. Inventor' collection of 40 computer graphics papers. Lauscher et al. (2018b) added argument annotation, using a variant of the claim/premise model: They distinguish between *OwnClaim* and *BackgroundClaim*, where the latter is about related work or conventional practices in the research field. Examples (Lauscher et al. 2018b, p. 41) with claims in italics:

(4.9) Own Claim:
"Furthermore, we show that *by simply changing the initialization and target velocity, the same optimization procedure leads to running controllers*."

(4.10) Background Claim:
"Despite the efforts, *accurate modeling of human motion remains a challenging task*."

The corpus (called SciArg) contains ca. 5400 Own Claims and 2800 Background Claims. For identifying them automatically, Lauscher et al. (2018a) use Bi-LSTMs to perform BIO tagging that assigns one of the three tags *OwnClaim, BackgroundClaim* and *Data* (corresponding to a premise) to each token; the F_1-score is 0.44.

Working in the medical domain, Mayer et al. (2020) produced a corpus of 500 abstracts of Randomized Control Trials from the MEDLINE database, which report the outcomes of medication tests. For manual annotation, the claim/premise model is extended by the notion of *major claim*, which is optionally present, functions like a summary and is supported by other claims. Generally, the claims appear at the beginning or the end of the text; a sample claim is (Mayer et al. 2020, p. 2110):

(4.11) ATP has beneficial effects on weight, muscle strength, and QOL in patients with advanced NSCLC.

Around 5.000 ACs have been labeled in the corpus. Similar to Lauscher et al. (2018a), BIO tagging is performed on token level for the target labels *claim* and *evidence* (i.e., the *major claim* category is fused with *claim*). A variety of word embedding models are combined with uni- or bidirectional LSTMs or GRUs (Cho et al. 2014), with and without a CRF as a last layer. Best performance was achieved with fine-tuned BioBERT (Lee et al. 2019) and SciBERT (Beltagy et al. 2019) embeddings, GRU and CRF layer, where the F_1 for the claim class ranges from 0.88 to 0.93 on different parts of the corpus.

For yet another scientific domain, we mention here the work of Accuosto and Saggion (2019) on the abstracts of computational linguistics papers; it will be discussed later in Sect. 5.3.2.

Peer Reviews Conceptually closely related to scientific writing is the genre of peer reviews. Hua et al. (2019b) obtained reviews from four conferences and annotated 400 of them with the genre-specific span types: *evaluation, request, fact, reference, quote,* and *non-argumentative*, yielding a total of around 10,000 spans. The biggest class is *evaluation* (close to 4000 spans), characterized as "subjective statements, often containing qualitative judgment", which effectively corresponds to claims. When the authors compared SVMs and various neural network classifiers, a BiLSTM-CRF model performed best, reaching 0.62 F_1 for the Evaluation class with jointly modeling ACS and ACTC (using different BIO tags for each class). An example for an evaluation in this dataset is:

(4.12) This paper shows nice results on a number of small tasks.

A second corpus was presented by Fromm et al. (2021). These authors collected 4000 reviews from different Computer Science conferences and annotated token spans with labels *pro, con* and *none*, which represent the stance toward accepting the paper. When projecting the spans to the sentence level, the best result from a variety of BERT models is a macro-F_1 score of 0.79.

Educational Text Essays written by students in response to a given prompt are a target of NLP primarily for the application of automatically scoring them, or for providing qualitative feedback to the author. A significant portion of essays in education are persuasive, which Burstein and Marcu (2003, p. 457) define as requiring "the writer to state an opinion on a particular topic, and to support the stated opinion to convince the reader that the perspective is valid and well-supported."

A frequently-used corpus in AM is the AAE Corpus by Stab and Gurevych (2017b). According to the annotation scheme, an essay can have one *major claim*, which expresses the author's stance with respect to the topic, and which is usually found in the first paragraph. Here is an example from (Stab and Gurevych 2017b, p. 628):

(4.13) (...) However, as far as I'm concerned, [cloning is an important technology for humankind]$_{MajorClaim}$ since [it would be very useful for developing novel cures]$_{Claim}$.

Then, the paragraphs between the introduction and the conclusion usually contain arguments related to the major claim. These consist of ('non-major') claims and premises, which are annotated as continuous token sequences, as done in the bracketed portions of the examples above. In total, the corpus has around 1500 claims and 750 major claims.

Stab and Gurevych (2017b) described a feature-based four-way classifier (*major claim, claim, premise, non-argumentative*). The feature set comprised positional, syntactic, and a variety of lexical features, and the token-based classification, implemented with a CRF, achieved an F_1 score of 0.867.

Starting with Persing and Ng (2016) and Eger et al. (2017), subsequent work on the AAE corpus developed end-to-end approaches that also involved relation identification; we will discuss several of them in Chap. 5.

Other corpora with educational text include Feedback, a 3000-text subset of the PERSUADE corpus (Crossley et al. 2022), which consists of 26,000 essays written by students from grades 6 through 12. In total, 15 prompts were used to elicit the essays. The Feedback subset has been annotated for a variety of AC types including *claim*. Finally, an example of a non-essay corpus is the set of 73 classroom discussion transcripts that Lugini and Litman (2018) used for ACTC.

Web Forums Over the years, a variety of forum web sites has been set up specifically for exchanging arguments about popular debatable issues, and these have been used as a natural source of data for argument mining.

In early work, Rosenthal and McKeown (2012) sought to detect claims in LiveJournal weblogs and in Wikipedia discussion pages. They define claims as "assertions by a speaker who is attempting to convince others that his opinion is true" (p. 30), and more specifically attend to the class of claims expressing opinionated beliefs, which are defined as "personal view[s] that others can disagree with" (p. 30). Table 4.1 shows examples, which demonstrate that especially the LiveJournal text can be very informal. Not surprisingly, it is not trivial to demarcate this class of claims precisely; when two annotators were asked to label sentences as claims (without considering the context) in each corpus, they achieved a Cohen κ of 0.50 for 663 LiveJournal sentences, and 0.56 for 997 Wikipedia discussion sentences.

The focus of the classification work was on measuring the utility of sentiment and so-called *committed belief* features. For the latter, the authors adopted the system by Prabhakaran et al. (2010), which tags individual words for the underlying type of belief:

Table 4.1 Examples of claims from two web forum corpora, adapted from Rosenthal and McKeown (2012, p. 31)

LiveJournal	1	oh yeah, you mentioned the race . . . that is so un-thanksgivish !
	2	A good photographer can do awesome work with a polaroid or 'phonecam.
	3	hugs I feel like I have completely lost track of a lot of stuff lately.
Wikipedia	4	The goal is to make Wikipedia as good as possible and, more specifically, this article as good as possible.
	5	This was part of his childhood, and should be mentioned in the article.
	6	If the book is POV or the writer has only a slender grasp of relevant issues, material can be wrong.

Doc#422 (forumpost, homeschooling) [*claim:* I try not to be anti-homeschooling, but... it's just hard for me.] [*premise:* I really haven't met any homeschoolers who turned out quite right, including myself.] I apologize if what I'm saying offends any of you - that's not my intention, [*rebuttal:* I know that there are many homeschooled children who do just fine,] but [*refutation:* that hasn't been my experience.]

Fig. 4.5 Sample annotation from the corpus of Habernal and Gurevych (2017, p. 169). Adapted from Habernal and Gurevych (2017). Copyright ©2017 Association for Computational Linguistics. All rights reserved

committed ("I know"), non-committed ("I may"), and not applicable ("I wish"). Rosenthal and McKeown report various experiments on in-domain and cross-domain classification, including feature impact measurements.

Habernal and Gurevych (2017) built a corpus containing various types of web discourse: newswire articles, blog posts, user comments on both of them, and forum posts. They applied BIO span tagging for a set of argument components that they derived from the Toulmin scheme (see Sect. 3.4.1): *backing, claim, premise, rebuttal, refutation* (and, in addition, *appeal to emotion*). See the example in Fig. 4.5, where the first statement constitutes the claim. For this category, human annotators achieved an agreement of 0.59 on span labeling, measured by Krippendorff's unitized α_U.

The automatic classification is performed not on token spans but on complete sentences; i.e., the problem is simplified to deciding whether a sentence hosts an argument component of a specific type. Habernal and Gurevych used an SVM^{hmm} with a rich feature set that is split into five groups:

- *Lexical:* word n-grams;
- *Structure and syntax:* initial and final tokens, relative positions, POS n-grams, dependency tree depth, constituency tree production rules, number of subclauses;
- *Topic and sentiment:* LDA topics and five sentiment categories $(-2, \ldots, 2)$;
- *Semantics and discourse:* semantic role labels, various coreference chain attributes, type of discourse relation, presence of connectives, attributions; and
- *Embeddings:* sums of word embedding vectors.

All features are considered not only for the current sentence but also for the four preceding and four subsequent sentences. The overall best results are achieved with the full feature set, yielding a macro-F_1 score of 0.25, in comparison to 0.60 obtained by human annotators. The classes Claim-B and Claim-I are among the top-performing classes, reaching 0.27 when omitting the lexical and structure/syntax features. As these numbers show, the problem tackled here is much harder than those we discussed before.

An interesting platform for argument mining is the *change my view* subreddit, where arguments are exchanged and also ranked for their persuasive effect; we will mention some work on this data in the next subsection, along with the popular eRuleMaking corpus of user comments by Park and Cardie (2018).

Wikipedia Switching the perspective to information-seeking argument mining (as introduced at the beginning of the chapter), Wikipedia text has been used for retrieving ACs by the IBM Debater team. In their scenario, the claim detection task started from a predefined *topic*, which Levy et al. (2014, p. 1489) defined as "a short phrase that frames the discussion" and a claim as "a general, concise statement that directly supports or contests the given topic", following Aharoni et al. (2014). The authors constructed a dataset on the basis of 32 debate motions from *Debatabase*. Then, 326 Wikipedia articles were identified as relevant to these topics, and therein, annotators labeled 976 topic-related claims, achieving a rather moderate agreement of $\kappa = 0.39$. More information about the corpus, as well as some examples for annotated claims, were given in the previous chapter (Sect. 3.6.2).

In this approach, annotated claims could be complete sentences or smaller units. The detection system thus needs to find, given a Wikipedia page and a topic, sentences and sub-sentences that qualify as a relevant claim. Levy et al. built a pipeline of three modules, where on average, the input to step 1 consisted of 1500 Wikipedia sentences.

1. *Classify sentences:* A logistic regression classifier identified sentences that contain a claim, using features that exploit topic relevance (cosine similarity between the topic phrase and subjects in the sentence) and various topic-independent features including morphosyntax, subjectivity, and sentiment. It passes the top scoring 200 sentences to the next component.
2. *Identify spans:* For each sentence, the 10 best candidate sub-sentences were identified using a maximum-likelihood model that primarily considers the tokens at the beginning and the end of the sequence. Then a logistic regression classifier selects the most probable claim, again looking at boundary tokens, along with a few other features.
3. *Rank claims:* The claims that have been identified in all the sentences are ranked by another logistic regression classifier. It considers the scores produced by the previous components and also re-computes some of the features that have been used in the preceding modules.

In subsequent work, Shnarch et al. (2017) added a pattern matching approach to the system, which identifies the most discriminative features for the claim identification task across different layers of analysis, and composes patterns out of these. The authors reported that adding the patterns improved the results of the previous approach significantly.

Working on a slightly bigger version of the IBM dataset, Lippi and Torroni (2015) addressed only the first step, i.e., sentence classification, and suggested a rather different approach. They started from the observation that argumentative sentences are often characterized by common 'rhetorical structures' and operationalized that intuition as the similarity between syntactic (constituency) parse trees. Their goal thus is to account for argumentative language irrespective of the domain, and to do so on the basis of syntactic

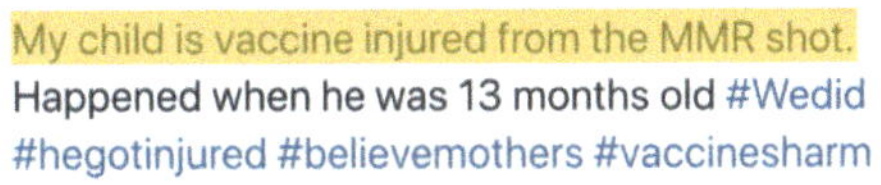

Fig. 4.6 Claim (highlighted) in a Tweet, from Wührl and Klinger (2021, p. 131), licensed under CC-BY 4.0 International

patterns. They obtained the parses from the Stanford CoreNLP suite (now Stanza[5]), and trained an SVM classifier that exploits a partial tree kernel to compute similarities. The authors conclude that they can obtain results that are competitive to those of Levy et al. (2014), even without considering topic similarity.

Twitter/X For many years, the Twitter platform offered relatively easy access to the posted data for research purposes, and thus the AM community began to study argumentative exchanges performed with short messages. An overview of the research between 2013 and 2020 was provided by Schaefer and Stede (2021). The annotation of ACs has usually been done on the level of whole Tweets (similar to the simplification of working on the sentence level in research discussed above); one exception with explicit AC segmentation is the small German corpus built by Schaefer and Stede (2020); the authors, however, report substantially lower human agreement for the AC level in comparison to that of full tweets. Likewise, claim detection as a BERT-based classification task on full tweets yielded a performance of 0.82 F_1, while a CRF finding AC spans achieved only 0.59.

Wührl and Klinger (2021) annotated a corpus of 1200 tweets on four topics of medical issues and their treatments: measles, depression, cystic fibrosis, and COVID-19. In addition to explicit claims (which are also marked with span annotations for the claim phrase, though with low inter-annotator agreement (IAA) in the same range as that obtained by Schaefer and Stede 2020), the authors also labeled tweets as containing an *implicit* claim. Both types of claim are characterized as statements that the author conveys as being true and that appear to be intentionally argumentative as opposed to just sharing an opinion. (Notice that many other annotation projects would treat *any* opinion as a claim.) The two classification settings for full tweets are binary claim/no-claim and ternary explicit/implicit/no-claim. Interestingly, in these experiments a Naïve Bayes classifier often beats a BERT model. The best result for the claim class in the binary setting is 0.70 F_1; in the ternary setting, the 'implicit' class achieves only 0.36, indicating the difficulty of this task (Fig. 4.6).

Feger and Dietze (2024b) use a dataset that is built on Twitter *conversations* constructed with the reply-to relation. 1700 tweets cover 200 conversations spanning six heterogeneous topics; six expert annotators had an agreement of 0.72 (Krippendorff's α). The annotation includes claims, though they are here called *inference*, which is defined as "a guess that you

[5] https://stanfordnlp.github.io/stanza/ (accessed January 15, 2026).

make or an opinion that you form based on the information that you have." The classifier is based on BERTweet (Nguyen et al. 2020) and achieves 0.85 macro-F_1 for detecting claims on the level of full tweets. Moving a step further, Feger and Dietze (2024a) show how the performance can be improved by utilizing contrastive learning in a Siamese network architecture that yields improved BERT embeddings.

As a rather special type of claim, Bhatti et al. (2021) built a corpus of 24,000 tweets where two opposing hashtags constitute the complete claim: #StandWithPP or #DefundPP, which address the planned parenthood debate in the US, and specifically the question whether it should receive further government funding. Example:

(4.14) God Has A Plan For Every Life #PraytoEndAbortion <u>#DefundPP</u> #DefendLife #innocent

As the claims are easy to identify, the classification task for Bhatti et al. targets the kinds of premises, which we will discuss in Sect. 4.2.4.

4.2.2 Subtypes of Claims

Generic Categories. As we mentioned in Chap. 1, coming from the perspective of argumentation theory, Eggs (2000) proposed three basic categories of argument: the *epistemic* argument (some proposition is true or false), the *ethical/aesthetical* argument (something is good or bad; beautiful or ugly), and the *deontic* argument (some action should be done or not done). These categories directly correspond to three types of claims that are often being distinguished in argument mining research. We quote from the definitions given by Park and Cardie (2018, p. 1625):

- *Fact:* stating facts or conditions as they are perceived, without distortion by personal feelings, prejudices, or interpretations;
- *Value:* giving value judgments that do not make claims about what should be done, and that cannot be directly proved by objective evidence;
- *Policy:* proposing a specific course of action to be taken (also not provable with objective evidence).

Park and Cardie worked with online comments on policy decisions, where it was sensible to distinguish a subtype of fact, which they call *testimony:* "an objective proposition about the author's personal state or experience". Unlike with general facts, it is often not possible to provide objective evidence for a testimony.

A domain-specific extension of the three claim classes was also made by Egawa et al. (2020), who analyzed the Reddit forum *change my view* (CMV). For these interactive discussions, the *Rhetorical Statement* category covers subjective value judgments in the form of figurative phrases, emotions, or rhetorical questions, such as "That's human nature!" or "What does that mean?"

Hidey et al. (2017) tackled the CMV text type with a different set of claim types: (i) An *Interpretation* expresses predictions or explanations of states of affairs (e.g., "I think she will win the election"). (ii) An *Evaluation-rational* expresses an opinion based on rational reasoning or on non-subjective evidence (e.g., "His political program is very solid"). (iii) An *Evaluation-emotional* expresses an opinion based on emotional reasons and/or subjective beliefs (e.g., "Going to the gym is an unpleasant activity"). (iv) *Agreement* or *Disagreement* express that the speaker shares/does not share to a certain degree the beliefs held by another speaker (e.g., "You are right").

Subtypes of claims are also of interest for the task of analyzing the quality of student essays. Carlile et al. (2018) aimed to study the degrees of persuasiveness in the early (and small) version of the AAE corpus by Stab and Gurevych (2014a) and labeled the claims with the *fact/value/policy* tags. Recently, Schaefer et al. (2023) slightly modified their definitions and made fine-grained claim annotations available for the full AAE2 corpus of 402 persuasive essays. A RoBERTa-base model achieved results of 0.759 F_1 for the subtypes of major-claims and 0.772 F_1 for claims. Facts turned out to be considerably more difficult to identify than policies and values.

Topical Aspects A different way of dividing the realm of claims pays attention to the topic under discussion and analyses (in analogy to aspect-based opinion mining) which aspect of the issue is being addressed by an argumentative utterance. Consequently, this line of work came to be called *aspect-based argument mining* (ABAM, Trautmann 2020).

Working on the task of summarizing argumentative dialogues, Misra et al. (2015) defined the *facet* of an argument as "a low level issue that often reoccurs in many arguments in support of the author's stance or in attacking the other author's position." For the issue of the death penalty, they give the examples arguing in favor by claiming that it deters crime, or by stating that it gives victims of the crimes closure.

In similar work, Hasan and Ng (2014) used data from the online debate platform *createdebate*, and they were interested in the reasons that debaters have provided for their stance. Taking posts from four different domains, annotators first marked sentences for containing a reason or not. Afterward, the reasons were grouped and a number of classes identified. For illustration, Fig. 4.7 shows the pro/con reason classes that were identified for the topic 'abortion'.

In the era before word embeddings and transformers, Hasan and Ng trained a maximum entropy classifier to decide which of the reasons from the predetermined set (if any) is present in a sentence. Features included uni- and bigrams, dependency relations, frame-semantic features, presence of quotations, and the position of the sentence in the post. The results for this multi-class problem varied between 19.5 and 32.7% accuracy, depending on the domain.

Gemechu and Reed (2019) took the idea of argument facets to the level of sentence analysis and proposed that a proposition expressed in an argumentative sentence can

Domain	Stance	Reason classes
ABO	*for*	[F1] Abortion is a woman's right (26%); [F2] Rape victims need it to be legal (7%); [F3] A fetus is not human (38%); [F4] Mother's life in danger (5%); [F5] Unwanted babies are ill-treated by parents (8%); [F6] Birth control fails at times (3%); [F7] Abortion is not murder (3%); [F8] Mother is not healthy/financially solvent (4%); [F9] Others (6%)
	against	[A1] Put baby up for adoption (9%); [A2] Abortion kills a life (29%); [A3] An unborn baby is a human and has the right to live (40%); [A4] Be willing to have the baby if you have sex (14%); [A5] Abortion is harmful for women (5%); [A6] Others (3%)

Fig. 4.7 Reason classes annotated in debate posts on abortion Hasan and Ng (2014, p. 753), used with permission

No	**Example**
1	**[Camping]**$_c$ [*is a great way*]$_{oc}$ to [bring]$_{oa}$ **[families]**$_a$ [together]$_{oa}$
2	**[Campers]**$_c$ [*have an opportunity*]$_{oc}$ to try some [interesting]$_{oa}$ **[food]**$_a$
3	When **[families]**$_c$ go **[camping]**$_c$, they put the **[jobs]**$_a$ and **[sporting events]**$_a$ [*on hold*]$_{oa}$
4	**[Housing]**$_c$ [*did collapse*]$_{oc}$
5	**[These countries, especially China]**$_c$, [*are taking*]$_{oc}$ **[Americans' jobs]**$_a$
6	**[We]**$_c$, [*are losing*]$_{oc}$ [our]$_a$ [*good*]$_{oa}$ **[jobs]**$_a$ so many of them
7	**[Our jobs]**$_c$, [*are fleeing*]$_{oc}$ **[the country]**$_a$
8	By putting aside these events, the **[family]**$_c$ [*has an opportunity*]$_{oc}$ to [bond]$_{oa}$ their [relationships]$_a$
9	**[Cooking]**$_c$ over a fire makes **[burgers]**$_c$ and **[potatoes]**$_c$ [*taste better*]$_{oc}$ than can be found at **[fast]**$_a$**[food]**$_a$**[place]**$_a$
10	**[Advertising]**$_c$ **[alcohol]**$_a$, **[cigarettes]**$_a$, **[goods]**$_a$ and **[services]**$_a$ with **[adult content]**$_a$ [*should be prohibited*]$_{oc}$
11	**[Modern society]**$_c$ [*needs*]$_{oc}$ **[advertising]**$_a$
12	**[Ads]**$_c$ will [*keep*] us [*well informed*]$_{oc}$ about [*new*]$_{oa}$ **[products]**$_a$ and **[services]**$_a$
13	**[advertising]**$_c$ **[cigarettes]**$_a$ and **[alcohol]**$_a$ [*will definitely affect*]$_{oc}$ our children [*in negative way*]$_{oc}$

Fig. 4.8 Annotation of (c)oncept, (a)spects, opinion on aspect (oa) and opinion on claim (oc), from Gemechu and Reed (2019, p. 518), licensed under CC-BY 4.0 International

contain four types of components: a concept, aspects thereof, and opinions on both of these entities. Figure 4.8 provides examples. The authors annotated material from three existing corpora (persuasive essays by Stab and Gurevych 2017a, argumentative microtexts by Peldszus and Stede 2016b, and 2016 US presidential debate by Lawrence and Reed 2017), resulting in 3000–4000 instances for each of the four types. Among several approaches, CNN-based sequence labeling yielded the best performance in detecting the units and their types, with F_1 scores of 0.67–0.83 across the datasets and types.

Another corpus annotated with such fine-grained information was built by Trautmann (2020). It consists of sentences that are labeled with ACs and their pro/con stance toward the (given) issue, and in addition with aspect terms within the ACs, defined as "the most important point(s) the argument unit is addressing". The final corpus has 4400 sentences on eight different issues (nuclear energy, gun control, school uniforms, etc.), and it contains 12,000 aspect instances of 4500 unique types. Trautmann used a BERT-large model to solve two different tasks:

1. Given pre-marked ACs, find aspects therein (binary token classification).
2. Given a sentence, find stance labels plus aspects (sequence labeling with five classes: NON-O, PRO-O, PRO-ASP, CON-O, CON-ASP). This is akin to a *nested named-entity recognition* task (Finkel and Manning 2009).

Table 4.2 Some of the claims quoted in Sect. 4.2.1 (some are abbreviated)

Claim	Genre	Source
These circumstances alone would have given him cause to feel apprehensive of the representatives of the State.	Court decision	Mochales Palau and Moens (2009)
Never put this cloth into the sun.	Instruction manual	Saint-Dizier (2012)
I favor the present depletion allowance.	Political debate	Haddadan et al. (2019)
But it's very good for us to see the breadth of subscriptions that we offer.	Company earning call	Alhamzeh et al. (2022)
By simply changing the initialization, the same optimization procedure leads to running controllers.	Scientific paper	Lauscher et al. (2018b)
This paper shows nice results on a number of small tasks.	Peer review	Hua et al. (2019b)
Cloning is an important technology for humankind.	Student essay	Stab and Gurevych (2017b)
I try not to be anti-homeschooling, but ... it's just hard for me.	Forum post	Habernal and Gurevych (2017)
Violent video games can increase children's aggression.	Wikipedia	Levy et al. (2014)
My child is vaccine injured from the MMR shot.	Twitter	Wührl and Klinger (2021)
#DefundPP	Twitter	Bhatti et al. (2021)

For Task 1, when testing on a domain that was not part of the training data, the model achieved an F_1 score of 0.75; for Task 2 the macro-F_1 was 0.37.

4.2.3 Summary: Varieties of Claims

We began Sect. 4.2.1 with the observation that claims are of central importance not only for argumentation as such, but also as a standalone task for various applications that are interested in collecting claims made in some specific discourse. Now, having discussed claim detection for a set of different genres, we can ask about generalizability: What do claims have in common, and how 'universal' can a claim classifier be?

Claims in Context Table 4.2 shows a subset of the examples of claims that we have quoted from the literature in the previous section. The collection reveals the difficulty of identifying any general characteristics of the language found in claims: While there are some tendencies (e.g., presence of modal verbs or of opinionated words), the range of formulations is wide. We observe:

- There are no *necessary* linguistic features that can be found in every claim.
- A statement functioning as a claim in context A may not be a claim in context B.

The second point can be illustrated with the presidential debates corpus of Haddadan et al. (2019). One of their examples is (p. 4687):

(4.15) [I disagree with Senator McCain in how to do it]$_{claim}$, because [the way Senator McCain has designed his plan, it could be a giveaway to banks if we're buying full price for mortgages that now are worth a lot less.]$_{premise}$

The connective *because* is a clear signal for linking the claim in the first statement to the premise in the second. However, the premise sentence also expresses a subjective belief, which in a different context could be backed up by a premise—and hence become a claim itself. Accordingly, the constellation of ACs present in the context can have an influence on the status of claims (and other ACs).

Overall, this situation makes claim detection quite different from a task like sentiment analysis, which can to a good extent—and with some reasonable degree of domain-independence—be tackled with lexicons of positive and negative words and some additional analysis of contextual polarity, or with transformer models that exploit the presence of such lexical regularities.

Claims within and Across Genres At the same time, arguing is obviously not an arbitrary linguistic activity: In Chap. 2, we showed the suggested features of claims compiled by Saint Dizier (2020); we mentioned above that Lippi and Torroni (2015) found common syntactic patterns of claims in their corpus; Nguyen and Litman (2015) used a corpus to automatically separate *domain language* from *argument language*; etc. Hence, an interesting question is to what extent the forms of claims are governed by the genre of the text material, or conversely, how well a classifier trained on one corpus can generalize to others.

An early cross-corpus study for claim identification was undertaken by Daxenberger et al. (2017). The authors used six different datasets[6] and mapped the existing annotations to the sentence level, for a common simplified setting. The goal was to measure the influence of different groups of features (structure, lexical, syntax, discourse, embeddings) and of machine learning approaches (three deep learning schemes, and a regularized logistic regression classifier).

For in-domain classification, the average performance of the best neural network and the logistic regression classifier was virtually the same. They obtained macro-F_1 scores

[6] AraucariaDB (Reed et al. 2008), essays from Stab and Gurevych (2017b), web discourse from Habernal and Gurevych (2017), online comments and Wikipedia talk pages from Biran and Rambow (2011), and argumentative microtexts from Peldszus and Stede (2016b).

Fig. 4.9 Claim classification results from Schaefer et al. (2022, p. 183). S1: in-domain / S2: train / test on union of all corpora / S3: train on three corpora, test on all four / S4: leave-one-out. Used with permission

		Claim Class			Macro
		F1	P	R	F1
S1)	CMV	0.72	0.74	0.69	0.79
	Essay	0.67	0.70	0.64	0.76
	Micro	0.73	0.82	0.69	0.82
	USDEB	0.73	0.75	0.71	0.78
S2)	All Corpora	0.72	0.72	0.72	0.78
S3)	No CMV	0.71	0.71	0.71	0.77
	No Essay	0.71	0.70	0.71	0.77
	No Micro	0.72	0.71	0.73	0.78
	No USDEB	0.49	0.72	0.37	0.65
S4)	CMV	0.46	0.56	0.39	0.62
	Essay	0.55	0.56	0.55	0.67
	Micro	0.59	0.52	0.68	0.71
	USDEB	0.37	0.75	0.25	0.58

ranging from 0.60 (Wikipedia TalkPages) to 0.80 (arg. microtexts); the average across the classes for the best system was 0.67, and the corresponding F_1 for the claim class was 0.43. Lexical (unigram), embedding, and syntax features were most predictive, whereas structural and discourse features did not help in most cases.

With cross-domain training and testing, performance drops were found throughout, most pronounced for the datasets that performed best in the in-domain setting. In leave-one-out experiments, the best average macro-F_1 across the corpora was 0.58, and for the claim class 0.32 (logistic regression). The best feature-based approach outperformed the deep learning approach in most of the cross-domain scenarios. However, the neural networks benefitted when trained on all datasets except one and tested on the excluded one, and yielded the best cross-domain results on average. Still, the best neural approach did not show benefits over training on good single-source datasets. Daxenberger et al. studied the six corpora further, and one of their conclusions was that it is difficult to predict cross-domain performance from lexical similarity of the datasets—hence, other factors must be at work in producing the differences.

In a later cross-domain study, Schaefer et al. (2022) used the RoBERTa-argument model that was fine-tuned on 25,000 non-/argumentative sentences by Stab et al. (2018b), and four datasets, two of which had not been available yet to Daxenberger et al. (AAE2 and microtexts, plus *change my view* subreddit by Tan et al. 2016 and USElecDeb60To16 by Haddadan et al. 2019). For comparability to the study of Daxenberger et al., all experiments were done on the sentence level, using 10-fold cross-validation.

Figure 4.9 shows the results. One outcome is that corpus size seems to matter most: Removing individual corpora from the training set while testing on all corpora (S3) shows that only the removal of the largest corpus (USElecDeb60To16) has a profound effect on the results. Also, in another experiment it was found that training on USElecDeb60To16 in a corpus train/test pair scenario consistently yields relatively good results (macro-F_1 0.64–0.67).

The RoBERTa model used by Schaefer et al. generally performed better than the systems of Daxenberger et al.. Also, for the in-domain results on AAE2 and microtexts, it is better or equal to the more complex system presented by Gupta et al. (2021). Gupta's system incorporates information on part-of-speech tags and on dependency syntax into a BERT model, aiming at combining the advantages of earlier feature-based classifiers and transformer models. Their cross-domain experiments covered seven datasets, including a new Twitter dataset. It was produced by re-annotating 1000 tweets for non-/claim from a dataset used for a CLEF shared task; in this process, the authors switched the original label in 11% of all tweets, which provides further evidence for the subjectivity that is inherent in claim annotation.

4.2.4 Identifying Premises

Detecting claims, the topic of the previous sections, is obviously a core task of argument mining, but in order to find a complete argument, there is at least one more component to be identified: the statement(s) that the author introduces to support the claim. In the argumentation literature, this is often called the *premises* of the argument. Notice that while claims can appear independently, a premise is a premise only because of it being linked to a claim. Therefore, the two tasks of identifying claims and premises are conceptually different.

Premises can be linked to the claim in two different ways, viz. as supporting or as attacking it. The latter, in monologue text amounts to a *counterconsideration*, a specific type of objection. Here is a simple example:

(4.16) You should buy that camera, because it has a brand-new excellent sensor. OK, it is quite expensive. But it's worth the money!

Our speaker, in giving their recommendation, imagines an 'opponent' pointing out the high price of the product. After quoting that potential counterargument, they refute it by emphasizing the good value one gets for the money here. Thus, the argument components to be detected are as follows:

- *A—Claim:* You should buy that camera.
- *B—Support:* That camera has a brand-new excellent sensor.
- *C—Objection:* That camera is quite expensive.
- *D—Support:* That camera is worth the money.

In dialogue, obviously, objections indicate actual disagreement between interlocutors, and therefore are very important to be identified properly. In the following, however, our main focus will be on monologue text and on supporting premises. They are often called *evidence* or—depending on the subtype—*justification*; in this section, we use these terms interchangeably with *support*.

The methods used to find premises depend heavily on the argument mining setting. In the following, we thus discuss discourse-based AM and information-seeking AM in turn.

Finding Premises in Discourse-based AM In discourse-based AM, as just illustrated with Example (4.16), the presence of a claim a condition for the presence of premises. Typically, these units are close to each other in the text. If we are certain that there is only one claim, it is sufficient to label each AC with its type, because the premises can only be linked to that single claim. If there can be more claims, then the relations between them and their premises need to be explicitly detected; this is why the topic of this section overlaps with that of Chap. 5 on mining argumentative relations.

Considering again Example (4.16), and its partitioning into ACs `A`, `B`, `C` and `D`, we notice the presence of certain words that serve to signal some important relationships. When we ignore the propositions themselves and reduce the text to the cue words and the punctuation, we get:

(4.17) `A`, because `B`. OK, `C`. But `D`!

Our text is 'easy' in the sense that the argumentative statuses of `A`, `B`, `C` and `D` are explicitly marked: *because* says that `B` is support for `A`; *OK*, in a context like this says that `C` is 'granted' and hence a counterconsideration; *but* says that the argumentative orientation is being switched at this point—since `C` is a counterconsideration, `D` must be a premise for `A`.

Because and *but* are examples of *connectives*, i.e., words that mark the connection between two adjacent portions of text (cf. Chap. 2). For our purposes, they can be exploited as hints to the links between ACs. Roughly:

- Causal connectives (*therefore, thus, because, …*) can mark a link between claim and premise.
- Additive connectives (*also, in addition, furthermore, …*) can mark a link between ACs of the same type, such as several supports.
- Contrastive connectives (*but, however, still, …*) can mark the transition from support to objection or vice versa.

In early argument mining work, Biran and Rambow (2011) found that plain single-sentence classification for identifying premises 'in isolation' is very difficult, but the presence of a claim and its location relative to the premise candidate are important features that can significantly boost performance. They collected connectives from an annotated text corpus[7] and used them as features for predicting support on online text (LiveJournal and Wikipedia talk pages).

In contrast to this data-driven approach, Eckle-Kohler et al. (2015) started from a pre-defined list of connectives (and a few other particles) and determined their potential utility. Working with a relatively small German corpus (88 documents, mostly news text), the aim was to determine which connectives correlate with claim, support and attack. The linear order of ACs is relevant because causal connectives signal directionality (e.g., 'claim *because* support' vs. 'support, *therefore* claim'). German connectives that in the data of Eckle-Kohler et al. frequently occur with claims are *also* ('therefore'), *doch* ('however'), *jedoch* ('though'), and *sondern* ('but'); in premises they found *denn* ('as'), *oder* ('or'), and *und* ('and'). A classifier using such groups of connectives can discriminate between claims and premises with accuracies around 0.7.

Short texts similar to our Example (4.16) are collected in the argumentative microtext corpus. They have been written by students for Part 1 (Peldszus and Stede 2016b) and by crowdworkers for Part 2 (Skeppstedt et al. 2018) who were instructed to take a position on a contentious issue and if possible also to consider 'the other side'. After segmenting into ACs, the manual annotations include labeling the distinction between *proponent* (the author's viewpoint: claim and supporting premises) and the imaginary *opponent* (objecting premises). For this classification task, Afantenos et al. (2018) used a feature-based log-loss stochastic gradient descent model (with lemmas, POS-tags, dependency tags, connectives, etc.) and obtained a macro-F_1 score of 0.78.

Mining Premises in Information-Seeking AM Recall that for the perspective of information-seeking AM, a topic/claim is given, and a—potentially large—set of documents is searched for relevant material that can be used as evidence for that claim. This setting was promoted originally by the IBM Debater team, as mentioned above for claim detection in Wikipedia. Correspondingly, Rinott et al. (2015) presented an approach to identifying claim-dependent support statements in Wikipedia text.

The following example by Rinott et al. (2015, p. 441) lists three statements that would ideally be classified as suitable evidence:

- *Topic:* Use of performance enhancing drugs (PEDs) in professional sports.
- *Claim:* PEDs can be harmful to athletes' health.
- *Evidence statements:*
  - (S1) A 2006 study examined 320 athletes for psychiatric side effects induced by anabolic steroid use. The study found a higher incidence of mood disorders in these athletes compared to a control group. [Study]
  - (S2) The International Agency for Research on Cancer classifies androgenic steroids as "probably carcinogenic to humans." [Expert]

[7] RST Discourse Treebank (Carlson et al. 2003).

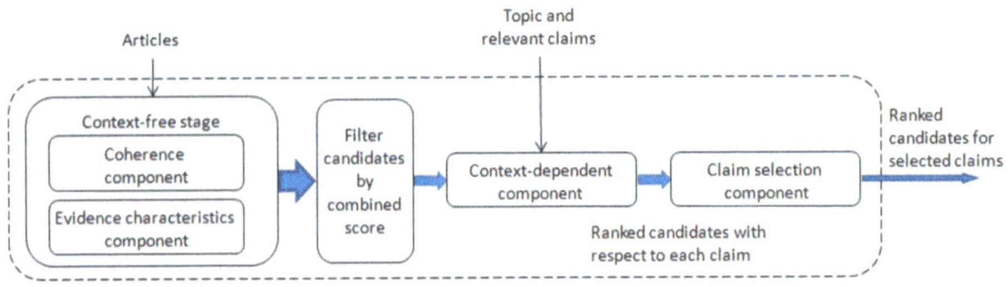

Fig. 4.10 System architecture of evidence detection system from Rinott et al. (2015, p. 443), used with permission

- (S3) Rica Reinisch, a triple Olympic champion and world record-setter at the Moscow Games in 1980, has suffered numerous miscarriages and recurring ovarian cysts following drug abuse. [Anecdotal]

Rinott et al. distinguished three different types of evidence, which are appended to the examples in brackets. We will discuss evidence types in depth in the next subsection, but in brief, *study* refers to results of a quantitative analysis of data, given as numbers, or as conclusions; *expert* refers to testimony by someone with known authority on the topic; and *anecdotal* is a description of an episode, centered on an individual or clearly located in place or in time.

The task is to go through all the relevant documents (in a dataset of 274 articles) and for each sentence to decide whether it constitutes evidence for the claim. Rinott et al. devised a modular system architecture shown in Fig. 4.10, responding to the observation that a target text segment should satisfy three criteria: it must be coherent; it must have characteristics of the desired evidence type; and finally, of course, it must support the claim. Of these, the first two aspects are context-independent. In the following, we briefly describe the corresponding modules of the system.

1. The *coherence* component makes sure that, for example, there are no unresolved anaphors (especially pronouns) in a sentence and that the first sentence does not start with a connective.
2. The *evidence characteristics* component estimates how well the candidate corresponds to the desired type of evidence. Study evidence, for example, is strongly associated with quantitative analysis of data, i.e., the presence of numbers, among other features. For each evidence type, the authors manually compiled a lexicon of words characterizing this type, and automatically expanded the sets. Other features are named entity types, regular expressions for finding quotations and verb/named entity patterns, and subjectivity.
3. The *context-dependent* component aims to detect whether the candidate indeed supports the provided claim in the context of the topic. Hence, it is trained on (topic, claim, evidence) triplets. The features include semantic relatedness (measured by cosine

similarity between TF-IDF vectors representing each text and by cosine similarity between their word embedding representations) and also sentiment agreement between candidate and claim.

4. Finally, the *claim selection* component aims to rank all input claims, according to the probability that evidence can indeed be found amongst top-ranking candidates for the claim. It uses several word lists, for example one of 'claiming words' ("lead", "result", "development", "significant", etc.)

All components employ a logistic regression classifier. The evaluation of this multi-component pipeline, done by the authors via mean reciprocal ranks, is complex and we do not reproduce it here. The authors conclude that assessing both the coherence and the evidence characteristics of candidates is of great importance. For the context-dependent stage, semantic relatedness turned out as the most valuable feature.

Subsequent work in this vein of finding arguments 'in the wild' addressed the question of scaling up, which means on the one hand the coverage of topics, and on the other hand the amount of text material that can be searched. Following up on the IBM Debater work, Ein-Dor et al. (2020) tackled the problem of finding sentences containing *study* and *expert* evidence (for a given claim) in a very large dataset of 400 million newspaper and journal articles. This classification problem has two characteristics:

- The label distribution is extremely skewed: the vast majority of sentences in the collection is not relevant.
- Precision is of much higher importance than recall: the debating system does not need a large number of evidence statements; but whatever it chooses to say should be appropriate.

Ein-Dor et al. selected some 250 claims for their train/development set and developed the following procedure to tackle the problem. It bears similarities to the *active learning* paradigm (Cohn et al. 1996), though Ein-Dor et al. (2020) discuss some differences. Figure 4.11 illustrates the procedure.

1. Build a small set of manually collected and labeled sentences. Here, they are taken from the Wikipedia corpus built earlier (Rinott et al. 2015).
2. Train a simple classifier that can generalize well from this dataset, and use it to predict the label of many relevant sentences in the large corpus (sentences that satisfy specific queries[8]). Here, the logistic-regression (LR) classifier of Rinott et al. is used.

---

[8] Query terms include the topic, certain named entities, sentiment words, certain connectives, and terms that are specific to the type of evidence sought. The retrieval step is based on some preprocessing and enrichment of the big document collection.

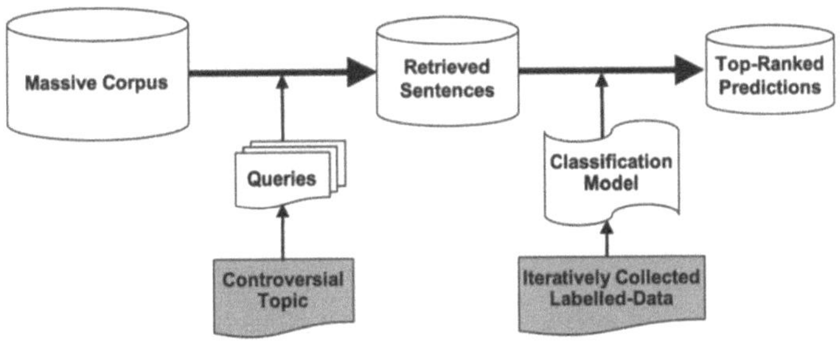

Fig. 4.11 End-to-end evidence retrieval in the system of Ein-Dor et al. (2020, p. 7686). Adapted from Ein-Dor et al. (2020). Copyright ©2020 Association for the Advancement of Artificial Intelligence (www.aaai.org). All rights reserved

3. LR yields a ranking over the predicted sentences. Take the top 40 sentences for *expert* and *study* evidence, and produce manual annotations (correct/incorrect) by crowdsourcing and majority voting. This increases the size of the dataset. The step of labeling the top predictions of the classifier has two benefits:

   - Since it yields a set of true-positive examples, the imbalance in the dataset becomes smaller.
   - It uncovers hard negative examples (the false positives), which are likely to be problematic for a 'real world' retrieval system that aims at high precision among its top-ranked predictions.

4. Iterate the previous step until a dataset with acceptable size and class distribution results.
5. Train a more powerful classifier on the dataset built so far. Here, a bidirectional LSTM with an additional attention layer, previously produced by the IBM group (Shnarch et al. 2017), is used. Again, perform manual annotation on the top 40 predictions for each claim and each evidence type. Iterate this step.

The procedure was stopped when a dataset of 200,000 manually-labeled sentences, including 33.5% positive examples, was produced. Experiments were run on this dataset (and some others) to compare an earlier BiLSTM approach to a BERT-based network. The BERT approach produced better results on the end-to-end sentence classification task, with precision reaching 0.95 for the top 40 candidates.

While Ein-Dor et al. (2020) worked with relatively homogeneous news and journal texts retrieved from the LexisNexis engine, Stab et al. (2018a) took the setting of argument search to more heterogeneous web documents. The authors selected eight contentious topics and submitted each name to a Google query. The 50 top-ranked pages were downloaded—a mix of news reports, editorials, blogs, debateforums, and encyclopedia articles. For the total of 25,000 sentences, annotators were given the topic and labeled each sentence as supporting, opposing or non-argumentative with respect to the topic.

For the computational classification task, Stab et al. were interested in integrating the topic information into the neural learner. They implemented two variants:

- An outer-attention BiLSTM learns an importance weighting of the input words depending on the given topic.
- In a contextual BiLSTM, topic information is added as an additional term to all four gates of an LSTM cell. Stab et al. experimented with restricting this to certain cells and found an improvement for adding the term at the i- and c-gates only.

For the evaluation setting, the authors measured cross-domain performance by taking the training and validation data from seven topics, and testing on the test set of the eighth topic. They found that multitask and transfer learning (with parameter transfer) can add to the performance of the classifier; overall, the best F_1 score they achieved for the three-label task (averaged over all train/test topic combinations) was 0.43.

4.2.5 Subtypes of Supporting Premises

While we have seen settings where both supporting and opposing premises were being mined for, many AM tasks in fact pay more attention to support (in line with the standard definition of an argument as a pair of a claim and a supporting premise). Therefore, similar to the efforts in developing claim typologies (Sect. 4.2.2), quite a bit of research has been done on differentiating different types of supporting material. This holds in particular for argumentation theory, where normative approaches seek to clearly demarcate the realm of arguments with acceptable backing. But the argument mining community, too, has embraced the task of annotating and recognizing separate classes.

We have seen for claims that topic-oriented and generic subtype inventories can be broadly distinguished. When we described work on aspect-based AM, we borrowed the terminology of the authors who stated that they analyse argumentative sentences—which in principle applies to both claims and premises. Hence, their techniques for extracting *facets* or *aspects* apply to premises, too; we will, however, not address them any further here.

Turning to generic inventories, Table 4.3 summarizes the labels that have been used in a number of studies.[9] We wish to demonstrate that some common categories emerge, though it has to be noted that we made some simplifications in the interest of brevity. Reynolds and Reynolds (2002) discuss the notion of evidence from the perspective of argumentation theory. *Statistical* evidence amounts to scientifically-established insights, while a *testimony* unfolds its authority through its source, which has to be a trustworthy person or institution, for instance an expert in the domain of the debated issue. Finally, they

[9] Several approaches also offer an *other* class to annotators, which we omit from the table.

Table 4.3 Types of *evidence* used in various studies (partly simplified)

Authors	Genre	Statistics, study	Testimony, expert	Anecdote, example	Common ground, fact	Assumption, opinion, analogy, reasoning
Reynolds and Reynolds (2002)		✓	✓	✓		✓
Al Khatib et al. (2016)	Editorial	✓	✓	✓	✓	✓
Rinott et al. (2015)	Wikipedia	✓	✓	✓		
Guo et al. (2023)	Wikipedia	✓	✓	✓		✓
Carlile et al. (2018)	Pers. Essays	✓	✓	✓	✓	
Schaefer et al. (2023)	Pers. Essays	✓	✓	✓	✓	
Hua and Wang (2017)	idebate.net	✓			✓	✓

distinguish *anecdotal* evidence (personal experience of the speaker) and *analogy*, where the similarity to a constellation in a different domain is being exploited. In the table, we lumped the latter label together with other subjective categories.

The richest inventory is used by Al Khatib et al. (2016) who work with news editorials—a genre that allows for a broad range of ways of backing up the author's position. Among the subjective labels in the rightmost column of the table, they use *assumption*, which represents any kind of subjective belief. The *common ground* refers to statements that can be assumed to be acceptable to most of the audience, as per the shared value or belief system. These categories were not of interest to Rinott et al. (2015), who worked on the IBM Debater project toward the goal of an automatic agent that can participate in a live debate on stage. For being persuasive in a competitive setting, 'objective' evidence is important, and hence the choice of Wikipedia as data source and of the three categories of support. Guo et al. (2023) build on the work of Rinott et al. and add *explanation*, which appears compatible to *opinion/reasoning*.

In the two annotation efforts on the AAE2 corpus of Stab and Gurevych (2017b), Schaefer et al. (2023) made some changes to the category definitions of Carlile et al. (2018) and furthermore distinguished 'real' examples from hypothetical situations (which is neglected in the table); the latter covers cases like the following:

(4.18) [If the health department actively recommends the vaccination,]$_{hypo}$ [we will be able to beat the disease by following their suggestion.]$_{claim}$

For capturing types of support in online arguments on a debate platform, Hua and Wang (2017) used *study* and *fact* as relatively objective categories, and *opinion* and *reasoning* (not distinguished in the table) as subjective ones.

On Twitter/X, conventions are somewhat different, and other types of evidence (beyond Table 4.3) become relevant. In the corpus compiled by Addawood and Bashir (2016), subjective claims are backed up by categories that combine purely-formal categories with some that represent an epistemic status:

- a link to content from a news media account,
- an expert opinion,
- a blog post,
- a shared picture, and
- other: links to audio, books, etc.

4.3 From Pipeline Systems to Joint Models

The previous sections explained the problem of detecting argument components, pointed out the sometimes sharp differences between various genres of text, and introduced some relevant corpora along with classification work that has been done with them. In this last section, we switch the perspective to the *methods* and analyze the AC classification tasks according to the technical approaches that are employed. In doing this we cannot aim for exhaustiveness; our categories will be in rough but not in perfect chronological order; and they also are not completely mutually exclusive. Nonetheless, the section should serve to provide some orientation on the implementation concepts and ideas that originated over the years.

Feature-based Supervised Text Classification In line with the dominating paradigm of NLP research in the early 2010s, argument mining started by regarding the problem as a supervised text classification task. This presupposes a clean pipeline approach where component segmentation is either being simplified to sentence-level AM, or it is a first task that precedes AC type classification. We mentioned a range of relevant approaches above, where different classifiers as well as different feature sets (such as lexical, positional/structural, syntactic) are being compared to each other (e.g., Stab and Gurevych 2014b). Some research in this period provided careful examination of linguistic properties of different argumentative discourse units—for a comprehensive overview, see (Janier and Saint-Dizier 2019).

Sequence Labeling As we have seen, for many types of text the AC boundaries cannot be presumed to coincide with sentence boundaries or syntactic clause boundaries. Then, token-level sequence labeling is needed, commonly framed as a BIO tagging task. Early classification approaches utilized conditional random fields (e.g., Goudas et al. 2014),

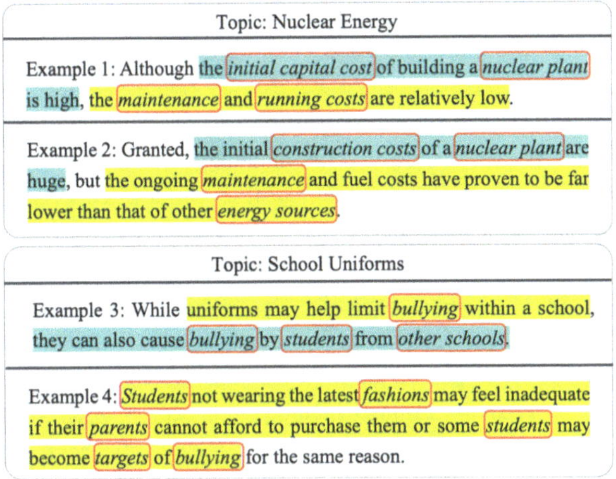

Fig. 4.12 Example annotations of ACs with stances 'pro' (*yellow*) and 'con' (*blue*) as well as aspect terms (italics in *red frames*), in the corpus of Trautmann (2020). Taken from Fu et al. (2023, p. 1423), licensed under CC-BY 4.0 International

which later were integrated as CRF layers into neural networks (e.g., as used by Schulz et al. 2018).

In *aspect-based* argument mining, BIO tagging becomes more complicated. In Sect. 4.2.2, we mentioned the corpus introduced by Trautmann (2020), which contains stance and aspect subsequences within argument components, yielding a two-level nested structure (Fig. 4.12). Building on the work of Trautmann, Fu et al. (2023) propose a *hierarchical enhancement framework*, a complex neural architecture consisting of four sequential components:

1. *Basic module* for determining AC boundaries and aspect terms: Given an input sentence and its topic, the enocder represents a token as a triple of BERT embedding, character representation and part-of-speech tag. A Semantic and Syntactic Fusion (SSF) component uses a graph attention network to capture long-distance dependencies within the sentence. A Star-Transformer for re-encoding the context and a CRF decoder complete the module.
2. *Argument unit enhancement module* for determining the stance of the ACs: It exploits correlations between stance and use of aspect terms by using a Batch-Level Heterogeneous Graph Attention Network (BHGAT), which aims to combine the strengths of sentence-level and corpus-level graph neural networks.
3. *Aspect term enhancement module* for improving aspect identification: It uses a Span Mask Interactive Attention (SMIA) component to make sure that only terms within an AC are being considered as aspect terms.
4. *Decision module* for creating the output: It fuses the probabilities resulting from the basic module with those of the two enhancement modules.

The approach lead to very good results on the corpora used by Trautmann (2020), and additional experiments reveal that the three modules SSF, BHGAT and SMIA indeed all contribute to the performance.

Multitask Learning As everywhere in NLP, manually annotating corpora is costly, and thus the AM community began to experiment with leveraging sets of similarly-annotated corpora as training data for the task that is then tested on one specific target corpus. One of the early approaches to this instance of multitask learning (MTL) for AC identification, as a token-level prediction task, was presented by Schulz et al. (2018). The authors showed that despite the heterogeneous features of different corpora (which we discussed in the previous sections) advantages can be gained by enlarging training data. Six datasets that use somewhat different types of argument components are regarded as separate learning tasks, and the label set for BIO tagging is $\{O\} \cup \{B, I\} \times T$, where T comprises all unit types used in the different corpora.

The authors use a BiLSTM with CRF layer to perform both single-task and MTL experiments. For the latter, they simulate data sparsity by sampling subsets from the corpora, and the sparse data is used as main task (to represent a realistic scenario), while all other datasets, representing separate auxiliary tasks, are used in their entirety for training. The main finding is that MTL performs particularly well (and better than single-task learning on that data) when only little training data is available for the main task.

Several similar studies have been conducted by other researchers, of which we discussed one already in Sect. 4.2.3: Restricted to claim identification, Schaefer et al. (2022) showed the effects of different ways of composing training sets on the classification performance for a certain target corpus.

More recent approaches involving MTL have been done with pretrained language models, which we will mention further below.

Cross-Lingual Transfer Another idea for tackling the sparse-data problem is to exploit corpora that are available in languages that are different from the target language of the specific research. Three approaches can be distinguished here.

- *Data transfer:* When machine translation had reached a mature state, it became an option to automatically or semi-automatically translate the corpora and to perform *annotation projection*, usually on the basis of automatic word alignment, to obtain a closely-related resource in another language. For example, the argumentative microtext corpus has been mapped to several other languages in this way, e.g., to Italian (Namor et al. 2019). For the AAE2 corpus, Eger et al. (2018) provide a human-translated German version, as well as machine-translated versions in German, Spanish, French and Chinese. For the task of token-level AC identification and typing (by sequence labeling), they find that for German, the automatic translation leads to almost the same result as the manual one; and that generally the results are competitive for all the automatically-produced target languages.

- *Model transfer:* This method originated with the availability of pretrained multilingual language models, which allow for learning annotations in one language and generating the predictions in a different one. Toledo-Ronen et al. (2020) tackle several AM tasks, including evidence detection (in the information-seeking AM setting). The IBM Debater English Wikipedia dataset (Rinott et al. 2015) as well as another large dataset are automatically translated into five European languages. The translations of the training subsets of the data were used for fine-tuning an mBERT model (Devlin et al. 2019), and the translations of the test subsets were used for evaluation. It turns out that for evidence detection, adding training data in the original language is helpful, while performance does not increase when adding other languages.
  Later work by Yeginbergen et al. (2024) automatically translated the AbstRCT corpus to Spanish, Italian, French and projected the annotations of claim and premise spans. They found that data transfer and sequence labeling by monolingual models clearly outperforms model transfer (training mBERT in English, evaluating on the three other languages). This is in contrast to earlier results on other NLP tasks that involve shorter spans, such as named-entity recognition (NER), where good results for model transfer have been obtained.
- *Few-shot prompting:* Yeginbergen et al. (2024) also ran experiments with the template-free 'EntLM' method for few-shot prompting in NER, proposed by Ma et al. (2022). It involves generating training samples by gathering class-specific 'label words', which are used as prediction targets in the position of the entity words. Working with the multilingual AbstRCT corpus, the goal is to predict the token labels *O, B C, B-P, I-C,* and *I-P* (C = claim, P = premise). As 'label words' they use the 10 most frequent words in the text spans for each of the five classes. Sample size is determined with a $k-$shot and $k-$percent scheme, with $k \in \{5, 10, 20, 50\}$, where either k samples are retrieved from the data, or the corresponding proportion (thus reflecting the distribution in the data). The experiments reveal, however, that a fine-tuned mBERT model is better than the EntLM-inspired few-shot prompting. Again, this may indicate greater difficulty of AM tasks in comparison to NER and similar problems.

Weakly-Supervised or Unsupervised Learning. AM tasks are generally difficult, and hence, before the eras of deep learning and pretrained language models, experiments with weakly- or unsupervised learning have been rather scarce. Exceptions include the work of Lawrence et al. (2014), who employed *topic modeling*, specifically Latent Dirichlet Allocation (LDA) (Blei et al. 2003), to determine the topical similarity of consecutive sentences in the text. The underlying assumption was that such similarity is indicative of an argumentative relation holding between the two sentences, while dissimilarity might indicate that the author is returning to a previous point, and thus the similarity measurement is made to all previous sentences. In this way Lawrence et al. were looking for hints on the overall argumentative structure.

LDA was also employed, though for a different purpose, by Nguyen and Litman (2015), who performed the standard AM tasks on the AAE1 corpus, and as a preparatory step used

LDA to separate the 'argument vocabulary' from the 'domain vocabulary' and then utilized the results for creating features for the supervised AC classifier.

Working also on the AAE corpus, Persing and Ng (2020) proposed an unsupervised approach to AM, which is, however, based on heuristics that exploit knowledge of the essay genre, i.e., of typical document structure and AC marking. After running a syntax parser, a small set of rules identifies boundaries of candidate ACs. We reproduce here the three tree-traversing rules for deciding on the location of the right boundary:[10]

- Exactly where the S node ends, or if S ends in a punctuation, immediately before the punctuation.
- If the S node ends in a (possibly nested) SBAR node, immediately before the n-th shallowest SBAR.
- If the S node ends in a (possibly nested) PP node, immediately before the n-th shallowest PP.

Then, another set of heuristics is used to label the candidates with their types; these make use of the position of the paragraph in the essay, the position of the sentence in the paragraph, and context token n-grams surrounding the candidate. This procedure, by design, achieves good precision but a low recall. Therefore, the next step is to use the generated set of all heuristically-identified instances as training data for a supervised classifier, which peruses features akin to those used originally by Stab and Gurevych (2017b). Note that the heuristic procedure could not distinguish well between 'real' non-argumentative units and those units that are argumentative but were not caught by the simple rules. For this reason, a self-training phase is added to improve the performance for non-ACs. In the end, the results of the system are competitive with two supervised baselines, but significantly lower than the state of the art at the time, the neural system by Eger et al. (2017) (which will be introduced in the next chapter, Sect. 5.4.1).

Early Deep Learning Models Among the first systems that demonstrated remarkable success on AM tasks without any manual feature engineering are BiLSTM neural network architectures. Earlier in this chapter, we mentioned their role in the AC segmentation study by Ajjour et al. (2017) and in the search for premise sentences implemented by Stab et al. (2018a) with word2vec (Mikolov et al. 2013) embeddings (Sect. 4.2.4).

Pretrained Language Models The advent of BERT (Devlin et al. 2019) marked the beginning of a new era in NLP, and hence also in AM. An early study was conducted on the open-domain argument search task by Reimers et al. (2019). For the UKP Sentential Argument Mining Corpus, they showed that contextualized word embeddings (BERT) in

[10] S and SBAR are nodes in the syntax tree that represent sentence-like structures; PP means prepositional phrase.

	Topic: Will artificial intelligence replace humans	Claim	Stance	Evidence
1	Job opportunities will grow with the advent of AI; however, some jobs might be lost because AI would replace them.	C_1	+1	
2	Any job that involves repetitive tasks is at risk of being replaced.	C_2	+1	
3	In 2017, Gartner predicted 500,000 jobs would be created because of AI, but also predicted that up to 900,000 jobs could be lost because of it.			E_1 | E_2
4	The number of industrial robots has increased significantly since the 2000s.			E_3
5	The low operating costs of robots make them competitive with human workers.			E_3
6	In the finance sector, computer algorithms can execute stock trades much faster than a human, needing only a fraction of a second.			E_3
7	As these technologies become cheaper and more accessible, they will be implemented more widely, and humans might be increasingly replaced by AI.	C_3	+1	
8	According to Harvard Business Review, most operations groups adopting RPA have promised their employees that automation would not result in layoffs.	C_4	-1	E_4
9	AI is incredibly smart, but it will never match human creativity.	C_5	-1	

Fig. 4.13 Example annotations from the IAM corpus. Solid lines represent boundaries between documents; evidence is related to the claim with the same index in the same document. Stance +1 denotes *pro topic*, −1 is *con*. Taken from Cheng et al. (2022, p. 2279), licensed under CC-BY 4.0 International

combination with adding topic information to the transformer network achieves much better results than the previous approach by Stab et al. (2018a), where the F_1 score for the argument class had been only 0.27.

The following years saw a flurry of activities performed with BERT, RoBERTa and other derived models; we already mentioned several of them earlier in this chapter. Some work uses the models more or less 'out of the box', while other work experiments with integrating linguistic information into the transformer network, such as part-of-speech tags and dependency-syntactic features in the approach of Gupta et al. (2021).

We add here a larger BERT/RoBERTa study in a line of research that we have not mentioned yet. Cheng et al. (2022) tackle the scenario that the IBM Debater project had defined (information-seeking AM with given topics) and introduce a large integrated corpus called IAM: 123 topics were gathered from online forums, then around 10 articles per topic were retrieved from Wikipedia, which results in a total of 1000 articles with 70,000 sentences. These have been manually annotated on the sentence level with claims and their stances toward the topic, as well as evidence premises that occur in a window of 20 sentences around the claim. The corpus contains 4900 claims and 9400 premises; examples are shown in Fig. 4.13. Note that claim and evidence can also occur in the same sentence (line 8) and the same evidence sentence can support multiple claims (line 3).

Classification is performed with a BERT-base-cased and a RoBERTa-base model, where the latter shows better performance throughout all the tasks and their combinations. Specifically, the authors test the single tasks as represented in the figure. For instance, for claim detection the macro-F_1 is 0.72, though F_1 for the *claim* class it is much lower (0.50). When combining claim and stance into a single 3-way classification task (*claim, no-claim, none*), the result beats a pipeline of the two separate classification runs. Similarly, for identifying claim-evidence pairs, a multitask approach beats the sequencing of claim

Table 4.4 Class distribution and classification result (RoBERTa) for evidence types on the extended IAM corpus. Adapted from Guo et al. (2023, p. 935)

Type	#Evidence	%Evidence	Classification F_1
Case	1073	12.8%	0.74
Expert	1538	18.3%	0.70
Research	1298	15.4%	0.78
Explanation	4234	50.4%	0.90
Other	264	3.1%	0.28

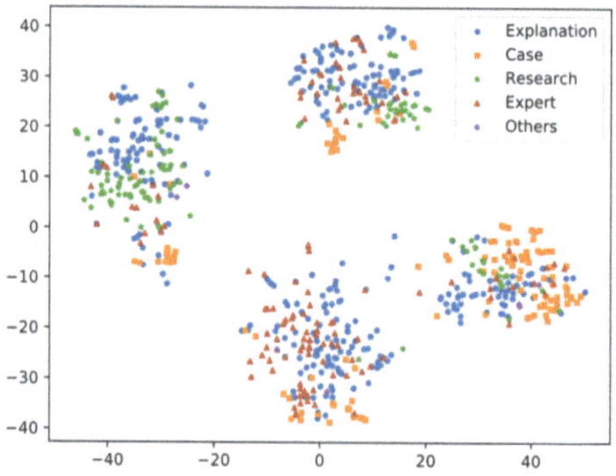

Fig. 4.14 t-SNE visualization of the evidence type clusters for four topics from the extended IAM corpus (Guo et al. 2023, p. 935), licensed under CC-BY 4.0 International

identification and subsequent classification of sentence pairs (given claim with all evidence candidates).

Afterwards, Guo et al. (2023) filtered the corpus for noisy material, and for the remaining 8300 evidence sentences, they added the fine-grained evidence types that we have already shown above at the end of Sect. 4.2.4. For their identification (on the manually-detected evidence sentences), a RoBERTa-base classifier achieves the results shown in Table 4.4, which also shows the class distribution.

For a closer look, the authors randomly selected four topics for a cluster analysis: *Should we support family education? / Should alcohol be forbidden? / Should intellectual property rights be abolished? / Should we fight for the Olympics?* Figure 4.14 provides a t-SNE[11] visualization, and Guo et al. observe that topics differ in terms of evidence type distribution and that furthermore, the types *case* and *research* form their own clusters within the topics.

Finally, we mention the study of Alhindi and Ghosh (2021), which was done on an unpublished corpus of 145 student essays. The authors combined ACS and ACTC in a token-wise classification task (using the types B-Claim, I-Claim, B-Premise, I-Premise, and O) and compared traditional feature-based CRF models, BiLSTM-CRF, and fine-tuned BERT models. Interestingly, the winning system was a BERT-based multitask learning approach, which combined the token type prediction with an auxiliary task, viz. the binary

[11] *t-distributed stochastic neighbor embedding* is a nonlinear dimensionality reduction technique that embeds high-dimensional data in a two-dimensional space.

classification of sentences as containing an AC or not. It beat a single-task BERT variant by 0.013 F_1 points (and both clearly outperformed the older models).

Prompting Generative LLMs A few years after the field was transformed by BERT, the generative large language models lead to a second methodological 'breakpoint'. We discuss here an extensive study by Chen et al. (2024), which continues the line of work on the IAM corpus and also adds various datasets from the IBM Debater project. The authors tackle the tasks we just discussed above: claim and evidence detection, evidence type classification, and stance detection (and in addition argument generation, which we ignore here). For the experiments, 500 samples are randomly drawn from each dataset.

The authors work with both open-source and proprietary LLMs, specifically with GPT-3.5 and different models from the Flan (Chung et al. 2024) and Llama (Touvron et al. 2023a) families. They compare zero-shot and various k-shot settings. We give just a glimpse of the results here: For the binary tasks of claim and evidence detection in the zero-shot setting, Flan-UL2 (20B) shows the best performance; the F_1 for claim detection on the IAM dataset is 0.84. Due to the different data size, this is not directly comparable to the figure we gave above for the RoBERTa-base result from Cheng et al. (2022), but the advantage for the LLM is clear. For the multi-class problem of evidence type classification on the IAM dataset (cf. Table 4.4 above), GPT-3.5-Turbo yields much better results than Flan-UL2; the macro-F_1 is 0.58.

A set of interesting experiments from the perspective of information-seeking AM was performed by Guida et al. (2025). They use the datasets of Boltužić and Šnajder (2014) and Hasan and Ng (2014) (see Sect. 4.2.2), where topics and arguments are assumed as given, and the problem is to detect their presence in user comments from online debate platforms. Specifically, there are six different topics (legalization of gay marriage, abortion, the Obama presidency, etc.) and 3–4 *pro* and *con* arguments per topic. In Fig. 4.7 above, the various arguments on the abortion topic have been shown. Guida et al. study three tasks: (i) given topic, argument and a comment, *classify* whether the comment mentions the argument; (ii) given the same, *extract* the specific text span from the comment that expresses the argument; (iii) identify the stance of the argument in the comment (support or attack the topic; this is a task discussed in the next chapter and will be ignored in the following).

The authors compared the performance of a fine-tuned RoBERTa model as baseline, a fine-tuned LLM (Llama3-8b-Instruct), and three commercial LLMs (Gemini1.5-f, GPT4o and GPT4o-m) as well as the Llama3 used with prompting. In a preparatory experiment on prompt design, they determined that for task (i) a structured prompt with detailed instructions but without role assignment performed best, while for extraction (ii), prompts combining structured step-by-step instructions with an explicit role assignment were optimal. These two successful prompt types were then used for the main experiment. The central results for the first two tasks include:

- *Binary classification:* All LLMs clearly beat the fine-tuned RoBERTa. The fine-tuned Llama3-8b-Instruct is overall best, achieving a macro-F_1 of 0.76. With prompting, Gemini1.5-f and GPT4o are significantly better than Llama3.
- *Extraction:* Here, too, the fine-tuned Llama3 wins, but closely followed by Gemini1.5-f, which clearly outperforms all other prompt-based models. Interestingly, the RoBERTa model is more competitive in this task: It is outperformed by the prompt-based models only in the five-shot setting, as opposed to the 0- and 1-shot.

Generally, Guida et al. found a high performance variance across the different topics. They performed an extensive error analysis with the best 5-shot model (Gemini) and found, for instance, that false positives account for a clear majority of the errors (especially for *con* arguments), thus showing a trend for the LLMs to over-predict sentences to be critical toward the topic.

Naturally, more work on fine-tuning or prompting LLMs for AM tasks has been conducted in the community in recent years—some of it, which explores the assignment of argumentative relations, will be discussed in the following chapter (Sect. 5.4.3).

4.4 Summary

This chapter began to explore the landscape of automatic argument mining with an examination of the *argumentative discourse unit*, a span of text whose communicative purpose is that it plays a role in an argument. Identifying it—and its precise boundaries—in text can be very difficult even for human readers, and it is no coincidence that throughout the chapter we often encountered research that is based on the simplification that the *sentence* is regarded as the candidate unit, which reduces the overall task to its classification: Is it argumentative? If yes, what does it do in the argument?

For the central part of an argument, the claim, we looked at a set of different text genres and found striking differences in the way claims are formulated. The difficult situation is aptly summarized by Saint Dizier (2020):

> "A claim must introduce a debate: it must therefore be based on some form of evaluation, a thesis, a belief, a position, a rhetorical question or an assumption. A claim states something that is plausible but which may be questioned, possibly in a number of ways, in particular if the claim has several facets. This specific character of a claim can be induced by listeners from pragmatic factors. In a number of circumstances, this specific character is linguistically marked."

We demonstrated in Sect. 4.2.3 that the linguistic marking can differ widely, and on top of this problem, as Saint-Dizier remarks, the marking is done by speakers or writers only "in a number of circumstances", which entails that in other circumstances the marking can be absent and the claim is merely implicit. Consider:

(4.19) A: Do you think I should buy the new Jonathan Franzen novel?
B: I started reading a week ago and basically cannot stop, it totally absorbs me!

Chances are that B is conveying a positive opinion on the novel in question, though without overtly using any standard 'sentiment word'. Speaker A would then induce, as Saint-Dizier puts it, that B is in fact recommending a purchase, or *claiming* that A ought to buy the book, which is the kind of speech act A expects in response to their question. Such implicit claims (and also premises) have received some attention in AM, and we will discuss this topic separately later in Sect. 8.3.

When we turned to premises, and especially types of evidence, the prospects for generalizability seemed better: Table 4.3 shows that there are recurring types of evidence in studies that work with different corpora from different genres. Correspondingly, in research on transferring argument component detection models to other domains, we noted that this sometimes turned out easier for evidence than for claims.

Early approaches to ACTC that classified individual sentences (or other units) had only limited success not only because of their dependence on feature engineering; they also generally did not take the context into consideration. And *context* here has two senses: On the one hand, the text surrounding an AC candidate can provide hints, and on the other hand, the fit between claim and premise can become part of the model. In various places we pointed out that joint models showed superior performance compared to pipeline-dependent single-task models; and the recently-invoked task of 'claim/evidence pair extraction' (at the end of the previous section) is one case in point.

This observation actually connects the chapter to the next one: for argumentative relations, there is in the same way the option to solve subtasks individually, or to address component and relation identification jointly, leading to *end-to-end* models. This trend started before the advent of LLMs, but of course has now accelerated.

Argument Relation Identification 5

Identifying the relations between argument components, the topic of this chapter, becomes relevant when the constellations between the ACs are ambiguous—for example when the same text has more than one claim and several premises that need to be linked to 'their' claim. Another constellation is *serial* argumentation, where a claim is supported by a premise, which in turn is supported by another AC. These situations occur typically in the document- or discourse-based setting of argument mining, which is therefore the primary perspective for the chapter.

Even in short texts, argument relations can establish relatively intricate constellations, with fairly long distances between the connected ACs. For illustration, in Fig. 5.1 we replicate from Hua and Wang (2022, p. 423) two examples of *support* structures in the genres of scientific peer review and eRulemaking online comment.

In the following, we first discuss the task of binary relatedness classification (Sect. 5.1), followed by that of identifying different types of relations (Sect. 5.2). Then, we take the step to building entire trees or graphs that aim to represent the full structure of argumentation in a text or part of a text (Sect. 5.3). Finally, we turn to end-to-end approaches that perform several of the above-mentioned tasks simultaneously (Sect. 5.4).

Throughout the chapter, besides introducing the tasks in general, we mention research that is interesting for historical or for methodological reasons, or because of using kinds of data that we so far have not mentioned in the book.

5.1 Determining Relatedness

Usually, merely knowing the relatedness of two ACs is not of much interest as a standalone problem, and therefore the ARI task (argument relation identification), also known as the linking task, usually arises as part of a pipeline of AM steps, where it is followed by

M. Stede et al., *Argument Mining*, Synthesis Lectures on Human Language Technologies, https://doi.org/10.1007/978-3-032-32291-3_5

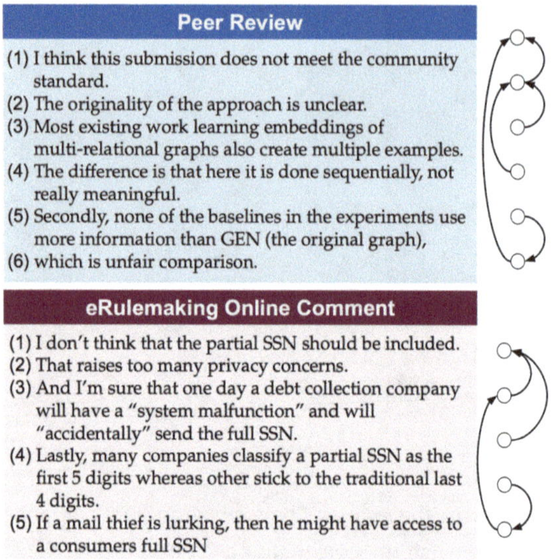

Fig. 5.1 Two examples of support relation constellations in short texts (Hua and Wang 2022, p. 423), licensed under CC-BY 4.0 International

argument relation type classification (ARTC), the topic of Sect. 5.2 below. ARI itself can be formulated as:

> Given two units that have been determined to be argumentative (and possibly have been classified for their type), are these units in some (unlabeled and undirected) argument relation to each other?

In settings where argument mining is performed on the sentence level rather than on arbitrary AC spans, ARI can be modeled in a more specific way by associating sentences with distances to their related sentences. For instance, Putra et al. (2021, p. 14) describe it for the genre of student essays:

> "Given an entire essay of N sentences as input, $s_1, \ldots, s_N$, a linking model outputs the distance $d_1, \ldots, d_N$ between each sentence s_i to its target. For instance, if a sentence is connected to its preceding sentence, the distance is $d = 1$. We consider those sentences that have no explicitly annotated outgoing links as linked to themselves ($d = 0$)."

ARI has frequently been observed as a particularly difficult task, because it amounts to finding the optimal structure in a potentially large search space of possible link combinations. Therefore, strategies for managing this search problem, with typically large class imbalances, are of particular interest in this section.

In the work of Stab and Gurevych (2014b) on the early and small version of the Persuasive Essay Corpus (PEC, 90 essays), the authors chose to ignore attack relations (which were rare in the data) and thus solved a binary ARI task that starts from given AC pairs and distinguishes support from non-support. The search space is kept small by working only on the paragraph level of the essays. In their feature-based support-vector machine (SVM) classification, the AC type (major claim, claim, premise) was one of the features, besides positional, syntactic and lexical features, where the latter includes a handcrafted list of discourse markers. The system is found to narrowly beat the majority baseline of 0.915 (F_1 for the non-support class). Interestingly, it turns out that the predicted type of the ACs does not yield a significant improvement when it is combined with all other features.

Using a similar feature-based approach on the English-language version of the argumentative microtext corpus, Peldszus and Stede (2015) faced a data imbalance of 464 related and 2000 unrelated pairs of argumentative discourse units. With 5–6 sentences, the texts are relatively short, and hence the search space is similar to that of the paragraphs in the Stab/Gurevych corpus. Peldszus and Stede, as part of a complete argument structure analysis, solved a directed version of the ARI task, trying to predict the "is-attached-to" relation. In this corpus, the baseline "attach to preceding segment" yields an F_1 value of 0.45 for this class, and a stochastic gradient descent (SGD) learner using similar features as those of Stab and Gurevych achieves 0.48.

Potash et al. (2017a) responded to the relatively low performances of early ARI classification with one of the first neural approaches to an argument mining problem. Working with both the AAE and microtext corpus, the authors assumed that AC detection has already been done and solved the tasks of predicting AC types (claim, major claim, premise) and link detection (i.e., establishing unlabeled relations). They propose that sequence-to-sequence attention modeling, specifically a Pointer Network (Vinyals et al. 2015) is well suited for this subproblem, as it can capture the sequential information of argument components, partly enforce the tree structure (the topic of Sect. 5.3), and jointly predict multiple subtasks with the hidden representations. For representing ACs, the system uses bag-of-words, GloVe embeddings, and positional features. Potash et al. reported results that outperform the previous work on the two corpora.

Subsequently, transformer models became popular for ARI. For example, Poudyal et al. (2020) made a corpus of court decisions available (from the European Court of Human Rights) that they labeled with ACs and support relations. After classifying AC types (premise, conclusion), they detect binary relatedness on sentence pairs. Here, the problem of the large search space is circumvented by considering only pairs that are at most five sentences apart; beyond this threshold, all material is predicted as unrelated. A RoBERTa model (Liu et al. 2019b) achieves a precision of 0.50 and a recall of 0.52, which echoes the earlier results on ARI, the obvious difference being that no feature engineering is being done.

Foreshadowing neural work on building complete structures that we will discuss later, we take a look at an alternative way of operationalizing the linking task, viz. seeing it as dependency parsing over segments (here: sentences). As an example, Putra et al. (2021) use the ICNALE-AS2R corpus of 434 essays (6000 sentences in total) written by English-as-a-foreign-language (EFL) learners, where sentences are annotated as non-/argumentative and linked with four different relations (support, attack, detail, restatement), though this particular paper ignores the labels and predicts merely the existence of a link.

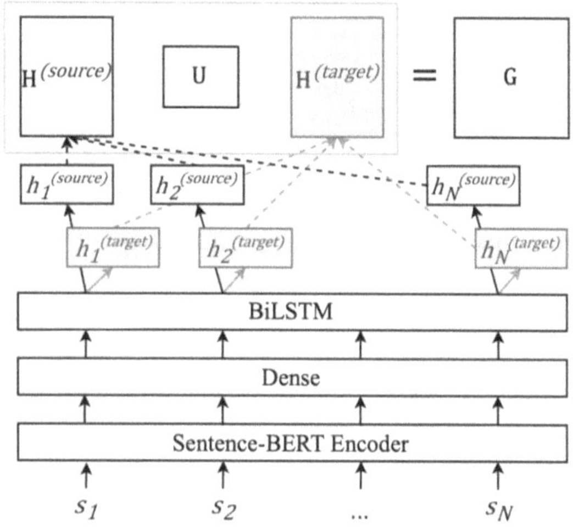

Fig. 5.2 Biaffine attention model for argument linking (Putra et al. 2021, p. 15), licensed under CC-BY 4.0 International

Figure 5.2 shows the system architecture used by Putra et al. The input sentences are encoded using sentence-BERT (Reimers and Gurevych 2019) and the embeddings are passed into a dense layer for dimensionality reduction. Next, a BiLSTM layer builds contextual sentence representations, which are passed into two different dense layers to encode the corresponding sentence when it acts as a source or target in a relation. Then, a biaffine transformation (Dozat and Manning 2017) is applied to all the source and target representations, which results in the final output matrix G, where each cell $g_{i,j}$ represents the probability of the source sentence s_i pointing to s_j. At last, G is being searched by a minimum-spanning tree algorithm that produces the output structure, where a sentence points to at most one other sentence (cf. Fig. 5.1 above for illustration).

Using this approach as a baseline, Putra et al. (2021) studied the effects of multitask and multi-corpora training. For multitask learning, they found that performance increases significantly when adding these two auxiliary tasks, which do not require extra annotation on the data:

- *Quasi-AC-type prediction:* Use the in- and out-degrees of the nodes in the dependency trees to encode attributes of ACs: *major claim* has only incoming links; non-leaf ACs have both outgoing and incoming links; leaf ACs have only outgoing links; non-ACs have neither incoming nor outgoing links.
- *Node depth prediction:* Six categories are used to differentiate places of nodes in the argumentative structure: depth 0 to depth 4, and depth 5+.

Further, the authors added the positions of sentences in the text as an extra feature to the network, by concatenating it to the initial sentence embeddings.

For multi-corpora training, Putra et al. (2021) emphasize the importance of selective sampling. The added corpus is AAE2 from Stab and Gurevych (2017b), which however differ from the texts in ICNALE-AS2R in terms of topics, length, proportion of non-ACs, and underlying relation types (AAE has only support and attack). The authors found that instead of taking all 400 AAE texts as additional training data, performance is better when excluding essays that are considerably longer than those in ICNALE-AS2R or contain more than two non-ACs. In this way the new training data retains some homogeneity.

Overall, with the various extra measures, the macro-F_1 for individual link predictions rose to 0.37 from 0.32, which indicates that, still, the linking task is generally very difficult on this corpus. Recall, however, that the setting is somewhat different from those in the work discussed before, as links now implicitly cover four quite different relation types.

5.2 Determining Relation Types

When establishing argument relations, in practice it is common to also determine their type, in order to get an informative representation of the arguments. This task of Argument Relation Type Classification (ARTC) can be run in a pipeline after ARI or—more frequently in implementations—in conjunction with ARI, when only the candidate ACs are given.

In the following we first discuss the most important argument relations *support* and *attack* and then introduce some work on methods of relation classification on different copora. The final subsection will take a look at additional, less common relations that have been used in some genre-specific argument corpora.

5.2.1 Support and Attack

Support As became clear throughout the previous chapters, *support* (in some approaches also called *inference*) is the most central—and often the only—relation that is being considered in AM corpora; after all, a minimal argument is commonly defined as combination of a claim with a supporting premise. One question that arises here is whether the support relation can be said to have meaningful subtypes: In Sects. 4.2.2 and 4.2.5, respectively, we discussed inventories of subtypes for claims and supporting premises; now we can ask, do these give rise to constraints of preferences on their combination in an argument?

In their work on LiveJournal (LJ) blogs and Wikipedia Talk (WT) pages, Biran and Rambow (2011) went through their annotated data, which on average contains 2.2 supporting statements per claim in WT, and 1.5 in LJ, and they found some patterns for claim and support pairs:[1]

[1] For reasons of space, we reproduce only one of the examples that the authors used to illustrate the claim (p. 364).

Fig. 5.3 Proportions of claim-premise types in Stab & Gurevych's AAE2 corpus, reannotated by Schaefer et al. (2023, p. 83), licensed under CC-BY 4.0 International

Claim Type	Premise Type	Proportion
Policy	Common-Ground	0.59
	Hypothetical-Instance	0.20
	Real-Example	0.11
	Statistics	0.09
	Testimony	0.01
Value	Common-Ground	0.47
	Hypothetical-Instance	0.24
	Real-Example	0.19
	Statistics	0.10
	Testimony	<0.01
Fact	Common-Ground	0.43
	Hypothetical-Instance	0.25
	Real-Example	0.17
	Statistics	0.15
	Testimony	<0.01
	other	<0.01

- Recommendation for action + motivation for proposed action;
  Claim: "I'd post an update with the new date immediately."
  Support: "In case anyone makes plans between now and when you post the reminder."
- Statement of like or dislike or of desires and longing + subjective reason for this;
- Statement of like or dislike or of desires and longing + claimed objective reason for this;
- Statement of subjectively perceived fact + proposed objective explanation;
- Claimed general objective statement + more specific objective statement that justifies the more general one.

The question of combination patterns was also briefly addressed by Park and Cardie (2014) in their study on the *verifiability* of argumentative statements. We mentioned it in Sect. 2.1 and give a slightly extended recapitulation of the proposed pairings here:

- Unverifiable claim + reason: "I don't like this wine, because it has so much tannin."
- Verifiable non-experiential ('public') claim + evidence: "I tell you Winston Churchill came to office in 1940. I saw it on Wikipedia!"
- Verifiable experiential ('private') claim + optional evidence: "I was not even close to the site of the accident. My mother showed me the new art exhibition downtown."

As a last example, some statistical patterns resulted from the annotation of fine-grained claim and evidence types in the AAE2 corpus, undertaken by Schaefer et al. (2023). In Fig. 5.3 we reproduce the proportions of evidence types per claim type, which shows a clear 'winner' for each type of claim.

These and other observations of patterns, however, did rarely translate into subtypes of the Support relation in actual corpus annotation and classification. One exception, which corresponds to some of the patterns given above, is the differentiation between relations *Reason* and *Evidence* in the CDTC corpus (Park and Cardie 2018, p. 1625):

- *Reason:* Proposition X is a reason for a proposition Y if X provides rationale for Y.
- *Evidence:* Proposition X is evidence for proposition Y if it proves whether proposition Y is true or not. The possible types of evidence ACs are limited to Testimony and Reference (see Sect. 4.2.5).

Occasionally, argument mining work on the support relation used classifiers trained on corpora that are annotated for *textual entailment* or TE (Dagan et al. 2013), which later was called *natural language inference* (NLI). Shared tasks on this problem have been popular for quite some time, independently of the AM community. NLI is defined as a directional relation between two text fragments, a *text* and a *hypothesis*; the relation holds whenever the truth of the hypothesis follows from that of the text. NLI is a fairly subjective annotation task and is only indirectly related to the strict notion of entailment in logic; nonetheless, it appeals to the notion of truth and thereby captures also a range of arguments that do not too heavily involve subjectivity (see the types above). While the idea of trying NLI modules on AM corpora seems tempting, early work (including Cabrio and Villata 2012 and Boltužić and Šnajder 2014) had only limited success; recently, interest has grown again with the advent of LLMs, which we discuss later.

Attack The attack relation, as the name suggests, inherently involves two parties who are arguing with each other, and where one may dispute the validity or the strength of an argument made by the other party. Consider:

(5.1) A: The world will collapse next year! A new epidemic has been forecasted on Telegram.
B. That's a silly argument. Don't believe everything you read there.

Though B is commenting here on A's argument as a whole, in argument mining the attack relation is predominantly used as linking two individual ACs (i.e., claims or premises), with the most usual configuration being that of a premise attacking a claim. Obviously, the clearest cases will be found in interactions, i.e., in spoken dialogue or in social media conversations.

Still, the notion applies to monologue text as well, as we illustrated already with example (4.16) in the previous chapter (Sect. 4.2.4), where a speaker advised to purchase a certain camera despite it also having a disadvantage (high price). Govier (2011) spoke of *counterconsiderations* that a speaker or writer can integrate into their argumentation, where they can either be merely a part of the author's unfolding decision process, or they can be used intentionally to anticipate (sometimes called *prebut*) a potential counterargument of the hearer or listener, which can then immediately be refuted, whereby the overall persuasive effect of the argumentation may increase. Not surprisingly, we therefore find attack relations for example in corpora with student essays (where it is taught to be important to also address 'the other side') and in scientific texts, where new claims need to be defended against potential objections that readers might have. For this genre, Mayer et al. (2020) in their annotation of medline abstracts, distinguish between the two relations *attack* and *partial attack*, which is characterized as not fully contradicting a statement but weakening the target statement by constraining its proposition. The authors give this example (p. 2110):

(5.2) [SLN biopsy is an effective and well-tolerated procedure.]$_1$ [However, its safety should be confirmed by the results of larger randomized trials and meta-analyses.]$_2$

Sentence 1 states a claim, which is generally upheld but toned down to some extent by sentence 2, thus forming a partial attack.

In the argumentative microtext corpus (Peldszus and Stede 2016b; Skeppstedt et al. 2018), the authors of the texts were specifically instructed to try to account for the other side in their short texts, and as a result, almost each of them actually contains an attack relation. In the annotations of this data, every AC is labeled for the side, i.e., whether it represents the stance of the author defending their claim, or that of an imagined opposing viewpoint. This type distinction is in addition to differentiating support and attack relations, and these distinctions are indeed independent, because, for example, the other side may in turn support their own counterconsideration with premises (see below in Sect. 5.3).

In the microtext corpus, *attack* is actually only a cover term for two subtypes of counterconsideration: the *rebuttal* and the *undercutter*. Peldszus and Stede (2013) illustrate the difference with this example:

(5.3) [We should tear the building down.]$_C$ [It is full of asbestos.]$_S$ [On the other hand, many people liked the view from the roof.]$_R$

(5.4) [We should tear the building down.]$_C$ [It is full of asbestos.]$_S$ [The building might be cleaned up, though.]$_U$

In Example 5.3, the third statement (R) *rebuts* the claim (C) by making a point that would invalidate the proposal of tearing the building down; it thus questions the validity of the claim. In contrast, the third statement of Example 5.4 (U) is directed toward the second (supporting) statement. It does not question the validity of the statement "full of asbestos" (i.e., it does not rebut it), but it questions the *relevance* of the support for the claim: Yes, there is asbestos, but that can be removed, and therefore we do not need to demolish the building. Thus the target of an *undercut* is actually not an individual statement but a relation between two of them.

Mayer et al. (2020) also distinguished undercut and rebut in their corpus of scientific abstracts, and more recently, Ye and Teufel (2024) dedicated a detailed study to the undercut relation. They collected data from Quora,[2] a platform that features answers to questions, where users often provide "a stand-alone cogently structured complete argument, often supplemented with explanations and supporting evidence" (Ye and Teufel 2024, p. 60), in contrast to other online venues that emphasize interactive exchange with often rather brief contributions. The QuoraAM dataset contains 400 arguments annotated with support and attack, where the latter can target either a proposition or a relation—in which case it functions as an undercut. This happens in 326 cases, about 25% of all attacks in the corpus. Ye and Teufel in turn identified three subcategories of undercut:

- *Rejection:* Deny the relevance of the target relation.
- *Low importance:* Question the importance of the target relation.
- *Alternative option:* State that the current solution is not the only option, or provide alternatives.

The authors perform automatic classification with a parser based on graph neural networks (GNNs). The F_1 score for the general attack relation is 0.40, with only a small difference between that of undercut and rebuttal. (The three subtypes of undercut were not actually used in the annotation.)

In some corpora, attack is a relatively rare relation in comparison to support. For example, in the AAE2 corpus by Stab and Gurevych (2017b), of 1400 relations only 160 are attacking. The combined microtext corpus (parts 1 and 2) has 780 supports and 388 attacks. In QuoraAM, there are 2752 instances of support and 1190 instances of attack. But there are also corpora with a relatively even distribution, such as the IBM corpus from the debate motions database (Bar-Haim et al. 2017a) or the UKP corpus of online comments (Stab et al. 2018b).

5.2.2 Corpora and Methods for Support/Attack Identification

Over the years, a number of studies have compared ranges of different methods for detecting support and attack relations across different corpora. We discuss some of them below in chronological order and quote their main results. Notice that numbers can hardly be compared across studies, due to different corpora being used, different setups of the task (binary versus ternary classification; use of context window to delimit the search space; etc.)—they are meant here merely as indicating the difficulty of the task.

Aker et al. (2017) worked with two datasets: AAE2 (Stab and Gurevych 2017b) and the IBM Wikipedia dataset of Aharoni et al. (2014) with annotations of claims and

[2] https://www.quora.com (accessed January 15, 2026).

evidence for given topics. The setup is to consider all claim/premise pairs in a dataset and classify for support versus attack; negative instances are sampled from the cross product of all claims and premises. The authors use eight different traditional supervised classifiers and a combination of six feature types: structural, lexical, part of speech (POS), indicator words, features of surrounding sentences, and word2vec embeddings (Mikolov et al. 2013). Experiments are run only within-domain; best results are in the range of 0.6 macro-F_1 (class-wise results are not given). Structural features like token frequencies and punctuation are generally most helpful, while the word embeddings do not help. Random Forest turns out as a successful classifier.

Cocarascu et al. (2020) turned to neural network methods and cross-domain test settings. They used ten corpora in total and compared non-neural baselines to four neural architectures, including an autoencoder and an attention architecture. The task is to take the given claim/premise pairs and to predict the relation type as support or attack. Features are POS tags, the output of a textual entailment classifier and a sentiment classifier, and (for comparison) non-contextualised versus contextualised (BERT) word embeddings. Training is done in different constellations on one or two datasets, the remaining corpora are used for testing. Findings include that the F_1 difference between the support and attack class can be enormous for several corpora; non-neural baselines perform weaker across the board; and BERT embeddings do not yield an advantage over non-contextualised ones. The best macro-averaged F_1 scores for the binary prediction range between 0.53 and 0.54.

Hua and Wang (2022) attended to the question of the distance between the related ACs and measured it in five corpora (AAE2, AbstRCT, ECHR, CDCP, and their new AMPERE++ corpus of scientific peer reviews). Figure 5.4 shows that the corpora differ in terms of the extent of that distance and also in skewedness: In AMPERE++ and CDCP, premises more often follow the claims they are supporting. For their system, they establish a context window of 20 sentences for candidate collection, which captures 98% of all relations in the dataset. Hua and Wang aim at an efficient and easily-adaptable technical approach. They use a RoBERTa encoder which reads the current *head* segment H_j as well as the surrounding segments in the context window. After encoding, each *tail* candidate representation H_i is concatenated with that of H_j to form the input to the output layer, which predicts support, attack, or no-relation. Hua and Wang conduct experiments with domain transfer and find that in many cases, adding domain-external training data yields

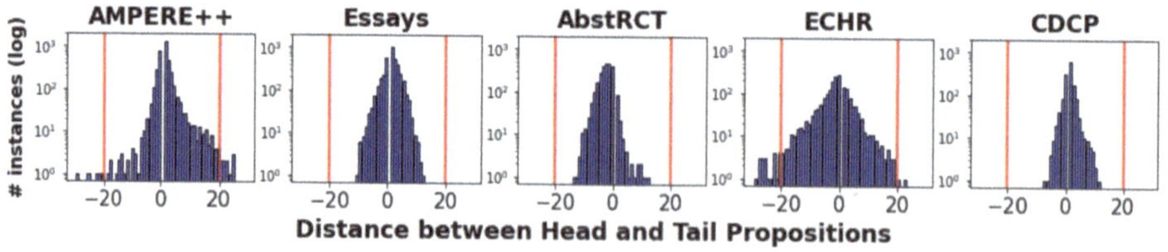

Fig. 5.4 Distribution of distance (number of sentences) between claim (*head*) and premise (*tail*) in various corpora. Positive values indicate that the premise linearly follows the claim. Hua and Wang (2022, p. 428), licensed under CC-BY 4.0 International

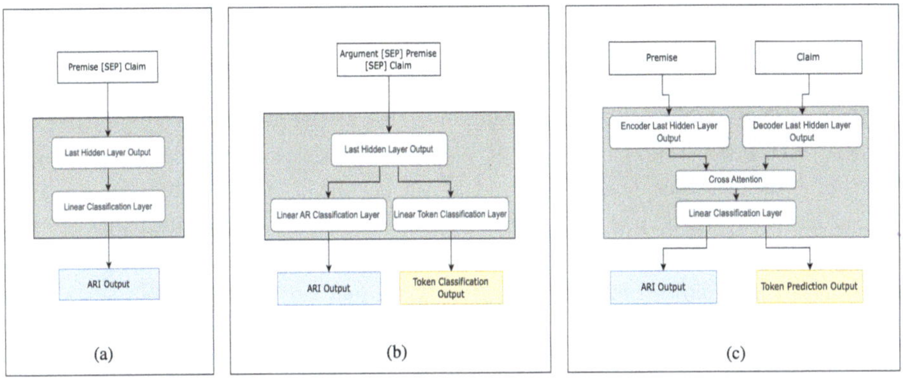

Fig. 5.5 Three modeling approaches used in the ARIES benchmark. The ARI output (in *light blue*) is evaluated, while token classification and prediction outputs (in *light yellow*) are auxiliary tasks. Gemechu et al. (2024, p. 4), licensed under CC-BY 4.0 International. (**a**) Sequence classification. (**b**) Token classification. (**c**) Sequence-to-sequence alignment

better results than the standard in-domain setting. In addition, they compare different active learning (Cohn et al. 1996) strategies for training data selection and show that preferring instances containing discourse markers (cf. Sect. 4.2.4) is beneficial.

Gemechu et al. (2024) present ARIES, a benchmark for the three-way support/attack/none classification of candidate pairs, which are supposed to be already classified as claims and premises. The authors use eight different datasets that are common in AM and compare three modeling approaches, which are depicted in Fig. 5.5. Sequence pair classification, the most popular approach so far, treats the two ACs as entire sequences of text. Token classification (inspired by Eger et al. 2017, cf. Sect. 5.4) is a multitask setup that predicts the actual span of a claim given a premise, or the other way round, while simultaneously predicting the relation between the two units. Sequence-to-sequence alignment is inspired by work on machine translation and takes the premise as input and the claim as expected output. This is done in two steps. First, sequence-to-sequence modelling attempts to improve the embedding representations of the input premise-claim pairs; afterwards, a relation classifier is trained on the resulting embeddings. Orthogonal to these three models, the three main transformer-based architectures are being tested: encoder-only (RoBERTa), decoder-only (DialoGPT, Zhang et al. 2020c), and encoder-decoder (T5). Gemechu et al. report within-dataset and cross-dataset (train on one, test on all others) results, where the former yield new state of the art performances for various datasets, and the latter generally reveals huge performance losses.

Ruiz-Dolz et al. (2024a) apply the task of support/attack/none classification across three domains and also three languages: financial market comments in English and Chinese, public debates in Catalan and English, and essays in English. The Chinese financial corpus is a new contribution, while the other four are established AM datasets. XLM-RoBERTa is used in different train/test data constellations, which include fine-tuning on the various combinations of source and target corpus. This covers changing the domain while holding the language constant, and vice versa.

The Role of Context We close this section by taking a brief look at the role of context in the ARI/ARTC tasks. The vast majority of research considers the two candidate ACs as the sole input to the classifier; see, e.g., Fig. 5.5 above. As one of the few exceptions, Hua and Wang (2022) emphasized that their RoBERTa model embeds a long context span in order to access also the surroundings of the two ACs. Also, as we mentioned, they point out the beneficial role of exploiting the presence of discourse markers for selecting instances in an active learning approach to ARI.

In earlier AM research on ARI, Nguyen and Litman (2016) had emphasized the importance of considering both information from the topic of the text and from the context surrounding the ACs. Regarding the context, they used LDA to differentiate between (topic-independent) 'argument words' on the one hand and 'domain words' on the other. They used the presence of argument words as binary features, and several features measuring the domain word overlap between the two segments. Their dataset is the AAE2 corpus, and here is an example, with argument words underlined and domain words in italics (Nguyen and Litman 2016, p. 1131).

(5.5) Essay 54. Topic: museum and art gallery will disappear soon?
Source/premise: more and more people can *watch exhibitions* through *television* or *internet* at *home* due to *modern technology*
Target/claim: some people think *museums* and *art galleries* will *disappear soon*

While adding only the topic features does not beat the authors' baseline, significantly better results (macro-F_1: 0.75) are achieved when also adding the output of two discourse parsers; one for PDTB relations (Prasad et al. 2008), one for RST structure (Mann and Thompson 1988). (In Sect. 5.3 we will return to the idea of integrating discourse structure information into AM.)

Following this theme, Opitz and Frank (2019) aimed to thoroughly disentangle the predictive effects of the material within the ACs from those of the context. They also worked with AAE2 and adopted a feature-based SVM classification approach following Stab and Gurevych (2017b). They compared the effects of using three different feature sets:

- *content-ignorant:* features computed from the contexts of the ACs (e.g., leading and trailing tokens surrounding the AC spans);
- *content-based:* features computed from the content of the ACs;
- *full access:* the union of both sets, plus information about discourse relations surrounding the ACs.

The individual features are inspired by those of Stab and Gurevych (2017b) and Aker et al. (2017), mentioned above. Opitz and Frank find that classifiers work best when focusing on the content-ignorant features, hence when ignoring the actual AC. They contend that this may be problematic, for instance in the context of cross-document linking, where determining the relevance of an AC should give most attention to its content. Nonetheless, the message here, too, is that context matters for identifying support and attack.

5.2.3 Other Relations

While support and attack, possibly with associated subtypes as discussed above, are clearly at the center of ARI/ARTC, some additional relations have occasionally been worked with. We discuss them in three groups.

Fine-Grained Argumentative Impact Inspired by the work of Freeman (2011), the argumenative microtext corpus of Peldszus and Stede (2016b) contains *linked* versions of both support and attack. These are constellations of two ACs, where one or each of them alone would possibly not be strong enough to successfully establish the argumentative relation, but the two of them in conjunction are. (For comparability with other datasets, however, in many corpus-based studies they often get 'de-linked' into two separate relation instances.) Here is an example from the annotation scheme description:

(5.6) [We should tear the building down.]$_{claim}$ [It is full of asbestos.]$_{p1}$. [All buildings with hazardous materials should be demolished.]$_{p2}$

While $p1$ can provide the evidence for the claim in its own right (inviting an inference on the reader's side), $p2$ can do so only if the contamination is already known to the reader. Hence, $p1$ and $p2$ form a linked-support for the claim.

Turning to arguments in dialogue, *Agree* and *Disagree* are sometimes used in AM as cross-turn relations with an argumentative impact. This can be done both for spoken dialogue and for interactions on social media. For example, Hou and Jochim (2017) use agreement and disagreement in their models of argumentative exchanges on the work on the Debatepedia platform.

Identity and Similarity Pure repetitions of statements might be regarded as just an ordinary fact of language use, but they can play an important role of realizing the authors' argumentative intent, as discussed by Koszowy et al. (2022) in their analysis of the *Rephrase* relation. A corpus where it appears relatively often is the US2016 transcripts of presidential candidate debates (see Sect. 5.3.3). Also, when Skeppstedt et al. (2018) annotated the Part 2 of the microtext corpus, among the 930 ACs they found 29 instances of *Restatement*, 19 of which were repetitions of the main claim of the text. Other work using *Restatement* includes that of Putra et al. (2021) on the student essay corpus ICNALE-AS2R, mentioned above.

The *Semantically-same* relation used in the SciArg corpus of scientific argumentation (Lauscher et al. 2018b) indicates a paraphrase relation similar to Restatement, but in SciArg it connects ACs that are possibly situated in different documents, which is different from an author intentionally re-iterating a claim or premise. Similarly, SciArg uses *Contradicts* to indicate the incompatibility of two statements. This is important, for example, when two claims about the same scientific matter are not compatible. A contradiction, too, may or may not be an intentional move of an author, whereas the standard *Attack* is generally produced to refute or weaken a claim.

Discourse Relations While the connection between argument and models of complete discourse structure will be covered below in Sect. 5.3.2, we mention here some work that uses individual discourse relations (cf. Sect. 2.5.2) as an extension of the analysis of argumentation.

In this vein, both the aforementioned ICNALE-AS2R corpus and the corpus of Accuosto and Saggion (2019) contain a *Detail* relation, which denotes an elaboration on a preceding AC. Elaborating is clearly not a genuinely-argumentative move—it can occur basically in any type of text—and hence is to be regarded as a general discourse relation. The same holds, e.g., for *Affiliation*, *Co-occurrence* and *Co-relevance*, which Liu et al. (2024a) use for the analysis of arguments in online financial forums.

A more comprehensive integration of argumentative relations and discourse relations is proposed for the application of essay scoring by Ren et al. (2025), who work with 226 essays in the Chinese language. The authors use rich inventories of both AC types and relations—though their categories do not always match with common accounts of discourse structure; for instance, one of their AC types is *Elaboration*, which in discourse research would always be treated as a relation between two units. Ren et al. use four discourse relations that can hold between ACs of the same type (e.g., *Contrast, Concession*) and ten different relations holding across AC types (e.g., *Detail, Restatement, Example*). Testing BERT, RoBERTA and various large language models, a fine-tuned Qwen LLM (Yang et al. 2025a) yields the best result, which is still relatively low, however (0.32 macro-F_1).

5.3 Building Argument Graphs

In the previous sections, we treated the task of linking argument components as a set of individual decisions: Pairs of ACs are being classified for standing in some argumentative relation or not, irrespective of what the other linking decisions in the surrounding context are. For many practical applications that is a suitable approach. For some tasks involving discourse-based AM, however, it may not be sufficient. Consider the case of an educational system that is supposed to evaluate a student's argumentative essay and give feedback on how well the author has built up their arguments throughout the text. This process may benefit from building a representation of the complete structure that connects the ACs in the text, where properties of this structure can contribute to the essay evaluation. Or, take the example of a social scientist who is interested in the unfolding discussion of a political issue on some social media channel. Mapping out how the participants respond to one another again yields a structural representation, now of the overall discussion over time. In both cases, the structure is technically a graph, where ACs constitute nodes, and argumentative relations make up the edges—albeit with different properties.

In this section, we first consider the structures that are commonly built for monologue text, followed by a digression to specific approaches that construct argument graphs on top of general-purpose representations of text structure as built by so-called discourse parsers. In the last subsection, we look at efforts on analyzing the structure of conversations, either spoken or on social media.

5.3.1 Monologue Text

Types of Structures To see the different factors that contribute to the overall structure of an argumentative text, we first look again at Example (4.16) from the previous chapter, repeated here, but with added subscripts indicating the types of components that we had assigned:

(5.7) [You should buy that camera,]$_{cl}$ because [it has a brand-new excellent sensor.]$_{sup}$ [OK, it is quite expensive.]$_{obj}$ [But it's worth the money!]$_{sup}$

In Chap. 4, we had analyzed the last sentence simply as providing support. But notice that we are missing something if our ARI module simply links it to the first sentence (claim). The statement has a tight connection to the preceding objection, rendering it much weaker than it first sounds. Its function can be described as *counter-attack*: The objection is in attack relation to the claim, and the last sentence in turn is in attack relation to the objection. Notice that making these decisions requires considering the argument as a whole, and evaluating the contributions of its individual steps.

Another phenomenon of argument structure is the *serialisation* of arguments that we had illustrated at the beginning of this chapter in Fig. 5.1: One AC supports an AC that in turn supports another AC (and so on). This is interesting on the one hand because it blurs the distinction between claim and premise (some units can have both functions, being related to more than one AC); on the other hand, it is unlikely that serializations of ACs in a text are not constrained by some overall well-formedness constraints: For reasons of cognitive processing ease, chains of adjacent ACs are more likely than arbitrary crossings of support chains where the reader would need to jump from one such chain to another while incrementally reading ACs.

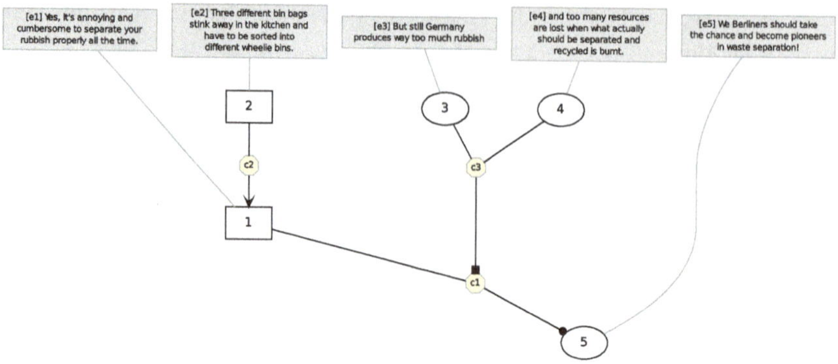

Fig. 5.6 Argument tree of a text in the argumentative microtext corpus (Peldszus and Stede 2016b). Elliptical nodes represent ACs from the proponent's view; rectangular nodes represent the opponent's view. Relations drawn with arrowhead are support; relations with circled head are attack (rebut or undercut, depending on the target). Used with Permission

In brief: While the previous section views AC linking as a pure bottom-up processing task, in this section we take the perspective of adding some top-down control that enforces certain properties of the desired target structure.

In their early AM work, Mochales Palau and Moens (2009) proposed to represent the argument structure in court decisions with trees rather than more general graphs, and experimented with context-free grammars for deriving the tree from the text. Subsequent work adopted the decision on trees, such as the annotation scheme of Peldszus and Stede (2013), which suggests a set of building blocks from which an arbitrarily complex tree can be constructed recursively. This scheme was used in the argumentative microtext corpus, and we show an example in Fig. 5.6. Likewise, trees are used in the AAE2 corpus of Stab and Gurevych (2017b), who posit (p. 627) that for the genre of essays, the tree-breaking property of a *divergent* argument, where a single premise is linked to two different claims, is unlikely to occur.

A different view is taken in the eRulemaking (CDCP) corpus. Niculae et al. (2017) argue that its social media texts are less well-formed than those in, e.g., the microtext or the AAE corpus, and that trees are not powerful enough to represent the structures adequately. Figure 5.7, taken from Bao et al. (2021), shows a sample text and annotation, where there is no single root (claim), and unit $AC2$ supports two other units, which is an instance of divergent argument. Niculae et al. report that 20% of the comments in the corpus give rise to such non-tree representations, and that 28% of the comments have no links at all. The annotator agreement in terms of Krippendorff's α is given as 0.65 for role assignment, and 0.44 for linking. A second corpus whose annotations allow for divergent arguments is AbstRCT (Mayer et al. 2020).

Besides trees and general graphs, a third type of representation, which was used by Habernal and Gurevych (2017) follows a modified Toulmin scheme, which we explained in Sect. 3.4.1. The key difference is in its static nature, i.e., the Toulmin scheme does not aim

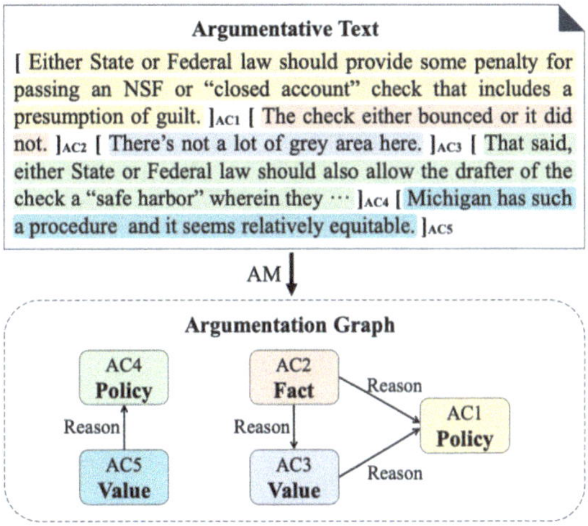

Fig. 5.7 Argumentation structure graph from the Cornell eRulemaking Corpus, adapted from Bao et al. (2021, p. 6354). Licensed under CC-BY 4.0 International

at recursively constructing complex configurations. The relational structure—involving claim, premise, backing, rebuttal and refutation—is hard-wired by the scheme, and hence text annotation consists in labeling ACs with their respective types, whereby the scheme gets instantiated.

Building Trees or Graphs Automatically Following early experiments on building argument trees with context-free grammars by Mochales Palau and Moens (2009) and Saint-Dizier (2012), a second phase of structure-building was based on segment-wise classification of ACs. Habernal and Gurevych (2017), for example, found that the vast majority of their web documents contained only one argument, and hence its analysis amounts to a single instantiation of the Toulmin scheme. The authors implemented BIO sequence tagging with 11 labels: *O* (not a part of any argument component), *Backing-B, Backing-I, Claim-B, Claim-I, Premise-B, Premise-I, Rebuttal-B, Rebuttal-I, Refutation-B, Refutation-I.* While the manual corpus annotation is on token level, for the automatic classification Habernal and Gurevych simplified the problem and projected the annotations to the sentence level; thus every sentence receives one of the labels given above. An SVM with a rich feature set is used for the labeling, and the authors found that best performance is reached when using the complete feature set, which also includes (less common) coreference and other discourse features, sentiment and topic distributions.

Turning to tree structures, in the spirit of the pipeline approach to AM, Peldszus and Stede (2015) proposed a four-stage approach to building argumentative structures for the microtext corpus:

1. Segmenting the text (ACS)
2. Classifying each AC on several dimensions, with bookkeeping of the resulting probabilities:

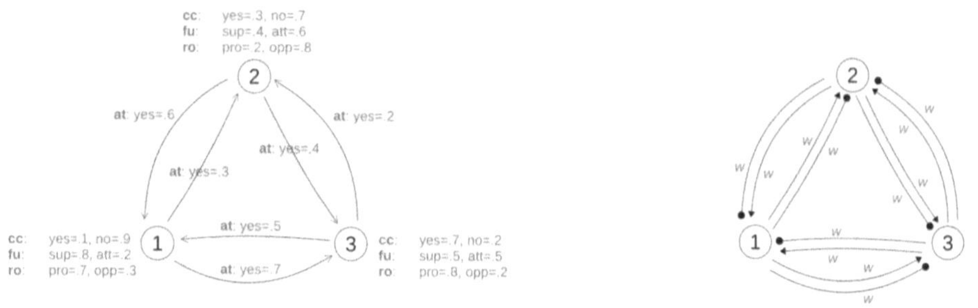

Fig. 5.8 An example evidence graph before (left) and after (right) combining the predicted probabilities of the different levels into a single edge score (values omitted here for readability), adapted from Peldszus and Stede (2015, p. 943)

- cc: is the AC the *central claim* of the text? (part of ACTC)
- role: does the AC represent the stance of the proponent (author) or the imagined opponent? (part of ACTC)
- attachment: for all target-AC candidates, is the AC linked to it in the argument structure? (ARI)
- function: does the AC have the function of supporting or attacking (an unspecified AC)? (ARTC)

3. Mapping the classification probabilities of the previous step to a fully-connected weighted graph (the *evidence graph*)
4. Decoding the optimal tree structure

A simplified example, with merely three ACs, is given in Fig. 5.8. On the left, there is a fully-connected directed graph that shows nodes and edges with the individual probabilites that have been computed for all ACs in step 2. A set of systematic rules maps the probabilities to weights that are then attached to the fully-connected multigraph on the right. Here, any pair of nodes is connected by four edges, which represent support and attack, respectively, in the two directions. Finally, in step 4, an implementation of the standard Minimum Spanning Tree (MST) algorithm (Chu and Liu 1965; Edmonds 1967) decoded the optimal structure. On the microtext corpus, the system achieved an F-score of 0.72 for identifying the argumentative relations and 0.87 for recognizing claims.

An alternative to building trees via MST decoding is *Integer Linear Programming* or ILP for short (Roth and Tau Yih 2004). This is an optimization technique operating over a set of linear equations, and thus presupposes that constraints enforcing global consistency can be formulated as numerical equations. Persing and Ng (2016) employed the approach for performing joint inference over the output of ACTC and ARTC systems on the early (small) version of the AAE Corpus, and Stab and Gurevych (2017b) applied it to the final corpus of 402 essays. For the argumentative microtext corpus, Afantenos et al. (2018) replicated the first two ILP approaches as well as the MST approach of Peldszus and

Stede (2015) (using improved versions of the base classifiers) and use three types of constraints:

- *Tree constraints*: All nodes have one or no outgoing edge; the root node has no outgoing edge; cycles are ruled out.
- *Relation labeling*: Every node has exactly one function (support or attack).
- *Interactions*: The root node (central claim) must be in proponent's voice; a support relation can hold only between nodes in the same voice; etc.

The comparative analysis by Afantenos et al. led to new state-of-the-art results for the microtexts and revealed that MST and ILP have similar performance there.

A shortcoming of the approaches discussed thus far is that they generally do not systematically incorporate the interdependencies between the various AM subtasks into the learning regime. This changed when neural networks entered the field, and this will be the topic of Sect. 5.4 below. But first, we take a look at experiments with incorporating information about discourse structure, in monologue text and in conversations.

5.3.2 Exploiting Discourse Structure Information

In Chap. 2, specifically in Sect. 2.5.2, we briefly introduced Rhetorical Structure Theory or RST (Mann and Thompson 1988). An RST analysis of a text is a tree structure that recursively connects adjacent text segments by means of a *coherence relation* such as Elaboration, Cause or Contrast. The proposed set of 25 relations is meant to be applicable to any kind of text; Fig. 2.2 showed an example of an RST analysis. A related approach is the Penn Discourse Treebank (Prasad et al. 2008), which also assigns coherence relations to adjacent text spans but does not build a tree structure over the individual relations; the associated computational task is called *shallow discourse parsing*.

Parallel Annotation: Arguments and RST Both for theoretical and for practical reasons (discourse parsing has reached a certain degree of robustness) it is interesting to study the relationship between the rhetorical and the argumentative structure of a text. For Part 1 of the argumentative microtext corpus, discourse structure has been annotated as additional layers, one of them being RST (Stede et al. 2016). Using this data, Peldszus and Stede (2016a) undertook a qualitative analysis of the correspondences between the argument and RST trees, and compared different ways of automatically mapping an RST tree to an argument structure tree according to the microtext scheme; however, the evaluation was done only on manually-annotated trees. As a next step, Hewett et al. (2019) used automatic discourse parsers following the two frameworks of RST and PDTB on the microtexts, and they added features of their output to the four base classifiers of the above-mentioned argument structure parser of Afantenos et al. (2018). It turned out that the PDTB features were more helpful than the RST ones, but combining both again improved the results.

For a different domain, a similar case study was done by Accuosto and Saggion (2019) on the SciDTB corpus of ACL anthology abstracts with RST trees. For 60 of those abstracts, the authors added argument structure information: types of ACs as well as relations (support, detail, additional, sequence). For the tasks of predicting (i) the AC type, (ii) the argumentative function (type of relation) and (iii) the target segments for attaching, individual models were trained with BiLSTMs on several types of word embeddings. Their performance is compared to encoders that have been trained with the RST annotations (broken down to labeling the individual discourse units with rhetorical relation and attachment target). Accuosto and Saggion found that the models with RST-trained encoders indeed performed better for all three argument structure task.

Recently, discourse structure information has been integrated also into neural end-to-end models (which we discuss in more detail below in Sect. 5.4). Using the RST-annotated microtext corpus, Chistova (2023) demonstrated that a biaffine dependency parsing model benefits from enhancing the dependency arc scores with discourse coefficients obtained from the RST tree. She uses on the one hand the RST adjacency matrix with the link information, and on the other hand the relation types, which are encoded into a scalar value with an additional trainable layer. In addition, Chistova augments the training data by pursuing the Russian version of the microtext corpus (Fishcheva and Kotelnikov 2019) and in addition running English–Russian machine translation both ways, resulting overall in four variants of the microtexts, on which the author conducted RST parsing. Chistova concludes that the paraphrases of the individual ADUs have a positive effect on AM performance, while the four alternative RST structures may in the end not be helpful.

Sun et al. (2024) propose the *DENIM* method for incorporating discourse structure information into a generative model (BART) that identifies claims and premises, as well as support and attack relations on the AAE2 and AbstRCT corpora. The authors use an RST parser but reduce the relation set to Expansion, Contingency, Comparison (the three broad classes of the PDTB framework). A discourse structure encoder (BART encoder followed by a relational graph convolutional network, RGCN) converts the RST tree into dense vectors, which then get disassembled and allocated to the transformer layers as prefixes. After conversion to supplementary key and value matrices, these prefixes influence the attention calculation and guide the generation mechanism. The experiments and ablation tests demonstrate that the discourse structure information leads to significant performance gains on both corpora, and especially on AbstRCT.

Mutlitask Learning with Discourse Information Another neural system, which uses discourse information in a reduced form (as compared to RST trees), has been proposed by Gemechu and Reed (2025). The authors map the annotations of four corpora to a common format that holds the information for the ACTC, ARI and ARTC tasks: the AAE and CDCP corpora representing monologue, and US2016 and QT30 representing dialogue (see also the next subsection). The argument component boundaries are assumed to be given.

A key idea is to move from a purely local identification of relations between ACs to a procedure that involves the overall argument structure of the text or dialogue. Motivated

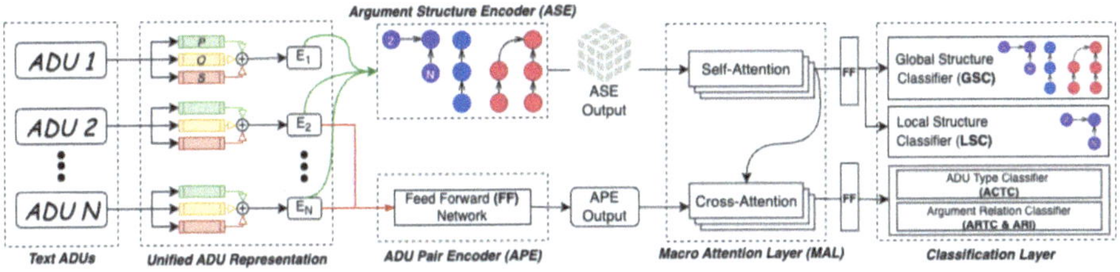

Fig. 5.9 System architecture of the CU-MAM system (Gemechu and Reed 2025, p. 19735), which solves the main tasks of learning ACTC and ARTC/ARI, as well as two auxiliary tasks of learning global and local argumentative text structure. Used under CC-BY 4.0 International

by the discourse structure theory of Grosz and Sidner (1986), the authors distinguish two kinds:

- *Global structure:* The set of all argument relations that hold between the ACs of a text. This structure represents the central purpose (author's intention) of the text
- *Local structure:* The set of argument relations that together form a segment of the text; a segment starts with a node that has no incoming edges (relations) and ends with a node that has no outgoing edge. This structure represents the purpose of the associated discourse segment.

Notice that local structure is defined by the constellation of argument relations, which means that its coverage need not necessarily correspond to a contiguous text portion. In a dialogue, for example, a local structure can also involve utterances from different speakers, which are (topically and) argumentatively related.

Figure 5.9 shows the system architecture proposed by Gemechu and Reed. On the left hand side, the input is a pre-segmented text whose ACs (here called ADUs) are represented with sentence embeddings (S) and with positional encoding of the linear order (O) of ADUs and the shift of participants (P) (for dialogue data). On the right hand side there are four classification layers; this includes two for the main tasks of ACTC and ARI/ARTC. In addition, two auxiliary tasks are learned, viz. the aforementioned global and local structures. The center of the architecture includes these components:

1. Argument structure encoder: A graph neural network (GNN) for the global and local structure. Starting from a fully-connected graph, during training it learns to encode the actual argument structure of a text.
2. AC (ADU) pair encoder: A feedforward layer is applied to the unified embeddings of two ACs in order to capture their relation.
3. Macro-attention layer: *(top)* Two self-attention layers attend to the argument graph from component (1), learning the local and global structures that are relevant to the ADU pair from component (2). *(bottom)* For contextualising AC and AR classifications within the

text structure, the outputs of the self-attention layers are fused with the AC pair output from component (2) using a cross-attention mechanism.

Gemechu and Reed (2025) report results that surpass those obtained by earlier work of Morio et al. (2020) and Bao et al. (2021) (see Sect. 5.4.2) on the AAE and CDCP corpora. Likewise, new best results for US2016 and QT30 (see Sect. 5.3.3) are reported; the authors attribute the gains to the incorporation of the text structure information.

5.3.3 Conversation Structure

Discourse structure arises not only in monologue text but also in dialogical interactions, though in a different way: There is no top-down well-formedness constraint ruling over the conversation (as is the case for the coherent monologue when modeled, e.g., with RST); instead, some kind of structure evolves locally and incrementally throughout the conversation.

Twitter Conversations Among the most simple forms of conversation is a pair of tweets where one is a response to the other. Argumentative relations across such pairs have been annotated for instance by Bosc et al. (2016), and in a smaller corpus study by Schaefer et al. (2025). The latter work showed that tweets issued by German members of parliament can contain fairly elaborate arguments, with support and attack relations holding both within tweets and between a 'root' tweet and a reply tweet.

An example of a large-scale study on longer Twitter conversation threads is the work by Ruckdeschel et al. (2024). They retrieved 2.5 million (German) tweets on the topic of nuclear energy using keyword search and then utilized the *reply-to* relation to build conversation chains; most of them turned out to be of length 6–10. With the help of English-language training datasets, they used the multilingual XLM-RoBERTa-large model to label the tweets for stance and topical aspects, and finally employed a pattern mining algorithm to extract recurring patterns over these annotations. In the end, the authors interpret alteration between pro and con stances in subsequent tweets of a chain as an attack relation, while identical stance is taken to indicate a support relation. The resulting dataset is then qualitatively interpreted for temporal dynamics of the nuclear energy debate in Germany.

Reddit Threads Chakrabarty et al. (2019) worked with the Change My View subreddit, where arguments are exchanged among discussants and rated for success (of changing the original author's view), cf. Sect. 4.2.2. They collected discussion threads with a total of 380 individual turns containing 2800 sentences. The authors employ principles of conversation structure to constrain the annotation of argumentative moves: In *intra-turn* relations (i.e., same author) a premise can support or attack a claim or another premise; in *inter-turn* relations (different authors), a claim can agree or disagree with another claim.

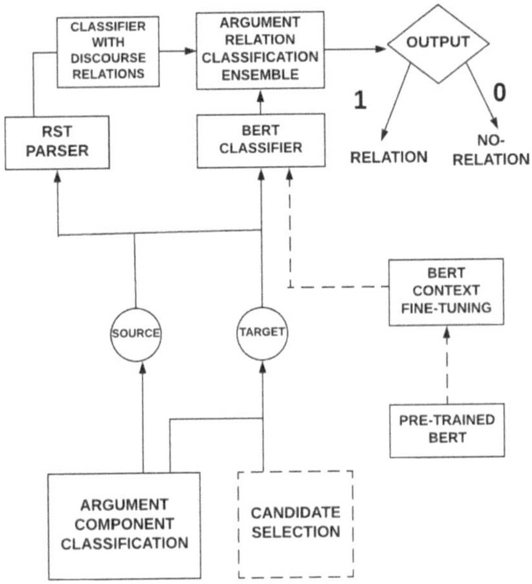

Fig. 5.10 Overview of the AMPERSAND discussion thread argument mining system. The *candidate selection* component is used only for intra-turn relations. Adapted from Chakrabarty et al. (2019, p. 2937). Licensed under CC-BY 4.0 International

The disagreement relation is split into rebut and undercut (see above), and an additional relation is *partial*, which denotes that a claim agrees to some extent with the target claim. Here is an example involving four participants (p. 2935); the name of the relation is followed by the index of the target AC.

(5.8) **A:** [I think the biggest threat to global stability comes from the political fringes.]$_{0:CLAIM}$ [It has been like that in the past.]$_{1:PREMISE}$
B: [Good arguments.]$_{2:AGREEMENT:0}$
C: [The only constant is change.]$_{3:REBUTTAL:0}$
D: [What happened in the past has nothing to do with the present.]$_{4:UNDERCUTTER:1}$

For fine-tuning a BERT model, a large amount of distant-labeled data is added to the reddit threads: Claim-premise pairs are found by searching for the tokens IMO and IMHO ('in my humble opinion') on social media, and assuming that the sentence following the token is a claim, which in turn is followed by a premise sentence. This may often not be the case, but the authors have retrieved 4.6 million such comments and assume that the noise will be tolerable for the model; this data is used for intra-turn relation classification. Similarly, for inter-turn relations, 97,000 distant-labeled inter-post pairs are retrieved from reddit posts where a user literally quotes another post, and the sentence following the quote is taken as commenting on it.

The overall approach is to first classify the ACs and then predict intra- and inter-turn outgoing relations, following the principles stated above. Figure 5.10 provides an overview. Following the ideas we discussed in Sect. 5.3.2, Chakrabarty et al. use an RST

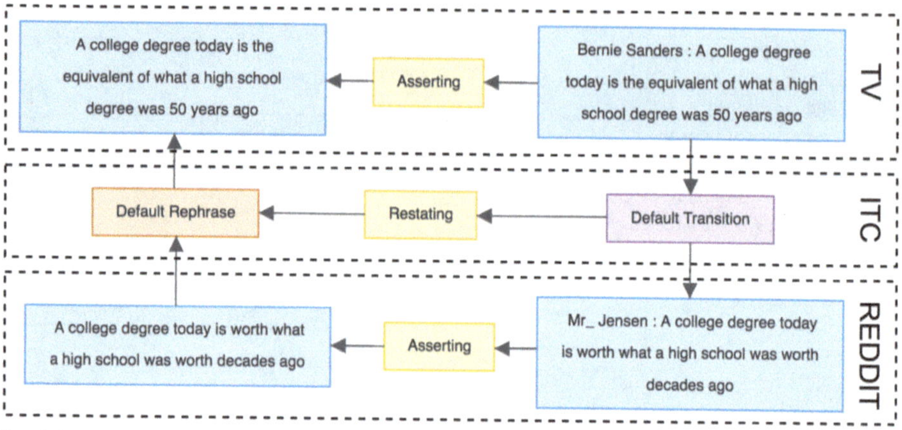

Fig. 5.11 Intertextual rephrase relation in the US2016 corpus. Top row represents a part of the TV debate annotation; bottom row the Reddit comment; middle row the layer of intertextual annotations. Adapted from Visser et al. (2020, p. 144). Licensed under CC-BY 4.0 International

parser to predict the discourse relation holding between a pair of ACs, and use it to train a classifier to decide whether an argument relation holds between these ACs. This classifier is ensembled with the predictions from the BERT classifier, with the rule that a relation holds when either one of the two classifiers predicts it. This ensemble turns out to be the most successful model variant; nonetheless, relation prediction remains difficult: the F_1 score for the *true* class is 0.25 (with predicted premises) for inter-turn relations and 0.28 for inter-turn relations (the recall in both cases is above 0.7—so precision is the key problem).

Spoken Dialogue The most detailed account of the argumentative moves in dialogical interaction is given by Inference Anchoring Theory (IAT), which we introduced in Sect. 3.4.3.

For this framework, Visser et al. (2020) present the US2016 corpus with transcripts of three TV debates among candidates for the 2016 US presidential election (60,000 tokens), as well as immediate reactions to the debate on Reddit (40,000 tokens). In total, there are 2700 support and 800 attack relations, as well as 600 rephrases. The corpus is unique in its interconnecting the TV and Reddit parts, which naturally is a one-way road: Reddit users can respond to comments made on TV (and to each other), but not vice versa. Visser et al. discuss four common patterns of this interaction, and we here illustrate one of them, viz. the intertextual rephrase (Fig. 5.11). In the top row, the locution of Bernie Sanders is analyzed as asserting (illocution) the proposition on the left hand side. Correspondingly, in the bottom row Mr. Jensen asserts a very similar proposition, which is connected via the Rephrase relation to that of Bernie Sanders. The Transition relation marks Mr. Jensen's statement as a dialogical reaction to Sanders; and the associated illocution is Restating.

The other three patterns capture situations where Reddit users accept and defend a statement of a candidate; or draw a conclusion from a candidate's statement; or disagree with it.

Subsequently, Ruiz-Dolz et al. (2021) used various transformer models to perform experiments on the US2016 corpus, and also tested them on a smaller corpus of BBC radio debates (*Moral Maze*). The task is to identify the relations *inference (support), conflict (attack), rephrase* and *none*. A RoBERTa-large model achieves a macro-F_1 of 0.70 on the US2016 data and 0.61 on the Moral Maze (which was not part of the training data). By far the most misclassifications occur between the classes *inference* and *none*.

Another large corpus of radio debates annotated according to IAT is QT30 (Hautli-Janisz et al. 2022), which contains 280,000 words from a British political talk show. Some AM research on this corpus was initiated as a shared task by Ruiz-Dolz et al. (2024b).

5.4 Joint Models and End-to-End Approaches

So far in this chapter, we discussed the subtasks of the relation identification problem in detail, and mentioned automatic approaches that predominantly focused on one or another subtask, in the spirit of the traditional AM pipeline paradigm. A thorough understanding of the nature of those tasks is important, but equally important is the insight that, ultimately, in understanding an argumentative text, the subtasks are not independent of each other. Carstens and Toni (2015), for instance, already argued emphatically that identifying ACs and ARs should not be seen as separate tasks, because one would lose important information on interdependencies. Furthermore, besides interacting tasks, the influence of sequentiality—the order of presenting the ACs in a text—was essentially ignored in early approaches. However, it took a number of years before the technology for efficiently creating *joint* models became available. In this last section, we therefore give an overview of such joint models, and in particular of end-to-end approaches that were developed from 2017 onward.

5.4.1 Early Neural Approaches

A key challenge for jointly modeling the individuation of argument components in text, their type assignment, and their combining in argumentative relations is the fact that the first task needs to be resolved on the level of single tokens, while the others are ideally done on the level of the component spans—i.e., after completing the first step. This is why some early ideas on joint models omitted the ACS step and assumed components as already given.

In Sect. 5.1 we mentioned the work of Potash et al. (2017b) who, in this vein, tackled AC classification and (unlabeled) linking with a pointer network and produced competitive results. At the same time, Niculae et al. (2017) went a step further and presented an

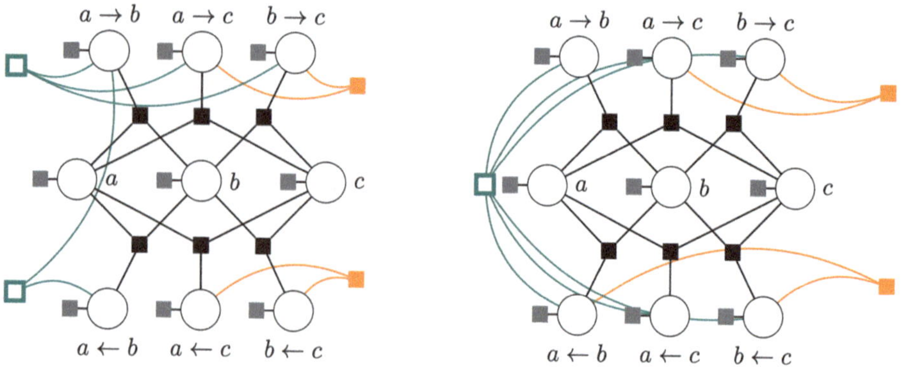

Fig. 5.12 Factor graph model (abbreviated) for the CDCP and AAE (here: 'UKP') corpora. Factors in boxes: *light grey* = unary; *black* = compatibility; *orange* = higher order; *hollow* = link structure. Niculae et al. (2017, p. 988), licensed under CC-BY 4.0 International. (**a**) CDCP. (**b**) UKP

approach that could be configured to handle trees and graphs alike, and the authors demonstrated this on the AAE and CDCP corpora—which assume trees with three AC types, and graphs with five fine-grained AC types, respectively. (An example graph from the CDCP corpus was shown earlier in Fig. 5.7.)

As indicated, Niculae et al. take AC segments as already given, and their system predicts their types as well as unlabeled relations among them. Besides the tree/graph flexibility, the approach is able to handle other differences between the datasets: CDCP has many unlinked ACs, while AAE does not allow them; AAE has support and attack relations, while CDCP has two types of support relations and no attack. Another central feature of the approach is its jointly modeling the ACTC and ARI tasks. We focus here on explaining this joint model, which is based on a *factor graph*, illustrated in Fig. 5.12 for a small example with three ACs.

The crucial step, in comparison to the evidence graph and ILP-based models we discussed in Sect. 5.3, is the ability to account for dependencies between the two decisions of AC typing and linking. The three nodes in the middle row of the graph represent the ACs *a*, *b* and *c*, while the other six nodes represent the potential directed links between any AC pair. All boxes depict *factors*, i.e., individual random variables:

- *Unary* factors (grey boxes to the left of each node): For a segment node, it is the vector of scores for each possible proposition type; for a link node, it holds the scores for the binary on/off decision. If all other factors were absent, these unary factors would amount to the customary independent classifiers for the respective task.
- *Compatibility* factors (black boxes): In a simple version, these are scores for joint assignment that capture information about the compatibility between types (e.g., in CDCP, a *fact* unit is unlikely to be linked to a *testimony* unit). Niculae et al. use an extended variant with three binary features:

  - bias: a constant *1* for learning the base score of the simple version,
  - adjacency: the two segments are adjacent or not,
  - order: the source precedes the target or not.
- *Second order* factors (orange boxes): Scores for local argument structures involving two links (hence the term *second order*). The model uses three types:
  - grandparent: $a \rightarrow b \rightarrow c$
  - sibling: $a \leftarrow b \rightarrow c$
  - co-parent: $a \rightarrow b \leftarrow c$
- *Constraint* factors (hollow boxes): They are parameter-free and encode well-formedness constraints for the resulting structures.

The second-order factors are partly corpus-specific: The CDCP example in the figure shows a co-parent (upper right) and a sibling (lower right); the latter cannot appear in trees and hence is absent in the AAE corpus, where a grandparent and a co-parent are shown. Constraint factors, too, can be corpus-specific, when they guarantee the tree structure in PE, or enforced transitivity (upper left) and prevented symmetry (lower left) in CDCP.

To perform the inference in the factor graph, Niculae et al. use the Alternative Directions Dual Composition (AD^3) algorithm (Martins et al. 2015), and two learning schemes are being compared: a structured SVM that uses the same feature set as done by Stab and Gurevych (2017b), and a feature-free neural network, specifically an LSTM operating on GloVe embeddings (Pennington et al. 2014). (This was one of the first attempts in argument mining to perform classification without feature engineering.)

The first finding is that training a structured objective beats the baseline models for the individual tasks on both corpora (and thus new SOTA results are achieved). Further, it turns out that the feature-based SVM outperforms the RNN model, which works well on the ACTC task but not on ARI. In response to this weakness on linking, Galassi et al. (2018) trained a residual network for the two tasks and reported a substantial improvement for link prediction, but lower results for ACTC.

While this first RNN-based attempt on *end-to-end* argument mining by Niculae et al. above yielded somewhat mixed results, Eger et al. (2017) successfully demonstrated the high potential of neural approaches, with a focus on the AAE2 corpus. Also, they extended the overall task to relation type classification, which the work we discussed just above had omitted.

Eger et al. compared several techniques. First, they tested variants of token-level *dependency parsing*, where all relevant information about the role of the encompassing span is encoded in the edge labels; see an example in Fig. 5.13 below, which will be explained shortly. It turned out, however, that neither the feature-based nor the two tested neural parsers lead to competitive results.

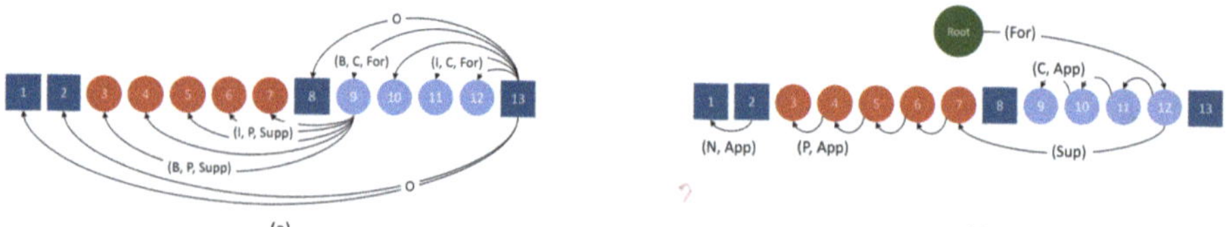

Fig. 5.13 Dependency representations for the sentence "Just because it killed much marine life, tourism has threatened nature.". (**a**) according to Eger et al. (2017), (**b**) according to Ye/Teufel. From Ye and Teufel (2021, p. 671), licensed under CC-BY 4.0 International

On the level of individual paragraphs,[3] Eger found the by far best-performing system—also beating the ILP approach of Stab and Gurevych (2017b)—to be a model built from a BiLSTM-CRF tagger for predicting the AC types, and a TreeLSTM model that makes use of dependency tree information for predicting the relations; hence a parser is needed in a preprocessing stage. The two tasks are de-coupled (in contrast to the dependency parsing approach, which fuses both into the edge labels) but many parameters are being shared and thus form a joint model.

When moving to the level of complete essays, a simpler tagger based on the named-entity recognition system of Ma and Hovy (2016), showed better performance than the TreeLSTM.

Overall, the main message of Eger et al.'s work was that feature engineering and constraint design, such as with ILP or in the approach by Niculae et al. (2017), now seemed to become unnecessary for argument mining. On the downside, when considering longer text, for the end-to-end scenario no single architecture was yet able to perform equally well on the two central tasks of component identification and linking—the different approaches each have one strength and one weakness.

5.4.2 Dependency Parsing

Notwithstanding the less encouraging result obtained by Eger et al. (2017), the notion of framing argument structure analysis as dependency parsing became popular in the subsequent years. Ye and Teufel (2021) revisited Eger's work, used a different parser and a different way of encoding the dependency information, and achieved new SOTA results on the AAE corpus. The parser was an adapted version of the biaffine dependency parser by Dozat and Manning (2018) (widely used for syntactic/semantic parsing). For the dependency encoding of text, Fig. 5.13 shows an example comparing the two approaches. The most crucial difference is that in the scheme of Eger et al., a token's parent is the first token of the parent *segment*, which creates relatively long distances between nodes

[3] Recall that in the AAE corpus every paragraph has its own argument structure.

and their parents. Ye and Teufel opt for the opposite approach and try to connect the vast majority of tokens to their neighbours:

- Within a segment (argumentative or not), each token except for the last one has its succeeding token as parent and is labeled with the component type (in the figure: P for premise and C for claim) and with *app* for *append*.
- If two components are linked by a relation, this is expressed with a labeled edge between the last token of the parent and last token of the child (in the example, the *Sup* edge from token 12 to token 7).
- A pseudo-token ROOT is added to the beginning of each argument. It represents the topic or the gist of the entire argument, so that the relationship between components and the topic can be modeled.

Ye and Teufel argue that this representation may be an important reason for the good results. Their F_1 scores of 0.73 for component identification and 0.46 for relations improve upon Eger et al.—but they also show that linking remains a difficult problem in AM. A second advantage, as Ye and Teufel surmise, is their using the more modern biaffine dependency parser and adapting it by replacing its embedding and BiLSTM layers with a pre-trained BERT encoder.

Around the same time, Bao et al. (2021) took up the goal of Niculae et al. (2017) to handle both tree and graph structures alike, and thus they also work with the two corpora CDCP and PE. They do not adapt an existing parser (like the works just discussed) but create their own transition-based parser. Importantly, its task is reduced to ACTC and ARI, i.e., they assume that ACs have been segmented already, and they do not classify the relation types.

The states of the parser are given by the tuple $(\sigma^t, \beta^t, D^t, \alpha^t)$, and are defined by the time step t, a stack σ for processed ACs, a buffer β for unprocessed ACs, a delay set D to record ACs that need to be removed subsequently, and an action list α to store past actions. At the beginning, all ACs are in the buffer, hence the initial state is: ([], $[c_1, c_2, \ldots, c_n]$, $\emptyset$, []). Six transition rules are defined to manipulate the state and process the input; for brevity, we list here just two rules as examples:

- *Shift:* When β^t is not empty and σ_1 is not in D^t, pop β_0 from β^t and move it to the top of σ^t.
- *Right-Arc:* When β^t is empty, remove σ_0 from σ^t and assign a link from σ_0 to σ_1.

The implementation uses BERT to represent each AC, where the token sequence is expanded with extra features: the bag of words vector for the AC, the position of the AC in the paragraph, and the type of the paragraph (in AAE: introduction, body, or conclusion). LSTMs encode parser states, and actions are predicted with a multi-layer perceptron. The authors implemented several recent systems as baselines and show that their new system is the most successful.

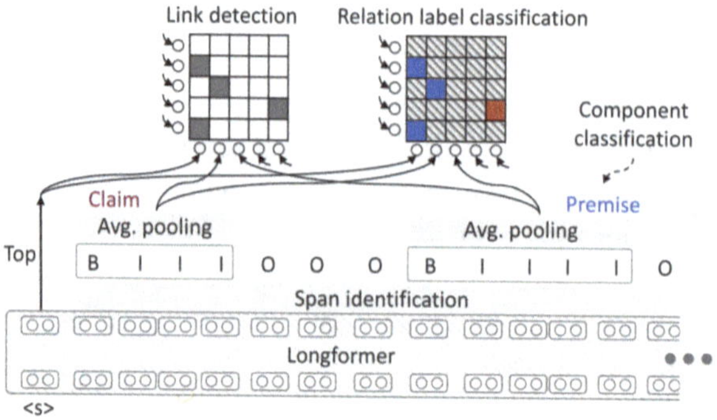

Fig. 5.14 Overview of the end-to-end system architecture by Morio et al. (2022, p. 644), licensed under CC-BY 4.0 International

Morio et al. (2020) focused solely on the graph structures in the CDCP corpus. Like Bao et al. (2021), they did not parse on token-level but on pre-segmented text and thus assume that ACs have already been identified. In contrast to Bao et al., Morio et al. in principle also classify relation types, though the authors explain that due to class imbalance in the data they only evaluate for the Evidence relation.

For encoding the AC segments, they use task-specific parameterization (TSP), where word forms, POS tags, GloVe and ELMo vectors are fed into a BiLSTM. Then, this shared encoder is followed by two task-specific attention-to-encoder layers, one for ACTC and one for ARI/ARTC. For edge prediction, the biaffine attention model by Dozat and Manning (2018) (which later had also been employed by Ye/Teufel, see above) is being extended to work on the segment level. Morio et al. model the three tasks jointly by minimizing the joint objective of AC type loss, edge loss, and relation label loss. The results are considerably better than those of Niculae and Galassi for ACTC and ARI.

In follow-up work, Morio et al. (2022) extended the 2020 system and conducted extensive experiments on using five different corpora[4] for training an end-to-end system that covers the full range from component segmentation to relation identification and typing. The divergences across the corpora presuppose a model flexible enough to deal with different notions of AC spans, different label type sets, and constraints on structure. The authors show that a combination of multitask pre-training on all five corpora and subsequent fine-tuning on the target corpus yields superior performance in comparison to training the same model on only the target corpus, with greater advantages gained for smaller target corpora. The model architecture is close to that of Morio et al. (2020), but with the older encoder replaced by a Longformer model; see Fig. 5.14.

[4] AAE (Stab and Gurevych 2017b), microtexts (Peldszus and Stede 2016b), CDCP (Niculae et al. 2017), AbstRCT (Mayer et al. 2020), AASD (Accuosto and Saggion 2019).

5.4.3 Generative Language Models

Early Approaches Generative models became highly influential in NLP in the early 2020s, and—motivated by their success for example in aspect-based sentiment analysis—Bao et al. (2022a) developed a new approach for end-to-end AM. The weakness of the dependency parsing approaches, they contended, is in their need for rather extensive pre- and postprocessing, which includes procedures for building the trees from the outputs of different network layers corresponding to the subtasks.

Bao et al. developed a sequence-to-sequence model that is in charge of producing output in this fashion:

(5.9) Source sequence: "I believe cloning is beneficial. For example, cloned organs can help patients."
Target Sequence: [3, 5, claim, 10, 14, premise, support]

where the numbers correspond to the token indices of the respective AC boundaries in the source sequence: The claim is "cloning is beneficial" and the supporting premise is "cloned organs can help patients".

The authors use a pretrained BART model to capture the dependencies between the target sequence and the input text, where the vanilla pointer mechanism (Vinyals et al. 2015) in the decoder generates the start and end indices in the target sequence. The pointer distribution is expanded with the distributions over all possible AC and AR type labels, in order to allow for their prediction being included.

Predicting the boundaries of augment components is generally more difficult than the boundaries in tasks like NER or sentiment aspect detection. To improve the predictions, Bao et al. therefore propose a *constrained* pointer mechanism (CPM), where they implement three constraints:

1. When decoding an end index, it should be greater than its associated start index
2. When decoding the start and end index of a source AC, they can not overlap with the target AC.
3. Valid pointer indices must be consistent with the type of the expected output for the current time step: AC and AR indices must be in their respective ranges.

These constraints are added to the basic model by means of a proxy distribution $\mathbf{Q}_t \in \mathbb{R}^{n_x+n_c+n_r}$ (where n_x, n_c and n_r are the numbers of input tokens, of AC types, and of AR types, respectively). It simulates the real pointer distribution with constraints that encode the values of valid and invalid pointer indices with 1 and 0, respectively. Figure 5.15 shows the series of $\mathbf{Q}_t$ distributions for example (5.9) given above. In $\mathbf{Q}_2$, the first three tokens (in I^x) cannot be predicted because of TS=3 in $\mathbf{Q}_1$, according to constraint (1) above. In $\mathbf{Q}_3$, only an AC type can be predicted; and so on. During training, $\mathbf{Q}_t$ is treated as the labels of an auxiliary binary classification task, so that the model is steered in the manner

PD	TS	I^x	I^c	I^r
Q_1	3	[1,1,1,1,1,1,1,1,1,1,1,1,1,1,1]	[0,0,0]	[0,0]
Q_2	5	[0,0,0,1,1,1,1,1,1,1,1,1,1,1,1]	[0,0,0]	[0,0]
Q_3	C.	[0,0,0,0,0,0,0,0,0,0,0,0,0,0,0]	[1,1,1]	[0,0]
Q_4	10	[1,1,0,0,0,1,1,1,1,1,1,1,1,1,1]	[0,0,0]	[0,0]
Q_5	14	[0,0,0,0,0,0,0,0,0,0,1,1,1,1,1]	[0,0,0]	[0,0]
Q_6	P.	[0,0,0,0,0,0,0,0,0,0,0,0,0,0,0]	[1,1,1]	[0,0]
Q_7	S.	[0,0,0,0,0,0,0,0,0,0,0,0,0,0,0]	[0,0,0]	[1,1]

Fig. 5.15 Proxy distributions $\mathbf{Q}_t$ for Example (5.9) with the target sequence (TS) [3, 5, *Claim*, 10, 14, *Premise, Support*]. I^x, I^c and I^r denote the range of the token indices, AC type indices and AR type indices. *C* Claim, *P* Premise, *S* Support. Taken from Bao et al. (2022a, p. 10441), licensed under CC-BY 4.0 International

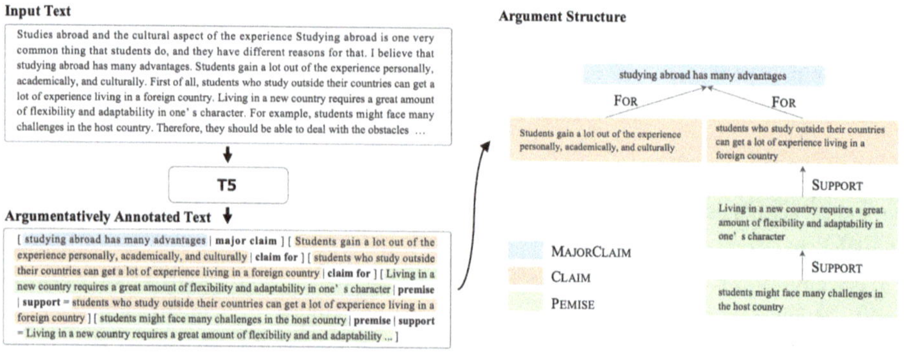

Fig. 5.16 Overview of the text-to-text generation approach by Kawarada et al. (2024, p. 2003), licensed under CC-BY 4.0 International

of multitask learning. And during inference, valid predictions are ensured by regarding $\mathbf{Q}_t$ as binary masks for setting the probabilities of all invalid pointer indices to zero.

Besides the CPM, Bao et al. proposed a second mechanism, a reconstructed positional encoding, in order to alleviate the order biases induced by the autoregressive generation paradigm in the BART model. Their experiments showed that the model outperforms baselines from previous work, including some that we discussed above (Eger et al. 2017; Ye and Teufel 2021).

Text-to-Text Generation The next 'wave' of approaches was driven by the techniques of LLM fine-tuning and prompting. When framing AM as a text generation task, two possibilities are to instruct the model to *add* annotations to a text or to *extract* portions of text. Following the first approach, Kawarada et al. (2024) extended the unprocessed input with annotations that determine the underlying argument structure; see Fig. 5.16. The technique is inspired by the 'Translation between Augmented Natural Languages' or TANL approach (Paolini et al. 2021), which had been previously applied to various information and relation extraction NLP tasks (e.g., NER, semantic role labeling, coreference resolution). Kawarada et. al. attribute the success of TANL to the implementation with the—at the time—powerful pretrained encoder-decoder model T5.

Kawarada et al. worked with the AAE, CDCP and AbstRCT corpora, mapped them to the argument-annotated versions of the texts and fine-tuned T5 individually for each corpus. The notation for an AC that does not depend on another one is $[\mathtt{s}^{src} \mid \mathtt{c}]$ where $\mathtt{s}^{src}$ is a text span and $\mathtt{c}$ a component type—in the figure, this is for example visible for the first sentence (the major claim). When an AC enters a relation, the notation is extended to $[\mathtt{s}^{src} \mid \mathtt{c} \mid \mathtt{r} = s^{tgt}]$ with two text spans (source, target) and with $\mathtt{r}$ denoting the relation type.

Notice that—since there are no indices for ACs involved in the scheme—there is a complication for this 'flat' annotation when the arguments of a relation are not adjacent to each other in the text. In that case, the authors duplicate the AC text span and insert it into the text where needed.

In the spirit of comparative studies on various LLMs, (Cabessa et al. 2025) (who had found in previous research that fine-tuning is more beneficial for AM than in-context learning) fine-tune eight open-weight LLMs on the AAE, AbstRCT and CDCP datasets. The authors follow an *extraction* approach that presupposes ACs to be already given in their input in this form:
<AC1> *text* </AC1>, <AC2> *text* </AC2>, ...

Prompts are designed to extract the desired information; for example, to accomplish ARI, the instruction to the model is to generate a list of AC pairs in this format:
`[[source_AC(i), target_AC(i)],..., [source_AC(i), target_AC(i)]]`
where `i` is the index for the AC as given in the input. Cabessa et al. use separate instructions for the three individual tasks AC, ARI, ARTC and also for combinations of them. As usually needed, the authors implemented some 'hallucination guardrails' to filter out predictions with incorrect formats or lengths. The authors report state-of-the-art results across all AM subtasks and datasets, and they attribute that to the LLM's ability to capture the sequentiality of arguments in the text and to leverage relevant contextual and structural information from the entire document.

Relation Classification As an example of a study that employs few-shot learning instead of fine-tuning the models, we mention Gorur et al. (2025), who work with a much larger set of corpora (eleven) than the research we described so far in this section, and the task in their experiments is relation identification. They work with Llama2-70B, Mistral-7B, Mixtral-8x7b and GPT-3.5-turbo.

The prompt includes, in the various experiments, one or two labelled examples of attack, support, and neither relation between arguments, followed by an unlabeled example for the LLM to classify (i.e., the desired output is just the name of the relation). The examples are randomly drawn from the datasets and fixed across the experiments.

It turns out that the LLMs beat the baseline of a fine-tuned RoBERTa model, with the Mixtral model achieving the highest micro-F_1 score of 0.82. Also, in an additional experiment, this model performed better on most datasets in the ARIES benchmark (Gemechu et al. 2024), which we discussed above in Sect. 5.2.2.

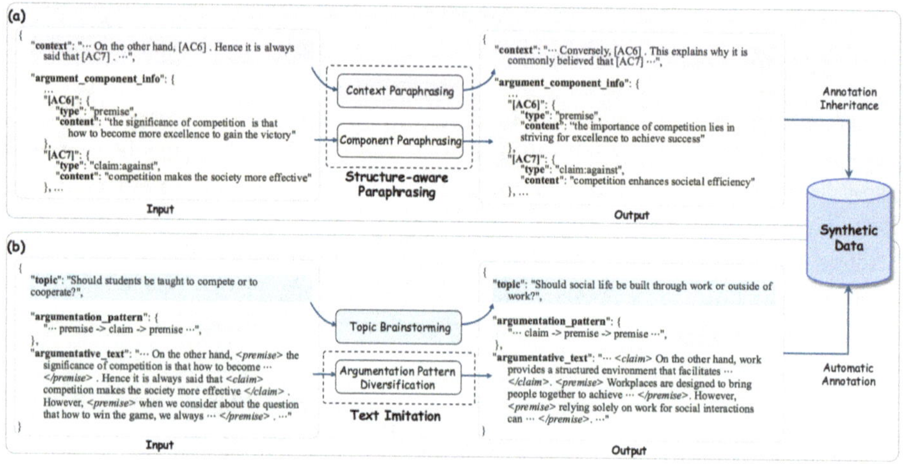

Fig. 5.17 Overview of the two data augmentation approaches by Bao et al. (2025a, p. 26596), licensed under CC-BY 4.0 International. (**a**) Quality-oriented synthesis (QOS). (**b**) Diversity-Oriented Synthesis (DOS)

Synthetic Training Data Yet another different perspective on exploiting the power of LLMs for argument mining is the automatic production of training data. One study following this idea, by Bao et al. (2025a), compares two complementary strategies: a structure-aware paraphrasing task that aims to preserve the quality of the original human-produced annotations, and a diversity-oriented task that focuses on the novelty of the generated material (in terms of topics and structures) and produces new annotations automatically. Figure 5.17 provides an overview.

Three established datasets (AAE by Stab and Gurevych 2017b; CDCP by Park and Cardie 2018; AbstRCT by Mayer et al. 2020) are being extended with these methods, using the GPT-4o model to produce new texts in sets of different sizes (so that the augmentation rates can also be compared). The AM tasks being evaluated are the identification of AC boundaries and their types, as well as the relation types between ACs. Various training settings (arising from combinations of the two augmentation approaches and the data sizes) are compared and evaluated on the test sets as used by Morio et al. (2022) (see previous section); results are shown to clearly improve on that previous work and on an LLM-based sequence-to-sequence approach proposed by Bao et al. (2025b).

5.5 Summary

We saw that complete argument structures have been studied primarily for the genres of student essay—where the application is to evaluate the quality and possibly provide feedback to the writer—and discussions on social media, where arguments are exchanged between different discussants and it can be illuminating to study the deliberative or confrontational patterns in the interaction. In either case, the basic building block is the establishing of a connection between an individual claim and a premise. For this step, spatial proximity is a constraining factor that is often exploited by fixing context window sizes for searching premises for a specific claim. Further, when fine-grained types of claim and premise are available, knowledge on the likelihood of the different type combinations can be used as a soft constraint.

Support and attack are the relations that most corpora have adopted, which is likely due to the roots in argumentation theory, where they are the key notions. Distinctions such as that between the *rebutting* and the *undercutting* attack are occasionally being accounted for; similarly, the *restatement* or the *contradiction* are sometimes added to the inventory. A few approaches go a step further and adopt relations from discourse coherence theory, thus blurring the distinction between the task of discourse parsing and that of argument mining. As we have seen, some studies have begun to explore the relationship between the two more systematically, and since discourse parsers have become more robust, their output has sometimes been used to inform AM systems.

For building a complete structure, a commitment has to be made on its formal properties. Student essays, for example, have been found to be well-described with tree structures, the reason being that their production is an exercise in 'good writing' with clearly-arranged arguments. The situation is very different in social media discussions, where by definition there can be no overall coherence in a thread that arises in a bottom-up way from individual locally-coherent exchanges. Either way, when non-trivial structures are built and paths of relations are established in a tree or graph, the originally quite fundamental distinction between claim and premise becomes blurry, as an argument component can play both roles at the same time.

We saw that when choosing tree structures, the analysis can exploit the property by using algorithms computing minimum-spanning trees, or—by extension—using dependency parsing strategies that can be implemented both in traditional symbolic systems and in neural networks.

The setting of information-seeking AM is by nature not much interested in complete structures but in topic-dependent (claim, stance, evidence) triples. The attack relation does not seem to play an interesting role; it is less relevant because the *pro* and *con* side are represented by the presence of claims with opposing stances (and their respective evidence premises). Nonetheless, knowing about more or less likely combinations, as we described for claim-evidence pairs, can be useful also for the attack relation, when more or less suitable counterarguments should be distinguished for a successful refutation of an argument made by the other side in a debate.

Similar to the previous chapter, we have moved here from discussing the nature of the ARI and ACTC tasks and their early AM approaches in a single-task pipeline manner, via joint models for some subtasks, to end-to-end approaches that can build full argument structures for a given text. Doing this with LLMs is at present clearly the dominating research theme. Problems with noise in the desired output formats, and thus the need for postprocessing, are likely to improve with new generations of models, and the most interesting question is likely to be the extent to which LLMs can perform argumentative reasoning—a topic that we will take up in Chap. 8.

Perspective Assessment

6

Chapters 4 and 5 have presented the core of argument mining, that is, the identification of argumentative structure in natural language texts. While this information constitutes the basis of any application dealing with arguments, many applications also need knowledge about the perspectives that mined arguments convey toward the controversial issues discussed. For example, existing argument search engines separately display pro and con arguments on an issue. Debating technologies should frame arguments in a way that supports their side convincingly, and the effectiveness of arguments may depend on whether the values they encode match those of their audience. In this chapter, we review NLP methods that assess the perspectives of arguments or argumentative texts. While the term *perspective* has been used in different, partly rather specific ways (Beigman Klebanov et al. 2010; Vilares and He 2017; Chen et al. 2019a), we here interpret it in a broad sense to cover different facets of texts that characterize how an argument pictures an issue and how it reflects the view of its author on the issue thereby. We illustrate the facets on two claims discussing whether to ban death penalty (also known as 'capital punishment'): [1]

(6.1) The death penalty legitimizes an irreversible act of violence by the state and will inevitably claim innocent victims.
(6.2) Capital punishment may brutalise society in a [...] more fundamental way, one that has implications for the state's relationship with all citizens.

First, perspective includes the author's *stance* toward an issue; both claims suggest a pro stance toward the ban. Assuming they come from different authors, we can say that they *agree* in their stance. Stance detection is a long-standing task in the NLP community, partly

[1] Both example claims are taken from https://www.bbc.co.uk/ethics/capitalpunishment/against_1.shtml (accessed December 8, 2025).

M. Stede et al., *Argument Mining*, Synthesis Lectures on Human Language Technologies, https://doi.org/10.1007/978-3-032-32291-3_6

treated independently from argument mining research (Küçük and Can 2020). While we briefly overview the spectrum of approaches below, we focus more on those that explicitly treat arguments in their modeling of stance. Second, perspective describes the way by which authors highlight specific *topical* aspects of an issue, such as "violence by the state" or "innocent victims" in the first claim. Often, this is to *frame* the issue in some way, here from the viewpoint of law. The notion of framing originates in political science where researchers have studied extensively how authors make certain aspects more salient through the selection, arrangement, and phrasing of content (Entman 1993). However, we restrict our view to the detection and analysis of frames using NLP methods. And third, some NLP research puts attention on the assessment of different *biases* that arguments may exhibit, from myside bias (Stanovich et al. 2013) to social bias (Fiske 1998). For example, discussing only pro arguments on the ban without looking at con arguments may be seen as myside-biased. Biases may arise from human *values* (Schwartz 1994) and *morals* (Haidt 2012); in this regard, the second claim puts higher value on a stable society than on the role of individuals related to the death penalty.

In the following, we subsequently present a selection of methods for each of the outlined aspects of perspectives. In particular, we start from the recognition of stance and agreement (Sect. 6.1), before we detail the identification of topics and frames (Sect. 6.2), and then the modeling of biases, values, and morals (Sect. 6.3).

6.1 Recognizing Stance and Disagreement

Stance constitutes one of the most central concepts of argumentation research: Any argument, implicitly or explicitly, reflects someone's position in favor of or against a controversial issue, even if not necessarily a fully decided one. The NLP task of stance classification (or stance detection) has been subject to much research in the last 15 years, not least reflected in shared tasks for several languages such as English (Mohammad et al. 2016), Chinese (Xu et al. 2016), and Arabic (Alturayeif et al. 2024) as well as for multiple modalities (Liu et al. 2023a). While variations exist, the task can basically be defined as: Given an argumentative text and a target (e.g., an issue or an entity), decide whether the text conveys a *pro* or *con* stance toward the target (or, sometimes also, *neutral* or *neither*). Stance forms the basis of another task, the recognition of agreement and disagreement (Stein et al. 2021): Two authors agree if they have the same stance toward an issue, and disagree otherwise.

In this section, we subsequently review a selection of NLP approaches to the classification of stance as well as to the prediction of agreement and disagreement. While both tasks have partly been studied within the argument mining community, ultimately stance and (dis)agreement imply an argumentative context by concept. Still, we put more focus below on those works that explicitly model arguments.

6.1.1 Classifying Stance of Claims and Arguments

For a meaningful comparison, we group approaches here by the context they use as the basis for classifying stance. Some assess the *individual* stance of a claim or argument toward some target, but there are also *collection-level* approaches that model the surrounding debate and those that *transfer* knowledge from other settings. We review the spectrum of research on all these in the following. For more comprehensive surveys of stance classification, see Küçük and Can (2020) and Li et al. (2025).

Individual Stance In early work, Somasundaran and Wiebe (2009) use integer linear programming (ILP) to determine the stance of posts from the debate portal convinceme.net (not online anymore).[2] The debates in their corpus are two-sided and oriented to two targets, such as *Blackberry* vs. *iPhone*. In this setting, concessions are relatively frequent: An author grants the 'opposing' product some advantage, but then gives more weighty arguments for the favored product. Therefore, the ILP approach exploits discourse features around the concession relation in addition to topic and subjectivity clues extracted from the training data. On the test set, it achieves an accuracy of 61.11–66.67% depending on the topic (and 100% on one small 4-instances topics). In follow-up work, Somasundaran and Wiebe (2010) study the role of argument-related terms, creating lexicons with phrases (e.g., "prove to be" or "threat against"). Combining these with modal verbs and sentiment-bearing words, they train a support vector machine (SVM) on 2232 debate posts from four domains (gun rights, gay rights, abortion, and creationism). In 10-fold cross-validation, their approach classifies 63.93% of all posts correctly, compared to a unigram SVM baseline with 62.50%. Accuracy varies across topics, though, with only 60.55% for abortion but 70.59% for gun rights. In general, the limited effectiveness in both studies already hints at the difficulty of stance classification, which may, to a good extent, be caused by the inherent subjectivity of the task.

Another pioneer exploration of stance classification comes from Faulkner (2014) who look at the genre of argumentative student essays. The authors present an approach to compute essay-level stance with two key ingredients:

1. *On-topicness Scoring.* One the one hand, the approach scores essay words for being on-topic. Faulkner uses a Wikipedia link-based measure to compute the similarity between words in the essay and words in the essay's prompt.
2. *Stance-oriented Dependency Parsing.* On the other hand, it extracts parse subtrees that match a *stance-attitude profile*, with the help of a dependency parser and two lexical

[2] Online debate portals are often used as a source of ground-truth stance information in NLP, as in the study at hand and further studies covered in this chapter. Some portals collect the most important arguments on an issue, directly grouping them by the stance they have on an issue. On others, two people debate with each other, where one takes the pro side and the other the con side.

DEPENDENCY TREE TRAVERSAL	POS-GENERALIZED SUB-TREE	STANCE-ATTITUDE PROFILE
"I <u>can</u> only say that this statement is completely **true**" 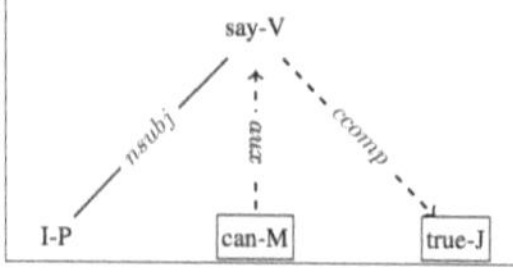	*can* → *V* → *true*	$S + A+$

Fig. 6.1 POS-generalized subtree from the approach of Faulkner (2014), with a sentence matching it. It reflects both positive stance and a positive attitude. Used with permission

resources of stance and attitudinal words. This records a positive/negative evaluation of a sentence's pro/con stance. Subtrees are generalized by means of their part-of-speech (POS) tags. An example is shown in Fig. 6.1.

On 1135 stance-annotated essays from the International Corpus of Learner English (ICLE) (Granger 2003), Faulkner demonstrates that an SVM trained on the topic-word model easily outperforms two baselines: bag-of-words and an implementation of the best-performing linguistic features from the earlier work of Somasundaran and Wiebe (2009). Adding the subtree features yielded another small improvement, resulting in an overall accuracy of 82%, suggesting that stance classification may be easier for texts that are longer and/or have a more explicit and conventionalized argumentative structure.

As a basis for community efforts on stance classification, the mentioned shared task of Mohammad et al. (2016) comes with a dataset of more than 4000 English-language tweets. Given a target (e.g., *Donald Trump*) and a tweet (e.g., "Jeb Bush is the only sane candidate in this republican lineup"), the goal is to assess whether the tweet is *in favor of* or *against* the target, or *neither*. Sobhani et al. (2016) employ a linear SVM for this task, using token and character *n*-grams, word2vec embeddings (Mikolov et al. 2013), and sentiment lexicons as features. On the test data, it reached a macro F_1-score of 0.5921, which beat the shared task winner (0.5603). In an article from the same author team building on this work, Mohammad et al. (2017) explore further approach variations. While not fully reaching the same macro F_1-score (0.583), the authors provide several insights into the relation between sentiment and stance, highlighting that knowing sentiment is not sufficient for knowing stance.

Simultaneously to Sobhani et al., Augenstein et al. (2016) propose a Bi-LSTM approach to the shared task, a rather early use of Bi-LSTMs in NLP. The approach concatenates target and tweet, such that the bidirectional encoder traverses the concatenated sequence in both directions. In their experiments, the authors also add weakly-supervised learning on automatically-labeled data for the test target (*Donald Trump*), which was allowed within the shared task and had been previously done by two best shared task participants (Wei et al. 2016; Zarrella and Marsh 2016). While Bi-LSTM alone achieved a macro F_1-score of 0.4901 only, the weak supervision boosted it to 0.5803, beating the task winners but not Sobhani et al..

Bar-Haim et al. (2017a) present one of the most pivotal works on stance classification. The authors establish the conceptual notion that the stance $s \in [-1, 1]$ of a claim c with respect to a controversial topic t emerges from the sentiment polarity $s_c \in [-1, 1]$ of c toward its target x_c, the sentiment polarity $s_t \in [-1, 1]$ of t toward its target x_t, and the contrastiveness $\mathcal{R}(x_c, x_t)$ of the targets. Here, x_c and x_t are said to be *contrastive* (-1), if a pro stance on x_c makes a con stance on x_t likely, and vice versa. Otherwise, they are called *consistent* $(+1)$. Based on these values, the authors propose to compute s as:

$$s := s_c \cdot \mathcal{R}(x_c, x_t) \cdot s_t$$

For illustration, consider the following examples from Bar-Haim et al.:

(6.3) Marketing promotes consumerism and waste. *pro toward* This house believes that advertising is harmful.
(6.4) Unity is seen as an essential feature of the nation and the nation-state. *con toward* This house would embrace multiculturalism.

In Example 6.3, both claim and topic convey negative sentiment, but their targets ("Marketing" and "advertising") are consistent, leading to a positive stance value. In Example 6.4, both claim and topic convey positive sentiment, but their targets ("Unity" and "multiculturalism") are contrastive, leading to a negative stance value. For development and evaluation, Bar-Haim et al. added stance and target annotations to the IBM dataset (Aharoni et al. 2014), where a *target* is a phrase that is assigned a positive or negative valence in a claim or claim-like topic. Their corpus was built by selecting debate topics from idebate.net and manually finding claim and evidence statements in Wikipedia articles. The version of this corpus used by Bar-Haim et al. encompasses 55 topics and 2394 claims (25 topics for training, 30 for testing). By definition, all claims in the dataset either support or contest the topic. Given the data, they propose to compute the input to the stance formula above in three steps:

1. *Target Identification.* To identify x_c and x_t, Bar-Haim et al. consider all noun phrases as candidates. They train a logistic regression classifier employing features such as a candidate's position in the parse tree, its relation to sentiment terms in the tree, whether the candidate is a Wikipedia title, and similar.
2. *Sentiment Classification.* To assess s_c and s_t, Bar-Haim et al. quantify sentiment based on terms from the sentiment lexicon of Hu and Liu (2004), polarity shifters, and their distance to the target.
3. *Contrastiveness Classification.* To determine $\mathcal{R}(x_c, x_t)$, Bar-Haim et al. train a random forest classifier that uses relatedness measures, polarity shifters, matches against Wikipedia headers, and similar.

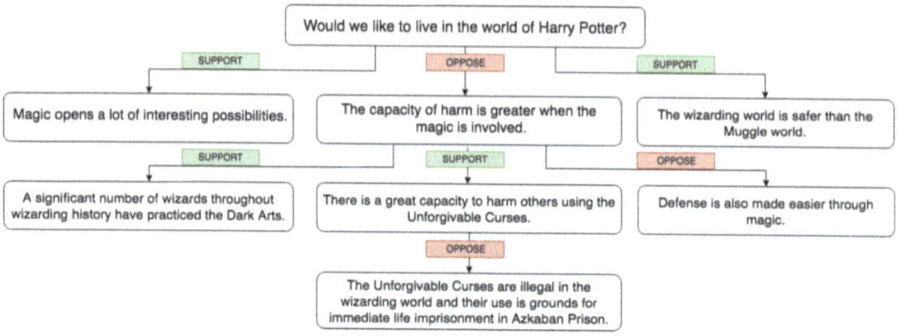

Fig. 6.2 Excerpt of the Kialo argument tree for the controversial topic "Would we like to live in the world of Harry Potter?", taken from Durmus et al. (2019). Licensed under CC-BY 4.0 International

The authors evaluate accuracy at different coverage values in [0, 1], where, for example, an 'accuracy@0.1' means that only the instances with top-10% absolute stance values are considered (others ignored). The idea behind is that, in many applications (e.g., debating technologies), it may be sufficient to rely on the instances with highest confidence. Indeed, on the test set, the approach achieved an accuracy@0.1 of 0.849 compared to 0.717 for an SVM with unigram and sentiment features. These values go down, the higher the coverage gets. For accuracy@1.0, both approach and baseline had the same limited value of 0.632.

In direct follow-up work, Bar-Haim et al. (2017b) point out that, by concept, hard cases are those where claims convey no sentiment. The authors therefore propose two extensions to improve the approach of Bar-Haim et al. (2017a): (1) For *lexicon expansion*, they train a linear SVM on the sentiment terms of Hu and Liu (2004), learning to map a term's word2vec embedding to a sentiment polarity (at an accuracy of 90.5%). Applying this classifier, the approach can find more sentiment terms. (2) For *context modeling*, they retrieve the neighboring sentences of a claim in its source Wikipedia article and use these as additional inputs to the polarity classification. On the experiment setup as above, the extended approach improved on all coverage levels, for example, with an accuracy@0.1 of 0.954 and an accuracy@1.0 of 0.691.

Some works combine the study of stance classification and other tasks. Among these, Durmus et al. (2019) classify both relative specificity and relative stance for claims within deep hierarchical argument trees, as they are found on online platforms such as kialo.com. Figure 6.2 visualizes an excerpt of such a tree. For pair of claims along the same path in the tree, the authors define the claim lower in the tree to be the more specific one. Fine-tuning and evaluating a specificity classifier based on a BERT encoder-only transformer (Devlin et al. 2019), it classified 84.91% of all pairs correctly, as opposed to feature-based logistic regression with 79.12%. For pairs of claims, the authors derive the stance of the lower claim toward the upper claim from the support and oppose relations along the path; for example, a path *(oppose, support, oppose)* indicates a pro stance. Here, fine-tuned BERT obtained an accuracy of 77.46%, the feature-based logistic regression only 63.27%.

Zhao et al. (2024) leverage the capabilities of large language models (LLMs) to generate a synthetic dataset for open-domain stance detection. Given a seed list of thematic categories (e.g., *politics* or *health*) and three geographic regions (America, Europe, and Asia), ChatGPT is first prompted to produce a total of 24k controversial claims, 40 per category-region pair. For example, one resulting claim for *health* and *Asia* is "Traditional Chinese medicine is more effective than modern medicine." 3000 of these claims then serve as the stance targets in the subsequent ChatGPT-based generation of stance-bearing texts (pro or con) of three types (e.g., *sharing individual experiences*). Neutral instances are create by combining texts with highly dissimilar targets, resulting in 27k texts for the 3000 claims, 9000 each per stance label. In experiments across six existing stance datasets, a RoBERTA transformer model (Liu et al. 2019b) fine-tuned on the dataset improved macro F_1-score in zero-shot stance detection by 14 points on average (0.6712 vs. 0.5328). While zero-shot ChatGPT was slightly stronger overall (0.6811), RoBERT beat ChatGPT on four datasets, suggesting that standard transformers can compete with LLMs, when learning from them.

Collection-Level Stance Hasan and Ng (2013) were the first to suggest moving beyond the language of a single claims or arguments, by also taking aspects of the *interaction* of debate participants into account. Their data is from createdebate.com (not online anymore) and comprises post-wise ideological debates on four topics: abortion, gay rights, Obama, and marijuana. The authors propose two features:

1. *Interaction Patterns.* Stance labels of posts in a sequence have interdependencies: In the data, 80% of the posts are followed by a reply with opposite polarity. Hasan and Ng use a CRF trained on post sequences to predict stance sequences.
2. *Ideology Patterns.* The stances of an author on different topics are not independent from each other. Thus, content from other posts of an author can be used to predict their stance on a given post. Hasan and Ng model this as conditional probabilities (e.g., that a pro stance on gay rights correlates with being pro-marijuana).

While both features might be less helpful with less heated debate topics, Hasan and Ng (2013) demonstrate how their constraints can be combined in an ILP inference problem, as input to stance classification. Their approach clearly beat different text-only classifiers by 8–14 points with accuracies of 69.9–75.4%, depending on the domain. This indicates the importance of debate context for the task.

Walker et al. (2012a) pursue a similar idea, modeling the structure of two-sided debates for stance classification, 2902 debates with 36k posts from convinceme.net in particular. Given a debate, the authors construct a graph where nodes indicate posts and edges indicate either rebuttals (which are explicitly marked as such on the platform) or author identity for two posts. Their approach then applies the MaxCut algorithm to partition the graph into two components based on different punishment weights assigned to rebuttal and identity edges respectively. A supervised JRIP classifier maps each component to one stance, using various features, such as post length, cue words, POS-generalized dependencies like those from Faulkner (2014), and rebuttal indicators. In experiments, the JRIP classifier alone achieved accuracy values between 46 and 72% across 14 debate topics. The MaxCut algorithm boosted many results beyond 80% with a peak at 88% for *iPhone vs. Blackberry*. Occasionally, it failed, though, with only 19% in the worst case (*Mac vs. PC*).

Another approach in this line of research is proposed by Ranade et al. (2013) who model user intents in two-sided debates, again for convinceme.net. Assuming two debating users to have opposite stances, their approach classifies each post to be positive about one stance, negative about the other, or neither. For classification of such topic-directed sentiment, it aggregates SentiWordNet sentiment values (Baccianella et al. 2010) toward targets found via dependency relations. On this basis, it computes sentiment scores for posts and whole arguments, combining subsequent posts of the same author. As a last step, the approach adjusts conflicting sentiment values computed for the same users. To this end, the debate is modeled as a graph like the one of Walker et al.. Then, a gradient *ascent* algorithm aims to maximize graph correctness by stepwise updating the values of the nodes to align neighboring values to each other. In their experiments, the overall approach classifies the stance of 74.4% of the posts correctly; an ablation without gradient ascent results in 70.3% only, underlining the impact of modeling user stance consistency.

Qiu and Jiang (2013) work with English and Chinese debate datasets, and are also interested in utilizing user interaction patterns for determining stance. In their unsupervised approach, they build a complete network based on user posts, representing the pro/con groups of users and the support/attack relations among them. Their main focus, however, is to pay attention to the topics mentioned in the posts, following the intuition that, given a contentious issue, the pro users tend to discuss different aspects of that issue than the con users do. Topic distribution, user identity, and user interaction are combined in a latent variable model inspired by latent Dirichlet allocation (Blei et al. 2003). The accuracies for stance identification ranged from 60 to 81% depending on the language and dataset.

Building on the ideas of Hasan and Ng (2013), Sridhar et al. (2015) collectively model the stance of authors based on their posts in online debates. They propose a probabilistic soft logic (PSL) (Bach et al. 2013) approach for collective and individual stance classifiers as well as for disagreement classifiers, and for both author-level and post-level stance. The PSL rules generalize over joint author and post variables X_1, X_2. Some are defined for all classifiers, such as $localPro(X_1) \rightarrow pro(X_1)$; others are specific, such as $disagree(X_1, X_2) \wedge pro(X_1) \rightarrow \neg pro(X_2)$ for collective classifiers. On the corpora of Walker et al. (2012b) and Hasan and Ng (2013), particularly the author-level disagreement classifiers seem strong: For author-level stance, they were best overall with 63.0–77.1% accuracy across the eight topics in the datasets. Interestingly, the same classifiers also did best for post-level stance, where they reached up to 80.5% accuracy.

Li et al. (2018) suggest to represent debate posts, information about post authors, their disagreements, and stance labels in the same embedding space. This space is optimized via a joint loss function that weighs similarities of authors and posts, authors and their profile attributes (e.g., gender), posts and their labels, and posts and other posts. The approach

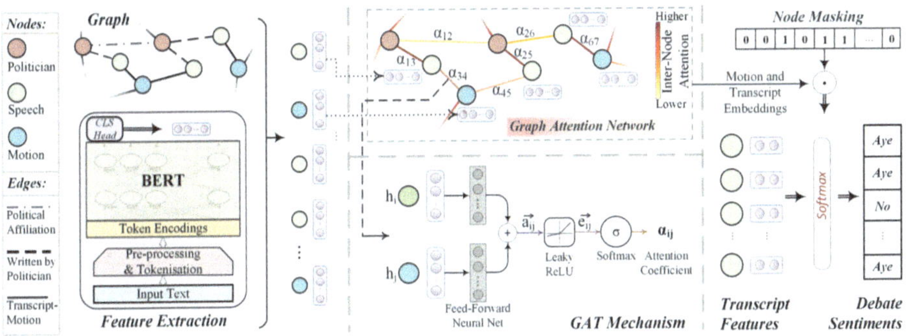

Fig. 6.3 Illustration of the approach of Sawhney et al. (2020): Speeches and motions of a debate are represented in a graph that is fed to a graph attention network (GAT) which learns to predict speaker stance based on the interactions of speeches and motions. Licensed under CC-BY 4.0 International

transfers the representations into a factor graph to model collective stance classification as an ILP problem. For inference, it defines constraints that ensure that authors, their attributes, and their posts are treated consistently. On the two portal-specific datasets in the corpus of Walker et al. (2012b), *createdebate.com* and *4forums.com* (not online anymore), the approach achieved accuracies of 75.2 and 84.9% respectively, further improving over the previous works above.

For the genre of parliamentary debates, Sawhney et al. (2020) propose a sophisticicated neural approach to collection-level stance classification. The approach jointly models both semantic language representations and relations between speeches, motions (i.e., debated issues), and political party members. Given a set of speech transcripts T from a set of speakers S of a set of parties P on a set of motions M, the task is to classify the stance of a speaker $s \in S$ based on their speech $t_s \in T$ on $m_t \in M$. To this end, the approach proceeds in three steps, as depicted in Fig. 6.3:

1. *Speech and Motion Encoding.* All speech transcripts and motions are encoded using contextualized embeddings as features. Sawhney et al. employ BERT for this purpose, fine-tuned on the ParlVote dataset of 33k transcripts of UK parliament debate speeches (Abercrombie and Batista-Navarro 2018).
2. *Debate Graph Creation.* Next, the approach creates a debate graph $G = (V, E)$ where $V = T \cup S \cup M$, and E consists of edges that model three types of context: (1) *speaker-self* edges between speakers $s \in S$ and their speeches $t_s \in T$; (2) *intra-party* edges between pairs of speakers $s_i, s_j \in S$ from the same party $p \in P$; and (3) *motion-level* edges between each $t \in T$ and the motion $m_t \in M$ it discusses.
3. *Graph Attention Network.* To predict 2-class stance (parliament votes *aye* and *no*), a graph attention network (Velickovic et al. 2018) is initialized with the speech/motion embeddings. The training on ground-truth stance labels of transcripts updates the representations by propagating information through all edges $e \in E$, computing attention weights α_{ij} for any neighboring nodes $v_i, v_j \in V$.

In experiments on ParlVote, Sawhney et al. (2020) compared their approach to multiple baselines, including a BERT-based classifier and latent DeepWalk (Perozzi et al. 2014) representations based on a speaker-speaker graph. The approach succeeded with an accuracy of 76%, while BERT reached 67% and DeepWalk 72%.

Sawhney et al. (2021) further extend the approach by modeling past speeches of speakers in addition, thereby establishing a dynamic graph model that changes over different time steps of a debate. The authors evaluated the extended approach on the same data, but with different splits for time modeling. On this data, BERT reached 67.31% accuracy, DeepWalk 70.12%, and the approach of Sawhney et al. (2020) 73.69%. The extended approach further improved this value to 75.07%.

Gambini et al. (2024) employ LLMs to assess the stance of a given Twitter user toward a given sentence, based on the user's Twitter timeline. First, their approach uses a zero-shot classifier to detect tweets matching the topic of the sentence. Then, another classifier assigns each a stance score on a 5-point scale from 1 (completely disagree) to 5 (completely agree) and uses different voting techniques to derive the user's stance from their tweets. In systematic experiments on nine datasets, the authors compared various transformer models and LLMs for each of the two classifiers. The strongest configuration used GPT-4 in both cases to reach an average F_1-score of 0.41 (five labels) of 0.62 (three labels) respectively. In comparison, Mixtral (Jiang et al. 2024) obtained 0.24 and 0.57, and DeBERTA (He et al. 2023) 0.29 and 0.53. All results suggest that there is still notable room for improvement left.

Stance Transfer Some research examines how to transfer knowledge from other sources to stance classification, be it via general transformer pretraining or fine-tuning on certain data. Among these, Allaway and McKeown (2020) tackle stance classification as a zero-shot task, ahead of the era of large language models (LLMs). To this end, they present the widely-used *VAried Stance Topics (VAST)* datatset with 3365 comments on 304 heuristically-extracted topics, taken from the reasoning comprehension corpus (Habernal et al. 2018c) (see Chap. 8). At a Krippendorff's α agreement of 0.427, crowdworkers assigned pro/con labels to each comment with respect to (a) the heuristic topics, (b) corrected topics, and (c) topics suggested by themselves. The authors add neutral examples by pairing comments with other topics. Their approach clusters all training comments to map the clusters to generalized topic representations. On these, a topic-grouped attention is trained capturing the similarity between topics. Given a new comment, the approach decides the stance label based on the comment's embedding and its topic-grouped attention. In experiments, the authors tested their approach against several baselines including the discussed Bi-LSTM of Augenstein et al. (2016) and ablations without topic-grouped attention. In the zero-shot setting, it largely improved over the Bi-LSTM (macro F_1-score of 0.666 vs. 0.428), but slightly only over the best ablation (0.661).

Schiller et al. (2021a) provide a benchmark that unifies the setting of 10 stance datasets to evaluate the robustness of classification methods. Following the transfer learning paradigm, the authors trained and tested a joint multitask learning approach on all

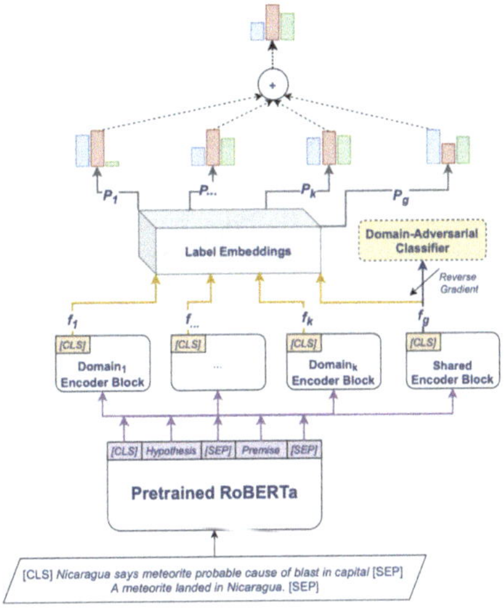

Fig. 6.4 Architecture of the cross-domain stance classification approach of Hardalov et al. (2021): A mixture-of-experts learns multiple domain-oriented stance representations that are combined into label embeddings, which can be mapped to the target labels. Licensed under CC-BY 4.0 International

datasets, starting from either BERT-large embeddings or the multitask-oriented MT-DNN embeddings (Liu et al. 2019a). On the benchmark, the authors opposed multitask to single-task learning for both encoders. While differences exist across the 10 datasets, overall the MT-DNN multitask variant performed strongest in the evaluation, with an average macro F_1-score of 0.6695, followed by BERT-large multitask (0.6585), MT-DNN single-task (0.6516), and BERT-large single-task (0.6181). For five of the six datasets where a direct comparison to the respective previous state of the art was possible, either variation also defined the new best approach.

In quite related work, Hardalov et al. (2021) look at 16 different stance datasets, but with the idea to evaluate classification performance *across* domains. The authors propose an unsupervised end-to end approach for cross-domain label-adaptive stance classification, illustrated in Fig. 6.4. Starting from a pretrained RoBERTa model, the approach employs an early mixture-of-experts architecture with one expert per domain, instantiated for four domains (debates, news, social media, various) in experiments. Their outputs go through a shared label embedding layer that produces the output label probabilities for each domain. A domain-adversarial training step optimizes all experts toward domain-invariant representations. To obtain the actual labels of an unseen domain from the label embeddings, the authors compare a *hard* mapping from learned meta-labels to target labels to two mappings that choose the most similar label names (*soft*) or the best match (*weak*) respectively. In in-domain experiments, the approach achieved an average macro F_1-score of 0.6555, beating multitask BERT (0.6311) and multitask RoBERTa (0.6512). Across domains, the weak mapping clearly outperformed the others, with 0.4920 compared to 0.4267 (soft) and 0.3278 (hard), but it technically is not fully unsupervised.

Saha et al. (2024) present a new twist to stance classification, namely, to generate explanations for the classified label. Somewhat comparable to the essay-oriented approach of Faulkner (2014) detailed above, their approach constructs a stance tree based on the discourse structure in a text. A trained predictor assigns a stance label with a confidence score to each claim-sentence relation in the tree, before irrelevant tree units are pruned, and disagreement indications are quantified based on the arguing lexicon of Somasundaran and Wiebe (2010). Using Dempster Shafer theory, the approach aggregates the results from these steps into a score that decides the final stance label. The individual stance-classified sentences in the tree then serve as the explanation of the label. For development and evaluation, the authors created a new dataset with 64k articles for 7k claims from createdebate.com and the *Room for Debate* of the NY Times. In a user study, human evaluators rated the informativeness of the explanations 3.5 on average, coverage 3.61, and overall quality 3.6 (all on a 1–5 scale). The authors evaluate their approach on five datasets, using different models for stance prediction including the approaches of Schiller et al. (2021a) and Hardalov et al. (2021). For both, they find that their approach mostly improves stance classification performance over the models in isolation.

Among LLM-based stance classification approaches, Zhang et al. (2024) evaluate the effectiveness of ChatGPT in comparison to various baselines including standard transformers, such as BERT, and existing approaches, such as Augenstein et al. (2016). The authors build on two datasets, the shared task dataset of Mohammad et al. (2016) and the P-stance dataset (Li et al. 2021). Even compared to fine-tuned versions of the baselines, ChatGPT achieved top macro F_1-scores on both datasets, 0.684 on the shared task data (best baseline: 0.673) and 0.828 on P-stance (best baseline: 0.814). It seems, though, that data contamination may be an issue here, which is not discussed in the paper. Besides, we observe that the numerical results still do not really go beyond those of the non-LLM approaches above. The authors conclude their study with a qualitative analysis of ChatGPT's explanations of its decisions. They observe that particularly cases that it cannot explain provide helpful insights.

Ajjour and Wachsmuth (2025) systematically explore four principled strategies of selecting few-shot examples for stance classification: *randomly*, by *diversity*, by *semantic similarity* to the instance to be classified, and by *stance-related similarity* to the instance. In experiments on three existing corpora (Bar-Haim et al. 2017a; Allaway and McKeown 2020; Chen et al. 2019a), the authors compared the strategies for four 7B LLMs: Llama 2 (Touvron et al. 2023b), Alpaca (Taori et al. 2023), Mistral (Jiang et al. 2023), and Vicuna (Chiang et al. 2023). For three of them, particularly stance-related priming performed strongly; for example, Vicuna reached a macro F_1-scores of 0.822 on the data of Bar-Haim et al. (2017a), 0.563 on VAST (Allaway and McKeown 2020), and 0.815 on the data of Chen et al. (2019a). Only Mistral worked better with the diversity strategy, resulting in values of 0.867, 0.577, and 0.845 respectively (the first and last beating the previous state of the art). Matching expectation, a full fine-tuning on task-specific training data further improved the results; for instance, for Mistral with diverse few-shots to 0.902, 0.674, and 0.908.

6.1.2 Predicting Agreement and Disagreement

Even though some approaches we just saw capture debate context, stance classification puts single claims or arguments into the focus. There is also research that explicitly targets the *agreement and disagreement* of two arguments in a debate or that asks whether two claims or arguments are on the *same side*. This way, the dependence on a specified topic is alleviated to some extent. We cover approaches to model *author agreement* here as well, which generalize over multiple arguments.

Agreement and Disagreement Menini et al. (2017) study agreement in US electoral manifestos. Their approach first applies an existing classifier (Zirn et al. 2016) to assign each sentence to one of seven macro-domains, such as *economy* or *social groups*. From the sentences of each domain, key concepts are extracted with a rule-based system and assigned a TF-IDF score. A clusterer then maps key concepts to GloVe embeddings (Pennington et al. 2014) and creates a graph, in which nodes denote key concepts and edges pair-wise embedding similarity, directed towards the higher-scored key concept. The clusters are used to find related statements in different parties' manifestos, before agreement is determined with an SVM classifier from prior work (Menini and Tonelli 2016). On the manifestos, the classifier reached an accuracy of 61.0% only. However, the retraining of Menini et al. (2017) on the manifesto data boosted it to 66.0% while still showing the difficulty of the data.

In contrast, Chen et al. (2018) look at agreement in online debates. Their approach combines two parallel Bi-LSTMs that use self-attention and cross-attention to encode a claim and a response to it. It then classifies the concatenation of the two encodings. On three datasets with arguments from different debate portals, the authors evaluate multiple approach ablations against different baselines. The full approach performed best on the datasets of Walker et al. (2012b) and Menini and Tonelli (2016) with accuracy values of 77.0 and 93.6%. While its accuracy of 76.9% was slightly beaten by a maximum entropy baseline (77.6%) on the dataset of Rosenthal and McKeown (2015), that baseline is rather theoretical, as it employs ground-truth annotations of conversational structure from the corpus.

Unlike the previous works, Xu et al. (2019) model (dis)agreement for any two *independent* utterances. To this end, the authors propose a reason comparing model that takes a topic T and two utterances P, Q with stance on the topic as input. The model then outputs one of three reason labels $\hat{\mathbf{y}}$ (agree, disagree, neither). Figure 6.5 illustrates its architecture, showing the four main steps of the approach:

1. *RNN Encoder.* First, Bi-LSTMs create encodings $\mathbf{H}$ of P and Q conditioned on the topic, in line with the idea of Augenstein et al. (2016) outlined above.
2. *Reason Encoders.* Two identical neural networks learn pairwise relations between all claims and reasons in each utterance, representing them in self-attention matrices $\mathbf{C}^P$

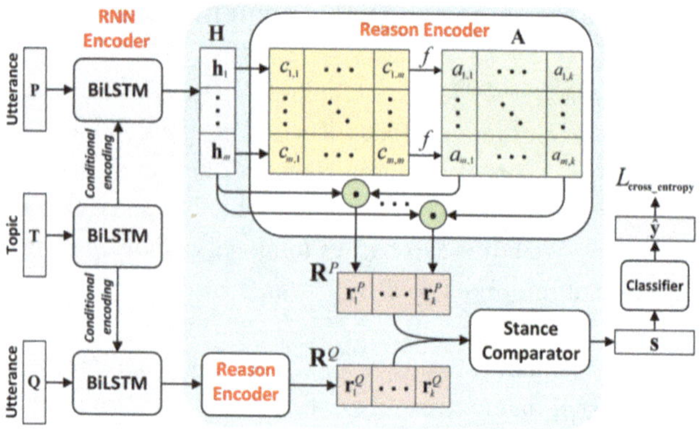

Fig. 6.5 Architecture of the approach of Xu et al. (2019): Utterance encodings are topic-conditioned, before reasons are encoded to compare stance and classify agreement. Licensed under CC-BY 4.0 International

and $\mathbf{C}^Q$ respectively. Via a weight matrix **A**, the representations are then mapped to reason encodings $\mathbf{R}^P$ and $\mathbf{R}^Q$.

3. *Stance Comparator*: The approach now computes similarities for all pairs of encoded reasons, $(\mathbf{r}_i^P, \mathbf{r}_j^Q)$, from the two utterances, and aggregates them via max-pooling into a similarity vector, **s**.
4. *(Dis)Agreement Classifier*: A two-layer feedforward network maps **s** to $\hat{\mathbf{y}}$, which is optimized end-to-end via a loss function for the entire architecture.

For evaluation, Xu et al. (2019) created 20k agreement, 20k disagreement, and 10k neither pairs from the Tweet stance dataset of Mohammad et al. (2016), on which basis they compared their approach to different baselines. Across all five topics in the dataset, it obtained the best macro F_1-score, ranging from 0.586 to 0.730. For comparison, a simple Bi-LSTM achieved values between 0.525 and 0.681.

To study (dis)agreement in settings where people use slang, sarcasm, and jokes, Pougué-Biyong et al. (2021) present a dataset of 42k comment-reply pairs from five Reddit forums. Crowdworkers labeled each pair for agreement, disagreement, or neither (while a fourth class *unsure* led to some pairs being discarded). As baselines, the authors compare nine transformer models from four model families: BERT, XLNet (Yang et al. 2019b), RoBERTa (Liu et al. 2019b), and DeBERTa. On an 80/10/10 split, the models all perform similar with accuracy values between 61.8% (BERT-base-cased) and 64.1% (DeBERTa-large). We come to this dataset further below again, in a study on human values. Here, we conclude that, despite the lower topic dependence, (dis)agreement classification seems not be easier than stance classification, judging based on the numerical results.

Same-Side Stance In a separated line of research, Stein et al. (2021) introduce the task of *same-side stance classification*: Given two arguments on the same topic, do they have the same stance or not? The authors deployed this task as a shared task, for which they sampled a dataset from the args.me corpus (Ajjour et al. 2019b): 61k argument pairs on abortion and 6k pairs on gay marriage, both more or less balanced (same side vs. not same side). They provided two training/test splits, one in-topic and cross-topic, for the nine teams that participated with 11 different approaches. In terms of accuracy, in-topic accuracy ranged between 50 and 77%, and the cross-topic accuracy was only a little lower (50–73%). For both settings, the best approach comes from Ollinger et al. (2021), which relies on a pretrained BERT-large model fine-tuned on the respective training sets. Ollinger et al. (2021) found that the model performs better when training is done only on argument pairs that do not exceed the 512 tokens context size of BERT.

The second best approach uses a fine-tuned BERT model as well (Körner et al. 2021a). In a later study, the same author group compares several transformer models on same-side stance classification (Körner et al. 2021b). In the standard setting, the lightweight ALBERT model pretrained on embedding matrix compression and sentence order prediction (Lan et al. 2020) was best overall, outperforming the model of Ollinger et al. in the cross-domain setting (74.2% accuracy) but not in-domain (73.7%). However, the authors doubted the generalization ability of the model, which is why they created alternative data splits that (a) avoid argument overlap in training and test pairs and (b) contain synthetically-created adversarial examples with modified versions of the original arguments (e.g., negated arguments). On the respective test sets, the ALBERT model achieved accuracies of (a) only 62.4% and (b) even only 43.4%, stressing that the task is far from being solved yet.

Author Agreement In a rather unusual work, Toledo-Ronen et al. (2016) construct an expert stance graph that serves as a knowledge resource, encoding the stance of more than 100k experts on 114 controversial concepts in the form of relations (e.g., *pro(Dawkins, atheism)*). For construction, the authors first manually derived 201 concepts (e.g., *atheism*) from Wikipedia's list of controversial topics and Wikipedia articles on controversies. For each concept term and thesaurus-like derivations (e.g., *atheist* for *atheism*), they then retrieved all Wikipedia categories containing any concept term (e.g., *American atheists*). All 4603 categories with at least five persons were kept and, if they really indicated group membership, manually labeled for their stance toward the concept at Cohen's $\kappa = 0.79$. Toledo-Ronen et al. also propose a simple rule-based algorithm that takes a category and an author as input and assigns a stance, depending on the indicator strings in the category, such as "critics of" or "anti". On a test split, the algorithm found pro experts with a recall of 0.618 at a precision of 0.898, and con experts with a recall of 0.581 at a precision of 0.976.

Sasaki et al. (2017) explore inter-topic preferences of Japanese Twitter users: if a user agrees with a stance on topic t, would the user agree with topic t'. Figure 6.6 gives an overview of their approach. Building on a corpus of 35B tweets, it first uses regular expressions to filter tweets with pro and con hashtags, in Japanese expressed as `#(.+)sansei` and `#(.+)hantai`, where `(.+)` matches any topic. To mine topic

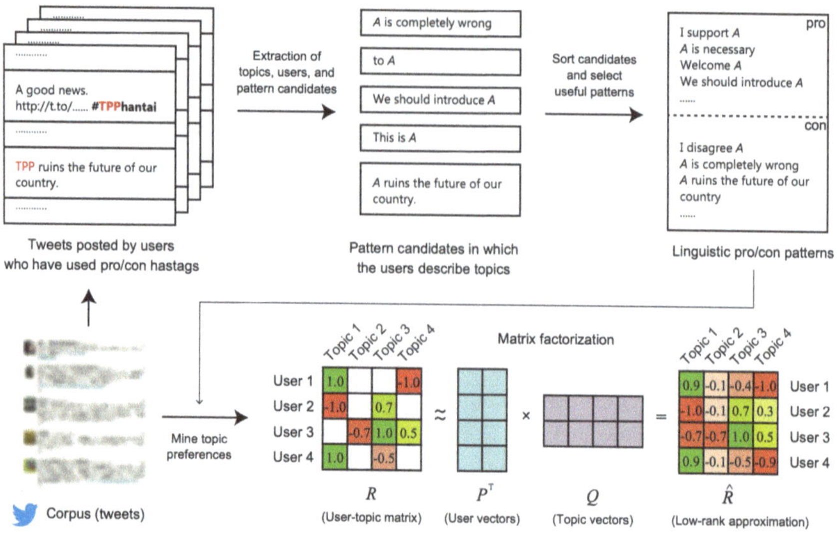

Fig. 6.6 Illustration of the approach of Sasaki et al. (2017): Given a Twitter corpus, it mines users' topic preferences based on hashtags and linguistic patterns. Then, it factorizes the resulting user-topic matrix to predict unknown topic preferences for users. Licensed under CC-BY 4.0 International

preferences from the tweets, it then applies simple linguistic patterns, such as "t is necessary" or "I don't want t'". To this end, 100 pro and 100 con patterns were derived from the filtered tweets in a semi-automatic process, resulting in 10M topic preferences for 273k users on 2323 topics. Based on the ratios of the users' pro and con views, a user-topic matrix is factorized to predict unknown preferences of users. In experiments, the authors evaluate the prediction of topic preferences depending on the number of known preferences of users. For users with at least five preferences, the approach obtained an accuracy of 82.1%; for those with 100+ preferences 94.0%.

6.2 Identifying Topics and Frames

Stance may be seen as the core concept in the context of perspective assessment. However, as we have extensively detailed in the previous section, stance is inherently relational, being bound to a controversial issue, that is, a topic at discussion. In other words, underlying the notion of stance are the question as to what the topics are that argumentation and debates actually consider, and how to identify and model the aspects of the topics that arguments convey a stance on. By emphasizing certain aspects and disregarding others, arguments *frame* a topic in a specific way (Entman 1993), often to explicitly or implicitly push forward a stance. The notion of *framing* is thus at the heart of perspectives as well. Some researchers see frames as topic-specific (de Vreese 2005). Others argue that there is a limited set of generic frames (Boydstun et al. 2014), which play a role across topics and argumentative settings.

We cover computational approaches in the context of the different outlined notions in this section, starting from the strand of NLP research on argumentation that deals with the modeling of topics, their aspects, and the keypoints built from them. Then we look more closely at computational methods to identify frames in arguments as well as those that analyze the framing emerging therefrom.

6.2.1 Modeling Topics and Keypoints

In the following, we first look at the modeling of *topics and issues*. Then, we discuss approaches to the identification of *topical aspects* as well as to the exhibition of *key points* from a set of arguments.

Topics and Issues Beigman Klebanov et al. (2010) picture perspectives as particular ways of thinking about issues influenced by beliefs or experiences. The authors shed light on the relation of stance to the issue discussed on four abstraction levels: perspective may simply refer to a person's specific *opinion about an issue* (e.g., on some death penalty legislation), to their *stance on the issue* (e.g., on death penalty), to their *stance on a general conflict* that covers multiple aspects (e.g., on how to deal with serious criminals), or to *cultural, regional, religious, or political traditions* that emanate from the person's life contingencies and that influence general patterns of discourse (e.g., how a person sees the value of an individual's life within society). On different datasets, the authors classify texts with respect to proxies of these abstraction levels in order to then analyze the importance of specific vocabulary choice for classification. They find that often very few words are needed to reach a classification accuracy that is not significantly worse than the best observed.

Bar-Haim et al. (2019) observe that, in a debate on a controversial issue, it is common to also consider alternative topics, make generalizations, or give specific examples. To teach this capability to machines, the authors introduce the task of *debate topic expansion*: finding concepts relevant to a concept debated. They distinguish *consistent* from *contrastive* expansions. Matching the idea behind contrastiveness of Bar-Haim et al. (2017a) (see Sect. 6.1), the former covers concepts for which it is likely to have the same stance on as for the given concept, and vice versa for the latter. Bar-Haim et al. (2019) create a dataset for the task in two steps:

1. *Candidate Extraction*. For a given Wikipedia concept, candidates for consistent cases are found using Hearst-like patterns (Hearst 1992), such as "X such as Y". Accordingly, patterns such as "X * better than * Y" find contrastive cases.
2. *Candidate Filtering*. Only candidates are kept that have an 80% uniform directionality with respect to the patterns, have a minimum distributional cosine similarity of 0.5,

Table 6.1 Positive (⇒) and negative (⇏) examples of *consistent* and *contrastive* debate topic expansions from the approach of Bar-Haim et al. (2019). Adapted from Bar-Haim et al. (2019). Licensed under CC-BY 4.0 International

Consistent expansions				Contrastive expansions			
#	Debate concept		Expansion concept	#	Debate concept		Expansion concept
1	Wind power	⇒	Renewable energy	11	Democracy	⇒	Dictatorship
2	Vegetarianism	⇏	Diet (nutrition)	12	Democracy	⇏	Socialism
3	Entrepreneurship	⇒	Startup company	13	Flat tax	⇒	Progressive tax
4	Abortion	⇏	Fetus	14	Flat tax	⇏	Value-added tax
5	Fast food	⇒	McDonald's	15	Global warming	⇏	Global cooling
6	Fast food	⇏	Restaurant	16	Carbon tax	⇒	Emission trading
7	Gender inequality	⇒	Gender pay gap	17	Boxing	⇏	Wrestling
8	Gender inequality	⇒	Social inequality	18	Polyamory	⇒	Monogamy
9	Organic food	⇏	Local food	19	Private university	⇒	Public university
10	Casino	⇒	Gambling	20	Recycling	⇒	Landfill

and match constraints of generalizations and specifications, such as that only the more specific concept may be a named entity.

Table 6.1 shows a set positive examples (candidates kept) and negative examples (others). On the final dataset with about 3000 pairs of concept and expansion, Bar-Haim et al. evaluate automatic topic expansion, combining a feature-based logistic regression classifier with a Bi-LSTM, distantly-supervised on retrieved sentences that match training concept pairs. At a precision@1 of 0.9, it reaches a recall@1 of only 0.248 for consistent expansions and 0.164 for contrastive expansions. At a precision@0.5, however, these values went up to 0.798 and 0.721 respectively.

More generally, Ajjour et al. (2023) explore the realm of topics actually studied in NLP research on argumentation, surveying 59 argument corpora. To organize the collected topics, the authors propose a hierarchical ontology of 1810 topics, derived from the World Economic Forum, the Wikipedia list of controversial topics, and *debatepedia.org* (not online anymore). While the surveyed corpora span 2259 different topic labels, Ajjour et al. find that they match only 646 of the taxonomy topics. Figure 6.7 visualizes an exemplary matching of arguments to the taxonomy topics. The authors analyze the distributions of topics in the corpora on this basis, to conclude that topic coverage is still limited with respect to the ontology and, notably, very skewed with some topics being highly overrepresented. The ontology thus also serves as a basis for future corpus acquisitions with increased topic coverage.

Topical Aspects Some research analyzes topics at a more fine-grained level, modeling the different aspects, or facets, that arguments may discuss for a given controversial issue. Among these, Misra et al. (2015) followed a semi-automatic process to identify the main

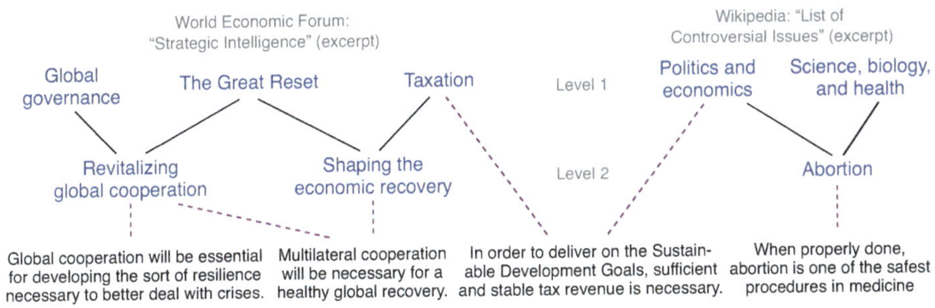

Fig. 6.7 Exemplary assignment of arguments (bottom) to the hierarchically organized topics in the topic ontology of Ajjour et al. (2023). Figure excerpt, licensed under CC-BY 4.0 International

facets of 85 dialogical argument chains in the Internet Argument Corpus (Walker et al. 2012b). After crowdworkers summarized all dialogues, three human annotators identified argumentative propositions in them, from which the 329 most frequent ones were kept. Using agglomerative clustering with cosine similarity, all arguments in the dialogues were then grouped hierarchically. For all proposition pairs within a cluster, crowdworkers assessed their similarity in terms of reflecting the same facet on a 6-point scale. In experiments, Misra et al. trained and evaluated featured-based support vector regression (SMO) and linear regression to predict similarity scores. Both seemed equally strong, for example, achieving a mean absolute error of 0.8019 (SMO) and 0.8003 (linear regression) respectively. In follow-up work, Misra et al. (2016) present the Argument Facet Similarity (AFS) corpus with 6000 arguments on three topics, annotated for the 6-point scores.

With a similar idea, Vilares and He (2017) explore how to detect main perspectives in terms of stance-bearing claims on specific aspects of a debated issue. The authors propose an unsupervised Bayesian modeling approach that distinguishes between *background words* (occurring across topics), *topic words* (specific to a topic), and *argument words* (expressing perspectives on a specific topic). Comparable to latent Dirichlet allocation (LDA) (Blei et al. 2003), the approach models sentences as a stochastic sample of topic and perspective words. In experiments on UK parliament debates from different domains (e.g., *treasury* or *environment*) covering various topics (e.g., *infrastructure* or *investment* for *treasury*), Vilares and He (2017) compare their approach against LDA and other baselines. In nearly all cases, it was found to be strongest, reliably grouping sentences on the same ground-truth topic into the same topic, and similar for perspectives. For the three most representative sentences per topic, human evaluators could identify perspectives up to 67% successfully.

Reimers et al. (2019) study how to identify similar arguments for the same topic, motivated by result presentation in argument search. First, the authors evaluate the classification of the relevance of sentences for a given topic on the corpus of Stab et al. (2018b) with eight topics and three classes (pro, con, no argument) and on the corpus of Shnarch et al. (2018) with 118 topics and two classes (evidence, no evidence). Comparing several contextualized embedding-based approaches, they find that giving the topic as input is crucial. On the former corpus, BERT-large performed best with an F_1-score of 0.6325 this way (0.5019 without the topic); on the latter corpus, BERT-base with 0.8137 (0.7928 without). In a second experiment, the authors evaluate whether agglomerative hierarchical clustering helps to identify similar arguments with BERT models fine-tuned on some topics for two corpora: the AFS corpus and their own extension of the corpus of Stab et al. (2018b) by annotation of four levels of similarity, used binarily though (similar, not similar). Compared to unsupervised embedding methods, fine-tuning notably pushes the F_1-score, for example from 0.6539 to 0.7401 on the extended corpus. Interestingly, clustering does not improve over simply assessing similarity directly.

Tackling the same task, Opitz et al. (2021) propose abstract meaning representation graphs for explainable argument similarity assessment. Given two arguments, their fully unsupervised approach parses concept relations (e.g., "fracking *contaminates* water") from them to build up their graphs whose similarity is computed from both concept overlap and relation overlap. Moreover, a T5 encoder-decoder transformer is fine-tuned on premise-conclusion pairs from the AAE2 corpus (Stab and Gurevych 2017b) to augment the arguments with explicit conclusions. On the extension of the data of Stab et al. (2018b), the best configuration of the approach focuses on concepts (rather than relations) in the augmented arguments, achieving an F_1-score of 0.6870 compared to the 0.6539 of Reimers et al. (2019) above. Without augmentation, the result was only slightly worse (0.6817), whereas adding relations rather seems to have negative effects (0.6621). In a qualitative analysis, the authors demonstrate how the graphs can be used to explain what makes arguments similar.

Trautmann (2020) introduce the two-stage task of *aspect-based argument mining* already discussed in Chap. 4: (a) extract all aspects from a set of topic-related arguments in terms of the subtopics covered and (b) segment arguments into spans with stances on specific aspects. Building on a corpus of 4396 sentence-level arguments on eight topics (Trautmann et al. 2020), the author provides 12,040 annotations of 4525 unique aspects. Table 6.2 shows the top-5 aspects per topic. Some aspects are also common across all topics, such "life" or "government". In experiments, Trautmann (2020) models both subtasks as sequence labeling problems and fine-tunes BERT (base and large), with or without a conditional random field (CRF) head. As a baseline, he considers POS patterns that were also used to create candidates for annotation. In aspect extraction, BERT-large was best in-domain (0.821), and BERT-CRF-large best across domains (0.756). The other BERT variants were close, while the patterns had only 0.610 and 0.640, respectively. In segmentation, BERT-large slightly beat BERT-CRF-large with 0.520 (in-domain) and 0.369 (cross-domain). The limited effectiveness underlines the difficulty of aspect extraction, though, possibly partly caused by the subjectivity of the task.

In the realm of perspectivism research (Plank 2022), Plenz et al. (2025) bring together topic-specific aspects and author stance by modeling an arguer's individual stances on different topic-related concepts as a *perspectived stance vector*. Concept candidates are derived from conceptnet.io and then filtered based on their stance-specific frequency in a set of arguments. To compute concept-related stance for an argument, the authors compare

Table 6.2 The top-five most common aspects per topic in the dataset of Trautmann (2020), along with their absolute counts. The table is an excerpt from the paper, licensed under CC-BY 4.0 International

Topic	Aspects (with # of occurrences)
Abortion	Child (28), life (26), woman (24), unsafe abortion (22), death (16)
Cloning	Animal (24), child (20), clone (20), disease (16), scientist (16)
Marijuana legaliz'n	Drug (51), marijuana (44), people (41), alcohol (37), medical marijuana (27)
Minimum wage	Worker (119), job (52), increase (46), employer (41), economy (39)
Nuclear energy	Energy (42), electricity (35), fossil fuel (34), environment (30), nuclear power plant (24)
Death penalty	Crime (62), deterrent (30), punishment (28), cost (27), criminal (27)
Gun control	Crime (56), gun (55), criminal (28), crime rate (25), gun control law (22)
School uniforms	Student (140), parent (77), child (66), kid (60), school (57)

three alternatives: a baseline that simply takes the argument's stance, RoBERTa transfer-learned on stance and human value data (Sobhani et al. 2016; Mohammad et al. 2017; Mirzakhmedova et al. 2024b), and GPT4o. The resulting vectors allow computing whether the arguers (or their arguments) agree or disagree, or are orthogonal to each other, for which the authors compare six different stance aggregation methods. In experiments on a debate dataset (Plenz et al. 2024), zero-shot GPT4o performed best in concept stance prediction, with a macro F_1-score of 0.502 compared to 0.432 for RoBERTa and 0.384 for the baseline. An aggregation of stance probability proved strongest, with an AUC score of 0.62 for agreement, 0.76 for disagreement, and 0.75 for orthogonality.

Key Points The transition between arguments on topical aspects and key points is not properly set in stone and certainly smooth; we follow Bar-Haim et al. (2020a) who loosely define the key points in a debate as a set of salient talking points that reocccur across arguments. The authors introduce key point analysis as the task to summarize an argument collection by a small number of high-level pro and con arguments that appear in different forms across the collection. The data they provide has 6515 crowdsourced arguments on 28 topics with 243 key points, taken from the IBM-ArgQ-Rank-30kArgs corpus (Gretz et al. 2020b). For example, "Homeschooling should be banned" comes with four pro points (matching arguments in parentheses):

(6.5) Mainstream schools are essential to develop social skills (61 arguments)
Parents are not qualified as teachers (20 arguments)
Homeschools cannot be regulated/standardized (15 arguments)
Mainstream schools are of higher educational quality (9 arguments)

Conceptually, key point analysis consists of two subtasks: the *generation* of the key points, and the *matching* of arguments with the key points. Bar-Haim et al. tackle the second only. They compare different ways to score a pair of argument and key point as well as different strategies to decide to which key point(s) each argument is assigned on this basis. A BERT model with a sigmoid output layer fine-tuned on the training data achieves the most accurate scores, outperforming unsupervised methods such as TF-IDF and BERT-based NLI. For the final matching, experiments on the validation set revealed that learning a minimum score threshold is favorable (the consequence is that some arguments will not be assigned to any key point). On the test set, using the top-1 key point was best in terms of accuracy, whereas using the top-2 key points (if both above threshold) was best in terms of F_1-score.

In follow-up work, Bar-Haim et al. (2020b) propose an approach that tackles both subtasks of key point analysis, and Friedman et al. (2021) present the results of a shared task on key point analysis that was carried out on the data of Bar-Haim et al. (2020a). Since the methodological parts ultimately aim at summarization, we detail these two works later in Chap. 9 on argument generation.

6.2.2 Detecting Frames and Framing

Computational research on frames and framing exists across disciplines and across areas of NLP; for a survey of 37 papers, we refer the reader to Ali and Hassan (2022). Here, we focus on those with at least a somewhat apparent relation to argumentation, grouped by *topic-specific* frames, *generic* frames, and *combinations*.

Topic-Specific Frames Tsur et al. (2015) investigate how to detect framing in 134k public statements of US congress members from 2010 to 2013. The authors developed a semi-automatic approach that combines LDA for topic modeling with a time-series analysis, in order to learn how politicians put forth agendas through specific framing over time. After initial tests, they ran LDA with 100 topics and 50 words per topic, and let human annotators manually validate and hierarchically organize the topics. On this basis, they focus on the 14 most salient topics in terms of conciseness, generality, and frequency, such as *health*, *energy*, and *economy/budget*. In their time-series analysis, Tsur et al. find interesting patterns in the way Democrats and Republicans respond to each other; for example, Democrats often answer with health-related statements to Republicans statements on the economy/budget frame.

Naderi and Hirst (2016) present the first approach to framing in the context of argument mining, in a focused study on *gay marriage*. The authors distinguish seven predefined frames, which are listed in Table 6.3 and underline the connection of many frames to either stance of the topic given. Their approach employs a multiclass SVM to assign each argument to one of the frames, modeling the argument using different features based on word2vec embeddings and syntactic embeddings (Wang et al. 2015) along with stance information. For training, the authors use 275 argumentative statements from forum posts included in the corpus of Boltužić and Šnajder (2014), 176 of them explicitly targeting the

Table 6.3 The seven predefined topic-specific frames in arguments on the topic *gay marriage*, taken from the study of Naderi and Hirst (2016)

#	Topic-specific frame on gay marriage
1	Gay couples can declare their union without resort to marriage.
2	Gay couples should be able to take advantage of the fiscal and legal benefits of marriage.
3	Gay marriage undermines the institution of marriage, leading to an increase in out of wedlock births and divorce rates.
4	It is discriminatory to refuse gay couples the right to marry.
5	Major world religions are against gay marriages.
6	Marriage is about more than procreation; therefore gay couples should not be denied the right to marry due to their biology.
7	Marriage should be between a man and a woman.

frame and 98 implicitly. They evaluate several approach ablations on 136 statements from the 2006 Canadian parliament, manually labeled for the seven frames in an annotation study ($\kappa = 0.46$). The best ablation achieved 73.5% accuracy (compared to 48.2% of a bag-of-words classifier) and combines word2vec cosine similarity with stance information.

Luo et al. (2020) look at the relation of stance and frames for debates on *global warming*, providing a dataset with 2k stance-labeled opinions on the topic, extracted from 56k news articles with a total of 500k opinions. Their BERT-based 3-class stance classifier (neutral, agree, disagree) obtained an average F_1-score of 0.73, as opposed to 0.60 for logistic regression. Based on the identified opinions, the authors analyze two linguistic framing devices, *affirming* of own opinions (with terms such as "point out, "confirm", or "expert") and *doubting* of opponent's opinions (with terms such as "pretend", "flawed", or "so-called"). Among other insights, they find that left-leaning news outlines affirm four times as much as they doubt, whereas right-leaning outlets show a near-equal distribution of the different devices.

In a focused analysis, Musi (2024) discusses the role of framing based on the example of `#genocide` hashtag in the Russia-Ukraine conflict. The author points out that both war parties have extensively used this hashtag in the beginning of the war; one mainly to justify their actions (Russia) and the other mainly to trigger third parties to intervene (Ukraine). For a sample of 100 tweets, she studies the discourse function and the position of the hashtag in the tweet, finding that it has an argumentative function in all cases, 67 times to express stance, and 33 times as an argument. In 75%, it is part of the content itself, and in 21% as a final label, both suggesting a clear use of the hashtag for framing. As such, the study showcases the inherent interaction of framing and social media mechanisms.

Generic Frames Research on the idea that there is a set of generic frames often starts from the *Policy Frames Codebook* proposed by Boydstun et al. (2014). Table 6.4 lists the 15 codebook frame definitions, summarized by Card et al. (2015). Card et al. introduced the *media frames corpus*, in which about 20k news articles on three topics (immigration,

Table 6.4 The 15 generic frames in the *Policy Frames Codebook* of Boydstun et al. (2014) along with summarized definitions. Table redrawn from Card et al. (2015)

Frame	Summarized definition
Economic	Costs, benefits, or other financial implications
Capacity and resources	Availability of physical, human or financial resources, and capacity of current systems
Morality	Religious or ethical implications
Fairness and equality	Balance or distribution of rights, responsibilities, and resources
Legality, constitutionality & jurisprudence	Rights, freedoms, and authority of individuals, corporations, and government
Policy prescription & evaluation	Discussion of specific policies aimed at addressing problems
Crime and punishment	Effectiveness and implications of laws and their enforcement
Security and defense	Threats to welfare of the individual, community, or nation
Health and safety	Health care, sanitation, public safety
Quality of life	Threats and opportunities for the individual's wealth, happiness, and well-being
Cultural identity	Traditions, customs, or values of a social group in relation to a policy issue
Public opinion	Attitudes and opinions of the general public, including polling and demographics
Political	Considerations related to politics and politicians, including lobbying, elections, and attempts to sway voters
External regulation & reputation	International reputation or foreign policy of the U.S.
Other	any coherent group of frames not covered by the above

smoking, and same-sex marriage) are labeled for span-level frames, about 3–10 in most cases. The unitized Krippendorff's α agreement was limited, though, ranging from 0.08 (same-sex marriage) to 0.23 (tobacco). Here is an excerpt from one article on immigration, copied from Naderi and Hirst (2017):

(6.3) [Immigrants say bias is 'swift kick' to citizenship]$_{\textit{Fairness and equality}}$

[When Eduardo Flores moved to Texas in 1981, he was content straddling two cultures: working in the United States but retaining his Mexican citizenship]$_{\textit{Cultural identity}}$. [Now, the anti-immigrant sentiment spawned by California's Proposition 187 is making him have second thoughts]$_{\textit{Cultural identity}}$: [Flores wants a claim on the rights available in his adopted land.]$_{\textit{No frame}}$ [Legal immigrants like Flores throughout the Southwest have been applying for citizenship at record levels, and many say they want the right to vote to stop the spread of laws like Proposition 187.]$_{\textit{Legality, constitutionality \& jurisprudence}}$

Following up on their topic-specific approach above, Naderi and Hirst (2017) derived datasets from the media frames corpus to tackle the computational classification of the five most frequent generic frames: *economic*, *legality, constitutionality & jurisprudence*, *policy prescription & evaluation*, *crime and punishment*, and *political*. The authors consider two settings, one with two topics (immigration and smoking) and the other with one topic only (immigration). For classification, they experiment with LSTMs, Bi-LSTMs, and GRUs (Cho et al. 2014), based on pre-trained and fine-tuned GloVe embeddings as well as embeddings trained from scratch. In both settings, the GRU with pretrained embeddings proved best. On the two-topics test set, it achieved an accuracy of 68.7%, being 1–4% points better than all LSTM variations and much better than a random forest TF-IDF baseline (54.2). On the one-topic test set, the gains are smaller with the pretrained GRU at 71.2% followed by a pretrained LSTM with 70.5% and random forest with 64.8%.

Hartmann et al. (2019) look at the transfer of frames in news articles (Card et al. 2015) to those in argumentative online forum discussions. For evaluation, they add annotations of the five most common frames to the corpus of Swanson et al. (2015). That corpus covers four topics (gay marriage, gun control, death penalty, and evolution) and also has quality-related argument annotations. For the transfer from news articles, Hartmann et al. (2019) propose two LSTM-based approaches: (a) a joint multitask learning approach that uses tweet frame information (Johnson et al. 2017) and the quality annotations as auxiliary tasks; and (b) an adversarial learning approach that uses unlabeled data from the target domain (forum discussions) to distinguish frames from domains. In experiments, adversarial learning performed best with macro and micro F_1-scores of 0.515 and 0.548 respectively. With 0.505 and 0.534, multitask learning only minimally improved over a single task LSTM baseline (0.503 and 0.521). All results show the difficulty of the transfer, though.

To facilitate multilingual studies of framing and persuasion, Piskorski et al. (2023) created a dataset with 1612 news articles of six languages (English, French, German, Italian, Polish, Russian). The articles are categorized into 14 generic frames of Card et al. (2015) (all but *other*), three genres (opinion, report, satire), and 23 persuasion techniques from related work on propaganda detection (Da San Martino et al. 2020) from six high-level groups: attack on reputation, justification, simplification, distraction, call, and manipulative wording. As baselines, they classify all categories using a multilingual pretrained transformer, XLM-RoBERTa-large (Conneau et al. 2020) with individual output layers for each task. In frame classification, it reached an overall micro F_1-score of 0.649. Notable differences exist across languages, with Russian appearing to be hardest (0.436) and English easiest (0.677). Partly, the differences may stem from the different numbers of articles per language, though.

Combinations of Frames Covering both topic-specific and generic frames, Ajjour et al. (2019a) present one of the most fundamental NLP works on framing in argumentation. The authors start from the observation that a frame, F, ultimately defines a subset of all arguments, A, in that framing selects specific arguments to emphasize a specific

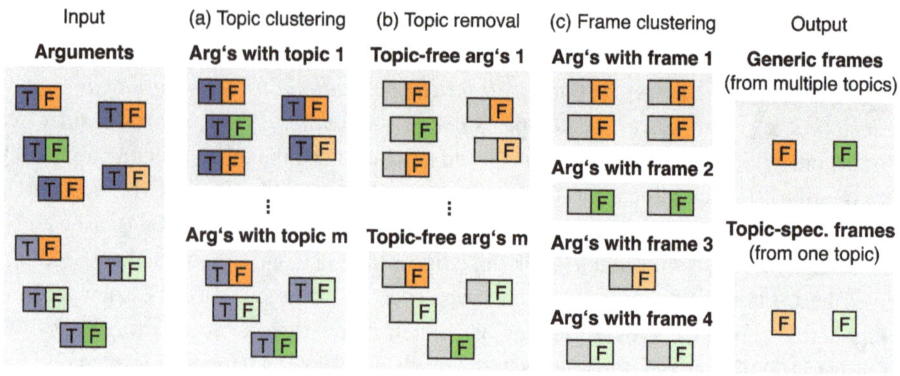

Fig. 6.8 Illustration of the unsupervised approach of Ajjour et al. (2019a) to detect *generic* and *topic-specific* frames: (**a**) Cluster arguments to find topics, T. (**b**) Remove topic information from arguments. (**c**) Cluster arguments to find frames, F. Licensed under CC-BY 4.0 International

perspective on a topic, T. For a given set A covering various topics and frames, they propose a fully unsupervised approach to frame identification that is illustrated in Fig. 6.8 and consists of three main steps:

1. *Topic clustering.* First, A is grouped into m clusters based on semantic similarity, each representing one topic, T. Ajjour et al. use k-means based either on TD-IDF vectors or on latent semantic analysis (LSA) vectors (Deerwester et al. 1990) (based on arguments or on debates), evaluating k from 0 to 1000.
2. *Topic removal.* Given the topic clusters, topic-specific features are identified for each cluster and removed from the respective arguments. Again, Ajjour et al. compare two ways: one removes the words with highest TD-IDF values, the other the arguments' conclusions (since they likely talk about the topic).
3. *Frame clustering.* Given the set of 'topic-free' arguments, the approach reclusters them. This time, each cluster is assumed to represent one frame, F. If F includes arguments from multiple topics, it is called generic, otherwise topic-specific. Ajjour et al. use k-means here as well, testing k from 1000 to 1600 based on some information about the frames in the data they work with.

Ajjour et al. evaluate their approach on a new dataset with all 12,326 arguments from *debatepedia.org*, covering 465 topics and 1639 frames derived from meta-information. The most common frames are *economics* (appearing for 119 topics) followed by *public opinion* and *environment*. Testing against the ground truth, the best topic clustering resulted in 310 clusters when using LSA on debates, with a B^3 F_1-score of 0.52. For topic removal, the authors measure B^3 F_1-score without the removed parts; here, simple TF-IDF is best with 0.45. The best frame clustering variations use different TF-IDF variations, resulting in B^3 F_1-scores of 0.28 (all frames), 0.28 (generic frames), and 0.48 (topic-specific frames).

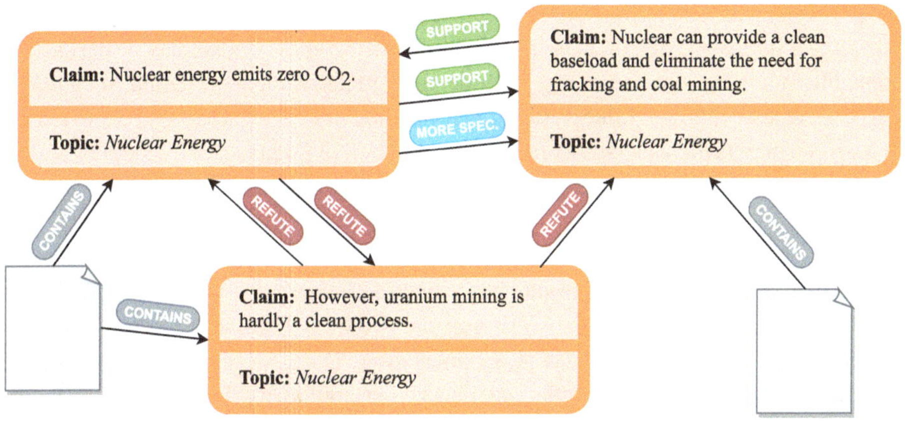

Fig. 6.9 Illustration of two documents and three claims in the multigraph for stance and frame classification created by the approach of Barrow et al. (2021). Licensed under CC-BY 4.0 International

Barrow et al. (2021), finally, tackle the classification of both stances and frames (called aspects there) on the collection level, that is, for all claims in a given corpus at the same time. Their approach automatically creates a directed multigraph for the corpus, where each node represents either a document or a claim. An edge from a claim to a document simply indicates that the claim comes from the document, whereas multiple edges may exist between claims, as depicted in Fig. 6.9. To determine edges, the authors trained and applied four RoBERTa classifiers on text pairs from existing datasets, namely for *relative stance*, *relative specificity*, *paraphrasing*, and *NLI*. Two further edges for *term similarity* and *topic similarity* were created using TF-IDF and LSA cosine similarity, respectively. For stance, Barrow et al. (2021) propose a relational graph convolutional network (Schlichtkrull et al. 2018), whereas they rely on unsupervised modularity-based community detection for frames (Clauset et al. 2004). On the stance datasets of Stab et al. (2018b) and Bar-Haim et al. (2017a), their approach achieved macro F_1-scores of 0.8340 and 0.6777 respectively, clearly beating a reimplementation of Schiller et al. (2021b) (0.7772 and 0.6138). Similarly, it had a superior B^3 F_1 of 0.5542 in frame identification on the data of Ajjour et al. (2019a). However, while all six edge types contribute to stance performance, only paraphrasing seems helpful for frame identification.

6.3 Assessing Biases, Values, and Morals

Arguments are inherently biased by nature. Not only do they push forward specific stances toward controversial issues, but the way in which an argument is framed may also induce lexical bias (how something is said) as well as informational bias (what is said, and what not) into the discussion of the issue (Fan et al. 2019). When we speak of the assessment of bias in argumentation, however, we rather mean the detection of *cognitive* biases that lead to explicit mispicturing of an issue, possibly crossing lines of what may be considered reasonable in a discussion (see Chap. 7 for details on reasonableness). Often, such biases emerge from the different value systems that humans have (Searle 2003); for example, some people may favor societal security while others strive for personal freedom of action. Human values are also the source of moral behaviors, such as being fair or caring for each other.

While particularly the detection and mitigation of social bias (Blodgett et al. 2020) and political bias (Feng et al. 2023) are studied in diverse regards in NLP, in what follows, we focus on work that explicitly deals with argumentative texts. First, we present approaches that detect and quantify certain bias in argumentation. Then, we discuss how to identify the human values and moral foundations underlying arguments. Both are rather young research lines in NLP research on argumentation.

6.3.1 Detecting and Quantifying Bias

We group the few computational bias assessment approaches for argumentation by either of two types of bias they address: *myside bias* and *social bias*.

Myside Bias Myside bias can be understood as a form of confirmation bias (Stanovich et al. 2013), describing that an argumentative text solely supports the stance of its author while disregarding opposing views. Stab and Gurevych (2016) present a computational approach to detecting myside bias in student essays, employing a feature-rich SVM. On the 402 essays in their AAE2 corpus (251 biased), the best feature set found combines bag-of-words, constituency tree rules, and indicator phrases of adversative transitions, such as concessions and dismissal. The respective SVM obtained an accuracy of 75.6%, compared to 62.4% of a majority baseline.

For both stance and myside bias classification, Wachsmuth et al. (2017a) propose the first NLP approach that jointly models the hierarchical overall structure (induced by argumentative discourse units (ADUs) and relations) and the sequential overall structure (induced by the text ordering) of argumentative texts. Figure 6.10 illustrates the two types of structure for an example text. To jointly model both types, the authors propose a kernel-based approach that builds on three elements:

1. *Positional Tree Representation.* Each input text is represented as a tree $T = (V, E)$, where each node $v \in V$ denotes an ADU and each edge $e = (v, v') \in E$ that the respective ADUs have a premise-conclusion relation. Node labels indicate the premise's (pro or con) stance toward the conclusion, and edge labels the relative position of the premise to the conclusion in the sequential text ordering.
2. *Adapted Route Kernel.* For structure representation, a route kernel (Aiolli et al. 2009) is employed, which extends a tree kernel (Collins and Duffy 2001) by edge labels

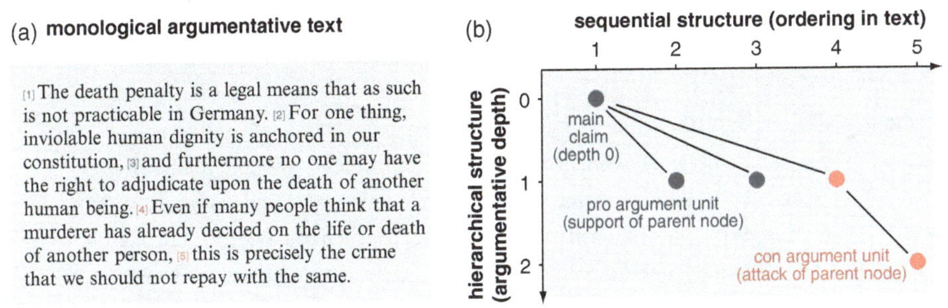

Fig. 6.10 Illustration of the joint structure modeled in the approach of Wachsmuth et al. (2017a). (**a**) Example text from the Arg-Microtexts corpus (Peldszus and Stede 2016b) with five ADUs. (**b**) The text's hierarchical and sequential structure. Licensed under CC-BY 4.0 International

indicating node positions relative to siblings, and which models a tree T by node label paths $\xi(v)$ and edge label paths $\pi(v)$ from the root to v. Wachsmuth et al. adjust the edge labeling according to their tree representation.

3. *Kernel Function.* Given the trees $T = (V, E)$ and $T' = (V, E')$ of two texts, the authors compute the trees' similarity following Aiolli et al. (2009) as

$$K_{\xi\pi}(T, T') = \Big(\sum_{v \in V} \sum_{v' \in V'} \frac{\delta(\xi(v), \xi(v')) \cdot \delta(\pi(v), \pi(v'))}{(|V| \cdot |V'|)^2}\Big)^d,$$

where δ is the identity function used to count matching node label and edge label paths. The sum of counts is normalized over all node pairs (v, v'). d is the kernel's polynomial degree determined experimentally ($d = 2$ was found to be best).

The function can be used for classification by any kernel-based classifier; Wachsmuth et al. employ an SVM. In their experiments, the authors compare the route kernel against a linear kernel (capturing node label distributions), a sequence kernel (node label sequences), and a tree kernel (hierarchical structure only) as well as token and part-of-speech n-grams. On the corpus of Peldszus and Stede (2016b), the route kernel performed best in stance classification, with an accuracy of 66.7% followed by token n-grams (65.2%) and tree kernels (59.8%). A combination of both achieved the top value (69.8%). For myside bias on the data of Stab and Gurevych (2016), the tree kernel alone basically solves the task with 97.4%. This results remains theoretical, though, as all experiments are carried out on ground-truth argument structure.

Unlike the previous works, Palomino et al. (2022) propose to model stance-related bias relatively, that is, to assess whether one argument is more biased than another. The authors carried out a crowdworking study in which participants assessed the bias of individual arguments and argument pairs of these arguments. Their results suggest that biased arguments are indeed easier to identify in comparison to other arguments, but relative and absolute differences also correlate to a good extent.

Table 6.5 The 10 most discriminating words for female/male genders and pro/con sides in debate portal arguments on abortion, from the study of Durmus and Cardie (2018b). Licensed under CC-BY 4.0 International

Combination		Top 10 most discriminating words
Female	Pro	Fetus, right, woman, sex, body, care, medical, emotion, really, alive
	vs. Con	baby, kill, cause, murder say, moral, wrong, abortion, human, womb
Male	Pro	Will, women, birth, pain, force, pregnancy, good, bad, society, reason
	vs. Con	human, unborn, kill, innocent, life, baby, development, crime, wrong, alive
Pro	Female	Sex, people, woman, adopt, care, choice, pregnancy, emotion, really, child
	vs. Male	moral, source, argument, will, human, conclusion, show, given, claim, logic
Con	Female	Baby, I'm, woman, don't, health, want, mother, birth, think
	vs. Male	human, argument, fetus, right, unborn, crime, case, moral, definition, claim

Social Bias NLP research has come up with diverse and partly debated notions of social bias (Blodgett et al. 2020). A coarse but common ground is that social bias refers to stereotypical thinking and/or prejudices against social groups (Fiske 1998). We cover here multiple works that treat social bias from different perspectives.

Durmus and Cardie (2018b) analyze linguistic differences that emerge from the gender and the stance of the writers of arguments. The authors analyze 1639 debates on abortion from debate.org (not online anymore), focusing on those writers identifying themselves as female (265) or male (648). Depending on the combination of gender and stance, arguments vary notably in the ratio of negations, question words, proper nouns, affect words, and much more. Exemplarily, Table 6.5 shows the most discriminating words within genders for different stances and within stances for different genders.

Spliethöver and Wachsmuth (2020) explicitly assess social bias in argumentative text corpora. To this end, they trained one GloVe embedding model separately for each of three debate portal corpora, the Internet Argument Corpus v2 (Abbott et al. 2016), the Webis-CMV-20 corpus (Al Khatib et al. 2020b), and the debate.org corpus of Durmus and Cardie (2019). For each model, they apply different variants of the WEAT social bias test (Caliskan et al. 2017), which mimics the implicit association test on human biases (Greenwald et al. 1998) by measuring embedding similarities of social group terms (e.g., words describing male people) and bias-related terms (e.g., negative words). In addition, they qualitatively analyze the cooccurrences behind the WEAT scores. Figure 6.11 illustrates the process. According to the results, all three corpora show social bias, mostly toward women and African-American people. However, some cooccurrences seem brittle, not always indicating associations between social groups and bias-related terms.

Similarly, Holtermann et al. (2022) observe that transformers such as BERT and RoBERTA increase in social bias (specifically, queerphobia and Islamophobia), when being fine-tuned on argument corpora (Ajjour et al. 2019b; Al Khatib et al. 2020b). They propose to combine the fine-tuning with an adapter-based debiasing approach (Lauscher et al. 2021) toward fair argumentative language modeling. Holtermann et al. evaluate

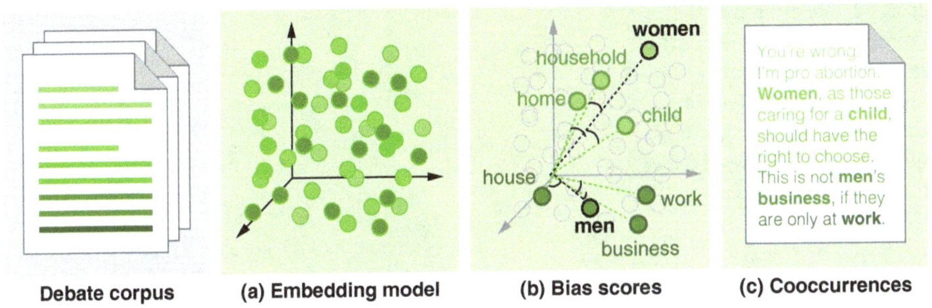

Fig. 6.11 Illustration of the social bias analysis of Spliethöver and Wachsmuth (2020): (**a**) Training an embedding model on a debate corpus, (**b**) computing bias scores for social groups, and (**c**) mining cooccurrences. Licensed under CC-BY 4.0 International

impact of debiasing for argument quality scoring on the corpora of Toledo et al. (2019) and Ng et al. (2020) (details on these corpora in Chap. 7). As a key result, they find that debiasing has no notable negative effect on quality assessment; in doubt, debiasing benefits performance rather than hurting it.

Muti et al. (2024) study the detection of implicit mysogyny in English and Italian argumentative texts. The authors propose to model the task as a reasoning problem: Given the claim of an argumentative message (e.g., "Women football commentators are annoying"), generate a warrant for the claim (e.g., "Women do not understand sport") and decide on this basis whether the message is mysogynistic. In experiments on a new Italian corpus and on the English SBIC+ corpus (Sap et al. 2020), Muti et al. prompted Llama3-8b (Touvron et al. 2023a) and Mistral-7B in zero-shot and few-shot settings. Few-shot Llama3-8B performed best in both languages, finding 73.8% of all Italian mysogyny cases and 71.9% of the English ones. However, an analysis of the generated warrant suggests that LLMs often fail to correctly infer the implicit assumptions underlying mysogynic texts.

The work of Falenska et al. (2024) is more in the line of Durmus and Cardie (2018b), investigating context of gender self-disclosures in the argumentative Reddit forum ChangeMyView, and their effect on interaction dynamics. The authors semi-automatically filtered 3235 forum comments with mentions of seven different genders. Analyzing the comments, they find that people mention their gender either to report personal experience or to increase credibility where gender is important. For controversial topics, however, the results suggest that self-disclosure negatively impacts the forum community's assessment of a comment. Looking at linguistic differences, Falenska et al. find that text of men receives higher toxicity scores, shows frequent use of nouns denoting certainty, and is semantically rich. Women's texts show more clarity in language use as well as positive emotions. The authors warn, though, that all results have a high variance and should not be overgeneralized.

Finally, Yang et al. (2025b) study for essay scoring to what extent prompted LLMs recognize the writers' demographics and introduce bias into the scoring process. Based on the 25k students essays in the PERSUADE corpus (Crossley et al. 2022), the authors asked

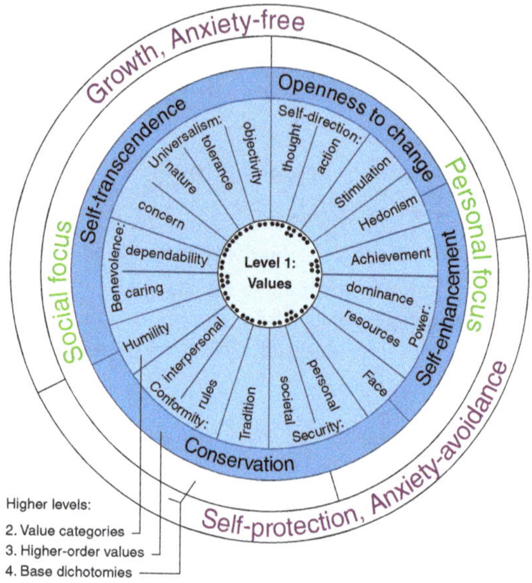

Fig. 6.12 Illustration of the hierarchical organization of the human values taxonomy of Kiesel et al. (2022). The 54 individual values are shown as black dots only. Licensed under CC-BY 4.0 International

GPT-4o assess gender and first-language background as well as to score the essays. While GPT-4o was often uncertain about gender, it predicted first-language background rather reliably, with accuracy ranging between 75.3 and 86.6% depending on the corpus subset considered. Worryingly, though, GPT-4o's essay scores seems biased against non-native speakers, particularly when it correctly predicts the language background. The authors conclude that a careful debiasing of LLMs is needed, when the models should be used for respective tasks.

6.3.2 Identifying Human Values and Morals

Human values and morals have an inherent connection, as morals can be understood to emerge out of values central to a person or society. We subsequently discuss argumentation-related approaches to the identification of *values* and *morals* here.

Values Kiesel et al. (2022) initialized the task of identifying human values behind arguments. The authors propose a taxonomy of 54 values, largely adopting theory from social science research (Schwartz et al. 2012). Figure 6.12 shows that the values can be grouped hierarchically into 20 categories of four higher-order-values: *openness to change*, *self-enhancement*, *conservation*, and *self-transcedence*. For example, the conservation category *societal security* consists of two values, *have a safe country* and *have a safe society*. Kiesel et al. created a corpus of 5270 arguments originating in four regions (Africa,

China, India, and USA) that are annotated binarily for all 54 values. Exemplarily, here is a pro argument on "South Africa's COVID-19 lockdown was too strict" with its three annotated values:

(6.7) *Argument:* The economic ramifications of the lockdown have been huge, and have been felt hardest by those who were already most vulnerable.
Values behind: Have a comfortable life, Have a stable society, Have equality

On an 85/5/10 corpus split, the authors trained and tested a baseline BERT classifier, reaching a mean label-wise macro F_1-score of 0.25 for the individual values, and 0.34 for the 20 categories (compared to an SVM with 0.20 and 0.30 respectively).

Kiesel et al. (2023) deployed human value identification as a shared task based on an extended version of the corpus above with 9324 arguments (Mirzakhmedova et al. 2024b), from which 8865 arguments are for the main experiments and 459 for an out-of domain study. The shared task considers the 20 value categories only, modeling the identification via separated binary tasks: Given an argument and a specific value, classify whether the argument resorts to the value. 39 teams participated in the shared task, which was won by Schroter et al. (2023). Their approach ensembles RoBERTa and DeBERTa and was pretrained on an argument quality dataset (Gretz et al. 2020b) that is also the source of many arguments in the shared task corpus and detailed in Chap. 7. It obtained a macro F_1-score of 0.56, as opposed to 0.42 of the BERT baseline (Kiesel et al. 2022). In a later paper of another team that reached 0.44, Ferrara et al. (2023) discuss that the complexity of the task emerges from classifying implicit aspects of arguments (the value categories). They point out that the task is even hard for humans and may call for a perspectivist approach. To a limited extent, this is supported by the corpus' moderate inter-annotator agreement of 0.41 in terms of Krippendorff's α (Mirzakhmedova et al. 2024b).

Combining research on human values and disagreement prediction, van der Meer et al. (2023) hypothesize that differences in personal values are indicative of disagreement in online discussions. Starting from the 43k comment-reply pairs with disagreement labels in the Reddit dataset of Pougué-Biyong et al. (2021), the authors collected up to 1000 posts of each active Reddit user represented in the dataset. On this basis, their approach proceeds in three steps that are illustrated in Fig. 6.13:

1. *Value Extraction.* Given a comment, the approach employs one binary classifier per value, trained on two value datasets (Qiu et al. 2022; Kiesel et al. 2022). van der Meer et al. consider the original 10 Schwartz values (on the right of the figure) and manually map the 20 categories of Kiesel et al. (2022) to them. For classification, they compare BERT and RoBERTa.
2. *Value Profile Estimation.* Given all comments of a user, the identified values are mapped to a value profile based on the values' relative frequency in the comments.
3. *Value Conflict Measuring.* The distance of the value profiles of two users reflects a potential value conflict. van der Meer et al. compute similarity in four ways: (1) inverse

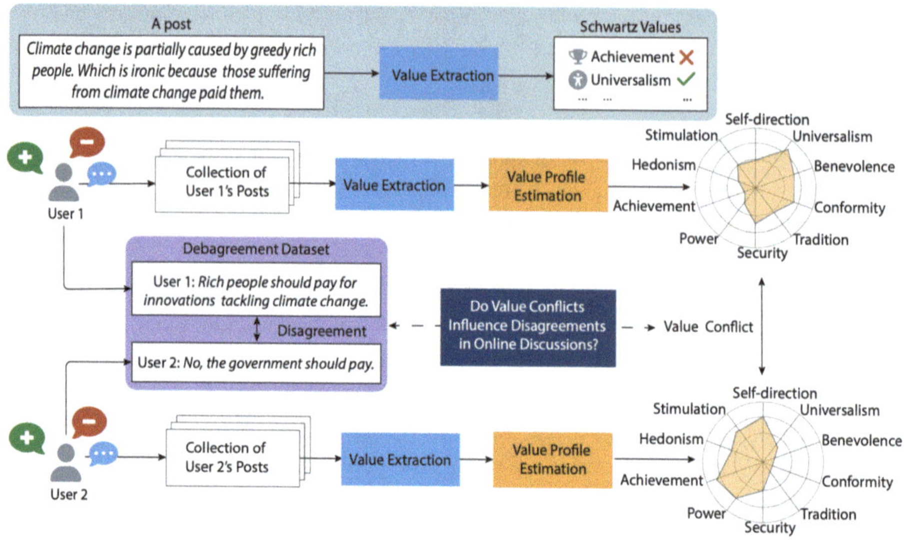

Fig. 6.13 Illustration of the approach of van der Meer et al. (2023): From two user posts, values are extracted to estimate profiles for predicting disagreement. Licensed under CC-BY 4.0 International

Kendall's τ of the users' value rankings derived from their profiles; (2) the *Manhattan distance* of the two profiles; (3) inverse *cosine similarity*; and (4) a *weighted cosine* derived from known value similarities (Schwartz 2012).

In their evaluation, van der Meer et al. observe high macro F_1-scores in value identification, with BERT being slightly better (0.79) than RoBERTa (0.78). To test their hypothesis, the authors quantify whether the measured value conflicts are higher for disagreeing comments than for agreeing comments. On average, however, value conflicts do not correlate with disagreement, rather rejecting the hypothesis. Some subcorpora show different results, though, such as the one on Brexit.

Morals A common typology of moral reasoning is the *moral foundation theory* (Haidt 2012). Originally, it distinguishes five foundations, each expressing a contrast between good and bad behavior: *care/harm*, *fairness/cheating*, *loyalty/betrayal*, *authority/subervsion*, and *purity/degradation*. Later, *liberty/oppression* was added as a sixth foundation (Graham et al. 2013). The authors of these theories observe that people put different importance on the different foundations depending on their background; for example, liberals prioritize individualizing morals (care and fairness), whereas conservatives have a less clear prioritization but with a tendency toward binding morals (loyalty, authority, and purity).

Johnson and Goldwasser (2018) model how politicians frame controversial issues in Twitter discourse in order to identify the moral foundations that politicians use to convey stance. The authors annotate a dataset of congressional tweets for the original $5 \cdot 2 = 10$

moral foundation labels, separately with a conservative and a liberal annotator (Cohen's $\kappa = 0.79$). Using PSL (Bach et al. 2013) based on this data, their weakly supervised approach employs logic rules that map unigram matches and the tweet authors' party affiliation to specific morals. In experiments, the approach achieved a macro F_1-score of 0.725 when using the *moral foundation lexicon* (Haidt and Graham 2007) for the unigrams, and 0.694 when using a hand-crafted list from the authors. In contrast, a unigram SVM obtained 0.219 only.

Kobbe et al. (2020) study the correlation of moral foundations with the stance and quality of arguments. As a basis, the authors extended all 320 arguments in the argument quality corpus of Wachsmuth et al. (2017c) (see Chap. 7) by manual annotations of the five original moral foundations, with Cohen's κ between 0.280 (purity) and 0.469 (care). For prediction, they look at multiple methods, including a sense-disambiguated unigram matcher for the moral foundation lexicon, a Sentence-BERT classifier (Reimers and Gurevych 2019) fine-tuned on lexicon-labeled Wikipedia abstracts, and a multilabel BERT classifier fine-tuned on the training set of the extended corpus. On the test set, multilabel BERT was strongest with a mean F_1-score of 0.308, opposed to 0.111 for the lexicon matcher and 0.252 for Sentence-BERT. Kobbe et al. observe notable Spearman's ρ correlations between moral framing and argument quality dimensions: 0.15–0.30 for ground-truth labels and 0.09–0.17 for predicted labels. On another argument quality dataset (Gretz et al. 2020b), the correlations are bit lower while stance shows almost no correlation with morals.

Given the known moral foundation preferences of people with different ideology, Alshomary et al. (2022a) study the persuasive effects of morally-framed arguments in a human evaluation study with conservatives and liberals. The core of the study is the generation of the arguments, which we detail further in Chap. 9. To inform generation, however, the authors also trained a BERT moral classifier. For this purpose, they labeled the aspect-controlled argument dataset of Schiller et al. (2021b) automatically, matching it against another moral foundation lexicon (Hulpus et al. 2020). On the dataset of Kobbe et al. (2020), it achieved a macro F_1-score of 0.40, outperforming the previous approaches. The moral foundations identified thereby then served for filtering ADUs for the arguments to be generated. In the evaluation study, Alshomary et al. (2022a) find that arguments controlled for morals are more effective than uncontrolled ones. For liberals, the morals matched their known preferences, whereas the effect was a bit more diverse for conservatives.

Farag et al. (2022) explore how to open up people's minds toward views that opposing views with dialogue-leading language models. Based on a new collection of 183 argumentative human-human dialogues, the authors develop two variants of a BART model for answer generation; the first variant uses retrieval-augmented generation based on Wikipedia articles, whereas the second was fine-tuned on the collected dialogues. In a user study, participants interacted with either variant, before they judged whether the opposite side had *good reasons*, *morality*, and *intellectual capabilities* (both for the human-human and the human-BART dialogues). While the humans had a positive impact on the perception of good reasons in 35%, the two BART variants managed this in 22 and 23% respectively, with the fine-tuned variant leading to better user experience. However, the success rate was notably lower for the other two dimensions; for morality in particular, the BART variants had no success at all (and also the humans in 13% only). These results give insights into what makes dialectical argumentation particularly hard in real life.

The reviewed works on morals are those that explicitly deal with argumentation and/or reasoning on controversial issues. Beyond them, related works discuss moral reasoning in the context of norms, intents, actions, and their consequences (Emelin et al. 2021) or in the context of moral dilemmas (Kumar and Jurgens 2025). We do not go into detail into this strand of research here, but refer the reader to a rather recent general survey covering 135 papers on modeling morality at the intersection of NLP, computational social science, and psychology (Reinig et al. 2024a).

6.4 Summary

By nature, natural language arguments take specific perspectives on the controversial issue they address, that is, the topic at discussion. Thereby, they inherently reflect the subjective viewpoints that their authors take within the discussion. As a matter of fact, NLP research on argumentation has been extensively considering various facets of perspective assessment since the early times. The respective literature specifies a variety of partly orthogonal and partly overlapping or even interchangeable terms and concepts, such as topic, issue, motion, aspect, facet, frame, framing, key point, stance, standpoint, stand, position, side, viewpoint, perspective, bias, values, morals, and more. Modeling at least some of these concepts is of central importance to the correct interpretation of the role of an argument in any practical application.

In this chapter, we have organized computational approaches to several perspective-related tasks, covering manifold techniques from early algorithmic methods to recent LLM-based end-to-end approaches. Some tasks tackle a specific concept, such as stance classification, whereas others build on one or multiple concepts, such as value-based disagreement prediction. As a conclusion, we now revisit the base concepts that make up a perspective from an NLP viewpoint. We slightly reorder them, to transition from content-related concepts to more subjectivity-related concepts. In line with previous research (Barrow et al. 2021), we see the core of a perspective as 3-tuple *(topic, frame, stance)*. At the same time, the manifestation of a perspective in an argument reflects the authors *biases* and *values*, implicitly or explicitly:

Topic Humans mostly state arguments in the context of the discussion of some controversial issue. Yet, the same argument may be relevant to different discussions, and may appear in very similar or even identical phrasing across different discussions. While, in many tasks, the issue is given as input, topics themselves can be modeled at different granularities and are related to other possibly-relevant topics. Some researchers have thus modeled the topic space of specific discussions or of argumentation as a whole, mostly in an unsupervised or weakly supervised fashion, as seen above. Ideas from the respective works may be of interest in any setting that is concerned with more than just the assessment of a single argument.

Frame Many arguments do not discuss a topic holistically, if that is even feasible in general. Rather, they emphasize a specific aspect of the topic (the frame), making it more salient, while concealing other aspects, putting them in the background. We have opposed the two main frame notions: generic frames that exist across topics, being somewhat universal in the discussion of controversies, as well as topic-specific frames, reflecting more fine-grained subtopics of a topic. NLP research has come up both with unsupervised, clustering-like approaches to open frame identification and with supervised classification approaches for a given frame typology. Usually, framing does not happen unconsciously of the author's side in a discussion, but it has a rhetorical function, namely, to purposefully to support the author's stance.

Stance At their core, arguments convey a pro or con stance toward the framed issue, even if not fully one-sided or phrased rather implicitly. The other way round, though, not all arguments necessarily convey a stance toward the *given* issue, which is why the stance classification task is often modeled with a third class (say, *neither*). We have provided an overview of the numerous existing approaches to the task. They cover techniques, ranging from standard text classification, to modeling sentiment polarity and contrastiveness, to accounting for debate structure and/or all its interactions. To this date, some of the most effective approaches treat the task at the collection level, classifying stance for all task instances simultaneously. In practice, what approach is most suitable also depends on what information is available.

Biases The perspectives that authors encode in their arguments may indicate cognitive biases, reflected in an overproportional one-sideness (myside bias) or an unfair treatment of social groups (social bias), for instance, of certain genders or ethnicities. So far, cognitive biases have been investigated sporadically only in NLP research that explicitly treats argumentation. However, there is extensive recent research on bias in the broader NLP community, much of which will be applicable to argumentative contexts as well, possibly with shifted findings though. We expect that more research on bias in argumentation will come up in the next years.

Values Biases specifically, but also the perspectives of arguments in general, are often rooted in the value systems of humans, which in turn emerge from the humans' background and experiences as well as from societal and cultural contexts. As we have summarized above, a still young but important research line in NLP has taken on the question as to what extent the underlying human values can be inferred from arguments. Values are often decisive for what arguments people find convincing or are at least open to listen to. Having information about the values of people involved in a discussion may thus be key to understand how to argue effectively with them. We will deepen these ideas in the following chapter on argument quality.

Overall, this chapter is meant to give readers an idea of what to pay attention to when it comes to assessing perspectives of arguments with computational methods. We stress again, though, that the views on perspective-related concepts and terminology in research are diverse and not fully consistent with each other. Deciding what concepts to model and how to model them should therefore depend on what information is important for the downstream task or application at hand.

Argument Quality Assessment 7

In some sense, the question about the quality of an argument is the 'ultimate' one for argument mining. Being able to reconstruct argumentative structures from a text (Chaps. 4–5) and learning about the perspectives that arguments convey toward a topic (Chap. 6) lays the ground to make arguments processable by machines. However, nearly all practical applications of NLP research on argumentation require some distinction of good from bad arguments, in order to focus on the strongest arguments or to identify weak arguments. Argument search engines aim to rank the best arguments highest, debating technologies aim to choose arguments that help convince their opponent or audience, argumentative writing assistance tools aim to spot the weak points to give feedback on, and so forth. In this chapter, we therefore discuss how to assess argument quality with computational means.

The notion of argument quality is complex, and its discussion remains controversial despite a long history. Aristotle (ca. 350 B.C.E./ translated 2007) already brought up the question of what makes a good speech in his book *On Rhetoric*, and other cultures deliberated on this matter even earlier, in the *Nyāya Sūtra* for example (Lloyd 2007). There are both normative and empirical views about what makes a good argument. They come with various argument quality dimensions, covering aspects of logic, rhetoric, dialectic, and combinations, many of which being inherently subjective. Some researchers suggest an absolute rating of argument quality, whereas others argue that arguments can only be compared relatively. Even if attempts to organize the different views have been made, the diversity of argument quality renders a uniform view infeasible. As a matter of fact, a plethora of computational assessment methods has come up in the last years, making argument quality one of the most studied argumentation-related topics in recent NLP research. Perelman and Olbrechts-Tyteca (1969) nicely stress the underlying conflict in a simple question: "Is a strong argument an effective argument which gains the adherence of the audience, or is it a valid argument, which ought to gain it?"

M. Stede et al., *Argument Mining*, Synthesis Lectures on Human Language Technologies, https://doi.org/10.1007/978-3-032-32291-3_7

We begin the chapter with a discussion of fundamental views of argument quality, from basic concepts to different perspectives and perceptions of quality (Sect. 7.1). On this basis, we survey NLP approaches to the absolute and relative assessment of logical, rhetorical, dialectical, and overall quality (Sect. 7.2). Finally, we look at recent trends in argument quality research: explicit treatments of subjectivity, the connection of argument quality to the deliberative quality of a discussion, and the rewriting of arguments to improve quality (Sect. 7.3). Most works we summarize here target what Wachsmuth et al. (2024) call *maximal quality* in their recent survey, that is, how an argument ideally should be. Some, however, rather model *minimal quality*, that is, what to expect at least from an argument. In this regard, it is noteworthy that a different research branch on argument quality focuses on what makes a *bad* argument, leading to the notion of *fallacies*. As fallacies are tightly related to failed or deceptive reasoning, we will discuss them afterwards in Chap. 8.

7.1 Modeling Argument Quality

The argument models we learned about in Chap. 3 define the roles and relations that the components of an argument should have. However, even if a real-world argument complies with any such model, it does not necessarily do so in a strong way. In this section, we discuss what *strong* may actually mean, how this differs between normative theory and empirical practice, as well as how and when it depends on the argumenative setting and the subjective perception of the participants therein. Not all of the quality dimensions that we cover are always relevant, but knowing what might be relevant is a prerequiste for realiably assessing argument quality, be it from a human perspective or with computational methods.

We start with basic concepts underlying any argument quality assessment. From that ground, we review the main perspectives on argument quality and manifold dimensions that operationalize the perspectives. As many dimensions are inherently subjective, we discuss the main influence factors of subjectiveness at the end.

7.1.1 Basic Concepts of Argument Quality

When humans argue, they rarely do so in a logically sound or valid way. They may give arguments that are well-reasoned or that are effective to persuade specific people, but most arguments are defeasible in nature (Walton 2006). Consider the following example argument that takes a pro stance on whether to ban plastic water bottles. It comes from the debate portal corpus of Habernal and Gurevych (2016a) and has already been given as an example by Wachsmuth et al. (2017c):

(7.1) Water bottles, good or bad? Many people believe plastic water bottles to be good. But the truth is water bottles are polluting land and unnecessary. Plastic water bottles should only be used in emergency purposes only. The water in those plastic are only filtered tap water. In an emergency situation like Katrina no one had access to tap water. In a situation like this water bottles are good because it provides the people in need. Other than that water bottles should not be legal because it pollutes the land and big companies get 1000% of the profit.

From a normative perspective, the argument does not really draw a valid conclusion from its premises, nor is it presented fully convincingly. However, the premises seem acceptable, and the way how the arguments anticipates counterconsiderations may add to its persuasive effect. At least, the annotators of the corpus of Habernal and Gurevych saw it as more convincing than the following argument:

(7.2) Estimates variously place worldwide bottled water sales at between $50 and $100 billion each year, with the market expanding at the startling annual rate of 7%. Bottled water is big business. But in terms of sustainability, bottled water is a dry well.

The two examples lead us to a few observations: There may be differences between *normative and empirical* views of what makes argumentation strong. We may assess them in *absolute or relative* terms. We can look at argument quality at different levels of *granularity*, from an argument's individual components to the surrounding debate as a whole, and we may do so in often *diverse and subjective* regards. Ultimately, how to assess argument quality depends on what the *goal* of argumentation is.

Normative vs. Empirical Assessment Argumentation theory and rhetoric have come up with different normative views of what makes a good argument. Normative views describe *how we should argue*, and are the basis for common argument models, such as the one of Toulmin (1958). However, Allwood (2016) points out that they often do not match *how we do argue*, and hence may not always serve as an adequate basis for understanding what makes argumentation effective in practice. The author brings about the question as to whether we should rather assess quality from a normative or from an empirical perspective. We discuss main theories of the logical cogency of arguments (Johnson and Blair 2006), their rhetorical effectiveness (Aristotle ca. 350 B.C.E./ translated 2007), and their dialectical reasonableness (van Eemeren and Grootendorst 2004) in the next subsection, also including study of how different they are to empirical practice (Wachsmuth et al. 2017b).

Absolute vs. Relative Assessment Both normative and empirical views of argument quality can be assessed in absolute terms and in relative terms. However, normative views integrate well with absolute ratings based on some predefined scale, as they imply that we can judge the extent to which an argument meets its aim. Common ranges include ordinal scales such as 1–3 (Wachsmuth et al. 2017c) or 1–5 (Ng et al. 2020) as well as real-valued scales such as [0, 1] (Toledo et al. 2019). Computationally, these scales speak for modeling quality assessment as a regression task (irrespective of the approach used). Habernal and Gurevych (2016b) observe that, in practice, absolute ratings of individual arguments may be hard for lack of comparison and potential bias of the judge. They argue that, empirically, relative comparisons of arguments hence tend to be easier, that is, deciding which of two arguments is better with respect to the criteria aimed for. A straightforward way to model a comparison computationally is to treat it as a pairwise classification task. Comparing the two alternatives, we note that, while both allow for ranking arguments, absolute ratings entail relative comparisons (assuming that ties are allowed), and only they imply a maximum and minimum. Relative comparisons, however, may be preferable in situations where it is sufficient to know which argument is best, even though it remains unclear how good the best argument actually is.

Granularity of Assessment Conceptually, argument quality can be assessed on four granularity levels: (1) We can look at the strength of individual *claims* that make up the premises and conclusions of arguments (Skitalinskaya et al. 2021). (2) Together, they form *arguments* whose quality may be rated (Toledo et al. 2019) or compared (Habernal and Gurevych 2016a). (3) Multiple arguments may be composed in the monological *argumentation* of an author (Persing and Ng 2015), or (4) in a dialogical *debate* whose winner is to be predicted (Zhang et al. 2016b).

Diversity and Subjectivity of Assessment Beyond the granularity question of what input assessed, a subsequent question regards under what aspects to assess the input. In particular, research has brought up different general perspectives on argument quality (logic, rhetoric, and dialectic) along with diverse quality dimensions for each perspective, both in theory and in practice (Wachsmuth et al. 2017c). Moreover, the perception of argument quality dimensions may be highly subjective (O'Keefe and Jackson 1995) and thus dependent on the views of the readers or audience of an argument. We detail both diversity and subjectivity in the following subsections.

Goal Dependence of Assessment What perspective and/or dimension to consider is affected by the goal of argumentation. As Tindale (2007) points out, arguments may aim to persuade audiences, to resolve disputes, to achieve agreement, to complete inquiries, and to recommend actions. Sometimes, we are simply interested in understanding each other better, or to deliberate jointly on a topic of interest. In certain situations, several dimensions may be relevant, but in others only specific ones. What an argument is meant to be used for thus must be known prior to assessment. Often, though, its purpose is defined by the genre of text in which the argument appears.

7.1.2 Argument Quality Perspectives and Dimensions

Argumentation theory and NLP have come up with different perspectives on argument quality and various quality dimensions that operationalize these perspectives. Wachsmuth et al. (2017c) provide a unifying taxonomy of the perspectives and dimensions that is often referred to in NLP research as the common ground of argument quality assessment, which is why we primarily build on their work here. Some researchers also propose extensions or refinements, and there are some criticisms to the taxonomy that we discuss afterwards. For simplicity, we mostly speak of quality on the level of single arguments the following, even if different granularities of assessment exist, as indicated above.

Argument Quality Perspectives In a strict sense, argumentation refers to the logical reasoning that happens in arguments from premises to conclusions. In a broader sense, however, the process of arguing does not only comprise arguments but also rhetorical aspects (how to present arguments to persuade others) and dialectical aspects (how to argue with others to resolve issues). Wachsmuth et al. adopt the view of Blair (2012) who distinguish three general perspectives on argument quality:

- *Logical Argument Quality.* The cogency of drawing the conclusion of an argument based on the given the premises of the argument;
- *Rhetorical Argument Quality.* The effectiveness of an argument in persuading a specific target audience;
- *Dialectical Argument Quality.* The reasonableness of an argument to resolve differences of opinions.

All three perspectives may notably or also just mildly affect the perceived (overall) quality of an argument, but not all of them are always relevant in all situations.

Argument Quality Dimensions In argumentation theory, the logical perspective on argument quality in natural language has been studied in separated but somewhat comparable work by multiple researchers, including Johnson and Blair (2006), Damer (2009), and Govier (2010). While the different authors analyze the influence factors of an argument's logical cogency at different level of detail and with slightly varying terms, what is common to their models is a distinction of three subdimensions that affect cogency. Wachsmuth et al. adds the idea that they are *local* to argument to later distinguish them from dialectical dimensions:

- *Cogency.* An argument's premises are acceptable, relevant, and sufficient, where:
- *(Local) Acceptability.* The premises are worthy being believed to be true;
- *(Local) Relevance.* The premises provide actual support for the conclusion;
- *(Local) Sufficiency.* Together, they provide enough support to draw the conclusion.

On the rhetorical side, some literature speaks of the *persuasiveness* of arguments. However, this term may refer not only to the success in achieving persuasion but also to the pure persuasion attempt (van Eemeren 2015). Instead, the preferred term is (persuasive or rhetorical) *effectiveness*. To model subdimensions of effectiveness, Wachsmuth et al. follow Aristotle (ca. 350 B.C.E./ translated 2007) who states: "In making a speech, one must study three points: the means of producing persuasion, the style or language to be used, and the proper arrangement of the various parts." The 'means' refer to logos (appeal to reason), ethos (appeal to character), and pathos (appeal to emotion), which the authors map to *cogency*, *credibility*, and *emotional appeal* respectively. While Aristotle presents various dimensions of style, they all cover aspects of either *clarity* or *appropriateness*. Wachsmuth et al. use these two style terms as the level of granularity in their unified view. Overall, they model six rhetorical dimensions (in addition to cogency):

- *Effectiveness.* The effectiveness of an argument is affected by its cogency as well as the following five dimensions:
- *Credibility.* The presentation of arguments and other content in a way that makes the author worthy of credence;
- *Emotional Appeal.* The successful creation of emotions that make the target audience more open to the author's arguments;
- *Clarity.* The use of correct and widely unambiguous language along with the avoidance of unnecessary complexity and deviation from the issue;
- *Appropriateness.* The use of language that is proportional to the issue and that supports the creation of credibility;
- *Arrangement.* The presentation of an argument's different parts in a proper order.

Dialectical quality, finally refers to an argument's impact in resolving differences of opinion. In their pragma-dialectical theory, van Eemeren and Grootendorst (2004) develop an idealized model for the evaluation of critical discussions. Even if discussion participants still aim at persuasion, the overarching goal is to achieve agreement on an issue, which requires strategic maneuvering between these two (van Eemeren and Houtlosser 2002). To this end, arguments needs to be *reasonable*, which does not only presuppose cogent arguments, but also requires *intersubjective acceptability* and *problem-solving validity* (van Eemeren 2015). The latter matches the concept of *dialectical relevance* (Walton 2006). Wachsmuth et al. brings these dimensions together with the notion of *dialectical sufficiency* of Damer (2009) and Blair (2012): the rebuttal of anticipated counters to an argument. On this basis, they model four dialectical quality dimensions (in addition to cogency and effectiveness) that they see as *global* within a discussion of a topic:

- *Reasonableness.* The reasonableness of an argument is affected by its cogency, effectiveness, and the following three dimensions:
- *(Global) Acceptability.* The consideration and presentation of the argument are intersubjectively acceptable to the discussion participants;

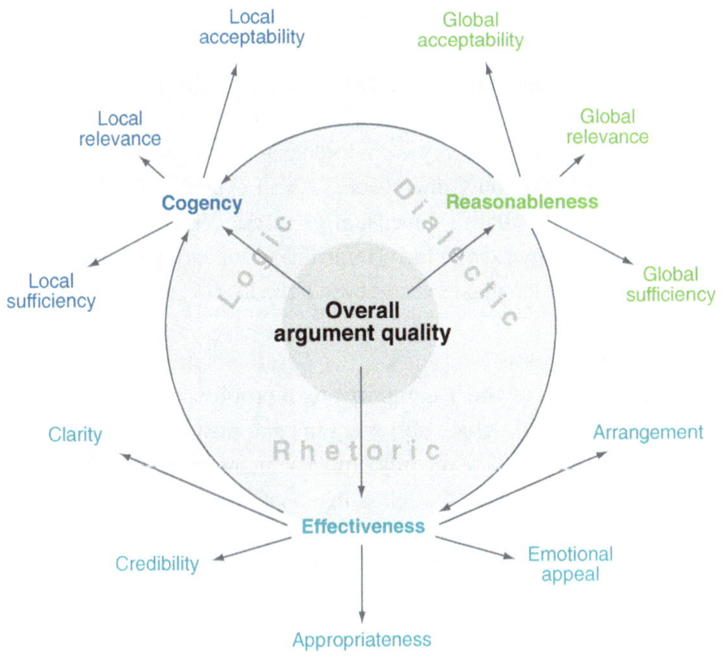

Fig. 7.1 Taxonomy of Wachsmuth et al. (2017c): *Overall argument quality* may be affected by logical *cogency*, rhetorical *effectiveness*, and dialectical *reasonableness* (each with subdimensions). Note that effectiveness subsumes cogency, and reasonableness subsumes both others. Not all dimensions are relevant in all settings. Licensed under CC-BY 4.0 International

- *(Global) Relevance.* The argument is valid for problem-solving in that it contributes to the resolution of the difference of opinions;
- *(Global) Sufficiency.* The argument adequately rebuts anticipated counters.

A Taxonomy of Argument Quality Building on the summarized connections between the outlined dimensions for all three general perspectives, Wachsmuth et al. organize their unified view of argument quality in the taxonomy in Fig. 7.1. The taxonomy's idea is that the overall quality of an argument *may* be affected by logical, rhetorical, and dialectical perceptions, not that it necessarily has to be. What perspectives and dimensions are important in practice depends on the setting. For instance, if an argument is meant to make people agree on a controversial issue, global acceptability is critical. If the argument merely seeks to persuade a specific target audience, this dimension may be well-negligible. Similarly, not all subdimensions are always in place when assessing one of the main dimensions. For example, an argument may be rhetorically effective, even if it is not cogent at all.

Moreover, it is important to see that the taxonomy captures argument quality only at certain level of abstraction and, hence, may not sufficiently detail aspects important in specific settings. Both in argumentation theory and in NLP practice, many more quality dimensions have been proposed, several of which we learn about in Sect. 7.2. However, under the assumption that the taxonomy is comprehensive, specific dimensions can always be mapped to one of the taxonomy dimensions. As an example, Persing and Ng (2013) introduce *thesis clarity* as a quality dimension to assess for argumentative essays, and Persing and Ng (2014) *prompt adherence* (referring to the essay's prompt). Wachsmuth et al. map both to *clarity*, which makes sense, even if the loss of specificity is rather obvious for prompt adherence.

Extensions and Criticisms of the Taxonomy As a proof of concept, Wachsmuth et al. present a small corpus of 320 debate portal arguments, manually annotated with scores from 1 (low) to 3 (high) for all 15 taxonomy dimensions by three annotators. Exemplarily, the Katrina example above received the following mean scores:

- *Logic.* Cogency 2.33, local acceptability 2.67, local relevance 3.0, local sufficiency 2.0
- *Rhetoric.* Effectiveness 2.0, credibility 2.33, emotional appeal 2.33, clarity 2.67, appropriateness 2.67, arrangement 2.33
- *Dialectic.* Reasonableness 2.67, global acceptability 2.67, global relevance 2.67, global sufficiency 1.67
- *Overall.* Overall argument quality 2.67

The absolute score scale fits the idea that the taxonomy reflects theoretical views of argument quality, but they already suggest that often no full agreement is observed (e.g., for this example, effectiveness received each score once). The arguments come from the aforemention corpus of Habernal and Gurevych (2016a), containing also relative argument convincingness comparisons made by crowdworkers. The crowdworkers gave justifications for their judgments, which Habernal and Gurevych (2016b) clustered into the 17 reasons in Table 7.1. Given the overlap in absolute and relative assessments, the two author teams joined forces to systematically analyze 736 argument pairs as to which reasons for relative differences correlate with which absolute differences of ratings (Wachsmuth et al. 2017b). Several of their observations match expectation. For example, if an argument was deemed *attacking/abusive*, it always received a lower score in *global acceptability* (Kendall's $\tau = 1.00$). If it was deemed *unclear*, it mostly received a lower *clarity* score ($\tau = 0.91$). Generally, the authors find many strong correlations, and *convincingness* itself correlates most with *overall argument quality* ($\tau = 0.64$). They conclude that theory and practice match more than expected, pointing out that theory can guide quality assessment in practice, whereas practice indicates what to focus on in theory.

Some taxonomy dimension have been further refined in later work. Two noteworthy studies in this regard are those of Yang et al. (2019a) and Ziegenbein et al. (2023). The former extend a news editorial corpus (Al Khatib et al. 2016) by 3591 manual

Table 7.1 The 17 reasons for convincingness differences found by Habernal and Gurevych (2016b)

Label	Argument A is more convincing than Argument B, because...
5-1	*B* is attacking/abusive.
5-2	*B* has language/grammar issues, or uses humour or sarcasm.
5-3	*B* is unclear/hard to follow.
6-1	*B* has no credible evidence/no facts.
6-2	*B* has less or insufficient reasoning.
6-3	*B* uses irrelevant reasons.
7-1	*B* is only an opinion/a rant.
7-2	*B* is non-sense/confusing.
7-3	*B* does not address the topic.
7-4	*B* is generally weak/vague.
8-1	*A* has more details/facts/examples, has better reasoning/is deeper.
8-4	*A* is objective/discusses other views.
8-5	*A* is more credible/confident.
9-1	*A* is clear/crisp/well-written.
9-2	*A* sticks to the topic.
9-3	*A* makes you think.
9-4	*A* is well thought through/smart.

sentence-level annotations of local acceptability on a 7-point Likert scale. Analyzing the data, they find meaningful correlations between acceptability and three attributes that the authors derive from truth theory: knowledge awareness, verifiability, and disputability. Their results shed light on the complex nature of local acceptability; Fig. 7.2 visually contrasts the reasons given for accepted as opposed to rejected arguments as word clouds. Ziegenbein et al. (2023), on the other hand, refine the rather generic quality dimension of appropriateness from Wachsmuth et al. (2017c) in a fine-grained taxonomy of 14 dimensions of (in)appropriateness, based on literature and empirical analyses. According to their model, what makes an argument inappropriate are the use of *toxic emotions*, a *missing commitment* to the discussion, a *missing intelligibility* of the argument's reasoning, or *other reasons* (e.g., detrimental orthography). Each of these has subdimensions, as illustrated in Fig. 7.3.

The unified view of argument quality by Wachsmuth et al. (2017c) is not fully undebated in the community, partly seen as too simplifying, not fully comprehensive, or not fully adequate in its details. As part of a survey of 32 argument quality datasets, Ivanova et al. (2024) propose an extension of the taxonomy by quality dimensions such as *strength*, *persuasiveness*, and *convincingness*. Wachsmuth et al. left out the three latter due to their ambiguous nature (as discussed above), but Ivanova et al. suggest that their widespread use justifies an explicit consideration. Ivanova and Gubelmann (2025) revisit

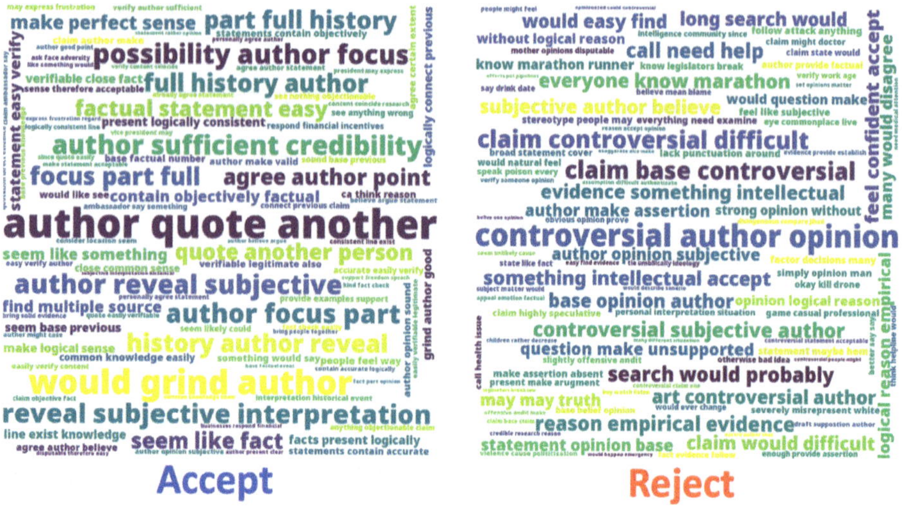

Fig. 7.2 Word clouds illustrating why an argumentative sentence is seen as acceptable (accept) or not (reject), from Yang et al. (2019a). Used with permission

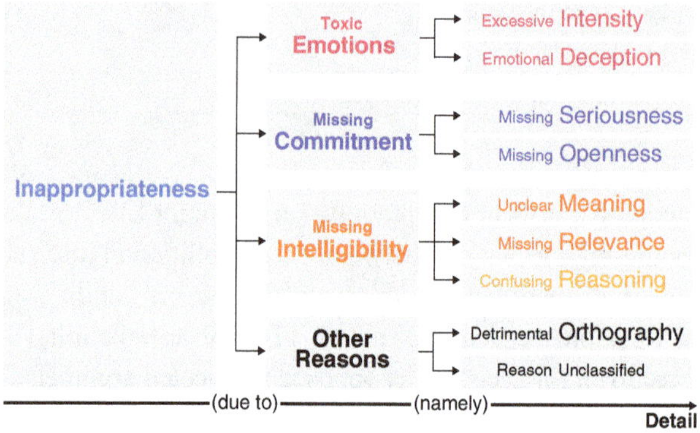

Fig. 7.3 Taxonomy of 14 fine-grained quality dimensions of argument (in)appropriateness from Ziegenbein et al. (2023). Rotated version of original figure, licensed under CC-BY 4.0 International

the taxonomy concept from a philosophical perspective. The authors argue that single arguments are hardly assessable in terms of dialectical quality without context as well as that the logical dimension *local acceptability* is dialectical in nature. They empirically underpin their claims based on correlations of respective dimensions in existing datasets. On this basis, they recommend to take local acceptability out of the assessment of logical quality and to assess logical quality at different granularity (arguments) than dialectical quality (argumentation). We note, though, that Wachsmuth et al. already point both to the dialectical side of local acceptability and to potential granularity differences of assessment. Still, the observations of Ivanova and Gubelmann are certainly valuable, emphasizing the complex relationship between logic and dialectic.

7.1.3 Subjectivity in the Perception of Argument Quality

The outlined argument quality views reflect properties that argumentation should aim toward in order to reach its goal. However, Clark and Schober (1992) stress "the common misconception that language use has primarily to do with words and what they mean. It doesn't. It has primarily to do with people and what *they* mean". Along these lines, even an argument that perfectly matches the requirements of a quality dimension targeted may have low or even zero impact in practice. This is because the perception of argument quality is, in many respects, inherently respective. It depends on the subjective weighting of the different aspects of a controversial issue of the *reader or audience* of an argument (Kock 2007). It may also be influenced by who is the *author or speaker* that communicates an argument as well as by the *situational context* in which the argument is made. We briefly sketch the role of these influence factors here, whereas approaches to modeling them follow later in Sect. 7.3.

Readers and Audiences When arguing, humans take into account who they argue with. In other words, argumentation mostly targets a particular audience, since different arguments and ways of arguing work for different readers or listeners, depending on their background, value system, and preconceived opinions. For illustration, let us look back at the first argument on banning plastic water bottles. The reference to Hurricane Katrina smartly anticipates potential emotions of American readers on the topic. But other readers may find it rather specific, or possibly even dislike a focus on rich countries in the discussion of environment-related issues. So, while the annotators of Habernal and Gurevych (2016a) saw the first argument as more convincing, some more market-critical readers may rather prefer the second argument, or they may find neither of them convincing, missing more profound logical reasoning.

In general, various audience traits may affect quality perception, from sociodemographic factors (e.g., gender or ethnicity) to cultural aspects (e.g., morals or values). Lukin et al. (2017) are the first to examine subjectiveness of argument quality in NLP, comparing the effect of different arguments on different readers. The authors profiled 637 crowdworkers on their prior beliefs and the Big-Five personality traits: openness, conscientiousness, extraversion, agreeableness, and neuroticism (Goldberg 1990). Then, they tested how often factual and emotional arguments led to stance change. While, on average, all arguments less affected entrenched than neutral readers, the difference was particularly strong for factual arguments. For open and agreeable readers, stance could be predicted much better than for neurotic readers.

El Baff et al. (2018) even argue that stance change is unlikely in general and therefore propose an alternative view of argument quality: A good argument challenges those readers with opposing prior stance and empowers those whose stance it matches—or challenges both sides. Stance change is the extreme case under this view, as depicted in Fig. 7.4. The authors present a corpus where 12 liberals and 12 conservatives each assessed such quality for 1000 news editorials from the (rather liberal) New York Times. Only 1% of all

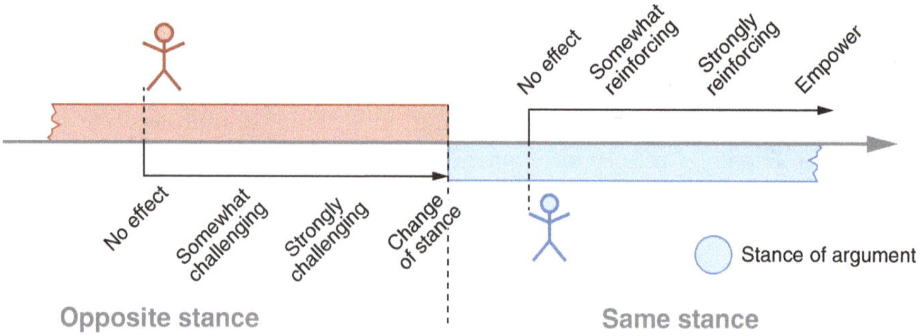

Fig. 7.4 Illustration of the stance-dependent argument quality view of El Baff et al. (2018): An argument may challenge those people whose stance it opposes to, and it may reinforce those people whose stance it matches. Licensed under CC-BY 4.0 International

editorials challenge both sides, while 5% challenge one side and empower the other. Most editorials reinforce the stance of both sides (44%) or reinforce one while having no effect on the other (38%).

Chen and Eger (2025) study to what extent emotional intensity affects the perceived convincingness of arguments. To this end, the authors let GPT-4o rewrite arguments from multiple sources with different emotional tone, which worked reliably according to human validation. Both human and LLM evaluators then assessed the convincingness of different rewrites. While the impact of emotional tone remained limited, a slight correlation of intensity and convincingness was found.

Authors and Speakers Not only the recipient of an argument plays a role for its perceived quality, but argumentation is also connected to the person who argues. In particular, an argument may have an entirely different impact, depending on who says or writes the argument. For instance, the initial argument on water bottles has been posted by some private person on an online debate portal. If this person would state their argument in a public debate, its impact may be limited. Instead, however, if former US president Barack Obama had stated exactly the same argument in the same debate, it may sway many more people, likely particularly those who generally sympathized with Obama or with his political leaning. And what if someone known to push toward free markets had stated the argument? NLP research on the impact of authorship in argumentation is limited so far, but Sect. 7.3 presents studies of the impact of modeling meta-information about a debater on quality assessment.

Situational Context The discussion of authors and audiences of arguments already hints on the role of the context in which an argument is made. Beyond logos, ethos, and pathos, Aristotle (ca. 350 B.C.E./ translated 2007) and other Greek philosophers refer to the notion of *kairos* in this regard: the time and location of an argument may strongly affect its impact, that is, when and where an arguer delivers it. The aforementioned reference to

Katrina likely seemed much more natural when the hurricane was still recent than it would today, and maybe more so in an explicit debate of the tackled issue than in everyday life argumentation. But there are other examples that highlight the critical role of kairos even more. We observe its impact, for instance, in times where war, or the fear of war, spreads across the world, and even people who have been opponents of any military defense and weaponry start advocating armament. The situational context of arguments is, if accessible at all, complex to model in NLP research and, in consequence, often disregarded. When it comes to practical applications of argumentation (see Chap. 10), it is nevertheless of key importance to be aware of its critical role.

7.2 Assessing Argument Quality

Given the basics of argument quality, we now look at the actual computational assessment of quality. Numerous assessment methods have come up in NLP research in the last years. They span a wide spectrum of individual or multiple quality dimensions for (or across) different argumentative settings and genres, using diverse computational models. Since a comprehensive treatment of the whole spectrum would exceed the extent of this book, we sample a selection of assessment methods based on popularity and technical diversity. For a clear structure, we organize them according to the main perspectives of argument quality laid out above, even though some methods have clear touching points with multiple perspectives.

Accordingly, the following pages subsequently discuss approaches to the assessment of logical, rhetorical, dialectical, and overall quality, respectively. In each case, we give an overview of the main ideas and discuss selected approaches in detail.

7.2.1 Assessing Logical Argument Quality

For a reliable assessment of logical argument quality, arguments should be *evaluable*, which we start from here. Then, we summarize existing approaches to *(local) sufficiency*, the core property of the reasoning within a cogent argument (see the taxonomy in Fig. 7.1) and the logical dimension most tackled so far in NLP. We end with the few approaches to *other* logical quality dimensions.

Evaluability Park et al. (2015) establish the notion that, for an argument to be evaluable, the connection of its premises to its conclusion must be clear. The authors formalize this notion in an argument model that specifies the required connections between two types of premises (*reason* or *evidence*) and four possible types of conclusions: A conclusion that makes a *policy* or *value* judgment requires propositional reasons as premises, whereas a conclusion that states a *fact* requires either factual reasons or evidence to support it. Only arguments that have *testimonial* conclusions do not require (but still can have) any

Table 7.2 Required and optional premise types for the evaluability of an argument, depending on the type of the argument's conclusion. The table is adapted from Park and Cardie (2018)

Conclusion type	Premise type	Connection
Policy	Reason	Required
Value	Reason	Required
Fact	Reason or evidence	Required
Testimony	Reason or evidence	Optional

premise type as support. In later work, Park and Cardie (2018) elaborate that, conceptually, any reliable argument quality assessment presupposes evaluability, since only evaluable arguments eventually reason properly. Table 7.2 summarizes the connections between premises and conclusions.

An operationalization of evaluability in the broader realm of argument quality assessment is done by Chen et al. (2022b) for product reviews. Based on the model of Park et al. (2015), their approach first identifies premises and conclusions of the mentioned types using the state-of-the-art biaffine parsing-based argument mining model of Morio et al. (2020). Employing the instances of each type as features, either a feedforward neural network (FNN) or a graph convolutional neural network (CNN) then classifies the helpfulness of the reviews. In experiments, Chen et al. observe that the features successfully boost effectiveness for both FNNs and CNNs.

Local Sufficiency The question whether an argument's premises suffice to draw its conclusion is at the heart of logical quality, as discussed. Stab and Gurevych (2017a) present the first computational approach that explicitly assesses sufficiency. The authors split the essays in the AAE2 corpus into 1029 paragraph-level arguments and asked human experts to classify each argument as being sufficient (66.2% of all arguments) or not (33.8%), following the definition of Johnson and Blair (2006). Stab and Gurevych compare a feature-rich support vector machine (SVM) with a CNN based on static word embeddings. With a macro F_1-score of 0.827, the CNN clearly beat the SVM and simpler baselines in 20-times repeated fivefold cross-validation. An error analysis reveals that lexical clues can be misleading, for instance, the term "example" led to wrong classifications of arguments as insufficient.

A rather unusual approach comes from Gurcke et al. (2021) who study whether conclusion *generation* benefits sufficiency assessment. In particular, the authors hypothesize that, only for a sufficient argument, it is well-possible to infer its conclusion from its premises. Their approach operationalize this hypothesis in two main steps:

1. *Conclusion Generation.* Given an argument with annotated components, the span of the original conclusion is masked in order to then reconstruct it by denoising the masked span with a generative transformer. In experiments, Gurcke et al. compare a zero-short

BART encoder-decoder transformer (Lewis et al. 2020) with a BART variant fine-tuned on the training data for conclusion generation.

2. *Sufficiency Assessment.* Next, the argument's premises are combined with both the original and the generated conclusion. Following the authors' hypothesis, the idea is that, only for a sufficient argument, the generated conclusion should be semantically similar to the original conclusion, as in the following example:

   (7.3) *Masked argument:* Second, <MASK> Averagely, public transports use much less gasoline to carry people than private cars. It means that by using public transports, the less gas exhaust is pumped to the air and people will no longer have to bear the stuffy situation on the roads, which is always full of fumes.
   Original conclusion: public transportation helps to solve the air pollution problems
   Generated conclusion (zero-shot): public transport is more efficient than private cars
   Generated conclusion (fine-tuned): using public transports will help to reduce the amount of pollution in the air

   The assessment is finally tackled by fine-tuning a transformer encoder with added classification head on the combined data, RoBERTa (Liu et al. 2019b) in the experiments. Gurcke et al. compare various subsets of premise and conclusion information given to assess the impact of conclusion generation.

Replicating the experimental set-up of Stab and Gurevych (2017a) for their approach, Gurcke et al. find that RoBERTa on the argument's plain text alone already obtains a macro F_1-score of 0.876, underlining the advantages of transformer-based models. More information slightly improves the F_1-score to 0.885. While the support of the hypothesis seems hence limited, the authors find that having only the premises (without any conclusion) already achieves 0.875, questioning whether the data purely encodes sufficiency or conflates it with other quality aspects. This observation stresses the difficulty of human judgment of quality dimensions.

Most recently, Liu et al. (2024b) propose a causality-driven approach that prompts large language models (LLMs) for sufficiency assessment. The approach first extracts claim-like premises, X, and a conclusion, Y, from an argument. Then, it generates context samples C that are logically inconsistent to the combination X and Y. Iteratively creating revisions R of C to meet the premises X, the approach then estimates the probability of the conclusion to hold under R. Figure 7.5 illustrates the process. The authors evaluate their approach for two 7B LLMs, Llama 2 (Touvron et al. 2023b) and Tulu (Wang et al. 2023b), on two logical fallacy corpora (Alhindi et al. 2022; Srivastava et al. 2023). Their results suggest that the causality-driven approach notably improves over zero-shot and one-shot LLMs as well as some natural language inference baselines. However, the best macro F_1-score on the two datasets varies from 0.612 to 0.734, suggesting that LLMs can barely solve the task yet.

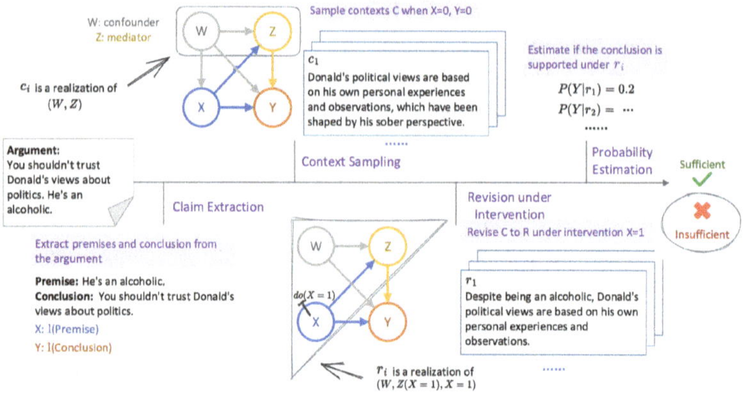

Fig. 7.5 Causality-driven LLM approach to sufficiency assessment of Liu et al. (2024b): Starting from the argument's premises and conclusion, inconsistent contexts are sampled and revised to predict the argument's local sufficiency on this basis.

Other Dimensions Some work also tackles the other logical quality dimensions in the taxonomy of Wachsmuth et al. (2017c). Local relevance, as one of them, has conceptual overlap with the relevance notion from information retrieval. Dumani and Schenkel (2019) present a systematic analysis of the performance of 196 standard retrieval methods in finding relevant premises for claims. According to their results, combining hand-crafted retrieval axioms with divergence from randomness beats common techniques such as BM25 (Robertson and Zaragoza 2009) and Doc2Vec similarity (Le and Mikolov 2014). In their core work on argument retrieval, Dumani et al. (2020) then formalize their idea of argument-related relevance in a probabilitistic ranking framework, thus defining an important basis for argument search.

Saveleva et al. (2021b) present an approach to cogency and all its subdimensions that models the graph structure of an argument. First, it parses discourse units and relations, for which the authors compare a joint model (Lin et al. 2014) to a combination of Bi-LSTM-CRF with fine-tuned XLNet (Yang et al. 2019b). A matrix representation of the graph emerging from the units and relations runs through a graph neural network (Velickovic et al. 2018) that takes BERT and GloVe embeddings (Pennington et al. 2014; Devlin et al. 2019) as additional features. The network is fine-tuned to predict either of the four quality dimensions. In experiments, the authors interpret the 3-point ratings in the corpus of Wachsmuth et al. (2017c) as nominal class labels. For local acceptability, the approach with BERT features has an accuracy of 85.0 compared to 80.6 of a majority classifier. For local relevance and sufficiency, GloVe features seem best (both 74.5, compared to 54.8). For cogency, solely relying on graph structure is strongest, boosting accuracy from 54.8 to 72.5.

7.2.2 Assessing Rhetorical Argument Quality

Rhetorical quality has been assessed at different granularity levels. Some works rate or compare individual online *arguments* in terms of effectiveness or subdimensions from the taxonomy in Fig. 7.1. A bulk of research deals with *argumentation-level quality*, often for essays where the clear target audience reduces subjectivity issues. Moreover, there are *debate-level* approaches that predict the winner of a debate.

Argument-Level Quality Habernal and Gurevych (2016a) stress the difficulty of rating argument effectiveness (called *convincingness* there) in absolute terms, due to lack of context, subjective beliefs, and similar. Opting for relative judgments instead, they gathered 16,927 argument pairs from two debate portals (*createdebate.com* and procon.org). Crowdsourcing was then employed to judge which argument of each pair is more convincing, followed by a filtering step that determined problematic pairs from annotation inconsistencies. The crowdworkers' reasons for their judgments are analyzed in a direct follow-up paper (Habernal and Gurevych 2016b) already mentioned above as part of the taxonomy discussion. In automated convincingness comparison, Habernal and Gurevych (2016a) compared a feature-rich SVM to a bidirectional LSTM. Interestingly, the SVM achieved a better accuracy (78%) than the LSTM (76%), but the authors point out that they did little optimization work on the LSTM, and that the feature engineering for the SVM was quite laborious.

Potash et al. (2017a) work on the same dataset. Observing that longer arguments are often more effective, they propose so called Siamese bag-of-words embeddings for the task: Their approach separately models the arguments to be compared, concatenates their GloVe embeddings, and then uses logistic regression for effectiveness classification. This leads to an accuracy of 82.5%. The authors also explore how to model the similarity of the arguments to Wikipedia articles with a memory network (Sukhbaatar et al. 2015), but do not manage to further improve the results (82.1%). Other works on the dataset of Habernal and Gurevych (2016a) also go into further directions, such as the approach of Simpson and Gurevych (2018). The authors demonstrate that a combination of Bayesian preference learning and active learning can be used to determine effective arguments in noisy, low-resource situations.

Even with relative comparisons, a remaining problem is that two arguments may cover different aspects of an issue that are hard to compare. As an alternative, Gleize et al. (2019) present a dataset of 5697 pairs of evidence sentences from Wikipedia where both may serve as premises to the same claim. Crowd annotators decided for each pair which sentence they would more likely use as evidence, with a Cohen's κ agreement of 0.33. For premise comparison, Gleize et al. use a Siamese neural network that computes an effectiveness probability for each argument. In training, the model is optimized to maximize the probability of the more effective argument and minimize the other. On the data of Habernal and Gurevych (2016a), they reach an accuracy of 81.0%, while clearly outperforming approaches like the one of Simpson and Gurevych (2018) on their own data.

To reduce subjectivity even further, Skitalinskaya et al. (2021) compare different revisions of the same claim-like argument. To this end, they create a corpus of 200k revision pairs from the claim edit history on the collaborative platform kialo.com. Human annotators corroborated the underlying assumption that a revision improves a claim for 93% of 315 sample claims (at $\kappa = 0.75$). The authors test different approaches for predicting the better revision, from simply taking the longer claim to Siamese bag-of-words (Potash et al. 2017a) and a Sentence-BERT classifier (Reimers and Gurevych 2019). In balanced settings, Sentence-BERT classifies up to 77.7% correctly, compared to 60.8% based on length only. Skitalinskaya et al. also combine Sentence-BERT with a ranking method, SVMRank (Joachims 2006), to rank entire revision histories with a Pearson correlation coefficient of 0.70.

Absolute assessment approaches exist for rhetorical quality as well. In two closely connected works, Persing and Ng (2017a,b) rate the persuasive effectiveness of 1208 arguments from idebate.net on a 6-point Likert scale. To this end, the authors model five weaknesses of arguments: grammar errors, lack of objectivity, inadequate support, unclear assertions, and unclear justifications. The approaches from both works employ various features to assess the weaknesses, from lexico-syntactic aspects (e.g., grammaticality and subjectivity indicators) to more semantic aspects (e.g., citations and subject matches). Persing and Ng (2017a) simply use supervised support vector regression for argument rating. In contrast, Persing and Ng (2017b) propose to cluster training arguments based on aggregated weakness assessments, using average effectiveness scores as cluster ratings, and then assign a test argument the rating of its closest cluster. In fivefold cross-validation, both approaches outperform simple feature-based baselines as well as adaptations of the approaches of Persing and Ng (2015) (see above) and Tan et al. (2016) (follows further below). Comparing the results across papers, the supervised approach wins over the clusting approach slightly only, for example, with an error rate of 0.721 compared to 0.744 in predicting the exact score. This suggests that an unsupervised assessment may be possible where training time is an issue.

Online arguments are also in the focus of the appropriateness taxonomy (Ziegenbein et al. 2023) outlined above. In experiments, the authors used encoder-only transformers to predict each of the 14 taxonomy dimensions for a given argument on some issue; specifically, DeBERTaV3-large (He et al. 2023) with a multi-label prediction loss. On their corpus of 2191 arguments, they compared DeBERTa in 5-times repeated fivefold cross-validation against ablations without issue (to test context importance) or with shuffled sentence ordering (to test coherence importance). The full model performed best for all but one dimension, with bigger gains over the shuffle ablation but small gains only over the issue ablation. The best F_1-score is 0.75 for both overall *inappropriateness* and *missing commitment* (as opposed to 0.32 and 0.40 of a majority baseline). Some dimensions seem harder, such as *confusing reasoning* with 0.62 only (majority 0.48), indicating what makes the task challenging.

Argumentation-Level Quality One of the first attempts to argumentation-related essay scoring comes from Persing et al. (2010) who assess the *organization* of essays, matching the arrangement dimension in the taxonomy presented: According to their definition, a well-organized essay introduces its thesis before it opposes pros and cons, and concludes. Their approach models an essay as a sequence of discourse functions, separately on the sentence level and on the paragraph level. To this end, it determines the k nearest-neighbor sequences in a training set and derive scores from these sequences. The scores and representations of discourse function subsequences are encoded in different kernels that are combined in a composite kernel and fed to an SVM. In experiments on 856 manually annotated student essays from the widely used ICLE corpus (Granger et al. 2009), the combined kernel was best compared to several ablations, with a mean squared error (MSE) of 0.175 on a 4-point scale.

In follow-up works, researchers from the same author team look at three further rhetorical dimensions (Persing and Ng 2013, 2014, 2015): *thesis clarity*, *prompt adherence*, and *argument strength*. The first two can be seen as specific aspects of the taxonomy dimension *clarity*, as discussed in Sect. 7.1. For argument strength, Persing and Ng (2015) define that a top-scored "essay makes a strong argument for its thesis and would convince most readers", which largely matches rhetorical effectiveness. In all three works, the authors engineer several task-specific surface-level features, less sophisticated than Persing et al. (2010), though. They systematically evaluate SVM regressors on feature ablations, finding more or less insightful features in the different cases: While proxies of argument structure prove strong for argument strength (the best MSE being 0.244 on a 4-point scale), the most discriminative feature of thesis clarity is simply the proportion of misspelled words (MSE 0.369).

Wachsmuth et al. (2016) go beyond heuristic argument concepts, explicitly studying the impact of argument mining on all four argumentation-related essay quality dimensions from the aforementioned works. Their study consists of three main steps:

1. *Mining Structure.* First, argumentative discourse units (ADUs) are classified on the sentence level. Wachsmuth et al. rely on the annotations in the corpus of Stab and Gurevych (2014a) to this end. Their mining approach uses an SVM based on several features such as token n-grams, the relative position of a sentence in an essay, or the similarity of the sentence to the essay's prompt. On the test set of Stab and Gurevych (2014a), it achieves a micro F_1-score of 0.726.
2. *Analyzing Structure.* The next step is to identify common paragraph-bounded sequences of ADUs (called *ADU flows*) or of different ADUs (*ADU change flows*). Wachsmuth et al. apply ADU mining to all 6085 essays from the ICLE corpus, finding that 25.1% of all paragraphs start with a conclusion followed by one or more premises, whereas the reverse ordering only covers 2.7%.
3. *Assessing Quality.* Finally, the mined structure is used to score each of the four quality dimensions. From their analysis, Wachsmuth et al. derive argument features for assessment, such as the distribution of different variants of *ADU flows* (e.g., ADU

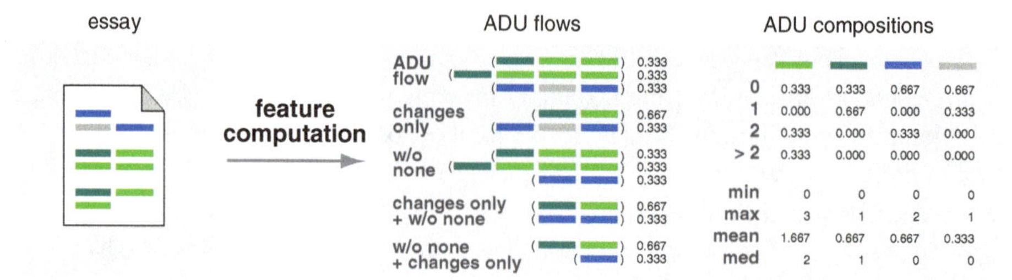

Fig. 7.6 Excerpt of the illustration of the features for scoring essay argumentation of Wachsmuth et al. (2016): The essay's argument structure is mapped to the distribution of different *ADU flows* and to frequency representations of the *ADU composition*. Licensed under CC-BY 4.0 International

change flows) and *ADU compositions* which capture the frequency of paragraphs with zero, one, two, or more of each of the ADU types. Figure 7.6 illustrates these two features. They are put into an SVM regressor for assessment.

In experiments, Wachsmuth et al. replicate Persing et al.'s set-ups and combine their features with different ablations of token and part-of-speech *n*-grams as well as discourse function flows, mimicking Persing et al. (2010). Matching intuition, argument mining helps most for structure-related tasks. The best feature combinations are state of the art for *organization* (MSE 0.164) and *argument strength* (MSE 0.226), but do not beat Persing and Ng in *thesis clarity* and *prompt adherence*.

More recently, Ding et al. (2023) take on the hypothesis that argument structure and rhetorical argument quality are related, but tackle it in a multitask learning fashion. Building on the 25k essays from the PERSUADE corpus (Crossley et al. 2022), the authors develop a token-level BIO tagging approach that jointly identifies span-level ADUs of seven types (lead, position, claim, counterclaim, rebuttal, evidence, and conclusion) and assesses 3-class effectiveness of each span (effective, adequate, or ineffective). Both of these are annotated in the corpus. In their evaluation, the authors compare the multitask approach to sequentially tackling the two tasks based on a LongFormer model (Beltagy et al. 2020), observing notable improvements, though room for improvement remains. They also find that information about the essay's prompt and the surrounding text further benefits span-level prediction accuracy.

Debate-Level Quality Zhang et al. (2016b) investigate how to use to NLP methods to predict the winner of 'Oxford-style debates', where two parties argue with each other in multiple rounds, before an audience decides about the winner. They present a corpus of 108 debates from Intelligence Squared, which consist of three rounds: the *introduction* of the main points of each side, the *discussion* with questions and attacks, and the *conclusion* with final remarks. In their approach, Zhang et al. model the conversational flow of ideas in four steps:

1. *Identifying Talking Points.* First, the most discriminating words of each side are determined. Per side, Zhang et al. take the 20 words in the introduction with highest z-scores in their probability distribution. For a debate on *Millenials don't stand a chance*, for example, this leads to talking points such as "debt" and "boomer" on the for side, and "economy" and "volunteer" on the against side.
2. *Modeling Talking Point Flow.* Debaters may promote own talking points, tackle the opponent's points, or discuss other points. Zhang et al. model the resulting flow by the time that each side spends on these three options in each round (quantified as the fraction of content words). For example, $f_{Disc}(For, Against)$ is the time that the for side spends on the other side's talking points in the discussion.
3. *Identifying Discussion Points.* Next, the approach identifies new points that arise in the discussion round. Zhang et al. consider all those words as discussion points that one side states and the other side adopts at least twice. Only 3% of all words match this criterion in the data, on average ten points per debate.
4. *Modeling Discussion Point Flow.* Analogous to talking points, Zhang et al. model the flow of discussion points based on the respective proportions.

In leave-one-out evaluation of debate winner prediction on the corpus, the authors compare the approach to a content baseline (bag-of-words and counts of words and turns per side) and an audience baseline (counts of audience applauses and laughters). Using the flow features in logistic regression yields an accuracy of 63% (65% after feature selection), better than both audience (60%) and content baseline (50%). Despite the limited accuracy, the general idea thus shows potential.

Potash and Rumshisky (2017) evolve the ideas of Zhang et al. on the same data. The authors also model talking points (based on TF-IDF), but rely a recurrent neural network (RNN) with LSTM units and attention to model the interaction of talking points. Besides, they add bag-of-words and GloVe embeddings as features. An interesting aspect is the regularization of the RNN based on applause and laughter counts, which the authors propose to convert to side preferences of the audiences and integrate these in the RNN's loss function. Replicating the setup of Zhang et al., the approach of Potash and Rumshisky boosts accuracy to 71.0%.

At a similar time, Wang et al. (2017) present another corpus of 118 Intelligence Squared debates. Their approach to predict debate winners on this data formalizes the effects of content and style (in terms of linguistic features) using latent variables that combine linguistic features with estimates of the persuasive strength of different latent topics, and that also model the interaction between the two. The idea behind persuasive strength is that the discussion of certain topics may help one side of the debate more. In leave-one-out experiments comparable to those above, the full approach predicts the winner correctly for 73.7% of the debates. While the different data prevents a real comparison, it thus seems slightly stronger than those above.

Li et al. (2020) study the role of argument structure in persuading the audience of an online debate between two parties, similar to the outlined approach of Wachsmuth

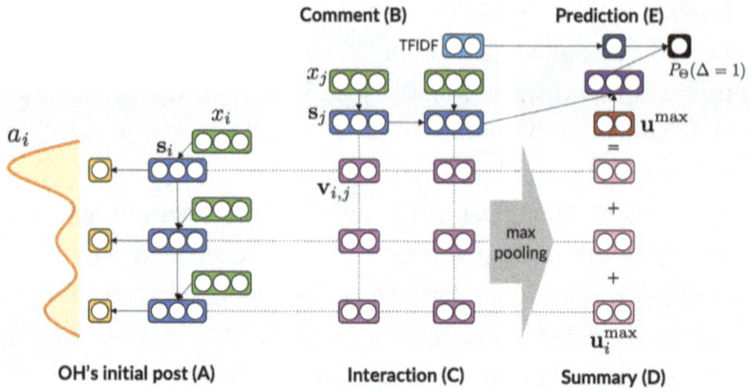

Fig. 7.7 The attentive interaction approach of Jo et al. (2018): A vulnerability value a_i is computed for the neural representation $\mathbf{s}_i$ of each sentence x_i of the opinion holder's post. Combining the values with interaction encodings $\mathbf{v}_{i,j}$ for the sentences of the posts and the replying comment, it uses summarized representations to predict delta awards. Licensed under CC-BY 4.0 International

et al. (2016). Specifically, Li et al. start from 77k debates from debate.org included in the corpus of Durmus and Cardie (2019). The authors employ the argument mining approach of Niculae et al. (2017) which builds on discussed the evaluability model of Park et al. (2015). For their approach, Li et al. derive features from mined arguments, such ADU n-grams and counts of convergent, divergent, and serial argument structures. A Bi-LSTM combines them with a BERT representation of the debate text. In fivefold cross-validation, the approach obtains an accuracy 77.3%, beating a majority baseline (62.6%) and various ablations.

Tan et al. (2016) consider the open-minded online debates in the Reddit forum ChangeMyView. There, a user initiates a discussion by posting their opinion on some topic, and others reply with opposing arguments. The opinion holder can assign *delta awards* to arguments that made them change their view. Rather than focusing on an approach, Tan et al. study how interaction dynamics and persuasion strategies correlate with the probability of these awards. Among other insights, they find that the probability notably grows with the number of challengers, peaking at about 0.40 for 128 challengers (e.g., opposed to 0.13 for 18 challengers). On average, replying three times to the opinion holder maximizes award probability (almost 0.06), whereas the probability drops to zero as of the fifth reply. Moreover, awarded replies tend not to be similar in linguistic style according to their analyses.

Jo et al. (2018) propose a computational approach to predicting whether a comment on ChangeMyView receives a delta award. Using the neural network architecture in Fig. 7.7, the approach models attentive interaction between an opinion holder's post and the comment based on *vulnerable regions* of the post, that is, sentences that may be important to address in a reply. It then transforms the vulnerability values and interaction encodings into summarized representations for prediction. For evaluation, Jo et al. build on the data of Tan et al., 18k discussions for training and 2k for testing. They cluster the data into 20 topical domains using latent Dirichlet allocation (Blei et al. 2003) to enable both in-domain and cross-domain tests. In-domain, one of their approach variations improves over a logistic regression baseline derived from Tan et al., with an AUC score of 72.0 compared to 70.9. Across domains, it performs slightly worse, though (69.4 vs. 69.6). Looking at the effectiveness results of all debate-level approaches, we conclude that a reliable winner prediction seems hard, at least purely based on its textual transcription only.

7.2.3 Assessing Dialectical Argument Quality

Few computational accounts specifically for the dialectical side of argument quality exist so far, but some works explicitly tackle the three *subdimensions of dialectical quality* from the taxonomy in Fig. 7.1: global acceptability, global relevance, and global sufficiency. Individual works are also related to some form of *reasonableness*.

Subdimensions of Dialectical Quality A pioneer approach to argument quality comes from Cabrio and Villata (2012) which aims at the globally acceptable arguments in an online debate. It combines textual entailment (Dagan et al. 2009) with the abstract argumentation framework of Dung (1995) (see Chap. 3) in two steps:

1. *Identifying Attack Relations.* Given the set of all arguments in a debate, the approach first identifies attack relations between the arguments. Cabrio and Villata apply a textual entailment method (Kouylekov and Negri 2010) to all pairs of arguments. They map contradictions to attack relations, and they also derive further attacks from entailment pairs: If argument A_1 attacks A_2 and A_2 entails A_3, then A_1 also attacks A_3, since A_3 is more specific than A_2.
2. *Determining Acceptable Arguments.* The identified attack relations define an abstract argumentation graph. In their approach, Cabrio and Villata follow the idea of Dung that A is acceptable if all arguments attacking it are rejected, and A is rejected if it at least one accepted argument A' attacks A.

To evaluate their approach, Cabrio and Villata collected 200 attack and support argument pairs from idebate.net. They used the arguments from nine topics for training and from ten other topics for testing. While textual entailment reached a limited accuracy of 67% (compared to a word-overlap baseline with 62%), still 75% of all arguments found to be acceptable also would be acceptable, if the method of Dung would have been applied to the ground-truth relations between arguments.

Wachsmuth et al. (2017e) explicitly tackle global relevance, hypothesizing that the relevance of an argument's conclusion depends on what other arguments reuse it as a premise. The rationale is that, by reusing an author's conclusion, others deem it relevant, no matter whether they build on it, refute it, or elsewise. To operationalize their hypothesis, Wachsmuth et al. proceed in the following steps:

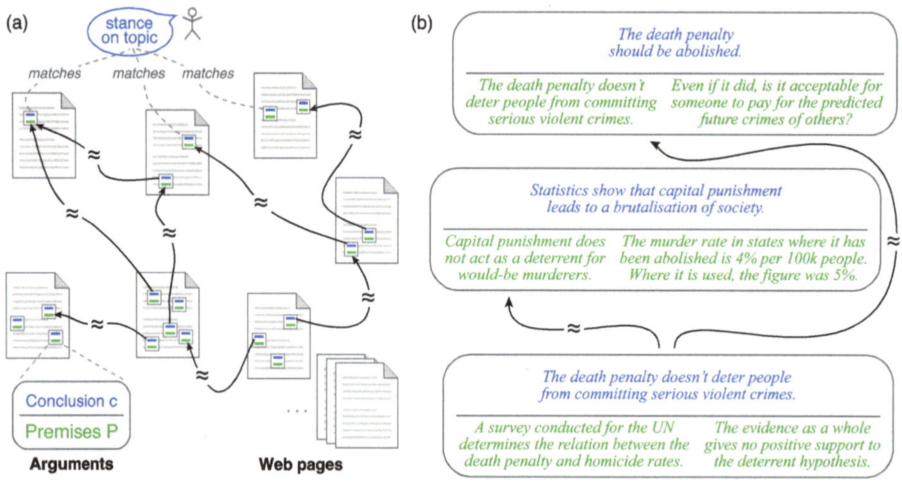

Fig. 7.8 (**a**) Argument reuse graph in the global relevance assessment approach of Wachsmuth et al. (2017e). (**b**) Example reuse of the conclusion of the argument at the bottom as a premise in two other arguments. Licensed under CC-BY 4.0 International

1. *Building a Reuse Graph.* Given a large collection of arguments, conclusion reuse defines a directed graph $G = (A, E)$ where each node $a \in A$ denotes an argument consisting of a conclusion and a set of premises, and each edge $(a, a') \in E$ represents the reuse of the conclusion of a as one of the premises in a'. Figure 7.8a illustrates the graph and Fig. 7.8b shows an example reuse. Wachsmuth et al. build a graph from 18k arguments of the AIFdb (corpora.aifdb.org), considering only the exact same phrasing of ADUs as reuse.
2. *Computing Conclusion Relevance.* The reuse graph constitutes the basis of computing relevance in the approach. In particular, Wachsmuth et al. adapt the unsupervised PageRank algorithm (Page et al. 1999) to score the relevance of a conclusion, c, recursively as a weighted sum of two parts, namely,

$$\hat{p}(c) \;:=\; (1-\alpha) \cdot \frac{p(d) \cdot |D|}{|A|} + \alpha \cdot \sum_{i} \frac{\hat{p}(c_i)}{|P_i|}.$$

   Here, the first part normalizes the PageRank score of the source document d of c based on the counts of documents, $|D|$, and arguments, $|A|$, as the ground relevance. The second part recursively adds relevance to c based on the score $\hat{p}(c_i)$ of each conclusion c_i that uses c as a premise, normalized by its number of premises, $|P_i|$. In their experiments, Wachsmuth et al. use a uniform ground relevance, as no PageRank document scores are available in their data.
3. *Deriving Argument Relevance.* The adapted PageRank allows computing a score for each ADU. To obtain a score for a whole argument, Wachsmuth et al. suggest to

aggregate the scores of the argument's premises. They compare four aggregation functions experimentally: minimum, average, maximum, and sum.

For evaluation, Wachsmuth et al. let seven human annotators rank arguments for 32 conclusions to compute average benchmark rankings. The authors compare their approach to other unsupervised baselines. With Kendall's $\tau = 0.28$ under the sum aggregation, it achieved the highest correlation with the benchmark rankings. In comparison, scoring an argument's relevance based on the frequency of its premises leads to $\tau = 0.10$ only. While the correlations are not strong, neither the arguments' content nor the way the arguments reason is considered. As such, the approach may seem suitable as for a preselection of the most relevant arguments.

Rebutting all counters to an argument that can be anticipated will often be hard to achieve. However, a step toward such global sufficiency is to avoid *myside bias*, that is, the ignorance of opposing views to an argument. In Chap. 6, we discussed two approaches to classifying myside bias in student essays (Stab and Gurevych 2016; Wachsmuth et al. 2017a), and point the reader there for more details.

Reasonableness of Arguments While we see approaches covering reasonableness as part of overall quality below, no NLP research has focused on reasonableness specifically so far. However, El Baff et al. (2020b) present an approach to assessing the dialectical quality view of El Baff et al. (2018) (see Sect. 7.1). In particular, the authors analyze the impact of linguistic style on the persuasive effect for conservatives and liberals in the US. To model style, they explore psychological word usage, word-emotion associations, evidence types, arguing words. and subjectivity words. On the 3-class task of the news editorial corpus of El Baff et al. (2018), they evaluate SVMs with according features, in comparison to content features (lemma n-grams). Emotion associations as well as arguing and subjectivity words predict comparably well whether liberals are challenged or reinforced, and a combination with content features works best (micro F_1-score of 0.54). Style helps little to assess the perception of conversatives, though, for which content seems more important.

In follow-up work, El Baff et al. (2020a) look at differences between ideologically lean and extreme readers as well as between different personality traits, determined using the Big-Five personality test (Goldberg 1990). They find that extreme readers are affected more by style, lean readers more by content. For personality differences, the results are not so clear, but some personality types seem more affected by style, such as those with high conscientiousness or with low extraversion.

7.2.4 Assessing Overall Argument Quality

Finally, some research models argument quality in overall terms. This includes approaches that assess specific *holistic quality* notions, as well as those that tackle the main or all dimensions of the argument quality taxonomy in Fig. 7.1.

Holistic Quality Assessment Toledo et al. (2019) propose both an absolute and a relative quality idea for 5k short crowdsourced arguments and 14k argument pairs built on this basis. For absolute scoring, the authors asked annotators whether they would recommend a given argument to a friend who prepares a speech on the respective topic, to then derive a numerical score from all "yes" answers. For relative comparison, in turn, they asked which of two stance-matching arguments the annotators would prefer to support or contest the topic. To assess quality, they fine-tune BERT with a regression head (for scoring) or classification head (for comparison) respectively. In cross-validation on their data and the data of Habernal and Gurevych (2016a), BERT is on par with Simpson and Gurevych (2018), achieving a Pearson correlation of 0.42–0.49 in scoring and an accuracy of 80–80% in comparison.

Gretz et al. (2020b) adopted the annotation process of Toledo et al. for an even bigger dataset of 30k arguments on 71 topics. To obtain reliable scores, they incorporate MACE annotator reliability (Hovy et al. 2013), either used directly to weigh the "yes" and "no" judgments (called *MACE-P*) or to build a weighted average (called *WA*). For scoring, they compare pretrained and fine-tuned BERT (with or without topic information) to different non-transformer baselines. On their data, fine-tuned BERT with topic information has the best Pearson correlation, 0.53 on MACE-P and 0.52 on WA. The other BERT variant comes close, though, whereas the baselines show notably lower correlations. Since the code of Gretz et al. is not open, Zelch et al. (2025b) study to what extent the reported results can be reproduced. While some configuration details had to be guessed, the authors managed to achieve nearly identical scores, 0.537 on MACE-P and 0.536 on WA.

For a cross-domain experiment on argument quality, Fromm et al. (2023) built own splits of the corpora of Habernal and Gurevych (2016a), Toledo et al. (2019), and Gretz et al. (2020b) as well as the corpus of Swanson et al. (2015) with 5k debate portal arguments judged binarily for easy interpretability. The authors relied on a BERT model with regression head for absolute scoring, which they fine-tuned on the training set of either corpus and then evaluated on each test set in terms of Pearson correlation. In-domain correlations ranged from 0.190 to 0.475. Matching expectation, cross-domain generalization worked comparably well for similar corpora, such as those of Toledo et al. and Gretz et al., with correlation reductions of 0.10. For other corpus pairs, it partly failed entirely, for example, with only 0.03 when training on the data of Habernal and Gurevych and testing on the data of Gretz et al..

Wang et al. (2023a) argue that previous approaches struggle with subtle differences between arguments. The authors propose an approach that employs contrastive learning to support the distinction of medium-quality arguments from high-quality and low-quality arguments in RoBERTa embeddings. On this basis, a graph neural network models discourse and logical structure for relativequality assessment. The approach is compared to LLMs such as GPT-3.5 with few-shot examples as well as simpler baselines and ablations on the dataset of Gretz et al. (2020b). In terms of Pearson correlation, it achieved 0.5603 compared to 0.5283 of a simple RoBERTa classifier and only 0.1896 of GPT-3.5 with three examples.

Beyond assessment itself, Elaraby et al. (2024) study whether LLMs can generate rationales for why an argument is of higher quality than another one. In their experiment, they prompt nine open-weight and closed LLMs to decide which argument of a pair is better and to provide a rationale for the decision, based on the datasets of Toledo et al. (2019) and Gretz et al. (2020b). Rather than evaluating assessment performance, however, they analyze the quality of the rationales, partly using human annotators and partly using GPT-4. Across all settings, Llama2-70B-Chat (Touvron et al. 2023a) performs strongest, beating GPT 3.5/4 as well as smaller versions of Llama and other LLMs. The annotators saw *contrastive* rationales as most persuasive, such as the following on an argument pair related to mandatory flu vaccination:

(7.4) The first argument emphasizes the importance of bodily autonomy and the limitation of state intervention in personal choices. It presents a clear ethical principle that can be applied consistently across different situations. The second argument highlights potential negative consequences of mandatory vaccination, which, while valid, may not be as persuasive as the ethical principle of bodily autonomy.

Lastly, Jin et al. (2025) discuss the lack of considering multiple perspectives in argument quality assessment. As an approach, the authors present a multi-persona LLM agent framework that first dynamically generates four diverse personas. On training data generated with hand-designed prompts, the persona generation is optimized to fit the given topic and argument. Then, one quality score is predicted for each persona, along with a rationale similar to those of Elaraby et al. (2024). The average score of the personas is then used as the final score. Personas and rationales come from GPT-4o-mini, whereas the quality assessment model is a fine-tuned LLama-3.1-8B. The authors carried out experiments on the datasets of Toledo et al. (2019) and Gretz et al. (2020b). They obtained Pearson correlations of 0.5353 and 0.6406 respectively, notably improving over the results above.

Taxonomy-based Quality Assessment Wachsmuth and Werner (2020) explore which of the 15 dimensions from the argument quality taxonomy can be assessed only based on features of the text. Their features model content, embeddings, style, structure, length, text quality, evidence, and subjectivity. In leave-one-topic-out validation on the 16 topics in the debate portal corpus of Wachsmuth et al. (2017c), they compare SVM regression using each feature type alone and all features. The authors observe the biggest gains for *local sufficiency*, *cogency*, and *overall quality*, but no dimension is predicted fully reliably. The dimension with the lowest observed mean absolute error on the given 3-point scale is *global sufficiency* (0.22), the one with highest is *local acceptability* (0.40). Subjectivity and length are the strongest features, the latter corroborating the observations on length by Potash et al. (2017a). In their analysis, Wachsmuth and Werner also find that the predictability of annotated quality scores depends notably on who annotated it.

Lauscher et al. (2020) look beyond debate portals, assessing the four main taxonomy dimensions (cogency, effectiveness, reasonableness, and overall quality) on a 5-point scale for a new corpus (Ng et al. 2020) of 5285 arguments from three genres: community question answering (CQA), debate forums, and product reviews. The authors propose two variants of a BERT-based multitask learning approach for assessment. To deal with the varying argument lengths (possibly exceeding the context size of BERT), the approach first transforms an argument into WordPiece tokens (Wu et al. 2016) and creates a pooled hidden representation from the sequence of tokens. This representation is input to either of the two multitask learning variants:

1. *Flat Multitask Learning.* This variant jointly optimizes individual regression heads for each of the four dimensions. To this end, the loss function sums up the losses of each of the four regression heads with equal weights.
2. *Hierarchical Multitask Learning.* This variant exploits the hierarchical relationship of overall quality and its three subdimensions. It first jointly learns regression heads for all subdimensions, analogous to the flat variant. For overall quality, it uses the scores of these heads as additional inputs for another regression head.

Lauscher et al. compare the two variants against a length-based predictor and different support vector regressors, including a reimplementation of the approach of Wachsmuth et al. (2016) (see above), and a single-task BERT variant. In in-genre experiments, flat multitask learning performs best on average in terms of Pearson correlation. All BERT variants clearly beat the other baselines, with the approach of Wachsmuth et al. (2016) being closest. Training on all genres further increases assessment performance, with correlations of 0.653–0.686 for CQA, 0.487–0.598 for debates, and 0.599–0.643 for reviews (depending on the quality dimension). Here, the hierarchical variant performs better, suggesting that it needs sufficient data. In Chap. 6, we have detailed a follow-up work, aimed at debiasing language models (Holtermann et al. 2022). Noteworthily, debiasing has no notable negative effect on quality assessment; in doubt, debiasing benefits performance rather than hurting it.

Marro et al. (2022) investigate both cogency and reasonableness on the AAE2 corpus (Stab and Gurevych 2014a). To this end, they extend the corpus by manual judgments of the two quality dimensions on a 5-point scale and classify the main rhetorical means (logos, ethos, or pathos). For cogency and rhetoric, they combine a LongFormer model with graph embeddings (Rozemberczki and Sarkar 2020) of the ground-truth argument relations and use an SVM for assessment. For reasonableness, they map the essay's argument components to cogency scores to then apply an expert-defined algorithm that derives a reasonable score from the scores of arguments and counterarguments. In experiments, the graph embedding-based SVM achieves a cogency macro F_1-score of 0.77, compared to 0.72 without embeddings. Reasonableness reaches 0.54 only, but compared to 0.18 of a majority baseline, the idea of the algorithm seems to work out to some extent.

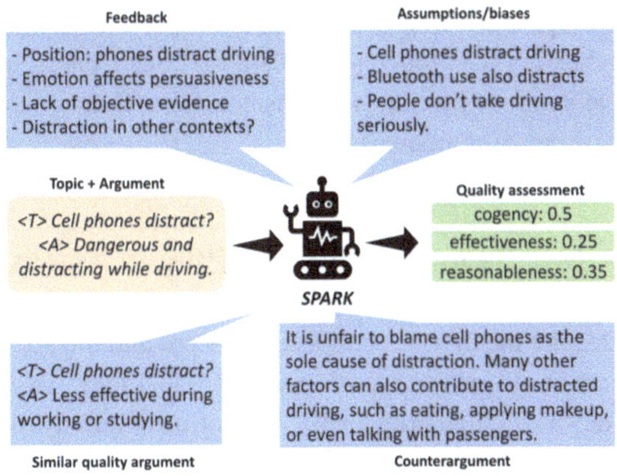

Fig. 7.9 Four types of context information generated by an LLM for assessing argument quality in the approach of Deshpande et al. (2024): *feedback* on the argument, *assumptions/biases* in the argument, a *similar quality argument*, and a *counterargument*. Licensed under CC-BY 4.0 International

Mirzakhmedova et al. (2024a) analyze the agreement of LLMs and humans in annotating all 15 dimensions of the quality taxonomy. On one hand, the authors asked novice annotators to re-assess all dimensions for the expert-annotated arguments in the corpus of Wachsmuth et al. (2017c). On the other hand, they repeatedly prompted two LLMs to do so, GPT-3.5 and PaLM-2 (Chowdhery et al. 2023). To quantify the reliability of LLM-based assessment, Mirzakhmedova et al. compute pairwise Krippendorff's α agreement for experts, novices, and the LLMs. PaLM-2 nearly perfectly agrees with itself, and also GPT-3 agrees more with itself than humans agree with each other. Comparing human with LLM annotations, the authors observe similar: the α values for human/LLM pairs are higher than for expert/novice pairs. They conclude that LLMs may be a valuable support of human quality annotation.

Deshpande et al. (2024) explore to what extent augmenting an argument by LLM-generated context information benefits the assessment of the argument's quality. Quality is considered in terms of cogency, effectiveness, and reasonableness. For a given argument on a given topic, their approach consists of two parts:

1. *Context Generation.* For augmentation, the approach prompts GPT-3.5 to generate four types of information: concise writing *feedback* in bullet point form; *assumptions* that the argument builds on, if any; an *argument of similar quality*; and a *counterargument* to the given argument. Figure 7.9 shows an example.
2. *Quality Assessment.* Deshpande et al. propose a dual BERT encoder with multi-head cross attention, where the argument and topic serve as the query and the information generated as the key and value. Via a mean pooler, the approach then feeds the representation into three regressions heads, one per quality dimension.

The authors carried out experiments on the corpus of Ng et al. (2020) and out-of-domain experiments on the corpus of Gretz et al. (2020b). Compared to three baseline transformer models (BERT, XLNet, GPT 3.5) and their dual architecture without context information, the approach improves in Pearson correlation by about 0.10 on all three dimensions, achieving 0.44 for cogency, 0.48 for effectiveness, and 0.44 for reasonableness. Especially the generated feedback seems helpful, and an ablation based only on the feedback proves best out-of-domain (0.29).

7.3 Beyond Argument Quality Assessment

Despite the diverse settings considered and the approaches pursued, the NLP methods we saw in the previous section all share that they assess or compare the quality of arguments (on some granularity level). The notion of quality that the methods reflect is encoded in the *ground-truth* annotations that they are trained and evaluated on. Ground truth is a brittle assumption here, though, given the inherent subjectivity of argument quality perception discussed in the beginning of the chapter.

In this section, we come to NLP research beyond this brittle assumption, accounting for subjectivity explicitly toward a more reliable and robust quality assessment. Moreover, we look beyond the idea that it is the quality of individual *arguments* that counts, namely, at deliberative settings where the collective quality of participants' arguments is in the focus. Finally, we review the few computational approaches that go beyond the restriction of an *assessment* to the actual improvement of argument quality. All of them constitute recent trends of argument mining research that are still evolving dynamically and, hence, up to a refined discussion in the future.

7.3.1 Assessing Argument Quality under Subjectivity

Multiple techniques for handling the inherent subjectivity of argument quality have come up. Some minimize subjectivity by focusing on *'objective' criteria*. Others explicitly *model context* relevant to subjectivity or *model perspectives* of people.

Focus on 'Objective' Criteria Assessing quality is a subjective action by nature, which is why we put *objective* in quotes here. The core idea meant here is to avoid relying on subjective human judgment for assessment, which may be particularly helpful where dialectical quality (beyond specific audiences) is of interest. Often, this leads to modeling structural properties induced by the set of all arguments in a given setting. We have already seen two such approaches in the part on assessing dialectical quality above: Cabrio and Villata (2012) derive the binary judgments of the acceptability of arguments directly from attack relations between the arguments, and evaluate the judgments against the formal framework of Dung (1995) on ground-truth arguments. In follow-up work, the authors also further extend their approach to bipolar argumentation frameworks (Cabrio and Villata 2017). In contrast, Wachsmuth et al. (2017e) model argument relevance based on the reuse of conclusions as premises in other arguments, as discussed. For evaluation, they approximate objective judgments by average judgments over several human evaluators.

Lawrence and Reed (2017) propose two further approaches of this fashion, one targeting the *centrality* of a claim within in a debate and the other the claim's *diviseness* of the two sides of an issue. For each, the authors define a normative formula for how to calculate a score based on ground-truth argument structure. To automatically compute centrality, they rank claims with TextRank (Mihalcea and Tarau 2004) on either of four measures: word overlap, WordNet distance (Miller 1995), word2vec similarity (Mikolov et al. 2013), and doc2vec (Le and Mikolov 2014) similarity. Diviseness computation builds on the same idea, but multiplies the centrality values with sentiment scores derived from SentiWordNet (Baccianella et al. 2010). In experiments on US presidential debates data, WordNet distance maximizes Kendall's τ correlation with the normative values for both centrality ($\tau = 0.656$) and diviseness ($\tau = 0.284$). How much the values match human perception is not studied.

As these studies suggest, there are two inherent limitations to an 'objective assessment': On the one hand, its evaluation either still requires subjective judgments or it needs to build on a normative view whose adequacy in practice may be hard to justify. On the other hand, not all quality dimensions are to open to a respective assessment, as some dimensions presuppose the idea of a specific target audience.

Explicit Context Modeling Ultimately, a reliable assessment of argument quality will often need awareness of who argues to whom, due to the influence of this context on the perception of quality that we discussed in Sect. 7.1. A number of NLP approaches have therefore explicitly modeled either or both sides of a discussion, the reader/audience and the author/speaker respectively. Some of these predict argument quality for specific audiences, such as the two consecutive approaches of El Baff et al. (2020b) and El Baff et al. (2020a) discussed above that predict the persuasive effect of news editorials separately for conservatives and liberatives. Others model features of the involved parties available in a given setting.

Durmus and Cardie (2018a) investigate to what extent modeling the prior beliefs of a reader improves quality prediction. The authors consider settings as those in the aforementioned *debate.org* corpus (Durmus and Cardie 2019), where users vote for the winner of a debate. Many users have profiles that include labels of their political and religious ideology as well as of their stances on 'big issues', such as *gay marriage* or *death penalty*. In experiments, Durmus and Cardie (2018a) match arguers' and voters' prior beliefs based on ideology and stances, and compare these user features to several linguistic features (e.g., TF-IDF or sentiment) for logistic regression. For religious ideology, user features (accuracy 62.97%) and linguistic features (61.10%) have a similar impact in predicting the winner, totaling to 64.56% when combined. For political ideology, however, the similarity in big issue stances of reader and arguer is much more important (73.96%) than the best features (56.88%) and dominates overall accuracy (74.53%). Later, Longpre et al. (2019) extend the work of Durmus and Cardie by looking specifically at voters undecided on the given debate topic. Interestingly, they find that audience features have notably less impact on the persuasive effect, largely being dominated by linguistic features.

Unlike the previous works, Luu et al. (2019) fully focus on the author's side, modeling how their ability to win debates evolves over time on *debate.org* as well as how the authors' language reflect this ability. To this end, they combine the Elo rating model for winner probability prediction (Elo 1978) with several linguistic features, such as post length, counts of emotional words, questions, hedging, and fighting words. In their experiments Luu et al. (2019) find that the authors indeed get better over time. The Elo model and the linguistic features are similarly important for prediction, together achieving around 80% accuracy in winner prediction.

Al Khatib et al. (2020b) study how to model prior beliefs, interests, and personality traits of the authors of arguments to predict whether their arguments are effective. To this end, they extend the aforementioned ChangeMyView corpus of Tan et al. (2016) by all posts on Reddit related to any author on ChangeMyView posting an opinion or arguing against it. Their approach models the following three aspects as a vector:

1. *Interests.* The author's interest in general topics, such as *politics* or *religion*. To model these, Al Khatib et al. categorize Reddit forums into 720 categories using SnooSnoop and then counts the author's posts for each category.
2. *Prior Beliefs.* The author's stances toward various topics. Al Khatib et al. consider each Wikipedia article title as a candidate topic, links topic mentions to the author's posts using Semanticizer, and then computes a stance value as the author's median sentiment on the topic using VADER (Hutto and Gilbert 2014).
3. *Personality Traits.* The author's behavioral attributes, such as *adventurous* or *self-conscious*. Al Khatib et al. model these by the distribution of words from the Linguistics Inquiry and Word Count (LIWC) tool (Pennebaker et al. 2015).

Figure 7.10 sketches the resulting vectors, which can then be used to compare any two authors. In experiments on the original and the extended ChangeMyView corpus, Al Khatib et al. evaluate their approach for argument effectiveness using logistic regression against features of Tan et al. (2016), such as bag-of-words and the interplay of ChangeMyView participants. While the approach falls behind Tan et al. (2016) on the original corpus (61.8% vs. 70.0%), it proves better on the extended corpus (61.1% vs. 57.8%). In both cases, it is stronger in predicting opinion holders that do not change their view; particularly, personality traits seem important.

In a later work from the same author team, Wiegmann et al. (2022) look at differences between authors on ChangeMyView that are successful and unsuccessful in terms of achieving persuasion. They model the authors' engagement and experience on the platform as well as their debate style. In empirical analyses, they observe that more engaging posts (those that receive more answers) tend to be more successful, whereas increasing experience mainly affects novice authors on the platform positively. The results on debate style are somewhat comparable to those of Luu et al. (2019) on *debate.org*, while

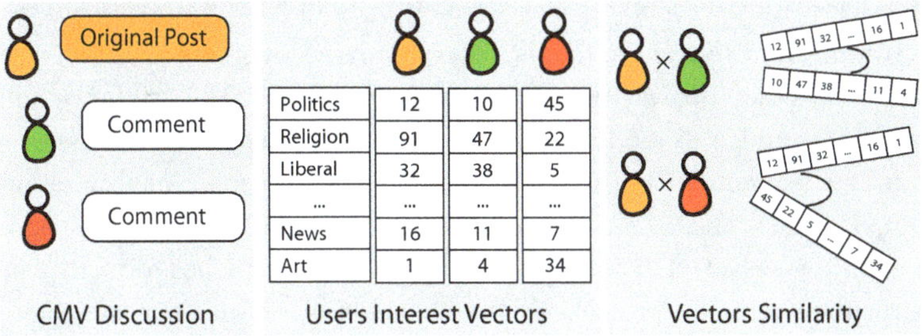

Fig. 7.10 Illustration of the interest vectors of users generated from their participation behavior on a debate portal in the approach of Al Khatib et al. (2020b). The vectors are employed to compute similarity between opinion holder and commenting users.

suggesting that the way debates frame their arguments varies notably between successful and unsuccessful authors.

Chen et al. (2022a) study culture-specific differences across argumentative learner essays as well as their impact on two argument quality dimensions: organization and argument strength. Analyzing the essays of learners with five different first languages in the ICLE corpus (Granger et al. 2009), the authors observe that Chinese and Italian learners use twice as many climactic arguments (where the conclusion is at the end) as Tswana, Swedish, and German learners. Chinese learners also exhibit notably more vertical structures (those with hierarchical reasoning chains), though horizontal structures are the majority in all cases. While there are little quality differences on average between more climactic and more anti-climactic essays, both organization and argument strength seem to profit from more vertical structures.

Looking at the behavior of debaters, Nabhani et al. (2025) assess the impact of storytelling in ChangeMyView discussions. The authors employ a RoBERTa-based story classifier (Antoniak et al. 2024) to measure correlations between storytelling and debater effectiveness. In the data of Tan et al. (2016) (see Sect. 7.2), They find that 5.06% of delta-awarded comments include storytelling compared to 4.63% for the other comments; a significant difference, but with low effect size. Interestingly, however, debaters who use storytelling more tend to be less effective on average.

With a similar idea, Quensel et al. (2025) investigate different subjectivity indicators in argument quality assessment. In particular, the authors fine-tuned RoBERTa classifiers for storytelling and emotions on training data of Falk and Lapesa (2022) and Troiano et al. (2019) respectively, where they model hedging based on a matching against different lexicons, such as the one of Islam et al. (2020). Both storytelling and hedging turn out to positively correlate with persuasive effect of posts in ChangeMyView discussions Tan et al. (2016); however, they the opposite holds for the quality of the short crowdsourced arguments of Toledo et al. (2019). Regarding the emotions, both datasets show comparable results: most emotions seem to affect quality rather negatively, but fear and sadness show a positive effect.

Perspective Modeling Recently, some research lines in NLP push forward the idea of perspectivism in subjective tasks, that is, to explicitly account for human label variation rather than to abstract it away via aggregation (Plank 2022). Strikingly, this notion exactly matches the idea to model the audience in argument quality assessment. While Wachsmuth and Werner (2020) already trained annotator-specific quality rating models (see above), Heinisch et al. (2023) are the first to explicitly model perspectivism for argument quality assessment. The authors compare five approaches to include subjective quality perception into the prediction: simple majority voting, per-annotator models, annotator-specific classification heads, shared RoBERTa encoders to integrate annotation-specific views, and separated RoBERTa encoders. On a corpus from their earlier shared task (Heinisch et al. 2022), where the conclusions are annotated for novelty and validity, the authors observe that modeling perspectives notably improves the assessment of the two dimensions. The shared RoBERTa encoder perform best, with an F_1-score of 0.6595 for validity (compared to 0.4763 of majority voting) and 0.6204 for novelty (compared to 0.4347).

To enable more perspectivism research on quality, Romberg et al. (2025) survey 103 argument quality-related datasets that provide the individual labels of different annotators. In a case study, they stress different perspectives for the main dimensions of the quality taxonomy (Wachsmuth et al. 2017c), looking at the Krippendorff's α agreement of experts (Wachsmuth et al. 2017c), crowdworkers (Wachsmuth et al. 2017b), and novices (Mirzakhmedova et al. 2024a). For overall quality exemplary, experts agree more with each other (0.443) than crowdworkers (0.140) and novices (0.233). The agreement across groups is even lower, between 0.083 (crowd/novice) and 0.180 (experts/crowd), underlining the importance of modeling perspectives.

7.3.2 Assessing Deliberative Quality

The study of deliberation has its orgins in political science and computational social science, which has led to the *discourse quality index*. Assessment there focuses on *deliberative quality* rather than argument quality. These two views of quality are not independent from each other; rather deliberative quality emerges from specific dimensions of argument quality. Some NLP research has been connecting *deliberative and argument quality* explicitly.

Discourse Quality Index The notion of deliberative quality comes from the discussion of deliberative democracy, which puts the discourse exchange in a community that precedes decision making into the focus (Bächtiger and Parkinson 2019). To foster such exchange, the contributions of participants in a discussion need to be constructive. Steenbergen et al. (2003) developed the *discourse quality index* (DQI, also known as *deliberative quality index*) to quantify the quality contributions. We summarize the updated version of Gerber et al. (2018) here, which models the adherence to deliberative norms using six quality dimensions on different ordinal scales:

1. *Justification rationality (0–3).* The extent to which reasons are provided for claims;
2. *Common good orientation (0–3).* The reference to common interests of groups;
3. *Interactivity (0–3).* The extent to which others' arguments are taken up;
4. *Respect (0–3).* The extent to which needs/rights of other groups are considered;
5. *Inquisitiveness (0–1).* The raising of informational or critical questions;
6. *Storytelling (0–1).* The communication via personal narratives or experiences.

Gerber et al. also provide the Europolis Corpus of about 1000 contributions from transcribed discussions of participants from 27 countries on climate change and immigration, annotated for the updated DQI. A similar corpus comes from Esau et al. (2021), which contains German deliberative discourse on three levels of formality.

Deliberative Quality Modeling A number of computational approaches to deliberative quality exist, but only some have a notable connection to NLP. Among these, Gold et al. (2017) present a visual analysis of the deliberative quality in political discussions about the restructuring of a German railway station. In their approach, the authors model *participation* based on the proportion of tokens of each participant, whereas they quantify *respect* in terms of linguistic indicators of interruptions. Furthermore, they see causal and other discourse connectives as indicators of *justifications*, and the distribution of speech acts to model *persuasiveness*. Due to the focus on visualization, an actual computational assessment does not take place.

Behrendt et al. (2024) look at how to assess 20 deliberative quality dimensions in online discussions. To this end, they combine a BERT-based encoder with fine-tuned adapters that predict an ordinal score for each dimension. Their approach then weighs all scores to obtain an overall score between 0 and 5. In experiments on a dataset of Facebook discussions of political news, the weighted average F_1-score for the different dimensions varies notably from 0.39 for *relevance* (a subdimension of rationality) to 0.98 for a *polite form of address* (a subdimension of civility). The overall score prediction is comparably accurate, with an F_1-score of 0.7815.

Deliberative vs. Argument Quality Based on a survey of NLP and political science research on argumentation, Vecchi et al. (2021) propose an integrated definition of deliberative and argument quality, discussing overlaps between the original DQI of Steenbergen et al. (2003) and the taxonomy of Wachsmuth et al. (2017c). For example the deliberative *justification level* matches the idea of *local sufficiency*, and *respect* resembles *global acceptability* in its practical manifestation. However, the authors also point out unique aspects. For example, *interactivity* is not covered by the taxonomy, which largely disregards dialogical aspects. Vice versa, the *arrangement* of arguments plays no role in the DQI, nor interestingly *credibility*, to name a few.

Falk et al. (2021) study the relation between argument quality and the need for moderation in deliberative discussions. Using the approach of Lauscher et al. (2020) detailed above, the authors score the cogency, effectiveness, reasonableness, and overall quality of 3k comments from the eRulemaking corpus of Park and Cardie (2018) to then analyze the discussion points where moderation happens. A bit counterintuitively at first sight, argument quality rather correlates negatively with the need for moderation according to their results. Falk et al. identify reasons such as the explanation of new arguments in the data, but they also suggest that argument quality may not fully suffice to model important triggers of moderation.

Turning their view to deliberative quality assessment of, Falk and Lapesa (2022) approach four quality dimensions on the corpus of Gerber et al. (2018), each as a multi-class classification task: justification, common good orientation, interactivity, and respect. The authors compare a gradient boost tree using text complexity and sentiment features to a fine-tuned RoBERTa classifier. Due to the class imbalance in the data, they augment the fine-tuning using easy data augmentation (Wei and Zou 2019). While the features fail on all dimensions with macro F_1-scores in 0.27–0.41, RoBERTa does much better; the standard RoBERTa is best for justification (0.74) and common good orientation (0.86), whereas the augmented RoBERTa outperforms it notably on interactivity (0.80 vs. 0.65) and respect (0.84 vs. 0.75).

Finally, Falk and Lapesa (2023) explicitly investigate the interaction of argument quality and deliberative quality. Their approach assesses eight dimensions of argument quality from four corpora (Swanson et al. 2015; Durmus and Cardie 2019; Ng et al. 2020; Gretz et al. 2020b) and 12 of deliberative quality (Gerber et al. 2018; Esau et al. 2021). Building on RoBERTa, it employs 20 respective adapters trained in a multitask fashion using adapter fusion (Pfeiffer et al. 2021). Compared to single-task models, the approach significantly improves quality assessment on four dimensions (e.g., from 0.49 to 0.59 macro F_1-score for *effectiveness*), while not leading to any (significant) F_1-score reductions. Ablations only based on deliberative quality or argument quality, respectively, achieve the best results for some other dimensions. In follow-up anlyses, the authors provide insights into specific interactions of the quality dimensions and their impact on moderation need prediction.

Vecchi et al. (2025) integrate deliberative quality and moderation with perspectivism considerations in a new dataset. The authors sampled 225 comments from discussion forums based on the output the approach of Falk and Lapesa (2023), and let 12 annotators label each comment for argument quality, deliberative quality, and moderation needs. On this basis, they study how labeling decisions correlate with annotators' background and values (derived from interviews). Among several insights, they find that annotators who favor diverse perspectives are more sensitive to problematic emotional appeals, while those who value logical arguments focus more on appropriateness and clarity. Moreover, annotators with moderation experience are less affected by misinformation in a comment than those without. Overall, their analysis clearly corroborates the need to model the audience in quality perception.

7.3.3 Improving Argument Quality

The first step to improve argument quality is to identify whether an argument *needs revision*. Some works also study how to provide feedback *suggesting improvements* to respective arguments, and some actually *optimize the quality* of arguments.

Revision Need Identification Skitalinskaya and Wachsmuth (2023) investigate on the Kialo data from their above-mentioned work (Skitalinskaya et al. 2021) how to identify an argumentative claim in need of revision. Comparing fine-tuned BERT, DeBERTa, and ELECTRA (Clark et al. 2020) to different embedding-based SVM variations in a balanced setting, DeBERTa performed best, with a limited accuracy of 67.1% though (a GloVe-based SVM even achieves only 54.9%). Subsequently, the authors tackle the task to suggest one of four possible improvements (clarification, grammar correction, link correction, and other), which turns out challenging as well, with 62.0% as the best result (again, for DeBERTa). The authors discuss reasons that make the two tasks challenging, the most apparent one being that it remains unclear when a claim is actually not improvable anymore.

Liu et al. (2023b) assess the quality of candidate argument revisions of college student essays. The authors emphasize that the quality of a revision depends on the surrounding context of the revised argument. To account for this issue, they design chain-of-thought prompts to make ChatGPT generate different types of context from a given essay that may help revision assessment (claims, reasoning, and evidence). On this basis, they evaluate RoBERTa variations on the task, using the revision and either context as input. Particularly, the generation of a reasoning context seems helpful, achieving an F_1-score of 0.7263, improving by a few points over a baseline that simply uses the actual surrounding sentences as context (0.6994).

With a similar idea, Afrin and Litman (2023) develop models to classify desirable revisions of the reasoning and evidence in essays of elementary, high-school, and college students. They explore the benefit of adding short or long essay context for the task as well as feedback given to the students before revision, all as input to a BERT-based Bi-LSTM classifier. In 10-fold cross-validation, the authors find that the combination of longer context and feedback mostly performs best, for example, with an F_1-score of 0.649 for the reasoning and of 0.587 for the evidence in elementary student essays (as opposed to 0.597 and 0.569 without context, respectively).

Improvement Suggestion Guerraoui et al. (2023) present a survey of feedback systems for argumentative writing support, some of which we see later in Chap. 10 as applications of argumentation. The authors organize the reviewed work according to four dimensions to be considered for feedback (depicted in Fig. 7.11): on what level of detail to give feedback on argumentation (called *richness*), how to present the feedback (*visualization*), how to communicate in the feedback process (*interactivity*), and how to adapt feedback to the arguer's background (*personalization*).

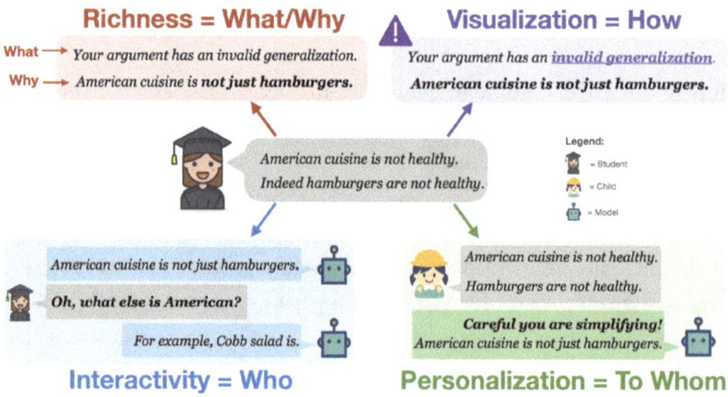

Fig. 7.11 Illustration of four dimensions of feedback to argumentation (richness, visualization, interactivity, personalization) from Guerraoui et al. (2023). Licensed under CC-BY 4.0 International

In comparably early computational work on the topic, Ke et al. (2018) explore how to assess different aspects of student essays to which to potentially give feedback. In particular, they propose a bi-directional LSTM with attention that jointly predicts the persuasive effectiveness of an argument in an essay as well as different mostly numerical attributes of argument components: specificity, eloquence, evidence, logos/ethos/pathos, the claim type, the premise type, and the component's strength. However, their approach does not actually give feedback itself. More recently, Liu et al. (2025) build on methods such as those on revision need identification above in an automated feedback system for student essays. The system provides 10 levels of revision feedback, four for describing the need for more evidence and three each on the need for more specific details and the need for more explanation, respectively. The authors carried out an extensive study with 406 students, consistently suggesting that the feedback provided affects the quality of essays positively.

Quality Optimization The first NLP approach that actually improves the quality of argumentative content comes from Skitalinskaya et al. (2023). Given a claim potentially along with context information, the task is to optimize the claim in terms of text and argument quality, while preserving the meaning as far as possible. As illustrated in Fig. 7.12, their approach proceeds in two main steps:

1. *Candidate Generation*. First, a language model rewrites the original claim into n candidate optimizations. For rewriting, Skitalinskaya et al. fine-tune BART on their claim revision data (Skitalinskaya et al. 2021). To increase diversity, their approach uses top-k sampling (Fan et al. 2018) to create $n = 10$ candidates.
2. *Candidate Reranking*. Then, a ranking model identifies the best among the candidates. For ranking, Skitalinskaya et al. learn a weighting of scores for three quality aspects: grammatical fluency, meaning preservation, and argument quality. For the latter, the

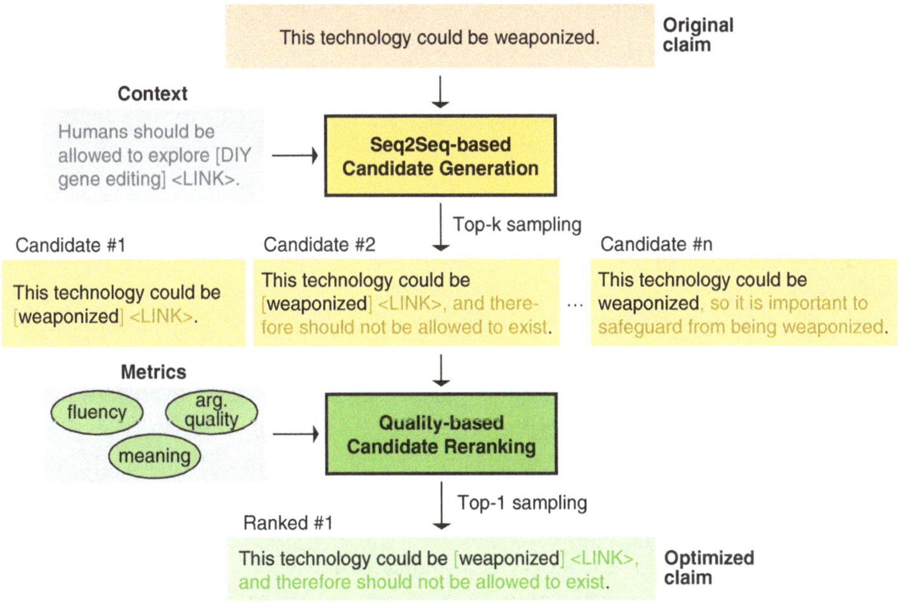

Fig. 7.12 Illustration of the claim optimization approach of Skitalinskaya et al. (2023): *n* candidates are generated from the original claim and context, using top-*k* sampling. The optimized claim is then selected based on quality metrics. Licensed under CC-BY 4.0 International

authors use the probabilities computed by their model from Skitalinskaya et al. summarized above. On the validation set, however, the best weighting basically discards meaning preservation (weight 0.01), while argument quality gets a slightly higher weight (0.56) than fluency (0.43).

In human evaluation on 600 test cases, the approach clearly improves over maximum likelihood generation and random sampling, and is also better than the authors' SVMRank method (Skitalinskaya et al. 2021). In a manual analysis of all 600 revisions, Skitalinskaya et al. (2023) identify eight types of optimizations: specification, simplification, reframing, elaboration, corroboration, neutralization, disambiguation, and copy editing. They find that their approach improves 60% of all claims and maintains quality for further 24%. A better *specification* of claims seems easier (65% improved), a *corroboration* by further evidence somewhat harder (53% improved). The following example compares how humans and the approach revise a claim on the censoring of Mark Twain's use of the N-word in Huckleberry Finn:

(7.5) *Original claim:* In Huckleberry Finn, Twain captured the essence of "[everyday midwest American English]<LINK>".

Human optimization (specification): In Huckleberry Finn, Twain captured the essence of "[everyday midwest American English]<LINK>". This quality makes it still relevant and worth teaching in the school system.
Approach optimization (elaboration): In Huckleberry Finn, Twain captured the essence of "[everyday midwest American English]<LINK>" by using the N-word in everyday conversation.

Building on the instruction-following capabilities of LLMs, El Baff et al. (2024) explore how to rewrite arguments to make them effective for readers of a specific ideology (American conservatives vs. liberals in particular). On arguments derived from the debate corpus of Durmus and Cardie (2019), the authors compare zero-shot and one-shot prompting to activation-based steering, that is, adjusting specific layer activations of an LLM to ideology-specific texts (Konen et al. 2024). According to automatic evaluation, all prompting methods improve arguments for liberals for both GPT-3.5 and Llama-2-7b; however, they rather reduce effectiveness (predicted with a trained classifier) for conservatives. Zero-shot prompting worked best for GPT-3.5, whereas steering created the top-scored rewrites for Llama-2-7b. In human evaluation, conservative evaluators preferred the original arguments in only 3% of the cases, liberals in only 8% (on average, the two LLMs were more on less on par). This suggests that LLM-based rewriting tends to be useful for optimizing arguments.

More targeted, Ziegenbein et al. (2024) study how to optimize the appropriateness of arguments. We detail their reinforcement learning approach to argument rewriting in Chap. 9. In a nutshell, the approach aligns the rewriting behavior of an instruction fine-tuned LLM. A reward model guides the LLM to achieve appropriateness while preserving semantic similarity. In experiments, Ziegenbein et al. evaluate different weightings of the two aspects, from prioritizing similarity to a full focus on appropriateness. They observe that the LLM (Llama 7B) adjusts arguments very well in line with the weighting. On 225 argument rewrites, human judges ranked the arguments with full appropriateness best, even better than expert rewrites. The experts achieved a strong balance between similarity and appropriateness, though.

Wang et al. (2025d) adapt the alignment method of Ziegenbein et al. (2024) to claim optimization (Skitalinskaya et al. 2023). The authors train a clarity scoring algorithm on a subset of the Kialo corpus of Skitalinskaya et al. (2021) and quantify meaning changes using Sentence-BERT cosine similarity. They evaluate the alignment method against supervised fine-tuning on claim-revision pairs as well as against zero-shot and few-shot prompting, all for three different 7B LLMs: Llama 2, Mistral (Jiang et al. 2023), and Qwen (Yang et al. 2024). On the Kialo data, the alignment method wins across models for most automatic measures (including a new sliding window-based metric). Depending on the LLM, it improves claims in 84.6–85.6% of all cases according to a ChatGPT-based judge. However, supervised fine-tuning comes close (83.3–85.4%), whereas the prompting methods fall far behind.

7.4 Summary

Whereas the first decade of NLP research on argumentation was primarily devoted to argument mining and perspective assessment, argument quality assessment is meanwhile studied similarly extensively. Not least, this is because of the pervasive importance of distinguishing good from bad arguments for nearly any technology that deals with arguments in practice. A reliable quality assessment depends on many factors, from the perspective of quality considered, to the argumentative genre tackled, to the way subjectiveness in quality perception is treated.

In this chapter, we have discussed how to *model quality* of arguments and how to *handle subjectivity* as part of the modeling. We have further surveyed several NLP approaches to *assessing quality* computationally along with the few that even aim to *improve quality*. For each of these aspects, we now shortly recap the state of the art discussed above to give a brief outlook on what is to come on this basis:

Modeling Quality Diverse dimensions of logical, rhetorical, and dialectical argument quality have been proposed that capture notions at different levels of granularity, from the acceptability of single premises to who argues more effectively in a dialogical debate. While further dimensions continue to come up, the general concept of argument quality has reached some common ground in the NLP community. For any dimension, arguments may be assessed absolutely on some scale or relatively to each other. What dimension to focus on, depends on the application: In writing support, for example, several logical and rhetorical quality dimensions are relevant. For discussions targeting agreement, a focus on dialectical quality may be preferable. Nevertheless, it is important to be aware that different quality dimensions may affect each other. In a position paper on state-of-the-art LLMs, Wachsmuth et al. (2024) hence propose to instruct them about quality dimensions and their interaction.

Handling Subjectivity Argument quality is inherently subjective, that is, humans perceive arguments differently, depending on their background, value system, and preconceived opinions. They may also be affected by *who* states an argument and in *what* situational context. Any computational approach to quality assessment should thus account for subjectiveness, be it by modeling the target audience as part of the assessment, by handling different perspectives explicitly, or simply by focusing a on specific audience. This is done only partially so far, and even then often only for Western-centric perspectives on English-language corpora, in line with general shortcomings of NLP research. Wachsmuth et al. (2024) stress that the shift to LLMs opens up new opportunities in this regard, by specifying context factors such as the audience in the prompt and by teaching LLMs systematically to deal with them.

Evaluating Quality The diversity and subjectivity of argument quality pose challenges for evaluation. This already becomes apparent in the many (largely English-language) argument quality datasets with limited inter-annotator agreement. Some studies we have reviewed above also suggest that quality dimensions may be conflated in ground-truth annotations, as further supported by differences between automatic and human judgments. A reliable evaluation needs to carefully model the quality dimensions considered, the target audience, and similar. New benchmarks that account for such aspects may be needed. However, a fully unified evaluation procedure may be infeasible, as it depends on the information available in a given setting.

Assessing Quality The spectrum of NLP techniques used for assessment that we have covered in this chapter is broad, ranging from standard supervised classification and regression, to Bayesian preference learning and graph-based analyses, to the fine-tuning, alignment, and prompting of language models. What technique to use, particularly depends on the available training data and the type of desired output. At the core of their position, Wachsmuth et al. (2024) state that existing approaches do not yet fully exploit the capabilities of state-of-the-art LLMs to push research forward on this task. In particular, the authors argue that the extensive literature on argumentation theory, along with the variety of available argument quality corpora, provide a strong basis to make LLMs experts in a reliable assessment of argument quality. We expect more research in this direction to follow soon.

Improving Quality So far, NLP research on argument quality only sporadically goes beyond assessment to actually improve quality. However, the general advancements in NLP research in the context of transformers and instruction-following LLMs have enabled strong text production and rewriting capabilities that can be well-exploited to automatically optimize arguments or to provide improvement suggestions to human users. We have summarized the few existing approaches to these tasks above, but also here it is likely that more is to come in the near future.

Overall, this chapter has aimed to comprehensively show both the potential and the complexity of NLP research on argument quality as well as its close connection to argumentation theory. The improvement of arguments further emphasizes that this research is not restricted to analysis tasks, but may also involve synthesis tasks—that provide new opportunities as well as additional challenges. We come back to both in Chap. 9, where we see how improving quality relates to other tasks in argument generation. Before, we look at argument *reasoning*, though, which involves elements of both assessment and generation, and goes down to the core of argumentation.

Argument Reasoning

8

Reasoning is the heart of argumentation—so much that some researchers might equate the terms *reasoning* and *argumentation* (Walton 1990). This is because, conceptually, an argument manifests a reasoning process (or process step) in natural language: the relation that it defines from one or more premises to a conclusion instantiates the act of giving a reason, or reasons, to support a claim. In a broader sense, though, argumentation comprises more than just reasoning. As the previous chapters on perspective and quality assessment have emphasized, subjective viewpoints and perceptions are inherent to argumentation, and rhetoric and dialectic are important in any real-world argumentation setting. Thus, reasoning can be understood as the part of argumentation that describes how people infer new (or hidden) information from given information through the use or exchange of arguments (Mercier and Sperber 2011). As such, reasoning is where the NLP tasks of analysis and synthesis meet. In this chapter, we discuss some main strands of NLP research that model key aspects of reasoning, given previously mined or otherwise structured arguments.

We note upfront that the recent breakthroughs on large language models (LLMs) have led to a (controversial) uptick in the use of the term *reasoning* in NLP. This term is overapplied with multiple ideas conflated: not everything termed reasoning nowadays in research has much to do with reasoning, not even the latest generation of 'reasoning-enhanced' LLMs (Guo et al. 2025). Even within argumentation, researchers refer to various aspects as reasoning, leading to a scattered view of what falls under the notion of *argument reasoning* (Lauscher et al. 2022). Towards a common denominator, we focus on three families of NLP tasks in the following that target a deeper understanding of the reasoning happening in arguments: identifying reasoning patterns, detecting fallacies, and reconstructing enthymemes.

In Sect. 8.1, we begin with the most common categorization of argument reasoning patterns, *argumentation schemes* (Walton 2008b; Rigotti and Greco Morasso 2010),

M. Stede et al., *Argument Mining*, Synthesis Lectures on Human Language Technologies, https://doi.org/10.1007/978-3-032-32291-3_8

whose basics we have already presented in Chap. 3. We discuss their identification with computational methods as well as their use in downstream tasks. As implied by the critical questions coming with each scheme, a scheme application may be failed or deceptive, which leads to the notion of *fallacies* (Hamblin 1970), originating in Aristotle's work on *Sophistical Refutations* (Aristotle ca. 350 B.C.E./ translated 1984). The detection of fallacious arguments is challenging, but has recently sparked increased interest (Sect. 8.2). Finally, we consider the reconstruction of implicit parts of arguments in Sect. 8.3, particularly evolving around *enthymemes*. Also originating with Aristotle (ca. 350 B.C.E./ translated 2007), this concept amounts to the (logically) missing premises (and, more broadly, also missing conclusions) needed for an argument to make sense.

8.1 Identifying Reasoning Patterns

Several times in this book we were concerned with assigning *types* to arguments or to their components. In Chap. 1, for example, we gave three types of what one can reasonably argue *for* (epistemic, ethical/aesthetical, and deontic arguments). Chapter 4 echoed these by three popular subtypes of claims (fact, value, and policy) used as conclusions in arguments, and it compared various proposals for typing premises. In this section, we move to the relation between premises and conclusion: On what 'grounds' does the conclusion become credible in the presence of the premises? The theory of argumentation schemes posits that there is, again, a set of categories that can characterize the underlying reasoning patterns that explain why (or why not) a particular constellation of inference works.

In the following, we give an overview of two specific reasoning pattern theories and their application in human annotation studies, before we discuss work on automatically detecting the schemes underlying the arguments in text. Then, we mention some applications that make use of scheme information.

8.1.1 Theory and Annotation Studies

Argumentation schemes are conventionalized or otherwise stereotypical patterns of reasoning that explain the plausibility of the relationship between premises and conclusions. Long studied in argumentation theory, this line of research has also been taken up by the argument mining community. A few different categorizations exist, each with their pros and cons. We look here specifically at *Walton's argumentation schemes*, as it has been most widely used in NLP, but we also cover the *argumentum model of topic*, and some *other schemes*.

Walton's Argumentation Schemes A catalogue of formalized reasoning patterns that became influential for argument mining is presented by Walton et al. (2008) who identify

65 distinct schemes. We already showed an example scheme earlier in Chap. 3. For illustration, we here reproduce one further scheme (p. 332):

Argument from Positive Consequences

Premise: If *A* is brought about, good consequences will plausibly occur.
Conclusion: *A* should be brought about.

An analogous scheme is formulated for the *argument from negative consequences* (negative consequences will plausibly occur; *A* should not be brought about.

Most schemes are abductive, reflect defeasible reasoning, but also deductive and inductive schemes exist. Each scheme comes with a small set of hand-defined (and often scheme-specific) *critical questions*. Assuming a (virtual) dialogue between proponent and opponent, the role of critical questions is as follows: When the proponent makes an argument of a specific scheme, the opponent may ask any critical question. Doing so diminishes the presumptive weight of the argument, until the proponent supplies an acceptable answer to the question. The argument from positive consequences has three critical questions:

Critical Questions of the Argument from Positive Consequences

1. How strong is the likelihood that the cited consequences will (may, must) occur?
2. What evidence supports the claim that the cited consequences will (may, must) occur, and is it sufficient to support the strength of the claim adequately?
3. Are there other opposite consequences (bad as opposed to good, for example) that should be taken into account?

The scheme catalogue is a structured taxonomy, not a loose list. Walton and Macagno (2015) discuss the motivation of the various dimensions that lead to such classifications and propose the taxonomy shown in Fig. 8.1 (though the authors note that it is not meant to be complete). A comprehensive explanation would exceed the space here, but the topmost division marks whether an argument is *source-based* (the support stems from the credibility of the person or entity who provides the opinion) or *not source-based* (the support stems from the subject matter or the reasoning). The argument from positive consequences, listed above, is a subtype of the class shown in the second row from the top.

An early corpus annotated with scheme information of this kind is AraucariaDB (Reed et al. 2008). It consists of 658 individual arguments (not complete texts) that were gathered from newspaper editorials, parliamentary records, judicial summaries, and online discussions. The authors note that scheme distribution varies somewhat between the genres; we will return to the corpus in the next subsection.

Reisert et al. (2018) start out from the Walton's schemes, but they propose a more fine-grained account of the logical reasoning, centering on just a single scheme. They analyze 90 texts from Part 1 of the AMT corpus (Peldszus and Stede 2016b), where the vast majority of conclusions are of type *policy* (see Chap. 4). The authors find that the most common argumentation scheme is that of positive/negative consequences (shown above).

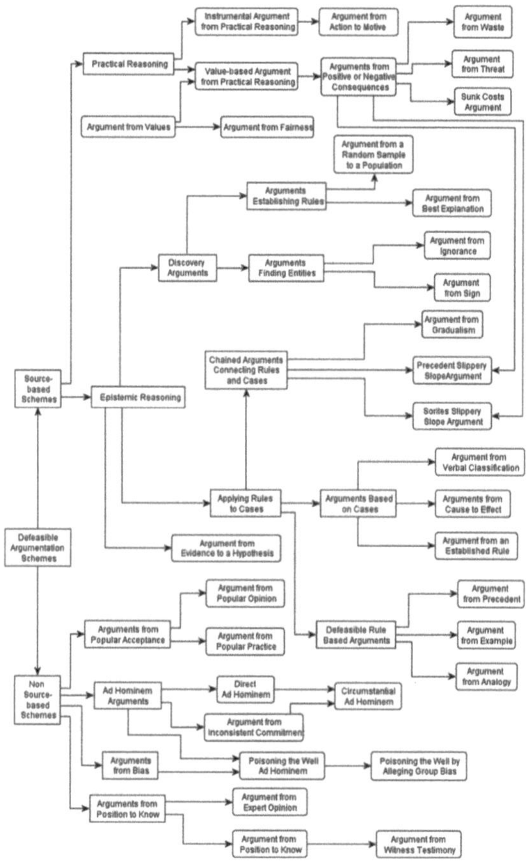

Fig. 8.1 Taxonomy of *source-based* and *non source-based* argumentation schemes proposed by Walton and Macagno (2015, p. 241). Used with permission

For this scheme, the authors create a set of 'argument templates' for support and attack relations. They used 20 texts to induce the template set, while the others were the basis for the subsequent annotation study. Figure 8.2 shows eight templates from the set. For example, the 'support' template AT-S_1 states:

> S_t, the target segment, implies/states that x, an entity/event, is GOOD and should be brought about. S_s, the source segment, implies/states that x is GOOD, because when x exists/happens (or existed/happened), y, a GOOD entity/event, will be (or was) PROMOTED (or NOT SUPPRESSED).

To illustrate the application of a template, AT-S_3 matches the support relation in the following example from the corpus. x is instantiated with "charge tuition fees" (BAD), and y with "right to education" (GOOD):

(8.1) S_1: German universities should not charge tuition fees.
S_2: Every German citizen has a right to education.

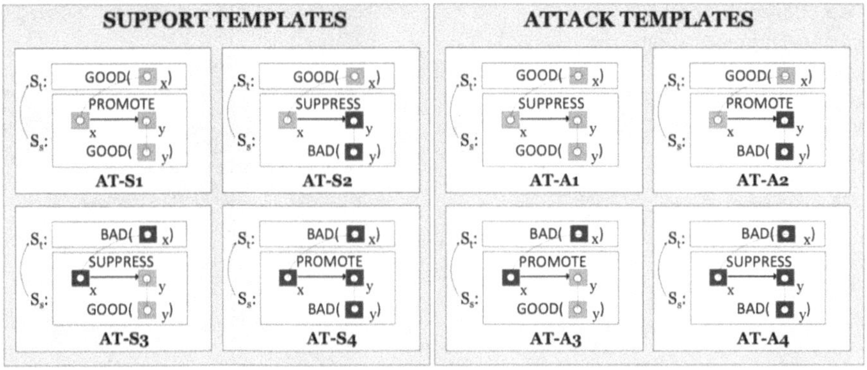

Fig. 8.2 Eight argument templates proposed by Reisert et al. (2018, p. 82) for the argument from consequences scheme, for each for support and attack.

For better coverage of the corpus texts, Reisert et al. define four additional template types besides *support* and *attack*. In their annotation study, two annotators labeled all 270 argumentative relations in the test set by selecting a template (if they found an appropriate one) and filling the slots with excerpts from the text. To deal with semantically-compatible but textually-different instantiations, they were afterwards asked as to whether they considered the other analysis as 'agreeable'. This led to an overall Cohen κ agreement of 0.80. The coverage of the template set was 74.6%; that is, for the other relations in the corpus, annotators could not identify a suitable template. Reisert et al. also sketch an implementation of automatic template instantiation, which however revealed the task to be quite difficult (best F_1 was 0.38).

Turning to the practicalities of the annotation task, Lawrence et al. (2019) present a decision tree rooted in the source/non-source dichotomy, which leads the annotator through a series of questions toward assigning a scheme; this process is called *argument scheme key (ASK)*. The procedure is implemented as an extension to the OVA annotation tool (see Chap. 10), which now smoothly integrates the labeling of argument components and relations with the scheme information. Visser et al. (2021) used it to annotate a part of the US2016 corpus of televised presidential debates, which we have described in Chap. 5. Adding to the existing annotations with the *inference anchoring theory* (see Chap. 3), they labeled both Walton's schemes and the 'periodic table of arguments' (see Chap. 3) in order to discuss and compare the respective annotation practices. For the Walton's schemes, they report an inter-annotator agreement of 0.72 in terms of Cohen κ.

Bezou-Vrakatseli et al. (2024) hand-picked 22 debates from kialo.com, which all deal with ethics-related topics. The authors extracted a subset of arguments from each debate. Following critical questions, they added implicit components where necessary—which was the case in more than half of the arguments. For example, in a debate on the topic "Should abortion be legal", they encountered the statement "Access to legal abortion improves the health and safety of pregnant people." To turn this into a complete argument,

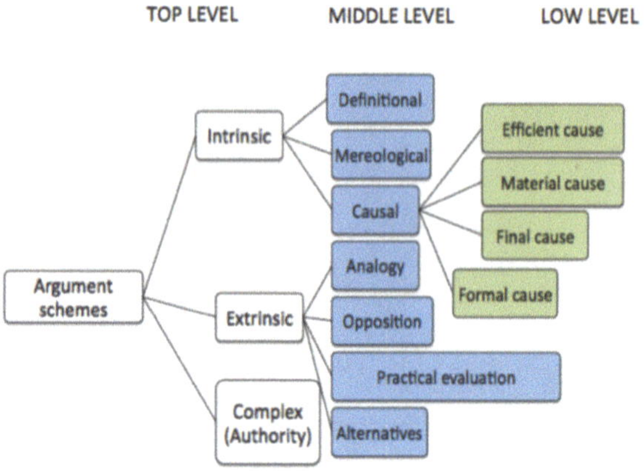

Fig. 8.3 Illustration of the taxonomy of argumentation schemes in the *Argumentum Model of Topics* (Musi et al. 2018, p. 1630). Used with permission

they spelled out the implicit claim, extending the statement by "...so pregnant people should have the right to choose abortion." Then, the authors annotated Walton's schemes using the aforementioned ASK (Lawrence et al. 2019), determining $\kappa = 0.52$ and finding two schemes to be particularly difficult for agreement: the *argument from cause to effect* and the *argument from alternatives*. They hypothesize that this is due to causality being difficult to distinguish from the presence of general argumentative reasoning on the one hand, and to alternatives often not being mutually exclusive on the other. The final corpus contains 686 arguments, annotated for eight different schemes, all of which occur at least 50 times.

The availability of corpora was further improved by Ruiz-Dolz et al. (2024). As we have detailed in Chap. 3, the authors used GPT-3.5 and GPT-4 to generate a bilingual corpus of 1893 textbook-like arguments in English and 1917 in Spanish that match 20 different Walton's schemes. Moreover, Ruiz-Dolz et al. (2025) introduce QT-Schemes, a corpus of 441 arguments from BBC political debates, annotated for 24 argumentation schemes by two experts that used Walton's descriptions as the main annotation guidelines. They obtained an agreement of $\kappa = 0.39$, again underlining the complexity of the task. To account for the fair agreement, the authors followed Walton and Macagno (2015) in grouping arguments according to their scheme 'families'.

Argumentum Model of Topics We presented the argumentum model of topics by Rigotti and Greco Morasso (2010) in Chap. 3. The scheme set of this model is much smaller, as Fig. 8.3 shows, and each scheme is accompanied by a set of inferential rules, as we will illustrate.

Musi et al. (2016) developed a first version of annotation guidelines, where the definitions refer to semantic properties of the participating entities rather than to the logical inference steps. They applied the approach to 30 texts from the AAE1 corpus of Stab and Gurevych (2014a). The authors report a low Fleiss κ of 0.10, but the study involved nine, only lightly-trained annotators. In a subsequent study (Musi et al. 2018), 40 texts from the AMT corpus were annotated in two steps: First, a scheme was selected from the middle level of the taxonomy, with the help of identification questions and additional information given in the annotation guidelines; and, second, one of the inference rules associated with the scheme was chosen. In the experiment, three annotators reached a Fleiss κ agreement of at least 0.30. The *practical evaluation* scheme proved to be one that often causes disagreement, being confused easily with *causal* or with *none*, that is, the absence of any scheme.

Other Schemes The approaches discussed above were designed with no specific domain or genre in mind, and thus aimed for wide applicability. Yet, this is not the only way of approaching the notion of argumentation schemes. We mention here the work of Green (2015) who studies scientific papers. Finding the schemes from the 'standard approaches' not to be directly applicable to her data, she devised 10 schemes on her own, which she determined to represent the major forms of argumentation for scientific claims in four papers from the genetics domain. Here are two examples (Green 2015, p. 18):

Failed to Observe Expected Cause

- *Premise:* G is missing from one or more individuals with property P.
- *Premise:* G may be a cause of P in some cases.
- *Conclusion:* G is not likely the cause of P in this case.
- Example: "We screened 24 unrelated affected Belgian and Dutch individuals with a moderate to severe hearing loss for mutations in CABP2 (...), but we could not identify a clear damaging mutation in any of them."

Failed Predicted Effect

- *Premise:* G was (previously considered to be) a candidate cause of P in some individuals.
- *Premise:* G is not predicted to have effect P.
- *Conclusion:* G may not be a cause of P.
- Example: "The second was a heterozygous missense variant (...) in exon 2 of PPM1K (...) on chromosome 4. It was not predicted to be damaging by MutationTaster, SIFT, or PolyPhen-2."

To evaluate the devised schemes in a pilot study, Green worked with 30 subjects and determined to what extent schemes were recognized, by means of test questions that had to be answered. Subsequently, a second pilot study (Green 2017a) tested whether six participants from biology and computer science research could consistently apply five common schemes, this time defined contextually with genetics-specific concepts. Green (2018) then presents an initial investigation of the automatic application of these schemes, in combination with semantic types such as genes, mutations, proteins, and phenotypes, as they can be detected by generic BioNLP tools.

8.1.2 Classifying Argumentation Schemes

In the early years of argument mining, identifying the reasoning patterns *underlying* the arguments found in text must have seemed like a relatively daunting task, but nonetheless *feature-based approaches* date back to 2011. Even with *LLM-based approaches* getting the most attention in the NLP field these days, only a few approaches to this task exist, possibly due to the relative scarcity of scheme-annotated corpora. Recently, researchers have started to intensify research on the task, though.

Feature-Based Approaches Feng and Hirst (2011) tackle the problem of automatically assigning one of the five most frequent schemes from Walton et al. (2008) to pairs of premise and conclusion (whose types are assumed as given already) taken from the AraucariaDB data (Reed et al. 2008): *argument from example*, *argument from cause to effect*, *argument from consequences*, *argument from verbal classification*, and *practical reasoning*. The approach uses positional features (absolute and relative, for premise and conclusion), length of the two components, the number of premises, as well as some scheme-specific features (largely cue phrases). In a separate experiment, the authors also measure the impact of additionally specifying the type of argumentation structure (linked vs. convergent) to the classifier. In one-against-others classification via a C4.5 decision tree, their approach produced rather promising results: For two schemes, the accuracy was above 90%, while for the other three the results ranged between 63% and 70%. Adding the linked/convergent feature generally helped, and most dramatically for arguments from example.

In an experiment on AIFdb data of Lawrence et al. (2012) (which includes the AraucariaDB), Lawrence and Reed (2016) also classify the presence of a scheme. In addition, they study the identification of scheme components (premise, conclusion) by means of similar features as those of Feng and Hirst (2011). Here, the F_1-score results vary widely between schemes and between classifiers (Naïve Bayes, SVM, Decision Tree), ranging from 0.57 to 0.91. One reason for the effectiveness differences across schemes is their varying tendency for overt linguistic marking: some co-occur often with particular connectives (e.g., "for example") or other expressions relatively often, while others do not.

From the perspective of essay scoring, Song et al. (2014) are interested in exploring the relationship between writers' use of scheme-relevant critical questions and essay quality. The authors found the scheme definitions by Walton (2008b) partly ambiguous and thus made modifications; ultimately, their study centered on their account of three schemes: *policy*, *causal*, and *sample*. We reproduce here the four critical questions that were used for one scheme:

Causal

- *Causal Mechanism:* Is there really a correlation [between events]? Is the correlation merely a coincidence (invalid causal relationship)? Are there alternative causal factors?

- *Causal Efficacy:* Is the causal mechanism strong enough to produce the desired effects?
- *Applicability:* Does this causal mechanism apply?
- *Intervening Factors:* Are there intervening factors that could undermine the causal mechanism?

The authors see references to critical questions as a positive feature. Accordingly, they approach the task of determining whether or not a sentence has such references. For each of two given writing prompts, 300 essays were manually annotated (260 for training, 40 for testing). Their approach employs a logistic regression classifier using n-gram, positional, and part-of-speech features, as well as lexical overlap between the sentence and the prompt. The crucial question for practical relevance is how well the model can generalize across prompts. When training and testing on data including both prompts, the system reached a Cohen's κ of 0.44 with the ground truth, but when training on one and testing on the other, the average was only 0.26.

LLM-Based Approaches On their dataset of ethics-related kialo.com arguments described above, Bezou-Vrakatseli et al. (2024) fine-tuned six pretrained language models. They found ERNIE (Zhang et al. 2019) to notably outperform BERT (Devlin et al. 2019), RoBERTa (Liu et al. 2019b), and others, achieving a macro-F_1 score of 0.63 when training and testing on the same topic. The *argument from expert opinion* was the most difficult to classify. The authors also ran cross-topic classification, where the macro-F_1 score for ERNIE (still the best model) dropped to 0.52.

In follow-up work, Bezou-Vrakatseli et al. (2025) systematically evaluate to what extent LLMs can classify the Walton's schemes on the data of both Ruiz-Dolz et al. (2024) and Bezou-Vrakatseli et al. (2024). They consider two open-weight and five closed-source LLMs of different size in zero-shot and few-shot prompting, with four different prompting variations: a *standard* prompt asking for the scheme, a prompt with *definitions* of the schemes, a prompt with LLM-generated scheme *descriptions*, and *chain-of-thought* (Wei et al. 2022) and giving scheme definitions. On the textbook-like arguments of Ruiz-Dolz et al. (2024), OpenAI's GPT-4o and Google's Gemini-1.5 achieve a perfect macro F_1-score in few-shot prompting (with standard or definition prompts) and still 0.99 in zero-shot prompting. On the different subsets data of Bezou-Vrakatseli et al. (2024), Anthropic's Claude-3.5 consistently performed best with a maximum macro F_1-score of 0.72 (with standard or description prompt). Among the two open-weight models, Mistral (Jiang et al. 2023) and Llama-3.2 (Touvron et al. 2023a), Mistral turned out stronger with values of 0.91 and 0.60 in the respective settings (both with chain-of-thought prompting).

8.1.3 Utilizing Argumentation Schemes

We close this section with an outline of a few areas of investigation where argumentation schemes fruitfully contribute to other research questions: *legal reasoning*, *educational contexts*, and *Wikipedia discussions*.

Legal Reasoning The application of argumentation schemes to legal procedures is a topic in the early survey on argument mining by Mochales Palau and Moens (2011). The authors establish mining techniques on the corpus of texts from the European Court of Human Rights (see Chap. 4). In the survey, they point out the importance of schemes as part of their definition of argument, though they do not yet tackle that particular task in their approach at the time.

In the argumentation community, the relationships between schemes and legal reasoning practices has received a lot of attention. As an example, we mention here the work of Bench-Capon and Atkinson (2022). The authors sketch the process of deciding a legal case as going through four stages, at which different reasoning styles are appropriate and where, accordingly, different argumentation schemes can be formulated to explain them. The key task is to determine whether certain terms of the law apply to the given case, which gives rise to a set of so-called *issues*. Resolving these is done on the grounds of *factors*, whose applicability is in turned governed by the previously-established *facts*. In chronological order, the stages are:

1. *Establishing Facts.* Given evidence, this stage clarifies 'what has happened' and provides the basis for the following steps. Here, the type of reasoning is not specific to the legal domain; it is therefore not addressed further by the authors.
2. *Ascribing Factors.* Given the facts, factors do not follow straightforwardly from facts. For example, when an accident happened at a public event, the organizer probably has taken security measures; but whether these have been 'adequate' (a factor) depends in part on what is considered as reasonable. The authors propose four applicable schemes, including one of *analogy*, which relates the situation to a similar one in a precedent case.
3. *Resolving the Issues.* Given the factors, one of the three schemes is the *knockout factor* scheme, which formalizes the situation where the preference for resolving an issue is obvious from the nature of the factors (and thus the situation does not need a precedence for resolving the issue).
4. *Deciding the Outcome.* Once the issues are resolved, they can form the leaves of a tree representing a logical model using the law represented as a set of rules. Here, standard reasoning applies, captured by a single straightforward scheme:

   Issue to Outcome

   - *Warrant Premise:* The law yields a rule $R : I_1, I_2, \ldots, I_n \rightarrow O$
   - *Issue Premise:* $I_1, I_2, \ldots, I_n$ are (not) satisfied
   - *Conclusion:* Outcome is (not) O

The scheme comes with three critical questions. As an example, we mention one that describes exceptions (where the argument is for O): "Is there an issue I_{n+1} which is satisfied and which provides an exception to R?" The authors hint at the possibility that the stage model is actually not restricted to legal proceedings but may apply to some domains of 'everyday reasoning', too.

Educational Contexts Not surprisingly, the adherence to argumentation schemes is often regarded as a feature of 'good' thinking, writing, and speaking, which is why they are studied as tools for education. In addition to the study of essay scoring by Song et al. (2014) that we detailed above, we mention two further examples here.

Macagno and Konstantinidou (2013) propose to employ schemes as didactic tools to convey knowledge. The authors discuss the role of belief change in science education and point out that introducing new concepts should not be regarded as simply replacing students' prior beliefs by new ideas. On the contrary, the prior understanding forms the ground of the teacher's arguments, which aim to lead the students to regard the new ideas as more convincing. The hypothesis is that argumentation schemes, due to their capacity for outlining the structure of implicit elements, can provide a transparent reconstruction of the hidden premises. Specifically, the authors conducted a case study using two schemes (*from cause to effect* and *from analogy*) to reconstruct the argumentative processes in a physics class.

Educational discourse is also studied by Anthony and Kim (2015) who selected nine schemes from Walton et al. (2008) for analyzing informal (oral) interactions on socioscientific issues among volunteer teacher education students. The authors illustrate in detail how they adapted the schemes to spoken conversation. They observe that the original scheme definitions are not straightforwardly applicable to their setting and that the purported universality of the schemes may have limits. An important observation is that interactions among classmates are of a specific kind where conflicts about standpoints are being deflected not necessarily via deliberative reasoning. Instead, students "were being successful by preferring schemes that serve to sustain a positive interactional relationship" (p. 107)—a dimension that is largely absent in the kinds of legal or political argumentation that the Walton's schemes have most often been applied to. Anthony and Kim conclude that the nine adapted schemes are sufficient to capture the arguing behavior in their setting, and that increasing the set would likely exacerbate the problem of ambiguities in the definitions.

Wikipedia Discussions Finally, we summarize the study of Schneider et al. (2013b) who use the scheme catalogue of Walton et al. (2008) to label 741 messages from 72 talk pages on Wikipedia (each discusses whether its associated Wikipedia article should be deleted). In a first annotation phase, the authors found 17 schemes to be applicable to this data. Then, two annotators labeled the arguments in each message for schemes ($\kappa = 0.48$). The most common schemes in the resulting corpus of 1213 arguments are shown in Fig. 8.4. The distribution reflects the focus on precedent and rules typical for the given genre as

More often given by	Can be prob.	Argumentation Scheme	Full corpus 72 debates (novices & experts)	Subcorpus 28 debates (novices & experts)	Subcorpus 28 debates (novices only)	χ^2	Sig. level
		Argument from Evidence to Hypothesis	19.29%	20.65%	21.51%		
		Argument from Rules	16.90%	18.66%	12.90%		
Experts		**Note**	**13.69%**	**10.14%**	**0.00%**	χ^2=3.66	p < .05
Novices	⚠	**Argumentation from Values**	**4.20%**	**4.17%**	**9.68%**	χ^2=5.13	p < .05
		Argument from Need for Help	4.12%	3.62%	2.15%		
		Argument from Bias	3.87%	4.53%	6.45%		
		No reason given	3.22%	3.62%	5.38%		
		Argument from Position to Know	3.05%	2.36%	4.30%		
Experts		**Argument from Precedent**	**3.05%**	**3.80%**	**0.00%**	χ^2=3.66	p < .1
	⚠	Argument from Ignorance	2.97%	3.08%	4.30%		
		Argument from Composition	2.56%	2.54%	2.15%		
Novices	⚠	**Argument from Cause to Effect**	**2.31%**	**2.72%**	**7.53%**	χ^2=5.59	p < .02
Novices	⚠	**Argument from Analogy**	**2.23%**	**2.36%**	**8.60%**	χ^2=9.86	p < .05
	⚠	Argument from Waste	2.23%	2.54%	1.08%		
	⚠	Practical Reasoning	2.23%	2.72%	3.23%		
		Arg. from Verbal Classification	2.06%	1.45%	2.15%		

Fig. 8.4 Distribution of the argumentation schemes included in the Wikipedia deletion discussion corpus of Schneider et al. (2013b, p. 28). Used with permission

well as a tendency to discuss Wikipedia articles in terms of values and community norms. The figure also shows differences in scheme usage between novice and expert participants. Generally, the study suggests that the most prevalent schemes are *Rules* and *Evidence to Hypothesis* (36% of the arguments), and that familiarity with community norms correlates with the novices' ability to craft persuasive arguments. Regarding the success of arguments in a discussion, the authors find that successful arguments tend to use rhetoric in line with the policies and values established in the community. Unsuccessful arguments are mostly based on personal preference or on inappropriate analogy to other cases.

8.2 Detecting Reasoning Flaws

Argumentation schemes define valid or plausible ways of reasoning, even if not always logically strong or rhetorically effective ones. According to the idea of critical questions (Walton 2008b), however, arguments may also fail to apply an argumentation scheme correctly, or they may even do so deceptively (i.e., on purpose). We speak of *fallacious arguments* in this case or just of *fallacies*. A fallacy is an argument with some (often hidden) flaw in its reasoning (Tindale 2007). Detecting such flaws can be seen as alternative approach to argument quality assessment (see Chap. 7), defining a good argument as one that is not fallacious (Hamblin 1970). While various types of fallacies exist and have been studied for millenia (Aristotle ca. 350 B.C.E./ translated 1984), few works from the early NLP research on argumentation deal with fallacies. The reason lies not only in the lack of ground-truth data, but also in the complexity of distinguishing good arguments from fallacies, as we exemplify below. With the rise of LLMs, however, in the last few years an increasing amount of work has investigated detecting and classifying fallacies.

In the following, we first briefly review part of the theory of fallacies along with case studies from practice. Then, we subsequently present computational approaches to the detection of specific types of fallacies, such as *ad-hominem arguments*, and to the classification of arguments into one of various fallacy types.

8.2.1 Theory and Annotation Studies

As a basis for the discussion of NLP research on fallacies, we here discuss the notion of *fallacies in theory* as well as some *case studies on fallacies*.

Fallacies in Theory Some of the earliest work on fallacies developed within the logic tradition of India from the *Nyāya Sūtra* (Lloyd 2007), discussing forms of faulty reasoning in the context of controversies. In the Western hemisphere, the study of fallacies independently began with Aristotle's work on *Sophistical Refutations* (Aristotle ca. 350 B.C.E./ translated 1984). Aristotle distinguishes 13 principal types of fallacies, six of which arise from the ambiguity of language and seven types that may even be present in perfectly clear language. An example fallacy type related to ambiguity is the *fallacy of equivocation*, that is, an argument that shifts the meaning of terms, concepts, or phrases during the process of arguing. Here is an example fallacy on the relationship between aging drivers and dementia, borrowed from Tindale (2007) whose treatment of fallacies we discuss below:

(8.2) Your claims about an increase of aging drivers with dementia fan the flames against older motorists. [...] You give the impression of a multitude of safe, younger drivers inundated by a growing minority of demented seniors at the wheel. The risk is worse because the signs of dementia "are so subtle." Anyone driving in a major city today does not have to look hard to find signs of demented drivers, but few of these are aged, and the indications are not so subtle. We have young and middle-aged (rarely old) drivers chatting obliviously on cellphones as they perilously negotiate crowded streets at hazardous speeds, we have the mid-30s executive in his/her SUV charging through red lights, we even have the youthful bicycle courier risking his life—and that of others—on the road.

Similarly, an example fallacy type independent of ambiguity consists in arguments *affirming the consequent*, which describes the fallacious inference of a premise from the truth of a conclusion. It may come with different interactions of the information involved, but here is one simple example, again taken from Tindale (2007):

(8.3) All people with conservative values support the war. Some religious leaders support the war. So, some religious leaders must have conservative values.

Nyāya Sūtra and *Sophistical Refutations* have remained the basis of all theory on fallacies for millennia. The literature was scattered from medieval times until Hamblin (1970)'s first comprehensive modern book of fallacies. As Hamblin puts it, in general, a fallacious argument "is one that seems to be valid but is not so". He starts his discussion from a presentation of Aristotle's list of fallacies, before he sheds light on various additional fallacies that came up later and on the Indian correspondents. Then, he moves to a discussion of arguments and dialectic. Hamblin equates the notions of fallacies and fallacious arguments.

While building on Hamblin's work, Tindale (2007), in his book on fallacies, questions this identification, since some fallacies do not meet the actual structure of arguments, but are rhetorical in nature. However, that debate is not integral to the chapter at hand, which is why we use the terms fallacy and fallacious argument interchangeably in the remainder, while reminding the reader of the slight simplification we are making. Tindale elaborates that, more precisely, many fallacies are failed instantiations of argumentation schemes. The author describes a fallacy as "a particular kind of egregious error, one that seriously undermines the power of reason in an argument by diverting it or screening it in some way." To account for both fallacies that are arguments and other fallacies, he loosely defines fallacies as patterns of reasoning within an argumentative discourse that look similar to argumentation schemes. Furthermore, Tindale suggests to keep the definition of a fallacy free of whether the writer aimed to deceive or simply failed to apply a scheme correctly. At the same time, he stresses that fallacies clearly can be used to undermine reason and to deceive others in debates.

In Table 8.1, we give a compressed overview of the types of fallacies that Tindale refers to when he speaks of scheme-like patterns of reasoning. The table gives two example types each for the nine groups of fallacies he distinguishes. Several of them are directly taken from the original list of Aristotle (ca. 350 B.C.E./ translated 1984), and most of them are also found in the work of Hamblin (1970). We note that a fully comprehensive overview of fallacies would exceed the space here and is also not really possible, due to the different organizations that exist in the literature. We will mention further concrete types of fallacies when we come to computational approaches to fallacy detection in the next section.

A core goal of Tindale is to highlight the complexity of distinguishing fallacies from valid or plausible ways of reasoning. He discards the idea of evaluating fallacious reasoning by "simply applying a label from a list that can be learned"—a fact to keep in mind for the computational approaches presented below. The author's argument is that, to assess whether an argumentative utterance is fallacious, it is generally important to consider the context in which it occurs, since correct and failed applications of schemes may be structurally identical and content-wise very similar. For illustration, let us look at two constructed instances of the argumentation scheme *denying the antecedent*, a correct one and a failed one:

Table 8.1 The nine fallacy groups (e.g., *fallacies of diversion*) covered by Tindale (2007), each with two selected fallacy types (e.g., *straw man* and *red herring*) and short descriptions of the types

Group	Selected fallacy types	Descriptions of fallacy types
Fallacies	Straw man	Attacking a distorted view of the opponent's position
of diversion	Red herring	Introducing an unrelated issue for distraction
Fallacies	Invalid syllogism	Denying the conclusion based on a denied premise
of structure	Affirming the consequent	Inferring a premise from the conclusion
Problems	Equivocation	Shifting the meaning of a term, concept, or phrase
with language	Begging the question	Circular reasoning with the conclusion as a premise
Ad hominem	Abusive ad hominem	Attacking the opponent instead of their position
arguments	Circumstantial ad hom.	Attacking the circumstances the opponent argues from
Ad	False authority	Referring to a person who is no (trustworthy) authority
verencundiam	Misuse of authority	Referring to a person who actually provides no support
Other 'ad'	Ad populum	Affirming the conclusion based on its popularity
arguments	Ad baculum	Affirming the conclusion based on evoking fear
Sampling	Hasty generalization	Inferring a general conclusion from specific cases
	Secundum squid	Ignoring appropriate exceptions to a general case
Correlation	Post hoc fallacy	Inferring a cause from the temporal order of actions
and cause	Slippery slope	Assuming that a course of actions causes bad effects
Analogical	False analogy	Reasoning analogically using superficial similarities
reasoning	Appeal to precedent	Assuming that an action will cause other (bad) actions

(8.4) *Correct argumentation scheme (denying the antecedent):* My flight won't be delayed tomorrow. I have received no indication to the contrary from the airline.

(8.5) *Failed argumentation scheme (fallacy):* My girlfriend won't give me a gift tomorrow. I have received no indication to the contrary from her.

In general, the context required may include who argues to whom, in what situation, and what background information is available in this situation to the opponents as well as to those evaluating the utterance. Tindale concludes from this observation that rhetorical and dialectical features are crucial to the evaluation, rather than focusing on a purely logical assessment.

In their critical discussion, Boudry et al. (2015) question classical theories and taxonomies of fallacies. Matching the conclusion of Tindale, Boudry et al. particularly reject the exclusive focus on inferential logical structure in fallacies, emphasizing that at least a pragma-dialectical approach is needed to model the notion of fallacies. Given that the close relation of most proposed fallacy types to correct applications of argumentation schemes, the authors describe the underlying dilemma as the so-called 'fallacy fork': If the notion of fallacies describes actual invalid forms of reasoning, then the authors see limited applicability of this notion in real life. If, however, the notion is sufficiently sophisticated to capture the complexity of real-life argumentation, then they do not see the notion as useful for discriminating good and bad reasoning. While Boudry et al. do not propose an operational solution, they suggest that, instead, an option may be to focus on the need for clarification in certain arguments rather than to focus on reasoning flaws.

Case Studies on Fallacies Nevertheless, there are several studies that analyze fallacious reasoning in real-world argumentation. Outside NLP, we exemplarily mention the work of Sahlane (2012) who manually analyzes different types of fallacies in opinionated editorials of four major US newspapers from the time before the US invaded Iraq in 2003. The author looks at *ad hominem*, *ad baculum*, and *secundum quid* fallacies (all listed in Table 8.1) as well as arguments *ad ignorantiam* (affirming a conclusion based on a rejection of its opposite) and different types of arguments *ad consequentiam* that point to negative consequences, such as the widely quoted *sunk cost fallacy* (recommending an action due to the resources invested already). He reveals the powerful and detrimental impact that fallacious reasoning may have, in the given case to build up a moral and legal basis for justifying the war.

As a first attempt to gather fallacy data for NLP research, Habernal et al. (2017) developed an online serious game called *Argotario*. In Argotario, users both write fallacious arguments themselves and classify arguments of others into six types: *ad hominem*, *red herring*, and *hasty generalization* (all listed above) as well as *irrelevant authority* (i.e., false authority), *appeal to emotion* (instead of giving real reasons), and *non-fallacious arguments*. Users are incentivized with an in-game point system and monetary rewards. In their user study, the authors collected 1160 hand-written English fallacies on predefined controversial issues this way, estimating gold labels using MACE (Hovy et al. 2013). In a second paper on *Argotario*, Habernal et al. (2018a) describe how they adapt the game to the German language, collecting 296 further arguments. The authors observe that users write largely clear and coherent arguments, while not always matching the type of fallacy aimed for.

Musi et al. (2022) introduce a corpus of 1135 fact-checked news articles from the COVID-19 pandemic with instances of 10 types of fallacies as well as their relations to claims in the articles and sources of mis-/disinformation. The authors' fallacy scheme builds on Tindale (2007), distinguishing four types of *fallacies of diversion* (e.g., *straw man* and *red herring*), five different types of fallacious reasoning (e.g., *false authority*, *hasty generalization*, and *false analogy*), and one *problem of language* (i.e., *vagueness*). For identification, two annotators went through 20 questions that stepwise test for the different types for each fact-checked claim in a news article, reaching a moderate Cohen's κ agreement of 0.52. The corpus covers 526 fallacies in total and is used in some of the methodological studies we summarize below. Musi et al. (2022) find that fallacies often reveal the cause of misleading claims, underlining the importance of their detection in practice.

Payandeh et al. (2024) study the impact of fallacies on LLMs' arguing behavior. In their agent setting, a 'persuader' tries to convince a 'debater' of a given claim. The persuader is optionally informed either by a 'logical helper' or by a 'fallacious helper'. The latter is prompted to craft deceptive arguments of eight types: *ad hominem*, *appeal to emotion*, *false information*, *cause fallacy*, *slippery slope*, *appeal to popular opinion*, *straw man*, or *false dilemma* (without explicit definitions). In experiments, the persuader convinced the debater in 29% (using GPT-3.5) and 37% (using GPT-4) respectively, when given no helper. Concerningly, the fallacious helper boosted these values to 37% and 67%, the logical only to 30% and 39%—a result that underlines the danger of misusing LLMs for manipulation.

8.2.2 Classifying Fallacies in Dialogical Argumentation

Some fallacy detection studies in NLP focus on dialogical settings, where the interaction of participants may give clues regarding what is fallacious. This includes argumentation in *discussion forums* as well as in *political debates*.

Discussion Forums Habernal et al. (2018b) present the first NLP approach to actually detecting fallacies, focusing on the rather specific idea of ad hominem arguments. While personal attacks and incivil language are a common phenomenon across the web (Coe et al. 2014), the authors look at 'open-minded' discussions on the Reddit forum *ChangeMyView*. In a discussion on this forum, one user posts their opinion on a controversial issue, and others argue against the opinion. Convincing arguments may receive a so-called 'delta award' from the opinion poster. Ad hominem arguments are rare on the forum (0.2%) and removed by the moderators, but Habernal et al. reached out to the moderators to get access. Given the resulting dataset of 3866 ad hominem arguments among 2M posts, the authors present three analyses:

1. *Recognition of Ad Hominem.* First, Habernal et al. trained and evaluated both a bidirectional LSTM and a convolutional neural network (CNN) on 7242 balanced instances to distinguish between ad hominem and delta-award arguments. For comparison, they carried out a crowdworking study on 100 balanced instances. The models achieved accuracies of 78.2% (Bi-LSTM) and 81.0% (CNN) respectively, whereas the crowdworkers did a bit better on average (87.0%).
2. *Typology of Ad Hominem.* In a second crowdworking study, seven participants marked the spans that cause ad hominem in 400 arguments. The authors then manually categorized all cases into 15 proposed subtypes of ad hominem. Among these, the most frequent are *vulgar insult*, *illiteracy insult* (e.g., "Reading comprehension is your friend"), *condescension* (e.g., "little buddy"), and *idiot insult*.
3. *Triggers of Ad Hominem.* Finally, Habernal et al. analyze what causes ad hominem. To this end, they employed a self-attentive LSTM (Lin et al. 2017) that distinguishes sequences of three dialogue turns that resulted in ad hominem from those that resulted in delta awards at an accuracy of 72.0%. Projecting the LSTM's attention weights

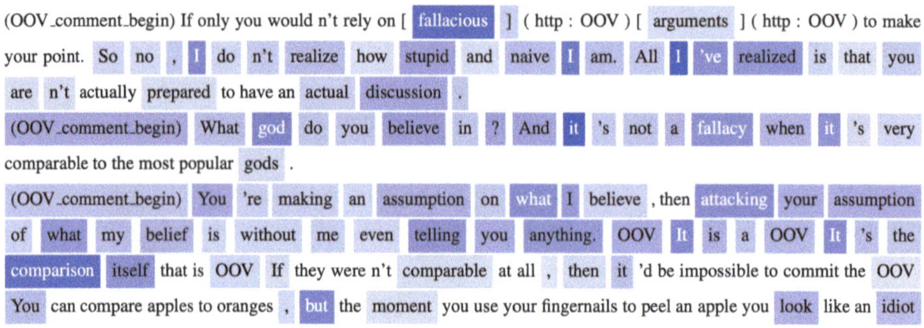

Fig. 8.5 Attention visualization of two dialogue posts classified as triggering ad hominem by the self-attentive LSTM of Habernal et al. (2018b). The darker the background color, the more the respective word added to the LSTM's classification decision.

back to the input texts, the authors manually examined what words occur in 191 true positives, 77 false positives, and 84 false positives. Figure 8.5 shows an example. They observe that most causes are topic-independent rhetorical devices and deal with meta-level argumentation rather than profanity.

Delobelle et al. (2019) present an approach to deciding whether a given post (without its discussion context) in the dataset of Habernal et al. (2018b) represents ad hominem or not. The approach inputs word2vec and doc2vec representations (Mikolov et al. 2013; Le and Mikolov 2014) of the post along with a bidirectional GRU representation (Cho et al. 2014) of its part-of-speech tags to a two-layer recurrent neural network (RNN). In experiments, the authors compare the RNN to the CNN of Habernal et al. (2018b), SVMs with TD-IDF and embedding representations as well as some ablations. On the test set, the RNN's accuracy (85.6%) improved over the CNN (81.0%) but not over the SVMs (90.0% with embeddings). However, it outperformed the latter clearly in terms of F_1-score (0.489 vs. 0.374).

Sahai et al. (2021) present a dataset of 1650 non-fallacious and 1708 fallacious comments from 10 different Reddit forums. The latter are classified into eight fallacy types: *ad verecundiam*, *ad populum*, *false dilemma*, *hasty generalization*, and *slippery slope* (all mentioned above) as well as *naturalistic fallacy* (discouraging actions that do not appear in nature), *ad antiquitatem* (discouraging an action since it has always been discouraged), and *appeal to worse problems* (justifying a problem by worse other problems). On the data, the authors tested the identification and classification of fallacies, at comment level and at token level. They compared fine-tuned BERT to a multi-granularity network (MGN) from related work on propaganda detection (Da San Martino et al. 2019) that jointly models information at both levels. Both approaches optionally employ the forum's title post or parent post as context respectively. At comment level, either of the MGN variations performed best, for example, with an F_1-score of 0.6969

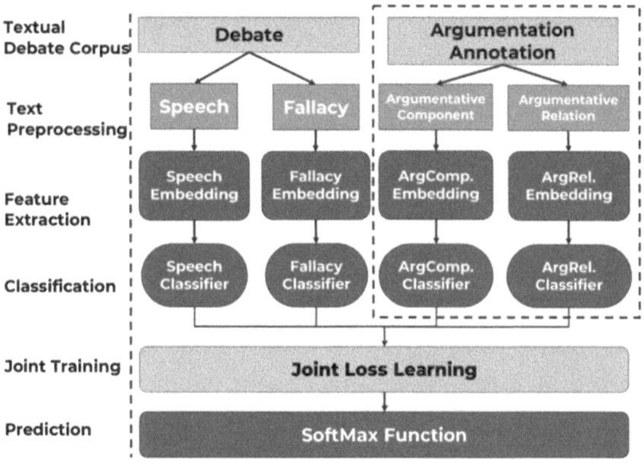

Fig. 8.6 Multitask fallacy classification architecture of Goffredo et al. (2022), with joint loss for debate speech, fallacy, component, and relation features. Used with permission. Copyright ©International Joint Conferences on Artificial Intelligence, ijcai.org

(base MGN) in identification and 0.4906 in joint identification and classification (MGN with title context). The base MGN was also strongest in token-level classification (.7586), whereas BERT with parent context succeeded in the joint setting (.4707).

For fallacy detection in Italian, Ramponi et al. (2025) present a dataset with human label variation, following the idea of perspectivism (Plank 2022). The dataset consists of 1440 tweets in which 11k spans are annotated for 20 fallacy types. Each post was annotated by two annotators, leading to variations and overlapping fallacy spans. The authors experimented with a supervised 'multi-view multi-label' (MVML) model that fine-tunes a transformer encoder with one separated decoder per annotator. For encoding, they used AlBERTo (Polignano et al. 2019) and UmBERTo (Parisi et al. 2020). As unsupervised alternatives, zero-shot versions of LLaMa-3-8B (Grattafiori et al. 2024) and Mixtral 8x7B (Jiang et al. 2023) were instructed with fallacy definitions. At post level, MVML-AlBERTo received the best F_1-score (0.443), while all others were about 20 points behind. Similar holds for the span level, where MVML-AlBERTo achieved 0.333 while the MVMD-UmBERTo landed at 0.073 and the zero-shot models at 0.034 and 0.042 only. The results underline the difficulty of predicting the fallacy classifications of different annotators simultaneously.

Political Debates To study fallacies in politics, Goffredo et al. (2022) introduce a dataset of 31 US Presidential Campaign debates, with 1628 annotated span-level fallacies of six types (and 14 subtypes): *ad hominem*, *appeal to emotion*, *ad veruncandiam*, *slippery slope*, *false cause*, and *slogan* (e.g., "Make America great again!"). Given a fallacious text span, the task is to decide which fallacy type it refers to. The authors propose a multitask learning approach with a joint loss function for four embedding-based features, analyzing the speech transcript and the fallacious span as well as mined argument components and relations. Figure 8.6 illustrates the architecture. Comparing multiple fine-tuned transformer models, a Longformer (Beltagy et al. 2020) achieved the highest macro F_1-score on the six types (0.84), largely improving over a standard fine-tuned BERT (0.55) and suggesting that all features have an impact. On the 14 subtypes, the macro F_1-

score was naturally notably lower (0.42), with varying scores per class between 0.00 (for the ad verencundiam subtype *false authority*) and 0.83 (for the emotion subtype *loaded language*).

In follow-up research, Goffredo et al. (2023) identify and classify fallacies token by token. The authors develop a similar multitask learning architecture as before, but with slightly different features: components, relations, and part-of-speech tags. The results again show some impact for all features, yielding a token-level macro F_1-score of 0.7394. Standard BERT comes close to the approach, though (0.7237).

Finally, Ruiz-Dolz and Lawrence (2023) evaluate the robustness of fallacy detection approaches. As a motivating example, the authors stress that an argument matching the ad hominem scheme is not necessarily fallacious, namely when the attack of the opponent's character is justified. To test such cases, they handcraft a small validation dataset with one pair of valid and fallacious argument each for seven different argumentation schemes, such as *argument from position to know* or *circumstancial ad hominem*. The scheme types correspond to the fallacy types in the two datasets merged for the evaluation: the Reddit data of Sahai et al. (2021) and the debate data of Goffredo et al. (2022). Ruiz-Dolz and Lawrence (2023) compare multiple models, including a fine-tuned RoBERTa and GPT-4. On the merged data, RoBERTa performed strongest overall, for example, with a macro F_1-score of 0.796 in a two-class setting (fallacy or not), while GPT-4 did much worse (0.511). However, while RoBERTa misclassifies six out of the 14 validation examples, GPT-4 gets 12 of them right in the two-class setting, indicating better generalization capabilities. Both largely fail, though, when it comes to identifying the exact fallacy type.

8.2.3 Classifying Fallacies in Monological Argumentation

In monological settings, fallacies need to be found based on the content of an argument itself, or by connecting to external sources. Most respective approaches deal with *education and news*, but some recent work also targets *scientific articles*.

Education and News Jin et al. (2022) focus on logical fallacies, presenting a new dataset of 2449 fallacies taken from three student quiz websites. The dataset covers educational examples of 13 fallacy types, most of which we have discussed above (e.g., *ad hominem* and *ad populum*), but also some others, such as the *fallacy of relevance*. An example for the latter is "Why should we be worrying about how the government treats Native people, when people in our city can't get a job". In addition, a news article dataset of 1109 span-level fallacies was manually created to test the generalizability of models trained on the educational data. The authors propose a structure-aware approach that masks parts of the content of candidate fallacies to identify whether its logical form matches the typical form of a specific fallacy type. For classification, an ELECTRA transformer model (Clark et al. 2020) for natural language inference (NLI) was fine-tuned on the data. In experiments, Jin et al. compared their approach to zero-shot and fine-tuned transformers. It obtained a micro

F_1-score of 0.5877 as opposed to, for example, 0.5331 of fine-tuned standard ELECTRA and 0.1367 of zero-shot GPT-2 (Radford et al. 2019). The approach is strong on fallacy types such as ad hominem (0.7865) and ad populum (0.7945), whereas it struggles with some others including the fallacy of relevance (0.3922). Moreover, generalization seems hard with a micro F_1-score of 0.2381 on the news articles.

Transitioning between fine-tuned transformers and LLMs, Alhindi et al. (2022) present an early instruction-based prompting approach to fallacy detection. For development and evaluation, the authors build on five different fallacy-related datasets, including Argotario (Habernal et al. 2017), a propaganda detection dataset (Da San Martino et al. 2019), the educational logical fallacies (Jin et al. 2022), COVID-19 news articles (Musi et al. 2022), and a new dataset of 477 fallacious and 301 non-fallacious segments from climate change-related news articles that follows the annotation scheme of Musi et al. (2022). They convert task instances into instruction-input-output triples to fine-tune a T5 encoder-decoder transformer (Raffel et al. 2020) on this basis. Here is one example created based on Argotario:

> *Instruction:* Given the question and answer below, which of the following fallacies occur in the answer: Ad hominem, Red Herring, Hasty Generalization, Irrelevant Authority, or Emotional Language?
>
> *Input:* Questions: Has anyone been on the moon? Answer: The moon is so far away, we should focus on our society.
>
> *Output:* Red Herring

In their evaluation on the test sets of all five datasets, Alhindi et al. trained their approach both on a single training set and on all training sets, and compared both variants against different baselines. The all-training-set variant did better with macro F_1-scores in the range of 0.20–0.66 across the datasets. The single-training-set variant reached 0.17–0.62, whereas a zero-shot question answering model from related work (Khashabi et al. 2020) largely failed (0.02–0.14).

Sourati et al. (2023) bring together fine-tuned transformers with case-based reasoning (Schank 1983), classifying arguments by retrieving and adapting similar existing fallacy cases. A retriever first identifies some $k > 0$ cases based on their embedding cosine similarity to the argument at hand. An adapter then uses self-attention to represent the combination of the argument and each of the cases. Given this representation, a feedforward network predicts the likelihood that the argument reflects the same fallacy type as the respective case. To enrich the case representation, the authors add either of four types of information to it, generated by a combination of ChatGPT and Codex (Chen et al. 2021): a counterargument to the fallacy, the fallacy's goal, an explanation of the fallacious reasoning, and an abstract structure specification similar to Jin et al. (2022). On the two datasets of Jin et al. (2022), Sourati et al. oppose the case-based reasoning approach for three transformers (BERT, RoBERTa, and ELECTRA) against fine-tuned standard transformers. Across the board, their approach beat the standard versions. The top micro F_1-scores were achieved by ELECTRA, with 0.657 on the educational data and 0.270 on news.

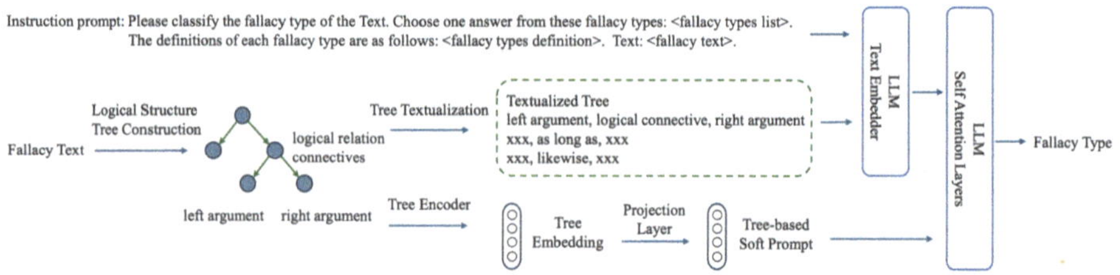

Fig. 8.7 Illustration of the fallacy detection approach of Lei and Huang (2024): From the logical structure tree of a fallacy, a tree textualization and tree-based soft prompt are computed that, together with an instruction, go into an LLM's representation.

To explicate the implicit logic of fallacies, Robbani et al. (2024) extended 400 fallacies from Jin et al. (2022) with annotations of structural claim-premise templates. The authors restrict their view to four fallacy types: *fallacy of credibility* (ad hominem-like argument, attacking the opponent's character), *false causality*, *false dilemma* (presenting two options while hiding others), and *faulty generalization*. Exemplary, here is an example of faulty generalization used in the paper:

(8.6) I took an [NLP class]$_{A'}$, an advanced course in Stanford. I suggest not taking [further advanced courses]$_A$ because they will hurt your [GPA]$_C$.

The example is a failed instance of an *argument from consequence* that matches the following ⟨claim, premise⟩ template of Reisert et al. (2018): ⟨*bad(A), A suppress C, good(C)*⟩ (*A* is bad and would suppress *C*, which is good). To stress the fallacy, the annotators of Robbani et al. added another premise template that explains the fallacy: ⟨*A′ suppress C, good(C)*⟩. Based on the data, Robbani et al. test to what extent different LLMs can automatically (a) select the right templates, (b) fill the template's slots, and (c) do both jointly. Mistral-7b (Jiang et al. 2023) performed best in template selection with an accuracy of 47%, clearly outperforming LLaMA-3-7b (34%), GPT-4o (38%) and GPT-3.5 (35%). While GPT-4o slight beat Mistral in slot filling (24% vs. 23%), Mistral also was first in the joint task (11% vs. 9% of GPT-4o). Still, the results indicate the difficulty of the task.

Lei and Huang (2024) observe that fallacies often use connectives to encode logical relations between argument components, while the components' semantics do not actually support these relations. The authors define a taxonomy of 10 common relations and respective connectives, such as *restatement* (connectives, e.g., include "specifically" or "moreover"), *contrast* (e.g., "but" or "rather than"), or *analogy* (e.g., "likewise" or "just as"). To distinguish valid from fallacious arguments, they propose an LLM-based approach with four main steps (depicted in Fig. 8.7):

1. *Logical Structure Tree Construction.* Given an argument, the approach derives a logical structure tree, T_{logic}, from its constituency tree, T_{con}. Traversing T_{con} from the root, it

looks for any of the taxonomy connectives. In case of a match, the connective defines an inner node of T_{logic}, and the approach recursively repeats the process for each of the two arguments related through the connective. Lei and Huang use the stanza library for constituency parsing (Qi et al. 2020).
2. *Textualized Tree Embedding.* T_{logic} is converted into a table-like text representation, where each table row is a triplet *(left argument, connective, right argument)*, ordered bottom-up. The approach then embeds this textualization using an LLM.
3. *Tree-based Soft Prompting.* In addition, T_{logic} is encoded as a soft prompt by mapping it to a tree embedding and then projecting it into the LLM's representation. For mapping, Lei and Huang embed each lowest-level triplet r as

$$e_s \;:=\; W^r \cdot (e_l \oplus e_c \oplus e_r) + b^r$$

where e_l, e_c, and e_r are the embeddings of the triplet components, initialized using RoBERTa, $\oplus$ denotes concatenation, and W^r and b^r are trainable parameters. The lower-level embeddings e_s then recursively become the embeddings e_l and e_r of higher-level triplets. The final projection has trainable parameters as well.
4. *Fallacy Training.* Given the embedded textualized tree, the tree-based soft prompt, and an embedded instruction (as shown in Fig. 8.7), the LLM is finally fine-tuned against gold fallacy type labels.

For evaluation, Lei and Huang used four of the above-mentioned fallacy detection and classification datasets (Habernal et al. 2017; Sahai et al. 2021; Alhindi et al. 2022; Jin et al. 2022). As LLMs, they compared Llama-2-6B (Touvron et al. 2023a) and Flan-T5-large (Chung et al. 2024) against baselines from previous works and standard alternatives (RoBERTa and GPT-3.5). Across all datasets and both tasks, the Llama-2 variant outperformed all others, followed by the Flan-T5 variant. For example, in identification on the data of Sahai et al. (2021), it obtained an F_1-score of 0.7672 compared to 0.7507 (Flan-T5), 0.6845 (GPT-3.5), and 0.6920 (Sahai et al. 2021). In classification on the data of Jin et al. (2022), it reached 0.6955 compared to 0.6937 (Flan-T5), 0.3130 (GPT-3.5), and 0.6200 (Alhindi et al. 2022).

A prompting-based approach to classifying logical fallacies comes from Jeong et al. (2025). Given an argument x to be classified, the approach first prompts an LLM to generate three types of context, following Sourati et al. (2023): a counterargument, an explanation, and a goal. For each context, another prompt asks for a query that analyzes x under that context. For each of the resulting augmentations, the approach computes the maximum likelihood of x having any of the set of given fallacy types according the given LLM. The likelihoods of all augmentations are then used in a final prompt that predicts the fallacy type. The authors evaluate their approach on five existing fallacy-related datasets, comparing different GPT and LLaMA variants in zero-shot classification, while also fine-tuning a RoBERTa model with the respective prompts as input and the fallacy type as output. In terms of macro F_1-score, GPT-4 won on two datasets with values

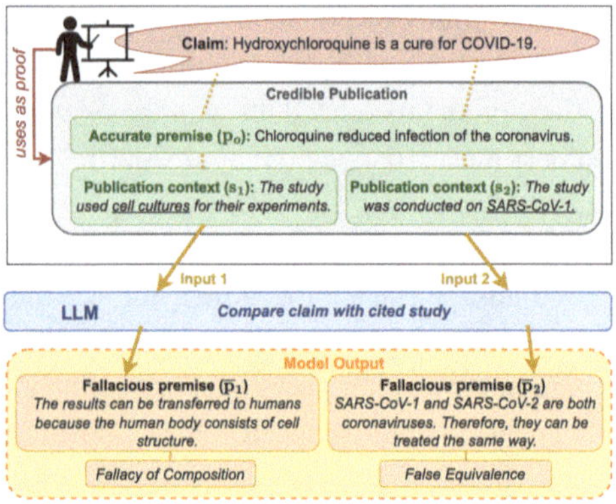

Fig. 8.8 Illustration of how an LLM reconstructs fallacious premises that a science article uses for a claim based on the given sources (Glockner et al. 2024). Licensed under CC-BY 4.0 International

of 0.83 (Habernal et al. 2017) and 0.76 (Musi et al. 2022), and RoBERTa on two others with 0.79 (Jin et al. 2022) and 0.74 (Alhindi et al. 2022). On the data of Da San Martino et al. (2019), no approach variant could compete with the state-of-the-art of Sourati et al. (2023), which achieved 0.91.

Scientific Articles Glockner et al. (2024) look at fallacies in scientific articles, many of which are implicit and arise from misrepresentation of cited literature. Building on a taxonomy of scientific fallacies (Cook et al. 2018), they consider nine fallacy types, some of which merge multiple types, observing their lack of distinguishability (e.g., *false cause* and simplifying *single cause* are merged into *causal simplification*). For development and evaluation, Glockner et al. introduce a dataset of 527 articles from a fact-checking website and 8695 source articles linked by them. For these links, the annotators reconstructed 435 fallacious premises used in 184 arguments (together with accurate premises) to infer a claim. Figure 8.8 illustrates the setting. In experiments, the authors assessed whether LLaMA-2-70B (Touvron et al. 2023a) and GPT-4 can reconstruct at least one premise of the same fallacious type under different prompt variants. The best GPT-4 variant achieved to do so in 31.7% of the cases, the best LLaMa variant only in 22.3%. LLaMa turned out to be slightly better in mimicking the human-written premises, for example, with a top BERTScore (Zhang et al. 2020b) of 0.627 compared to 0.619 (GPT-4). However, human validation still found the GPT-4 premises to be of higher quality on average.

In direct follow-up work, Glockner et al. (2025) extend their dataset by grounding all fallacies explicitly in the passages of misrepresented scientific studies that reveal the fallacy. This enables the development and exploration of retrieval models for revealing fallacies. The authors evaluate how such passage retrieval affect LLMs in reconstructing fallacies as well as fact-checking models. They benchmark various models for the different tasks, finding that existing retrieval approaches and LLMs struggle to reconstruct the fallacies from the evidence given in the passages.

8.3 Reconstructing Implicit Reasoning

Regardless of whether humans argue in a valid way, correctly applying argumentation schemes, or they mistakenly or deceptively argue fallaciously, it is rare that they make all the components of their arguments explicit during reasoning. This is because some components may be clear or taken for granted, or because they are hidden for rhetorical reasons (Al Khatib et al. 2016). Argumentation theory has extensively studied this phenomenon under the notion of *enthymemes*, that is, arguments in which a premise is left unstated (Aristotle ca. 350 B.C.E./ translated 2007). However, not only the premise may be implicit, but particularly conclusions are often clear from context (Habernal and Gurevych 2015) and, hence, not repeated or even explicated at all. For humans, enthymematic reasoning often feels perfectly natural. For machines, it can make the comprehension of arguments even more challenging.

We review a few NLP approaches to the detection and reconstruction of implicit argument components in the following. Starting from the basics of implicit reasoning, we discuss NLP research on its detection and reconstruction. Then we move to more formal approaches to the modeling and handling of implicitness.

8.3.1 Theory of Implicit Reasoning

As a basis for the computational approaches presented in this section, we first briefly discuss the notions of *enthymemes and implicit argument components*, what their role in *human communication* is, and how to *reconstruct* them.

Enthymemes and Implicit Argument Components Conceptually, an enthymeme is an argument with one or more unstated premises (Aristotle ca. 350 B.C.E./ translated 2007), even though some researchers also use the term to refer to the implicit premise itself (Feng and Hirst 2011). Enthymemes can be understood by a hearer only if they consider the given conclusion and premise, and reconstruct a 'hidden' premise that provides the link between the two. Often, the so-called *minor premise* is stated and the *major premise* remains unstated. Here is a classical example:

(8.7) *Stated minor premise:* Socrates is human.
Unstated major premise: All humans are mortal.
Stated conclusion: Therefore, Socrates is mortal.

Enthymemes are a natural phenomenon, as already pointed out by Aristotle (ca. 350 B.C.E./ translated 2007): When a (logically necessary) premise represents a fact that can be assumed to be known to the hearer, the speaker can leave this premise implicit in an argument. The hearer then needs to activate their common knowledge to perform the reconstruction (Walton 2008b). In real-world settings, it may even be counterproductive to make too much explicit. Consider the following claim in a debate on whether or not to ban the death penalty in the US:

(8.8) The death penalty kills innocent people.

While this claim may require to be backed up further by evidence, we can understand itself as a premise of an enthymematic argument in favor of banning the death penalty. In particular, the respective argument leaves the major premise unstated, say, that "killing innocent people conflicts with basic values". Making this premise explicit does not only seem pointless; it may even seem odd, as most humans would see it as an indisputable fact anyway. Interestingly, the argument actually leaves the conclusion conveying the stance toward the ban implicit as well, which again seems natural, as it is clear from the context. A more comprehensively spelled-out version of the argument may hence be:

(8.9) *Stated minor premise:* The death penalty kills innocent people.
Unstated major premise: Killing innocent people conflicts with basic values.
Unstated conclusion: Therefore, the death penalty should be banned.

Enthymemes in Human Communication It is, of course, not coincidence that Aristotle (ca. 350 B.C.E./ translated 2007) brought up the notion of enthymemes in his study of rhetoric. As McBurney (1936) analyzes, enthymemes are central to the goal of arguments to have a persuasive effect on their audience in that enthymemes allow the audience to engage. Just like in the example above, the unstated premise may often refer to a shared belief or value and, therefore, makes the audience follow the argument's point without pushing them to do so. Walker (1994) further evolves the notion of engagement toward understanding enthymemes as a dialogical relation between the writer of an argument and their audience. Upon constructing an argument, the writer needs to put themselves into how the audience thinks. Walker stresses the ethical side of enthymematic reasoning in this regard, given its close connection to manipulation, although noting that it is only one under several persuasion techniques. Ultimately, he pictures an enthymeme as a "stylistically intensified argumentative turn that serves not only do draw conclusions but also, and decisively, to foreground stance and motivate identification with that stance."

In line with the dialogical understanding of enthymemes, Walton (2008a) develops a theory of enthymemes that builds on three bases: First, both the arguer and the audience commit to a set of statements that they take for granted and that may be further extended during the dialogue; an unstated premise is usually taken from the audience's commitment set. Second, the argumentation schemes that the arguer makes use of need to fit those that the audience understands and accepts; only then the enthymematic argument may prove effective. For example, some but not all people may be open to arguments from expert opinion, and some may struggle with following particular reasoning schemes. And third, there is also common knowledge that the two sides share. This knowledge can be kept implicit in any argument.

In a way, Breitholtz (2021) brings together the views of McBurney (1936) and Walton (2008a) is his theory of the interaction of enthymemes and patterns of reasoning in dialogue. The author stresses that enthymeme-like inferences are the very core of the pragmatic concept of implicature, making them common in conversation and rhetorical speeches. He elaborates that they are needed to provide structure in discourse and to communicate implicit information. As a matter of fact, an analysis of the interaction of the participants of a dialogue is critical to understanding what information is communicated implicitly and how this is realized linguistically.

Enthymeme Reconstruction Vassiliev (2001) point out that the process of reconstructing enthymemes may appear easy at first sight in that no special scholarly skills are needed. However, complexity arises from the individual understanding that a listener perceiving an argument has of what is left implicit. The author delineates four types of understanding: (1) 'reference recognition' refers to getting what the speaker actually says; (2) 'designation comprehension' captures that speaker and listener may share, or not share, understanding of key aspects of the argument; (3) 'sense decoding' describes that the listener reconstructs premises that make the argument coherent according to their background; and (4) 'sense comparison' is about the listener's evaluation of the reconstructed premise. All these may affect the listener's interpretation of the argument. In addition, Vassiliev emphasizes that listeners may only partially reconstruct arguments according to their needs in the given situation.

Walton and Reed (2005) promote the idea that argumentation schemes play an important role for enthymeme reconstruction. In particular, the authors suggest that, once the scheme of an argument is determined, it becomes much more straightforward to see what is left implicit. One example they give is the following:

(8.10) *Enthymematic argument:* The corporate income tax should be abolished; it encourages waste and high prices.

Knowing that this is an argument from (negative) consequences, the authors infer that the unstated major premise must be roughly the following, even though the exact phrasing may be up for discussion:

(8.11) *Unstated premise:* Wastc and high priccs arc (gcncrally) bad things.

They further argue that implicit premises often follow from the goal of the practical reasoning happening (e.g., to support the ban of taxes in the given case).

Challenging much enthymeme research, Paglieri and Woods (2011) raise the question as to whether Aristotle's original idea that reconstruction solves a deficiency in enthymemes is justified. Starting from the premise that an uttered argument is not the same as a meant argument, the authors develop the notion that the utterance 'advances' the meant argument. They lay out that, in many cases, no reconstruction will be needed, as

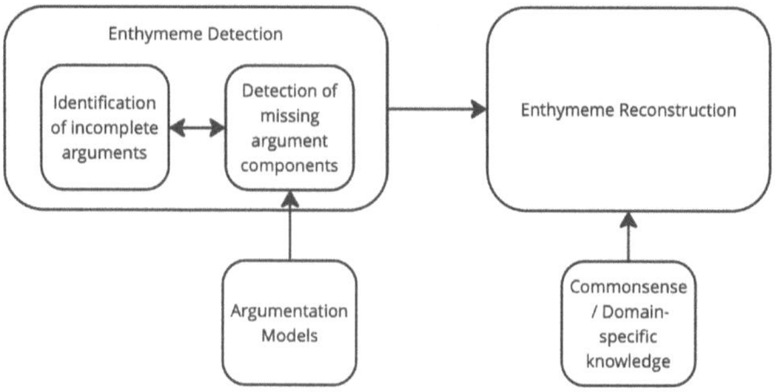

Fig. 8.9 Enthymeme reconstruction pipeline according to Sviridova et al. (2026): Step 1 (*enthymeme detection*) has two subtasks, one of which needs an argumentation model, whereas Step 2 (*enthymeme reconstruction*) needs external knowledge. Used with permission

the audience will just understand what was meant. At the same time, they acknowledge that enthymematic arguments often allow for multiple reconstructions with different results. However, they point to the importance of *parsimony* in this regard: "the costs of understanding an enthymeme need to be lower than the benefits of uttering the argument" explicitly, that is, reconstruction tends to be short and straightforward. The authors conclude that, instead of seeing enthymeme reconstruction as a problem per se, research should focus on those cases where the enthymematic argument actually seems obscure or otherwise problematic.

8.3.2 Detecting and Reconstructing Implicit Reasoning

We now come to computational approaches as well as underlying annotation studies. Sviridova et al. (2026) recently organized literature on the topic by the steps in the pipeline shown in Fig. 8.9. For *enthymeme detection*, the authors observe that detecting missing components requires an argumentation model, whereas identifying incomplete arguments may work without. Matching theory, they argue that *enthymeme reconstruction* nearly always requires external commonsense or domain knowledge to model the shared human background in the reasoning. In what follows, we start with works that primarily target enthymeme detection, but then we separately review a specific task studied notably in this context: *warrant classification*. Finally, we look at NLP research on the *reconstruction of implicit argument components*.

Enthymeme Detection As a first attempt, Wyner et al. (2010, 2016) provide a manual pilot study on implicit major premises in online discussions. The authors first annotated the premises in a variant of 'controlled English' (i.e., a simplified and semi-formalized language, see Kuhn 2014) in order to define propositional logic axioms on this basis that explicate the stances of discussion participants. Overall, this illustrates the kind of knowledge required for an in-depth treatment of enthymemes.

In another pilot study, Rajendran et al. (2016) connect enthymematic reasoning to opinion mining in product reviews. They propose to model the handling of 'implicit opinions' (statements that look like facts but contain an implicit evaluation) as a type of enthymeme reconstruction. Their idea is to classify an opinion statement as to whether it is implicit or explicit, and to regard an explicit statement together with the overall judgment on the product (as derived from the rating given with the review) as complete arguments: "The reviewer likes a product *x* because of some reason *y*." Implicit opinions, on the other hand, when combined with the conclusion can create an enthymeme. Then, common knowledge is necessary to complete the argument—which is the major problem left unsolved in the authors' study.

Taking a more general perspective, Boltužić and Šnajder (2016) tackle the task of matching a given user claim to an appropriate main claim, with the idea to explore the 'gap' between the two claims. The authors propose to fill the gap by making implicit major premises explicit (i.e., enthymeme reconstruction). Given claim pairs collected by Hasan and Ng (2014), they let annotators write missing major premises, following the instruction to formulate statements that 'bridge the gap'. They regard the number of major premises as a measure of the size of the inferential gap—in their corpus, the average is 2.7. To gather evidence for this hypothesis, they ran a crowdsourcing study in which they obtained judgments on the semantic similarity between the user claim and the main claim. Indeed, the study yielded a statistically significant (though weak) negative correlation between semantic similarity and gap size. Next, Boltužić and Šnajder turned to the question as to whether the annotated gold premises can support their actual task. Their approach computes cosine similarity between the average word embeddings of the claims. Among various ways of making use of the major premises, they find that combining the premises with the main claim, and then running the similarity computations, works best.

Focusing on manual annotation of enthymemes, Razuvayevskaya and Teufel (2017) explore how to reach sufficient inter-annotator agreement in enthymeme detection. Concretely, they look at 'a fortiori arguments', that is, arguments in which a smaller case is argued for or against by referring to a larger case. A common way to encode such arguments is the 'let alone' construction, as in "This does not apply to Germany, let alone Europe." In their study, the authors develop 11 relation categories for the scaling happening in such arguments, such as *part of*, *precondition of*, or *more extreme case than* relations. For the case that the category can be detected, they provide suggestions on how to explicate the implicit components.

Warrant Classification To lay the ground for enthymeme reconstruction, Habernal et al. (2018c) propose the *argument reasoning comprehension task*. Essentially, the tasks consists in choosing the right warrant for a given claim-reason pair out of two candidate variants that directly oppose to each other, as in the following example:

Claim: Russia cannot be a partner.
Reason: Cooperating with Russia on terrorism ignores Russia's overall objectives.
Warrant candidate 1: Russia has the same objectives of the US.
Warrant candidate 2: Russia has the opposite objectives of the US.

In a multistage crowdsourcing process, the authors collected 1970 task instances with handwritten warrants for arguments from the New York Times Room for Debate, as the one seen. They also developed a Bi-LSTM model that uses 'intra-warrant attention' to directly model the interaction of the two candidates with the given claim-reason pair. On their test set, it achieved a limited accuracy of 56.0%, indicating the difficulty of the task while still outperforming all its ablations.

Habernal et al. (2018d) deployed argument reasoning comprehension as a shared task, providing the topic and some additional information as input along with claim, reason, and the two warrants. 20 teams participated in the shared task with various approaches, covering bidirectional LSTMs, GRUs, CNNs, SVMs, and more. The winning approach, GIST (Choi and Lee 2018), achieved an accuracy of 71.2%, clearly outperforming all other teams; the second best obtained 60.6% (Zhao et al. 2018). GIST uses transfer learning from NLI, pretraining the tree-LSTM model of Chen et al. (2017) on 500k premise-hypothesis NLI instances. Different pretrained units then take different pairs of task inputs (e.g., warrant 1 + reason), while standard LSTM units complement them with individual representations of the different inputs. The output of these units is combined in a feedforward network for prediction.

Later, an approach that explicitly models knowledge from knowledge bases was proposed by Botschen et al. (2018). In particular, the approach extends the baseline of Habernal et al. (2018c) by event-based frames from FrameNet (Baker et al. 1998) as well as fact-based entities from Wikidata. The rationale is that FrameNet may help identify entities that refer to the same frame, while Wikidata gives additional information on the entities. The approach proceeds in two steps:

1. *Frame Identification and Entity Linking.* Given a claim, a reason, and the two warrant candidates, the approach automatically annotates frames and entities in them, both using methods from own previous work. On the task data, Botschen et al. found an average of 6.6 frames and 0.7 entities. Figure 8.10 shows exemplary results of this annotation.
2. *Semantic Enrichment.* Next, the approach maps frames and entities to pretrained TransE embeddings for multi-relational data (Bordes et al. 2013). It then combines these embeddings with the word embeddings of the intra-warrant attention approach of Habernal et al. (2018c). The result goes into a Bi-LSTM to compute attention weights between the two warrants.

In experiments, Botschen et al. (2018) compare their approach to a reimplementation of Habernal et al. (2018c) as well as approach ablations. Using only FrameNet reached the maximum observed accuracy of 61.04%, while the full approach remained with a

Fig. 8.10 Illustration of frame and entity annotations automatically created by the argument reasoning comprehension approach of Botschen et al. (2018). Licensed under CC-BY 4.0 International

maximum of 59.04%. Given these results, the authors question the importance of external world knowledge for the argument reasoning comprehension task, rather seeing a logic-based analysis of the reasoning chain as key.

Niven and Kao (2019), authors from the fourth-best team in the shared task with 59.0% (Niven and Kao 2018), were the first to evaluate transformers on argument reasoning comprehension. In particular, they developed a BERT-based approach that separately encodes each warrant together with claim and reason to predict a probability for each of them on this basis. This alone sufficed to reach an accuracy of 67.1% on the task, in some runs even up to 77%. However, the authors observe that an uneven distribution of cue words in the warrants (e.g. "not") allowed BERT to exploit spurious correlations. To probe its 'actual' effectiveness on the task, they created an adversarial dataset by negating the claim of each instance and inverting the label of each warrant. On this dataset, the same approach obtained only 50% accuracy (and a maximum of 53%). Niven and Kao argue that this is how it should be, if little to no knowledge about the context of an argument is accessible.

Building on the preceding work, António Rodrigues et al. (2020) sought to reproduce the results of six approaches that participated in the shared task and whose source code was available. Among these are the four top-scoring approaches, three of which we have mentioned above. While GIST (Choi and Lee 2018) roughly achieved the same accuracy (71.4%) on the original data of Habernal et al. (2018c), the results of Zhao et al. (2018) and Niven and Kao (2018) even increased in the reproduction to 64.2% and 62.3% respectively. However, on the adversarial data of Niven and Kao (2019), the two top approaches indeed failed with 50.0% and 46.6%. The approach of Niven and Kao (2018) still reached 55.5%, but the results generally corroborate the findings of Niven and Kao (2019).

Half a decade later, Behzadidoost et al. (2025) followed up with argument reasoning comprehension. Their approach begins by augmenting all training instances by an equal number of meaningless synthetically-modified instances in which parts of the input are distorted through ordering changes. Then, it fine-tunes a pretrained RoBERTa encoder using contrastive learning on pairs of positive and negative instances drawn from both the original and the modified data. The encoder is optimized based on the sum of the contrastive loss and the classification loss on the task. On the shared task test set, the approach yielded an accuracy of 76.8%—to our knowledge, the best accuracy reported at the time of writing.

Reconstruction of Implicit Components The reconstruction of implicit premises and/or conclusion ultimately constitutes a text generation task. As such, there is a conceptual overlap between the contents of this very subsection and some aspects of argument generation (Chap. 9). Moreover, it may yield insights into the quality of the respective arguments, hence having intersection points with aspects of argument quality assessment as well (Chap. 7). For completeness, we also briefly include two works below that are covered more thoroughly in other chapters.

One of these works comes from Alshomary et al. (2020b) who infer the target of an implicit argument conclusion from the argument's premises. In a nutshell, their core approach first identifies the premise targets using a neural sequence tagger (Akbik et al. 2018) learned on target-annotated claims (Bar-Haim et al. 2017a). Trained via contrastive learning, it then predicts the embedding of the conclusion target from the premise targets and matches this embedding against a pool of targets (for details, see Chap. 9). In experiments, Alshomary et al. (2020b) evaluate this approach against a ranking alternative that predicts and picks the most representative premise target (along with other baselines). On a debate portal argument dataset (Wang and Ling 2016) and two argument variations from the AAE2 corpus (Stab and Gurevych 2017b), the approach largely beat the ranker in terms of BLEU and METEOR score. While humans more often found the ranked targets to be fully adequate conclusion targets than the predicted targets (55% vs. 50%), only the approach can infer new targets. It did so in 12–25% of the cases, depending on the dataset.

The approach of Gurcke et al. (2021) that we detailed already in Chap. 7 goes one step beyond in that it generates the entire conclusion from an argument's premises, employing a fine-tuned BART transformer (Lewis et al. 2020). Technically, the conclusion is not implicit originally, but the authors mask it before generation. The underlying hypothesis is that a comparison of the two conclusion variants enables a more effective assessment of the argument's logical sufficiency. In the generation experiments, human evaluators saw the generated conclusions on par with the original ones in terms of being *likely* (mean score of 2.96 vs. 2.98 on a 5-point scale) and *sufficiently* drawn from the premises (2.87 vs. 2.92). Only in terms of *novelty*, the generated conclusions fell notably behind (3.47 vs. 3.79).

As a basis for reconstruction research, Becker et al. (2020) extended the 112 arguments in the AMT corpus (Peldszus and Stede 2016b) by implicit knowledge, phrased as simple natural language statements. To this end, annotators analyzed 719 pairs of argument components that are either neighbors in the text or have an argumentative relation. For example, for the two components "Capital punishment is not a solution" and "as it cannot be ruled out that the judicial process may make mistakes.", annotators added "In a judicial process it is decided about capital punishment." In a subsequent step, each statement was categorized into one of four semantic types: *states*, *events*, *generic sentences*, and *generalizing sentences*.

In follow-up work, Becker et al. (2021) explore to what extent language models can reconstruct such knowledge. The authors created instances for model fine-tuning from two corpora that explain the connections between sentences (Camburu et al. 2018; Bhakthavatsalam et al. 2020). For evaluation, Becker et al. used the respective test sets as well as, as an out-of-domain set, the corpus of Becker et al. (2020). According to human judges, BART performed best compared to GPT-2 and XLNet (Yang et al. 2019b), generating premises that are nearly always grammatical and often coherent in their context. However, given the diverse possibilities of completing enthymemes discussed above, the resulting matches of references were limited, for example, with BLEU-1 scores between 0.0114 and 0.1271. At the same time, effectiveness remained rather stable out-of-domain.

Chakrabarty et al. (2021b) explicitly tackle the task of inferring the implicit premise of enthymemes. The authors propose a BART-based approach that uses transfer learning to leverage commonsense knowledge and abductive reasoning in narrative text where the task is: Given two observations, O_1 and O_2, generate a plausible explanatory hypothesis, H (Bhagavatula et al. 2020). Here is an example:

O_1: Jenny cleaned her house and went to work, leaving the window just a crack open.
O_2: When Jenny returned home she saw that her house was a mess!
H: A thief broke into the house by pulling open the window.

The transfer learning approach consists of the following three steps:

1. *Fine-Tuning for Abductive Reasoning.* First, the BART model is fine-tuned on the data of Bhagavatula et al. (2020) to predict H from O_1 and O_2. Exploiting the capabilities of encoder-decoder transformers, Chakrabarty et al. encode the input as "O_1 `[SEP]` O_2" and the output as "O_1 And since H O_2".
2. *Fine-Tuning for Commonsense Knowledge.* Next, BART is further fine-tuned on output of the PARA-COMET model (Gabriel et al. 2021), which generates nine types of discourse-aware commonsense inferences from narratives. Chakrabarty et al. focus on the inference of intentions of persons, which they derive from $O1$ to obtain triples "O_1 `<Intention>` O_2". Given this input, BART is trained to output "O_1 And since H O_2" again.
3. *Inference-Time Decoding.* Given the conclusion and a premise of an enthymematic argument, the fine-tuned BART model generates an output that is supposed to represent the implicit premise. Chakrabarty et al. employ beam search with a width of 5 for generation.

The authors evaluated their approach to premise reconstruction on three datasets (Boltužić and Šnajder 2016; Habernal et al. 2018c; Becker et al. 2020). Compared to a zero-shot BART, the approach achieved notable gains in all cases, for example, from 0.4696 to 0.6775 in terms of BERTScore on the data of Boltužić and Šnajder (2016). Both fine-tuning steps were helpful according to ablation tests. Human evaluators judged many more generated premises to be plausible for the full approach (e.g., 66% on the same data) than for the ablation without PARA-COMET (48%).

Finally, Stahl et al. (2023) study the detection and reconstruction of enthymematic arguments in learner essays. Their focus is a sophisticated approach to the automatic creation of a corpus for both tasks, which removes components of argument to obtain enthymemes. As a first step, it filters high-quality arguments from the essays, based on an approximative reimplementation of the essay scoring approach of Wachsmuth et al. (2016) (see Chap. 7). Only those components are candidates for being removed that are (a) classified to be argumentative with the model of Chen et al. (2022a), and (b) do not result in unnatural arguments if removed. The latter is checked via BERT's next-sentence prediction for the neighboring sentences. The candidates are ranked by centrality using a variation of LexRank (Erkan and Radev 2004; Alshomary et al. 2020a) as well as by quality reduction in order to obtain enthymemes that actually show quality deficiencies. Stahl et al. conducted baseline experiments with a DeBERTa model (He et al. 2023) for detection and an adaption of the approach of Gurcke et al. (2021) for reconstruction. The former obtained an F_1-score of 0.68 and the latter a BERTScore of 0.252, both suggesting that more advanced approaches are needed for the two tasks.

8.3.3 Formalizing Implicit Reasoning

In this subsection, we first discuss approaches to *formalizing implicit reasoning* using knowledge resources. Then we look at the use of *formal argumentation* to manage enthymemes. Further related work can be found in Sviridova et al. (2026)'s survey coverage of argument explicitation and enthymeme reconstruction.

Modeling Implicit Knowledge Saadat-Yazdi et al. (2023) approach the argument relation identification task (see Chap. 5) as a search for a series of (implicit) inferences that can be chained together to connect two argument components. This generalizes the notion of warrants in Toulmin (1958)'s model (Chap. 3) to encompass components connected not only by support but also by attack and neutral relations. Using COMET-ATOMIC$^{20}_{20}$ (Hwang et al. 2021) for social commonsense, their ARGCON approach finds all knowledge graph paths that connect the two components. For each component, ARGCON generates a graph with *causes*, *hinderedBy*, *isAfter*, and *isBefore* relations to then merge the graphs. Additional paths can be generated in an optional link inference step using LINK, a fine-tuned BERT model. In experiments, the authors compare their knowledge-enhanced RoBERTa-based Siamese models to a RoBERTa baseline on three datasets. Knowledge here means all graph paths that connect the two components in ARGCON (or in ARGCON+LINK). The approaches outperform the baseline overall, with macro F_1-scores of 0.70, 0.76, and 0.49 on student essays (Opitz and Frank 2019), Debatepedia (Paul et al. 2020), and the M-Arg Presidential Debate corpus (Mestre et al. 2021) respectively. However, noisy connections reduced precision from knowledge-enhanced approaches. In M-Arg, knowledge provided a substantial advantage for some topics but the baseline was superior in the "Why They Should Be Elected" topic.

Delas et al. (2024) use argumentation schemes in a two-step process to reconstruct enthymemes. First, their approach classifies premises by argumentation scheme. Then, it pairs up all premises fitting a given argumentation scheme and sends the resulting pairs to an argument validator. They experiment with a corpus of LLM-generated, human-validated argumentation schemes (Ruiz-Dolz et al. 2024) (see above). As a baseline, they pair all premises (regardless of suitability for a given scheme) as input to the argument validator. Their approach significantly outperforms the baseline (macro F_1-score 0.78 vs. 0.51) in part by minimizing false positives.

Hunter (2022) considers knowledge resources that could be used in logic-based argumentation to resolve enthymemes that arise due to similar concepts (e.g., "showery" and "rainy") or different terms expressing the same concept (e.g., "dad" and "father"). He notes four types of semantic distance measures to address this: word embeddings, semantic networks, ontologies (description logic), and lexical analysis. He proposes using semantic distance based on GloVe embeddings (Pennington et al. 2014), with the caveat that words may only be appropriate to swap in some contexts or not at all. He argues for lazy substitution and provides some proofs about substitution concluding that "substitutions and abduction of default knowledge are well-integrated with respect to the logical language" (Hunter 2022, p. 5734). Since substitutions can introduce inconsistency, he then tests consistency via a call to the SAT solver PySAT (Ignatiev et al. 2018). While the resulting arguments might be different from the intended arguments, he envisions that this approach could help bridge argument mining and deductive, logic-based argumentation, supporting applications such as explanations, fusion, or updating an argument graph.

Enthymemes in Formal Argumentation 'Dialogue games' have been used to study enthymemes in arguments (see Walton and Krabbe 1995 for an influential perspective on dialogue from argumentation theory). A dialogue game has a logic (typically classical logic) and a finite set of moves (e.g., *assert* and *why*) that agents take turns in making. Each agent's perception of what common knowledge can be assumed may be imperfect. In this context, agents aim to agree upon an intended explicit argument based on the actually expressed implicit 'real' argument.

Black and Hunter (2008) develop a procedure for generating enthymematic inquiry dialogues between two agents. Each agent has a personal knowledge base and their own co-base that represents their (imperfect perception about what common knowledge is shared in their interlocatur's personal knowledge base. Agents have their own commitment

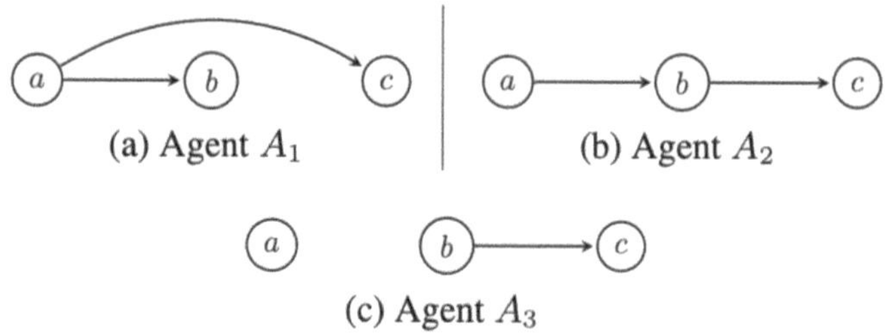

Fig. 8.11 Illustration of the disagreement between three agents, A_1–A_3, arising from three enthymemes, a, b, c. The disagreement is modeled via abstract argumentation frameworks. Adapted from Mailly (2016). Copyright ©2016 Association for the Advancement of Artificial Intelligence (www.aaai.org). All rights reserved

store containing the statements to which they have agreed. These dialogues construct an argument for a specific belief using five moves (*open*, *posit*, *quiz*, *agree*, and *close*) in which agents share beliefs. Under the assumptions of the authors, dialogues always terminate, even though decoding an enthymeme may take repeating posit and quiz cycles.

Mailly (2016) considers enthymemes as sources of mistaken attacks in abstract argumentation frameworks. He presents a motivating example of three enthymematic arguments that generate three different argumentation frameworks shown in Fig. 8.11. The difference arises because three agents each make their own interpretation of the defeater attacks between the arguments by using personal beliefs (based in the example on source credibility and taxonomic issues). Using Dung's semantics (see Chap. 3), Agent A_1's argumentation framework accepts a, Agent's A_2's framework accepts a and c, and Agent A_3's framework accepts a and b. Mailly considers how the agents could come to an agreement. There is not a single outcome: If A_1 and A_3 consider Agent A_2 trustworthy, they would need to update their argumentation frameworks if A_2 shares "c should be accepted". If the agents vote, Agents A_1 and A_3's rejection of c would mean that A_2 should update their argumentation framework. The author introduces 'questionable attacks', distinguished from 'certain attacks', in argumentation frameworks. This helps formalize a process for revising the argumentation frameworks from the motivating example.

Envisioning dialogues between humans and agents, Xydis et al. (2020) aim to bridge between formal and informal argumentation. They consider missing inferences, not only missing premises, and hence model enthymemes as disjoint unions of directed trees. To help dialogue participants recover from misunderstandings, they enable moves targeting an earlier locution, rather than replying only to the immediate previous move, such as asking "what did you think I meant by". Some of the additional moves allow participants to provide their own interpretation of an enthymeme (*assumed*), which another participant can correct (*meant*) and confirm (*agree*). Forward chaining to resolve inferences is another strength of their approach.

Xydis et al. (2021) develop a simple enthymeme dialogue system enabling participants to arrive at missing inferences. Here, their focus is soundness and completeness, so they simplify their previous proposal, using just three moves: *assert*, *and-so* (requesting the inference be supplied), and *hence* (supplying the inference). To show that their system generates arguments corresponding to Dung's framework, they formalize it within the ASPIC+ framework (see Chap. 3).

8.4 Summary

Reasoning is not only a key topic of current mainstream NLP research, but also the core of argumentation. Consequently, methods that model, assess, or reconstruct the reasoning are undoubtedly important for a comprehensive computational treatment of argumentative texts. Nonetheless, reasoning-related tasks are still comparably understudied in NLP research on argumentation. One main reason lies in the complexity of acquiring sufficient reliable data to study reasoning, which is why we have covered several data and annotation-oriented studies above. Another reason may be a missing shared view of what *argument reasoning* refers to exactly.

In this chapter, we have presented theories and computational methods for those aspects of argumentation that are typically seen as reasoning-related. Common ways of reasoning are described by *argumentation schemes*, those that are flawed by *fallacies*. To distinguish between correct and failed or deceptive applications of a scheme, the *critical questions* associated to argumentation schemes are the key. Knowing the scheme then helps to identify and reconstruct *enthymemes*. All of these may need to be handled to successfully apply *formal reasoning* to natural language. We briefly review all named aspects in the following:

Argumentation Schemes An argumentation scheme describes a formalized reasoning pattern that explains the plausibility of drawing the conclusion of an argument given the argument's premises. As such, a scheme models common inference mechanisms of arguments, which ultimately are the core of what argumentation is all about. Various deductive, inductive, and particularly abductive schemes have been proposed over the years. Most known is the catalogue of 65 schemes by Walton et al. (2008), but some researchers intentionally deviate from those. A surprisingly-limited number of NLP approaches exists so far for classifying an argument's scheme; some of them are based on features, others on language modeling.

Fallacies Fallacies denote failed or deceptive applications of argumentation schemes. Similar to the schemes, large and varying catalogues of fallacy types exist. Not all types technically fulfill the criteria of being (fallacious) arguments. Moreover, far from all flaws they exhibit refer to the logic in their reasoning, but many are clearly rhetorical in nature. Detecting fallacies can be understood as an alternative view of argument quality; however, one that is computationally challenging, as many fallacy types are often not reflected in surface-level text features. Still, this task has received increased attention, particularly following the rise of transformer-based methods.

Critical Questions Following the view of Walton et al. (2008), each argumentation scheme comes with a small set of critical questions that reflect the constraints that an argument needs to fulfill to be a valid instance of the respective scheme. Critical questions are therefore important to distinguish valid arguments from fallacies. Likewise, explicating the answer to a critical question brings to light implicit information underlying the argument. As such, critical questions also hint at the enthymematic reasoning happening in many arguments.

Enthymemes Conceptually, enthymemes are specifically arguments that leave one or more premises implicit. Many real-world arguments also leave their conclusion implicit, though. It is often easy for the target audience of an enthymematic argument to understand it properly, and making the implicit components explicit may sound odd. From a computational perspective, however, it can be important to explicate what is left unstated, which is why enthymeme detection and reconstruction have seen notable interest. Especially the latent knowledge of pretrained language models often provides a suitable starting point for completing enthymematic arguments.

Formal Reasoning Ultimately, a full specification of the knowledge in and underlying arguments creates the basis for applying formal reasoning techniques to natural language argumentation. When sufficiently specified, models such as the abstraction argumentation framework of Dung (1995) and its variants can be applied to natural language reasoning. We have discussed initial works that go in this direction.

Overall, the study of argument reasoning marks the turning point where NLP research on argumentation transitions from analysis to synthesis. Analyzing the structure and perspective of arguments defines the basis for the study, whereas reasoning itself implies that new knowledge or new information is synthesized. While still comparably underresearched, schemes, fallacies, and enthymemes are getting more attention, not least with the rise of reasoning-enhanced LLMs (Guo et al. 2025). In the long term, we expect argument reasoning research to increasingly integrate with research on reasoning in LLMs. In this regard, Gemechu et al. (2025) recently created a benchmark with a total of sixteen different argument reasoning tasks, covering serial, linked, convergent and divergent reasoning variations. Their baseline experiments suggest that LLMs still show limited effectiveness on reasoning tasks. We expect notable improvements in future work, though. We move fully to the synthesis side in the next chapter, presenting the state of the art of another topic resurging in interest: argument generation.

9 Argument Generation

Both the mining of arguments from natural language text (Chaps. 4 and 5) and the assessment of their properties (Chaps. 6 and 7) imply *analysis* tasks: NLP methods infer information from input texts. In the context of argument quality and reasoning, Chaps. 7 and 8 already covered some more synthesis-oriented tasks, the rewriting of argumentative text to improve its quality and the reconstruction of argument components left implicit in a text, respectively. In this chapter, we fully turn our view to situations in which new argumentative content is to be produced, be it single claims, complete arguments, or longer argumentative texts. That is, we consider *synthesis* tasks in detail here (even if, seen strictly, they lie outside the scope of a book called *Argument Mining*): NLP methods produce new text from information or other input texts. We cover all such methods under the term *argument generation*.

Historically, argument generation is one of the argumentation tasks studied earliest in NLP, tracing back to the beginning of the millenium (Zukerman et al. 2000). As for text generation in general, however, comparably limited substantial progress happened until the advent of transformer-based language models made generation one of the major topics in NLP research (Zhou et al. 2025a). This shift has also increasingly put argument generation into the focus of the community (Wang et al. 2023a). While a need for machine-generated arguments may seem unexpected at first sight, the applications are manifold (details in Chap. 10): Technologies such as Project Debater may compose and create arguments to use in a debate. Support tools may rewrite human-written arguments to optimize impact. Counterarguments may be generated to automatically fight online misinformation, and speeches or debates may be summarized to face information overload and ease opinion formation.

We organize this chapter along the three general techniques of how to generate argumentative texts: One technique is to produce new argumentative content from existing content or from scratch (Sect. 9.1). Another is to rewrite an argumentative input text into

M. Stede et al., *Argument Mining*, Synthesis Lectures on Human Language Technologies, https://doi.org/10.1007/978-3-032-32291-3_9

a respective output text, either in order to adjust certain properties of the input text or to obtain a counterargument to it (Sect. 9.2). Lastly, both monological argumentative texts and dialogical or multi-party debates may be summarized, which shares characteristics of both other ways while having a unique goal (Sect. 9.3). We conclude with the key points to consider in argument generation (Sect. 9.4).

9.1 Composing and Creating Argumentative Text

First, we look at NLP methods that produce new argumentative content, either by *composing* the content from structured information and existing text segments, or by *creating* arguments and their components from scratch. A clear delineation between composition and creation is not straightforward, given that any language production composes bigger utterances from smaller ones (with a single word as the minimum linguistically independent utterance). This brings up the question as to when content is 'new enough' to be called *new*. As a working solution, we here see argumentative content as new, if the argument components it subsumes have not been expressed before, as far as known. *Before*, in turn, refers to the data available in a given setting, meaning that it is directly accessible or implicitly stored in a model.

In the following, we start with composition-based approaches, before we delve into the creation of new content of increasing size: from single argumentative discourse units (ADUs) and arguments to longer argumentative texts. Later, in Chap. 10, we also see IBM's Project Debater, an advanced real-world application that builds on many of the ideas covered in this section.

9.1.1 Composition of Arguments from Existing Content

The composition of arguments starts from a *knowledge base* or from a *retrieval* step that finds text to be included. Given ADUs can also be composed under guiding principles from *rhetoric*. Most of the respective approaches we discuss here rather come from the times of rule-based and simple statistical NLP methods. However, also more recent works exist that bridge to today's language modeling concepts.

Knowledge-Based Composition Early work in text generation was concerned with systems that are able to produce short texts from a collection of structured data or from knowledge represented in a suitable formalism, such as description logic or Bayesian belief networks. Zukerman et al. (2000) employ such networks to show how the logical structure of an argument can be constructed systematically by combining knowledge about argument structures with a model of hearer beliefs, which the argument should try to influence. Grasso et al. (2000) pursue a different path, embedding argument generation into a dialogue system that aims to convince users to eat more healthy food. A knowledge

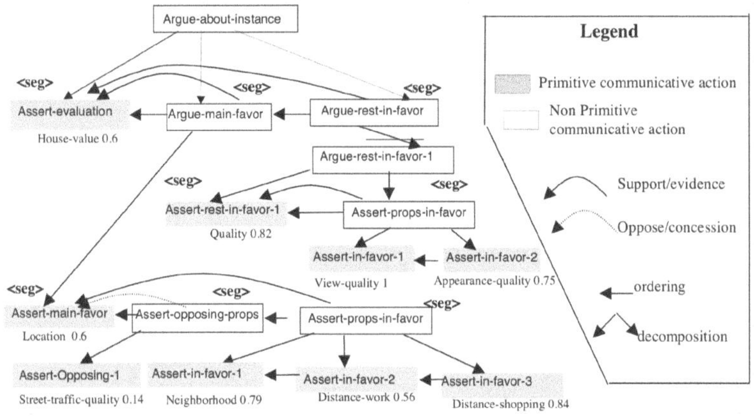

Fig. 9.1 Sample text plan produced by the generator of Carenini (2001): The chosen strategy *argue-about-instance* first asserts the overall evaluation computed for a house, then provides the main argument in favor, followed by positive observations. Decomposition stops at the gray boxes, which correspond to speech acts with attribute and value. Used with permission

base encodes information on what kinds of food have positive or negative effects on health, and a dynamic network models perspectives and values associated with topics, as they develop in a dialogue.

In a similar fashion, Carenini (2001) aims to influence a user's attitude toward a given entity, studied for the real estate domain. A knowledge base covers features of a set of houses (e.g., size, location, and price), and a user model represents preferences (e.g., that location is important). On this basis, an algorithm computes how valuable each house is for the user, and how valuable the different attributes are, following the three common phases of complete text generation systems (Reiter and Dale 2000):

1. *Text Planning.* The ADUs to be expressed are selected and organized in a hierarchical text plan, which determines the order in which they will appear. Carenini implements several argumentation strategies that specify how to order positive and negative ADUs. Strategies are coded as operators that decompose abstract goals into concrete ones. Figure 9.1 shows a sample text plan.
2. *Microplanning.* The text plan is distributed into a sequence of sentence plans, with linguistic information and lexical choices for expressing the ADUs. As part of this, Carenini's approach converts the speech act objects into linguistic predicate/argument structures. The mapping uses a lexicon, and the choices among near-synonyms are made on the basis of the values associated with attributes.
3. *Realization.* Each sentence plan is converted to a well-formed sentence in natural language: words are inflected properly, and appropriate function words are inserted. Carenini chooses specific connectives to indicate a continuing or changing argumenta-

tive orientation, and then connects the different ADUs to produce the final output. Here is a sample output (entity marked in italic):

(9.1) *House 2-33* is an interesting house. In fact, it has a reasonable location in the safe Eastend neighborhood. Even though the traffic is intense on 2nd street, *house 2-33* is reasonably close to work. And also it offers an easy access to the shops. Furthermore, the quality of *house 2-33* is good. *House 2-33* offers an excellent view. And also it looks beautiful.

Further knowledge-based attempts include the GenIE system of Green et al. (2011) for composing genetic counseling letters. GenIE plans a text using a hand-crafted discourse grammar along the lines of the rhetorical structure theory (RST) (Mann and Thompson 1988), which we briefly introduced in Chap. 2. For material that needs more motivation, a separate argument generation module inserts argumentation schemes as a small RST tree into the overall text plan, for instance an effect-to-cause scheme. In later work, Green (2017b) extends the ideas of GenIE to provide feedback to learners based on a comparison of generated and learner arguments.

Retrieval-Based Composition The aforementioned approaches involve much manual labor, because only a few components for the generation process are reusable or standardized. Even if knowledge representations avoid hard-wiring domain specific information, the actual knowledge acquisition process has to be restarted for any new domain. An alternative is to combine argument mining with argument generation: find textual material that can be recomposed in new text.

Along these lines, Ashley and Walker (2013) propose to compose legal arguments by recombining parts of related arguments from 35 legal decisions on vaccine injuries, manually annotated for propositional inference structures and domain-specific entity relations. The authors envisage that a retrieval engine may find relevant components to produce new arguments. In another work, Reisert et al. (2015) instantiate Toulmin arguments (see Chap. 3) using an input motion as the claim. Data, warrant, and backing for the claim are retrieved from a preprocessed knowledge base of promote and suppress relations and integrated using hand-crafted rules.

Sato et al. (2015) provide one of the first fully-implemented retrieval-based argument generators: A user enters a claim (e.g., "This house should ban gambling in the city.") and a stance toward it, and the system generates three argumentative paragraphs on different aspects of the motion. The paragraphs are produced by selecting (and partly modifying) syntactically-parsed sentences from 10 million news articles. Manual work is involved only in some built-in lexicons for epistemic verbs, evaluative modifiers, and similar. The system works as follows:

1. *Motion analysis.* The input motion is divided into keyphrases capturing the motion topic, the predicate used in the topic, polarity, and further components.
2. *Aspect selection.* Aspects that foster evaluative judgments are deemed relevant. The system retrieves five sentences that match the given stance and contain affect relations between the motion and aspects from a dictionary. For the motion above, a candidate is "Gambling increases the number of crimes", as "increase" belongs to the semantic class *affect*, and "crime" is commonly evaluated as negative.
3. *Sentence retrieval.* Given a query built from the motion and the aspect phrases, relevant sentences are retrieved and filtered that have the right polarity and contain either promote or suppress relationships.
4. *Sentence ordering.* To build a paragraph, sentences are arranged such that the paragraph starts with a claim sentence and is followed by support sentences. To determine claims, a binary classifier is run on the sentences (see Chap. 4). The ordering of supporting sentences aims to maximize local coherence. Finally, details such as dates or proper names are eliminated to avoid inconsistencies.

For 50 claims from *Debatabase*, human judges scored all 150 paragraphs from 0 (makes no sense) to 4 (sounds natural). 86 received label 0, indicating that the overall problem is difficult. Errors came particularly from polarity computation, complex claims given as input by the user, and erroneous sentence retrieval.

Rhetoric-Based Recomposition Some researchers pay attention to rhetoric beyond the hand-crafted patterns in the works above (usually taken from guides to good writing). Wachsmuth et al. (2018a) suggest following Aristotle's means of persuasion (logos, ethos, and pathos) when selecting, arranging, and (re-)phrasing existing ADUs in a new text. To gather data, they conducted a study with 26 human 'composers' who recombined claims, supporting premises, and opposing premises on 10 topics from the arg-microtext corpus (Peldszus and Stede 2016b). The authors instructed the composers to select and arrange ADUs, combining the ADUs with discourse connectives. The goal was to obtain new logos-oriented arguments (defined as making rational and logical conclusions toward the intended stance regarding the topic) and pathos-oriented arguments (appealing to emotions of the reader regarding the topic), respectively. Wachsmuth et al. found the selection agreement to be significantly higher within the logos-/pathos-oriented texts than between them, indicating that people can sense the means of persuasion. The most popular arrangement pattern was *(claim, opposing ADU, three supporting ADUs)*.

Based on the study results, El Baff et al. (2019) present a topic-agnostic argument composition approach that abstracts ADUs into ADU types using k-means clustering based on style features. Given an ADU pool for a controversial topic (e.g., "Should all universities in Germany charge tuition fees?"), a stance (e.g., *against*), and a means of persuasion (e.g., *pathos*), two ADU-level language models and a regression model realize the concept of Wachsmuth et al. (2018a) in three computational steps:

1. *Selection.* The approach first trains a n-gram language model that predicts probabilities of ADU type sequences. At inference time, it uses all ADU sequences matching the top type sequence as candidates. 2-grams worked best for El Baff et al. with six clustered types and sequences of five ADUs.
2. *Arrangement.* In training, the approach learns an n-gram language model that predicts probabilities of ADU *role* sequences (where roles are *claim*, *pro premise*, and *con premise*). During inference, only those candidates are kept that match the top ADU role sequence. ADU role 3-grams proved best for El Baff et al..
3. *Phrasing.* In training, a regression model learns to assess the coherence of adjacent ADUs, approximated by embedding similarity. In inference, the approach takes the candidate with maximum aggregate coherence. El Baff et al. predict coherence for ADU 2-grams. Exemplarily, their approach composes the following pathos-oriented argument against tuition fees (connectives added for readability):

(9.2) Education must not be a question of money in a wealthy society such as Germany *(claim)*. One could argue that an increase in tuition fees would allow institutions to be better equipped *(con)*. But studying and taking higher degrees must remain a basic right for everyone *(pro)*, and longer durations of studies are costly *(pro)*. The universities in Germany should not under any circumstances charge tuition fees *(pro)*.

While rhetorical considerations play a role in many recent argument creation and rewriting approaches (see further below), only few works have pursued similar ideas for recomposition. A notable exception is the moral framing approach of Alshomary et al. (2022a) which composes topic and stance-specific arguments that match a chosen subset of the five morals from the moral foundation theory of Haidt (2012): *care*, *fairness*, *loyalty*, *authority*, and *purity*. To this end, the approach retrieves topic-specific sentences via the Project Debater API (see Chap. 10), filters those that fit the chosen moral foundations, extracts ADUs from the sentences, and generates a narrative from the ADUs that fits the topic and stance (again employing the API). Figure 9.2 illustrates the approach for a pro argument on globalization.

9.1.2 Creation of New Argumentative Discourse Units

The smallest possible argumentative content to be created is a single ADU, that is, a claim or a premise. We here distinguish approaches as to whether they *invent* new ADUs, *reconstruct* implicit ADUs, or obtain them via *conditioned generation*. While we will see some more classically algorithmic approaches below, most exploit the capabilities of neural transformers or large language models (LLMs) in some way.

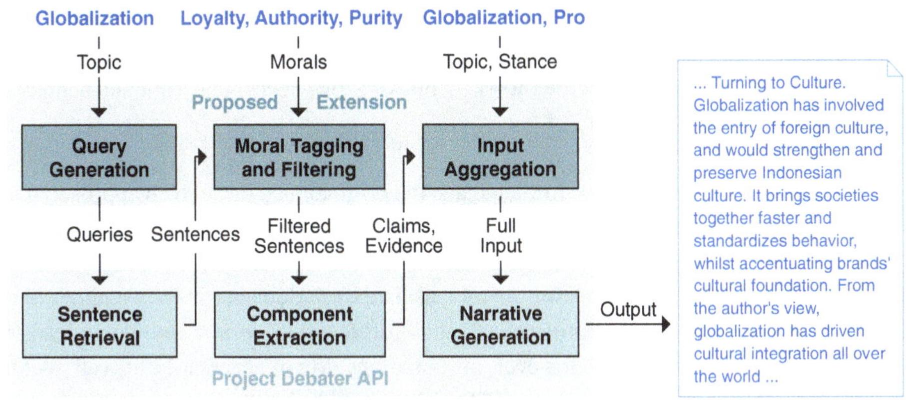

Fig. 9.2 Composition of a *pro globalization* argument by the approach of Alshomary et al. (2022a), matching the morals *loyalty*, *authority*, and *purity*. The figure is taken from Alshomary et al. (2022a). Licensed under CC-BY 4.0 International

ADU Invention One of the first research lines on ADU creation comes from the Project Debater team and extends purely compositional elements. In particular, Bilu and Slonim (2016) seek to minimize human intervention in inventing new claims. The basic idea is to construct claims by 'recycling' linguistic predicates found in the claims of other arguments, which the authors illustrate with the example: Given the claim "banning violent video games is a violation of free speech" for the topic *banning violent video games*, its predicate may be transferred to the topic *internet censorship* to generate "internet censorship is a violation of free speech." Thus, a key task in their approach is to learn the contexts allowing or disallowing a candidate recombination. The proposed claim invention approach works in three steps:

1. *Predicate Lexicon Acquisition.* Given a set of claims, extract the verb from each of them and a concatenation of its right-modifiers, which together form a predicate, p. p is added to the lexicon, if and only if it contains at least one sentiment word, thereby focusing on predicates with a clear stance toward their topic. Concretely, Bilu and Slonim obtain 1203 lexicon entries this way, starting from the Wikipedia claims in the corpus of Aharoni et al. (2014).
2. *Claim Candidate Invention.* Given a target topic t, all predicates p in the lexicon are sorted by similarity to t. For the top-k predicates, a claim candidate is created by combining the predicate with t as subject (as in the example above). This may require morphological adjustments (e.g., singular/plural matching). In their work, Bilu and Slonim use a similarity measure involving word embeddings and the SimpleNLG realization engine for adjustments (Gatt and Reiter 2009). They generate 28 candidate claims each for 67 motion topics from *idebate.org*.
3. *Claim Candidate Ranking.* Finally, the candidate claims are ranked based on their scores assigned by a logistic regression classifier, trained on human assessments of claims. Bilu

and Slonim use 15 features for the classifier capturing three concepts: the generality of the predicate, its relevance to t, and the linguistic likelihood of the claim. The classifiers are trained on assessments of crowdworkers on Amazon Mechanical Turk and achieved an accuracy of 75.0%.

In later work, Bilu et al. (2019) further shape the original idea through an approach that invents argumentative claims *from first principles*, inspired by how professional human debaters reuse principled ideas in various contexts. Here is an example: "banning a product or a service may lead to the creation of a black market." Debaters may instantiate this principled idea in many meaningful claims, such as "*banning pornography* may lead to the creation of a black market." However, instantiations do not necessarily fit well, as for *banning breastfeeding* in the given case. To guide the instantiation, Bilu et al. experiment with Naïve Bayes classifiers and recurrent neural networks based on topic similarity and predicate similarity.

In a rather unusual work with important practical implications, Evgrafova et al. (2025) study to what extent LLM-generated definitions of controversial issues are biased by the data the LLMs have been trained on, such that they convey stance as in "abortion is the act of deliberately killing a fetus." The authors fine-tune Llama-3-7b-Instruct (Touvron et al. 2023a) on different neutral or slang language dictionaries. In experiments, the resulting fine-tuned LLMs are prompted to generate definitions for a number of controversial issues from the args.me corpus (Ajjour et al. 2019b) and from the IBM keypoint dataset discussed below (Friedman et al. 2021). The results demonstrate that the stance-related bias in the definitions is indeed bigger when the training data is not neutral. A subsequent manual analysis of 1000 definitions reveals that the biased models produce more polarized but less plausible definitions.

ADU Reconstruction In many settings, the argumentative content to be generated is not isolated from surrounding context. Rather, a specific claim or premise may be missing or left implicit on purpose. A number of works in the last years have taken on the task to reconstruct such ADUs, or parts of the information they contain. We have touched on this task already at the end of Chap. 8 in the context of enthymemes and their role in reasoning. Now, we turn our view to computational methods.

For reconstruction, multiple researchers have leveraged the text generation capabilities of transformers. Chakrabarty et al. (2021b) model the inference of implicit premises of a given argument as a sequence-to-sequence problem (as we have detailed in Chap. 8). For inference, they propose to fine-tune a BART model (Lewis et al. 2020) on both abductive reasoning (Bhagavatula et al. 2020) and commonsense knowledge from the PARA-COMET model (Gabriel et al. 2021). In experiments on three datasets, the fine-tuned BART clearly outperforms zero-short BART, creating plausible premises in 56–66% of the cases according to human evaluation.

In contrast, Gurcke et al. (2021) reconstruct the conclusions of arguments from the arguments' premises as a pre-step for argument sufficiency assessment (as detailed in Chap. 7), modeling reconstruction as a fill-in-the-blank problem. In their manual evaluation on student essays, the conclusions generated by a fine-tuned BART model compete with human conclusions in relevance and likeliness, but fall a bit behind in novelty. Other researchers have followed the fill-in-the-blank model, for example, to tackle enthymeme reconstruction explicitly (Stahl et al. 2023).

One of the few attempts to operationalize reconstruction from the time before transformers came up is the contrastive learning approach of Alshomary et al. (2020b) to inferring the topic targeted by an implicit conclusion from the premises. For example, if one premise is that "human life is invaluable" and another one that "the risk of executing the innocent can never be eliminated", then it may be reasonable to infer that the conclusion target is *death penalty*, say, in a conclusion stating that "the *death penalty* should be abolished." Alshomary et al. compare two alternative variants to infer targets. One variant ranks the premises' targets by their likelihood of representing a conclusion target. For cases such as the given example, however, this is insufficient, since the actual target never appears in the premises. The other variant aims to tackle this issue by predicting the conclusion target in a learned embedding space. Conceptually, it carries out four main steps:

1. *Target Identification.* A target tagger is learned on a target-annotated ADU dataset and applied to identify all premise targets, p_i, and all conclusion targets, c_j, in a training set for the task. In their experiments, Alshomary et al. train a neural sequence tagger (Akbik et al. 2018) on respective data of Bar-Haim et al. (2017a), and use two essay datasets (Stab and Gurevych 2017b) as well as one debate portal dataset (Wang and Ling 2016).
2. *Target Embedding Learning.* All targets are represented in a default embedding space (e.g., c as $\mathbf{c}$). Each set of premise targets of an argument, $\mathbf{p}_1, \ldots, \mathbf{p}_k$, together with the argument's conclusion target, $\mathbf{c}$, define a positive training instance. $\mathbf{p}_1, \ldots, \mathbf{p}_k$ together with another random conclusion target, $\mathbf{c}'$, define an associated negative instance. Then, training instance pairs are used for contrastive learning, namely, to train a triplet neural network (Hoffer and Ailon 2015) that learns a transformed embedding space in which the distance of the mapped mean embeddings $f(\mathbf{s}_1), \ldots, f(\mathbf{s}_l)$ derived from $\mathbf{p}_1, \ldots, \mathbf{p}_k$ to $f(\mathbf{c})$ are minimized and their distance to $f(\mathbf{c}')$ is maximized. Figure 9.3 illustrates this idea.
3. *Target Inference.* To obtain the actual conclusion target from its predicted embedding, a pool of candidate targets is mapped to the learned embedding space. The candidate target closest to $f(\mathbf{c})$ is taken. In this neuro-symbolic way, it is ensured that the inferred conclusion target is always a meaningful target. Alshomary et al. simply use all targets from the training set as the candidate pool.

In automatic evaluation based on the three mentioned datasets, the embedding learning variant proves stronger than the premise target ranking variant, and a hybrid of the two (that prefers a premise target if the predicted target is too different) even stronger. On average,

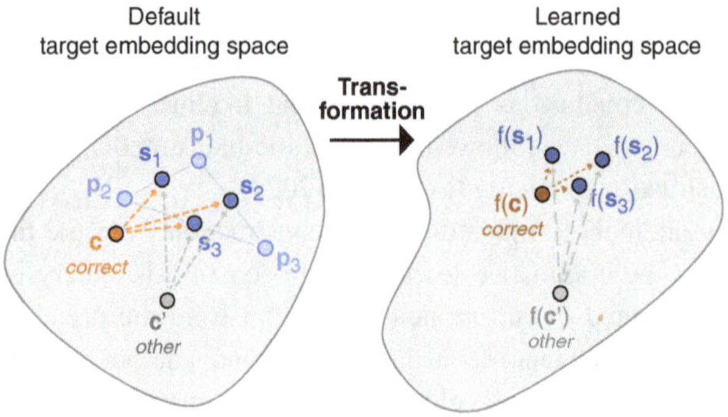

Fig. 9.3 Illustration of the embedding learning approach of Alshomary et al. (2020b): The distance from the averages $\mathbf{s}_1, \mathbf{s}_2, \ldots$ of the premise targets $\mathbf{p}_1, \mathbf{p}_2, \ldots$ to the correct conclusion target $\mathbf{c}$ is minimized; the distance to other targets $\mathbf{c}'$ is maximized. Licensed under CC-BY 4.0 International

however, humans slightly prefer the ranking approach, possibly because its targets have a more obvious connection to the premise targets.

Conditioned ADU Generation In general, conditioned text generation aims to guide the creation of a text so that certain specified criteria are met. Specifically, Park et al. (2019) generate claims on a given topic using an encoder-decoder language model with gated recurrent units (GRUs) for context modeling (Cho et al. 2014). To force different perspectives, the encoder outputs multiple latent mechanisms and the decoder generates multiple candidate claims accordingly. Each candidate that is optimal with respect to one mechanism is chosen.

Alshomary et al. (2021a) go beyond, making perspectives *audience-aware*. The authors condition the way claims are stated on the beliefs of a given audience, where the audience is identified by its stances on different general controversial issues given on debate.org, such as *environmental protection*. Deriving an audience-specific bag of words from the stances, they input it to the plug-and-play language model (Dathathri et al. 2020) to generate claims on given topics. Experiments show limitations of representing an audience by a few words, while the general idea works well. For the topic *whaling*, for example, the environmental protection output is: "Whaling is a very dangerous and cruel practice. It causes great harm to the environment, animals that are caught in it have their lives cut short by being eaten alive."

Gretz et al. (2020a) compare variants of GPT-2 (Radford et al. 2019) for topic-specific claim generation, fine-tuned on different topic-claim datasets. They observe both plausible outputs (e.g., "A proper democracy is good for the country") and implausible ones (e.g., "free newspapers reduce crime"). From both, they derive strategies as to when to prefer claim generation and when claim retrieval. Saha and Srihari (2023) address factuality issues of BART-generated claims, by representing facts about the topic discussed in an encoding stage. Given a stance and either of six argumentation schemes covered in the crowdsourced dataset of Kondo et al. (2021), their approach creates an argument template from the inputs and integrates it with the fact encoding to generate arguments. Experiments showed promising results, but indicated some tradeoff between the control of factuality, stance, and schemes.

Following up on the perspective-oriented approach of Park et al. (2019), Cao et al. (2025) propose a preference optimization approach to generating diverse claims. An instruction fine-tuning stage first teaches an LLM to generate claims that are relevant and stance-consistent. For preference optimizations, the authors mined claims on given controversial issues and quantified their perspective diversity based on differences in cosine similarity to the discussed controversial issue. Using direct preference optimization (DPO) (Rafailov et al. 2024), the LLM then learns to favor diversity-oriented claims. In experiments on the PERSPECTRUM dataset (Chen et al. 2019b) and data from the Reddit forum *ChangeMyView* (Hayati et al. 2024), the authors evaluate their approach using Llama-3-8B-Instruct (Touvron et al. 2023a) and Qwen-2.5-7B-Instruct (Yang et al. 2024). In automatic evaluation it overall seems to best balance between diversity, stance, and argument quality compared to the base models and closed models such as GPT-4. According to human judges, GPT-4 and the approach seem largely on par across various dimensions.

9.1.3 Creation of New Arguments and Argumentative Texts

A few researchers have recently turned the view to creating full arguments or longer argumentative texts. Approaches for arguments mostly employ some form of *conditioned generation*. Longer texts are so far tackled with *planning-based generation*, integrating traditional discourse ideas into language modeling processes.

Conditioned Argument Generation Schiller et al. (2021b) investigate how to control the aspects discussed in an argument. The authors train an aspect detector based on an extension of the argument corpus of Stab et al. (2018b), where all aspects of the eight covered topics are annotated (e.g., "bullying", "individuality", or "expensive" for the topic *gun control*). Using the detector, they gather aspect-specific data from Reddit and CommonCrawl that they use to fine-tune a controlled transformer model (Keskar et al. 2019) to generate an argument for a given *(topic, stance, aspect)* tuple. In their evaluation, they demonstrate how aspect-specific arguments can be generated. For example, the output argument to "School uniforms are expensive and affect pupil's individuality" for the aspect "expensive" starts as follows: "The cost of the uniform is not that much more than a regular shirt and shorts [. . .]."

The work of Al Khatib et al. (2021) can be seen as an extension of the above-mentioned research on knowledge-based argument composition to neural methods. In particular, to control for the plausibility and topical relevance of arguments, the authors study how to infuse argumentation knowledge into the text generation process of a pretrained language model, GPT-2 in particular. To this end, instances from knowledge graphs containing promote and suppress relations or causal relations are encoded into texts that are then used to fine-tune GPT-2. While the arguments generated in their experiments often turned out plausible and relevant to the topic, they sometimes became socially biased and factually incorrect.

Li et al. (2024b) seek to control LLMs to create arguments that support an input argument. The core idea is to let two LLMs (prompted to have varying stances) debate on the argument and eventually summarize their main point. The points are used as ground-truth outputs in an instruction fine-tuning stage. In the evaluation, an LLM fine-tuned this way outperforms different default LLMs in generating high-quality and stance-adherent arguments.

A technically up-to-date approach comes from Mouchel et al. (2025) who tackle factuality issues in argument generation explicitly through a reinforcement learning-based preference optimization method. It aligns the behavior of an LLM to avoid 13 types of logical fallacies (e.g., *faulty generationalization*, *ad-hominem*, and *ad populum*). Given a topic and a stance on the topic, it proceeds in three main steps:

1. *Supervised Fine-Tuning.* On a training set of fallacy-free arguments, an LLM is fine-tuned using maximum likelihood estimation. In their experiments, Mouchel et al. consider Llama-2-7B (Touvron et al. 2023a) and Mistral-7B (Jiang et al. 2023), fine-tuning them using low-rank adaptation (LoRA) (Hu et al. 2022).
2. *Preference Data Collection.* For preference optimization, ChatGPT is prompted with fallacy definitions and few-shot examples to generate fallacies of the 13 types for the training topics. Pairs of fallacy-free and fallacious arguments then become preference examples. Specifically, Mouchel et al. create 7872 fallacies for an existing dataset of 1968 arguments (Saha et al. 2021), following the fallacy distribution in the data of Jin et al. (2022).
3. *Reinforcement Learning.* On the preference data, a reward model is trained to predict reward values for given arguments. This model is used to align the fine-tuned LLM toward generating fallacy-free arguments. Mouchel et al. realize the model with Electra (Clark et al. 2020). While common preference methods such as proximal policy optimization (PPO) (Schulman et al. 2017) and DPO would apply, they propose to balance a contrastive preference optimization (CPO) loss (Xu et al. 2024) with a classification loss that guides the LLM to avoid the different fallacy types.

In experiments, both LLaMA-2-7B and Mistral-7B aligned in this manner create fallacious arguments in less than 20% of the cases, compared to around 30% if aligned with methods such as PPO, DPO, or CPO alone.

Planning-Based Text Generation Goldfarb-Tarrant et al. (2020) discuss how to achieve a globally-coherent narrative in story generation by planning its plot structure. While not specifically for argumentative text, their approach involves an 'Aristotelian rescoring' step, following Aristotle's layout of four main story elements: *event choice and arrangement*, *character*, *relevant content*, and *diction*. Technically, it is a learned classifier that distinguishes good from bad plot structures based on element-specific features derived from the plots, such as inter-sentence and intra-sentence event ordering or character entity sequences. In automatic and human evaluation, a fine-tuned BART transformer using the 'Aristotelian plots' beat most baselines in terms of overall quality and topic relevance of the created stories, but its scores are not significantly better than those of simpler BART variants.

More focused on argumentative text, Bao et al. (2022b) introduce the task of generating a persuasive essay for a given writing prompt. The authors propose a transformer architecture with one encoder but two decoders: The first decoder plans the perspectives and aspects to be discussed along with lexical diversity considerations, and the second one incorporates this information in the form of attention to generate the essay word-by-word. According to human evaluation on a new dataset of 11k English essays from essayforum.com, the approach outperformed standard transformer architectures in relevance, coherence, and content richness, but still shows room for improvement, particularly for coherence.

Xiao et al. (2024) aim to tackle these limitations by first generating an ordered list of claims to be made. The order is informed by logical abstractions of training texts, obtained automatically using GPT-4 (OpenAI et al. 2024). They pursue a similar process to generate supporting evidence for each claim, and a final model takes the claims and evidence to generate an essay. In the evaluation, humans clearly preferred the generated essays over those of Bao et al. (2022b). While essays generated by ChatGPT had even higher relevance, credibility of evidence, rhetoric, and persuasiveness, the approach of Xiao et al. (2024) beat it in the validity of reasoning.

A prompting-based approach to planning-based generation not only for essays is proposed by He et al. (2024), which combines ideas similar to those of the previous approaches with a dialectical planning strategy that considers potential rebuttals to the arguments made. The hand-defined strategy follows notions from theory such as the model of Toulmin (1958). Given a writing prompt, it proceeds in three steps:

1. *Sketch Planning.* An LLM is prompted in two consecutive steps to draft a major claim $\tilde{c}^m$ (the essay's thesis) and n claims $\tilde{c}_i$ supporting $\tilde{c}^m$. He et al. evaluate three LLMs in a zero-shot setting: Baichuan-7B for Chinese (Yang et al. 2023), LLaMA-7B for English, and GPT-3.5 for both. They use rather minimalist prompts, such as "Write a concise, contentious, and coherent Thesis Statement (major claim) given the writing prompt", and create $n = 3$ claims per essay.
2. *Dialectical Planning.* Next, the LLM is prompted to challenge each claim $\tilde{c}_i$ with an overriding rebuttal r_i^o, which functions as feedback to $\tilde{c}_i$. Given $\tilde{c}_i$ and r_i^o, the LLM is hence prompted again to optimize $\tilde{c}_i$ into c_i. Afterwards, an undercutting rebuttal r_i^u is created accordingly, but instead of simply refining c_i again, an explicit counter-rebuttal r_i^c is obtained from the LLM. Moreover, k evidence statements e_{ij} are generated for

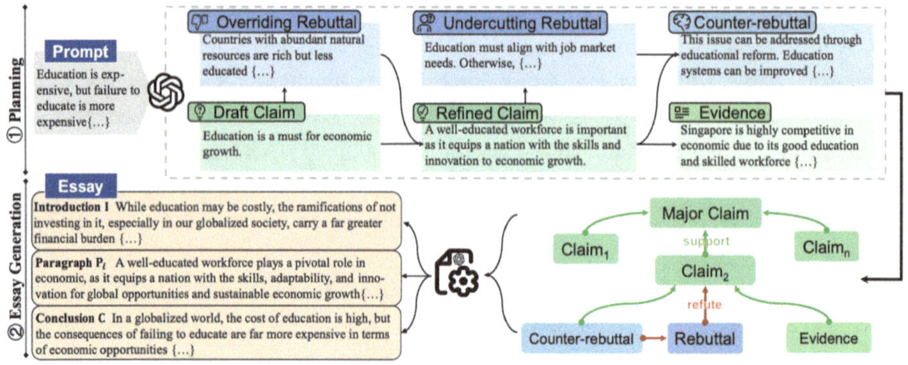

Fig. 9.4 Overview of the essay generation approach of He et al. (2024): *(1) Planning:* A preliminary outline of claims, evidence, and rebuttals to be discussed in the essay is prepared. *(2) Essay Generation:* The prepared information is grouped into introduction, argument paragraphs, and conclusion, which are then generated by an LLM. Licensed under CC-BY 4.0 International

each c_i. Finally, the major claim $\tilde{c}^m$ is revised into c^m to account for the changes made. He et al. use similarly simple prompts again, and create $k = 2$ evidence statements per claim.

3. *Essay Generation.* Given all generated statements, the LLM is prompted to draft the introduction of the text, one paragraph per claim c_i, and a conclusion. The introduction is based on the writing prompt and the major claim c^m, and the conclusion on c^m and on all claims c_i. The paragraph prompts in turn contain c_i and all related information, that is, each e_{ij}, r_i^u, and r_i^c. Once all parts are drafted, they are used for the final generation of the entire text. Here, He et al. give additional instructions, such as "You should adequately rebut and address the rebuttal according to Counter_rebuttal to further support the claim" or "Write a coherent and persuasive body paragraph in favor of the claim."

Figure 9.4 illustrates the steps for an example prompt. He et al. carried out experiments on (a) the dataset of Bao et al. (2022b), (b) a new Chinese essay dataset, and (c) two new editorial datasets (one English, one Chinese). They did not compare to the previous approaches but to well-known prompting strategies, such as chain-of-thought (Wei et al. 2022) and tree-of-thought (Yao et al. 2024). Across all models, the approach was mostly best according to GPT-4-based assessments of cogency, persuasiveness, and reasonableness. Also, humans ranked the resulting essays highest in 68% of the cases, followed by tree-of-thought in 19%. The authors point out, though, that aspects such as factuality are not accounted for at all. This exemplifies the many challenges still to be tacked in generating longer argumentative texts.

Inspired by the behavior of human debaters, Zhao et al. (2025) proposes a dynamic essay planning and generation approach that employs agent-based prompting in three steps: First, a chain-of-thought-based 'host' agent analyzes the given essay topic to come up with a central opinion. Next, two persona-prompted agents (an 'attacker' and a 'defender') debate on a logically-coherent hierarchical argument tree that guides the host in organizing the essay with arguments from different perspectives. Prompted to follow 13 situation elements and rhetorical skills from the rhetorical situation theory of Bitzer (1968), such as *audience-specific group characteristics* or *causal reasoning*, the host then step-by-step generates the introduction, arguments, and conclusion of the essay. On four datasets, the authors compare their approach to Bao et al. (2022b), He et al. (2024), and other baselines, reporting consistently higher results for automatic and manual evaluation of relevance, logic, complexity, persuasiveness, and rhetoric (often with small margins only, though).

9.2 Rewriting and Countering Arguments

The methods discussed so far target the composition and creation of *new* argumentative content largely from scratch, given basic information such as topic and stance. We now turn our view to two other tasks, the rewriting of arguments to (better) match specified criteria as well as the countering of an argument with another argument. Even though many techniques we learned about above equally apply to these tasks, these tasks come with one important difference: For both, an argument is given as the input to adhere to. This shifts the focus from deciding what to argue about to optimizing how to argue about it (or, to how to argue against it). Still, the tasks entail very different goals, leading in turn to different techniques and ways of integrating information from the argument with knowledge from other sources.

We begin with approaches to the rewriting of single claims and full arguments. Afterwards, we consecutively look at the two main ways to create counterarguments: either argumentative content retrieved from other sources is composed and rewritten in a new text (similar to the first works we saw in Sect. 9.1), or counterarguments are generated using language modeling at the core (as the last works in Sect. 9.1).

9.2.1 Goal-Oriented Claim and Argument Rewriting

NLP research on the computational rewriting of argumentative content so far pursues either of two goals: to create an output whose stance opposes the input, or to create an optimized version of the input. We summarize approaches to the former under *claim inversion*, and to the latter under *claim and argument optimization*. They cover a broad spectrum of techniques, from linguistic rules to reinforcement-learning.

Claim Inversion The first to consider the rewriting of argumentative content have been Bilu et al. (2015) who deal with the task of claim negation, that is, to assert the opposite of a claim in a plausible way for the given topic. As main challenges, they point out grammar correctness, clarity and coherence, the actual opposition of the original claim, and the usability of the negation as a plausible claim for the topic. They propose a rule-based low-level editing approach based on part-of-speech information, aiming to insert "not", "n't", "does not", or similar at linguistically correct positions, as in "affirmative action is *not* effective." On the Wikipedia claim dataset of Aharoni et al. (2014), 96% of the resulting negations were grammatically correct according to human annotators, but only 50% actually seemed usable.

Hidey and McKeown (2019) pursue a similar idea with the generation of a contrastive claim to an input claim via minimal edits. However, the authors consider actual content edits, such as the replacement of *Hillary Clinton* by *Bernie Sanders* in "Hillary Clinton should be president." Their approach extends a sequence-to-sequence model with bidirectional GRU units and attention by mechanisms to account for the number of edits, the output length, and information about the discussion context. They trained it on a dataset of Reddit posts containing the acronym *FTFY* ("fixed that for you") with both intended and other claim rewrites as well as on a set of crowdsourced claim rewrites. Compared to the base model, human evaluators saw improvements in terms of coherence and contrast while fluency remained stable. However, fluency and coherence still fell short compared to human rewrites.

In related research areas, some works tackle contrastive stance generation on a higher level. Among these, Chen et al. (2018) "flip" the media bias of news headlines on political events from right to left or vice versa. They model the task as a style transfer problem, seeing bias as the style to be changed and the event as the content to be maintained. Their approach to the task employs a cross-aligned autoencoder (Shen et al. 2017), trained jointly for both transfer directions on paired headlines from news articles on the same event by media outlets of opposite political leaning. While the approach cannot compete with the capabilities of current language models in correct and fluent text generation, it still shows the potential of the idea in general. For example, "Obama accepts nomination, says his plan leads to a 'better place'." is flipped into "Obama blasted re-election, saying it a 'very difficult' to go down."

Claim and Argument Optimization Optimizing argumentative content means to improve it with respect to some desired property while preserving its general meaning as far as possible. Chakrabarty et al. (2021a) study how to make claim-like arguments more trustworthy by toning down emotionally-loaded language, such as appeals to fear. To this end, they propose a low-level connotation reframing and fine-tune BART on paired data from ChangeMyView. In the data, emotionally-loaded connotations (e.g., "Every nation with *territorial claims...*") have been automatically replaced by more neutral ones (e.g. "Every nation with *sovereign competence...*"). To control for meaning, their approach generates multiple candidates and then picks the one that most likely entails the input argument, according to a RoBERTa model (Liu et al. 2019b) trained on the Multi-NLI dataset (Williams et al. 2018). In human evaluation, the approach clearly outperformed simpler BART variants and style transfer approaches from related work in fluency, meaning preservation, and trustworthiness. While human rewrites seemed notably stronger in these dimensions, the approach beat them in terms of the reduction of appeals to fear.

Quite related is the approach of Skitalinskaya et al. (2023) that we described in detail at the end of Chap. 7. The authors fine-tune a BART model on human revisions of argumentative claims (taken from the debate portal kialo.com) to improve claim quality with minimal meaning changes. Similar to Chakrabarty et al. (2021a), they sample multiple candidate optimizations, but the clue of their approach is to then rank the candidates based on a weighted mix of fluency, meaning preservation and argument quality. In experiments, this ranking outperforms maximum likelihood generation and existing argument ranking methods. Human judges identified 60% of all its rewrites to improve quality and further 24% to maintain quality. Particularly, the specification of facts by examples or discussions works well, whereas a corroboration through external evidence seems harder.

The ability to rewrite text toward a specified criterion is a key strength of instruction-following LLMs. Ziegenbein et al. (2024) present a technically sophisticated approach that builds on this strength to transform inappropriate arguments into appropriate ones, following the notion of appropriateness from argumentation theory (see Chap. 7). An exemplary inappropriate argument on whether news reporters should go to jail for what they write from the data of Ziegenbein et al. (2023) is the following (potentially inappropriate parts marked in italic):

(9.3) *You have all missed the point. Confidential sources within the Government that leak classified information are not covered by the freedom of the press.* When a court order is issued there is more at stake than a news story. Often the court order compromises one case to resolve another. When you have someone that leaks vital information that threatens the welfare of the American People (nuclear secrets etc.) you might give up a case against a *squealer* to get the name of the *mole*. Freedom of the press means you can publish what you want. It doesn't mean that you are free of the consequences. Geraldo got thrown out of Iraq for airing the American battle plans for Bagdad before the battle. *He should been hung.*

Unlike the rewriting tasks above, inappropriateness rewriting may require bigger content changes. Moreover, the high rewriting effort makes parallel training data at a bigger scale practically infeasible. To deal with these challenges, the approach of Ziegenbein et al. (2024) aligns the behavior of an LLM using reinforcement learning where PPO guides the LLM to obtain appropriateness while maintaining semantic similarity. Its process is illustrated in Fig. 9.5 and consists of the following parts:

1. *Initial LLM.* For reinforcement learning, an initial pretrained LLM π^{PRT} that rewrites an argument x into an improved version $\hat{y}$ is needed. For lack of training data, Ziegenbein et al. suggest to obtain π^{PRT} from prompting. They experimentally

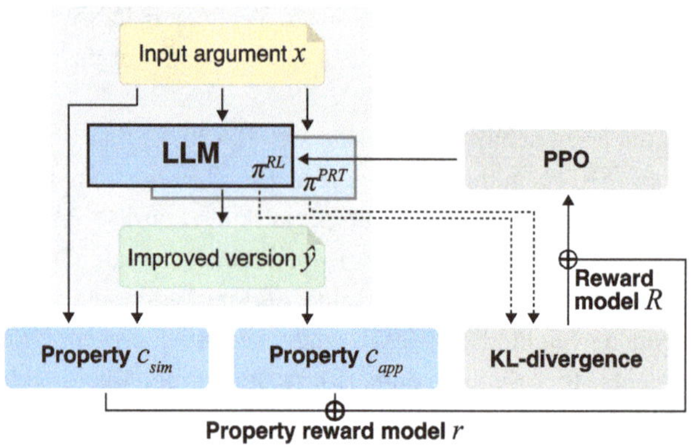

Fig. 9.5 Inappropriateness rewriting approach of Ziegenbein et al. (2024): The behavior of LLM π^{RL} is aligned using *PPO* to generate a more appropriate version $\hat{y}$ of an input argument x. PPO's reward model R is based on the similarity c_{sim} of x and $\hat{y}$, the classified appropriateness c_{app} of $\hat{y}$, and the KL-divergence of π^{RL} from the initial LLM π^{PRT}. Licensed under CC-BY 4.0 International

compare zero-shot and few-shot prompting as well as instruction fine-tuning according to Taori et al. (2023) for four LLMs with 6–7 billion parameters: OPT (Zhang et al. 2022b), BLOOM (BigScience Workshop 2024), GPT-J (Wang and Komatsuzaki 2021), and LLaMA (Touvron et al. 2023a). In an automatic pre-evaluation, the instruction fine-tuned LLaMA was best and, hence, used as π^{PRT}. The given instruction is fairly simple: "Rewrite the following argument to be more appropriate and make only minimal changes to the original argument."

2. *Reward Model.* The PPO optimization process builds on a property reward r that trades the appropriateness c_{app} of $\hat{y}$ against the similarity c_{sim} of x and $\hat{y}$:

$$r(x, \hat{y}) := \alpha \cdot c_{\text{sim}}(x, \hat{y}) + (1 - \alpha) \cdot c_{\text{app}}(\hat{y})$$

Following Schulman et al. (2017), r is regularized by Kullback-Leibler divergence in the reward model R. The authors score c_{app} using a classifier from prior work (Ziegenbein et al. 2023) and quantify c_{sim} as BERTScore (Zhang et al. 2020b).

3. *LLM Alignment.* Given R with a defined weight α, the rewriting behavior of π^{PRT} is stepwise aligned by PPO to learn the final rewriting model π^{RL}. Ziegenbein et al. (2024) employ LoRA for the alignment and run the reinforcement learning process for 25,000 steps. They compare four α values: 0.4 (similarity first), 0.5 (balanced), 0.6 (appropriateness first), and 1.0 (full focus on appropriateness).

In the manual evaluation of 225 arguments, for which they have expert rewrites, the human scores of appropriateness and similarity strongly correlate with α and $1 - \alpha$ respectively, underlining that the alignment works highly reliably. While the expert rewrites achieve a good balance, π^{RL} with $\alpha = 1.0$ is best in appropriateness and $\alpha = 0.4$ is best in similarity. Intriguingly, the evaluators preferred those with $\alpha = 1.0$ (followed by $\alpha = 0.6$) among the different rewrites, clearly outperforming the expert rewrites, and even more so those of the non-aligned LLM π^{PRT}. The results suggests that the chosen value of α is directly reflected in the obtained output. For the argument above, for example, a preference toward appropriateness ($\alpha = 0.6$) leads to the following rewrite (text changes marked in italic except for removed parts):

(9.4) When a court order is issued there is more at stake than a news story. Often the court order compromises one case to resolve another. *While* freedom of the press *allows journalists* to publish information *without fear of government interference it does not* mean that *they* are free *from legal or other* consequences. *Geraldo was ultimately expelled from* Iraq for airing the American battle plans for Baghdad before the battle.

Huber and Niklaus (2025) present 57 lexical, syntactic, semantic, and pragmatic metrics to assess quality-oriented rewriting of argumentative text. Using these metrics, the authors systematically evaluate the rewrites of six prompted LLMs on three datasets for this family of tasks. Aside from some model-specific findings, they find that LLMs generally tend to shorten arguments, reduce reading ease, rarely delete or add entire sentences, make the arguments' tone more negative, but still ultimately make the arguments more coherent and persuasive. On average, human evaluators preferred the rewritten arguments in 79% of the cases. Exemplary results on the lexical level included that perceived quality correlates somewhat positively with average word length but negatively with sentence length. On the syntactic level, merging of sentences seems to have a positive effect, whereas little meaningful correlations could be found for semantics and pragmatics. Even though a comparison to the above-mentioned rewriting methods is missing, the papers' findings thus yield notable insights into what is important in argumentative rewriting.

9.2.2 Retrieval-Based Counterargument Generation

According to argumentation theory, a counterargument may attack an argument's conclusion, one or more of the argument's premises, or the reasoning from premises to conclusion (Walton 2009). Building on retrieved information has the advantage that the counterargument is rooted in existing sources, which supports factuality and/or traceability. While not being actual generation, one possibility is the *direct retrieval of counters*, which is why we shortly discuss it here. Then, we go into detail into *generation based on retrieval.*

Direct Retrieval of Counters Wachsmuth et al. (2018b) study how to retrieve the argument that best counters a given argument from a pool of arguments, without any additional knowledge. Their simplifying hypothesis is that a counterargument has high topic similarity to an argument while having the opposite stance. In their approach, the authors operationalize the hypothesis by learning a function that weighs different word and embedding similarity measures. They evaluate different retrieval settings, finding that the best counterargument can be found in about 3 out of 4 cases among all arguments with opposite stance, and in about 1 out of 3 cases among an average of 2801 candidates (while being ranked in the top 15 on average).

Starting from general web documents, Jo et al. (2021b) retrieve counterevidence to a given statement (e.g., "vegan diets suffer from poor nutrition"). For each candidate counterevidence statement (e.g., "veganism reduces the risk of diabetes"), a natural language inference (NLI) model enhances the RoBERTA representations of the two statements with knowledge from a structured knowledge graph, Wikidata (Vrandečić and Krötzsch 2014) or CauseNet (Heindorf et al. 2020) respectively. On data from ChangeMyView and Kialo, the NLI model outperforms RoBERTa and is on par with LogBERT, a BERT-based argument relation classifier (Devlin et al. 2019) based on logical mechanisms from own related work (Jo et al. 2021a). The authors conclude that a combination of both may be best for counterargument generation.

Generation Based on Retrieval The first NLP approach to the actual generation of counterarguments comes from Hua and Wang (2018). It combines a retrieval component with a neural sequence-to-sequence model that has one encoder and two decoders. The former ranks evidence sentences from Wikipedia articles that match the noun phrases of any sentence of the argument to be countered. The encoder represents both the argument and the evidence sentences, before one decoder generates keyphrases to be used for countering. The other encoder then combines the argument with attention to these keywords to generate the output counterargument. While the approach improves over a standard sequence-to-sequence model in informativeness and relevance (not in grammaticality) in their human evaluation on ChangeMyView arguments, it cannot compete yet with a retrieval-only baseline.

Hua et al. (2019a) evolve the idea further in the integrated CANDELA approach for the retrieval-based counterargument generation to an argument (called input statement), such as: "The wage gap isn't about gender. [...] So one factor definitely the fact that there are some government jobs that are seriously dominated by women and happen to pay really low [...]". CANDELA decomposes the counterargument generation process into five steps, as illustrated in Fig. 9.6:

1. *Passage Retrieval.* Given a text collection, the top-k passages are retrieved that match queries based on the content words of any input statement sentence, similar to Hua and Wang (2018). Hua et al. indexed a pool of 12 million articles, about half of them from Wikipedia (with roughly 43M passages) and the other from four major American news portals (77M passages), taken from commoncrawl.org. BM25 ranking (Robertson et al. 1994) is done for $k = 20$ passages.

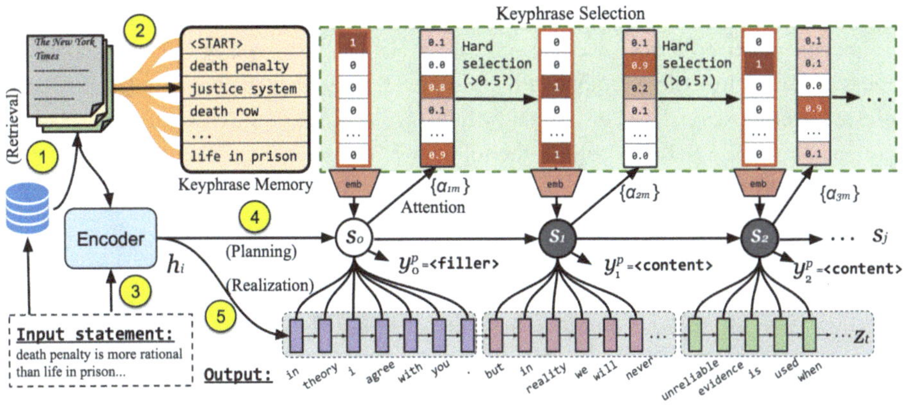

Fig. 9.6 CANDELA approach for retrieval-based counterargument generation of Hua et al. (2019a): (1) Passages are retrieved based on stance and relevance to the input statement. (2) Keyphrases are extracted from the passages. (3) Input statement and passages are encoded. (4) A planner decodes sentence representations, predicting argumentative functions and selecting keyphrases per sentence. (5) A content realizer decodes the counterargument.

2. *Keyphrase Selection.* Noun and verb phrases are extracted from the retrieved passages and stored in a keyphrase memory. Hua et al. take all phrases with at most 10 tokens that contain at least one of the input statement's topic signature words (Lin and Hovy 2000) or a Wikipedia article title.
3. *Input Encoding.* The retrieved passages are further filtered and ranked based on their keyphrase overlap with the input statement. Only those passages are kept that do not overlap much with higher-ranked passages and do not have the same stance to the input statement. The input statement and the remaining passages are then encoded. Hua et al. use the stance scoring model of Bar-Haim et al. (2017a) and a bidirectional LSTM with attention for encoding.
4. *Text Planning.* Sentence representations for the output counterargument are generated one after the other, based on a set of keyphrases and a predicted argumentative function (*content* or *filler sentence*). To foster coherence, each representation is required to have a minimum keyphrase similarity to its predecessor. Hua et al. train a sentence-level LSTM for generation and learn attention weights to score keyphrase similarity. They decide the argumentative function using hand-defined rules based on the content words and topic signature words.
5. *Content Realization.* The counterargument is generated token by token based on the current sentence representation and previous tokens. Hua et al. train another LSTM model for this purpose and use sentence-level beam search (beam width 5), ranking sentences based on the number of generated keyphrases.

A human evaluation on ChangeMyView arguments similar to the one from the previous work revealed that CANDELA outperforms the model of Hua and Wang (2018) clearly in terms of grammaticality, appropriateness, and content richness. While the retrieval-only baseline still received higher average scores, CANDELA was nearly on par in appropriateness and also strong in grammaticality. Moreover, its generated counterarguments were preferred over those retrieved or written by humans in 39.2% of the cases. For the example argument above, CANDELA outputs the following (integrated key phases italicized, filler sentence underlined):

(9.5) the problem with this argument is that the *wage gap* does not have to do with the *gender pay gap*. It is a fact that women are more likely to be able to *take care of their children* than their *male counterparts*. This is not to say that it is unfair to assume that women are being paid less than men, but that does not mean that it is not the case that *women are discriminated against*. It is not a matter of the wage gap, it is a matter of opinion. It is the job of the employer to make sure that the job is not the same as the other.

In follow-up work, Hua and Wang (2019) further optimize the integration of sentence-level content and style within argument generation, and also test their generation concept on other tasks, such as the creation of Simple Wikipedia text.

Yeginbergen et al. (2025) study the integration of external knowledge into the counter-argument generation processes of LLMs toward improved factuality. Their straightforward retrieval-augmented generation (RAG) approach sends five auto-generated queries to the AI-based search engine cohere.com, asking for information to question the veracity of a given claim. The results are then incorporated as context in a prompt for generating a three-sentence counterargument. For evaluation, the authors constructed a new dataset by creating counterarguments with CANDELA for arguments from ChangeMyView and then summarizing them with Llama-3.1-70B. In experiments, they compared two LLMs, Command R+ (CohereForAI 2024) and Mistral-7B-Instruct, to ablations without external knowledge. According to automatic metrics (e.g., BLEU and ROUGE) and LLM-as-a-judge tests, Command R+ with external knowledge was strongest overall, while both LLMs slightly improved over their ablation. Somewhat worryingly, though, humans ranked the factuality of the ablations better, whereas the approach seemed to rather benefit the persuasiveness and topic relatedness of the generated counterarguments.

9.2.3 Counterargument Generation Based on Language Modeling

As an alternative to the retrieval of argumentative knowledge or content, the capabilities of language models may be leveraged for counterargumentation. Research has consecutively come with *fine-tuned* and *prompting-based* approaches in this regard, roughly in line with the general transition in NLP from pretrained transformers to instruction-following and aligned LLMs.

Fine-Tuned Countering Focusing on the way countering works, Alshomary et al. (2021c) seek to generate arguments that attack the weakest premise of an argument. To this end, they train a weak-premise ranking model based on the ChangeMyView data of Jo et al. (2020). Given a training set of correct and incorrect argument-counterargument pairs, they employ the ranking model to encode the argument's weakest premise and then fine-tune the embeddings of a GPT transformer jointly for two tasks on this basis: language modeling and counterargument classification. In their evaluation, human judges saw the counterarguments of their approach as notably better compared to a simple fine-tuned GPT model. Compared to the retrieval-based approach of Hua and Wang (2019), the judges also deemed grammatical correctness (in terms of relevance and stance), and content richness to be better, but generally saw notable room for improvement for both approaches, particularly for correctness.

Alshomary and Wachsmuth (2023) further study the counterargument task but with a different hypothesis, namely, that the key to effective generation is to explicitly model and attack the conclusion of the input argument. Notably, the conclusion may not be explicit in many arguments, such as in the following:

(9.6) *Argument:* In my opinion AGI needs the algorithms that make us intelligent and by having these missing pieces they will be a generally intelligent entity. I hear arguments that an AGI needs to have a subjective experience like a human being in order to be generally intelligent and I find this theory to be lackluster if the laws of physics can be computed than so can the algorithms that make general intelligence. After all we are information processing systems however, i am trying to explore all avenues of thought, even play devil's advocate and not get caught in some sort of echo chamber or even worse a spirit of the age.

The approach of Alshomary and Wachsmuth jointly generates multiple candidate conclusions and counterarguments and then outputs the counterargument that most opposes to its conclusion. In detail, it consists of two main steps:

1. *Candidate Generation.* At training time, a model is trained that, given the input argument's premises, generates the argument's conclusion as well as a counterargument to the argument. At inference time, a diverse set of such candidates is generated. Alshomary and Wachsmuth explore two alternative BART-based models for candidate generation: *joint-one-seq* has one decoder that sequentially generates the conclusion and the counterargument, whereas *joint-two-decoders* has two decoders, one for the conclusion and one for the counterargument (with a weighted loss, optimized experimentally). To promote diversity, the conclusions are started with Wikipedia concepts extracted from the premises following Ein Dor et al. (2018), and nucleus sampling is used (Holtzman et al. 2020).
2. *Stance Ranking.* At training time, a classifier learns to predict the stance of a sentence toward a conclusion along with a probability. At inference time, for each candidate,

stance is predicted once for each counterargument sentence. The average probability defines the stance score of a counterargument, and the one with maximum opposite stance to the conclusion is taken. Alshomary and Wachsmuth train the classifier on pairs of claim and counter-claim from kialo.com.

In their experiments on the same ChangeMyView data above, both approach variants beat a simple fine-tuned BART model as well as the approach of Alshomary et al. (2021c). While the outputs of the joint-two-decoders variant did not convince the human judges, joint-one-seq generates the best counterarguments (though the differences are rather small), particularly the stance ranking seems important. For the argument above, it outputs the following conclusion and counterargument:

(9.7) *Conclusion:* Scientific law is the only thing that can make AGI generally intelligent. *Counterargument:* The problem with AGI is that we don't really know what it is that makes us intelligent. we have no idea how it works, what it's like to be an AGI, how it's different from a human being, or how it will work in the real world.

Finally, Purkayastha et al. (2023) introduce the notion of *jiu-jitsu argumentation* to counterargument generation, that is, to identify an arguer's attitudes, and to then align the counterargument with these attitudes instead of invalidating them. They consider this notion for the specific task of rebutting scientific peer-reviews. While the core of their work is dataset construction, they present simple end-to-end baseline experiments on zero-shot, few-shot, and fully fine-tuned generation using BART, PEGASUS (Zhang et al. 2020a), and T5 (Raffel et al. 2020). In automatic evaluation, BART does best in many cases, but all models plateau at two shots already. This suggest that a generalization of jiu-jitsu argumentation is not straightforward, but a more sophisticated modeling of the notion is needed.

Prompting-Based Countering The fine-tuned approaches above all rely on standard transformers for language modeling. Having instruction-following LLMs, research also examines the potential of prompting for counterargument generation. Among these, Lin et al. (2023) propose a multistep approach based on chain-of-thought. At training time, LLaMA-7B is fine-tuned with LoRA on ChangeMyView input-output instances for counterargument-related instructions, such as "Can we believe this statement?". Moreover, a filtering model is learned on respective preference data to rank multiple counterargument candidates by quality. At inference time, the LLM is first prompted to generate multiple counterarguments, given few-shot chain-of-thought instructions, such as "This argument has a logical fallacy. (*1*) The subtext of this argument is that unintelligent people cannot be wealthy. (*2*) However, intelligence is not the sole determining factor." The final counterargument is determined using the filtering model. According to human judges, the approach created the best counterarguments in 62% of the cases compared to an instruction fine-tuned Alpaca (Taori et al. 2023) and to a LLaMA baseline, showing advantages in persuasiveness, logic, and appropriateness while being on par in grammaticality and content richness.

Hu et al. (2024) fully rely on prompting, decomposing the counterargument generation process into four consecutive steps that generate (1) a claim, (2) a reasoning for the claim, (3) a concession of the claim, and (4) the final argument based on the output of the three preceding steps. Moreover, their approach includes an agent-based refinement module. In particular, an evaluation agent is first persona-prompted to act as a lecturer that provides feedback on relevance, logical consistency, coherence of structure, and persuasion. A refinement agent then revises the counterargument based on the feedback. This process is repeated for a defined number of iterations (three in the experiments). In human evaluation, the approach succeeded clearly over a simple end-to-end prompting baseline and a chain-of-thought baseline in terms of appropriateness, content richness, and overall quality (all with notable room for improvement, though). Interestingly, the validity of the generated counterarguments was seen better without the refinement module.

Verma et al. (2025) use argument-counterevidence pairs from Hua et al. (2019a) to either prompt or fine-tune five different LLMs, such that they generate counterarguments with either of three styles: plain, reciprocity, and justification. The styles are specified with hand-crafted descriptions as part of the prompt, such as "Use a writing style that asks questions designed to elicit opinions or information from the user." for reciprocity. Analyzing the resulting arguments with human judges, the authors find that justification leads to the best arguments and reciprocity to the worst arguments across LLMs and five quality dimensions: content, grammaticality, logic, relevance, and overall effectiveness. However, even the arguments of the best-performing LLM (GPT-3.5-turbo) are not seen as strong as human-written alternatives.

Finally, Dönmez and Falenska (2025) study the style of counterarguments generated by three different LLMs (Llama2-7B, Mistral-6B-instruct, and GPT-3.5) in response to ChangeMyView arguments from Tan et al. (2016) (see Sect. 7.2) via the prompt: "You have one chance to change my view. Answer:". Building on the communicative action theory of Habermas (1984), the authors analyze the presence of nine pragmatic social dimensions in the counterarguments using an existing classifier (Choi et al. 2020): knowledge, power, status, trust, support, similarity, identity, fun, and conflict. While humans exhibit all dimensions rather evenly in about 15–20% of their arguments according the results, all three LLMs express trust overwhelmingly often (>90%), as in "I understand your perspective". Further findings include that GPT-3.5's output shows higher reciprocity. In direct follow-up work, Dönmez et al. (2025) oppose LLM-generated to human-written counterarguments in the same setting in terms of argument and deliberative quality (see Sect. 7.3) as well as linguistic style. Based on the output of the argumentative and deliberative quality assessment method of Falk and Lapesa (2023), the authors find, among other insights, that LLM-generated counterarguments refer less to other discussion participants, show less implicit respect, and less negative emotion. In contrast, they seem to be more interactive, more reasonable, and of higher overall argument quality according to the method. Style-wise, the LLMs produce more emotional arguments, whereas the human arguments show more lexical diversity and variance.

9.3 Summarizing Arguments and Debates

So far, this chapter has discussed NLP methods that aim at the production or optimization of new (or newly composed) argumentative content—be it arguments, counterarguments, the components they are built from, or similar. In practice, such methods come into play when humans shall be supported in their writing processes, or when technologies shall argue somewhat autonomously. However, also in scenarios focused on the understanding and assessment, argument generation methods may be important, namely those where the sheer amount of arguments and debates makes it infeasible to read everything. These scenarios call for *summarization*. Summarization is one of the most widely studied downstream tasks in NLP, but we will see below that it has specific challenges in the context of argumentation. The underlying techniques share aspects both with the composition and creation of argumentative texts (Sect. 9.1) and with the rewriting or arguments (Sect. 9.2). What makes them unique is the goal to boil down single arguments as well as whole debates to main gists or key points, rather than creating anything completely new.

In what follows, we first present research on the summarization of single arguments and monological argumentative texts, covering both extractive and abstractive approaches to this task. We then come to the question how to summarize the arguments by two or more people in a debate, which—in line with related problems from other areas of NLP—implies a multi-document summarization task.

9.3.1 Summarization of Individual Arguments

Matching general NLP literature, we distinguish between *extractive* and *abstractive* argument summarization. Even though many approaches are hybrid, the focus of the former type is on identifying and recomposing the ADUs that make up an argument's gist, whereas the latter reformulates the gist in (more or less) its own words.

Extractive Argument Summarization Alshomary et al. (2020a) seek to extract two-sentence summaries that may serve as snippets in argument search. They hypothesize that the most representative sentences are those that cover the argument's claim and main reason. Their unsupervised approach adapts the LexRank method (Erkan and Radev 2004) which scores the importance of a sentence based on its similarity to other important sentences in the same text. The similarities induce a graph that can be traversed with PageRank (Page et al. 1999) for scoring. The approach models representativeness by the centrality of a sentence in its discussion context and by its argumentativeness. Given an argument, it proceeds as follows:

1. *Graph Construction.* Each graph node represents one sentence s_i from the discussion, in which the argument appears, and is assigned a weight $arg(s_i)$ indicating argumentativeness. Edges between the nodes of two sentences s_i and s_j represent their similarity $sim(s_i, s_j)$. Alshomary et al. simply compute $arg(s_i)$ based on the occurrence of words from a discourse lexicon. $sim(s_i, s_j)$ is quantified as the cosine similarity of the sentences' universal sentence embeddings (Cer et al. 2018). In experiments, they use debate portal arguments from the args.me corpus (Ajjour et al. 2019b); the respective debate constitutes the context.
2. *Sentence Scoring.* Once all similarity and argumentativeness scores are given, the approach quantifies the representativeness of any sentence s_i using PageRank as

$$P(s_i) := (1-d) \cdot \sum_{s_j \neq s_i} \frac{sim(s_i, s_j)}{\sum_{s_k \neq s_j} sim(s_j, s_k)} P(s_j) + d \cdot \frac{arg(s_i)}{\sum_{s_k} arg(s_k)},$$

   where the first term models centrality, the second argumentativeness, and d weighs the two terms. The computation starts with equal scores for all sentences. The scores are then updated iteratively during graph traversal until near-convergence. Alshomary et al. use the LexRank default weight $d = 0.15$.
3. *Summary Construction.* The two sentences of the given argument with the highest score are used for the summary. Alshomary et al. return the sentences in their original ordering for coherence, without any further rephrasing.

Figure 9.7 visualizes the graph constructed in the first step for a debate excerpt. In experiments on 50 test arguments, the approach determines 44% of all summary sentences correctly, compared to 36% of LexRank and 40% of the extractive summarizer BertSum (Liu 2019). Human evaluators saw the representativeness of its summaries as best, but favored BertSum's summaries in terms of readability, possibly because the approach tends to favor longer sentences.

In follow-up work, Alshomary et al. (2022b) extend their idea to make the summaries of different arguments from the same context 'contrastive', such that a summary highlights what is unique to the respective argument: Adjusting the formula above, a third term negatively scores the similarity of a sentence to sentences from other arguments. Alternatively, the authors also propose an adaptation of a feature-based contrastive summarizer (Bista et al. 2020), which aims to make a summary as distinguishable as possible to other summaries and as indistinguishable as possible to other sentences in the argument. In human evaluation on the same data, the extended approach was best in contrastiveness, but created less representative summaries than the approach of Alshomary et al. (2020a). The feature-based summarizer won in representativeness and was second in contrastiveness.

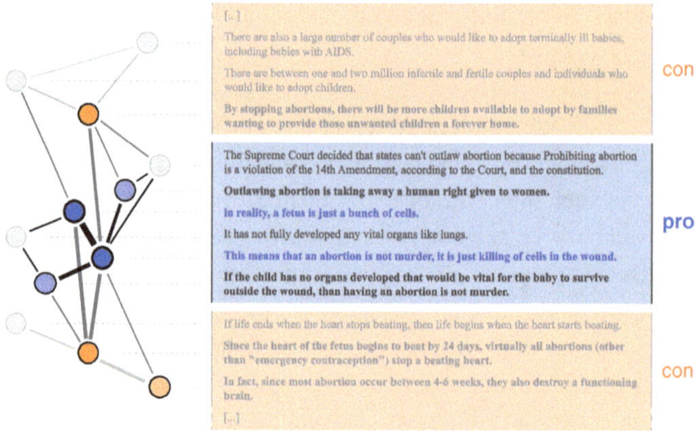

Fig. 9.7 Illustration of sentence scoring in the extractive summarizer of Alshomary et al. (2020a) for a *pro* argument in a discussion of abortion. Black borders define argumentative sentences (bold text). Edge width reflects similarity, node saturation the score. Used with permission

For the domain of legal case decisions, Xu et al. (2021) propose to extract argument triples as summaries that cover the issue addressed in the case, the court's conclusion on the issue, and the reasons the court gives for the conclusion. The authors compare n-gram-based and BERT-based convolutional neural networks with an embedding-based LSTM and a RoBERTa classifier for the extraction. They carried out experiments on a corpus with about 120k sentences, from which only about 6% contain issues, reasons, or conclusions. RoBERTa was strongest, with an average F_1-score of 0.27 only, likely caused by the high data imbalance. Reasons seemed harder to identify, whereas conclusions appeared a little easier.

Abstractive Argument Summarization One of the earliest NLP works on argument summarization is the approach of Wang and Ling (2016) who combine an importance-based sampling method with an attention-based LSTM for sequence-to-sequence generation. The sampling method ensures that a fixed number k of text units of the input argument is used ($k = 5$ sentences are used in the experiments). The units are ordered by importance, which is predicted based on various surface-level text features. In automatic evaluation on data from *idebate.org* where one-sentence claims summarize an average of 7.7 one-sentence arguments, the approach achieves a BLEU score of 25.84 compared to 13.39 of LexRank and to 15.09 of another extractive summarizer (Sipos et al. 2012).

In a similar vein, Syed et al. (2021) investigate how to summarize longer monological argumentative texts into a single (possibly implicit) conclusion, combining ideas from both extractive and abstractive summarization. An example for the arguments considered is the following on the topic "Is Feminism a Force For Good?":

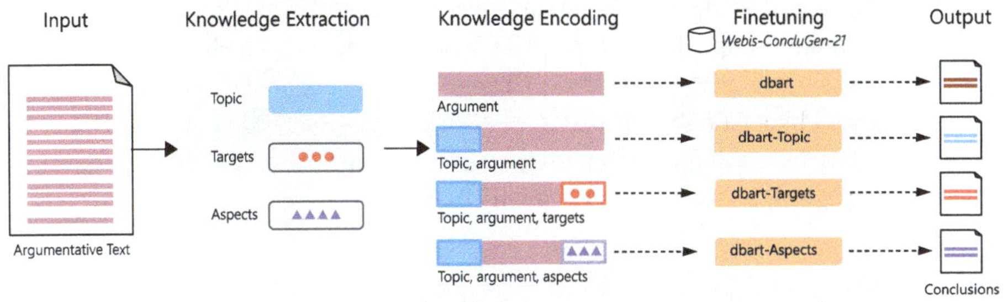

Fig. 9.8 The three training steps of the abstractive summarizer of Syed et al. (2021) to output informative conclusions for an argumentative text (1) Different types of knowledge are extracted from the text. (2) Different knowledge subsets are encoded using control codes. (3) One transformer-based summarizer is fine-tuned on each configuration. Licensed under CC-BY 4.0 International

(9.8) Feminism as a 'linguistic term' often misses clarity, universal definition and regularly incorporates opposite goals at the same time in regard to key feminist issues as gender equality, gender-neutrality, non-binary and gender-related rights. The linguistic term thereby clouds public debate and hampers the setting of clear social and political goals in society.

As a baseline, they paraphrase the top-scored sentence of the approach of Alshomary et al. (2020a) using PEGASUS. However, their own approach is more controlled, encoding knowledge extracted from the input argument in a fine-tuned abstractive summarizer. It proceeds in three steps that are depicted in Fig. 9.8:

1. *Knowledge Extraction.* To foster informativeness, knowledge is inferred from the argument, namely the discussed topic, the premise targets (in the example above: "Feminism as a 'linguistic term'" and "The linguistic term"), and the aspects covered in the argument (e.g., "gender equality" or "social and political goals"). Syed et al. simply use the title of the debate the argument comes from, while employing the target identifier of Alshomary et al. (2020b) and the aspect identifier of Schiller et al. (2021b), both of which we have seen in Sect. 9.1.
2. *Knowledge Encoding.* Different knowledge subsets are encoded together with the argument using control codes, for example in the form "<|`TOPIC`>Is Feminism a Force For Good? <|`ARGUMENT`> Feminism as a 'linguistic term' often misses...". In their experiments, Syed et al. explore four configurations: all knowledge, topic only, topic plus targets, and topic plus aspects.
3. *Fine-Tuning.* One sequence-to-sequence model is fine-tuned on all training instances of the respective encoding and then applied to summarize a given argument. Syed et al. use a distilled BART model for this purpose, shrinked and fine-tuned according to Shleifer and Rush (2020).

Human judges evaluated the validity and informativeness of the conclusions generated by each configuration, a simple fine-tuned BART baseline, and the paraphrasing baseline on three input types: ChangeMyView posts, ChangeMyView comments, and mixed debate portal arguments. Interestingly, the BART baselines largely succeeded in validity and the paraphrasing baseline in informativeness. However, the approach configurations seemed the best midway, without a clear winner among them.

9.3.2 Summarization of Argument Collections and Debates

The summarization of multiple arguments targets the consolidation of important points across them, rather than the boiling down of each argument to its gist. Some approaches aim for a *key point analysis* of argument from different sources, whereas others deal with the *summarization of debates* on a given topic. They all share that they address situations in which the spectrum of points is not in advance, but discovered in the summarization process.

Key Point Analysis As discussed in Chap. 6 on perspective assessment already, Bar-Haim et al. (2020a) introduce a dataset for key point analysis, the task to summarize a collection of arguments by a small set of high-level arguments that appear in different forms in the collection. The data they provide includes 6515 crowdsourced arguments on 28 topics with 243 key points. While the authors skip the *generation* of the key points, only *matching* arguments with key points, Bar-Haim et al. (2020b) present an overall approach to key point analysis studied for three datasets: the data of Bar-Haim et al. (2020a), comments of respondents to the *Austin Community Survey*, and a review dataset (Ganesan et al. 2010). Given a collection of arguments, it obtains and matches key points in three steps:

1. *Key point extraction.* Assuming that all key points are among the collected arguments, a set of candidates is extracted based on conciseness and argument quality. For conciseness, Bar-Haim et al. consider only one-sentence arguments with a certain maximum length (10–12 tokens depending on the dataset) that do not start with a pronoun. Argument quality is scored using the assessment method of Gretz et al. (2020b) discussed in Chap. 7. Only key points above a score tuned on the validation set are kept (0.35–0.70 depending on the dataset).
2. *Key point selection.* The final key points are filtered from the candidates based on their commonness and their diversity. Bar-Haim et al. match all arguments to candidates using best match matching with thresholding (0.856–0.999 depending on the dataset). Then, candidates that themselves are matched to a higher-scored candidates are filtered out, and the associated arguments are re-assigned.
3. *Key point matching.* Analogous to Bar-Haim et al. (2020a), a score is computed for each pair of argument and key point, from which a matching is derived. Bar-Haim

et al. (2020b) compare best-match matching with and without thresholding for four fine-tuned models: BERT, XLNet (Yang et al. 2019b), RoBERTa, and ALBERT (Lan et al. 2020).

On the data of Bar-Haim et al. (2020a), matching works best using ALBERT best-match matching with thresholding in terms of both accuracy and F_1-score. To evaluate the overall approach, the authors compute the precision of matching all test set arguments from the three datasets to the top-scored key points according to human judges. For IBM-ArgQ-Rank-30kArgs, using the top-5 key points lead to a precision of 0.752 and using the top-10 to 0.792. For the other datasets (which are less argumentative in nature), the respective computed values were notably lower, though, ranging between 0.454 and 0.514.

Friedman et al. (2021) carried out a shared task on the data of Bar-Haim et al. (2020a), treating the two subtasks separately. Among the six approaches competing in the generation task, Bar-Haim et al. (2020b) was best. However, among the 18 approaches competing in the matching task, it was only 13th. The top approach there (and the second best in the generation task) comes from Alshomary et al. (2021b) who combine ideas from conclusion target inference (Alshomary et al. 2020b) with the extractive summarization approach of Alshomary et al. (2020a) (both detailed above). In particular, for generation, the approach of Alshomary et al. (2021b) scores arguments as candidate key points using PageRank and selects the top-ranked arguments including diversity considerations similar to Bar-Haim et al. (2020b). For the matching, it uses contrastive learning to obtain an embedding space, in which an argument is similar to the correct key point and different to others.

In parallel, two recent works evolved key point analysis into the LLM era. On the one hand, Altemeyer et al. (2025) compare three zero-shot LLM approaches: The first generates candidate key points with an LLMs to then match arguments with the candidates using either of the two mentioned approaches Bar-Haim et al. (2020b) and Alshomary et al. (2021b); the second clusters arguments with another approach from the shared task (Li et al. 2023) to then generate a summary for each cluster with an LLM; and the third directly generates all key points for the arguments with an end-to-end LLM. In experiments, the authors measure the coverage and redundancy of the key points of each approach with four different LLMs: GPT-4o, Llama-3.3-70b, Qwen-2.5-72b, and Qwen3-32b. Qwen3-32b proved best across all approaches. On average, the two shared task winners were largely on par and slightly better than Li et al. (2023). Simple-end-to-end summarization performed strongest, though. On the other hand, Gurjar et al. (2025) present an LLM benchmark for argument summarization. The authors argue that the data of Friedman et al. (2021) is not representative of online user discussions and limited in argument length and diversity. Instead, they constructed a new dataset by crawling 12k ChangeMyView arguments, extracting 3k key points from them with an LLM, and manually validating a sample of them. On average, the arguments have 4.27 ADUs (compared to 1.22 for the shared task data), and map to 2.80 key points (compared to 0.76). An automatic evaluation of different baseline LLMs suggests that the task is harder on the new dataset and still leaves much room for new approaches in future research.

Summarization of Debates In early work, Egan et al. (2016) considered the idea to summarize key points for multi-party debates. Given a debate transcript, their approach proceeds in several steps: Using dependency information, all points made are first extracted as subject-verb-object triples (e.g., *(the world, created, in six days)*). Then, similar triples are unified (e.g., those that differ only in the personal pronoun used) or filtered out if blacklisted (e.g., those whose subject is "that"). The remaining points are clustered. A representative is chosen based on bigrams and lengths, and low-level rephrased in a rule-based manner to make it self-contained (e.g., "But, was the world created in six days." is changed to "The world was created in six days"). All representatives are output as a plain list or grouped by predefined categories (e.g., *points of disagreement*). In a human evaluation on five debates from the Internet Argument Corpus (Walker et al. 2012b), both variations outperform an extractive text summarizer (Nenkova et al. 2006) in terms of content, punctuation, readability, and organization. The grouped variation was preferred.

Syed et al. (2023) propose to create individual summaries for the different frames covered in a multi-party debate. Their fully-unsupervised approach builds on a given frame taxonomy, specifically on the 15 topic-independent frames of Boydstun et al. (2014), such as *quality of life*, *economic*, or *cultural identity* (see Chap. 6). Given a debate, each post is seen as one argument and mapped to one of the frames based on its similarity to the frames' descriptions. For each frame, the arguments are then ranked separately by topical relevance and by informativeness using different retrieval model variations (compared experimentally), and a final ranking is obtained from reciprocal rank fusion (Cormack et al. 2009). The top-k arguments per frame are used for the summary, where the choice of k is left to the user. According to human judgments, the best approach variations show gains over a supervised frame assignment baseline in terms of frame and topic relevance (Heinisch and Cimiano 2021), but the ultimate usefulness of the summaries is not evaluated.

Toward assessing the capabilities of LLMs in creating structured summaries of debates, some other researchers have provided annotated datasets. Among these, Roush and Balaji (2020) derive extractive summaries together with their sources from publicly-available data of the *National Speech and Debate Association*. As baseline results, they compare three transformer-based models on the data, achieving high ROUGE-L scores of up to 57.21 using a Longformer-based model (Beltagy et al. 2020). Li et al. (2024a) connect debate summarization to keypoint analysis by providing LLM-generated stance-specific summaries from the ground-truth keypoints of Bar-Haim et al. (2020b), which have been assessed by human evaluators. In their baseline experiments, FlanT5-3B (Chung et al. 2024) outperformed FlanT5-large and PEGASUS with ROUGE-L scores between 38.01 and 45.08.

9.4 Summary

Argument generation has become one of the main topics studied in NLP research on argumentation. Its potential for practical applications such as writing assistance and debating technologies has long been known, and we look at a number of such applications in the following chapter. However, only the recent advancements in text generation, above all enabled by transformer-based language models and their extensions, have actually enabled substantial progress on this topic.

In this chapter, we have seen that argument generation covers a variety of *tasks* with different *inputs* and desired *outputs*. To tackle the tasks, different types of *knowledge* may be accessed in different ways, and different *techniques* may be used to generate the output. We now revisit the spectrum explored in research for these dimensions so far, in order to guide researchers and practitioners regarding what to consider when tackling a new argument generation task. While the granularity of argumentative content dealt with may vary (both in inputs and in outputs) from single ADUs and arguments to monological argumentative texts and dialogical debates, we speak only of arguments in the following for brevity:

Task On a broad level, we have discussed five general tasks in the three sections above: the *composition* of arguments from existing content, the *creation* of new arguments, the goal-oriented *rewriting* of arguments, the *countering* of an argument by another argument, and the *summarization* of arguments. As in any NLP area, the task specifies what output to create from what input.

Input Composition and creation may come with a specified *topic* as input only, often at least accompanied by a target *stance*, though. The other tasks start from one more *arguments* to modify, build on, or adhere to. We have also sketched settings where annotated *argument structure* is presupposed or where additional meta-information is given, such as the *target audience* to address. Whatever input is required at training time, naturally also needs to be available (or computable) at inference time.

Output The output to be generated is not only dependent on the mentioned *inputs*, but may also have to be optimized toward specified target criteria. This includes general text quality criteria, such as *coherence*, *factuality*, or *freedom of social bias*, but also argumentation-specific criteria, such as *argument quality* dimensions or *rhetoric principles* to follow. A control for the respective criteria usually requires their explicit treatment with a suitable generation technique.

Knowledge With the (possible) exception of summarization, all generation tasks share that the desired output adds something new beyond the input. To this end, some form of knowledge or information needs to be modeled or accessed in some way. Existing approaches connect to *knowledge bases* for this purpose, *retrieve* unstructured or semi-structured information from external sources, represent knowledge in a latent way in a *language model*, or similar. The clue often lies in a task-specific combination of different ways and their integration with the input.

Techniques Various techniques have been employed for argument generation, as discussed. In the last years, the focus is clearly on sequence-to-sequence generation using *language models*. In line with general NLP research, diverse ways to steer the models' behavior toward target criteria have been proposed, from *fine-tuning* and *instruction fine-tuning* to *alignment* and advanced *prompting* strategies. However, to ensure an accurate encoding of content and argumentative structure, we have seen that more 'traditional' techniques, such as *retrieval-based* composition or even *planning-based* text organization, are still preferred to this day.

A facet of argument generation that we have touched rather superficially only in this chapter are its ethical implications. Automatic methods that can automatically create, rewrite, or summarize arguments entail many potential benefits for individuals and society, from the fostering of critical thinking through showing new perspectives, to supporting the writing of strong and appropriately-phrased arguments, to easing the understanding of complex argumentative discussions. However, they can also easily be misused for doubtful use cases, such as the spread of convincingly-phrased misinformation or the mass manipulation of individuals through a targeted adjustment of argumentative style. In times where LLM-based tools and applications are used increasingly in everyday life as well as in sensitive domains, such misuse may cause serious harms. It is thus imperative to prevent misuse to the extent possible and to create awareness for the potential dangers of respective technologies otherwise.

Finally, while we have aimed to provide an adequate picture of the status quo of argument generation in this chapter, we point out that research on this family of tasks is still young and dynamically evolving. Particularly, the most evolutions of instruction-following LLMs only start to find their way into argument generation approaches, enabling various new techniques such as self-refinement, critique-based prompting, and specialized instruction fine-tuning. We will sketch some recent endeavors toward LLM-based argumentation and debating systems in our final outlook in Chap. 11, including new directions of evaluation coming up in this regard. Moreover, while most past and contemporary generation approaches that we cover in this book show great potential in general, many of them work far from perfectly or come with key limitations, as we have indicated in several places. It is thus likely that the state of the art is soon up to revision and refinement on its way toward a reliable generation of argumentative content that meets the criteria aimed for.

Tools & Applications 10

This chapter discusses tools for working with arguments as well as applications that use or could use argument mining. In our usage, *tools* process arguments as input or output for well-defined tasks within argumentation theory; they may be relevant for tasks such as creating corpora or assessing argument quality. By *applications* we mean complete argumentation systems designed to support or interact with human users to achieve a specific goal that substantively involves argument or controversy in some way.

In selecting tools, our goal is to raise awareness of key functionality available from computer support tools used in argumentation theory and computational argumentation. In selecting applications, our emphasis is on diversity and showcasing ideas. Argument mining is used for a number of user-facing applications, studied in the field of human-centered artificial intelligence and presented at venues in computational argumentation, human-computer interaction, natural language processing, and information retrieval. The centrality of arguing makes it difficult to draw firm boundaries. The technologies used in current applications also vary, particularly in the extent to which argument mining and NLP are used. Some applications integrate argument mining; others suggest how NLP research could be integrated into human-facing systems. Technology readiness varies across applications, ranging from an unimplemented idea to a proof-of-concept to a fully implemented system in routine use. Where possible, we present fully implemented, currently available systems. Yet we also include defunct systems that illustrate important past work as well as emerging systems.

The potential real-world impact of argument mining is immense, given the wide range of human activities that rely on reasoning or exchange of views. For argument mining to have an impact beyond the research community, it must be integrated into human-facing systems, which will require collaboration, especially for these applications to move into wide use. Existing applications can help argument mining researchers understand what can

M. Stede et al., *Argument Mining*, Synthesis Lectures on Human Language Technologies, https://doi.org/10.1007/978-3-032-32291-3_10

be done with arguments once they are extracted or otherwise formalized. Understanding real-world needs may also inspire future argument mining tasks.

In Sect. 10.1 we discuss tools for working with arguments that can be useful for understanding arguments by visualizing or solving them. The remainder of the chapter concerns applications. We divide these by envisioning a rough lifecycle: one might first find, then understand, then create arguments. Thus we cover applications for *finding* arguments (Sect. 10.2); *understanding* arguments (Sect. 10.3); and finally *creating* arguments, both writing monologues (Sect. 10.4) and contributing to deliberative and other types of dialogues (Sect. 10.5). We close by discussing IBM Debater, an end-to-end system incorporating argument mining in an autonomous debating system (Sect. 10.6), and summarizing the chapter (Sect. 10.7).

10.1 Tools for Working with Arguments

Tools process arguments as input or output for well-defined tasks within argumentation theory. Here we discuss argument mapping tools for working with informal arguments and argument solvers for manipulating abstract and formal arguments.

10.1.1 Argument Mapping Tools

Numerous tools for argument mapping (introduced in Sect. 3.1) are available. While even explicitly mapping an argument on paper can enable a clearer understanding of a topic, many tools offer additional computational support such as calculating acceptable sets of arguments (see Sect. 3.5.2). A quick visual overview of several styles of argument mapping can be found in Benetos (2023)'s review of interfaces for computer-supported argumentation.

Next we briefly review seven representative argument mapping tools. This is just a small selection of a diverse and crowded field of tools, which we present in alphabetical order. For more comprehensive reviews of tools, see Scheuer et al. (2010), Sinikallio et al. (2025), both of which cover computer-supported learning, and Schneider et al. (2013a), which focuses on web-based tools.

The Adelard Safety Case Editor (ASCE) ASCE[1] (Emmet and Cleland 2002) is primarily used in safety assurance, and can use the common formats of Goal Structuring Notation and Claims-Argument-Evidence.

Argunet Argunet[2] (Schneider et al. 2007) is an open source (GNU General Public License v2) cross-platform editor that can be used as standalone system or with a shared

[1] https://www.adelard.com/asce/ (accessed January 18, 2026).

[2] http://www.argunet.org/editor/ (accessed January 18, 2026).

server. In Argunet, sentences are the basic elements, which are connected together into arguments. Support and conflict relationships are visually distinguished, and the user can add descriptions for any inference patterns they wish. Individual arguments appear in argument maps which may be part of larger debates. The debating system can be used by multiple users and maps made in Argunet can be displayed online with a JavaScript widget. While still a strong tool, since 2018, developers have moved their focus to Argdown, which we discuss next.[3]

Argdown Argdown[4] is a markdown-like syntax. For instance, support (+) and attack (−) relationships can be processed to draw an argument map. Argdown is designed for Web and document publishing using markdown parsers, pandoc, Visual Studio Code, or static site generators.

DebateGraph DebateGraph[5] is an online mapping tool that has been used by media organizations to help users browse complex ideas, integrated with rich media. Maps can be viewed graphically or in outline format. Maps can include issues, positions, supportive arguments, and opposing arguments.

MonkeyPuzzle MonkeyPuzzle[6] (Douglas and Wells 2017) is a free open source online argument mapping tool which can also be run as a standalone Java application. It is based on Araucaria[7] (Reed and Rowe 2004).

Online Visualization of Argument (OVA) OVA[8] (Snaith et al. 2010) facilitates analysis of web pages. Various semantics can be automatically applied to compute acceptable sets of arguments. It has been adapted into OVA+ (Janier et al. 2014) to provide particular support for a dialogue-based argument annotation system called Inference Anchoring Theory (see Sect. 3.4.3). It has also been widely used for applications (Lawrence et al. 2017a).

Rationale Rationale[9] (van Gelder 2007) and its cousin bCisive[10] are commercial argument mapping tools created by the Australian Austhink company and overseen by the

[3] http://www.argunet.org/2018/10/26/new-beginning-introducing-argdown/ (accessed January 18, 2026).

[4] https://argdown.org (accessed January 18, 2026).

[5] http://debategraph.org/ (accessed January 18, 2026).

[6] http://arg.napier.ac.uk/projects/monkeypuzzle/ (accessed January 18, 2026).

[7] http://araucaria.arg.tech/doku.php (accessed January 18, 2026).

[8] http://ova.arg-tech.org (accessed January 18, 2026).

[9] https://www.rationaleonline.com (accessed January 18, 2026).

[10] https://www.bcisiveonline.com (accessed January 18, 2026).

Dutch parent company Critical Thinking Skills BV. Rationale is an online system focused on teaching critical thinking as well as essay writing while bCisive is designed for business decision making. Maps can be public or private. Different types of argument maps are supported; for instance, in writing-oriented maps, concepts might connected with words such as *but*, *however*, and *because*.

10.1.2 Research Prototype Tools for Corpus Creation and Development

Argument mining research groups have developed argument-specific tools for corpus creation and development. These tools, while not widely available, may inspire future development.

The Argument Analysis Wall This (Bex et al. 2013) enabled multiple analysts to collaborate in real-time manual mapping of radio debates from the BBC's Moral Maze radio program, as shown exemplarily in Fig. 10.1. The resulting corpora jumpstarted early argument mining on dialogues and brought visibility to the Argument Web (Reed et al. 2017).

Fig. 10.1 Analysts mapping a British Broadcasting Corporation (BBC) radio debate in real time on the Argument Analysis Wall at the Center for Argument Technology, Dundee, Scotland. Photo via https://www.arg.tech/index.php/argument-analysiswall-analysis-in-real-time/ (accessed January 16, 2026); online representation of the resulting argument map is available at http://aifdb.org/argview/789 (accessed January 16, 2026), used with permission

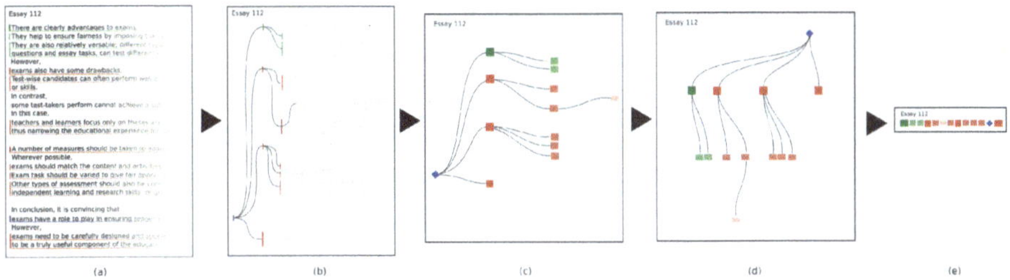

Fig. 10.2 An ArguLine (image e, right) summarizes an essay with a compact abstraction (Kiesel et al. 2021a). Used with permission

The Visual Analysis of Essay Argumentation This (Kiesel et al. 2021a) combines visual analytics with argument mapping, providing interactive interfaces that support quality assurance for corpus annotation of argumentative essays. Here we mention two key visualizations. *ArguLines* are single-line summaries that compress a single argument's structure; Fig. 10.2 illustrates how they are derived from a given text. Another visualization, the *Argument Unit Occurrence Tree* (not shown) aggregates larger numbers of arguments with histogram summaries, easing the identification of patterns and variation in argument structures.

10.1.3 Computational Argumentation Reasoning Tools

Here we briefly mention several tools that support visualization and solving formal representations of arguments. As mentioned in Sect. 3.5, argument solvers can compute the acceptability for argumentation frameworks.

The Online Argument Structures Tool (TOAST) TOAST[11] (Snaith and Reed 2012) is an online implementation of the ASPIC+ (Sect. 3.5.2) theory of structured argumentation. Given a knowledge base, rules, preferences and contrariness, TOAST converts the ASPIC+ formal representation into a Dung-style (Sect. 3.5.1) argumentation framework and solves it.

PyArg PyArg[12] (Odekerken et al. 2023) is a flexible tool for visualizing and evaluating formal arguments including abstract argumentation frameworks and ASPIC+ argumentation theories. It has a Python package and web interface.

[11] http://toast.arg-tech.org/ (accessed January 18, 2026).

[12] https://pyarg.npai.science.uu.nl/ (accessed January 18, 2026).

XRAY XRAY[13] (Xia et al. 2025) also visualizes and evaluates formal arguments. It emphasizes a provenance and game-based views for argumentation frameworks.

10.2 Support for Finding Arguments and Evidence

Here we discuss applications that help people find arguments and evidence. We focus on argument search and evidence collection from texts.

10.2.1 Argument Search Systems

Argument search systems are a popular and important application envisioned for argument mining. Likewise, argument-based search for scientific literature is a long-standing vision.

args.me: Debate Search args.me (Wachsmuth et al. 2017d)[14] is a prototype argument search engine. Arguments were crawled from five debate portals (see Ajjour et al. 2019b) and mapped to the args.me model which includes the conclusion, premises, and stances as well as context for the argument. Ranking uses a BM25 variant.[15] The interface shows pro vs. con (see Fig. 10.3) or all arguments in rank order. Subsequently, args.me added dynamic topic views based on offline topic modeling (Ajjour et al. 2018). An analysis of users' search query logs found that the corpus responded well for some queries, yet some searched topics were not well-covered (Ajjour et al. 2019b). The presented argument snippets are extractive summaries, created with the approach of Alshomary et al. (2020a) discussed in Sect. 9.3.

ArgumenText: Web Search ArgumenText (Stab et al. 2018a) used supervised argument mining to extract arguments from CommonCrawl,[16] a large public web archive dataset. ArgumenText retrieves arguments related to the user's query and presents pro and

[13] https://github.com/idaks/xray deployed at https://xray-n7sd5.ondigitalocean.app (accessed January 18, 2026).

[14] https://www.args.me/ and API https://www.args.me/api-en.html (accessed January 18, 2026).

[15] The team's related work investigated ranking ("PageRank for argument relevance counts any use of a conclusion as a premise as a support of relevance" (Wachsmuth et al. 2017e, page 1118)) and extracting snippets that encapsulate the differences between arguments (Alshomary et al. 2022b). They also presented an early information retrieval evaluation (Potthast et al. 2019). For more on ranking see the Touché Lab on Argument Retrieval at CLEF 2020-2025, https://touche.webis.de (accessed January 5, 2025).

[16] https://commoncrawl.org (accessed January 18, 2026).

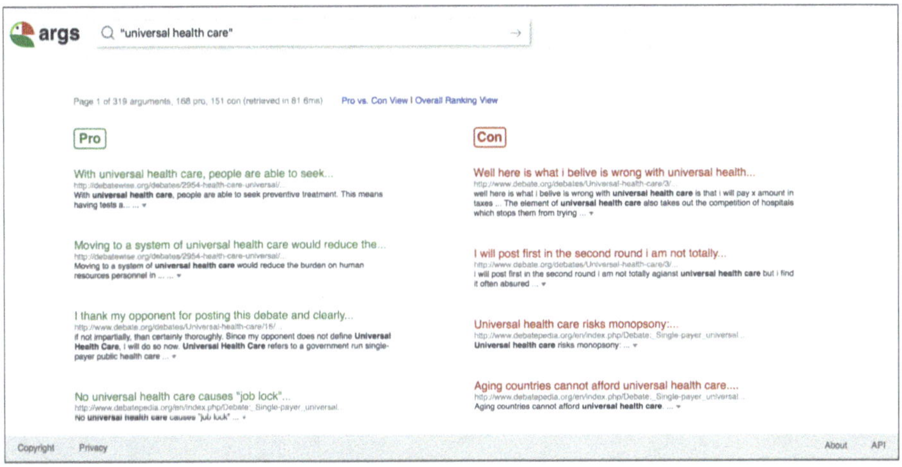

Fig. 10.3 Interface of the argument search engine *args.me* from Wachsmuth et al. (2017d, page 56), licensed under CC-BY 4.0 International

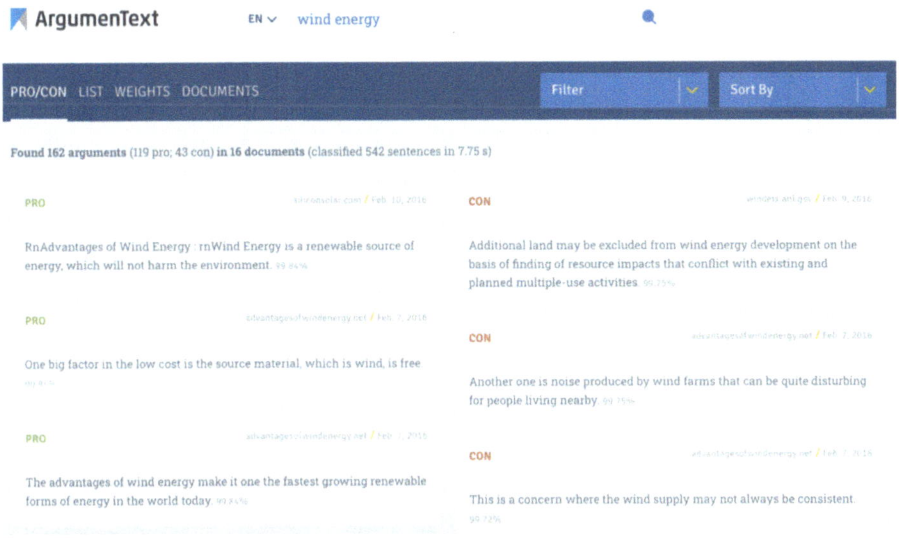

Fig. 10.4 Interface of ArgumenText from Daxenberger et al. (2020, page 117), licensed under CC-BY 4.0 International

con arguments as shown in Fig. 10.4. The system demo previously included an API. Daxenberger et al. (2020) mention its use cases such as deep analysis of customer feedback (see Arzt et al. 2021; Skiera et al. 2022) and investment decision support (mining news to get a balanced view of technology).

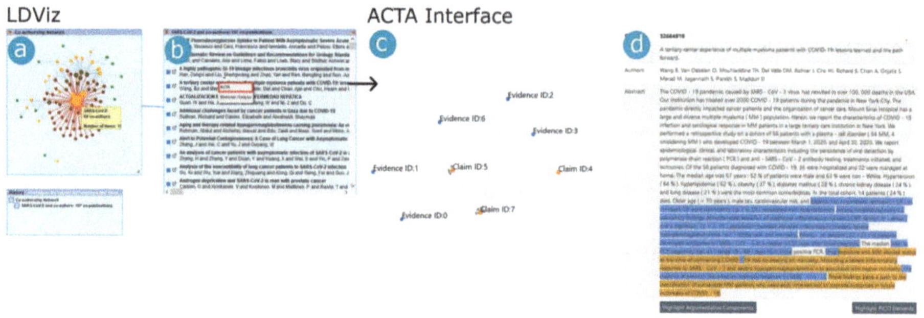

Fig. 10.5 A multi-step exploratory visualization process (**a–d**) leads to an argumentative graph (**c**) and an ACTA interface (**d**) showing the claim, evidence, and PICO elements, from Menin et al. (2021, page 1318), licensed under CC-BY 4.0 International

Summetix[17] is a spin out company from the Technical University Darmstadt commercializing this line of work, with a public demo[18] that searches documents from their university open access repository TUprints and the open access publisher MDPI.

ACTA: Exploratory Search of COVID-19 Literature Argumentative Clinical Trial Analysis (ACTA) facilitated exploratory search of the COVID-19 literature (Menin et al. 2021). COVID-on-the-Web[19] used entity detection and ACTA's argument mining to enhance the CORD-19 corpus[20] (Wang et al. 2020) as RDF-structured linked data. This was combined with a visualization interface (LDViz),[21] based on the Multidimensional Graph Explorer) enabling multi-step exploration as shown in Fig. 10.5.

10.2.2 Evidence Support

Several prototype interfaces aim to help users collect or visualize evidence.

EDoHa: Document-based Evidence Collection Designed for humanities and social science researchers, Evidence Detection fOr Hypothesis vAlidation (EDoHa)[22] (Stahlhutt et al. 2018; Stahlhut 2019) aims to "enabl[e] a user to validate their hypotheses with evidence they annotated in a collection of documents". EDoHA has two views: Document view (Fig. 10.6) supports evidence annotation. It uses a pre-trained model to suggest

[17] https://www.summetix.com/company/ (accessed January 18, 2026).

[18] https://www.argumentsearch.com (accessed January 18, 2026).

[19] https://github.com/Wimmics/CovidOnTheWeb (accessed January 18, 2026).

[20] https://github.com/allenai/cord19 (accessed January 18, 2026).

[21] LDViz demo https://youtu.be/Cn_IWQ7yVvE (accessed January 18, 2026).

[22] https://github.com/UKPLab/EDoHa (accessed January 18, 2026).

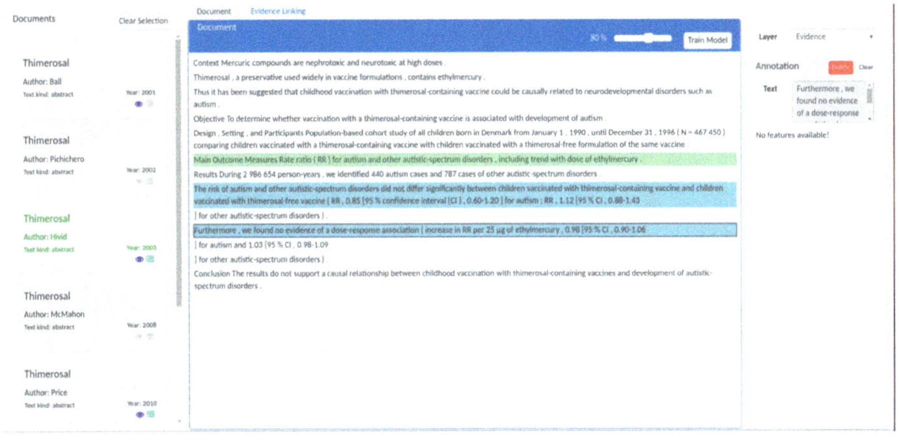

Fig. 10.6 EDoHA document view from https://github.com/UKPLab/EDoHa (accessed January 18, 2026), used with permission

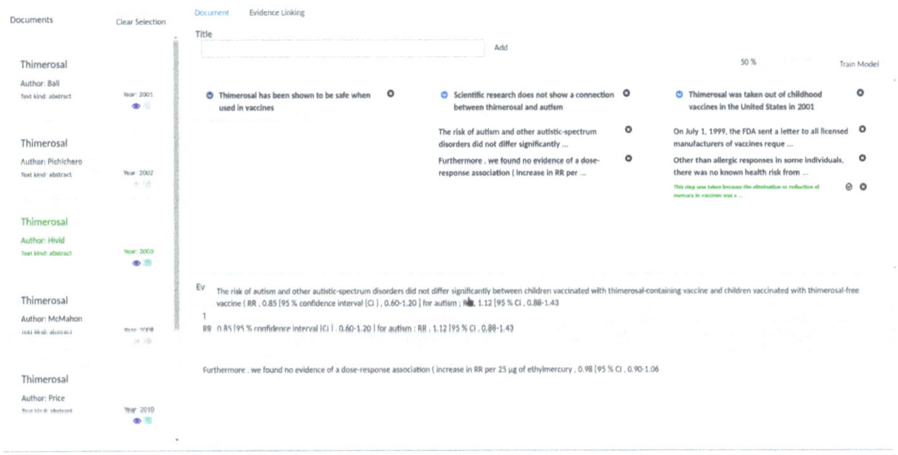

Fig. 10.7 EDoHA linking view from https://github.com/UKPLab/EDoHa (accessed January 18, 2026), used with permission

sentences; once the user annotates sentences, the model can be retrained on the user's data. Evidence Linking view (Fig. 10.7) supports the user in grouping evidence into groups.

ACTA: Claim-Evidence Visualization of Biomedical Literature We return to ACTA[23] (Mayer et al. 2019; Molinet et al. 2022; Cardellino et al. 2024) which provides claim-evidence visualizations from argument mining of biomedical literature (Fig. 10.8).

[23] https://ns.inria.fr/acta/ and a demo for ACTA2.0 https://www.youtube.com/watch?v=OX59bWWL6WA (both accessed January 18, 2026).

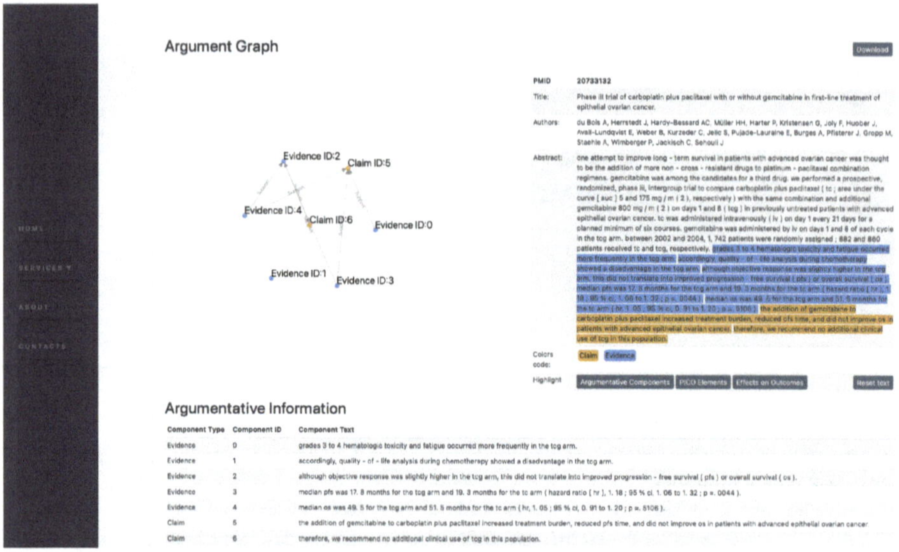

Fig. 10.8 ACTA's argument graph for the PubMed document PMID 20733132 from https://ns.inria.fr/acta/browse/?ids=20733132 (accessed January 18, 2026)

They use PICO elements—Patient/Problem/Population, Intervention, Comparison or Control, and Outcome(s)—which are widely used for forming biomedical literature searches. They provide an API and JSON export of the data.

10.3 Support for Understanding Arguments

Moving from tools to applications, we first discuss applications that help people understand arguments, by surfacing diverse perspectives, visualizing stance and polarization, and making rhetoric visible. Related reviews consider mass online deliberation (Shortall et al. 2022) and online arguing tools (Schneider et al. 2013a), argument mining for social good (Vecchi et al. 2021) and how NLP can support deliberation in online political discussions (Behrendt et al. 2025).

10.3.1 Surfacing Diverse Perspectives

Argument mining could be useful in surfacing diverse perspectives.

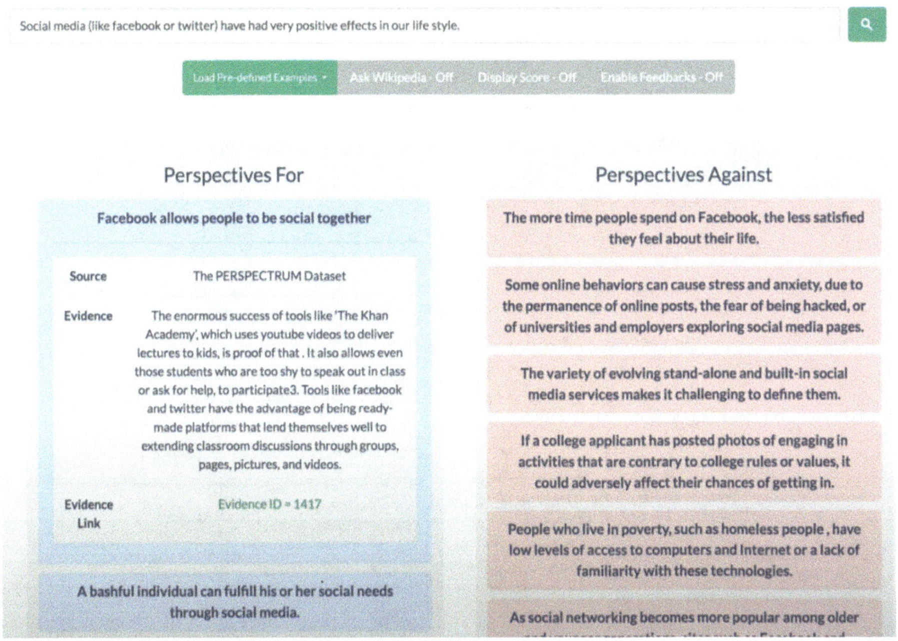

Fig. 10.9 Screenshot from the PerspectroScope Demo (Chen et al. 2019a), (timepoint 2:22) from https://youtu.be/MXBTR1Sp3Bs?t=142 (accessed January 18, 2026). Used with permission

PerspectroScope PerspectroScope[24] (Chen et al. 2019a) aims to present diverse evidence in search results as shown in Fig. 10.9. It relies on a crowdsourced dataset, augmented with paraphrasing and web search, called Perspectum (Chen et al. 2019b). Perspectum envisioned a system highlighting a range of perspectives, as shown in Fig. 10.10 (Chen et al. 2019b).

Dispute Finder Dispute Finder (Ennals et al. 2010b)[25] was a web browser plugin designed for skeptical readers and activists. It highlighted "known disputed claims that frequently appear on the web" (Ennals et al. 2010b, page 341) as the user was browsing. Clicking on a highlighted claim showed a popup with articles for and against the claim as shown in Fig. 10.11. The plugin also enabled users to mark disputed claims, add paraphrases of claims, and add evidence for or against a claim.

[24] PerspectroScope code: https://github.com/CogComp/perspectroscope (accessed January 18, 2026).

[25] Code archive https://github.com/robennals/think-link and short 2010 demo https://www.youtube.com/watch?v=jsUKhNICeqg (both accessed January 18, 2026).

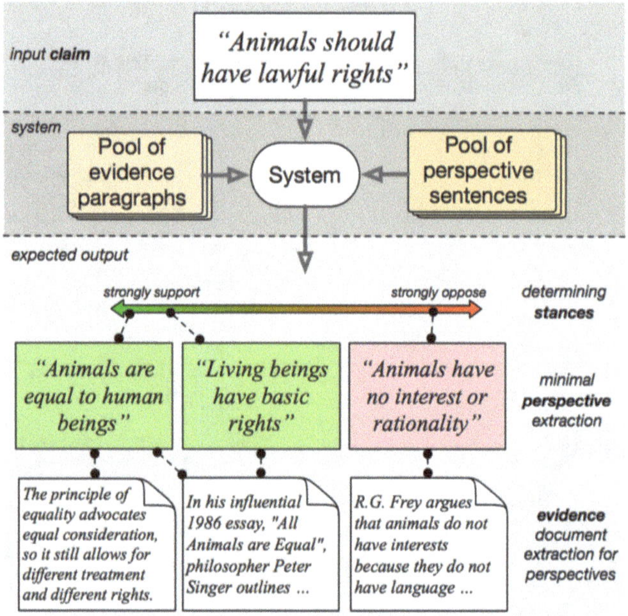

Fig. 10.10 Envisioning the PerspectroScope (from the Perspectum system demo) (Chen et al. 2019b, page 542), licensed under CC-BY 4.0 International

Fig. 10.11 DisputeFinder (Ennals et al. 2010b, page 341), used with permission

Dispute Finder used textual entailment to check its knowledge base. The disputed claim knowledge base drew from user submissions as well as online databases from Snopes[26] and Politifact[27] Subsequent work (Ennals et al. 2010a) expanded the corpus of disputed claims using hand-crafted patterns and a Naive Bayes classifier.

---

[26] https://www.snopes.com (accessed January 18, 2026).

[27] https://www.politifact.com (accessed January 18, 2026).

In their user study, users preferred article lists that highlighted who disagreed with a claim as more useful summaries than argumentation graphs (Ennals et al. 2010b, pages 347-8). They also prototyped search engine and voice interfaces.[28]

10.3.2 Visualizing Stance and Polarization

For social media discussions, visualizing stance and polarization can be helpful.

SAGESSE: Stance in Reddit Discussion Threads SAGESSE[29] (Almerge et al. 2025) creates argument maps from Reddit while retaining each discussion thread's reply structure. Pro and con messages are summarized as shown in Fig. 10.12, with neutral (blue) replies hidden by default. Node size in the argument map indicates more child replies in the Reddit thread. Their LLM-based pipeline includes claim extraction and stance detection.

Polviz: Polarization in Social Media Diaz et al. (2024) introduce the Polviz analytics framework and an interface[30] which supports interactive exploration of social media discussions. As shown in Fig. 10.13, users can explore three interlinked views that show the topics as hierarchical tree and nested view, and, for geolocated messages, a map of denier and believer locations.

10.3.3 Making Rhetoric Visible

Ethos mining is an emerging area making rhetoric visible (Budzyńska and Koszowy 2020; Duthie et al. 2016) for instance to find ad hominem arguments. Rhetorical structures are also important in scientific arguing (Teufel 2014).

LEPAn: Rhetorical Analytics of Annotated Arguments Gajewska et al. (2024) develop an analytics dashboard called LEPAn[31] to analyze rhetorical arguments (logos, ethos, and pathos). For instance, ethos-based arguments from two Reddit discussions are summarized as shown in Fig. 10.14 with the most-supported "heroes" and least-supported "villans" from ethotic arguments. LEPAn has been used to compare patterns of two existing

[28] Prototypes are shown in the Online Deliberation Emerging Tools 2010 presentation video https://www.youtube.com/watch?v=l-X21HRUhuE (accessed January 18, 2026); possible applications for a corpus of disputed claims are also briefly discussed in (Ennals et al. 2010a, pages 71-2).

[29] https://modemos.epfl.ch/sagesse/ (accessed July 8, 2025).

[30] https://cs.uns.edu.ar/~dku/vis/polviz-climate-change/ (accessed January 18, 2026).

[31] https://lepan-v01.streamlit.app/ (accessed January 18, 2026); find documentation and related tools via https://newethos.org/technologies/ (accessed January 18, 2026).

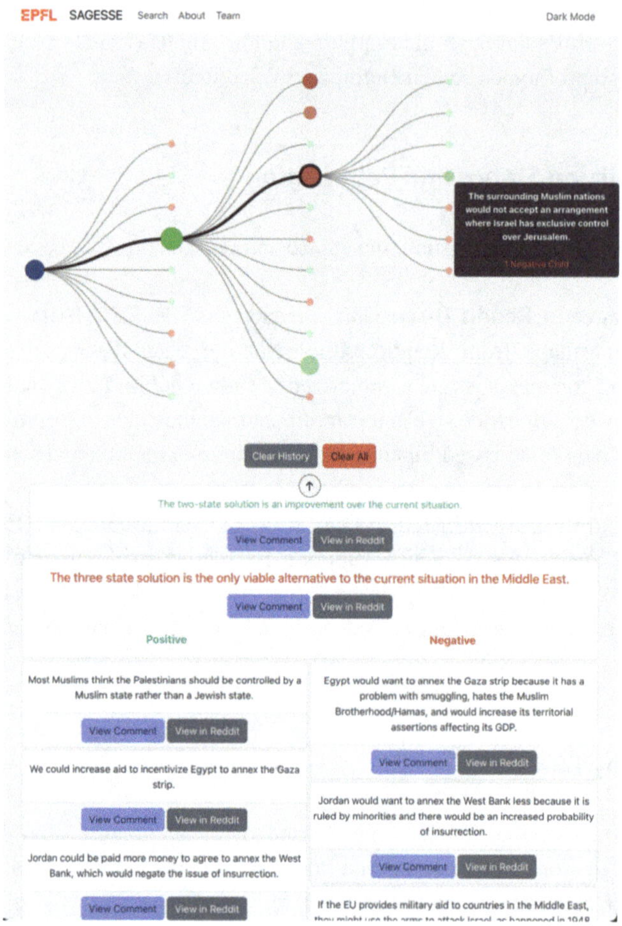

Fig. 10.12 Reddit data transformed into an argument map with SAGESSE from Almerge et al. (2025, 1027), used with permission

manually annotated datasets (PolarIs1 and US2016reddit) (Budzynska et al. 2024), leading to insights in argumentation theory.

ArguminSci: Rhetorical Analytics in Science ArguminSci[32] (Lauscher et al. 2018a) displays arguments automatically mined from scientific papers. Figure 10.15 shows two tabs from the web application: argument components (background claim, own claim, data) and discourse roles (background, challenge, approach, outcome, future work). Three other tabs, not shown, display citation contexts, subjective aspects (e.g., advantage, novelty,

[32] https://github.com/anlausch/ArguminSci (accessed January 18, 2026).

Fig. 10.13 Polviz interface (Diaz et al. 2024, p. 342), used with permission

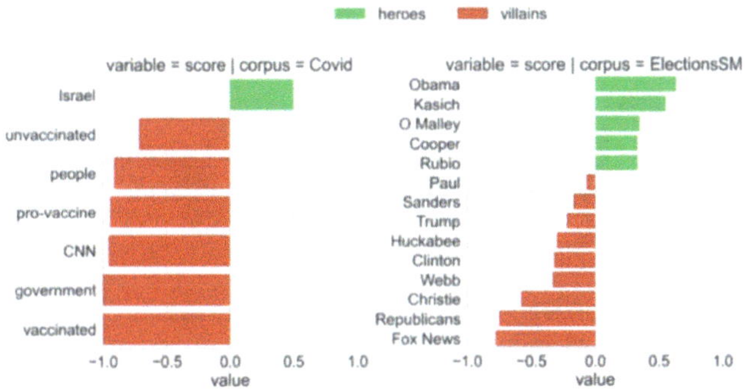

Fig. 10.14 LEPAn (Gajewska et al. 2024, 352) counts the "heroes" and "villains" who are mentioned the most in positive and negative ethotic arguments, respectively, here summarizing two Reddit discussions. Used with permission

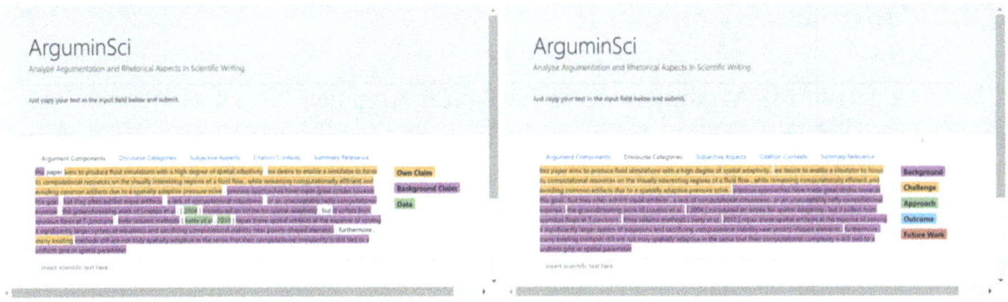

Fig. 10.15 Part of the ArguminSci web interface from (Lauscher et al. 2018a, page 26), licensed under CC-BY 4.0 International

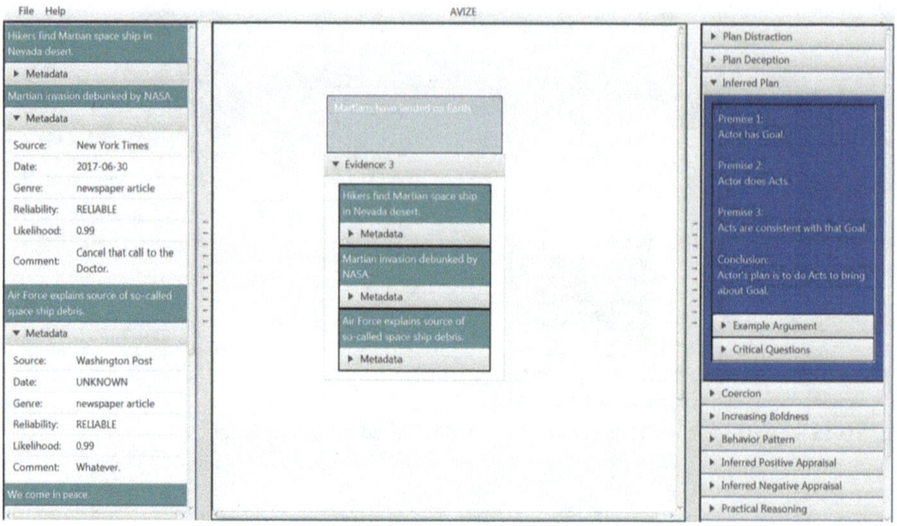

Fig. 10.16 Selecting evidence in AVIZE (Green et al. 2018, page 50), used with permission

common practice, limitation), and the degree of relevance for summarization. Besides the web-based user interface, a command line interface and API are also available.

10.4 Support for Writing Monological Arguments

Numerous work has applied argumentation mining to creating arguments, largely in the guise of writing support.[33] Guerraoui et al. (2023)[34] survey NLP-based systems for argument writing support to students.

10.4.1 Constructing Arguments

AVIZE: Constructing Arguments from Evidence Argument Visualization and Evaluation (AVIZE)[35] (Green et al. 2018) aim to help users "construct and challenge their own arguments based upon evidence of varying plausibility from sources of varying reliability". It contains argument schemes customized for the domain of international politics. Users can both collect evidence (Fig. 10.16) and organize it (Fig. 10.17) in AVIZE.

[33] Browse the prototypes of Bern University of Applied Sciences' Human-Centered AI-based System Lab for a wide range of examples: https://haislab.com/services/ (accessed January 18, 2026).

[34] See also their accompanying website https://kmilia.github.io/teach_me_how_to_argue/index.html (accessed January 18, 2026).

[35] https://github.com/greennl/AVIZE (accessed January 18, 2026).

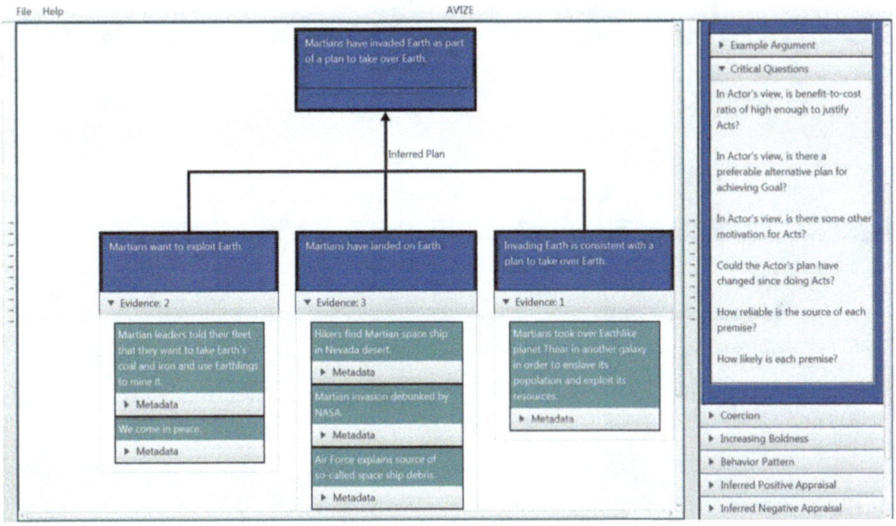

Fig. 10.17 Using the Inferred Plan argument scheme to build a plan in AVIZE (Green et al. 2018, page 51), used with permission

Vincent AI: Generating Legal Arguments Vincent AI from vLex is a RAG-based LLM-based legal information system. Its "Build an Argument" feature generates persuasive arguments in a litigation context[36] Given a jurisdiction, the facts of the case, and the goals, Vincent AI suggests several possible lines of argument. The user then specifies which lines of argument to pursue. Vincent AI suggests an argument and provides the legal texts from which it was generated.

10.4.2 Critiquing and Revising Arguments

Test Your Argument: A Quiz for Improving Humans' Arguing Skills In the realm of critiquing arguments, *Test Your Argument* (Lawrence et al. 2018)[37] accompanied the BBC's Moral Maze radio program, discussed briefly above. This educational online quiz was developed to help people make better arguments. The user is stepped through the process of creating and strengthening an argument with multiple choices at each stage (Fig. 10.18).

---

[36] Documentation https://support.vlex.com/features/vincent/build-an-argument and demo video https://vimeo.com/showcase/11016912/video/1036077068 (accessed January 18, 2026).

[37] http://tya.arg.tech/index.html (accessed January 18, 2026).

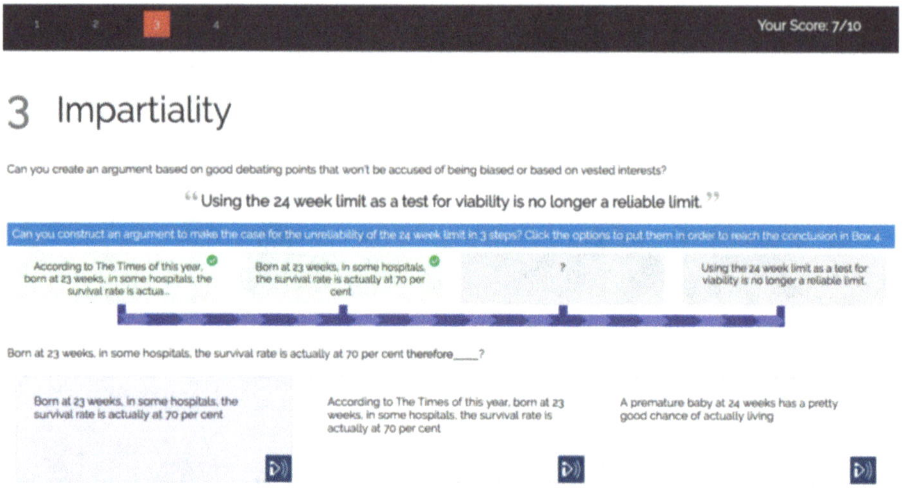

Fig. 10.18 Part of "Test Your Argument" from (Lawrence et al. 2018, page 466), used with permission

Fig. 10.19 Argumentative Sparks in VISAR (Zhang et al. 2023b, page 6), used with permission

VISAR: A Human-AI Argumentative Writing Assistant LLMs with chain-of-thought prompting power Zhang et al. (2023b)'s writing assistant VISAR.[38] A text draft and tree are kept in sync. Both of these outline the main arguments, key points, supporting evidence, discussion points, and counterarguments. Users can request help from the LLM in generating counterarguments, logical weaknesses, or supporting evidence as shown in Fig. 10.19.

ArgRewrite: Essay Revision Support ArgRewrite[39] (Zhang et al. 2016a) incorporates argument mining output in a web interface that supports essay revision. ArgRewrite

[38] See their paper's online supplement in the ACM Digital Library page for Zhang et al. (2023b) for a video demo.

[39] https://argrewrite.cs.pitt.edu (accessed January 18, 2026).

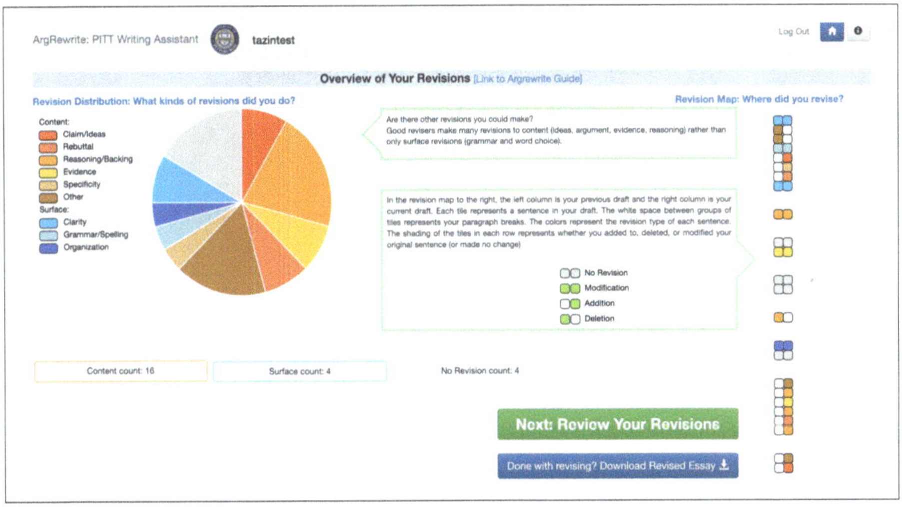

Fig. 10.20 Part of the ArgRewrite interface from page 4 of https://argrewrite.cs.pitt.edu/files/ArgrewriteGuide.pdf, used with permission

automatically identifies an essay's thesis, rebuttal, reasoning, and evidence and tracks revisions between two successive versions of an essay. Users are shown an overview (as shown in Fig. 10.20); the same color scheme is used for a sentence-by-sentence view. A user evaluation (Afrin et al. 2021) found that detailed sentence-level revision feedback was the most helpful of four ArgRewrite versions tested.

10.5 Support for Argumentative Dialogues

We review a few systems that support taking part in arguments, scaffolding deliberative arguing or enabling dialogue with argumentation systems.

10.5.1 Support for Deliberative Arguing

ConsiderIt ConsiderIt (Kriplean et al. 2012)[40] is a scalable debate forum collecting pros and cons, for and against a given proposal. It has been used for civic engagement, strategic planning and community visioning, and decentralized decision-making. Forums can be

[40] https://consider.it with open source code https://github.com/Considerit/ConsiderIt (accessed January 18, 2026).

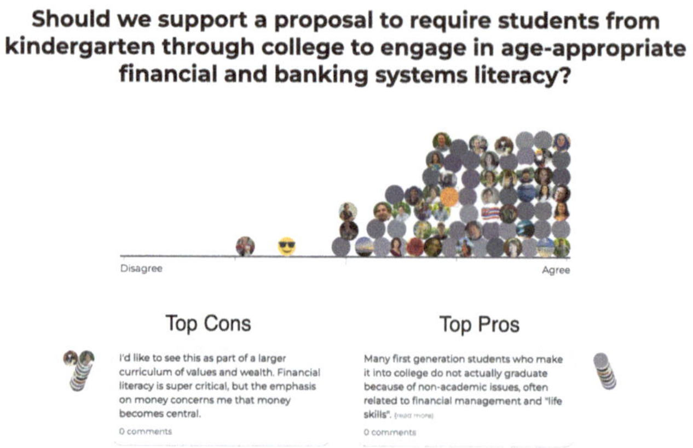

Fig. 10.21 ConsiderIt example from https://consider.it/examples/community_visioning (accessed January 18, 2026), used with permission

private or public, with both free and fee-based versions available. Figure 10.21 shows an example which can also be examined interactively online.[41]

BCause and AM4DSP: Human-AI Collaborative Structuring of Deliberation Forums BCause[42] (Anastasiou and De Liddo 2026) is a human-AI system using the Issue-Based Information System (IBIS) model of argumentation (Sect. 3.4.4). To help structure deliberation in a discussion forum, BCause uses pre-trained models to structure text. Humans can correct and adjust machine annotations. Earlier versions of BCause were used to support real world deliberations (Anastasiou et al. 2023). Lately, AM4DSP (Elguendouze et al. 2025) builds on BCause, incorporating more sophisticated NLP. In Fig. 10.22 text is compared to the given text to highlight it as supporting, attacking, or attacked by the given (grey) text.

10.5.2 Argumentation-Based Dialogue Systems

Here we discuss argumentation systems that foreground the interaction between human and computer, for behavior change or learning.

Dialogue systems, chatbots, and other approaches can provide an interactive experience from an argument base. Castagna et al. (2024) survey chatbots using computational argumentation.

[41] https://ainaalohafutures.consider.it/should-we-support-a-proposal-to-require-students-from-kindergarten-through-college-to-engage-i-rethinking-education-15168?tab=Education (accessed January 18, 2026).

[42] https://bcause.app (accessed January 18, 2026).

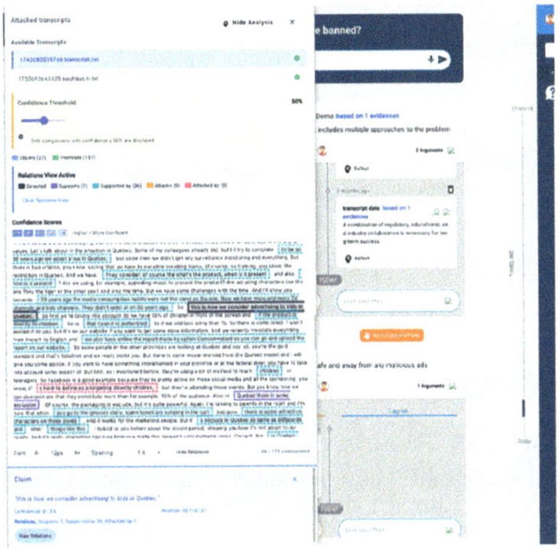

Fig. 10.22 AM4DSP (Elguendouze et al. 2025) builds on BCause's user interface, incorporating more sophisticated NLP, licensed under CC-BY 4.0 International

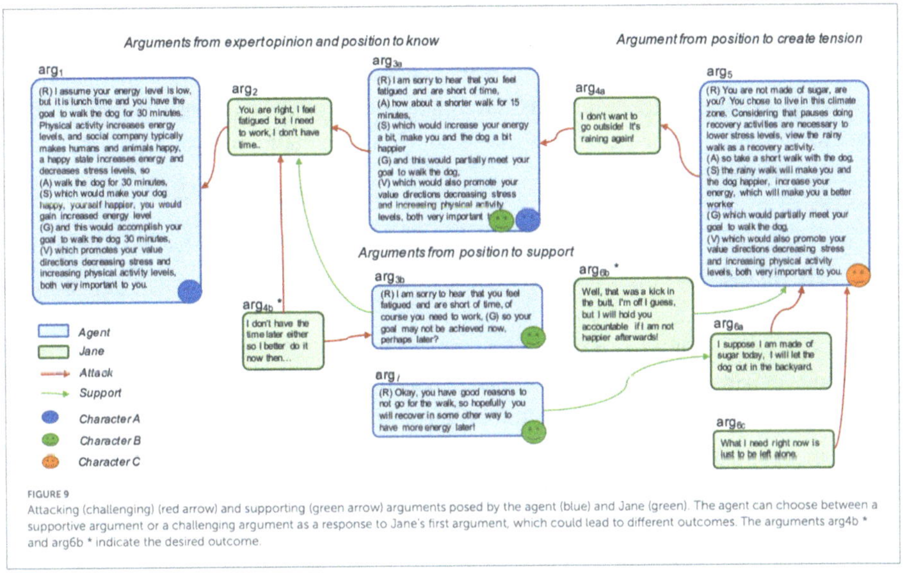

Fig. 10.23 STAR-C's dialogue generation will adapt responses to the user (Kilic et al. 2023, page 17), licensed under CC-BY 4.0 International

STAR-C: Argument Generation Supporting Behavior Change The STAR-C project is developing an argumentative digital coach as part of a long-term population health project in the Swedish county of Västerbotten (Kilic et al. 2023). To support behavior change, the coach will use both supportive and challenging responses in dialogues, adapting to the user and the situation, as shown in Fig. 10.23. It is based on a bipolar argumentation framework (Sect. 3.5.2), incorporating dialogue types, argument schemes (Sect. 3.3), and value-based argumentation.

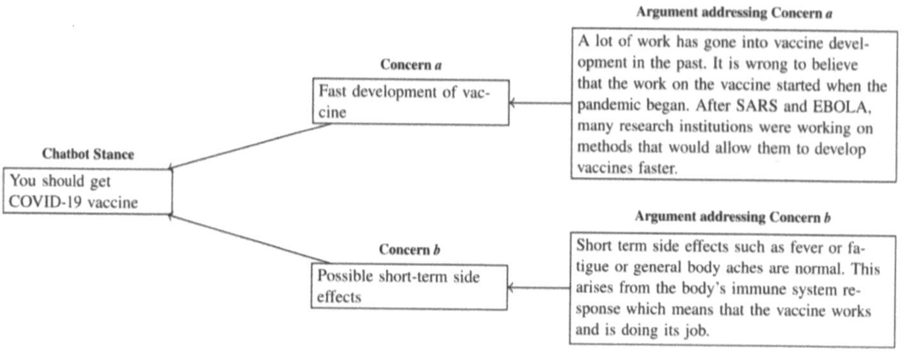

Fig. 10.24 Part of the "concern-argument graph" about COVID-19 vaccination from (Chalaguine and Hunter 2021) used to determine the chatbot's responses, used with permission

A Chatbot Built on Argument Graphs An argument graph such as the one shown in Fig. 10.24 helps the chatbot in Chalaguine and Hunter (2021) respond to concerns about COVID-19 vaccination. This "concern-argument graph" simplifies traditional argument graphs by grouping counterarguments into related concerns. Users who chatted with the system were more persuaded than those who viewed a static webpage with the most persuasive arguments.

10.6 IBM Debater: An Autonomous Debating System

We end by discussing the IBM Debater. In February 2019, Project Debater, IBM's autonomous debating system, faced human debate champion Harish Natarajan in front of a live public audience.[43] The debate topic—subsidizing preschools—and their positions (Project Debater pro, Natarajan con) were assigned just 15 minutes before the moderator called for opening speeches. The audience said Project Debater "better enriched [their] knowledge".[44] Yet human Natarajan was declared the winner: "Support for preschool subsidies dropped from 79 to 62 percent, and opposition more than doubled from 13 to 30 percent." (Grant 2023, page 102). Yet the imbalanced views of the audience complicate evaluation; as Slonim et al. (2021, page 381) note, "Project Debater had a potential of 21% of the audience to convince, whereas H. Natarajan had a potential of 87%".

Argument mining was essential to the Project Debater system (Slonim et al. 2021) (Fig. 10.25) that Natarajan debated, which drew on a corpus of millions of newspaper articles that it chunked and indexed before the debate. Once given its topic and position,

[43] The debate was hosted by Intelligence Squared U.S., which is now known as Open to Debate; see https://opentodebate.org/debaters/ibm-project-debater/ (accessed January 18, 2026) and https://www.youtube.com/watch?v=m3u-1yttrVw (accessed January 18, 2026).

[44] See minute 54 of the debate video.

Fig. 10.25 Moderator John Donvan (left), IBM Project Debater (center), and Harish Natarajan (right) February 11, 2019. Photo from https://www.flickr.com/photos/ibm_research_zurich/32216085047/ (accessed January 27th, 2026), used under CC-BY-ND 2.0 Generic

Project Debater developed corpus-based arguments using claim detection, evidence detection, and stance detection. In the same process, the system also identified "claims the opponent may use" [page 380] (Slonim et al. 2021) and evidence that could be used in rebuttal.

Project Debater also relied in part on an argument knowledge base of texts drawing on first principles (Bilu et al. 2019). These texts, designed for reuse across debates, were previously custom-written or custom-edited. A feature-based classifier determines which classes of "principled arguments, counter-arguments, and commonplace examples" [page 380] (Slonim et al. 2021) the system might use for a given debate.

For rebuttals, the system first identified claims in the opponent's speeches (after speech-to-text). Then it compared them to claims mined from the corpus, found in the argument knowledge base, or previously used in debates on iDebate.[45] Rebuttals could also draw on stock responses to key sentiment terms (e.g., "harmful") from the argument knowledge base.

IBM currently licenses Project Debater technologies "for both business and academic use"[46] Use cases and public demonstrations for Project Debater are discussed in an EMNLP demo paper presenting the APIs (Bar-Haim et al. 2021).

---

45 The International Debate Education Association has renamed their database Debatabase; it is now available at https://idebate.net/resources/debatabase (accessed January 18, 2026).

46 https://research.ibm.com/haifa/dept/vst/debater.shtml (accessed January 18, 2026).

10.7 Summary

This chapter first covered three types of tools: argument mapping tools for working with informal arguments; research prototype tools used for corpus creation and development; and argument solvers for manipulating formal arguments. Then we turned to various applications—for *finding* arguments; *understanding* arguments; *writing* monological arguments; and *participating in* argumentative dialogues. We closed by discussing the IBM Debater, an end-to-end system incorporating argument mining in an autonomous debating system.

Conclusions 11

In this final chapter, we first look back and survey the landscape of argument mining (AM) research that we have covered in all the preceding chapters (Sect. 11.1). Then we look forward by pointing to areas and aspects of AM that may become more important in the future (Sect. 11.2), before we reflect on possible ethical implications of AM research and conclude the book (Sect. 11.3).

11.1 Summary

As the 'sum total' of the chapters in this book demonstrates, AM has become a somewhat unwieldy research area of natural language processing (NLP)—or its own research field if you will—in the sense that it has many different facets that can be explored and possibly developed into entire subareas. As usual in NLP, this diversification has been over the years mainly driven by the availability of annotated corpora: Where there is data, labeled with some interesting argument-related phenomenon, the machine learning community will pick it up and compare their methods; leaderboards spring up; perhaps shared tasks are organized at workshops. As a result, a research field does not grow in a top-down fashion by carefully-meditated decisions on how the overall 'big' problem should ideally be handled, but much more as a result of individual bottom-up activities, which in NLP often relate to data availability.

Nonetheless, at the beginning of Chap. 4, we pointed out a rough division of the core argument *mining* tasks into two research lines that correspond to two separate practical goals: *information-seeking AM* and *discourse-based AM*. In the following, we structure our summary of the book first along this division, before turning to the follow-up tasks that the two lines actually share. In the interest of brevity, we limit the discussion to monological arguments and do not explicitly discuss the specific requirements for AM on dialogue (or

M. Stede et al., *Argument Mining*, Synthesis Lectures on Human Language Technologies, https://doi.org/10.1007/978-3-032-32291-3_11

multi-logue). The tasks we enumerate are a superset of what is usually done in a specific application; at the same time, our brief summary invariably makes many simplifications.

11.1.1 Information-Seeking 'Core' Argument Mining

In the information-seeking approach, the starting point is a given controversial topic, and the (interim) goal is a collection of argumentative material pertaining to that topic. The topic is not just a phrase describing it (*climate change, tuition fees, …*) but should be concrete enough to warrant the retrieval of truly relevant material, and can be formulated as a question, such as "Are fossil fuels primarily responsible for climate change?", "Should tuition fees be capped at private universities?", and so on. The tasks to be tackled in information-seeking AM are:

1. **Prepare the Corpus for Argument Component Retrieval:** We saw that one popular source for finding arguments and argument components (ACs) is Wikipedia, but much other material from the web has also been used. The corpus needs to be preprocessed, possibly indexed for topic areas and the like.
2. **Retrieve Claim Candidates from Corpus (Sect. 4.2.1):** Typically, the first step is to retrieve *claims* that pertain to the given topic, that is, sentences that (i) address the topic and (ii) have the features of argumentative claims.
3. **Detect the Support and Stance of Claims (Sects. 5.2.1 and 6.1):** For each claim, it is usually important to determine whether its stance is *pro* or *contra* with respect to the topic as posed, or whether it can be used for *support* or *attack*.
4. **Retrieve Evidence Candidates from Corpus (Sect. 4.2.4):** For each candidate claim, compatible *evidence* needs to be looked for that either supports or attacks the claim (i.e., stance is in agreement or disagreement).
5. **Filter Argument Component Candidates:** If the set of claims produced in Step 2 is large, the ACs can be *ranked* for topic relevance, target stance, potential strength, and the like.

Information-seeking AM is typically a means to an end; this research line got started when the 'end' was defined by the IBM Debater team as an artificial agent that is able to conduct an argumentative exchange with a human 'opponent'. This requires the AC candidates to be arranged in rhetorically-effective ways, and/or to be selected such that a felicitous response to arguments introduced by the opponent can be given. Tasks that we will discuss below in Sects. 11.1.3 and 11.1.4 are relevant here.

11.1.2 Discourse-Based 'Core' Argument Mining

In the discourse-based approach, the challenge is not to find ACs 'in the wild' of a potentially very large document collection, but to give a precise account of the argumentation that is undertaken in a single text or dialogue. A small example of the discourse-based AM scenario was discussed at the beginning of the book; see Fig. 1.1 in Sect. 1.2.

Like in information-seeking AM, there are prototypical *settings* where discourse-based AM is embedded: analyzing student essays for grading or for giving feedback; mapping out the structure of a social media discussion; and similar. The individual tasks are:

1. **Select the Target Text:** Depending on the setting, the target text T is either already given, or needs to be identified by a classifier that judges the type of text.
2. **Separate Argumentative from Non-Argumentative Content (Sect. 4.1.1):** Unless T is short and/or simple (e.g., a tweet), the *argumentative discourse units* (ADUs, usually sentences or smaller units) need to be identified in the text.
3. **Label Argument Components with their Types (Sect. 4.2):** Depending on the setting, maybe the type *claim* is the only unit type of interest; or a larger set of fine-grained AC types (such as different kinds of *evidence*) is to be determined. Given such a target inventory, assign a type to each AC, thus yielding a set of *typed argument components* for the text.
4. **Assign Relations to Argument Component Pairs (Sects. 5.1 and 5.2):** If the setting suggests there is only one claim, all premises have *pro* stance, and there is no recursive constellation, then all ACs are implicitly linked to the single claim; no extra work is needed. Otherwise, relations need to be explicitly assigned to AC pairs. For the inventory, the minimum is *support*, but fine-grained distinctions, such as that between *rebut* and *undercut* attacks are also possible.
5. **Fix the Formal Type of Overall Structure (Sect. 5.3):** Depending on the setting, the target of 'core' AM can be a tree (i.e., no AC is in a directed relation to more than one other AC) or a general graph, or merely a set of individual *(claim, premise)* pairs.
6. **Build the Overall Structure (Sect. 5.3):** Depending on the setting, there can be different kinds of hard or soft constraints on how the structure can be formed. A suitable formalism (e.g., a minimum-cost optimization or a parsing algorithm) is used to connect the ACs and the already-established argument relations (ARs) into a single 'coherent' structure, which may involve selecting a subset from the previously-established ARs.

These steps need not be done in exactly this order, and they may be combined in multiple ways (e.g., ADU segmentation and AC type assignment can be done jointly).

11.1.3 Perspectives, Quality, and Reasoning

Beyond the 'core' tasks described above, the subsequent steps are of potential relevance to information-seeking AM and to discourse-based AM alike. These tasks, which do not suggest a sequential order, can be:

- **Determine Fine-Grained Topics (Sect. 6.2.1):** In both information-seeking AM and discourse-based AM, identifying fine-grained topics can be relevant. For instance, an AC may *expand* a topic, or it may address a specific subtopic or *aspect* or *facet.*
- **Detect the Framing of Argument Components (Sect. 6.2.2):** 'Framing' is a contested term and can be operationalized in different ways. In practice, it often refers to the *perspective* from which an argument is addressed. For example, arguments on climate change mitigation can be given from economic, resource-oriented, global-fairness, or other perspectives.
- **Identify Biases and Underlying Values (Sect. 6.3):** A complete constellation of arguments on a given topic can exhibit *biases* such as *myside* (failure to address the opposing viewpoint) or *social* biases (use of value-laden or judgmental terms in referring to a situation or its participants). Similarly, one can determine the *human values* underlying a presented argument (using taxonomies from the social sciences).
- **Assess the Quality of Arguments (Chap. 7):** Broadly distinguishing *logic*, *rhetoric*, and *dialectic*, one can determine whether an argument is cogent, effective, and/or reasonable.
- **Identify Underlying Reasoning Patterns (Chap. 8):** Argumentation theory has proposed inventories of *argumentation schemes* that capture the stereotypical reasoning pattern between premise and claim. Examples include the 'argument from positive consequences' and the 'argument from example'.
- **Detect Misguided Reasoning (Sect. 8.2):** Reasoning is not always sound and not always acceptable. Inventories of common *informal fallacies* have been proposed (e.g., the 'ad hominem' argument, which attacks the opponent instead of their position, and is often but not always fallacious). This step aims at detecting their presence in argumentation.
- **Reconstruct Enthymemes (Sects. 8.3 and 9.1.2):** In interdependent steps, one can infer the scheme for each relation and make explicit the propositions that are only implicitly conveyed: the reconstruction of *enthymemes*. This task can for instance be solved by selecting a proposition from a given pool of candidates. But enthymemes can also be produced from scratch using text generation techniques.

11.1.4 Generation

Besides argument mining as a language *understanding* problem, the community is also interested in the *generation* of argumentative text. Generation can be either be from scratch or in combination with some of the steps from information-seeking AM or discourse-based AM discussed above. Often, automatic generation has particular benefits when *tailoring* text to a particular audience (and their values, beliefs, etc.). Prominent lines of research include:

- **Recombine Argumentative Text (Sect. 9.1.1):** Given a set of arguments, a text can be built by selecting and recombining the surface units, possibly with giving attention to rhetorics (such as the role of linear order). The units to be recombined can vary from individual words to full ACs.
- **Generate Arguments from Scratch (Sect. 9.1.2 and 9.1.3):** The traditional 'text generation pipeline' involves a sequence of decision-making steps that map some formal specification of 'content' to a natural language text: planning the rough structure of the text; planning the distribution of information to individual sentences; selecting suitable words; arranging them so the sentences are grammatically correct. Meanwhile, language models often take over many or all of these steps.
- **Rewrite Arguments (Sect. 9.2.1):** Going beyond mere recombination, arguments can be rewritten, to achieve a change in strength, in perspective, and the like.
- **Generate Counterarguments (Sect. 9.2.2):** Especially for an information-seeking AM scenario, an important task is to understand an argument produced by the opponent and to then generate an effective counterargument to it, for instance on the basis of retrieving a set of AC candidates.
- **Summarize Arguments (Sect. 9.3):** Summarization can be done by extraction (select certain units from a text) or by abstraction (actively reformulate certain units from the text). It can be applied to individual arguments or to complete exchanges (debates).

Contemporary techniques for generation tasks that go beyond recombining include controlling instruction-following large language models (LLMs) in various ways, for instance, by mimicking the above-mentioned text planning pipeline.

11.2 Outlook

So far, this book has primarily covered the past development of the argument mining field, from its early endeavors to the current state of the art. Here and there, we have also mentioned recent trends and anticipated what might happen. We now share our brief, speculative outlook on *future research* on argument mining. We touch particularly on the role of argument mining for *LLMs* and *AI technology*. We point out that our view is speculative and opinionated: it may not be shared by all researchers.

11.2.1 Argument Mining in Future Research

Argument mining has become an integral part of NLP research and continues to evoke much interest. As we have discussed above, the early years of argument mining research predominantly targeted the core tasks of identifying argument components (see Chap. 4), their relations (Chap. 5), and the perspectives they convey (Chap. 6). Meanwhile, quality assessment (Chap. 7) and argument generation (Chap. 9) are being studied at least equally intensively as the core mining tasks. Recent trends suggest that reasoning-related concepts (Chap. 8)—such as argumentation schemes (Ruiz-Dolz et al. 2024), fallacies (Mouchel et al. 2025), and enthymemes (Sviridova et al. 2026)—will eventually become the focus of attention.

In their survey, Lauscher et al. (2022) found that, over time, more and more NLP methods have started to use knowledge of different types (from linguistic and world knowledge to argumentation and task-specific knowledge) for computational argumentation. They propose a *unified knowledge representation space* that aggregates and consolidates all argumentation-relevant knowledge. With the rise in LLMs, such representations have become much more feasible. In particular, Wachsmuth et al. (2024) suggest to instruction fine-tune LLMs toward argumentation knowledge, enabling treatment of some of the most challenging aspects of argumentation, particularly treatment of the subjectivity inherent to arguments, their perception, and related questions of perspectivism (Romberg et al. 2025). The first argumentative LLMs have already been proposed in recent work (Stahl et al. 2025), achieving decent effectiveness even on unseen and challenging argumentation-related NLP tasks. However, an evaluation shows that argumentative reasoning is still beyond the capabilities of LLMs (Gemechu et al. 2025).

Beyond the tasks we covered in detail in this book, there are other topics that argument mining research has touched upon, which we expect to develop considerably in the future. Multimodal argumentation is among these topics. Some initial studies consider images in NLP research on argumentation (Kiesel et al. 2021b; Liu et al. 2022; Carnot et al. 2023), and selected work has analyzed voice-based argumentation (Mirkin et al. 2018; Lavee et al. 2019) and the use of voice interaction with arguments (Kiesel et al. 2020). Some studies also show the impact of debating beyond argumentation tasks, for example, to improve the reasoning capabilities of vision-language models (Adhikari and Lapata 2025). As in this work, LLMs and their multimodal derivatives bring new opportunities for multimodality, and will likely boost multimodal NLP research on argumentation in the near future.

Another topic is the long-envisioned full integration of argument mining with computational methods of reasoning and formal argumentation from the artificial intelligence (AI) community. We mentioned early work in the intersection of these areas in Chap. 7 on argument quality (Cabrio and Villata 2012), but more recent lines of research target the integration. As one example, in Chap. 8 we discussed the work of Hunter (2022) who envisions combining argument mining and logic-based argumentation to reconstruct enthymemes in order to support automatic explanations, fusions, and updates of argument graphs. Recently, Sanayei et al. (2025) also studied to what extent LLMs can assess formal reasoning in line with computational argumentation theory, finding promising results for shorter arguments but clear limitations for longer discourse. Similarly, Zhou et al. (2025b) explore different ways of quantiying uncertainty in the construction of bipolar argumentation frameworks with LLMs. Their results on claim verification suggest that prompting for uncertainty quantification seems more effective than may be expected. Again, these works indicate the potential of LLMs for future argument mining research.

11.2.2 Argument Mining and Large Language Models

We started the summary above by pointing out the 'power of corpus annotation' for steering the field by making data available for supervised classification. In recent years, however, pretrained language models have changed the landscape. A lot of research now aims at reducing or outright eliminating the need for supervised classification, instead using the capabilities of LLMs to tackle core tasks of argumentation. We have covered a number of such LLM-based approaches throughout this book.

For example, we presented how LLMs can create contextual information that helps to model causality within argument quality assessment (Liu et al. 2024b) as well as how LLMs can give a hypothetical context for an argument on which basis argument quality can be assessed (Deshpande et al. 2024). We also reviewed research on the ability of LLMs to identify the rationales underlying arguments and their impact on the perceived strength (Elaraby et al. 2024). Other studies systematically evaluate the ability of LLMs to deal with argumentation schemes (Bezou-Vrakatseli et al. 2025), explicitly teach LLMs to deal with fallacies (Lei and Huang 2024), and analyze the dangers of feeding fallacious reasoning into LLMs for their behavior (Payandeh et al. 2024). Researchers have combined classical discourse planning with LLMs' text generation capabilities to produce meaningful longer argumentative texts (He et al. 2024), aligned the rewriting behavior of LLMs for precise improvements of argument quality (Ziegenbein et al. 2024), and optimized LLMs aiming to avoid fallacies in their output (Mouchel et al. 2025).

In recent work, Stahl et al. (2025) studied to what extent the instruction fine-tuning process of LLMs can be specialized in order to enable them to deal with any argumentation task. Starting from seed instructions derived from existing argument mining, assessment, and generation tasks, their approach *ArgInstruct* augments them by tens of thousands of synthetic tasks. An LLM trained on these develops strong generalization skills across argumentation tasks, even unseen ones. Other researchers propose LLM-based evaluation frameworks to automatically guide debating systems toward generating high-quality arguments (Wang et al. 2025a), infer deeper logical interpretations from arguments with LLMs (Wang et al. 2025b), and use LLMs to reconstruct the discourse structure underlying opinionated articles (Wang et al. 2025c). More research that exploits, optimizes, and/or evaluates LLMs specifically for argumentation is likely in the future.

However, one central question sparking substantial interest lately in the realm of LLMs still needs to be connected more closely to argument mining research. The (hypotheticallyemerging) *reasoning* capabilities of LLMs (Guo et al. 2025) are assumed, studied, questioned, or otherwise dealt with in much recent research. Considering reasoning in the classical sense—that is, the process of abstracting from the instance level, carrying out inference on the type level, and reinstantiating the inferred knowledge—we conclude that LLMs, as of this writing, do not actually reason (Shojaee et al. 2025). LLMs mimic reasoning very well in many situations, though, and it is as yet unclear whether this mimicry may be brought to a state in which it is indistinguishable from 'real' reasoning. Needless to say, argument mining research can inform the evolution of LLMs toward argumentation well, as it actually deals with the fundamental principles of reasoning. It should thus play an important role in this process, and can contribute evaluation metrics (e.g., Gemechu et al. 2025). So far, this combination of research lines is still underexplored and deserves much more attention in the future.

11.2.3 Argument Mining and Artificial Intelligence Technology

Integrating argument mining into AI technology is now feasible and, in our view, future work in the field could benefit from considering the potential applicability and integration of argument mining research. Some integration opportunities were mentioned earlier in the book when we discussed quality assessment (Chap. 7), reasoning (Chap. 8), and applications (Chap. 10). We now highlight three particularly promising directions for argument mining and AI technology: The full integration of argument mining with computational argumentation, the leveraging of dialectical argumentation theory-inspired argument mining for conversational AI, and cross-field collaborations on human-computer AI.

The first direction, the full integration of argument mining with methods of reasoning and formal argumentation from the AI community, was mentioned in the opening to this section. Numerous computational argumentation reasoning tools (Sect. 10.1.3) calculate acceptability of arguments in a formal framework. Argument mining can be the input to these tools, creating a full pipeline integrating NLP with symbolic AI. Steps in this direction were envisioned in earlier work such as Wyner et al. (2016) and Cabrio and Villata (2017). The formal argumentation community has recently shown increased interest in language technologies and pipelining from argument mining; for instance, identifying guardrails for bringing semantic distance into logical frameworks (Hunter 2022) and managing challenges in instantiation within formal argument frameworks (Ben-Naim et al. 2024).

Second, by drawing on research on dialogue from the argumentation AI community, the field of argument mining can inspire improvements in conversational technology. In a position paper, Musi et al. (2025) argue that conversational technology should present diverse viewpoints to foster deliberation and improve users' critical thinking. They prototyped this approach in several LLM systems, adding four conversation 'parrot' partners—Socratic, Cynical, Eclectic, and Aristotelian Parrots—who challenge users' views. Whereas Musi et al. draw on pragma-dialectics theories (van Eemeren and Grootendorst 2004) for promoting ideal critical discussions, multiple theories from AI research on argumentation can be relevant. Most obvious are dialogue games, which AI research has long used to grapple with language from both formal and informal argumentation perspectives. Some of the work we discussed in Sect. 8.3.3, while still far from core NLP approaches, leverages dialogue games. For instance, dialogue game research in informal argumentation enumerated various types of dialogue (inquiry, eristic, etc.) (Walton and Krabbe 1995), beyond the persuasion dialogues which have been emphasized in many conversational AI approaches. Conversational systems could benefit from increased attention to bridging argument mining drawing on dialectical argumentation theory.

Third, argument mining can power human-facing AI systems such as search engines, writing assistants, and the like, as we discussed in Chap. 10. Search engines have recieved dedicated attention in the past few years through collaboration between argument mining and information retrieval in the Touché CLEF series of shared tasks,[1] an area that could be further developed into more widely deployed systems. Additionally, collaboration between human-computer interaction and NLP researchers would, in our view, benefit these research areas as well as society. One example is the role that argument mining may take within explainable AI technology, as is already being studied in bigger projects.[2] Reasoning and argument have obvious application in AI for social good and AI in computational social science. Perspective taking is one example. Consider PerspectroScope, showcased in Sect. 10.3.1. Implemented by combining argument mining and AI technology, PerspectroScope combines argument mining (Chen et al. 2019b) and a search interface (Chen et al. 2019a) to display diverse perspectives on a topic.

11.3 Ethical Implications

The given summary and outlook underline the ongoing evolution of argument mining research. We thus conclude the book with a look at ethical implications in terms of the promises and risks that come with argument mining. On this basis, we point to important resources for action before we finally close the discussion.

11.3.1 Promises and Risks

Widescale deployment of computational argumentation technologies built on argument mining brings great opportunity. The notion of *argument checking*—generalizing fact

---

[1] Touché CLEF shared task series, https://touche.webis.de (accessed January 5, 2025).

[2] See, for example, ANTIDOTE, https://www.chistera.eu/projects/antidote, and TRR 318 "Constructing Explainability", https://trr318.upb.de (both accessed January 18, 2026).

checking—has great potential for improving human capacity to reason (Brave et al. 2022; Plug and Wagemans 2020). Argument summarization can enable rapid e-consultation for public involvement in government.[3] Argument search has the potential to promote perspective taking and overcome individuals' filter bubbles, so that society can discuss a shared reality (Wachsmuth et al. 2017d).

But risks also increase as argument mining becomes more effective. Technologies built on argument mining can threaten individuals' autonomy. Increased power of personalization of arguments is a particular risk, especially considering adversarial commercial incentives for an 'attention economy' and individual-level persuasion. Already, without argumentation, general LLMs are very persuasive according to findings from research on argumentation (Hinton and Wagemans 2023; Altay et al. 2022), psychology (Costello et al. 2024; Bai et al. 2025), and communication (Dehnert and Mongeau 2022; Huang and Wang 2023). Human-computer interaction research has found that people are even more likely to change their perspective when deception is involved (Danry et al. 2025) . So far, there is only limited work tackling deception in the context of argumentation (Contro et al. 2025), making this an area urgent for prioritization: Overcoming deceptive reasoning is a keystone to ethical reasoning (Stevens 2025), while language models generally suffer from the racial and socioeconomic biases common to other data-driven technology (see e.g., Benjamin 2019; D'Ignazio and Klein 2020; West et al. 2019). Writing support from general-purpose LLMs also risks reducing learning (Kosmyna et al. 2025) whereas incorporating argument maps can support learning (Twardy 2004).

We believe that ethics should be an explicit concern of the argument mining community: Considering not only the immediate research but also its downstream application is important. This includes unintended uses and weaponization. Sociocultural issues must be considered, such as further excluding or disadvantaging historically disadvantaged groups—a topic that has received increased attention in NLP lately, but has only been sporadically dealt with in argument mining research (e.g., Spliethöver and Wachsmuth 2020; Holtermann et al. 2022). Environmental impacts, particularly the energy consumption of large models, also need attention.

Considering ethics requires more than a singular, once-and-done momentary effort: Ethics must be woven integrally into education, professional development, and research. Case studies can be an effective pedagogical tool—discussing disasters and near-miss disasters from the NLP community and its downstream applications.[4] Given the rapid

---

[3] Lugano Digital Day September 3, 2019, Speech by Crowd, summarized 2400 public comments on autonomous vehicles into pro and con narratives https://www.ictjournal.ch/news/2019-11-25/a-lugano-ibm-teste-lia-pour-synthetiser-le-debat-public, video at https://www.youtube.com/watch?v=h7EyaLY34dU (both accessed January 5, 2026).

[4] Two recent examples: Maia Szalavitz. Love is a drug. A.I. chatbots are exploiting that. June 3, 2025, *The New York Times*. https://www.nytimes.com/2025/06/03/opinion/chatbots-ai-addiction-love.html and Zeynep Tufekci, Musk's chatbot started spouting Nazi propaganda. That's not the scariest part.

evolution of the field and the fast deployment of technology from the lab to the real world, professional development is an increasing need.

This holds particularly for NLP research on argumentation, given the immediate persuasive effect arguments may have on people (see Sect. 7.1.1) and the power coming from LLMs being able to generate effective and potentially manipulative arguments fully automatically (see Chap. 9).

11.3.2 Resources for Action

Professional conferences and academic research conferences can foreground ethics in NLP and argumentation at their events. Specifically, research conferences can draw on exemplars and resources from a number of recently-established ACL groups and events:

1. Ethics tutorials[5] such as the 2023 European ACL meeting tutorial "Understanding Ethics in NLP Authoring and Reviewing" (Benotti et al. 2023)[6] and the 2025 ACL meeting tutorial "Navigating Ethical Challenges in NLP: Hands-on strategies for students and researchers" (Benotti et al. 2025) provide content designed and licensed for reuse.
2. The ACL Ethics Committee[7] shepards additional resources such as the ACL ethics reading list.[8]
3. The ACL Rolling Review Responsible NLP Research checklist[9] provides questions for authors and peer reviewers to consider around "responsible research, [...] research ethics, societal impact and reproducibility".

Cross-pollination of ethics processes can also come from cognate conference communities, including but not limited to the following:

1. The code of ethics from the Association for Computing Machinery (ACM)[10] was incorporated into the ACL code of ethics.[11]

July 11, 2025, *The New York Times*. https://www.nytimes.com/2025/07/11/opinion/ai-grok-x-llm.html (both accessed January 5, 2026).

[5] https://ethics.aclweb.org/tutorials/ (accessed January 5, 2026).

[6] See associated online resources https://github.com/acl-org/ethics-tutorial (accessed January 5, 2026).

[7] https://ethics.aclweb.org/committee/ (accessed January 5, 2026).

[8] https://ethics.aclweb.org/resources/ethics-reading-list/ (accessed January 5, 2026).

[9] https://aclrollingreview.org/responsibleNLPresearch/ (accessed January 5, 2026).

[10] https://www.acm.org/code-of-ethics (accessed January 5, 2026).

[11] https://www.aclweb.org/portal/content/acl-code-ethics (accessed January 5, 2026).

2. The machine learning community around Neural Information Processing Systems (NeurIPS) shares widely influential ethics guidelines and the process of developing their paper checklist.[12]
3. The International AAAI Conference on Web & Social Media (ICWSM) paper checklist[13] modifies the NeurIPS checklist from a computational social science perspective.
4. Ethics and conduct guidelines from the ACM Special Interest Group on Computer-Human Interaction (SIGCHI) checklist[14] are useful for work related to human factors.
5. Several AI-related conferences focus on ethics, including the ACM Conference on Fairness, Accountability, and Transparency (FAccT) and the AAAI/ACM Conference on AI, Ethics, and Society (AIES).

In the pursuit of ethics, argument mining could benefit from collaboration with philosophy, the broader argumentation theory community, and emerging work on AI ethics and the social impacts of AI.

1. The *Ethics of Argumentation* (Stevens 2025) foregrounds the reciprocal impact that arguers have on each other. Its relational perspective of ethical arguing could be particularly valuable for future treatment of non-human agents, including LLMs as arguers.
2. The Ethics of Argumentation Speaker Series[15] has been meeting monthly under the aegis of The Argumentation Network of the Americas since 2021. Their YouTube channel hosts over 50 recorded lectures.
3. Applying moral philosophy, computational ethics (Awad et al. 2022) envisions formalizing ethics algorithmically.
4. The Center for Humans & Machines at the Max Planck Institute for Human Development is dedicated to studying the social impact of AI and digital technology. Its director, Iyad Rahwan, led early efforts in argumentation and AI; his recent review (Bonnefon et al. 2024) examined roles for machines as moral agents, moral patients, and moral proxies.
5. Virtue argumentation (Aberdein and Cohen 2024; Aberdein 2025) applies the study of character traits and dispositions to think about good arguers (not just good arguments). Virtue-based thinking can also be applied to systems. For instance, in applying virtue ethics to argument search contexts, philosopher and information scientist Tim

[12] Ethics guidelines: https://neurips.cc/public/EthicsGuidelines (accessed January 5, 2026); paper checklist process: https://neuripsconf.medium.com/introducing-the-neurips-2021-paper-checklist-3220d6df500b (accessed January 5, 2026).

[13] https://www.overleaf.com/project/66aced0e9d61256497102d9e (accessed January 5, 2026).

[14] https://sigchi.org/about/ethics-and-conduct/ (accessed January 5, 2026).

[15] Series: https://www.argnet.org/ethics-of-arg.html. YouTube video archive: https://www.youtube.com/@ethicsofargumentationspeak1772/videos (accessed January 10, 2026).

Gorichanaz concluded that online search systems should "help [...] us establish a shared reality and promoting dialog in knowledge-conducive ways" (Gorichanaz 2024).

11.3.3 Final Thoughts

Arguers can do each other "a lot of good—or a lot of harm" because in arguing we influence each others' beliefs, attitudes, emotions, and decisions (Stevens 2025, page 1). Advancing argument mining research and technologies reponsibly toward social good will require interdisciplinary effort. We believe that the interdisciplinary knowledge of the argument mining community (in our lived experience and our publishing record) should be used to also proactively foster collaboration with the broader AI ethics community, with the broader argumentation theory community, and between these groups. In the coming years, drawing on argumentation's deep philosophical roots could help develop principles for ethical argument mining. In times when pervasive AI technologies are said to 'reason', responsible NLP research on argumentation is more important than ever before.

Selected Corpora

A

In this appendix, we present a selection of corpora that are relevant for a number of argument mining tasks discussed throughout the book. For each corpus entry, we first highlight the types and counts of documents within the corpus, and then we separately detail annotation tasks carried on the corpus. For some corpora, different names are used in the literature; we also list such alternatives where applicable.

A.1 Corpora for Argument Representation

Here, we present a select number of corpora that are useful for classic argument mining tasks, aimed at extracting a full representation of argument structure from a text.

A.1.1 Argument-Annotated Essays (Version 1)

Argument-annotated essays version 1 (AAE1) (Stab and Gurevych 2014a), consists of 90 essays taken from the *essayforum* website.
Alternative names: Persuasive Essay Corpus (PEC)
Genre: Online discussions
Document type: Essays
Document count: 90

Argument Component Segmentation and Classification
In Stab and Gurevych (2014a) essays are segmented into their argumentative components. Annotators first identified the major claim of the essay, and then the claims and premises in each paragraph. Because there are no predefined markables in the data, annotators had to

M. Stede et al., *Argument Mining*, Synthesis Lectures on Human Language Technologies, https://doi.org/10.1007/978-3-032-32291-3

determine the boundaries of argument components themselves, performing a segmentation of the argumentative text. A modification of Krippendorff's α (α_U) that allows for disagreement in span boundaries was used to capture annotation performance in both the segmentation of argumentative units and their classification.
Annotators: 3 non-expert annotators
Agreement type: Krippendorff's α_U
Annotator agreement: "Major Claim": 0.7726, "Claim": 0.6033, "Premise": 0.7594
Link: https://tudatalib.ulb.tu-darmstadt.de/items/a52f7fef-4388-420c-91f0-ac03dac26bbb

Argument Component Relation Annotation
In Stab and Gurevych (2014a), classified argument components (premises, claims, and major claims) are linked by either support or attack relations. Annotators first linked claims and premises within each paragraph, before linking claims to major claims with either a support or attack relation.
Annotators: 3 non-expert annotators
Agreement type: Krippendorff's α
Annotator agreement: "Support": 0.8120, "Attack": 0.8066
Link: https://tudatalib.ulb.tu-darmstadt.de/items/a52f7fef-4388-420c-91f0-ac03dac26bbb

Argumentum Model of Topics
In Musi et al. (2016), a subset of 30 essays from AAE1 were annotated using an annotation scheme based on the Argumentum Model of Topics for a pilot study. Several student annotators were given a set of identification questions for a group of argument schemes from the Argumentum Model of Topics, and asked to identify which question most closely matches argumentative components linked by a support relation (annotators could select no argument).
Annotators: 9 graduate students with no specific background in linguistics or argumentation
Agreement type: Fleiss' κ
Annotator agreement: 0.1
Link: Unavailable

A.1.2 Argument-Annotated Essays (Version 2)

Argument-annotated essays version 2 (AAE2) (Stab and Gurevych 2017b), consists of 402 essays taken from the *essayforum* website.
Alternative names: Persuasive Essay Corpus (PEC)
Genre: Online discussions
Document type: Essays
Document count: 402

Coarse-Grained Argument Component Classification
In Stab and Gurevych (2017b), 402 persuasive essays were segmented into their argumentative components by annotators, which were then classified as either major claim, claim, or premise. Annotation was performed by three non-native speakers, one of which was an expert, and annotation was performed using the brat rapid annotation tool. Annotator agreement was reported for a random subset of 80 essays that all three annotators labelled, a modification of Krippendorff's α (α_U) that allows for disagreement in span boundaries was used to capture annotation performance in both the segmentation of argumentative units and their classification.
Annotators: 3, 1 of which was an expert
Agreement type: Krippendorff's α_U
Annotator agreement: "Major Claim": 0.810, "Claim": 0.584, "Premise": 0.824
Link: https://tudatalib.ulb.tu-darmstadt.de/items/9177c48c-8bd5-4881-9cb4-0632b5941464

Argument Component Relation Classification
In Stab and Gurevych (2017b), a set of 4922 previously annotated argumentative units from 402 persuasive essays were annotated with their argumentative relations. Pairs were obtained by considering all pairs of argumentative components that occur within a paragraph as markable. All pairs were annotated by 3 annotators, who could either label relations as support or attack.
Annotators: 3, 1 of which was an expert
Agreement type: Fleiss' κ
Annotator agreement: "Support": 0.708, "Attack": 0.737
Link: https://tudatalib.ulb.tu-darmstadt.de/items/9177c48c-8bd5-4881-9cb4-0632b5941464

Myside Bias
In Stab and Gurevych (2016), 402 persuasive essays are annotated as either positive or negative, where positive indicates the say includes an opposing an argument, and negative if it only includes arguments supporting the author's standpoint. The existing AAE2 corpus was used to derive initial document-level annotations, previously annotated argument structures include arguments annotated with support or attack relationships within essays and so could be re-used. To verify these automatically derived annotations, a subset of 80 essays were annotated by 3 independent annotators and agreement was reported which showed the derived annotations were reliable.
Annotators: 3
Agreement type: Krippendorff's α
Annotator agreement: 0.787
Link: https://tudatalib.ulb.tu-darmstadt.de/items/ecb6f8cf-0bf3-4843-b299-8c1d9819cee9

Sufficiency

In Stab and Gurevych (2017a), each paragraph from 402 persuasive essays was considered as an argument, resulting in 1029 arguments ready for annotation. Then, 3 non-native speakers with excellent English proficiency independently annotated all arguments as either sufficient (premises provide enough evidence to accept or reject the claim) or insufficient. An evaluation set of 433 arguments was annotated by all three annotators to compute agreement.

Annotators: 3 non-native speakers with excellent English proficiency

Agreement type: Fleiss' κ

Annotator agreement: 0.7672

Link: https://tudatalib.ulb.tu-darmstadt.de/items/5d6a075e-697d-4f82-977f-b2cb16aa8542

Fine-Grained Claim-Type Classification

In Schaefer et al. (2023), 402 essays were annotated with a fine-grained classification of their claims types. Claims in the essay had previously been extracted in Stab and Gurevych (2017b). Annotation was performed by 3 experts (including 1 author), who were able to label claims as one of 3 types: policy, value, or fact. Annotation proceeded in stages, with agreement computed at each stage to improve guidelines, final annotator agreement was computed over a set of 40 essays that all annotators labelled.

Annotators: 3 experts

Agreement type: Krippendorff's α

Annotator agreement: "Policy": 0.78, "Value": 0.52, "Fact": 0.34, "Overall": 0.52

Link: https://github.com/discourse-lab/arg-essays-semantic-types

Fine-Grained Premise-Type Classification

In Schaefer et al. (2023), 402 essays were annotated with a fine-grained classification of their premise types. Premises in the essay had previously been extracted in Stab and Gurevych (2017b). Annotation was performed by 3 experts (including 1 author), who were able to label premises as one of 6 types: testimony, statistics, hypothetical-instance, real-example, common-ground, or other. Annotation proceeded in stages, with agreement computed at each stage to improve guidelines, final annotator agreement was computed over a set of 40 essays that all annotators labelled. The number of occurrences of the "testimony" and "other" class was too small to compute inter-annotator agreement.

Annotators: 3 experts

Agreement type: Krippendorff's α

Annotator agreement: "Statistics": 0.16, "Hypothetical-Instance": 0.70, "Real-Example": 0.58, "Common-Ground": 0.42, "Overall": 0.53

Link: https://github.com/discourse-lab/arg-essays-semantic-types

Cogency and Reasonableness
In Marro et al. (2022), the arguments contained in 402 persuasive essays were annotated with scores for their cogency and reasonableness. An argument is cogent if it has individually acceptable premises that are relevant and sufficient to draw the arguments conclusions. An argument is reasonable if it contributes to the resolution of an issue in a way that is acceptable to the target audience. The previously annotated argument components and relations in the AEE2 corpus were used to aid in annotation. Cogency was scored on a 3-point scale (originally a 5-point scale which was reduced after experimentation) for the premises of a given argument. Reasonableness was computed on a 5-point scale for a whole argumentation graph, taking into consideration the reasonableness of counterarguments and rebuttals. Annotation was carried out by 3 English speakers who were experts in argument mining. Agreement was calculated over a subset of 33 essays.
Annotators: 3 English speakers who were experts in argument mining
Agreement type: Fleiss' κ
Annotator agreement: "Cogency": 0.86, "Reasonableness Counterargument": 0.78, "Reasonableness Rebuttal": 0.84
Link: https://doi.org/10.18653/v1/2022.findings-emnlp.306

Rhetorical Strategy
In Marro et al. (2022), 402 essays were annotated at the argument level with their rhetorical strategy: either *ethos*, *logos*, or *pathos*. Annotation was carried out by 3 English speakers who were experts in argument mining. Agreement was calculated over a subset of 33 essays.
Annotators: 3 English speakers who were experts in argument mining
Agreement type: Fleiss' κ
Annotator agreement: 0.85
Link: https://doi.org/10.18653/v1/2022.findings-emnlp.306

A.1.3 Argumentative Microtexts Corpus (Part 1)

A dataset of 112 short texts in German (with English translation), consisting of 22 texts written by the author as a proof of concept, and a further 90 texts created during a controlled text generation experiment (Peldszus and Stede 2016b). Versions of this corpus in various other languages are available, as well as additional annotation layers (discourse structure, enthymemes).
Alternative names: AMT, MT corpus
Genre: Debate
Document type: Microtexts
Document count: 112

Argumentation Structures
In Peldszus and Stede (2016b), 112 short texts (written in German) were annotated by their argumentation structure based on Freeman's theory of the macro-structure of argumentation. The annotation scheme argumentative roles, argumentative functions, and the identification of central claims, which together form a fully linked argumentative structure. Annotation was carried out on the original German version of the texts (and later projected to the English version) by 3 annotators, and agreement was computed over a subset of 8 texts.
Annotators: 3
Agreement type: Fleiss' κ
Annotator agreement: 0.83
Link: https://angcl.ling.uni-potsdam.de/resources/argmicro.html

Argumentum Model of Topics
In Musi et al. (2018), 112 short texts were annotated with their argument schemes based on the Argumentum Model of Topics. Annotation involved two tasks, first annotators had to, given a support or rebut relation that already existed in the original Microtexts corpus, identify the argument scheme among 8 possible schemes (or none if no reasoning was present). Second, annotators had to identify the associated inference rule of any identified argument scheme, these inference rules have forms such as "if the effects the case, the cause is probably the case" or "if the cause is the case, the effect is the case". Annotation was performed by 6 annotators (all students with relevant backgrounds), and agreement was computed over two sets of 20 microtexts that had each been annotated by 3 annotators.
Annotators: 6 annotators, including 4 students with a background in linguistics and argumentation, and 2 PhD students with a background in natural language processing
Agreement type: Fleiss' κ
Annotator agreement: 0.296
Link: https://angcl.ling.uni-potsdam.de/resources/argmicro.html

A.1.4 Argumentative Microtexts Corpus (Part 2)

Second part of the microtexts corpus, which contains additional arguments that were written by crowd-sourced workers, who had to produce a short text that argued for or against a general debate topic (Skeppstedt et al. 2018). Every worker was given one of 26 prompts and wrote no more than one text for the experiment. Low quality texts were filtered out, and grammatical errors and misspellings fixed.
Alternative names: AMT, MT corpus
Genre: Debate
Document type: Microtexts
Document count: 171

Argumentation Structures

In Skeppstedt et al. (2018), 171 short texts were annotated with full argumentative structure by 2 annotators. Annotator agreement was not computed, as annotators followed a similar annotation scheme to the first version of the argumentative microtexts corpus (Peldszus and Stede 2016b). Their annotation resulted in the identification of 932 argumentative units, connected by 467 convergent support relations, 23 example support relations, 137 rebutting attack relations, 77 undercutting attack relations, 57 linked support or attack relations, and 29 restatement relations. Notably, restatement relations did not occur in the first version of the microtexts corpus.

Annotators: 2 annotators, one who was a co-author of the work
Agreement type: Not reported
Annotator agreement: Not reported
Link: https://angcl.ling.uni-potsdam.de/resources/argmicro.html

A.1.5 Cornell eRulemaking

A dataset of 731 comments on the Consumer Debt Collection Practices rule (Park and Cardie 2018).

Alternative names: CDCP corpus
Genre: Online Discussions
Document type: Posts/comments
Document count: 731

Elementary Unit Classification

In Park and Cardie (2018), a dataset of 731 comments were annotated at the sentence/clause level with their argument components, resulting in 4931 argument components in the final labelling. Argument components were one of 4 "Elementary Units": fact, testimony, value, policy, or reference. Annotation was performed by 2 annotators, while a 3rd annotator was used to resolve disagreements and produce the final gold label. Annotator agreement was reported between the 2 primary annotators.

Annotators: 2
Agreement type: Krippendorff's α
Annotator agreement: 64.8%
Link: https://huggingface.co/datasets/DFKI-SLT/cdcp

Support Relation Classification

In Park and Cardie (2018), a dataset of 731 comments that were previously annotated with their argument components, were annotated again with the relation between their argument components, resulting in 1221 relations in the final labelling. Argument relations were one of 2 support relations: reason or evidence. Annotation was performed by 2 annotators,

while a 3rd annotator was used to resolve disagreements and produce the final gold label. Annotator agreement was reported between the 2 primary annotators.
Annotators: 2
Agreement type: Krippendorff's α
Annotator agreement: 44.1%
Link: https://huggingface.co/datasets/DFKI-SLT/cdcp

A.1.6 Integrated Argument Mining (IAM) Corpus

A dataset of 69,666 sentences from 1010 articles, primarily sourced from English Wikipedia, covering 123 topics (Cheng et al. 2022).
Genre: Debate
Document type: Wikipedia articles
Document count: 1010

Claim and Evidence Identification
In Cheng et al. (2022), 69,666 sentences from 1010 Wikipedia articles were annotated with a scheme to support a variety of argument mining tasks. The annotation process was two-staged: first, annotators identified claims and their stances (+1 for supporting, -1 for contesting the topic), and second, annotators linked claims to evidence through claim-evidence pairs (CEPs). Evidence was searched within 10 to 15 sentences preceding and after the claim.
Annotators: Each sentence was labelled by 2 paid professional data annotators. A third professional annotator was also used in a confirmation phase to resolve disagreement.
Agreement type: Cohen's κ
Annotator agreement: 0.44
Link: https://github.com/LiyingCheng95/IAM

A.1.7 IBM Debater: Claims and Evidence Dataset (Version 1)

A dataset of 586 Wikipedia articles on controversial topics (Aharoni et al. 2014).
Genre: Debate
Document type: Wikipedia articles
Document count: 586

Claim and Evidence Identification
In Aharoni et al. (2014), 586 Wikipedia articles were annotated to derive a set of 2683 argument elements made up of context-dependent claims and context-dependent evidence. The annotation process was meticulous, and involved 20 well-trained annotators who followed several steps. First, 5 annotators in a search team were given a topic and

independently searched for related articles. Second, 5 annotators independently detected candidate context-dependent claims from the articles. Third, in a "Claim confirmation" stage, 5 annotators examined these candidates and rejected/accepted them (agreement was reported for this stage). In a fourth stage, 5 annotators detected candidate context-dependent evidence related to accepted context-dependent claims. In a fifth stage, "Evidence confirmation" was performed in the same manner as "Claim confirmation", with 5 annotators accepting/rejecting candidate context-dependent evidence.
Annotators: 20 well-trained annotators
Agreement type: Cohen's κ
Annotator agreement: "Claim confirmation": 0.39, "Evidence confirmation": 0.4
Link: https://research.ibm.com/haifa/dept/vst/debating_data.shtml

A.1.8 IBM Debater: Claims and Evidence Dataset (Version 2)

A dataset of 547 Wikipedia articles associated with 58 different topics (Rinott et al. 2015).
Genre: Debate
Document type: Wikipedia articles
Document count: 547

Evidence Identification
In Rinott et al. (2015) (following a similar process to Aharoni et al. (2014)), 547 Wikipedia articles were annotated to derive a set of context-dependent evidence. In the first stage, 5 annotators read the article and marked all context-dependent evidence candidates, in a second stage, 5 annotators confirmed or rejected each candidate and performed a fine-grained classification of the type of evidence (study, expert or anecdotal). Context-dependent evidence candidates and their type were determined by majority vote.
Annotators: 15 annotators involved across all stages
Agreement type: Not reported
Annotator agreement: Not reported
Link: https://research.ibm.com/haifa/dept/vst/debating_data.shtml

A.1.9 NLAS-Multi Corpus

A corpus of 3810 textbook-like natural arguments in English and Spanish (Ruiz-Dolz et al. 2024). The arguments instantiate one of 20 different argumentation schemes, on 50 different topics, and can have a pro/con stance. Arguments were generated using a combination of GPT-3.5-turbo and GPT-4 applying prompting techniques.
Genre: Generated argumentation
Document type: Argument schemes
Document count: 3810

Argument Scheme Validation

In Ruiz-Dolz et al. (2024), 5 annotators validated 3810 generated argument schemes against their reported type, topic, and stance. Validation proceeded in stages, at the final stage (based on feedback from previous stages) 1917/2000 arguments generated were valid. Annotator agreement was also computed for a 10% subset of the total number of samples for both the English and Spanish examples. 4 of the 5 annotators annotated the English generated samples, while 2 of the 5 annotators annotated Spanish generated samples.

Annotators: 5 professional linguists trained in argumentation theory

Agreement type: Cohen's κ

Annotator agreement: "English": 0.65, "Spanish": 0.22

Link: https://doi.org/10.5281/zenodo.8364002

A.1.10 Dr. Inventor

A dataset of 40 publications from computer graphics. The dataset was introduced by Fisas et al. (2015, 2016) with several layers of annotation for discourse relations and citation contexts.

Genre: Scientific publications

Document type: Scientific publications

Document count: 40

Toulmin-Style Component Classification

In Lauscher et al. (2018b), scientific publications were annotated with their argumentative components by 4 annotators (1 expert and 3 non-expert). Component types were based on the Toulmin model and a preliminary study, resulting in three argumentative components: own claim, background claim, and data. Annotator agreement was computed using F1, and was reported in a bar chart that gives approximate values. Annotator agreement was computed for 5 iterations of the task, and for both a weak and strict interpretation of the spans of the argument components.

Annotators: 1 expert and 3 non-expert annotators

Agreement type: F1

Annotator agreement: "Approximate 5th iteration weak": 75% "Approximate 5th iteration strict": 60%

Link: http://data.dws.informatik.uni-mannheim.de/sci-arg/compiled_corpus.zip

Dung-Style Relation Classification

In Lauscher et al. (2018b), previously annotated argument components from 40 scientific publications were annotated with their relation to each other by 4 annotators (1 expert and 3 non-expert). Relations were based on those described in Dung (1995) and included the three relations of supports, contradicts, and semantically the same (argument coreference).

Annotator agreement was computed using F1, and was reported in a bar chart that gives approximate values. Annotator agreement was computed for 5 iterations of the task, and for both a weak and strict interpretation of the spans of the argument components.
Annotators: 1 expert and 3 non-expert annotators
Agreement type: F1
Annotator agreement: "Approximate 5th iteration weak": 45%, "Approximate 5th iteration strict": 35%
Link: http://data.dws.informatik.uni-mannheim.de/sci-arg/compiled_corpus.zip

A.1.11 Swedish News Editorials Corpus

Corpus of 30 Swedish newspaper editorials from 6 newspapers, published between May-September 1973 (Lindahl et al. 2019).
Genre: News
Document type: News editorials
Document count: 30

Component Segmentation and Identification
In Lindahl et al. (2019), arguments were segmented into argument components, and their types (premises/conclusion) identified. These argument components were linked into full structures, for a downstream argument scheme annotation task. Annotation was performed using Araucaria. No predefined markers were used in the dataset to distinguish arguments, so annotators determined the boundaries of arguments themselves, because of this fuzziness agreement is measured using an equation based on the Sørensen-Dice coefficient which accounts for overlap in argument segments. Various combinations of agreement are reported in the paper, here we report the overall agreement for conclusions, for arguments where at least one premise matched (regardless of conclusion), and arguments were all premises matched (regardless of conclusion).
Annotators: 2 master's students with solid training in linguistic analysis
Agreement type: Modified Sørensen-Dice coefficient, with a hyperparameter that is more permissive of span overlap
Annotator agreement: "Matching conclusions": 0.34, "At least one matching premise": 0.12, "All premises match": 0.03
Link: Unavailable

Argument Schemes
In Lindahl et al. (2019), arguments were identified and then classified according to one of the 30 most common Walton-style argument schemes. Annotation was performed using Araucaria. Agreement over scheme is reported for arguments which match in both conclusion and premises for a previous annotation task.
Annotators: 2 master's students with solid training in linguistic analysis

Agreement type: Modified Sørensen-Dice coefficient, with a hyperparameter that is more permissive of span overlap
Annotator agreement: "Within matching conclusion": 0.22, "Within all arguments": 0.02
Link: Unavailable

A.1.12 Language of Opposition Corpus

A dataset argumentative exchanges in online technical discussions. Collected from the Technorati platform between 2008 and 2010, it comprises four discussion threads, each consisting of one original blog post and its first 100 user comments (Ghosh et al. 2014). The corpus targets technical blog discussions hosted on Technorati, a platform aggregating blog content. The four discussion threads address four topics: (1) Android vs. iPhone: Debates comparing the two smartphone platforms; (2) iPad Usefulness: Discussions on the practical value of the iPad; (3) Twitter as a Microblogging Platform: Arguments about Twitter's role and impact; (4) Corporate Layoffs/Outsourcing: Opinions on corporate employment practices.
Genre: Online Discussions
Document type: Posts/comments
Document count: 404

Callouts and Targets
In Ghosh et al. (2014), 404 posts/comments are annotated according to a scheme based on Pragmatic Argumentation Theory (PAT), which frames arguments as interactions between Callouts and Targets. A Callout is a subsequent action that expresses an explicit stance or rationale toward a Target, defined as a prior action in the discussion. Five graduate students with strong humanities backgrounds were trained as annotators to perform an annotation study that followed a three-step process: (1) segmenting the text into Argumentative Discourse Units (ADUs), (2) classifying each segment as a Callout or Target, and (3) linking each Callout to its most recent Target. Agreement is reported separately for each topic in the corpus. The agreement reported below is agreement across the whole annotation task (segmentation and type classification).
Annotators: 5 graduate students with strong humanities backgrounds
Agreement type: Krippendorff's α
Annotator agreement: "Android": 0.64, "iPad": 0.73, "Layoffs": 0.87, "Twitter": 0.82
Link: https://salts.rutgers.edu/identifying-the-language-of-opposition-in-online-interactions/

Stance/Relation Classification
In Ghosh et al. (2014), 404 posts/comments are annotated according to a scheme based on Pragmatic Argumentation Theory (PAT), which frames arguments as interactions between Callouts and Targets. A Callout is a subsequent action that expresses an explicit stance or

rationale toward a Target, defined as a prior action in the discussion. Five graduate students with strong humanities backgrounds were trained as annotators to perform the annotation. In this task, annotators had to perform a fine-grained classification of relations between callouts and targets, as either agree, disagree, or other. A range of agreement values across threads was reported.
Annotators: 5 graduate students with strong humanities backgrounds
Agreement type: Fleiss' κ
Annotator agreement: 0.45-0.55
Link: https://salts.rutgers.edu/identifying-the-language-of-opposition-in-online-interactions/

Rationale Identification
In Ghosh et al. (2014), 404 posts/comments are annotated according to a scheme based on Pragmatic Argumentation Theory (PAT), which frames arguments as interactions between Callouts and Targets. A Callout is a subsequent action that expresses an explicit stance or rationale toward a Target, defined as a prior action in the discussion. Five graduate students with strong humanities backgrounds were trained as annotators to perform the annotation. In this task, annotators had to identify the stance and rationale of callouts towards their targets, including the exact boundaries of the text segments. No agreement reported, although for 50% of callouts the stance and rationale were easily identified by the annotators.
Annotators: 5 graduate students with strong humanities backgrounds
Agreement type: Not reported
Annotator agreement: Not reported
Link: https://salts.rutgers.edu/identifying-the-language-of-opposition-in-online-interactions/

A.1.13 US2016

A corpus of transcripts from television debates leading up to the 2016 presidential election and online reactions from the Reddit social media platform, the whole corpus consists of 97,999 words (Visser et al. 2020). Specifically, the corpus is composed of 2 sub-corpora, one sub-corpus contains transcripts of 3 debates (the first Republican primary debate, the first Democrat primary debate, and the first general election debate between Clinton and Trump), a second sub-corpus contains several Reddit mega-threads on the topics of the previous 3 debates.
Genre: Political debates
Document type: Transcripts and Posts/Comments
Document count: 97,999 words/tokens across all documents

Inference Anchoring Theory

In Visser et al. (2020), 3 presidential debates and Reddit mega-threads that discussed them were annotated according to Inference Anchoring Theory (IAT) by 4 well-trained annotators. Annotation proceeded in stages, although sometimes later stages helped to inform a change in a previous stage, first annotators identified locutions segmenting the text into argumentative discourse units. Then annotators proceeded to identify functional transitions between locutions in the dialogue, as well as the illocutionary intention of locutions. Where relevant, annotators reconstructed the propositional content of a locution, as well as inferences between propositions. Propositions could also be related to each other by a conflict or rephrase relation. Agreement was calculated over a 10.5% subset of the debates sub-corpus annotated by 4 annotators, and a 12.6% subset of the Reddit sub-corpus was annotated by 2 annotators.

Annotators: 4

Agreement type: Cohen's κ

Annotator agreement: 0.61

Link: https://corpora.aifdb.org/US2016

Argument Schemes (Periodic Table of Arguments)

In Visser et al. (2019), 3 debate transcripts (the debate sub-corpus of US2016) is annotated with a layer of argument schemes according to the Periodic Table of Arguments (PTA). Annotation according to the PTA involves 3 subtasks to identify 3 distinguishing characteristics of arguments, which re-use previous Inference Anchoring Theory annotations from the original US2016 corpus (documented in (Visser et al. 2020)). The first annotation task involves distinguishing first-order and second-order arguments, which is a classification over the inference relation between two propositions. An inference relation is first-order if it connects two propositions which both contain a subject-predicate pair, otherwise the inference relation is second order if its premise is a locution. The second annotation task involves distinguishing predicate and subject arguments, where an inference relation is classified as a predicate argument if the propositions involved share the same subject term to which different predicates are applied and is a subject argument in the opposite case. Finally, propositions were also annotated as either fact, value or policy. Annotation was performed by 2 annotators, and agreement was calculated over a 10% sample of the corpus annotated by both annotators.

Annotators: 2

Agreement type: Cohen's κ

Annotator agreement: "First/second-order arguments": 0.658, "Predicate/subject arguments": 0.851, "Fact/value/policy": 0.778

Link: https://corpora.aifdb.org/US2016G1tvWAGEMANS

A.1.14 USElecDeb60To16

A dataset of 39 political debate transcripts from the last 50 years of US presidential campaigns (Haddadan et al. 2019). Debate transcripts were collected from the Commission on Presidential Debates, and include presidential debates from Kennedy vs Nixon in 1960 to Clinton vs Trump in 2016. The total number of speech turns in the dataset is 6601.
Genre: Political Debates
Document type: Transcripts
Document count: 39

Argument Component Segmentation
In Haddadan et al. (2019) 39 political debate transcripts are segmented in argumentative and non-argumentative text by 3 annotators. Each transcript was independently annotated by at least 2 annotators, and 19 debates were annotated by all 3 annotators to compute agreement.
Annotators: 3 annotators, 2 expert annotators were also used in a reconciliation phase
Agreement type: Fleiss' κ
Annotator agreement: 0.57
Link: https://github.com/ElecDeb60To16/Dataset

Argument Component Type Classification
In Haddadan et al. (2019), argumentative and non-argumentative segments of text in 39 political debate transcripts are annotated by their type: either "claim" or "premise". Each transcript was independently annotated by at least 2 annotators, and 19 debates were annotated by all 3 annotators to compute agreement.
Annotators: 3 annotators, 2 expert annotators were also used in a reconciliation phase
Agreement type: Fleiss' κ
Annotator agreement: 0.4
Link: https://github.com/ElecDeb60To16/Dataset

Fallacy Detection
In Goffredo et al. (2022), 31 political debates are annotated at the span level with 6 types of fallacies (ad hominem, appeal to emotion, appeal to authority, slippery slope, false cause, and slogan) which were selected based on an exploratory study on the dataset by an expert. Annotators selected spans which they determined contained a fallacy, of the 6 possible fallacies 4 were present in the final dataset which consisted of 1628 annotated fallacious arguments. Agreement was calculated based on the 3 annotators annotation of 9 sections from 5 debates.
Annotators: 3 annotators with a background in computational linguistics
Agreement type: Krippendorff's α

Annotator agreement: "Ad Hominem": 0.5315, "Appeal to Authority": 0.5806, "Appeal to Emotion": 0.4604, "Slogans": 0.5995
Link: https://github.com/pierpaologoffredo/IJCAI2022

A.1.15 The Web Discourse Corpus

A dataset of 5444 documents containing web discourse on controversial topics (Habernal and Gurevych 2017). Documents covered 5 different topics and varied in type, including forum posts, comments, articles, and blog posts.
Genre: Online Discussions
Document type: Posts/Comments
Document count: 5444

Toulmin Component Classification
In Habernal and Gurevych (2017), 5444 documents containing web-based discourse on controversial documents were annotated at the span level with their argumentative components. These argument components were derived from Toulmin's model, and annotators could choose to label spans as either claim, premise, backing, rebuttal, and refutation. Annotation was performed in stages, with discussions around problematic cases occurring early leading to a refinement of annotation guidelines. Annotators determined spans themselves (argument segmentation) and the gold label was obtained by majority vote on overlapping spans, and problematic cases resolved through further discussion. Agreement was reported using Krippendorff's α. Agreement varied significantly on both the topic discussed in the document and the type of the document. A joint agreement across all types of documents, all topics, and all kinds of argumentative components was reported, which we list here.
Annotators: All documents were annotated by three independent annotators who participated in two training sessions
Agreement type: Krippendorff's α
Annotator agreement: 0.48
Link: https://tudatalib.ulb.tu-darmstadt.de/items/d4a7ac0c-e7a8-466a-855a-917e42a24342

A.1.16 Webis-Editorials Corpus

A dataset of 300 news editorials from Aljazeera.com, foxnews.com, and theguardian.com. News editorials were selected based on publication date (similar publication date), had more than 5 comments, and contained at least 250 words. 100 news editorials were taken from each of the chosen websites.
Genre: News

Document type: News editorials
Document count: 300

Argumentative Discourse Unit Classification
In Al Khatib et al. (2016), 300 news editorials are annotated at the span level with their argumentative discourse unit. Each editorial was annotated by 3 annotators (out of 4 total annotators), and text was pre-segmented into text spans (annotators did not determine spans themselves). Annotators could label spans as one of 6 possible argumentative discourse unit types (common ground, assumption, anecdote, testimony, statistics, or other), they could also label spans as having no type, or as a continuation of the previous span.
Annotators: 4 crowd annotators from upwork.com
Agreement type: Fleiss' κ
Annotator agreement: "Common ground": 0.114, "Assumption": 0.613, "Anecdote": 0.399, "Testimony": 0.591, "Statistics": 0.582, "Other": 0.152, "No unit": 0.365, "Continued": 0.684, "Overall": 0.560
Link: https://webis.de/data/webis-editorials-16.html

A.1.17 Wikipedia Deletion Discussion Corpus

A dataset of 72 debates about the deletion of Wikipedia articles, that began or were relisted on Janurary 29th, 2011 (Schneider et al. 2013b). The 72 debates contain a total of 741 messages contributed by 244 users.
Genre: Revisions
Document type: Posts/comments
Document count: 741

Argument Scheme Identification
In Schneider et al. (2013b), 741 comments on Wikipedia debate/discussion pages were annotated with their argument schemes (as well as labels no reason was given or no argument present). Annotation proceeded in several rounds, in the second round the overall prevalence of various argument schemes was determined, this was used to guide annotation in a third and fourth round. In the fourth and final round two annotators annotated the corpus, agreement was reported for this fourth and final round of annotation.
Annotators: 2 student annotators (one graduate and one undergraduate)
Agreement type: Cohen's κ
Annotator agreement: 0.48
Link: Unavailable

A.2 Corpora for Argument Perspective Assessment

Here, we present a select number of corpora that are useful for computational assessment of perspective/stance.

A.2.1 IBM Debater: Claims and Stance Dataset

An updated version of the IBM Debater – Claims and Evidence dataset (see A.1.8), which contains 2394 claims on 55 controversial topics (Bar-Haim et al. 2017a).
Genre: Debate
Document type: Claims
Document count: 2394

Claim Stance Classification
In Bar-Haim et al. (2017a), first each of the 55 topics in the dataset were annotated by one of the authors for its target and sentiment. Then for the main annotation task, each claim was independently labelled with stance by 5 annotators who were provided with the target of the topic. Annotators first identified the target (positive/negative assertion) and sentiment of the claim, before determining if the claim target was the same or contrasted with the topic target. To obtain a final gold label, overlapping claim targets were clustered together, if no cluster contained the majority of the annotations then the claim was labelled as incompatible, if a majority was found then the minority annotations were discarded and the majority labels selected. Specific annotator agreement was reported, but the majority cluster was found for 98.5% of annotated claims, and for 92.5% of the claims most of the annotators agreed on the exact boundaries of the target.
Annotators: At least 5 annotators labelled each claim
Agreement type: Not reported
Annotator agreement: Not reported
Link: https://research.ibm.com/haifa/dept/vst/debating_data.shtml

A.2.2 Semeval-2016 Task 6 Dataset

A dataset of 4870 English tweets on a variety of controversial issues. Distributed by Mohammad et al. (2016) for the purposes of a shared task on stance detection.
Genre: Online discussions
Document type: Posts/comments
Document count: 1870

Stance Detection

In Mohammad et al. (2016), a dataset of 4870 English tweets is annotated with stance towards six commonly known targets in the United States ('Atheism', 'Climate Change is a Real Concern', 'Feminist Movement', 'Hillary Clinton', and 'Legalization of Abortion'). Targets were compiled by the authors, who also compiled a list of hashtags used when tweeting about the chosen targets. These hashtags were further distinguished by whether they expressed a pro/con/ambiguous stance towards the target. The selected hashtags were used to compile a list of tweets; the hashtags were then removed as the dataset was distributed for the purposes of a shared task and classification would be simplified by their inclusion. Crowd workers from *CrowdFlower* were presented with tweet-target pairs and asked to label the tweets stance (with the hashtag removed), each tweet was annotated by at least 8 respondents. For the final dataset, only instances with an agreement greater than or equal to 60% were kept. The number of tweets labelled with a neutral stance was less than 1%.

Annotators: 8 crowd workers per tweet
Agreement type: Overall agreement
Annotator agreement: 81.85%
Link: https://www.saifmohammad.com/WebPages/StanceDataset.htm

A.2.3 Argument Reasoning Comprehension (ARC)

A collection of 5000 randomly sampled NYTimes Room for Debate comments (Habernal et al. 2018c).
Genre: Online discussions
Document type: Posts/comments
Document count: 5000

Stance Classification

In Allaway and McKeown (2020), 3365 comments on 304 topics are annotated with their stance, a subset of the ARC corpus. Annotators were first asked to list all topics related to the comment and then provided with an automatically generated topic for the comment. Topics were extracted heuristically partly based on the original stance-position annotations in the ARC corpus (Habernal et al. 2018c). If an annotator disagreed that a topic applied to a given comment they could correct it, otherwise each annotator proceeded to annotate the stance of the comment towards the topic. Stance was labelled on 5 point scale, which was then mapped to a 3-point pro/con/neutral label. Each topic-comment pair was annotated by 3 crowd workers (Mechanical Turk), and the gold label taken by majority vote. Poor quality annotations were filtered out manually and by using MACE. The resulting dataset contains three kinds of annotation: stance labels on extracted topics provided to annotators, labels on topics corrected by annotators, and lists of possible topics provided by the annotators for each comment.

Annotators: 3 crowd workers per topic-comment pair
Agreement type: Krippendorff's α
Annotator agreement: 0.427
Link: https://github.com/emilyallaway/zero-shot-stance

A.3 Corpora for Argument Quality Assessment

Here, we present a select number of corpora that are useful for computational argument quality assessment.

A.3.1 GAQ Corpus

A corpus of arguments collected from three kinds of forums: debate forums, community questions and answers (CQA) forums, and review forums (Ng et al. 2020). 2100 arguments in the corpus are from debate forums (ConvinceMe and Change My View), 2085 arguments in the corpus are from CQA forums (Yahoo! Answers), and 1100 arguments in the corpus are from review forums (restaurant reviews from the Yelp-Challenge-Dataset). Curation was aided by experts.
Genre: Online discussions
Document type: Pro/con arguments
Document count: 5285

Theory-Driven Argument Quality Assessment
In Ng et al. (2020), arguments are annotated along 3 argument quality dimensions (cogency, reasonableness, and effectiveness) as well as for overall quality along a 5 point scale (very low/low/medium/high/very high quality or cannot judge). Subdimensions of the 3 argument quality dimensions are not scored, but are used to guide annotation. Annotation was performed by two groups, a set of four expert annotators with a deep understanding of argumentation theory, and a set of crowd annotators who were fluent in English. Agreement was measured along each quality dimension by comparing annotations between the set of experts and set of crowd annotators in arguments that were annotated by both groups within each category of text (CQA or debate or review).
Annotators: 4 expert annotators, and an unspecified number of crowd annotators
Agreement type: Krippendorff's α
Annotator agreement: "CQA Cogency": 0.42, "CQA Effectiveness": 0.52, "CQA Reasonableness": 0.52, "CQA Overall": 0.53, "Debates Cogency": 0.14, "Debates Effectiveness": 0.11, "Debates Reasonableness": 0.21, "Debates Overall": 0.19, "Reviews Cogency": 0.32, "Reviews Effectiveness": 0.32, "Reviews Reasonableness": 0.31, "Reviews Overall": 0.33
Link: https://github.com/grammarly/gaqcorpus

A.3.2 IBM-ArgQ-Rank-30kArgs

A crowd-curated dataset of 30,497 arguments (Gretz et al. 2020b). Arguments were collected using the Figure Eight platform. 71 common controversial topics were selected, and 280 contributors were presented with a topic and asked to create one pro/con argument for each topic. Length limits were placed during argument creation to limit the effect of length-bias on quality scoring, additionally annotators received extra payment for high-quality arguments. A small number of the arguments in the dataset were also collected/created by a set of experts.
Genre: Debate
Document type: Pro/con arguments
Document count: 30,497

Individual Binary Argument Quality
In Gretz et al. (2020b), arguments from are annotated with a binary quality score (1 or 0) by crowd annotators. 10 annotators annotated each argument, with an answer of yes/no (1 or 0) if they would recommend the argument be used as is by a person in a hypothetical speech on the topic. Poorly performing annotators, and those who failed test questions, were filtered out. To obtain a continuous quality score, scores were aggregated using two methods, MACE-P and WA (details in paper). Annotator agreement by crowd annotators is not reported in the paper, however the continuous scoring functions (MACE-P and WA) were assessed using several methods that compare predicted scores to a gold-standard pairwise annotation.
Annotators: 10 crowd annotators per argument
Agreement type: Not reported
Annotator agreement: Not reported
Link: https://huggingface.co/datasets/ibm-research/argument_quality_ranking_30k

A.3.3 UKPConvArg

A dataset of 16,081 argument pairs collected from 16 debates on 2 debate portals (*createdebate.com* and *procon.org*) (Habernal and Gurevych 2016a). A debate has a prompt, each prompt has two topics (one for each stance on the prompt) an argument is a single comment addressing the debate prompt, and an argument pair is an ordered set of two argument belonging to the same topic.
Genre: Debate
Document type: Argument pairs
Document count: 16,081

Pairwise Quality Assessment
In Habernal and Gurevych (2016a), argument pairs are annotated with a label indicating which argument was more convincing. For a given argument pair A1 and A2, workers could either label A1>A2, A2>A1 or A1=A2. Each annotator also had to provide a reason for their labelling. Agreement was not reported, but several quality control measures were used for the selection of annotators.
Annotators: All pairs were annotated by 5 crowd workers, in total 3900 workers participated
Agreement type: Not reported
Annotator agreement: Not reported
Link: https://github.com/UKPLab/acl2016-convincing-arguments

Reason Unit Classification
In Habernal and Gurevych (2016b), a bottom-up approach was used to annotate reasons given for why one argument in a pair of arguments was more convincing than another. Pairs of arguments and their reasons were obtained from a subset of 9,111 argument pairs from UKPConvArg1. From a pilot study, 19 distinct labels for reasons were obtained, for the final annotation study performed by crowd workers, these labels were decomposed into a hierarchy to be more suitable for non-experts. The annotated dataset was released as UKPConvArg2.
Annotators: All pairs were annotated by 5 crowd workers, in total 3900 workers participated
Agreement type: Not reported
Annotator agreement: Not reported
Link: https://github.com/UKPLab/emnlp2016-empirical-convincingness

A.4 Corpora for Argument Reasoning

Here, we present a select number of corpora that are useful for computational analysis of argument reasoning.

A.4.1 ElecDeb60To16-Fallacy

See the fallacy detection annotation task described in A.1.14.

A.4.2 EthiX

The EthiX Dataset (Bezou-Vrakatseli et al. 2024), is a curated collection of 686 arguments from ethical debates on the Kialo platform.

Genre: Online discussions
Document type: Posts/comments
Document count: 686

Argument Scheme Identification
In Bezou-Vrakatseli et al. (2024) arguments are annotated arguments with their argument scheme according to Walton's taxonomy (e.g., argument from example, values, positive/negative consequences, cause-to-effect, expert opinion, alternatives, analogy), with Argument Scheme Key (ASK) guidelines to aid consistent labeling. Annotation was performed by the authors, and agreement measured with another PhD student who was not an expert in argumentation.
Annotators: Authors and a PhD student in explainable AI, trained with workshops and examples.
Agreement type: Cohen's κ
Annotator agreement: 0.523
Link: https://github.com/ElfiaBv/EthiX

A.4.3 Logic

A dataset of 2449 common fallacy examples sourced from various online educational materials (Jin et al. 2022). Some instances were collected manually (around 600), while others (around 1700) were obtained by automatically crawling three student quiz websites (*Quizziz*, *study.com*, and *ProProfs*).
Genre: Fallacies
Document type: Fallacies
Document count: 2449
Link: https://github.com/causalNLP/logical-fallacy

A.4.4 LogicClimate

A dataset of 1079 climate change news articles, consisting of all climate change news articles from the *Climate Feedback* website up until October 2021 (Jin et al. 2022).
Genre: News
Document type: News editorials
Document count: 2079

Fallacy Detection
In Jin et al. (2022), climate change news articles are annotated with text spans that contain logical fallacies. Two annotators who were native English speakers, worked through every sentence in each article, and label all logical fallacies where applicable. When labelling

a text span as a logical fallacy, annotators had to pick between 1 of 13 possible logical fallacies. For the final ground-truth label, annotations were merged (text-spans), and where there was a divergent opinion, annotators consulted expert reviews on the site. If disagreement continued annotators had a discussion to resolve the divergent label. Annotator agreement was not reported, but prior to the annotation task the annotators achieved an accuracy of 85% on a test set.
Annotators: 2 expert trained annotators who are native English speakers
Agreement type: Not reported
Annotator agreement: Not reported
Link: https://github.com/causalNLP/logical-fallacy

A.5 Corpora for Argument Generation

Here, we present a select number of corpora that are useful for the automatic generation of arguments.

A.5.1 ArgEssay

A dataset of 11,282 prompt-essay pairs collected from *Essay Forum* (Bao et al. 2022b). A prompt essay pair consists of an essay writing prompt along with an argumentative essay that attempts to answer or discuss the prompt. The dataset is intended to support argument generation tasks, particularly the generation of argumentative essays.
Genre: Essays
Document type: Prompt-essay pairs
Document count: 11,282

Argument Quality Assessment
In Bao et al. (2022b), a dataset of prompt-essay pairs is used to evaluate the ability of several computational models in their performance of automatic essay generation. Part of the evaluation was performed human annotators, who gave scores from 1-5 (worst to best) for generated essays from 50 different prompts on quality dimensions of relevance, coherence, and content richness. No annotator agreement was reported, this human annotation is not publicly available, but the full ArgEssay dataset was made available by Bao et al. (2022b).
Annotators: 3
Agreement type: Not reported
Annotator agreement: Not reported, annotation was done to support downstream evaluation
Link: Unannotated dataset is https://github.com/HITSZ-HLT/AEG

A.5.2 ClaimRev (Version 1)

A dataset of 124,312 claim revision chains sourced from the debate website *kialo* (Skitalinskaya et al. 2021). On *kialo* users are allowed to revise their claims, and other users are able to suggest revisions to claims. ClaimRev of two corpora, a base corpus obtained by scraping all 1628 debates from *kialo* until June 26th 2021 for revisions, and an extended corpus that contains non-consecutive version pairs. The extended version was obtained by taking original sets of revision pairs, such as [version1, version2] and [version2, version3], and adding all possible non-consecutive pairs ([version1, version3] in the previous example).
Genre: Revisions
Document type: Claim revision chains
Document count: 124,312

Relative Quality Assessment
In Skitalinskaya et al. (2021), a randomly sampled set of 315 claim revision pairs was annotated by the authors to test the hypothesis that later versions have an increase in quality to previous versions. Their hypothesis was supported with the results that 93% of later versions had an improved overall argument quality in comparison to previous versions.
Annotators: 2 authors of the paper (experts)
Agreement type: Cohen's κ
Annotator agreement: 0.75
Link: https://github.com/GabriellaSky/claimrev

Revision Label Agreement
In Skitalinskaya et al. (2021), a random sampled set of 440 claim revision pairs were annotated by authors of the paper by their type (such as "Claim Clarification") to compare with original labels provided by *kialo*. Agreement was reported between the annotators, and between the annotators and the original labels.
Annotators: 2 authors of the paper (experts)
Agreement type: Cohen's κ
Annotator agreement: "Annotator agreement": 0.84, "Agreement with original labels": 0.82
Link: https://github.com/GabriellaSky/claimrev

Taxonomical Argument Quality Assessment
In Skitalinskaya et al. (2021), a randomly sampled set of 315 claim revision pairs was annotated by the authors to explore whether the type of revision had an effect on one of 15 argument quality dimensions. The authors observed strong correlations between some revision types and quality dimensions (such as "Corrected/Added Links" and the logical dimensions of "Cogency" and "Local Sufficiency").
Annotators: 1 author of the paper (expert)

Agreement type: None, only one annotator.
Annotator agreement: None, only one annotator
Link: https://github.com/GabriellaSky/claimrev

A.5.3 ClaimRev (Version 2)

A second version of ClaimRev was created by automatically deriving all possible claim optimization pairs from the original dataset of 124,312 claim revision chains (Skitalinskaya et al. 2023), filtering out infrequent labels, and adding the debate topic and previous claim as context to each claim-revision pair.
Genre: Revisions
Document type: Claim optimization pairs
Document count: 198,089
Link: https://github.com/GabriellaSky/claim_optimization

A.5.4 KPA Shared Task Dataset

A dataset of 24,093 argument and key point pairs. The arguments were curated by filtering low-quality arguments out of the IBM-ArgQ-Rank-30kArgs dataset (see A.3.2) to obtain a set of 7000 arguments on 28 topics. Then an annotation task was performed in Bar-Haim et al. (2020a) (details below) to map 378 expert written key points to each of the arguments. The final dataset contains 24,093 pairs, made up of 6,515 arguments and 243 key points.
Genre: Debates
Document type: Pro/con arguments
Document count: 7000

Key Point Assignment
In Bar-Haim et al. (2020a), a set of 7000 arguments was mapped to a set of 378 key points (curated by an expert on the 28 topics the arguments addressed). Each argument was labelled by 8 crowd annotators from Figure Eight, who were asked to check all relevant key points for the argument (or none). Various quality control measures were employed (such as test questions, and relying on annotators used in previous work). Inter-annotator agreement for the crowd annotators was reported, along with the agreement of 100 of the final key point labelings with an expert.
Annotators: 8 crowd annotators per argument, 1 expert for final evaluation
Agreement type: Cohen's κ
Annotator agreement: "Crowd": 0.5, "Expert": 0.82
Link: https://research.ibm.com/haifa/dept/vst/debating_data.shtml

References

Rob Abbott, Brian Ecker, Pranav Anand, and Marilyn Walker. Internet Argument Corpus 2.0: An SQL schema for dialogic social media and the corpora to go with it. In *Proceedings of the Tenth International Conference on Language Resources and Evaluation (LREC 2016)*, pages 4445–4452. European Language Resources Association (ELRA), 2016. ISBN 978-2-9517408-9-1. URL https://aclanthology.org/L16-1704/.

Gavin Abercrombie and Riza Batista-Navarro. 'Aye' or 'no'? Speech-level sentiment analysis of Hansard UK parliamentary debate transcripts. In Nicoletta Calzolari, Khalid Choukri, Christopher Cieri, Thierry Declerck, Sara Goggi, Koiti Hasida, Hitoshi Isahara, Bente Maegaard, Joseph Mariani, Hélène Mazo, Asuncion Moreno, Jan Odijk, Stelios Piperidis, and Takenobu Tokunaga, editors, *Proceedings of the Eleventh International Conference on Language Resources and Evaluation (LREC 2018)*, pages 4173–4180, Miyazaki, Japan, May 2018. European Language Resources Association (ELRA). URL https://aclanthology.org/L18-1659/.

Andrew Aberdein. The virtue approach to argument. In *The Routledge Handbook of Argumentation Theory*, pages 102–111. Routledge, 2025. https://doi.org/10.4324/9781003666851-13.

Andrew Aberdein and Daniel H. Cohen. Virtue theories of argument. *Inquiry: Critical Thinking Across the Disciplines*, 33(2):117–142, 2024. https://doi.org/10.5840/inquiryct20244115. https://doi.org/10.5840/inquiryct20244115.

Pablo Accuosto and Horacio Saggion. Transferring knowledge from discourse to arguments: A case study with scientific abstracts. In Benno Stein and Henning Wachsmuth, editors, *Proceedings of the 6th Workshop on Argument Mining*, pages 41–51, Florence, Italy, August 2019. Association for Computational Linguistics. https://doi.org/10.18653/v1/W19-4505.

Aseel Addawood and Masooda Bashir. "What is your evidence?" A study of controversial topics on social media. In Chris Reed, editor, *Proceedings of the Third Workshop on Argument Mining (ArgMining2016)*, pages 1–11, Berlin, Germany, August 2016. Association for Computational Linguistics. https://doi.org/10.18653/v1/W16-2801.

Ashutosh Adhikari and Mirella Lapata. Debating for better reasoning in vision-language models. In Christos Christodoulopoulos, Tanmoy Chakraborty, Carolyn Rose, and Violet Peng, editors, *Findings of the Association for Computational Linguistics: EMNLP 2025*, pages 15766–15784, Suzhou, China, November 2025. Association for Computational Linguistics. https://doi.org/10.18653/v1/2025.findings-emnlp.853.

M. Stede et al., *Argument Mining*, Synthesis Lectures on Human Language Technologies, https://doi.org/10.1007/978-3-032-32291-3

Stergos Afantenos, Andreas Peldszus, and Manfred Stede. Comparing decoding mechanisms for parsing argumentative structures. *Argument & Computation*, 9(3):177–192, 2018. https://doi.org/10.3233/AAC-180033.

Tazin Afrin and Diane Litman. Predicting desirable revisions of evidence and reasoning in argumentative writing. In Andreas Vlachos and Isabelle Augenstein, editors, *Findings of the Association for Computational Linguistics: EACL 2023*, pages 2550–2561, Dubrovnik, Croatia, May 2023. Association for Computational Linguistics. https://doi.org/10.18653/v1/2023.findings-eacl.193.

Tazin Afrin, Omid Kashefi, Christopher Olshefski, Diane Litman, Rebecca Hwa, and Amanda Godley. Effective interfaces for student-driven revision sessions for argumentative writing. In *Proceedings of the 2021 CHI Conference on Human Factors in Computing Systems*, pages 1–13, Yokohama Japan, May 2021. Association for Computing Machinery. https://doi.org/10.1145/3411764.3445683.

Ehud Aharoni, Anatoly Polnarov, Tamar Lavee, Daniel Hershcovich, Ran Levy, Ruty Rinott, Dan Gutfreund, and Noam Slonim. A benchmark dataset for automatic detection of claims and evidence in the context of controversial topics. In Nancy Green, Kevin Ashley, Diane Litman, Chris Reed, and Vern Walker, editors, *Proceedings of the First Workshop on Argumentation Mining*, pages 64–68, Baltimore, Maryland, June 2014. Association for Computational Linguistics. https://doi.org/10.3115/v1/W14-2109.

Fabio Aiolli, Giovanni Da San Martino, and Alessandro Sperduti. Route kernels for trees. In *Proceedings of the 26th Annual International Conference on Machine Learning*, pages 17–24, 2009. https://doi.org/10.1145/1553374.1553377.

Yamen Ajjour and Henning Wachsmuth. Exploring LLM priming strategies for few-shot stance classification. In Elena Chistova, Philipp Cimiano, Shohreh Haddadan, Gabriella Lapesa, and Ramon Ruiz-Dolz, editors, *Proceedings of the 12th Argument Mining Workshop*, pages 11–23, Vienna, Austria, July 2025. Association for Computational Linguistics. https://doi.org/10.18653/v1/2025.argmining-1.2.

Yamen Ajjour, Wei-Fan Chen, Johannes Kiesel, Henning Wachsmuth, and Benno Stein. Unit segmentation of argumentative texts. In Ivan Habernal, Iryna Gurevych, Kevin Ashley, Claire Cardie, Nancy Green, Diane Litman, Georgios Petasis, Chris Reed, Noam Slonim, and Vern Walker, editors, *Proceedings of the 4th Workshop on Argument Mining*, pages 118–128, Copenhagen, Denmark, September 2017. Association for Computational Linguistics. https://doi.org/10.18653/v1/W17-5115.

Yamen Ajjour, Henning Wachsmuth, Dora Kiesel, Patrick Riehmann, Fan, Giuliano Castiglia, Rosemary Adejoh, Bernd Fröhlich, and Benno Stein. Visualization of the topic space of argument search results in Args.Me. In Eduardo Blanco and Wei Lu, editors, *Proceedings of the 2018 Conference on Empirical Methods in Natural Language Processing: System Demonstrations*, pages 60–65, Brussels, Belgium, November 2018. Association for Computational Linguistics. https://doi.org/10.18653/v1/D18-2011.

Yamen Ajjour, Milad Alshomary, Henning Wachsmuth, and Benno Stein. Modeling frames in argumentation. In *Proceedings of the 2019 Conference on Empirical Methods in Natural Language Processing and the 9th International Joint Conference on Natural Language Processing (EMNLP-IJCNLP)*, pages 2922–2932, Hong Kong, China, November 2019a. Association for Computational Linguistics. https://doi.org/10.18653/v1/D19-1290.

Eddo Rigotti and Andrea Rocci. Sens–non-sens–contresens. Tentative d'une définition explicative. *Studies in Communication Sciences: Journal of the Swiss Association of Communication and Media Research*, 1(2), 45–80, 2001. https://doi.org/10.5169/SEALS-791150

Yamen Ajjour, Henning Wachsmuth, Johannes Kiesel, Martin Potthast, Matthias Hagen, and Benno Stein. Data acquisition for argument search: The args.me corpus. In *KI 2019: Advances in*

Artificial Intelligence - 42nd German Conference on AI, Kassel, Germany, September 23-26, 2019, Proceedings, pages 48–59, 2019b. https://doi.org/10.1007/978-3-030-30179-8_4.

Yamen Ajjour, Johannes Kiesel, Benno Stein, and Martin Potthast. Topic ontologies for arguments. In Andreas Vlachos and Isabelle Augenstein, editors, *Findings of the Association for Computational Linguistics: EACL 2023*, pages 1411–1427, Dubrovnik, Croatia, May 2023. Association for Computational Linguistics. https://doi.org/10.18653/v1/2023.findings-eacl.104.

Alan Akbik, Duncan Blythe, and Roland Vollgraf. Contextual string embeddings for sequence labeling. In *Proceedings of the 27th International Conference on Computational Linguistics*, pages 1638–1649, Santa Fe, New Mexico, USA, August 2018. Association for Computational Linguistics. URL https://aclanthology.org/C18-1139/.

Ahmet Aker, Alfred Sliwa, Yuan Ma, Ruishen Lui, Niravkumar Borad, Seyedeh Ziyaei, and Mina Ghobadi. What works and what does not: Classifier and feature analysis for argument mining. In Ivan Habernal, Iryna Gurevych, Kevin Ashley, Claire Cardie, Nancy Green, Diane Litman, Georgios Petasis, Chris Reed, Noam Slonim, and Vern Walker, editors, *Proceedings of the 4th Workshop on Argument Mining*, pages 91–96, Copenhagen, Denmark, September 2017. Association for Computational Linguistics. https://doi.org/10.18653/v1/W17-5112.

Khalid Al Khatib, Henning Wachsmuth, Johannes Kiesel, Matthias Hagen, and Benno Stein. A news editorial corpus for mining argumentation strategies. In *Proceedings of COLING 2016, the 26th International Conference on Computational Linguistics: Technical Papers*, pages 3433–3443. The COLING 2016 Organizing Committee, 2016. URL https://aclanthology.org/C16-1324/.

Khalid Al Khatib, Henning Wachsmuth, Matthias Hagen, and Benno Stein. Patterns of argumentation strategies across topics. In *Proceedings of the 2017 Conference on Empirical Methods in Natural Language Processing*, pages 1362–1368. Association for Computational Linguistics, 2017. https://doi.org/10.18653/v1/D17-1141.

Khalid Al Khatib, Viorel Morari, and Benno Stein. Style analysis of argumentative texts by mining rhetorical devices. In Elena Cabrio and Serena Villata, editors, *Proceedings of the 7th Workshop on Argument Mining*, pages 106–116, Online, December 2020a. Association for Computational Linguistics. URL https://aclanthology.org/2020.argmining-1.12.

Khalid Al Khatib, Michael Völske, Shahbaz Syed, Nikolay Kolyada, and Benno Stein. Exploiting personal characteristics of debaters for predicting persuasiveness. In *Proceedings of the 58th Annual Meeting of the Association for Computational Linguistics*, pages 7067–7072, Online, July 2020b. Association for Computational Linguistics. https://doi.org/10.18653/v1/2020.acl-main.632.

Khalid Al Khatib, Lukas Trautner, Henning Wachsmuth, Yufang Hou, and Benno Stein. Employing argumentation knowledge graphs for neural argument generation. In Chengqing Zong, Fei Xia, Wenjie Li, and Roberto Navigli, editors, *Proceedings of the 59th Annual Meeting of the Association for Computational Linguistics and the 11th International Joint Conference on Natural Language Processing (Volume 1: Long Papers)*, pages 4744–4754, Online, August 2021. Association for Computational Linguistics. https://doi.org/10.18653/v1/2021.acl-long.366.

Alaa Alhamzeh, Romain Fonck, Erwan Versmée, Elöd Egyed-Zsigmond, Harald Kosch, and Lionel Brunie. It's time to reason: Annotating argumentation structures in financial earnings calls: The FinArg dataset. In Chung-Chi Chen, Hen-Hsen Huang, Hiroya Takamura, and Hsin-Hsi Chen, editors, *Proceedings of the Fourth Workshop on Financial Technology and Natural Language Processing (FinNLP)*, pages 163–169, Abu Dhabi, United Arab Emirates (Hybrid), December 2022. Association for Computational Linguistics. https://doi.org/10.18653/v1/2022.finnlp-1.22.

Tariq Alhindi and Debanjan Ghosh. "Sharks are not the threat humans are": Argument component segmentation in school student essays. In Jill Burstein, Andrea Horbach, Ekaterina Kochmar, Ronja Laarmann-Quante, Claudia Leacock, Nitin Madnani, Ildikó Pilán, Helen Yannakoudakis, and Torsten Zesch, editors, *Proceedings of the 16th Workshop on Innovative Use of NLP for Building Educational Applications*, pages 210–222, Online, April 2021. Association for Computational Linguistics. URL https://aclanthology.org/2021.bea-1.22.

Tariq Alhindi, Smaranda Muresan, and Daniel Preotiuc-Pietro. Fact vs. opinion: The role of argumentation features in news classification. In Donia Scott, Nuria Bel, and Chengqing Zong, editors, *Proceedings of the 28th International Conference on Computational Linguistics*, pages 6139–6149, Barcelona, Spain (Online), December 2020. International Committee on Computational Linguistics. https://doi.org/10.18653/v1/2020.coling-main.540.

Tariq Alhindi, Tuhin Chakrabarty, Elena Musi, and Smaranda Muresan. Multitask instruction-based prompting for fallacy recognition. In Yoav Goldberg, Zornitsa Kozareva, and Yue Zhang, editors, *Proceedings of the 2022 Conference on Empirical Methods in Natural Language Processing*, pages 8172–8187, Abu Dhabi, United Arab Emirates, December 2022. Association for Computational Linguistics. https://doi.org/10.18653/v1/2022.emnlp-main.560.

Mohammad Ali and Naeemul Hassan. A survey of computational framing analysis approaches. In Yoav Goldberg, Zornitsa Kozareva, and Yue Zhang, editors, *Proceedings of the 2022 Conference on Empirical Methods in Natural Language Processing*, pages 9335–9348, Abu Dhabi, United Arab Emirates, December 2022. Association for Computational Linguistics. https://doi.org/10.18653/v1/2022.emnlp-main.633.

Emily Allaway and Kathleen McKeown. Zero-shot stance detection: A dataset and model using generalized topic representations. In Bonnie Webber, Trevor Cohn, Yulan He, and Yang Liu, editors, *Proceedings of the 2020 Conference on Empirical Methods in Natural Language Processing (EMNLP)*, pages 8913–8931, Online, November 2020. Association for Computational Linguistics. https://doi.org/10.18653/v1/2020.emnlp-main.717.

Jens Allwood. Argumentation, activity and culture. In *6th International Conference on Computational Models of Argument (COMMA 16)*, page 3, Potsdam, Germany, 2016. https://doi.org/10.3233/978-1-61499-686-6-3.

Nicolas Almerge, Matteo Santelmo, Ilker Gül, Amin Asadi Sarijalou, Rémi Lebret, Léo Laugier, and Karl Aberer. SAGESSE: A system for argument generation, extraction and structuring of social exchanges. In *Proceedings of the Eighteenth ACM International Conference on Web Search and Data Mining*, pages 1024–1027, 2025. https://doi.org/10.1145/3701551.3704122.

Milad Alshomary and Henning Wachsmuth. Conclusion-based counter-argument generation. In Andreas Vlachos and Isabelle Augenstein, editors, *Proceedings of the 17th Conference of the European Chapter of the Association for Computational Linguistics*, pages 957–967, Dubrovnik, Croatia, May 2023. Association for Computational Linguistics. https://doi.org/10.18653/v1/2023.eacl-main.67.

Milad Alshomary, Nick Düsterhus, and Henning Wachsmuth. Extractive snippet generation for arguments. In *Proceedings of the 43rd International ACM SIGIR conference on research and development in Information Retrieval, SIGIR 2020, Virtual Event, China, July 25-30, 2020*, pages 1969–1972. Association for Computing Machinery, 2020a. https://doi.org/10.1145/3397271.3401186.

Milad Alshomary, Shahbaz Syed, Martin Potthast, and Henning Wachsmuth. Target inference in argument conclusion generation. In *Proceedings of the 58th Annual Meeting of the Association for Computational Linguistics*, pages 4334–4345, Online, July 2020b. Association for Computational Linguistics. https://doi.org/10.18653/v1/2020.acl-main.399.

Milad Alshomary, Wei-Fan Chen, Timon Gurcke, and Henning Wachsmuth. Belief-based generation of argumentative claims. In Paola Merlo, Jorg Tiedemann, and Reut Tsarfaty, editors, *Proceedings of the 16th Conference of the European Chapter of the Association for Computational Linguistics: Main Volume*, pages 224–233, Online, April 2021a. Association for Computational Linguistics. https://doi.org/10.18653/v1/2021.eacl-main.17.

Milad Alshomary, Timon Gurcke, Shahbaz Syed, Philipp Heinisch, Maximilian Spliethöver, Philipp Cimiano, Martin Potthast, and Henning Wachsmuth. Key point analysis via contrastive learning and extractive argument summarization. In Khalid Al-Khatib, Yufang Hou, and Manfred Stede, editors, *Proceedings of the 8th Workshop on Argument Mining*, pages 184–189, Punta Cana, Dominican Republic, November 2021b. Association for Computational Linguistics. https://doi.org/10.18653/v1/2021.argmining-1.19.

Milad Alshomary, Shahbaz Syed, Arkajit Dhar, Martin Potthast, and Henning Wachsmuth. Counter-argument generation by attacking weak premises. In *Findings of the Association for Computational Linguistics: ACL-IJCNLP 2021*, pages 1816–1827, 2021c. https://doi.org/10.18653/v1/2021.findings-acl.159.

Milad Alshomary, Roxanne El Baff, Timon Gurcke, and Henning Wachsmuth. The moral debater: A study on the computational generation of morally framed arguments. In Smaranda Muresan, Preslav Nakov, and Aline Villavicencio, editors, *Proceedings of the 60th Annual Meeting of the Association for Computational Linguistics (Volume 1: Long Papers)*, pages 8782–8797, Dublin, Ireland, May 2022a. Association for Computational Linguistics. https://doi.org/10.18653/v1/2022.acl-long.601.

Milad Alshomary, Jonas Rieskamp, and Henning Wachsmuth. Generating contrastive snippets for argument search. In Francesca Toni, Sylwia Polberg, Richard Booth, Martin Caminada, and Hiroyuki Kido, editors, *Computational Models of Argument - Proceedings of COMMA 2022, Cardiff, Wales, UK, 14-16 September 2022*, volume 353 of *Frontiers in Artificial Intelligence and Applications*, pages 21–31. IOS Press, 2022b. https://doi.org/10.3233/FAIA220138.

Sacha Altay, Marlène Schwartz, Anne-Sophie Hacquin, Aurélien Allard, Stefaan Blancke, and Hugo Mercier. Scaling up interactive argumentation by providing counterarguments with a chatbot. *Nature Human Behaviour*, 6(4):579–592, April 2022. https://doi.org/10.1038/197s41562-021-01271-w.

Moritz Altemeyer, Steffen Eger, Johannes Daxenberger, Yanran Chen, Tim Altendorf, Philipp Cimiano, and Benjamin Schiller. Argument summarization and its evaluation in the era of large language models. In Christos Christodoulopoulos, Tanmoy Chakraborty, Carolyn Rose, and Violet Peng, editors, *Proceedings of the 2025 Conference on Empirical Methods in Natural Language Processing*, pages 35478–35499, Suzhou, China, November 2025. Association for Computational Linguistics. https://doi.org/10.18653/v1/2025.emnlp-main.1797.

Nora Alturayeif, Hamzah Luqman, Zaid Alyafeai, and Asma Yamani. StanceEval 2024: The first Arabic stance detection shared task. In Nizar Habash, Houda Bouamor, Ramy Eskander, Nadi Tomeh, Ibrahim Abu Farha, Ahmed Abdelali, Samia Touileb, Injy Hamed, Yaser Onaizan, Bashar Alhafni, Wissam Antoun, Salam Khalifa, Hatem Haddad, Imed Zitouni, Badr AlKhamissi, Rawan Almatham, and Khalil Mrini, editors, *Proceedings of the Second Arabic Natural Language Processing Conference*, pages 774–782, Bangkok, Thailand, August 2024. Association for Computational Linguistics. https://doi.org/10.18653/v1/2024.arabicnlp-1.88.

Leila Amgoud, Claudette Cayrol, Marie Christine Lagasquie-Schiex, and Pierre Livet. On bipolarity in argumentation frameworks. *International Journal of Intelligent Systems*, 23(10):1062–1093, 2008. https://doi.org/10.1002/int.20307.

Bilal Amjarso. *Mentioning and Then Refuting an Anticipated Counterargument: A Conceptual and Empirical Study of the Persuasiveness of a Mode of Strategic Manoeuvring*. PhD thesis, University of Amsterdam, Amsterdam, 2010. URL https://hdl.handle.net/11245/1.329753.

Lucas Anastasiou and Anna De Liddo. From shallow discourse to structured deliberation: The BCause approach. In Carmelo Ardito, Simone Diniz Junqueira Barbosa, Tayana Conte, André Freire, Isabela Gasparini, Philippe Palanque, and Raquel Prates, editors, *Human-Computer Interaction – INTERACT 2025*, pages 94–99, Cham, 2026. Springer Nature Switzerland. https://doi.org/10.1007/978-3-032-05008-3_19.

Lucas Anastasiou, Aldo de Moor, Barbara Brayshay, and Anna De Liddo. A tale of struggles: An evaluation framework for transitioning from individually usable to community-useful online deliberation tools. In *The 11th International Conference on Communities and Technologies (C&T)*, pages 144–155, Lahti Finland, May 2023. Association for Computing Machinery. https://doi.org/10.1145/3593743.3593771.

Robert Anthony and Mijung Kim. Challenges and remedies for identifying and classifying argumentation schemes. *Argumentation*, 29:81–113, 2015. https://doi.org/10.1007/s10503-014-9335-1.

Maria Antoniak, Joel Mire, Maarten Sap, Elliott Ash, and Andrew Piper. Where do people tell stories online? Story detection across online communities. In Lun-Wei Ku, Andre Martins, and Vivek Srikumar, editors, *Proceedings of the 62nd Annual Meeting of the Association for Computational Linguistics (Volume 1: Long Papers)*, pages 7104–7130, Bangkok, Thailand, August 2024. Association for Computational Linguistics. https://doi.org/10.18653/v1/2024.acl-long.383.

João António Rodrigues, Ruben Branco, João Silva, and António Branco. Reproduction and revival of the argument reasoning comprehension task. In Nicoletta Calzolari, Frédéric Béchet, Philippe Blache, Khalid Choukri, Christopher Cieri, Thierry Declerck, Sara Goggi, Hitoshi Isahara, Bente Maegaard, Joseph Mariani, Hélène Mazo, Asuncion Moreno, Jan Odijk, and Stelios Piperidis, editors, *Proceedings of the Twelfth Language Resources and Evaluation Conference*, pages 5055–5064, Marseille, France, May 2020. European Language Resources Association. ISBN 979-10-95546-34-4. URL https://aclanthology.org/2020.lrec-1.622/.

Aristotle. Sophistical refutations. In Jonathan Barnes, editor, *Complete Works of Aristotle, Volume 1: The Revised Oxford Translation*. Princeton University Press, ca. 350 B.C.E./ translated 1984. Translated by William A. Pickard-Cambridge.

Aristotle. *On Rhetoric: A Theory of Civic Discourse*. Oxford University Press, Oxford, UK, ca. 350 B.C.E./ translated 2007. Translated by George A. Kennedy.

Ron Artstein and Massimo Poesio. Inter-coder agreement for computational linguistics. *Computational Linguistics*, 34(4):555–596, 2008. https://doi.org/10.1162/coli.07-034-R2

Steven Arzt, Andreas Poller, and Gisela Vallejo. Tracing contacts with mobile phones to curb the pandemic: Topics and stances in people's online comments about the official German contact-tracing app. In *Extended Abstracts of the 2021 CHI Conference on Human Factors in Computing Systems*, pages 1–7, Yokohama Japan, May 2021. Association for Computing Machinery. https://doi.org/10.1145/3411763.3451631.

Kevin D. Ashley and Vern Walker. Toward constructing evidence-based legal arguments using legal decision documents and machine learning. In *Proceedings of the International Conference on Artificial Intelligence in Law*, pages 176–180, 2013. https://doi.org/10.1145/2514601.2514622.

Isabelle Augenstein, Tim Rocktäschel, Andreas Vlachos, and Kalina Bontcheva. Stance detection with bidirectional conditional encoding. In Jian Su, Kevin Duh, and Xavier Carreras, editors, *Proceedings of the 2016 Conference on Empirical Methods in Natural Language Processing*, pages 876–885, Austin, Texas, November 2016. Association for Computational Linguistics. https://doi.org/10.18653/v1/D16-1084.

John L. Austin. *How to Do Things with Words*. Harvard University Press, Cambridge, MA, 1975.

Edmond Awad, Sydney Levine, Michael Anderson, Susan Leigh Anderson, Vincent Conitzer, M. J. Crockett, Jim A. C. Everett, Theodoros Evgeniou, Alison Gopnik, Julian C. Jamison, Tae Wan Kim, S. Matthew Liao, Michelle N. Meyer, John Mikhail, Kweku Opoku-Agyemang, Jana Schaich Borg, Juliana Schroeder, Walter Sinnott-Armstrong, Marija Slavkovik, and Josh B. Tenenbaum. Computational ethics. *Trends in Cognitive Sciences*, 26(5):388–405, May 2022. https://doi.org/10.1016/j.tics.2022.02.009.

Moshe Azar. Argumentative text as rhetorical structure: An application of Rhetorical Structure Theory. *Argumentation*, 13:97–114, 1999. https://doi.org/10.1023/A:1007794409860.

Stefano Baccianella, Andrea Esuli, and Fabrizio Sebastiani. SentiWordNet 3.0: An enhanced lexical resource for sentiment analysis and opinion mining. In Nicoletta Calzolari, Khalid Choukri, Bente Maegaard, Joseph Mariani, Jan Odijk, Stelios Piperidis, Mike Rosner, and Daniel Tapias, editors, *Proceedings of the Seventh International Conference on Language Resources and Evaluation (LREC'10)*, pages 2200–2204, Valletta, Malta, May 2010. European Language Resources Association (ELRA). URL https://aclanthology.org/L10-1531/.

Stephen H. Bach, Bert Huang, Ben London, and Lise Getoor. Hinge-loss Markov random fields: Convex inference for structured prediction. In *Proceedings of the Conference on Uncertainty in Artificial Intelligence*, pages 32–41, 2013. https://www.auai.org/uai2013/prints/papers/176.pdf

Andre Bächtiger and John Parkinson. *Mapping and measuring deliberation: Towards a new deliberative quality*. Oxford University Press, Cambridge, MA, USA, 2019. https://doi.org/10.1093/oso/9780199672196.001.0001.

Hui Bai, Jan G. Voelkel, Shane Muldowney, Johannes C. Eichstaedt, and Robb Willer. LLM-generated messages can persuade humans on policy issues. *Nature Communications*, 16:6037, July 2025. https://doi.org/10.1038/s41467-025-61345-5.

Collin F. Baker, Charles J. Fillmore, and John B. Lowe. The Berkeley FrameNet project. In *36th Annual Meeting of the Association for Computational Linguistics and 17th International Conference on Computational Linguistics, Volume 1*, pages 86–90, Montreal, Quebec, Canada, August 1998. Association for Computational Linguistics. https://doi.org/10.3115/980845.980860.

Jianzhu Bao, Chuang Fan, Jipeng Wu, Yixue Dang, Jiachen Du, and Ruifeng Xu. A neural transition-based model for argumentation mining. In Chengqing Zong, Fei Xia, Wenjie Li, and Roberto Navigli, editors, *Proceedings of the 59th Annual Meeting of the Association for Computational Linguistics and the 11th International Joint Conference on Natural Language Processing (Volume 1: Long Papers)*, pages 6354–6364, Online, August 2021. Association for Computational Linguistics. https://doi.org/10.18653/v1/2021.acl-long.497.

Jianzhu Bao, Yuhang He, Yang Sun, Bin Liang, Jiachen Du, Bing Qin, Min Yang, and Ruifeng Xu. A generative model for end-to-end argument mining with reconstructed positional encoding and constrained pointer mechanism. In Yoav Goldberg, Zornitsa Kozareva, and Yue Zhang, editors, *Proceedings of the 2022 Conference on Empirical Methods in Natural Language Processing*, pages 10437–10449, Abu Dhabi, United Arab Emirates, December 2022a. Association for Computational Linguistics. https://doi.org/10.18653/v1/2022.emnlp-main.713.

Jianzhu Bao, Yasheng Wang, Yitong Li, Fei Mi, and Ruifeng Xu. AEG: Argumentative Essay Generation via a dual-decoder model with content planning. In Yoav Goldberg, Zornitsa Kozareva, and Yue Zhang, editors, *Proceedings of the 2022 Conference on Empirical Methods in Natural Language Processing*, pages 5134–5148, Abu Dhabi, United Arab Emirates, December 2022b. Association for Computational Linguistics. https://doi.org/10.18653/v1/2022.emnlp-main.343.

Jianzhu Bao, Yuqi Huang, Yang Sun, Wenya Wang, Yice Zhang, Bojun Jin, and Ruifeng Xu. Exploring quality and diversity in synthetic data generation for argument mining. In Christos Christodoulopoulos, Tanmoy Chakraborty, Carolyn Rose, and Violet Peng, editors, *Proceedings of the 2025 Conference on Empirical Methods in Natural Language Processing*, pages 26592–26615, Suzhou, China, November 2025a. Association for Computational Linguistics. https://doi.org/10.18653/v1/2025.emnlp-main.1351.

Jianzhu Bao, Mohan Jing, Kuicai Dong, Aixin Sun, Yang Sun, and Ruifeng Xu. UniASA: A unified generative framework for argument structure analysis. *Computational Linguistics*, 51(3):739–784, Sep. 2025b. https://doi.org/10.1162/coli_a_00553.

Roy Bar-Haim, Indrajit Bhattacharya, Francesco Dinuzzo, Amrita Saha, and Noam Slonim. Stance classification of context-dependent claims. In *Proceedings of the 15th Conference of the European Chapter of the Association for Computational Linguistics: Volume 1, Long Papers*, pages 251–261, Valencia, Spain, April 2017a. Association for Computational Linguistics. URL https://aclanthology.org/E17-1024/.

Roy Bar-Haim, Lilach Edelstein, Charles Jochim, and Noam Slonim. Improving claim stance classification with lexical knowledge expansion and context utilization. In Ivan Habernal, Iryna Gurevych, Kevin Ashley, Claire Cardie, Nancy Green, Diane Litman, Georgios Petasis, Chris Reed, Noam Slonim, and Vern Walker, editors, *Proceedings of the 4th Workshop on Argument Mining*, pages 32–38, Copenhagen, Denmark, September 2017b. Association for Computational Linguistics. https://doi.org/10.18653/v1/W17-5104.

Roy Bar-Haim, Dalia Krieger, Orith Toledo-Ronen, Lilach Edelstein, Yonatan Bilu, Alon Halfon, Yoav Katz, Amir Menczel, Ranit Aharonov, and Noam Slonim. From surrogacy to adoption; from bitcoin to cryptocurrency: Debate topic expansion. In Anna Korhonen, David Traum, and Lluís Màrquez, editors, *Proceedings of the 57th Annual Meeting of the Association for Computational Linguistics*, pages 977–990, Florence, Italy, July 2019. Association for Computational Linguistics. https://doi.org/10.18653/v1/P19-1094.

Roy Bar-Haim, Lilach Eden, Roni Friedman, Yoav Kantor, Dan Lahav, and Noam Slonim. From arguments to key points: Towards automatic argument summarization. In Dan Jurafsky, Joyce Chai, Natalie Schluter, and Joel Tetreault, editors, *Proceedings of the 58th Annual Meeting of the Association for Computational Linguistics*, pages 4029–4039, Online, July 2020a. Association for Computational Linguistics. https://doi.org/10.18653/v1/2020.acl-main.371.

Roy Bar-Haim, Yoav Kantor, Lilach Eden, Roni Friedman, Dan Lahav, and Noam Slonim. Quantitative argument summarization and beyond: Cross-domain key point analysis. In Bonnie Webber, Trevor Cohn, Yulan He, and Yang Liu, editors, *Proceedings of the 2020 Conference on Empirical Methods in Natural Language Processing (EMNLP)*, pages 39–49, Online, November 2020b. Association for Computational Linguistics. https://doi.org/10.18653/v1/2020.emnlp-main.3.

Roy Bar-Haim, Yoav Kantor, Elad Venezian, Yoav Katz, and Noam Slonim. Project Debater APIs: Decomposing the AI grand challenge. In Heike Adel and Shuming Shi, editors, *Proceedings of the 2021 Conference on Empirical Methods in Natural Language Processing: System Demonstrations*, pages 267–274. Association for Computational Linguistics, November 2021. https://doi.org/10.18653/v1/2021.emnlp-demo.31.

Pietro Baroni, Marco Romano, Francesca Toni, Marco Aurisicchio, and Giorgio Bertanza. Automatic evaluation of design alternatives with quantitative argumentation. *Argument & Computation*, 6(1):24–49, 2015. https://doi.org/10.1080/19462166.2014.1001791.

Pietro Baroni, Dov M. Gabbay, Massimiliano Giacomin, and Leendert van der Torre, editors. *Handbook of Formal Argumentation*, volume 1. College Publications, Milton Keynes, UK, 2018. ISBN 978-1-84890-275-6.

Joe Barrow, Rajiv Jain, Nedim Lipka, Franck Dernoncourt, Vlad Morariu, Varun Manjunatha, Douglas Oard, Philip Resnik, and Henning Wachsmuth. Syntopical graphs for computational argumentation tasks. In Chengqing Zong, Fei Xia, Wenjie Li, and Roberto Navigli, editors, *Proceedings of the 59th Annual Meeting of the Association for Computational Linguistics and the 11th International Joint Conference on Natural Language Processing (Volume 1: Long Papers)*, pages 1583–1595, Online, August 2021. Association for Computational Linguistics. https://doi.org/10.18653/v1/2021.acl-long.126.

Maria Becker, Alexis Palmer, and Anette Frank. Argumentative texts and clause types. In Chris Reed, editor, *Proceedings of the Third Workshop on Argument Mining (ArgMining2016)*, pages 21–30, Berlin, Germany, August 2016. Association for Computational Linguistics. https://doi.org/10.18653/v1/W16-2803.

Maria Becker, Katharina Korfhage, and Anette Frank. Implicit knowledge in argumentative texts: An annotated corpus. In Nicoletta Calzolari, Frédéric Béchet, Philippe Blache, Khalid Choukri, Christopher Cieri, Thierry Declerck, Sara Goggi, Hitoshi Isahara, Bente Maegaard, Joseph Mariani, Hélène Mazo, Asuncion Moreno, Jan Odijk, and Stelios Piperidis, editors, *Proceedings of the Twelfth Language Resources and Evaluation Conference*, pages 2316–2324, Marseille, France, May 2020. European Language Resources Association. ISBN 979-10-95546-34-4. URL https://aclanthology.org/2020.lrec-1.282/.

Maria Becker, Siting Liang, and Anette Frank. Reconstructing implicit knowledge with language models. In Eneko Agirre, Marianna Apidianaki, and Ivan Vulić, editors, *Proceedings of Deep Learning Inside Out (DeeLIO): The 2nd Workshop on Knowledge Extraction and Integration for Deep Learning Architectures*, pages 11–24, Online, June 2021. Association for Computational Linguistics. https://doi.org/10.18653/v1/2021.deelio-1.2.

Maike Behrendt, Stefan Sylvius Wagner, Marc Ziegele, Lena Wilms, Anke Stoll, Dominique Heinbach, and Stefan Harmeling. AQuA – Combining experts' and non-experts' views to assess deliberation quality in online discussions using LLMs. In Annette Hautli-Janisz, Gabriella Lapesa, Lucas Anastasiou, Valentin Gold, Anna De Liddo, and Chris Reed, editors, *Proceedings of the First Workshop on Language-driven Deliberation Technology (DELITE) @ LREC-COLING 2024*, pages 1–12, Torino, Italia, May 2024. ELRA and ICCL. URL https://aclanthology.org/2024.delite-1.1/.

Maike Behrendt, Stefan Sylvius Wagner, Carina Weinmann, Marike Bormann, Mira Warne, and Stefan Harmeling. Natural language processing to enhance deliberation in political online discussions: A survey, June 2025. https://doi.org/10.48550/arXiv.2506.02533.

Rashid Behzadidoost, Habib Izadkhah, and Farnaz Mahan. A combined multi-margin contrastive learning with granulated data for warrant identification in computational argumentation. *Information Sciences*, 699:121756, 2025. https://doi.org/10.1016/j.ins.2024.121756.

Beata Beigman Klebanov, Eyal Beigman, and Daniel Diermeier. Vocabulary choice as an indicator of perspective. In Jan Hajič, Sandra Carberry, Stephen Clark, and Joakim Nivre, editors, *Proceedings of the ACL 2010 Conference Short Papers*, pages 253–257, Uppsala, Sweden, July 2010. Association for Computational Linguistics. URL https://aclanthology.org/P10-2047/.

Iz Beltagy, Kyle Lo, and Arman Cohan. SciBERT: A pretrained language model for scientific text. In Kentaro Inui, Jing Jiang, Vincent Ng, and Xiaojun Wan, editors, *Proceedings of the 2019 Conference on Empirical Methods in Natural Language Processing and the 9th International Joint Conference on Natural Language Processing (EMNLP-IJCNLP)*, pages 3615–3620, Hong Kong, China, November 2019. Association for Computational Linguistics. https://doi.org/10.18653/v1/D19-1371.

Iz Beltagy, Matthew E. Peters, and Arman Cohan. Longformer: The long-document transformer, 2020. https://doi.org/10.48550/arXiv.2004.05150.

Jonathan Ben-Naim, Victor David, and Anthony Hunter. Understanding enthymemes in argument maps: Bridging argument mining and logic-based argumentation, August 2024. https://doi.org/10.48550/arXiv.2408.08648.

Trevor Bench-Capon and Katie Atkinson. Using argumentation schemes to model legal reasoning, 2022. Presented at the Fourth European Conference on Argumentation, Rome 2022. arXiv preprint arXiv:2210.00315. https://doi.org/10.48550/arXiv.2210.00315.

Kalliopi Benetos. Digital tools for written argumentation. In Otto Kruse, Christian Rapp, Chris M. Anson, Kalliopi Benetos, Elena Cotos, Ann Devitt, and Antonette Shibani, editors, *Digital Writing Technologies in Higher Education*, pages 81–99. Springer International Publishing, Cham, 2023. https://doi.org/10.1007/978-3-031-36033-6_6.

Ruha Benjamin. *Race after Technology: Abolitionist Tools for the New Jim Code.* Polity, Medford, MA, 2019. ISBN 978-1-5095-2643-7.

Luciana Benotti, Karën Fort, Min-Yen Kan, and Yulia Tsvetkov. Understanding ethics in NLP authoring and reviewing. In *Proceedings of the 17th Conference of the European Chapter of the Association for Computational Linguistics: Tutorial Abstracts*, pages 19–24, Dubrovnik, Croatia, May 2023. Association for Computational Linguistics. https://doi.org/10.18653/v1/2023.eacl-tutorials.4.

Luciana Benotti, Fanny Ducel, Karën Fort, Guido Ivetta, Zhijing Jin, Min-Yen Kan, Seunghun J. Lee, Minzhi Li, Margot Mieskes, and Adriana Pagano. Navigating ethical challenges in NLP: Hands-on strategies for students and researchers. In Yuki Arase, David Jurgens, and Fei Xia, editors, *Proceedings of the 63rd Annual Meeting of the Association for Computational Linguistics (Volume 5: Tutorial Abstracts)*, pages 7–8, Vienna, Austria, July 2025. Association for Computational Linguistics. https://doi.org/10.18653/v1/2025.acl-tutorials.5.

Jamal Bentahar, Bernard Moulin, and Micheline Bélanger. A taxonomy of argumentation models used for knowledge representation. *Artificial Intelligence Review*, 33(3):211–259, 2010. https://doi.org/10.1007/s10462-010-9154-1.

Philippe Besnard, Alejandro Garcia, Anthony Hunter, Sanjay Modgil, Henry Prakken, Guillermo Simari, and Francesca Toni. Introduction to structured argumentation. *Argument & Computation*, 5(1):1–4, January 2014. https://doi.org/10.1080/19462166.2013.869764.

Gregor Betz. Assessing the epistemological relevance of Dung-style argumentation theories. *Annals of Mathematics and Artificial Intelligence*, 78(3):303–321, December 2016. https://doi.org/10.1007/s10472-015-9484-4.

Gregor Betz and Sebastian Cacean. *The Moral Controversy about Climate Engineering - an Argument Map.* Karlsruhe Institute of Technology, February 2011. https://doi.org/10.5445/IR/1000022371.

Gregor Betz and Sebastian Cacean. *Ethical Aspects of Climate Engineering.* KIT Scientific Publishing, June 2012. ISBN 978-3-86644-856-8. https://doi.org/10.5445/ksp/1000028245.

Floris Bex, John Lawrence, Mark Snaith, and Chris Reed. Implementing the Argument Web. *Communications of the Association for Computing Machinery*, 56(10):66–73, 2013. https://doi.org/10.1145/2500891.

Elfia Bezou-Vrakatseli, Oana Cocarascu, and Sanjay Modgil. EthiX: A dataset for argument scheme classification in ethical debates. In *Proceedings of the European Conference on Artificial Intelligence (ECAI)*, pages 3628–3635. IOS Press, 2024. https://doi.org/10.3233/FAIA240919.

Elfia Bezou-Vrakatseli, Oana Cocarascu, and Sanjay Modgil. Can large language models understand argument schemes? In Wanxiang Che, Joyce Nabende, Ekaterina Shutova, and Mohammad Taher Pilehvar, editors, *Findings of the Association for Computational Linguistics: ACL 2025*, pages 13666–13681, Vienna, Austria, July 2025. Association for Computational Linguistics. https://doi.org/10.18653/v1/2025.findings-acl.702.

Chandra Bhagavatula, Ronan Le Bras, Chaitanya Malaviya, Keisuke Sakaguchi, Ari Holtzman, Hannah Rashkin, Doug Downey, Wen Tau Yih, and Yejin Choi. Abductive commonsense reasoning. In *International Conference on Learning Representations*, 2020. URL https://iclr.cc/virtual_2020/poster_Byg1v1HKDB.html.

Sumithra Bhakthavatsalam, Chloe Anastasiades, and Peter Clark. GenericsKB: A knowledge base of generic statements, 2020. https://doi.org/10.48550/arXiv.2005.00660.

Muhammad Mahad Afzal Bhatti, Ahsan Suheer Ahmad, and Joonsuk Park. Argument mining on Twitter: A case study on the Planned Parenthood debate. In Khalid Al-Khatib, Yufang Hou, and Manfred Stede, editors, *Proceedings of the 8th Workshop on Argument Mining*, pages 1–11, Punta Cana, Dominican Republic, November 2021. Association for Computational Linguistics. https://doi.org/10.18653/v1/2021.argmining-1.1.

Yonatan Bilu and Noam Slonim. Claim synthesis via predicate recycling. In *Proceedings of the 54th Annual Meeting of the Association for Computational Linguistics (Volume 2: Short Papers)*, pages 525–530. Association for Computational Linguistics, 2016. https://doi.org/10.18653/v1/P16-2085.

Yonatan Bilu, Daniel Hershcovich, and Noam Slonim. Automatic claim negation: Why, how and when. In *Proceedings of the 2nd Workshop on Argumentation Mining*, pages 84–93, Denver, CO, June 2015. Association for Computational Linguistics. https://doi.org/10.3115/v1/W15-0511.

Yonatan Bilu, Ariel Gera, Daniel Hershcovich, Benjamin Sznajder, Dan Lahav, Guy Moshkowich, Anael Malet, Assaf Gavron, and Noam Slonim. Argument invention from first principles. In Anna Korhonen, David Traum, and Lluís Màrquez, editors, *Proceedings of the 57th Annual Meeting of the Association for Computational Linguistics*, pages 1013–1026, Florence, Italy, July 2019. Association for Computational Linguistics. https://doi.org/10.18653/v1/P19-1097.

Or Biran and Owen Rambow. Identifying justifications in written dialogs by classifying text as argumentative. *International Journal of Semantic Computing*, 5(4):363–381, 2011. https://doi.org/10.1142/S1793351X11001328.

Umanga Bista, Alexander Mathews, Aditya Menon, and Lexing Xie. SupMMD: A sentence importance model for extractive summarization using maximum mean discrepancy. In Trevor Cohn, Yulan He, and Yang Liu, editors, *Findings of the Association for Computational Linguistics: EMNLP 2020*, pages 4108–4122, Online, November 2020. Association for Computational Linguistics. https://doi.org/10.18653/v1/2020.findings-emnlp.367.

Lloyd F. Bitzer. The rhetorical situation. *Philosophy & Rhetoric*, 1(1):1–14, 1968. ISSN 0031-8213. URL http://www.jstor.org/stable/40236733.

Elizabeth Black and Anthony Hunter. Using enthymemes in an inquiry dialogue system. In *Proceedings of the 7th International Joint Conference on Autonomous Agents and Multiagent Systems - Volume 1*, AAMAS '08, pages 437–444, Richland, SC, 2008. International Foundation for Autonomous Agents and Multiagent Systems. ISBN 978-0-9817381-0-9. URL https://www.ifaamas.org/Proceedings/aamas08/proceedings/pdf/paper/AAMAS08_0222.pdf.

J. Anthony Blair. *Groundwork in the Theory of Argumentation*. Springer Netherlands, 2012. https://doi.org/10.1007/978-94-007-2363-4.

David M. Blei, Andrew Y. Ng, and Michael I. Jordan. Latent Dirichlet allocation. *Journal of Machine Learning Research*, 3(Jan):993–1022, March 2003. ISSN 1532-4435. URL https://jmlr.org/papers/v3/blei03a.html.

Su Lin Blodgett, Solon Barocas, Hal Daumé III, and Hanna Wallach. Language (technology) is power: A critical survey of "bias" in NLP. In Dan Jurafsky, Joyce Chai, Natalie Schluter, and Joel Tetreault, editors, *Proceedings of the 58th Annual Meeting of the Association for Computational Linguistics*, pages 5454–5476, Online, July 2020. Association for Computational Linguistics. https://doi.org/10.18653/v1/2020.acl-main.485.

Filip Boltužić and Jan Šnajder. Back up your stance: Recognizing arguments in online discussions. In Nancy Green, Kevin Ashley, Diane Litman, Chris Reed, and Vern Walker, editors, *Proceedings of the First Workshop on Argumentation Mining*, pages 49–58, Baltimore, Maryland, June 2014. Association for Computational Linguistics. https://doi.org/10.3115/v1/W14-2107.

Filip Boltužić and Jan Šnajder. Fill the gap! Analyzing implicit premises between claims from online debates. In Chris Reed, editor, *Proceedings of the Third Workshop on Argument Mining (ArgMining2016)*, pages 124–133, Berlin, Germany, August 2016. Association for Computational Linguistics. https://doi.org/10.18653/v1/W16-2815.

Jean-François Bonnefon, Iyad Rahwan, and Azim Shariff. The moral psychology of artificial intelligence. *Annual Review of Psychology*, 75:653–675, January 2024. https://doi.org/10.1146/annurev-psych-030123-113559.

Antoine Bordes, Nicolas Usunier, Alberto Garcia-Duran, Jason Weston, and Oksana Yakhnenko. Translating embeddings for modeling multi-relational data. In C.J. Burges, L. Bottou, M. Welling, Z. Ghahramani, and K.Q. Weinberger, editors, *Advances in Neural Information*

Processing Systems, volume 26, pages 2787–2795. Curran Associates, Inc., 2013. URL https://papers.neurips.cc/paper_files/paper/2013/hash/1cecc7a77928ca8133fa24680a88d2f9-Abstract.html.

Tom Bosc, Elena Cabrio, and Serena Villata. DART: A dataset of arguments and their relations on Twitter. In Nicoletta Calzolari, Khalid Choukri, Thierry Declerck, Sara Goggi, Marko Grobelnik, Bente Maegaard, Joseph Mariani, Helene Mazo, Asuncion Moreno, Jan Odijk, and Stelios Piperidis, editors, *Proceedings of the Tenth International Conference on Language Resources and Evaluation (LREC'16)*, pages 1258–1263, Portorož, Slovenia, 2016. European Language Resources Association (ELRA). URL https://aclanthology.org/L16-1200/.

Teresa Botschen, Daniil Sorokin, and Iryna Gurevych. Frame- and entity-based knowledge for common-sense argumentative reasoning. In Noam Slonim and Ranit Aharonov, editors, *Proceedings of the 5th Workshop on Argument Mining*, pages 90–96, Brussels, Belgium, November 2018. Association for Computational Linguistics. https://doi.org/10.18653/v1/W18-5211.

Maarten Boudry, Fabio Paglieri, and Massimo Pigliucci. The fake, the flimsy, and the fallacious: Demarcating arguments in real life. *Argumentation*, 29:431–456, 2015. https://doi.org/10.1007/s10503-015-9359-1.

Amber E. Boydstun, Dallas Card, Justin Gross, Paul Resnick, and Noah A. Smith. Tracking the development of media frames within and across policy issues. American Political Science Association 2014 annual meeting paper, Jun. 2014. https://doi.org/10.1184/R1/6473780.v1.

Ruben Brave, Federica Russo, Ondrej Uzovic, and Jean Wagemans. Can an AI analyze arguments? Argument-checking and the challenges of assessing the quality of online information. In Christo El Morr, editor, *AI and Society: Tensions and Opportunities*, pages 267–281. Chapman and Hall/CRC, October 2022. https://doi.org/10.1201/9781003261247-20.

Ellen Breitholtz. *Enthymemes and Topoi in Dialogue: The Use of Common Sense Reasoning in Conversation*. Brill, 2021. ISBN 9789004436787. URL http://www.jstor.org/stable/10.1163/j.ctv1sr6hws.

Gerhard Brewka and Stefan Woltran. Abstract dialectical frameworks. In *Proceedings of the Twelfth International Conference on Principles of Knowledge Representation and Reasoning*, KR'10, pages 102–111, Toronto, Ontario, Canada, May 2010. AAAI Press. ISBN 978-1-57735-451-2. URL https://cdn.aaai.org/ocs/1294/1294-7400-1-PB.pdf.

Gerhard Brewka, Sylwia Polberg, and Stefan Woltran. Generalizations of Dung frameworks and their role in formal argumentation. *IEEE Intelligent Systems*, 29(1):30–38, January 2014. https://doi.org/10.1109/MIS.2013.122.

Gerhard Brewka, Stefan Ellmauthaler, Hannes Strass, Johannes P Wallner, and Stefan Woltran. Abstract dialectical frameworks. An overview. *Journal of Applied Logics*, 4(8):2263–2317, 2017.

Georg Brun and Gregor Betz. Analysing practical argumentation. In Sven Ove Hansson and Gertrude Hirsch Hadorn, editors, *The Argumentative Turn in Policy Analysis: Reasoning about Uncertainty*, volume 10, pages 39–77. Springer International Publishing, Cham, 2016. https://doi.org/10.1007/978-3-319-30549-3_3.

Katarzyna Budzyńska and Marcin Koszowy. An empirical turn in studying ethos in argumentation. In *International Workshop on Computational Argumentation and Cognition at the 24th European Conference on Artificial Intelligence (ECAI 2020) (COGNITAR 2020)*, Spain, 2020. URL https://cognition.ouc.ac.cy/cognitar/abstracts/an_empirical_turn_in_studying_ethos_in_argumentation.pdf.

Katarzyna Budzyńska and Chris Reed. Speech acts of argumentation: Inference anchors and peripheral cues in dialogue. In *Computational Models of Natural Argument: Papers from the 2011 AAAI Workshop (WS-11-10)*, pages 3–10, 2011. URL https://cdn.aaai.org/ocs/ws/ws0755/3940-16678-1-PB.pdf.

Katarzyna Budzynska, Mathilde Janier, Chris Reed, Patrick Saint-Dizier, Manfred Stede, and Olena Yaskorska. A model for processing illocutionary structures and argumentation in debates. In Nicoletta Calzolari, Khalid Choukri, Thierry Declerck, Hrafn Loftsson, Bente Maegaard, Joseph Mariani, Asunción Moreno, Jan Odijk, and Stelios Piperidis, editors, *Proceedings of the Ninth International Conference on Language Resources and Evaluation, LREC 2014, Reykjavik, Iceland, May 26-31, 2014*, pages 917–924. European Language Resources Association (ELRA), 2014. URL https://aclanthology.org/L14-1599/.

Katarzyna Budzynska, Marcin Koszowy, Ewelina Gajewska, Maciej Kulik, and Maciej Uberna. A computational method for quantitative analysis of ethos. In *Ethos, Technology, and AI in Contemporary Society*. Routledge, 2024. https://doi.org/10.4324/9781032688503-7.

Jill Burstein and Daniel Marcu. A machine learning approach for identification of thesis and conclusion statements in student essays. *Computers and the Humanities*, 37(4):455–467, 2003. https://doi.org/10.1023/A:1025746505971.

Jérémie Cabessa, Hugo Hernault, and Umer Mushtaq. Argument mining with fine-tuned large language models. In Owen Rambow, Leo Wanner, Marianna Apidianaki, Hend Al Khalifa, Barbara Di Eugenio, and Steven Schockaert, editors, *Proceedings of the 31st International Conference on Computational Linguistics*, pages 6624–6635, Abu Dhabi, UAE, January 2025. Association for Computational Linguistics. URL https://aclanthology.org/2025.coling-main.442/.

Elena Cabrio and Serena Villata. Combining textual entailment and argumentation theory for supporting online debates interactions. In *Proceedings of the 50th Annual Meeting of the Association for Computational Linguistics (Volume 2: Short Papers)*, pages 208–212. Association for Computational Linguistics, 2012. URL https://aclanthology.org/P12-2041/.

Elena Cabrio and Serena Villata. Natural language argumentation for text exploration. In Jaap van den Herik and Joaquim Filipe, editors, *Agents and Artificial Intelligence*, pages 133–150, Cham, 2017. Springer International Publishing. https://doi.org/10.1007/978-3-319-53354-4_8.

Elena Cabrio and Serena Villata. Five years of argument mining: A data-driven analysis. In *Proceedings of the Twenty-Seventh International Joint Conference on Artificial Intelligence, IJCAI-18*, pages 5427–5433, Stockholm, 2018. https://doi.org/10.24963/ijcai.2018/766.

Aylin Caliskan, Joanna J. Bryson, and Arvind Narayanan. Semantics derived automatically from language corpora contain human-like biases. *Science*, 356(6334):183–186, 2017. https://doi.org/10.1126/science.aal4230.

Oana-Maria Camburu, Tim Rocktäschel, Thomas Lukasiewicz, and Phil Blunsom. e-SNLI: Natural language inference with natural language explanations. In *Proceedings of the 32nd International Conference on Neural Information Processing Systems*, NIPS'18, pages 9560–9572, Red Hook, NY, USA, 2018. Curran Associates Inc. URL https://proceedings.neurips.cc/paper_files/paper/2018/hash/4c7a167bb329bd92580a99ce422d6fa6-Abstract.html.

Yilin Cao, Ruike Zhang, Penghui Wei, Qingchao Kong, and Wenji Mao. Perspective-driven preference optimization with entropy maximization for diverse argument generation. In Christos Christodoulopoulos, Tanmoy Chakraborty, Carolyn Rose, and Violet Peng, editors, *Findings of the Association for Computational Linguistics: EMNLP 2025*, pages 22479–22496, Suzhou, China, November 2025. Association for Computational Linguistics. https://doi.org/10.18653/v1/2025.findings-emnlp.1223.

Dallas Card, Amber E. Boydstun, Justin H. Gross, Philip Resnik, and Noah A. Smith. The Media Frames Corpus: Annotations of frames across issues. In Chengqing Zong and Michael Strube, editors, *Proceedings of the 53rd Annual Meeting of the Association for Computational Linguistics and the 7th International Joint Conference on Natural Language Processing (Volume 2: Short Papers)*, pages 438–444, Beijing, China, July 2015. Association for Computational Linguistics. https://doi.org/10.3115/v1/P15-2072.

Cristian Cardellino, Theo Collias, Benjamin Molinet, Erwan Hain, Wei Sun, Rodrigo Agerri, Serena Villata, and Elena Cabrio. ANTIDOTE: ArgumeNtaTIon-Driven explainable artificial intelligence fOr digiTal mEdicine. In Ulle Endriss, Francisco S. Melo, Kerstin Bach, Alberto Bugarín-Diz, José M. Alonso-Moral, Senén Barro, and Fredrik Heintz, editors, *27th European Conference on Artificial Intelligence, 19–24 October 2024, Santiago de Compostela, Spain – Including 13th Conference on Prestigious Applications of Intelligent Systems (PAIS 2024)*, volume 392, pages 4455–4458. IOS Press, October 2024. https://doi.org/10.3233/FAIA241028.

Henrique Lopes Cardoso, Rui Sousa-Silva, Paula Carvalho, and Bruno Martins. Argumentation models and their use in corpus annotation: Practice, prospects, and challenges. *Natural Language Engineering*, 29(4):1150–1187, July 2023. https://doi.org/10.1017/S1351324923000062.

Giuseppe Carenini. GEA: A complete, modular system for generating evaluative arguments. In Vassil N. Alexandrov, Jack J. Dongarra, Benjoe A. Juliano, René S. Renner, and C. J. Kenneth Tan, editors, *Computational Science — ICCS 2001*, pages 959–968, Berlin, Heidelberg, 2001. Springer Berlin Heidelberg. https://doi.org/10.1007/3-540-45545-0_108.

Winston Carlile, Nishant Gurrapadi, Zixuan Ke, and Vincent Ng. Give me more feedback: Annotating argument persuasiveness and related attributes in student essays. In Iryna Gurevych and Yusuke Miyao, editors, *Proceedings of the 56th Annual Meeting of the Association for Computational Linguistics (Volume 1: Long Papers)*, pages 621–631, Melbourne, Australia, July 2018. Association for Computational Linguistics. https://doi.org/10.18653/v1/P18-1058.

Lynn Carlson, Daniel Marcu, and Mary Ellen Okurowski. Building a discourse-tagged corpus in the framework of Rhetorical Structure Theory. In Jan van Kuppevelt and Ronnie Smith, editors, *Current and New Directions in Discourse and Dialogue*, pages 85–112. Kluwer, Dordrecht, 2003. https://doi.org/10.1007/978-94-010-0019-2_5.

Miriam Louise Carnot, Lorenz Heinemann, Jan Braker, Tobias Schreieder, Johannes Kiesel, Maik Fröbe, Martin Potthast, and Benno Stein. On stance detection in image retrieval for argumentation. In Hsin-Hsi Chen, Wei-Jou (Edward) Duh, Hen-Hsen Huang, Makoto P. Kato, Josiane Mothe, and Barbara Poblete, editors, *46th International ACM SIGIR Conference on Research and Development in Information Retrieval (SIGIR 2023)*, pages 2562–2571. Association for Computing Machinery, July 2023. https://doi.org/10.1145/3539618.3591917.

Jean-Claude Carron. Rhetoric: Overview. In Maryanne Cline Horrowitz, editor, *New Dictionary of the History of Ideas (Vol. 5)*, pages 2122–2126. Charles Scribner's Sons, 2005.

Lucas Carstens and Francesca Toni. Towards relation based Argumentation Mining. In *Proceedings of the 2nd Workshop on Argumentation Mining*, pages 29–34, 2015. https://doi.org/10.3115/v1/W15-0504.

Federico Castagna, Nadin Kökciyan, Isabel Sassoon, Simon Parsons, and Elizabeth Sklar. Computational argumentation-based chatbots: A survey. *Journal of Artificial Intelligence Research*, 80: 1271–1310, August 2024. https://doi.org/10.1613/jair.1.15407.

Daniel Cer, Yinfei Yang, Sheng-yi Kong, Nan Hua, Nicole Limtiaco, Rhomni St. John, Noah Constant, Mario Guajardo-Cespedes, Steve Yuan, Chris Tar, Brian Strope, and Ray Kurzweil. Universal sentence encoder for English. In Eduardo Blanco and Wei Lu, editors, *Proceedings of the 2018 Conference on Empirical Methods in Natural Language Processing: System Demonstrations*, pages 169–174, Brussels, Belgium, November 2018. Association for Computational Linguistics. https://doi.org/10.18653/v1/D18-2029.

Tuhin Chakrabarty, Christopher Hidey, Smaranda Muresan, Kathy McKeown, and Alyssa Hwang. AMPERSAND: Argument mining for PERSuAsive oNline discussions. In Kentaro Inui, Jing Jiang, Vincent Ng, and Xiaojun Wan, editors, *Proceedings of the 2019 Conference on Empirical Methods in Natural Language Processing and the 9th International Joint Conference on Natural Language Processing (EMNLP-IJCNLP)*, pages 2933–2943, Hong Kong, China, November 2019. Association for Computational Linguistics. https://doi.org/10.18653/v1/D19-1291.

Tuhin Chakrabarty, Christopher Hidey, and Smaranda Muresan. ENTRUST: Argument reframing with language models and entailment. In *Proceedings of the 2021 Conference of the North American Chapter of the Association for Computational Linguistics: Human Language Technologies*, pages 4958–4971, Online, June 2021a. Association for Computational Linguistics. https://doi.org/10.18653/v1/2021.naacl-main.394.

Tuhin Chakrabarty, Aadit Trivedi, and Smaranda Muresan. Implicit premise generation with discourse-aware commonsense knowledge models. In Marie-Francine Moens, Xuanjing Huang, Lucia Specia, and Scott Wen-Tau Yih, editors, *Proceedings of the 2021 Conference on Empirical Methods in Natural Language Processing*, pages 6247–6252, Online and Punta Cana, Dominican Republic, November 2021b. Association for Computational Linguistics. https://doi.org/10.18653/v1/2021.emnlp-main.504.

Lisa Chalaguine and Anthony Hunter. Addressing popular concerns regarding COVID-19 vaccination with natural language argumentation dialogues. In Jiřina Vejnarová and Nic Wilson, editors, *Symbolic and Quantitative Approaches to Reasoning with Uncertainty*, Lecture Notes in Computer Science, volume 12897, pages 59–73, Cham, 2021. Springer International Publishing. https://doi.org/10.1007/978-3-030-86772-0_5.

Guizhen Chen, Liying Cheng, Anh Tuan Luu, and Lidong Bing. Exploring the potential of large language models in computational argumentation. In Lun-Wei Ku, Andre Martins, and Vivek Srikumar, editors, *Proceedings of the 62nd Annual Meeting of the Association for Computational Linguistics (Volume 1: Long Papers)*, pages 2309–2330, Bangkok, Thailand, August 2024. Association for Computational Linguistics. https://doi.org/10.18653/v1/2024.acl-long.126.

Mark Chen, Jerry Tworek, Heewoo Jun, Qiming Yuan, Henrique Ponde de Oliveira Pinto, Jared Kaplan, Harri Edwards, Yuri Burda, Nicholas Joseph, Greg Brockman, Alex Ray, Raul Puri, Gretchen Krueger, Michael Petrov, Heidy Khlaaf, Girish Sastry, Pamela Mishkin, Brooke Chan, Scott Gray, Nick Ryder, Mikhail Pavlov, Alethea Power, Lukasz Kaiser, Mohammad Bavarian, Clemens Winter, Philippe Tillet, Felipe Petroski Such, Dave Cummings, Matthias Plappert, Fotios Chantzis, Elizabeth Barnes, Ariel Herbert-Voss, William Hebgen Guss, Alex Nichol, Alex Paino, Nikolas Tezak, Jie Tang, Igor Babuschkin, Suchir Balaji, Shantanu Jain, William Saunders, Christopher Hesse, Andrew N. Carr, Jan Leike, Josh Achiam, Vedant Misra, Evan Morikawa, Alec Radford, Matthew Knight, Miles Brundage, Mira Murati, Katie Mayer, Peter Welinder, Bob McGrew, Dario Amodei, Sam McCandlish, Ilya Sutskever, and Wojciech Zaremba. Evaluating large language models trained on code, 2021. https://doi.org/10.48550/arXiv.2107.03374.

Qian Chen, Xiaodan Zhu, Zhen-Hua Ling, Si Wei, Hui Jiang, and Diana Inkpen. Enhanced LSTM for natural language inference. In Regina Barzilay and Min-Yen Kan, editors, *Proceedings of the 55th Annual Meeting of the Association for Computational Linguistics (Volume 1: Long Papers)*, pages 1657–1668, Vancouver, Canada, July 2017. Association for Computational Linguistics. https://doi.org/10.18653/v1/P17-1152.

Sihao Chen, Daniel Khashabi, Chris Callison-Burch, and Dan Roth. PerspectroScope: A window to the world of diverse perspectives. In Marta R. Costa-jussà and Enrique Alfonseca, editors, *Proceedings of the 57th Annual Meeting of the Association for Computational Linguistics: System Demonstrations*, pages 129–134, Florence, Italy, July 2019a. Association for Computational Linguistics. https://doi.org/10.18653/v1/P19-3022.

Sihao Chen, Daniel Khashabi, Wenpeng Yin, Chris Callison-Burch, and Dan Roth. Seeing things from a different angle: Discovering diverse perspectives about claims. In Jill Burstein, Christy Doran, and Thamar Solorio, editors, *Proceedings of the 2019 Conference of the North American Chapter of the Association for Computational Linguistics: Human Language Technologies, Volume 1 (Long and Short Papers)*, pages 542–557, Minneapolis, Minnesota, June 2019b. Association for Computational Linguistics. https://doi.org/10.18653/v1/N19-1053.

Wei-Fan Chen, Henning Wachsmuth, Khalid Al Khatib, and Benno Stein. Learning to flip the bias of news headlines. In *Proceedings of the 11th International Conference on Natural Language Generation*, pages 79–88. Association for Computational Linguistics, 2018. https://doi.org/10.18653/v1/W18-6509.

Wei-Fan Chen, Mei-Hua Chen, Garima Mudgal, and Henning Wachsmuth. Analyzing culture-specific argument structures in learner essays. In Gabriella Lapesa, Jodi Schneider, Yohan Jo, and Sougata Saha, editors, *Proceedings of the 9th Workshop on Argument Mining*, pages 51–61, Online and in Gyeongju, Republic of Korea, October 2022a. International Conference on Computational Linguistics. URL https://aclanthology.org/2022.argmining-1.4/.

Yanran Chen and Steffen Eger. Do emotions really affect argument convincingness? A dynamic approach with LLM-based manipulation checks. In Wanxiang Che, Joyce Nabende, Ekaterina Shutova, and Mohammad Taher Pilehvar, editors, *Findings of the Association for Computational Linguistics: ACL 2025*, pages 24357–24381, Vienna, Austria, July 2025. Association for Computational Linguistics. https://doi.org/10.18653/v1/2025.findings-acl.1250.

Zaiqian Chen, Daniel Verdi do Amarante, Jenna Donaldson, Yohan Jo, and Joonsuk Park. Argument mining for review helpfulness prediction. In *Proceedings of the 2022 Conference on Empirical Methods in Natural Language Processing*, pages 8914–8922, Abu Dhabi, United Arab Emirates, December 2022b. Association for Computational Linguistics. https://doi.org/10.18653/v1/2022.emnlp-main.609.

Liying Cheng, Lidong Bing, Ruidan He, Qian Yu, Yan Zhang, and Luo Si. IAM: A comprehensive and large-scale dataset for integrated argument mining tasks. In Smaranda Muresan, Preslav Nakov, and Aline Villavicencio, editors, *Proceedings of the 60th Annual Meeting of the Association for Computational Linguistics (Volume 1: Long Papers)*, pages 2277–2287, Dublin, Ireland, May 2022. Association for Computational Linguistics. https://doi.org/10.18653/v1/2022.acl-long.162.

Wei-Lin Chiang, Zhuohan Li, Zi Lin, Ying Sheng, Zhanghao Wu, Hao Zhang, Lianmin Zheng, Siyuan Zhuang, Yonghao Zhuang, Joseph E. Gonzalez, Ion Stoica, and Eric P. Xing. Vicuna: An open-source chatbot impressing GPT-4 with 90%* ChatGPT quality, March 2023. URL https://lmsys.org/blog/2023-03-30-vicuna/.

Elena Chistova. End-to-end argument mining over varying rhetorical structures. In Anna Rogers, Jordan Boyd-Graber, and Naoaki Okazaki, editors, *Findings of the Association for Computational Linguistics: ACL 2023*, pages 3376–3391, Toronto, Canada, July 2023. Association for Computational Linguistics. https://doi.org/10.18653/v1/2023.findings-acl.209.

Kyunghyun Cho, Bart van Merriënboer, Caglar Gulcehre, Dzmitry Bahdanau, Fethi Bougares, Holger Schwenk, and Yoshua Bengio. Learning phrase representations using RNN encoder–decoder for statistical machine translation. In Alessandro Moschitti, Bo Pang, and Walter Daelemans, editors, *Proceedings of the 2014 Conference on Empirical Methods in Natural Language Processing (EMNLP)*, pages 1724–1734, Doha, Qatar, October 2014. Association for Computational Linguistics. https://doi.org/10.3115/v1/D14-1179.

HongSeok Choi and Hyunju Lee. GIST at SemEval-2018 task 12: A network transferring inference knowledge to argument reasoning comprehension task. In Marianna Apidianaki, Saif M. Mohammad, Jonathan May, Ekaterina Shutova, Steven Bethard, and Marine Carpuat, editors, *Proceedings of the 12th International Workshop on Semantic Evaluation*, pages 773–777, New Orleans, Louisiana, June 2018. Association for Computational Linguistics. https://doi.org/10.18653/v1/S18-1122.

Minje Choi, Luca Maria Aiello, Krisztián Zsolt Varga, and Daniele Quercia. Ten social dimensions of conversations and relationships. In *Proceedings of The Web Conference 2020*, WWW '20, pages 1514–1525, New York, NY, USA, 2020. Association for Computing Machinery. https://doi.org/10.1145/3366423.3380224.

Aakanksha Chowdhery, Sharan Narang, Jacob Devlin, Maarten Bosma, Gaurav Mishra, Adam Roberts, Paul Barham, Hyung Won Chung, Charles Sutton, Sebastian Gehrmann, Parker Schuh, Kensen Shi, Sashank Tsvyashchenko, Joshua Maynez, Abhishek Rao, Parker Barnes, Yi Tay, Noam Shazeer, Vinodkumar Prabhakaran, Emily Reif, Nan Du, Ben Hutchinson, Reiner Pope, James Bradbury, Jacob Austin, Michael Isard, Guy Gur-Ari, Pengcheng Yin, Toju Duke, Anselm Levskaya, Sanjay Ghemawat, Sunipa Dev, Henryk Michalewski, Xavier Garcia, Vedant Misra, Kevin Robinson, Liam Fedus, Denny Zhou, Daphne Ippolito, David Luan, Hyeontaek Lim, Barret Zoph, Alexander Spiridonov, Ryan Sepassi, David Dohan, Shivani Agrawal, Mark Omernick, Andrew M. Dai, Thanumalayan Sankaranarayana Pillai, Marie Pellat, Aitor Lewkowycz, Erica Moreira, Rewon Child, Oleksandr Polozov, Katherine Lee, Zongwei Zhou, Xuezhi Wang, Brennan Saeta, Mark Diaz, Orhan Firat, Michele Catasta, Jason Wei, Kathy Meier-Hellstern, Douglas Eck, Jeff Dean, Slav Petrov, and Noah Fiedel. PaLM: Scaling language modeling with pathways. *Journal of Machine Learning Research*, 24(240):1–113, January 2023. URL https://jmlr.org/papers/v24/22-1144.html.

Yoeng-Jin Chu and Tseng-Hong Liu. On the shortest arborescence of a directed graph. *Science Sinica*, 14:1396–1400, 1965.

Hyung Won Chung, Le Hou, Shayne Longpre, Barret Zoph, Yi Tay, William Fedus, Yunxuan Li, Xuezhi Wang, Mostafa Dehghani, Siddhartha Brahma, Albert Webson, Shixiang Shane Gu, Zhuyun Dai, Mirac Suzgun, Xinyun Chen, Aakanksha Chowdhery, Alex Castro-Ros, Marie Pellat, Kevin Robinson, Dasha Valter, Sharan Narang, Gaurav Mishra, Adams Yu, Vincent Zhao, Yanping Huang, Andrew Dai, Hongkun Yu, Slav Petrov, Ed H. Chi, Jeff Dean, Jacob Devlin, Adam Roberts, Denny Zhou, Quoc V. Le, and Jason Wei. Scaling instruction-finetuned language models. *Journal of Machine Learning Research*, 25(70):1–53, 2024. URL http://jmlr.org/papers/v25/23-0870.html.

Herbert H. Clark and Michael F. Schober. Asking questions and influencing answers. In Judith M. Tanur, editor, *Questions about Questions: Inquiries into the Cognitive Bases of Surveys*, pages 15–48. Russell Sage Foundation, New York, 1992. URL https://www.jstor.org/stable/10.7758/9781610445269.8.

Kevin Clark, Minh-Thang Luong, Quoc V. Le, and Christopher D. Manning. ELECTRA: Pre-training text encoders as discriminators rather than generators. In *International Conference on Learning Representations*, 2020. URL https://iclr.cc/virtual_2020/poster_r1xMH1BtvB.html.

Aaron Clauset, M. E. J. Newman, and Cristopher Moore. Finding community structure in very large networks. *Phys. Rev. E*, 70:066111, Dec 2004. https://doi.org/10.1103/PhysRevE.70.066111.

Oana Cocarascu, Elena Cabrio, Serena Villata, and Francesca Toni. Dataset independent baselines for relation prediction in argument mining. In Henry Prakken, Stefano Bistarelli, Francesco Santini, and Carlo Taticchi, editors, *Computational Models of Argument: Proceedings of COMMA 2020*, pages 45–52. IOS Press, Dordrecht, 2020. https://doi.org/10.3233/FAIA200490.

Kevin Coe, Kate Kenski, and Stephen A. Rains. Online and uncivil? Patterns and determinants of incivility in newspaper website comments. *Journal of Communication*, 64(4):658–679, Jun 2014. https://doi.org/10.1111/jcom.12104.

CohereForAI. Command-R model card, 2024. URL https://huggingface.co/CohereForAI/c4ai-command-r-v01.

David A Cohn, Zoubin Ghahramani, and Michael I Jordan. Active learning with statistical models. *Journal of Artificial Intelligence Research*, 4:129–145, 1996.

Michael Collins and Nigel Duffy. Convolution kernels for natural language. In *Advances in Neural Information Processing Systems 14*, pages 625–632. MIT Press, 2001. URL http://papers.nips.cc/paper/2089-convolution-kernels-for-natural-language.pdf.

Alexis Conneau, Kartikay Khandelwal, Naman Goyal, Vishrav Chaudhary, Guillaume Wenzek, Francisco Guzmán, Edouard Grave, Myle Ott, Luke Zettlemoyer, and Veselin Stoyanov.

Unsupervised cross-lingual representation learning at scale. In Dan Jurafsky, Joyce Chai, Natalie Schluter, and Joel Tetreault, editors, *Proceedings of the 58th Annual Meeting of the Association for Computational Linguistics*, pages 8440–8451, Online, July 2020. Association for Computational Linguistics. https://doi.org/10.18653/v1/2020.acl-main.747.

Jack Contro, Simrat Deol, Yulan He, and Martim Brandão. ChatbotManip: A dataset to facilitate evaluation and oversight of manipulative chatbot behaviour, June 2025. https://doi.org/10.48550/arXiv.2506.12090.

John Cook, Peter Ellerton, and David Kinkead. Deconstructing climate misinformation to identify reasoning errors. *Environmental Research Letters*, 13(2):024018, 2018. https://doi.org/10.1088/1748-9326/aaa49f.

Gordon V. Cormack, Charles L A Clarke, and Stefan Buettcher. Reciprocal rank fusion outperforms condorcet and individual rank learning methods. In *Proceedings of the 32nd International ACM SIGIR Conference on Research and Development in Information Retrieval*, SIGIR '09, page 758–759, New York, NY, USA, 2009. Association for Computing Machinery. https://doi.org/10.1145/1571941.1572114.

Thomas H. Costello, Gordon Pennycook, and David G. Rand. Durably reducing conspiracy beliefs through dialogues with AI. *Science*, 385(6714):eadq1814, September 2024. https://doi.org/10.1126/science.adq1814.

Scott A. Crossley, Perpetual Baffour, Yu Tian, Aigner Picou, Meg Benner, and Ulrich Boser. The persuasive essays for rating, selecting, and understanding argumentative and discourse elements (PERSUADE) corpus 1.0. *Assessing Writing*, 54:100667, 2022. https://doi.org/10.1016/j.asw.2022.100667.

Giovanni Da San Martino, Seunghak Yu, Alberto Barrón-Cedeño, Rostislav Petrov, and Preslav Nakov. Fine-grained analysis of propaganda in news articles. In Kentaro Inui, Jing Jiang, Vincent Ng, and Xiaojun Wan, editors, *Proceedings of the 2019 Conference on Empirical Methods in Natural Language Processing and the 9th International Joint Conference on Natural Language Processing (EMNLP-IJCNLP)*, pages 5636–5646, Hong Kong, China, November 2019. Association for Computational Linguistics. https://doi.org/10.18653/v1/D19-1565.

Giovanni Da San Martino, Alberto Barrón-Cedeño, Henning Wachsmuth, Rostislav Petrov, and Preslav Nakov. SemEval-2020 Task 11: Detection of propaganda techniques in news articles. In Aurelie Herbelot, Xiaodan Zhu, Alexis Palmer, Nathan Schneider, Jonathan May, and Ekaterina Shutova, editors, *Proceedings of the Fourteenth Workshop on Semantic Evaluation*, pages 1377–1414, Barcelona (online), December 2020. International Committee for Computational Linguistics. https://doi.org/10.18653/v1/2020.semeval-1.186.

Ido Dagan, Bill Dolan, Bernardo Magnini, and Dan Roth. Recognizing textual entailment: Rational, evaluation and approaches. *Natural Language Engineering*, 15(4):i–xvii, 2009. https://doi.org/10.1017/S1351324909990209.

Ido Dagan, Dan Roth, Mark Sammons, and Fabio Massimo Zanzotto. *Recognizing Textual Entailment: Models and Applications*. Morgan and Claypool, 2013. https://doi.org/10.1007/978-3-031-02151-0.

T. Edward Damer. *Attacking Faulty Reasoning: A Practical Guide to Fallacy-Free Arguments*. Wadsworth, Cengage Learning, Belmont, CA, 6th edition, 2009.

Valdemar Danry, Pat Pataranutaporn, Matthew Groh, and Ziv Epstein. Deceptive explanations by large language models lead people to change their beliefs about misinformation more often than honest explanations. In *Proceedings of the 2025 CHI Conference on Human Factors in Computing Systems*, CHI '25, pages 1–31, New York, NY, USA, April 2025. Association for Computing Machinery. https://doi.org/10.1145/3706598.3713408.

Sumanth Dathathri, Andrea Madotto, Janice Lan, Jane Hung, Eric Frank, Piero Molino, Jason Yosinski, and Rosanne Liu. Plug and play language models: A simple approach to controlled text generation. In *International Conference on Learning Representations*, 2020. URL https://iclr.cc/virtual_2020/poster_H1edEyBKDS.html.

Martin Davies, Ashley Barnett, and Tim van Gelder. Using computer-aided argument mapping to teach reasoning. In Anthony Blair, editor, *Studies in Critical Thinking*. Windsor Studies in Argumentation, 2019. URL https://ecampusontario.pressbooks.pub/criticalthinking1234/chapter/introduction/.

Johannes Daxenberger, Steffen Eger, Ivan Habernal, Christian Stab, and Iryna Gurevych. What is the essence of a claim? Cross-domain claim identification. In Martha Palmer, Rebecca Hwa, and Sebastian Riedel, editors, *Proceedings of the 2017 Conference on Empirical Methods in Natural Language Processing*, pages 2055–2066, Copenhagen, Denmark, September 2017. Association for Computational Linguistics. https://doi.org/10.18653/v1/D17-1218.

Johannes Daxenberger, Benjamin Schiller, Chris Stahlhut, Erik Kaiser, and Iryna Gurevych. ArgumenText: Argument classification and clustering in a generalized search scenario. *Datenbank Spektrum*, 20:115–121, 2020. https://doi.org/10.1007/s13222-020-00347-7.

Claes H. de Vreese. News framing: Theory and typology. *Information Design Journal and Document Design*, 13(1):51–62, 2005. https://doi.org/10.1075/idjdd.13.1.06vre.

Daya Guo, Dejian Yang, Haowei Zhang, Junxiao Song, Peiyi Wang, Qihao Zhu, Runxin Xu, Ruoyu Zhang, Shirong Ma, Xiao Bi, Xiaokang Zhang, Xingkai Yu, Yu Wu, Z. F. Wu, Zhibin Gou, Zhihong Shao, Zhuoshu Li, Ziyi Gao, Aixin Liu, Bing Xue, Bingxuan Wang, Bochao Wu, Bei Feng, Chengda Lu, Chenggang Zhao, Chengqi Deng, Chong Ruan, Damai Dai, Deli Chen, Dongjie Ji, Erhang Li, Fangyun Lin, Fucong Dai, Fuli Luo, Guangbo Hao, Guanting Chen, Guowei Li, H. Zhang, Hanwei Xu, Honghui Ding, Huazuo Gao, Hui Qu, Hui Li, Jianzhong Guo, Jiashi Li, Jingchang Chen, Jingyang Yuan, Jinhao Tu, Junjie Qiu, Junlong Li, J. L. Cai, Jiaqi Ni, Jian Liang, Jin Chen, Kai Dong, Kai Hu, Kaichao You, Kaige Gao, Kang Guan, Kexin Huang, Kuai Yu, Lean Wang, Lecong Zhang, Liang Zhao, Litong Wang, Liyue Zhang, Lei Xu, Leyi Xia, Mingchuan Zhang, Minghua Zhang, Minghui Tang, Mingxu Zhou, Meng Li, Miaojun Wang, Mingming Li, Ning Tian, Panpan Huang, Peng Zhang, Qiancheng Wang, Qinyu Chen, Qiushi Du, Ruiqi Ge, Ruisong Zhang, Ruizhe Pan, Runji Wang, R. J. Chen, R. L. Jin, Ruyi Chen, Shanghao Lu, Shangyan Zhou, Shanhuang Chen, Shengfeng Ye, Shiyu Wang, Shuiping Yu, Shunfeng Zhou, Shuting Pan, S. S. Li, Shuang Zhou, Shaoqing Wu, Tao Yun, Tian Pei, Tianyu Sun, T. Wang, Wangding Zeng, Wen Liu, Wenfeng Liang, Wenjun Gao, Wenqin Yu, Wentao Zhang, W. L. Xiao, Wei An, Xiaodong Liu, Xiaohan Wang, Xiaokang Chen, Xiaotao Nie, Xin Cheng, Xin Liu, Xin Xie, Xingchao Liu, Xinyu Yang, Xinyuan Li, Xuecheng Su, Xuheng Lin, X. Q. Li, Xiangyue Jin, Xiaojin Shen, Xiaosha Chen, Xiaowen Sun, Xiaoxiang Wang, Xinnan Song, Xinyi Zhou, Xianzu Wang, Xinxia Shan, Y. K. Li, Y. Q. Wang, Y. X. Wei, Yang Zhang, Yanhong Xu, Yao Li, Yao Zhao, Yaofeng Sun, Yaohui Wang, Yi Yu, Yichao Zhang, Yifan Shi, Yiliang Xiong, Ying He, Yishi Piao, Yisong Wang, Yixuan Tan, Yiyang Ma, Yiyuan Liu, Yongqiang Guo, Yuan Ou, Yuduan Wang, Yue Gong, Yuheng Zou, Yujia He, Yunfan Xiong, Yuxiang Luo, Yuxiang You, Yuxuan Liu, Yuyang Zhou, Y. X. Zhu, Yanping Huang, Yaohui Li, Yi Zheng, Yuchen Zhu, Yunxian Ma, Ying Tang, Yukun Zha, Yuting Yan, Z. Z. Ren, Zehui Ren, Zhangli Sha, Zhe Fu, Zhean Xu, Zhenda Xie, Zhengyan Zhang, Zhewen Hao, Zhicheng Ma, Zhigang Yan, Zhiyu Wu, Zihui Gu, Zijia Zhu, Zijun Liu, Zilin Li, Ziwei Xie, Ziyang Song, Zizheng Pan, Zhen Huang, Zhipeng Xu, Zhongyu Zhang and Zhen Zhang. DeepSeek-R1 incentivizes reasoning in LLMs through reinforcement learning. *Nature* 645(8081):633–638, 2025. https://doi.org/10.1038/s41586-025-09422-z.

Scott Deerwester, Susan T. Dumais, George W. Furnas, Thomas K. Landauer, and Richard Harshman. Indexing by latent semantic analysis. *Journal of the American Society for Information Science*, 41(6):391–407, 1990. https://doi.org/10.1002/(SICI)1097-4571(199009)41:6<391::AID-ASI1>3.0.CO;2-9.

Marco Dehnert and Paul A Mongeau. Persuasion in the age of artificial intelligence (AI): Theories and complications of AI-based persuasion. *Human Communication Research*, 48(3):386–403, June 2022. https://doi.org/10.1093/hcr/hqac006.

Zvonimir Delas, Brian Plüss, and Ramon Ruiz-Dolz. An argumentation scheme-based framework for automatic reconstruction of natural language enthymemes. In *Computational Models of Argument*, pages 61–72. IOS Press, 2024. https://doi.org/10.3233/FAIA240310.

Pieter Delobelle, Murilo Cunha, Eric Massip Cano, Jeroen Peperkamp, and Bettina Berendt. Computational ad hominem detection. In Fernando Alva-Manchego, Eunsol Choi, and Daniel Khashabi, editors, *Proceedings of the 57th Annual Meeting of the Association for Computational Linguistics: Student Research Workshop*, pages 203–209, Florence, Italy, July 2019. Association for Computational Linguistics. https://doi.org/10.18653/v1/P19-2028.

Darshan Deshpande, Zhivar Sourati, Filip Ilievski, and Fred Morstatter. Contextualizing argument quality assessment with relevant knowledge. In Kevin Duh, Helena Gomez, and Steven Bethard, editors, *Proceedings of the 2024 Conference of the North American Chapter of the Association for Computational Linguistics: Human Language Technologies (Volume 2: Short Papers)*, pages 316–326, Mexico City, Mexico, June 2024. Association for Computational Linguistics. https://doi.org/10.18653/v1/2024.naacl-short.28.

Jacob Devlin, Ming-Wei Chang, Kenton Lee, and Kristina Toutanova. BERT: Pre-training of deep bidirectional transformers for language understanding. In Jill Burstein, Christy Doran, and Thamar Solorio, editors, *Proceedings of the 2019 Conference of the North American Chapter of the Association for Computational Linguistics: Human Language Technologies, Volume 1 (Long and Short Papers)*, pages 4171–4186, Minneapolis, Minnesota, June 2019. Association for Computational Linguistics. https://doi.org/10.18653/v1/N19-1423.

Gabriela Andrea Diaz, Dana Urribarri, María Luján Ganuza, Carlos Chesñevar, Elsa Estevez, and Ana Maguitman. Polviz: Assessing opinion polarization in social media through visual analytics and argumentation. In *Proceedings of the 17th International Conference on Theory and Practice of Electronic Governance*, ICEGOV '24, pages 337–347, New York, NY, USA, December 2024. Association for Computing Machinery. https://doi.org/10.1145/3680127.3680212.

Catherine D'Ignazio and Lauren F. Klein. *Data Feminism*. Strong Ideas. MIT Press, March 2020. ISBN 978-0-262-04400-4. https://doi.org/10.7551/mitpress/11805.001.0001.

Yuning Ding, Marie Bexte, and Andrea Horbach. Score it all together: A multi-task learning study on automatic scoring of argumentative essays. In Anna Rogers, Jordan Boyd-Graber, and Naoaki Okazaki, editors, *Findings of the Association for Computational Linguistics: ACL 2023*, pages 13052–13063, Toronto, Canada, July 2023. Association for Computational Linguistics. https://doi.org/10.18653/v1/2023.findings-acl.825.

Esra Dönmez and Agnieszka Falenska. "I understand your perspective": LLM persuasion through the lens of communicative action theory. In Wanxiang Che, Joyce Nabende, Ekaterina Shutova, and Mohammad Taher Pilehvar, editors, *Findings of the Association for Computational Linguistics: ACL 2025*, pages 15312–15327, Vienna, Austria, July 2025. Association for Computational Linguistics. https://doi.org/10.18653/v1/2025.findings-acl.793.

Esra Dönmez, Maximilian Maurer, Gabriella Lapesa, and Agnieszka Falenska. AI argues differently: Distinct argumentative and linguistic patterns of LLMs in persuasive contexts. In Christos Christodoulopoulos, Tanmoy Chakraborty, Carolyn Rose, and Violet Peng, editors, *Proceedings of the 2025 Conference on Empirical Methods in Natural Language Processing*, pages 34583–34614, Suzhou, China, November 2025. Association for Computational Linguistics.

John Douglas and Simon Wells. Monkeypuzzle: Towards next generation, free & open-source argument analysis tools. In Floris Bex, Floriana Grasso, and Nancy L. Green, editors, *Proceedings of the 17th Workshop on Computational Models of Natural Argument Co-Located with ICAIL 2017, London, UK, July 16, 2017*, volume 2048 of *CEUR Workshop Proceedings*, pages 50–53. CEUR-WS.org, 2017. URL https://ceur-ws.org/Vol-2048/paper09.pdf.

Dov Gabbay, Massimiliano Giacomin, Guillermo R. Simari, and Matthias Thimm, editors. *Handbook of Formal Argumentation*, volume 2. College Publications, S.l., 2021. ISBN 978-1-84890-336-4. URL http://www.collegepublications.co.uk/downloads/handbooks00006.pdf.

Timothy Dozat and Christopher D. Manning. Deep biaffine attention for neural dependency parsing. In *International Conference on Learning Representations*, 2017. URL https://openreview.net/forum?id=Hk95PK9le.

Timothy Dozat and Christopher D. Manning. Simpler but more accurate semantic dependency parsing. In Iryna Gurevych and Yusuke Miyao, editors, *Proceedings of the 56th Annual Meeting of the Association for Computational Linguistics (Volume 2: Short Papers)*, pages 484–490, Melbourne, Australia, July 2018. Association for Computational Linguistics. https://doi.org/10.18653/v1/P18-2077.

Lorik Dumani and Ralf Schenkel. A systematic comparison of methods for finding good premises for claims. In *Proceedings of the 42nd International ACM SIGIR Conference on Research and Development in Information Retrieval*, SIGIR'19, pages 957–960, New York, NY, USA, 2019. Association for Computing Machinery. https://doi.org/10.1145/3331184.3331282.

Lorik Dumani, Patrick J. Neumann, and Ralf Schenkel. A framework for argument retrieval. In Joemon M. Jose, Emine Yilmaz, João Magalhães, Pablo Castells, Nicola Ferro, Mário J. Silva, and Flávio Martins, editors, *Advances in Information Retrieval*, pages 431–445, Cham, 2020. Springer International Publishing. https://doi.org/10.1007/978-3-030-45439-5_29.

Phan Minh Dung. On the acceptability of arguments and its fundamental role in nonmonotonic reasoning, logic programming and n-person games. *Artificial Intelligence*, 77(2):321–357, September 1995. https://doi.org/10.1016/0004-3702(94)00041-X.

Esin Durmus and Claire Cardie. Exploring the role of prior beliefs for argument persuasion. In *Proceedings of the 2018 Conference of the North American Chapter of the Association for Computational Linguistics: Human Language Technologies, Volume 1 (Long Papers)*, pages 1035–1045, New Orleans, Louisiana, June 2018a. Association for Computational Linguistics. https://doi.org/10.18653/v1/N18-1094.

Esin Durmus and Claire Cardie. Understanding the effect of gender and stance in opinion expression in debates on "abortion". In Malvina Nissim, Viviana Patti, Barbara Plank, and Claudia Wagner, editors, *Proceedings of the Second Workshop on Computational Modeling of People's Opinions, Personality, and Emotions in Social Media*, pages 69–75, New Orleans, Louisiana, USA, June 2018b. Association for Computational Linguistics. https://doi.org/10.18653/v1/W18-1110.

Esin Durmus and Claire Cardie. A corpus for modeling user and language effects in argumentation on online debating. In Anna Korhonen, David Traum, and Lluís Màrquez, editors, *Proceedings of the 57th Annual Meeting of the Association for Computational Linguistics*, pages 602–607, Florence, Italy, July 2019. Association for Computational Linguistics. https://doi.org/10.18653/v1/P19-1057.

Esin Durmus, Faisal Ladhak, and Claire Cardie. Determining relative argument specificity and stance for complex argumentative structures. In Anna Korhonen, David Traum, and Lluís Màrquez, editors, *Proceedings of the 57th Annual Meeting of the Association for Computational Linguistics*, pages 4630–4641, Florence, Italy, July 2019. Association for Computational Linguistics. https://doi.org/10.18653/v1/P19-1456.

Mihai Dusmanu, Elena Cabrio, and Serena Villata. Argument mining on Twitter: Arguments, facts and sources. In Martha Palmer, Rebecca Hwa, and Sebastian Riedel, editors, *Proceedings of the 2017 Conference on Empirical Methods in Natural Language Processing*, pages 2317–2322, Copenhagen, Denmark, September 2017. Association for Computational Linguistics. https://doi.org/10.18653/v1/D17-1245.

Rory Duthie, Katarzyna Budzynska, and Chris Reed. Mining ethos in political debate. In *Computational Models of Argument*, pages 299–310. IOS Press, 2016. https://doi.org/10.3233/978-1-61499-686-6-299.

Judith Eckle-Kohler, Roland Kluge, and Iryna Gurevych. On the role of discourse markers for discriminating claims and premises in argumentative discourse. In *Proceedings of the 2015 Conference on Empirical Methods in Natural Language Processing*, pages 2236–2242, 2015. https://doi.org/10.18653/v1/D15-1267.

Jack Edmonds. Optimum branchings. *Journal of Research of the National Bureau of Standards*, 718:233–240, 1967.

Charlie Egan, Advaith Siddharthan, and Adam Wyner. Summarising the points made in online political debates. In Chris Reed, editor, *Proceedings of the Third Workshop on Argument Mining (ArgMining2016)*, pages 134–143, Berlin, Germany, August 2016. Association for Computational Linguistics. https://doi.org/10.18653/v1/W16-2816.

Ryo Egawa, Gaku Morio, and Katsuhide Fujita. Corpus for modeling user interactions in online persuasive discussions. In Nicoletta Calzolari, Frédéric Béchet, Philippe Blache, Khalid Choukri, Christopher Cieri, Thierry Declerck, Sara Goggi, Hitoshi Isahara, Bente Maegaard, Joseph Mariani, Hélène Mazo, Asuncion Moreno, Jan Odijk, and Stelios Piperidis, editors, *Proceedings of the Twelfth Language Resources and Evaluation Conference*, pages 1135–1141, Marseille, France, May 2020. European Language Resources Association. ISBN 979-10-95546-34-4. URL https://aclanthology.org/2020.lrec-1.143/.

Steffen Eger, Johannes Daxenberger, and Iryna Gurevych. Neural end-to-end learning for computational argumentation mining. In Regina Barzilay and Min-Yen Kan, editors, *Proceedings of the 55th Annual Meeting of the Association for Computational Linguistics (Volume 1: Long Papers)*, pages 11–22, Vancouver, Canada, July 2017. Association for Computational Linguistics. https://doi.org/10.18653/v1/P17-1002.

Steffen Eger, Johannes Daxenberger, Christian Stab, and Iryna Gurevych. Cross-lingual argumentation mining: Machine translation (and a bit of projection) is all you need! In Emily M. Bender, Leon Derczynski, and Pierre Isabelle, editors, *Proceedings of the 27th International Conference on Computational Linguistics*, pages 831–844, Santa Fe, New Mexico, USA, August 2018. Association for Computational Linguistics. URL https://aclanthology.org/C18-1071/.

Ekkehard Eggs. Vertextungsmuster Argumentation: Logische Grundlagen. In Klaus Brinker, editor, *Text- und Gesprächslinguistik*, volume 16 of *Handbücher zur Sprach- und Kommunikationswissenschaft*, pages 397–414. Walter de Gruyter, Berlin, 2000. https://doi.org/10.1515/9783110194067-041.

Liat Ein Dor, Alon Halfon, Yoav Kantor, Ran Levy, Yosi Mass, Ruty Rinott, Eyal Shnarch, and Noam Slonim. Semantic relatedness of Wikipedia concepts – benchmark data and a working solution. In Nicoletta Calzolari, Khalid Choukri, Christopher Cieri, Thierry Declerck, Sara Goggi, Koiti Hasida, Hitoshi Isahara, Bente Maegaard, Joseph Mariani, Hélène Mazo, Asuncion Moreno, Jan Odijk, Stelios Piperidis, and Takenobu Tokunaga, editors, *Proceedings of the Eleventh International Conference on Language Resources and Evaluation (LREC 2018)*, pages 2571–2575, Miyazaki, Japan, May 2018. European Language Resources Association (ELRA). URL https://aclanthology.org/L18-1408/.

Liat Ein-Dor, Eyal Shnarch, Lena Dankin, Alon Halfon, Benjamin Sznajder, Ariel Gera, Carlos Alzate, Martin Gleize, Leshem Choshen, Yufang Hou, Yonatan Bilu, Ranit Aharonov, and Noam Slonim. Corpus wide argument mining—a working solution. *Proceedings of the AAAI Conference on Artificial Intelligence*, 34(05):7683–7691, Apr. 2020. https://doi.org/10.1609/aaai.v34i05.6270.

Roxanne El Baff, Henning Wachsmuth, Khalid Al-Khatib, and Benno Stein. Challenge or empower: Revisiting argumentation quality in a news editorial corpus. In *Proceedings of the 22nd*

Conference on Computational Natural Language Learning, pages 454–464, Brussels, Belgium, October 2018. Association for Computational Linguistics. https://doi.org/10.18653/v1/K18-1044.

Roxanne El Baff, Henning Wachsmuth, Khalid Al Khatib, Manfred Stede, and Benno Stein. Computational argumentation synthesis as a language modeling task. In *Proceedings of the 12th International Conference on Natural Language Generation*, pages 54–64, Tokyo, Japan, October - November 2019. Association for Computational Linguistics. https://doi.org/10.18653/v1/W19-8607.

Roxanne El Baff, Khalid Al Khatib, Benno Stein, and Henning Wachsmuth. Persuasiveness of news editorials depending on ideology and personality. In Malvina Nissim, Viviana Patti, Barbara Plank, and Esin Durmus, editors, *Proceedings of the Third Workshop on Computational Modeling of People's Opinions, Personality, and Emotion's in Social Media*, pages 29–40, Barcelona, Spain (Online), December 2020a. Association for Computational Linguistics. URL https://aclanthology.org/2020.peoples-1.4.

Roxanne El Baff, Henning Wachsmuth, Khalid Al Khatib, and Benno Stein. Analyzing the persuasive effect of style in news editorial argumentation. In *Proceedings of the 58th Annual Meeting of the Association for Computational Linguistics*, pages 3154–3160, Online, July 2020b. Association for Computational Linguistics. https://doi.org/10.18653/v1/2020.acl-main.287.

Roxanne El Baff, Khalid Al Khatib, Milad Alshomary, Kai Konen, Benno Stein, and Henning Wachsmuth. Improving argument effectiveness across ideologies using instruction-tuned large language models. In Yaser Al-Onaizan, Mohit Bansal, and Yun-Nung Chen, editors, *Findings of the Association for Computational Linguistics: EMNLP 2024*, pages 4604–4622, Miami, Florida, USA, November 2024. Association for Computational Linguistics. https://doi.org/10.18653/v1/2024.findings-emnlp.265.

Mohamed Elaraby, Diane Litman, Xiang Lorraine Li, and Ahmed Magooda. Persuasiveness of generated free-text rationales in subjective decisions: A case study on pairwise argument ranking. In Yaser Al-Onaizan, Mohit Bansal, and Yun-Nung Chen, editors, *Findings of the Association for Computational Linguistics: EMNLP 2024*, pages 14311–14329, Miami, Florida, USA, November 2024. Association for Computational Linguistics. https://doi.org/10.18653/v1/2024.findings-emnlp.836.

Sofiane Elguendouze, Lucas Anastasiou, Erwan Hain, Elena Cabrio, Anna De Liddo, and Serena Villata. AM4DSP: Argumentation mining in structured decentralized discussion platforms for deliberative democracy. In *Proceedings of the 2025 Conference on Empirical Methods in Natural Language Processing: System Demonstrations*, pages 796–805, 2025. https://doi.org/10.18653/v1/2025.emnlp-demos.61.

Arpad E. Elo. *The Rating of Chessplayers, Past and Present.* Acro Publishing, Inc., New York, 1978. ISBN 9780668047210.

Denis Emelin, Ronan Le Bras, Jena D. Hwang, Maxwell Forbes, and Yejin Choi. Moral stories: Situated reasoning about norms, intents, actions, and their consequences. In Marie-Francine Moens, Xuanjing Huang, Lucia Specia, and Scott Wen-Tau Yih, editors, *Proceedings of the 2021 Conference on Empirical Methods in Natural Language Processing*, pages 698–718, Online and Punta Cana, Dominican Republic, November 2021. Association for Computational Linguistics. https://doi.org/10.18653/v1/2021.emnlp-main.54.

Luke Emmet and George Cleland. Graphical notations, narratives and persuasion: A pliant systems approach to hypertext tool design. In *Proceedings of the Conference on Hypertext and Hypermedia*, pages 55–64, 2002. https://doi.org/10.1145/513338.513354.

Rob Ennals, Dan Byler, John Mark Agosta, and Barbara Rosario. What is disputed on the web? In *Proceedings of the 4th Workshop on Information Credibility*, WICOW '10, pages 67–74, New

York, NY, USA, April 2010a. Association for Computing Machinery. https://doi.org/10.1145/1772938.1772952.

Rob Ennals, Beth Trushkowsky, and John Mark Agosta. Highlighting disputed claims on the web. In *Proceedings of the 19th International Conference on World Wide Web*, pages 341–350, Raleigh North Carolina USA, April 2010b. Association for Computing Machinery. https://doi.org/10.1145/1772690.1772726.

Robert M. Entman. Framing: Toward clarification of a fractured paradigm. *Journal of Communication*, 43(4):51–58, 1993. https://doi.org/10.1111/j.1460-2466.1993.tb01304.x.

Günes Erkan and Dragomir R. Radev. LexRank: Graph-based lexical centrality as salience in text summarization. *Journal of Artifical Intelligence Research*, 22(1):457–479, December 2004. https://doi.org/10.1613/jair.1523.

Katharina Esau, Dannica Fleuß, and Sarah-Michelle Nienhaus. Different arenas, different deliberative quality? Using a systemic framework to evaluate online deliberation on immigration policy in germany. *Policy & Internet*, 13(1):86–112, 2021. https://doi.org/10.1002/poi3.232.

Natalia Evgrafova, Loic De Langhe, Véronique Hoste, and Els Lefever. Stance-aware definition generation for argumentative texts. In Elena Chistova, Philipp Cimiano, Shohreh Haddadan, Gabriella Lapesa, and Ramon Ruiz-Dolz, editors, *Proceedings of the 12th Argument Mining Workshop*, pages 168–180, Vienna, Austria, July 2025. Association for Computational Linguistics. https://doi.org/10.18653/v1/2025.argmining-1.16.

Jeanne Fahnestock. *Rhetorical Style: The Uses of Language in Persuasion.* Oxford University Press, Oxford, 2011. ISBN 9780199764129. https://doi.org/10.1093/acprof:oso/9780199764129.001.0001.

Agnieszka Falenska, Eva Maria Vecchi, and Gabriella Lapesa. Self-reported demographics and discourse dynamics in a persuasive online forum. In Nicoletta Calzolari, Min-Yen Kan, Veronique Hoste, Alessandro Lenci, Sakriani Sakti, and Nianwen Xue, editors, *Proceedings of the 2024 Joint International Conference on Computational Linguistics, Language Resources and Evaluation (LREC-COLING 2024)*, pages 14606–14621, Torino, Italia, May 2024. ELRA and ICCL. URL https://aclanthology.org/2024.lrec-main.1272/.

Neele Falk and Gabriella Lapesa. Scaling up discourse quality annotation for political science. In Nicoletta Calzolari, Frédéric Béchet, Philippe Blache, Khalid Choukri, Christopher Cieri, Thierry Declerck, Sara Goggi, Hitoshi Isahara, Bente Maegaard, Joseph Mariani, Hélène Mazo, Jan Odijk, and Stelios Piperidis, editors, *Proceedings of the Thirteenth Language Resources and Evaluation Conference*, pages 3301–3318, Marseille, France, June 2022. European Language Resources Association. URL https://aclanthology.org/2022.lrec-1.353/.

Neele Falk and Gabriella Lapesa. Bridging argument quality and deliberative quality annotations with adapters. In *Findings of the Association for Computational Linguistics: EACL 2023*, pages 2469–2488, Dubrovnik, Croatia, May 2023. Association for Computational Linguistics. https://doi.org/10.18653/v1/2023.findings-eacl.187.

Neele Falk, Iman Jundi, Eva Maria Vecchi, and Gabriella Lapesa. Predicting moderation of deliberative arguments: Is argument quality the key? In *Proceedings of the 8th Workshop on Argument Mining*, pages 133–141, Punta Cana, Dominican Republic, November 2021. Association for Computational Linguistics. https://doi.org/10.18653/v1/2021.argmining-1.13.

Angela Fan, Mike Lewis, and Yann Dauphin. Hierarchical neural story generation. In Iryna Gurevych and Yusuke Miyao, editors, *Proceedings of the 56th Annual Meeting of the Association for Computational Linguistics (Volume 1: Long Papers)*, pages 889–898, Melbourne, Australia, July 2018. Association for Computational Linguistics. https://doi.org/10.18653/v1/P18-1082.

Lisa Fan, Marshall White, Eva Sharma, Ruisi Su, Prafulla Kumar Choubey, Ruihong Huang, and Lu Wang. In plain sight: Media bias through the lens of factual reporting. In Kentaro Inui, Jing Jiang, Vincent Ng, and Xiaojun Wan, editors, *Proceedings of the 2019 Conference on*

Empirical Methods in Natural Language Processing and the 9th International Joint Conference on Natural Language Processing (EMNLP-IJCNLP), pages 6343–6349, Hong Kong, China, November 2019. Association for Computational Linguistics. https://doi.org/10.18653/v1/D19-1664.

Youmna Farag, Charlotte Brand, Jacopo Amidei, Paul Piwek, Tom Stafford, Svetlana Stoyanchev, and Andreas Vlachos. Opening up minds with argumentative dialogues. In Yoav Goldberg, Zornitsa Kozareva, and Yue Zhang, editors, *Findings of the Association for Computational Linguistics: EMNLP 2022*, pages 4569–4582, Abu Dhabi, United Arab Emirates, December 2022. Association for Computational Linguistics. https://doi.org/10.18653/v1/2022.findings-emnlp.335.

Adam Robert Faulkner. *Automated Classification of Argument Stance in Student Essays: A Linguistically Motivated Approach with an Application for Supporting Argument Summarization*. PhD thesis, City University of New York, 2014. URL https://academicworks.cuny.edu/gc_etds/204.

Marc Feger and Stefan Dietze. BERTweet's TACO fiesta: Contrasting flavors on the path of inference and information-driven argument mining on Twitter. In Kevin Duh, Helena Gomez, and Steven Bethard, editors, *Findings of the Association for Computational Linguistics: NAACL 2024*, pages 2256–2266, Mexico City, Mexico, June 2024a. Association for Computational Linguistics. https://doi.org/10.18653/v1/2024.findings-naacl.146.

Marc Feger and Stefan Dietze. TACO – Twitter arguments from COnversations. In Nicoletta Calzolari, Min-Yen Kan, Veronique Hoste, Alessandro Lenci, Sakriani Sakti, and Nianwen Xue, editors, *Proceedings of the 2024 Joint International Conference on Computational Linguistics, Language Resources and Evaluation (LREC-COLING 2024)*, pages 15522–15529, Torino, Italia, May 2024b. ELRA and ICCL. URL https://aclanthology.org/2024.lrec-main.1349/.

Marc Feger, Katarina Boland, and Stefan Dietze. Limited generalizability in argument mining: State-of-the-art models learn datasets, not arguments. In Wanxiang Che, Joyce Nabende, Ekaterina Shutova, and Mohammad Taher Pilehvar, editors, *Proceedings of the 63rd Annual Meeting of the Association for Computational Linguistics (Volume 1: Long Papers)*, pages 23900–23915, Vienna, Austria, July 2025. Association for Computational Linguistics. https://doi.org/10.18653/v1/2025.acl-long.1164.

Shangbin Feng, Chan Young Park, Yuhan Liu, and Yulia Tsvetkov. From pretraining data to language models to downstream tasks: Tracking the trails of political biases leading to unfair NLP models. In Anna Rogers, Jordan Boyd-Graber, and Naoaki Okazaki, editors, *Proceedings of the 61st Annual Meeting of the Association for Computational Linguistics (Volume 1: Long Papers)*, pages 11737–11762, Toronto, Canada, July 2023. Association for Computational Linguistics. https://doi.org/10.18653/v1/2023.acl-long.656.

Vanessa Wei Feng and Graeme Hirst. Classifying arguments by scheme. In Dekang Lin, Yuji Matsumoto, and Rada Mihalcea, editors, *Proceedings of the 49th Annual Meeting of the Association for Computational Linguistics: Human Language Technologies*, pages 987–996, Portland, Oregon, USA, June 2011. Association for Computational Linguistics. URL https://aclanthology.org/P11-1099/.

Alfio Ferrara, Sergio Picascia, and Elisabetta Rocchetti. A discussion on open issues regarding human value detection in arguments. In D. Calvanese, C. Diamantini, G. Faggioli, N. Ferro, S. Marchesin, G. Silvello, and L. Tanca, editors, *SEBD 2023: 31st Symposium of Advanced Database Systems*, volume 3478 of *CEUR Workshop Proceedings*, pages 120–132. CEUR-WS.org, 2023. URL https://ceur-ws.org/Vol-3478/paper36.pdf.

Jenny Rose Finkel and Christopher D. Manning. Nested named entity recognition. In Philipp Koehn and Rada Mihalcea, editors, *Proceedings of the 2009 Conference on Empirical Methods in Natural Language Processing*, pages 141–150, Singapore, August 2009. Association for Computational Linguistics. URL https://aclanthology.org/D09-1015/.

Beatriz Fisas, Horacio Saggion, and Francesco Ronzano. On the discoursive structure of computer graphics research papers. In Adam Meyers, Ines Rehbein, and Heike Zinsmeister, editors, *Proceedings of the 9th Linguistic Annotation Workshop*, pages 42–51, Denver, Colorado, USA, June 2015. Association for Computational Linguistics. https://doi.org/10.3115/v1/W15-1605.

Beatriz Fisas, Francesco Ronzano, and Horacio Saggion. A multi-layered annotated corpus of scientific papers. In Nicoletta Calzolari, Khalid Choukri, Thierry Declerck, Sara Goggi, Marko Grobelnik, Bente Maegaard, Joseph Mariani, Helene Mazo, Asuncion Moreno, Jan Odijk, and Stelios Piperidis, editors, *Proceedings of the Tenth International Conference on Language Resources and Evaluation (LREC'16)*, pages 3081–3088, Portorož, Slovenia, May 2016. European Language Resources Association (ELRA). URL https://aclanthology.org/L16-1492/.

Irina Fishcheva and Evgeny Kotelnikov. Cross-lingual argumentation mining for Russian texts. In *Analysis of Images, Social Networks and Texts*, pages 134–144, Cham, 2019. Springer International Publishing. https://doi.org/10.1007/978-3-030-37334-4_12.

Susan T. Fiske. Stereotyping, prejudice, and discrimination. In *The Handbook of Social Psychology*, volume 1-2, pages 357–411. McGraw-Hill, New York, NY, US, 4 edition, 1998. ISBN 978-0-19-521376-8.

James B. Freeman. *Dialectics and the Macrostructure of Argument.* Foris, Berlin, 1991.

James B. Freeman. *Argument Structure: Representation and Theory*, volume 18 of *Argumentation Library*. Springer, 2011. ISSN 978-94-007-0356-8. https://doi.org/10.1007/978-94-007-0357-5.

Roni Friedman, Lena Dankin, Yufang Hou, Ranit Aharonov, Yoav Katz, and Noam Slonim. Overview of the 2021 key point analysis shared task. In Khalid Al-Khatib, Yufang Hou, and Manfred Stede, editors, *Proceedings of the 8th Workshop on Argument Mining*, pages 154–164, Punta Cana, Dominican Republic, November 2021. Association for Computational Linguistics. https://doi.org/10.18653/v1/2021.argmining-1.16.

Michael Fromm, Evgeniy Faerman, Max Berrendorf, Siddharth Bhargava, Ruoxia Qi, Yao Zhang, Lukas Dennert, Sophia Selle, Yang Mao, and Thomas Seidl. Argument mining driven analysis of peer-reviews. *Proceedings of the AAAI Conference on Artificial Intelligence*, 35(6):4758–4766, May 2021. https://doi.org/10.1609/aaai.v35i6.16607.

Michael Fromm, Max Berrendorf, Evgeniy Faerman, and Thomas Seidl. Cross-domain argument quality estimation. In *Findings of the Association for Computational Linguistics: ACL 2023*, pages 13435–13448, Toronto, Canada, July 2023. Association for Computational Linguistics. https://doi.org/10.18653/v1/2023.findings-acl.848.

Yujie Fu, Yang Li, Suge Wang, Xiaoli Li, Deyu Li, Jian Liao, and JianXing Zheng. Hierarchical enhancement framework for aspect-based argument mining. In Houda Bouamor, Juan Pino, and Kalika Bali, editors, *Findings of the Association for Computational Linguistics: EMNLP 2023*, pages 1423–1433, Singapore, December 2023. Association for Computational Linguistics. https://doi.org/10.18653/v1/2023.findings-emnlp.99.

Saadia Gabriel, Chandra Bhagavatula, Vered Shwartz, Ronan Le Bras, Maxwell Forbes, and Yejin Choi. Paragraph-level commonsense transformers with recurrent memory. In *Proceedings of the Thirty-Fifth AAAI Conference on Artificial Intelligence, AAAI 2021*, pages 12857–12865. AAAI Press, 2021. https://doi.org/10.1609/AAAI.V35I14.17521.

Ewelina Gajewska, Katarzyna Budzynska, and Barbara Konat. Analytics for rhetorical arguments in discussions on polarised issues. In *Computational Models of Argument*, pages 351–352. IOS Press, 2024. https://doi.org/10.3233/FAIA240335.

Andrea Galassi, Marco Lippi, and Paolo Torroni. Argumentative link prediction using residual networks and multi-objective learning. In Noam Slonim and Ranit Aharonov, editors, *Proceed-*

ings of the 5th Workshop on Argument Mining, pages 1–10, Brussels, Belgium, November 2018. Association for Computational Linguistics. https://doi.org/10.18653/v1/W18-5201.

Margherita Gambini, Caterina Senette, Tiziano Fagni, and Maurizio Tesconi. Evaluating large language models for user stance detection on X (Twitter). *Machine Learning*, 113:7243–7266, 2024. https://doi.org/10.1007/s10994-024-06587-y.

Kavita Ganesan, ChengXiang Zhai, and Jiawei Han. Opinosis: A graph based approach to abstractive summarization of highly redundant opinions. In Chu-Ren Huang and Dan Jurafsky, editors, *Proceedings of the 23rd International Conference on Computational Linguistics (COLING 2010)*, pages 340–348, Beijing, China, August 2010. COLING 2010 Organizing Committee. URL https://aclanthology.org/C10-1039/.

Alejandro J. García and Guillermo R. Simari. Defeasible logic programming: DeLP-servers, contextual queries, and explanations for answers. *Argument & Computation*, 5(1):63–88, January 2014. https://doi.org/10.1080/19462166.2013.869767.

Albert Gatt and Ehud Reiter. SimpleNLG: A realisation engine for practical applications. In Emiel Krahmer and Mariët Theune, editors, *Proceedings of the 12th European Workshop on Natural Language Generation (ENLG 2009)*, pages 90–93, Athens, Greece, March 2009. Association for Computational Linguistics. URL https://aclanthology.org/W09-0613.

Debela Gemechu and Chris Reed. Decompositional argument mining: A general purpose approach for argument graph construction. In Anna Korhonen, David Traum, and Lluís Màrquez, editors, *Proceedings of the 57th Annual Meeting of the Association for Computational Linguistics*, pages 516–526, Florence, Italy, July 2019. Association for Computational Linguistics. https://doi.org/10.18653/v1/P19-1049.

Debela Gemechu and Chris Reed. CU-MAM: Coherence-driven unified macro-structures for argument mining. In Wanxiang Che, Joyce Nabende, Ekaterina Shutova, and Mohammad Taher Pilehvar, editors, *Proceedings of the 63rd Annual Meeting of the Association for Computational Linguistics (Volume 1: Long Papers)*, pages 19731–19749, Vienna, Austria, July 2025. Association for Computational Linguistics. https://doi.org/10.18653/v1/2025.acl-long.969.

Debela Gemechu, Ramon Ruiz-Dolz, and Chris Reed. ARIES: A general benchmark for argument relation identification. In Yamen Ajjour, Roy Bar-Haim, Roxanne El Baff, Zhexiong Liu, and Gabriella Skitalinskaya, editors, *Proceedings of the 11th Workshop on Argument Mining (ArgMining 2024)*, pages 1–14, Bangkok, Thailand, August 2024. Association for Computational Linguistics. https://doi.org/10.18653/v1/2024.argmining-1.1.

Debela Gemechu, Ramon Ruiz-Dolz, Henrike Beyer, and Chris Reed. Natural language reasoning in large language models: Analysis and evaluation. In Wanxiang Che, Joyce Nabende, Ekaterina Shutova, and Mohammad Taher Pilehvar, editors, *Findings of the Association for Computational Linguistics: ACL 2025*, pages 3717–3741, Vienna, Austria, July 2025. Association for Computational Linguistics. https://doi.org/10.18653/v1/2025.findings-acl.192.

Marlené Gerber, André Bächtiger, Susumu Shikano, Simon Reber, and Samuel Rohr. Deliberative abilities and influence in a transnational deliberative poll (EuroPolis). *British Journal of Political Science*, 48(4):1093–1118, 2018. https://doi.org/10.1017/S0007123416000144.

Debanjan Ghosh and Beata Beigman Klebanov. Automatic evaluation of argumentative writing by young students, July 2024. US Patent 12,046,155.

Debanjan Ghosh, Smaranda Muresan, Nina Wacholder, Mark Aakhus, and Matthew Mitsui. Analyzing argumentative discourse units in online interactions. In Nancy Green, Kevin Ashley, Diane Litman, Chris Reed, and Vern Walker, editors, *Proceedings of the First Workshop on Argumentation Mining*, pages 39–48, Baltimore, Maryland, June 2014. Association for Computational Linguistics. https://doi.org/10.3115/v1/W14-2106.

Martin Gleize, Eyal Shnarch, Leshem Choshen, Lena Dankin, Guy Moshkowich, Ranit Aharonov, and Noam Slonim. Are you convinced? Choosing the more convincing evidence with a Siamese network. In *Proceedings of the 57th Annual Meeting of the Association for Computational Linguistics*, pages 967–976, Florence, Italy, July 2019. Association for Computational Linguistics. https://doi.org/10.18653/v1/P19-1093.

Max Glockner, Yufang Hou, Preslav Nakov, and Iryna Gurevych. Missci: Reconstructing fallacies in misrepresented science. In Lun-Wei Ku, Andre Martins, and Vivek Srikumar, editors, *Proceedings of the 62nd Annual Meeting of the Association for Computational Linguistics (Volume 1: Long Papers)*, pages 4372–4405, Bangkok, Thailand, August 2024. Association for Computational Linguistics. https://doi.org/10.18653/v1/2024.acl-long.240.

Max Glockner, Yufang Hou, Preslav Nakov, and Iryna Gurevych. Grounding fallacies misrepresenting scientific publications in evidence. In Luis Chiruzzo, Alan Ritter, and Lu Wang, editors, *Proceedings of the 2025 Conference of the Nations of the Americas Chapter of the Association for Computational Linguistics: Human Language Technologies (Volume 1: Long Papers)*, pages 9732–9767, Albuquerque, New Mexico, April 2025. Association for Computational Linguistics. https://doi.org/10.18653/v1/2025.naacl-long.491.

Pierpaolo Goffredo, Shohreh Haddadan, Vorakit Vorakitphan, Elena Cabrio, and Serena Villata. Fallacious argument classification in political debates. In Lud De Raedt, editor, *Proceedings of the Thirty-First International Joint Conference on Artificial Intelligence, IJCAI-22*, pages 4143–4149. International Joint Conferences on Artificial Intelligence Organization, 7 2022. https://doi.org/10.24963/ijcai.2022/575. Main Track.

Pierpaolo Goffredo, Mariana Chaves, Serena Villata, and Elena Cabrio. Argument-based detection and classification of fallacies in political debates. In Houda Bouamor, Juan Pino, and Kalika Bali, editors, *Proceedings of the 2023 Conference on Empirical Methods in Natural Language Processing*, pages 11101–11112, Singapore, December 2023. Association for Computational Linguistics. https://doi.org/10.18653/v1/2023.emnlp-main.684.

Valentin Gold, Mennatallah El-Assady, Tina Bögel, Christian Rohrdantz, Miriam Butt, Katharina Holzinger, and Daniel Keim. Visual linguistic analysis of political discussions: Measuring deliberative quality. *Digital Scholarship in the Humanities*, 32(1):141–158, 2017. https://doi.org/10.1093/llc/fqv033.

Lewis R. Goldberg. An alternative "description of personality": The Big-Five factor structure. *Journal of Personality and Social Psychology*, 59(6):1216–1229, 1990. https://doi.org/10.1037/0022-3514.59.6.1216.

Seraphina Goldfarb-Tarrant, Tuhin Chakrabarty, Ralph Weischedel, and Nanyun Peng. Content planning for neural story generation with Aristotelian rescoring. In Bonnie Webber, Trevor Cohn, Yulan He, and Yang Liu, editors, *Proceedings of the 2020 Conference on Empirical Methods in Natural Language Processing (EMNLP)*, pages 4319–4338, Online, November 2020. Association for Computational Linguistics. https://doi.org/10.18653/v1/2020.emnlp-main.351.

Tim Gorichanaz. Virtuous search: A framework for intellectual virtue in online search. *Journal of the Association for Information Science and Technology*, 75(5):538–549, 2024. https://doi.org/10.1002/asi.24832.

Deniz Gorur, Antonio Rago, and Francesca Toni. Can large language models perform relation-based argument mining? In Owen Rambow, Leo Wanner, Marianna Apidianaki, Hend Al-Khalifa, Barbara Di Eugenio, and Steven Schockaert, editors, *Proceedings of the 31st International Conference on Computational Linguistics*, pages 8518–8534, Abu Dhabi, UAE, January 2025. Association for Computational Linguistics. URL https://aclanthology.org/2025.coling-main.569/.

Theodosis Goudas, Christos Louizos, Georgios Petasis, and Vangelis Karkaletsis. Argument extraction from news, blogs, and social media. In Aristidis Likas, Konstantinos Blekas, and Dimitris Kalles, editors, *Proceedings of the Hellenic Conference on Artificial Intelligence*, pages 287–299, 2014. https://doi.org/10.1007/978-3-319-07064-3_23.

Trudy Govier. *A Practical Study of Argument.* Wadsworth, Cengage Learning, Belmont, CA, 7th edition, 2010.

Trudy Govier. More on counter-considerations. In *Proceedings of the Conference of the Ontario Society for the Study of Argumentation*, pages 1–10, 2011.

Jesse Graham, Jonathan Haidt, Sena Koleva, Matt Motyl, Ravi Iyer, Sean P Wojcik, and Peter H Ditto. Moral foundations theory: The pragmatic validity of moral pluralism. In *Advances in Experimental Social Psychology*, volume 47, pages 55–130. Elsevier, 2013. https://doi.org/10.1016/B978-0-12-407236-7.00002-4.

Sylviane Granger. The International Corpus of Learner English: A new resource for foreign language learning and teaching and second language acquisition research. *TESOL Quarterly*, 37(3):538–546, 2003. https://doi.org/10.2307/3588404.

Sylviane Granger, Estelle Dagneaux, Fanny Meunier, and Magali Paquot, editors. *International Corpus of Learner English.* version 2, Presses universitaires de Louvain, 2009. ISBN 978-2-87463-143-6.

Adam Grant. *Think again: The power of knowing what you don't know.* Penguin, 2023. ISBN 9781984878106.

Floriana Grasso, Alison Cawsey, and Ray Jones. Dialectical argumentation to solve conflicts in advice giving: A case study in the promotion of healthy nutrition. *International Journal of Human-Computer Studies*, 53(6):1077–1115, 2000. https://doi.org/10.1006/ijhc.2000.0429.

Aaron Grattafiori, Abhimanyu Dubey, Abhinav Jauhri, Abhinav Pandey, Abhishek Kadian, Ahmad Al-Dahle, Aiesha Letman, Akhil Mathur, Alan Schelten, Alex Vaughan, Amy Yang, Angela Fan, Anirudh Goyal, Anthony Hartshorn, Aobo Yang, Archi Mitra, Archie Sravankumar, Artem Korenev, Arthur Hinsvark, and Arun Rao et al. The Llama 3 herd of models, 2024. https://doi.org/10.48550/arXiv.2407.21783.

Edouard Grave, Piotr Bojanowski, Prakhar Gupta, Armand Joulin, and Tomas Mikolov. Learning word vectors for 157 languages. In *Proceedings of the International Conference on Language Resources and Evaluation (LREC 2018)*, 2018. URL https://aclanthology.org/L18-1550.pdf.

Nancy Green. Representation of argumentation in text with Rhetorical Structure Theory. *Argumentation*, 24:181–196, 2010. https://doi.org/10.1007/s10503-009-9169-4.

Nancy Green. Identifying argumentation schemes in genetics research articles. In Claire Cardie, editor, *Proceedings of the 2nd Workshop on Argumentation Mining*, pages 12–21, Denver, CO, June 2015. Association for Computational Linguistics. https://doi.org/10.3115/v1/W15-0502.

Nancy Green. Manual identification of arguments with implicit conclusions using semantic rules for argument mining. In Ivan Habernal, Iryna Gurevych, Kevin Ashley, Claire Cardie, Nancy Green, Diane Litman, Georgios Petasis, Chris Reed, Noam Slonim, and Vern Walker, editors, *Proceedings of the 4th Workshop on Argument Mining*, pages 73–78, Copenhagen, Denmark, September 2017a. Association for Computational Linguistics. https://doi.org/10.18653/v1/W17-5109.

Nancy Green. Proposed method for annotation of scientific arguments in terms of semantic relations and argument schemes. In Noam Slonim and Ranit Aharonov, editors, *Proceedings of the 5th Workshop on Argument Mining*, pages 105–110, Brussels, Belgium, November 2018. Association for Computational Linguistics. https://doi.org/10.18653/v1/W18-5213.

Nancy Green, Rachael Dwight, Kanyamas Navoraphan, and Brian Stadler. Natural language generation of biomedical argumentation for lay audiences. *Argument & Computation*, 2(1):23–50, 2011. https://doi.org/10.1080/19462166.2010.515037.

Nancy L. Green. Argumentation scheme-based argument generation to support feedback in educational argument modeling systems. *International Journal of Artificial Intelligence in Education*, 27(3):515–533, 2017b. https://doi.org/10.1007/s40593-016-0115-y.

Nancy L. Green, Michael Branon, and Luke Roosje. Argument schemes and visualization software for critical thinking about international politics. *Argument & Computation*, 10(1):41–53, December 2018. https://doi.org/10.3233/aac-181003.

Anthony G. Greenwald, Debbie E. McGhee, and Jordan L. K. Schwartz. Measuring individual differences in implicit cognition: The implicit association test. *Journal of Personality and Social Psychology*, 74(6):1464–1480, 1998. https://doi.org/10.1037/0022-3514.74.6.1464.

Wayne Grennan. *Informal Logic: Issues and Techniques*. McGill-Queen's University Press, 1997.

Shai Gretz, Yonatan Bilu, Edo Cohen-Karlik, and Noam Slonim. The workweek is the best time to start a family – a study of GPT-2 based claim generation. In *Findings of the Association for Computational Linguistics: EMNLP 2020*, pages 528–544, Online, November 2020a. Association for Computational Linguistics. https://doi.org/10.18653/v1/2020.findings-emnlp.47.

Shai Gretz, Roni Friedman, Edo Cohen-Karlik, Assaf Toledo, Dan Lahav, Ranit Aharonov, and Noam Slonim. A large-scale dataset for argument quality ranking: Construction and analysis. In *Proceedings of the Thirty-Fourth AAAI Conference on Artificial Intelligence*, volume 34, issue 05, pages 7805–7813. AAAI, 2020b. https://doi.org/10.1609/aaai.v34i05.6285.

Barbara Grosz and Candace Sidner. Attention, intentions, and the structure of discourse. *Computational Linguistics*, 12(3):175–204, 1986.

Camelia Guerraoui, Paul Reisert, Naoya Inoue, Farjana Sultana Mim, Keshav Singh, Jungmin Choi, Irfan Robbani, Shoichi Naito, Wenzhi Wang, and Kentaro Inui. Teach me how to argue: A survey on NLP feedback systems in argumentation. In Milad Alshomary, Chung-Chi Chen, Smaranda Muresan, Joonsuk Park, and Julia Romberg, editors, *Proceedings of the 10th Workshop on Argument Mining*, pages 19–34, Singapore, December 2023. Association for Computational Linguistics. https://doi.org/10.18653/v1/2023.argmining-1.3.

Matteo Guida, Yulia Otmakhova, Eduard Hovy, and Lea Frermann. LLMs for argument mining: Detection, extraction, and relationship classification of pre-defined arguments in online comments. In Jonathan K. Kummerfeld, Aditya Joshi, and Mark Dras, editors, *Proceedings of the 23rd Annual Workshop of the Australasian Language Technology Association*, pages 176–191, Sydney, Australia, November 2025. Association for Computational Linguistics. URL https://aclanthology.org/2025.alta-main.12/.

Jia Guo, Liying Cheng, Wenxuan Zhang, Stanley Kok, Xin Li, and Lidong Bing. AQE: Argument quadruplet extraction via a quad-tagging augmented generative approach. In Anna Rogers, Jordan Boyd-Graber, and Naoaki Okazaki, editors, *Findings of the Association for Computational Linguistics: ACL 2023*, pages 932–946, Toronto, Canada, July 2023. Association for Computational Linguistics. https://doi.org/10.18653/v1/2023.findings-acl.59.

Shreya Gupta, Parantak Singh, Megha Sundriyal, Md. Shad Akhtar, and Tanmoy Chakraborty. LESA: Linguistic encapsulation and semantic amalgamation based generalised claim detection from online content. In Paola Merlo, Jorg Tiedemann, and Reut Tsarfaty, editors, *Proceedings of the 16th Conference of the European Chapter of the Association for Computational Linguistics: Main Volume*, pages 3178–3188, Online, April 2021. Association for Computational Linguistics. https://doi.org/10.18653/v1/2021.eacl-main.277.

Timon Gurcke, Milad Alshomary, and Henning Wachsmuth. Assessing the sufficiency of arguments through conclusion generation. In *Proceedings of the 8th Workshop on Argument Mining*, pages 67–77, Punta Cana, Dominican Republic, November 2021. Association for Computational Linguistics. https://doi.org/10.18653/v1/2021.argmining-1.7.

Omkar Gurjar, Agam Goyal, and Eshwar Chandrasekharan. ArgCMV: An argument summarization benchmark for the LLM-era. In Christos Christodoulopoulos, Tanmoy Chakraborty, Carolyn Rose, and Violet Peng, editors, *Proceedings of the 2025 Conference on Empirical Methods in*

Natural Language Processing, pages 21881–21894, Suzhou, China, November 2025. Association for Computational Linguistics. https://doi.org/10.18653/v1/2025.emnlp-main.1110.

Jürgen Habermas. *Theorie des kommunikativen Handelns*. Suhrkamp, Frankfurt, 1981.

Jürgen Habermas. *The Theory of Communicative Action, Vol. 1, Reason and the Rationalization of Society*. Polity, 1984. https://doi.org/10.2307/2185595.

Ivan Habernal and Iryna Gurevych. Exploiting debate portals for semi-supervised argumentation mining in user-generated Web discourse. In Lluís Màrquez, Chris Callison-Burch, and Jian Su, editors, *Proceedings of the 2015 Conference on Empirical Methods in Natural Language Processing*, pages 2127–2137, Lisbon, Portugal, September 2015. Association for Computational Linguistics. https://doi.org/10.18653/v1/D15-1255.

Ivan Habernal and Iryna Gurevych. Which argument is more convincing? Analyzing and predicting convincingness of Web arguments using bidirectional LSTM. In *Proceedings of the 54th Annual Meeting of the Association for Computational Linguistics (Volume 1: Long Papers)*, pages 1589–1599. Association for Computational Linguistics, 2016a. https://doi.org/10.18653/v1/P16-1150.

Ivan Habernal and Iryna Gurevych. What makes a convincing argument? Empirical analysis and detecting attributes of convincingness in Web argumentation. In Jian Su, Kevin Duh, and Xavier Carreras, editors, *Proceedings of the 2016 Conference on Empirical Methods in Natural Language Processing*, pages 1214–1223, Austin, Texas, November 2016b. Association for Computational Linguistics. https://doi.org/10.18653/v1/D16-1129.

Ivan Habernal and Iryna Gurevych. Argumentation mining in user-generated Web discourse. *Computational Linguistics*, 43(1):125–179, 2017. https://doi.org/10.1162/COLI_a_00276.

Ivan Habernal, Raffael Hannemann, Christian Pollak, Christopher Klamm, Patrick Pauli, and Iryna Gurevych. Argotario: Computational argumentation meets serious games. In Lucia Specia, Matt Post, and Michael Paul, editors, *Proceedings of the 2017 Conference on Empirical Methods in Natural Language Processing: System Demonstrations*, pages 7–12, Copenhagen, Denmark, September 2017. Association for Computational Linguistics. https://doi.org/10.18653/v1/D17-2002.

Ivan Habernal, Patrick Pauli, and Iryna Gurevych. Adapting serious game for fallacious argumentation to German: Pitfalls, insights, and best practices. In Nicoletta Calzolari, Khalid Choukri, Christopher Cieri, Thierry Declerck, Sara Goggi, Koiti Hasida, Hitoshi Isahara, Bente Maegaard, Joseph Mariani, Hélène Mazo, Asuncion Moreno, Jan Odijk, Stelios Piperidis, and Takenobu Tokunaga, editors, *Proceedings of the Eleventh International Conference on Language Resources and Evaluation (LREC 2018)*, pages 3329–3335, Miyazaki, Japan, May 2018a. European Language Resources Association (ELRA). URL https://aclanthology.org/L18-1526/.

Ivan Habernal, Henning Wachsmuth, Iryna Gurevych, and Benno Stein. Before name-calling: Dynamics and triggers of ad hominem fallacies in Web argumentation. In *Proceedings of the 2018 Conference of the North American Chapter of the Association for Computational Linguistics: Human Language Technologies, Volume 1 (Long Papers)*, pages 386–396. Association for Computational Linguistics, 2018b. https://doi.org/10.18653/v1/N18-1036.

Ivan Habernal, Henning Wachsmuth, Iryna Gurevych, and Benno Stein. The argument reasoning comprehension task: Identification and reconstruction of implicit warrants. In *Proceedings of the 2018 Conference of the North American Chapter of the Association for Computational Linguistics: Human Language Technologies, Volume 1 (Long Papers)*, pages 1930–1940. Association for Computational Linguistics, 2018c. https://doi.org/10.18653/v1/N18-1175.

Ivan Habernal, Henning Wachsmuth, Iryna Gurevych, and Benno Stein. SemEval-2018 task 12: The argument reasoning comprehension task. In Marianna Apidianaki, Saif M. Mohammad, Jonathan May, Ekaterina Shutova, Steven Bethard, and Marine Carpuat, editors, *Proceedings of the 12th International Workshop on Semantic Evaluation*, pages 763–772, New Orleans, Louisiana, June 2018d. Association for Computational Linguistics. https://doi.org/10.18653/v1/S18-1121.

Ivan Habernal, Daniel Faber, Nicola Recchia, Sebastian Bretthauer, Iryna Gurevych, Indra Spiecker genannt Döhmann, and Christoph Burchard. Mining legal arguments in court decisions. *Artificial Intelligence and Law*, 32:1–38, 2024. https://doi.org/10.1007/s10506-023-09361-y.

Shohreh Haddadan, Elena Cabrio, and Serena Villata. Yes, we can! Mining arguments in 50 years of US presidential campaign debates. In *Proceedings of the 57th Annual Meeting of the Association for Computational Linguistics*, pages 4684–4690, Florence, Italy, July 2019. Association for Computational Linguistics. https://doi.org/10.18653/v1/P19-1463.

Jonathan Haidt. *The Righteous Mind: Why Good People are Divided by Politics and Religion.* Vintage, 2012. ISBN 9780307455772.

Jonathan Haidt and Jesse Graham. When morality opposes justice: Conservatives have moral intuitions that liberals may not recognize. *Social Justice Research*, 20:98–116, 2007. https://doi.org/10.1007/s11211-007-0034-z.

Charles L. Hamblin. *Fallacies*. Methuen, London, UK, 1970.

Momchil Hardalov, Arnav Arora, Preslav Nakov, and Isabelle Augenstein. Cross-domain label-adaptive stance detection. In Marie-Francine Moens, Xuanjing Huang, Lucia Specia, and Scott Wen-Tau Yih, editors, *Proceedings of the 2021 Conference on Empirical Methods in Natural Language Processing*, pages 9011–9028, Online and Punta Cana, Dominican Republic, November 2021. Association for Computational Linguistics. https://doi.org/10.18653/v1/2021.emnlp-main.710.

Jelena Mitrović, Cliff O'Reilly, Miljana Mladenović, and Siegfried Handschuh. Ontological representations of rhetorical figures for argument mining. *Argument & Computation*, 8(3):267–287, 2017. https://doi.org/10.3233/AAC-170027.

Randy Allen Harris, Chrysanne Di Marco, Sebastian Ruan, and Cliff O'Reilly. An annotation scheme for Rhetorical Figures. *Argument & Computation*, 9(2):155–175, 2018. http://doi.org/10.3233/AAC-180037.

Mareike Hartmann, Tallulah Jansen, Isabelle Augenstein, and Anders Søgaard. Issue framing in online discussion fora. In Jill Burstein, Christy Doran, and Thamar Solorio, editors, *Proceedings of the 2019 Conference of the North American Chapter of the Association for Computational Linguistics: Human Language Technologies, Volume 1 (Long and Short Papers)*, pages 1401–1407, Minneapolis, Minnesota, June 2019. Association for Computational Linguistics. https://doi.org/10.18653/v1/N19-1142.

Kazi Saidul Hasan and Vincent Ng. Stance classification of ideological debates: Data, models, features, and constraints. In Ruslan Mitkov and Jong C. Park, editors, *Proceedings of the Sixth International Joint Conference on Natural Language Processing*, pages 1348–1356, Nagoya, Japan, October 2013. Asian Federation of Natural Language Processing. URL https://aclanthology.org/I13-1191/.

Kazi Saidul Hasan and Vincent Ng. Why are you taking this stance? Identifying and classifying reasons in ideological debates. In Alessandro Moschitti, Bo Pang, and Walter Daelemans, editors, *Proceedings of the 2014 Conference on Empirical Methods in Natural Language Processing (EMNLP)*, pages 751–762, Doha, Qatar, October 2014. Association for Computational Linguistics. https://doi.org/10.3115/v1/D14-1083.

Annette Hautli-Janisz and Miriam Butt. On the role of discourse particles for mining arguments in german dialogs. In *Proceedings of the COMMA 2016 workshop 'Foundations of the Language of Argumentation'*, pages 10–17, 2016. https://www.ling.uni-potsdam.de/comma2016/pdf/FLA16-proceedings.pdf#page=15.

Annette Hautli-Janisz, Zlata Kikteva, Wassiliki Siskou, Kamila Gorska, Ray Becker, and Chris Reed. QT30: A corpus of argument and conflict in broadcast debate. In Nicoletta Calzolari, Frédéric Béchet, Philippe Blache, Khalid Choukri, Christopher Cieri, Thierry Declerck, Sara Goggi, Hitoshi Isahara, Bente Maegaard, Joseph Mariani, Hélène Mazo, Jan Odijk, and Stelios Piperidis, editors, *Proceedings of the Thirteenth Language Resources and Evaluation Conference*, pages 3291–3300, Marseille, France, June 2022. European Language Resources Association. URL https://aclanthology.org/2022.lrec-1.352/.

Shirley Anugrah Hayati, Minhwa Lee, Dheeraj Rajagopal, and Dongyeop Kang. How far can we extract diverse perspectives from large language models? In Yaser Al-Onaizan, Mohit Bansal, and Yun-Nung Chen, editors, *Proceedings of the 2024 Conference on Empirical Methods in Natural Language Processing*, pages 5336–5366, Miami, Florida, USA, November 2024. Association for Computational Linguistics. https://doi.org/10.18653/v1/2024.emnlp-main.306.

Pengcheng He, Jianfeng Gao, and Weizhu Chen. DeBERTaV3: Improving DeBERTa using ELECTRA-style pre-training with gradient-disentangled embedding sharing. In *The Eleventh International Conference on Learning Representations*, 2023. URL https://iclr.cc/virtual/2023/poster/11295.

Yuhang He, Jianzhu Bao, Yang Sun, Bin Liang, Min Yang, Bing Qin, and Ruifeng Xu. Decomposing argumentative essay generation via dialectical planning of complex reasoning. In Lun-Wei Ku, Andre Martins, and Vivek Srikumar, editors, *Findings of the Association for Computational Linguistics ACL 2024*, pages 12305–12322, Bangkok, Thailand and virtual meeting, August 2024. Association for Computational Linguistics. https://doi.org/10.18653/v1/2024.findings-acl.731.

Marti A. Hearst. Automatic acquisition of hyponyms from large text corpora. In *COLING 1992 Volume 2: The 14th International Conference on Computational Linguistics*, 1992. URL https://aclanthology.org/C92-2082/.

Stefan Heindorf, Yan Scholten, Henning Wachsmuth, Axel-Cyrille Ngonga Ngomo, and Martin Potthast. CauseNet: Towards a causality graph extracted from the web. In *Proceedings of the 29th ACM International Conference on Information & Knowledge Management*, CIKM '20, pages 3023–3030, New York, NY, USA, 2020. Association for Computing Machinery. https://doi.org/10.1145/3340531.3412763.

Philipp Heinisch and Philipp Cimiano. A multi-task approach to argument frame classification at variable granularity levels. *it - Information Technology*, 63(1):59–72, 2021. https://doi.org/10.1515/itit-2020-0054.

Philipp Heinisch, Anette Frank, Juri Opitz, Moritz Plenz, and Philipp Cimiano. Overview of the 2022 validity and novelty prediction shared task. In Gabriella Lapesa, Jodi Schneider, Yohan Jo, and Sougata Saha, editors, *Proceedings of the 9th Workshop on Argument Mining*, pages 84–94, Online and in Gyeongju, Republic of Korea, October 2022. International Conference on Computational Linguistics. URL https://aclanthology.org/2022.argmining-1.7/.

Philipp Heinisch, Matthias Orlikowski, Julia Romberg, and Philipp Cimiano. Architectural sweet spots for modeling human label variation by the example of argument quality: It's best to relate perspectives! In Houda Bouamor, Juan Pino, and Kalika Bali, editors, *Proceedings of the 2023 Conference on Empirical Methods in Natural Language Processing*, pages 11138–11154, Singapore, December 2023. Association for Computational Linguistics. https://doi.org/10.18653/v1/2023.emnlp-main.687.

A. Francisca Snoeck Henkemans. State-of-the-Art: The structure of argumentation. *Argumentation*, 14(4):447–473, 2000. https://doi.org/10.1023/A:1007800305762.

Freya Hewett, Roshan Prakash Rane, Nina Harlacher, and Manfred Stede. The utility of discourse parsing features for predicting argumentation structure. In Benno Stein and Henning Wachsmuth, editors, *Proceedings of the 6th Workshop on Argument Mining*, pages 98–103, Florence, Italy, August 2019. Association for Computational Linguistics. https://doi.org/10.18653/v1/W19-4512.

Christopher Hidey and Kathy McKeown. Fixed that for you: Generating contrastive claims with semantic edits. In Jill Burstein, Christy Doran, and Thamar Solorio, editors, *Proceedings of the 2019 Conference of the North American Chapter of the Association for Computational Linguistics: Human Language Technologies, Volume 1 (Long and Short Papers)*, pages 1756–1767, Minneapolis, Minnesota, June 2019. Association for Computational Linguistics. https://doi.org/10.18653/v1/N19-1174.

Christopher Hidey, Elena Musi, Alyssa Hwang, Smaranda Muresan, and Kathy McKeown. Analyzing the semantic types of claims and premises in an online persuasive forum. In Ivan Habernal, Iryna Gurevych, Kevin Ashley, Claire Cardie, Nancy Green, Diane Litman, Georgios Petasis, Chris Reed, Noam Slonim, and Vern Walker, editors, *Proceedings of the 4th Workshop on Argument Mining*, pages 11–21, Copenhagen, Denmark, September 2017. Association for Computational Linguistics. https://doi.org/10.18653/v1/W17-5102.

Martin Hinton and Jean H.M. Wagemans. How persuasive is AI-generated argumentation? An analysis of the quality of an argumentative text produced by the GPT-3 AI text generator. *Argument & Computation*, 14(1):59–74, February 2023. https://doi.org/10.3233/AAC-210026.

David Hitchcock. Informal logic and the concept of argument. In Dale Jacquette, editor, *Philosophy of Logic*, Handbook of the Philosophy of Science, pages 101–129. North-Holland, Amsterdam, January 2007. https://doi.org/10.1016/B978-044451541-4/50007-5.

David Hitchcock and Jean H. M. Wagemans. The pragma-dialectical account of argument schemes. In Eveline T. Feteris, Bart Garssen, Francisca Snoeck Henkemans, editors, *Keeping in Touch with Pragma-dialectics*, pages 185–205. John Benjamins Publishing Company, 2011. https://doi.org/10.1075/z.163.13hit.

Elad Hoffer and Nir Ailon. Deep metric learning using triplet network. In *International Workshop on Similarity-Based Pattern Recognition*, pages 84–92. Springer, 2015. https://doi.org/10.1007/978-3-319-24261-3_7.

Carolin Holtermann, Anne Lauscher, and Simone Ponzetto. Fair and argumentative language modeling for computational argumentation. In Smaranda Muresan, Preslav Nakov, and Aline Villavicencio, editors, *Proceedings of the 60th Annual Meeting of the Association for Computational Linguistics (Volume 1: Long Papers)*, pages 7841–7861, Dublin, Ireland, May 2022. Association for Computational Linguistics. https://doi.org/10.18653/v1/2022.acl-long.541.

Ari Holtzman, Jan Buys, Li Du, Maxwell Forbes, and Yejin Choi. The curious case of neural text degeneration. In *Proceedings of the 8th International Conference on Learning Representations*. OpenReview.net, 2020. URL https://openreview.net/forum?id=rygGQyrFvH.

Robert E. Horn. Infrastructure for navigating interdisciplinary debates: Critical decisions for representing argumentation. In *Visualizing Argumentation: Software Tools for Collaborative and Educational Sense-making*, pages 165–184. Springer, 2003. https://doi.org/10.1007/978-1-4471-0037-9_8.

Yufang Hou and Charles Jochim. Argument relation classification using a joint inference model. In Ivan Habernal, Iryna Gurevych, Kevin Ashley, Claire Cardie, Nancy Green, Diane Litman, Georgios Petasis, Chris Reed, Noam Slonim, and Vern Walker, editors, *Proceedings of the 4th Workshop on Argument Mining*, pages 60–66, Copenhagen, Denmark, September 2017. Association for Computational Linguistics. https://doi.org/10.18653/v1/W17-5107.

Dirk Hovy, Taylor Berg-Kirkpatrick, Ashish Vaswani, and Eduard Hovy. Learning whom to trust with MACE. In Lucy Vanderwende, Hal Daumé III, and Katrin Kirchhoff, editors, *Proceedings of the 2013 Conference of the North American Chapter of the Association for Computational Linguistics: Human Language Technologies*, pages 1120–1130, Atlanta, Georgia, June 2013. Association for Computational Linguistics. URL https://aclanthology.org/N13-1132/.

Edward J Hu, Yelong Shen, Phillip Wallis, Zeyuan Allen-Zhu, Yuanzhi Li, Shean Wang, Lu Wang, and Weizhu Chen. LoRA: Low-rank adaptation of large language models. In *International Conference on Learning Representations*, 2022. URL https://iclr.cc/virtual/2022/poster/6319.

Minqing Hu and Bing Liu. Mining opinion features in customer reviews. In *Proceedings of the 19th National Conference on Artifical Intelligence*, AAAI'04, pages 755–760. AAAI Press, 2004. ISBN 0262511835. URL https://cdn.aaai.org/AAAI/2004/AAAI04-119.pdf.

Zhe Hu, Hou Pong Chan, and Yu Yin. AMERICANO: Argument generation with discourse-driven decomposition and agent interaction. In Saad Mahamood, Nguyen Le Minh, and Daphne Ippolito, editors, *Proceedings of the 17th International Natural Language Generation Conference*, pages 82–102, Tokyo, Japan, September 2024. Association for Computational Linguistics. https://doi.org/10.18653/v1/2024.inlg-main.8.

Xinyu Hua and Lu Wang. Understanding and detecting supporting arguments of diverse types. In Regina Barzilay and Min-Yen Kan, editors, *Proceedings of the 55th Annual Meeting of the Association for Computational Linguistics (Volume 2: Short Papers)*, pages 203–208, Vancouver, Canada, July 2017. Association for Computational Linguistics. https://doi.org/10.18653/v1/P17-2032.

Xinyu Hua and Lu Wang. Neural argument generation augmented with externally retrieved evidence. In *Proceedings of the 56th Annual Meeting of the Association for Computational Linguistics (Volume 1: Long Papers)*, pages 219–230, Melbourne, Australia, July 2018. Association for Computational Linguistics. https://doi.org/10.18653/v1/P18-1021.

Xinyu Hua and Lu Wang. Sentence-level content planning and style specification for neural text generation. In Kentaro Inui, Jing Jiang, Vincent Ng, and Xiaojun Wan, editors, *Proceedings of the 2019 Conference on Empirical Methods in Natural Language Processing and the 9th International Joint Conference on Natural Language Processing (EMNLP-IJCNLP)*, pages 591–602, Hong Kong, China, November 2019. Association for Computational Linguistics. https://doi.org/10.18653/v1/D19-1055.

Xinyu Hua and Lu Wang. Efficient argument structure extraction with transfer learning and active learning. In Smaranda Muresan, Preslav Nakov, and Aline Villavicencio, editors, *Findings of the Association for Computational Linguistics: ACL 2022*, pages 423–437, Dublin, Ireland, May 2022. Association for Computational Linguistics. https://doi.org/10.18653/v1/2022.findings-acl.36.

Xinyu Hua, Zhe Hu, and Lu Wang. Argument generation with retrieval, planning, and realization. In Anna Korhonen, David Traum, and Lluís Màrquez, editors, *Proceedings of the 57th Annual Meeting of the Association for Computational Linguistics*, pages 2661–2672, Florence, Italy, July 2019a. Association for Computational Linguistics. https://doi.org/10.18653/v1/P19-1255.

Xinyu Hua, Mitko Nikolov, Nikhil Badugu, and Lu Wang. Argument mining for understanding peer reviews. In Jill Burstein, Christy Doran, and Thamar Solorio, editors, *Proceedings of the 2019 Conference of the North American Chapter of the Association for Computational Linguistics: Human Language Technologies, Volume 1 (Long and Short Papers)*, pages 2131–2137, Minneapolis, Minnesota, June 2019b. Association for Computational Linguistics. https://doi.org/10.18653/v1/N19-1219.

Guanxiong Huang and Sai Wang. Is artificial intelligence more persuasive than humans? A meta-analysis. *Journal of Communication*, 73(6):552–562, December 2023. https://doi.org/10.1093/joc/jqad024.

Thomas Huber and Christina Niklaus. CLEAR: A comprehensive linguistic evaluation of argument rewriting by large language models. In Christos Christodoulopoulos, Tanmoy Chakraborty, Carolyn Rose, and Violet Peng, editors, *Findings of the Association for Computational Linguistics: EMNLP 2025*, pages 19548–19568, Suzhou, China, November 2025. Association for Computational Linguistics. https://doi.org/10.18653/v1/2025.findings-emnlp.1065.

Ioana Hulpus, Jonathan Kobbe, Heiner Stuckenschmidt, and Graeme Hirst. Knowledge graphs meet moral values. In Iryna Gurevych, Marianna Apidianaki, and Manaal Faruqui, editors, *Proceedings of the Ninth Joint Conference on Lexical and Computational Semantics*, pages 71–

80, Barcelona, Spain (Online), December 2020. Association for Computational Linguistics. URL https://aclanthology.org/2020.starsem-1.8/.

Anthony Hunter. Understanding enthymemes in deductive argumentation using semantic distance measures. *Proceedings of the AAAI Conference on Artificial Intelligence*, 36(5):5729–5736, June 2022. https://doi.org/10.1609/aaai.v36i5.20515.

C.J. Hutto and Eric Gilbert. VADER: A parsimonious rule-based model for sentiment analysis of social media text. *Proceedings of the International AAAI Conference on Web and Social Media*, 8(1):216–225, May 2014. https://doi.org/10.1609/icwsm.v8i1.14550.

Jena D. Hwang, Chandra Bhagavatula, Ronan Le Bras, Jeff Da, Keisuke Sakaguchi, Antoine Bosselut, and Yejin Choi. (COMET-) ATOMIC 2020: On symbolic and neural commonsense knowledge graphs. *Proceedings of the AAAI Conference on Artificial Intelligence*, 35(7):6384–6392, May 2021. https://doi.org/10.1609/aaai.v35i7.16792.

Alexey Ignatiev, Antonio Morgado, and Joao Marques-Silva. PySAT: A Python toolkit for prototyping with SAT Oracles. In Olaf Beyersdorff and Christoph M. Wintersteiger, editors, *Theory and Applications of Satisfiability Testing – SAT 2018*, volume 10929, pages 428–437. Springer International Publishing, Cham, 2018. https://doi.org/10.1007/978-3-319-94144-8_26.

Jumayel Islam, Lu Xiao, and Robert E. Mercer. A lexicon-based approach for detecting hedges in informal text. In Nicoletta Calzolari, Frédéric Béchet, Philippe Blache, Khalid Choukri, Christopher Cieri, Thierry Declerck, Sara Goggi, Hitoshi Isahara, Bente Maegaard, Joseph Mariani, Hélène Mazo, Asuncion Moreno, Jan Odijk, and Stelios Piperidis, editors, *Proceedings of the Twelfth Language Resources and Evaluation Conference*, pages 3109–3113, Marseille, France, May 2020. European Language Resources Association. ISBN 979-10-95546-34-4. URL https://aclanthology.org/2020.lrec-1.380/.

Rositsa V Ivanova and Reto Gubelmann. The shift from logic to dialectic in argumentation theory: Implications for computational argument quality assessment. In Owen Rambow, Leo Wanner, Marianna Apidianaki, Hend Al-Khalifa, Barbara Di Eugenio, and Steven Schockaert, editors, *Proceedings of the 31st International Conference on Computational Linguistics*, pages 4789–4802, Abu Dhabi, UAE, January 2025. Association for Computational Linguistics. URL https://aclanthology.org/2025.coling-main.321/.

Rositsa V Ivanova, Thomas Huber, and Christina Niklaus. Let's discuss! Quality dimensions and annotated datasets for computational argument quality assessment. In Yaser Al-Onaizan, Mohit Bansal, and Yun-Nung Chen, editors, *Proceedings of the 2024 Conference on Empirical Methods in Natural Language Processing*, pages 20749–20779, Miami, Florida, USA, November 2024. Association for Computational Linguistics. https://doi.org/10.18653/v1/2024.emnlp-main.1155.

Mathilde Janier and Patrick Saint-Dizier. *Argument Mining: Linguistic Foundations*. ISTE/Wiley, London/Hoboken, 2019. ISBN 978-1-786-30303-5.

Mathilde Janier, John Lawrence, and Chris Reed. OVA+: An argument analysis interface. In *Proceedings of the Conference on Computational Models of Argument*, pages 463–464, 2014. http://doi.org/10.3233/978-1-61499-436-7-463.

Jiwon Jeong, Hyeju Jang, and Hogun Park. Large language models are better logical fallacy reasoners with counterargument, explanation, and goal-aware prompt formulation. In Luis Chiruzzo, Alan Ritter, and Lu Wang, editors, *Findings of the Association for Computational Linguistics: NAACL 2025*, pages 6918–6937, Albuquerque, New Mexico, April 2025. Association for Computational Linguistics. https://doi.org/10.18653/v1/2025.findings-naacl.384.

Albert Q. Jiang, Alexandre Sablayrolles, Arthur Mensch, Chris Bamford, Devendra Singh Chaplot, Diego de las Casas, Florian Bressand, Gianna Lengyel, Guillaume Lample, Lucile Saulnier, Lélio Renard Lavaud, Marie-Anne Lachaux, Pierre Stock, Teven Le Scao, Thibaut Lavril, Thomas Wang, Timothé Lacroix, and William El Sayed. Mistral 7B, 2023. https://doi.org/10.48550/arXiv.2310.06825.

Albert Q. Jiang, Alexandre Sablayrolles, Antoine Roux, Arthur Mensch, Blanche Savary, Chris Bamford, Devendra Singh Chaplot, Diego de las Casas, Emma Bou Hanna, Florian Bressand, Gianna Lengyel, Guillaume Bour, Guillaume Lample, Lélio Renard Lavaud, Lucile Saulnier, Marie-Anne Lachaux, Pierre Stock, Sandeep Subramanian, Sophia Yang, Szymon Antoniak, Teven Le Scao, Théophile Gervet, Thibaut Lavril, Thomas Wang, Timothé Lacroix, and William El Sayed. Mixtral of experts, 2024. https://doi.org/10.48550/arXiv.2401.04088.

Bojun Jin, Jianzhu Bao, Yufang Hou, Yang Sun, Yice Zhang, Huajie Wang, Bin Liang, and Ruifeng Xu. A multi-persona framework for argument quality assessment. In Wanxiang Che, Joyce Nabende, Ekaterina Shutova, and Mohammad Taher Pilehvar, editors, *Proceedings of the 63rd Annual Meeting of the Association for Computational Linguistics (Volume 1: Long Papers)*, pages 12148–12170, Vienna, Austria, July 2025. Association for Computational Linguistics. https://doi.org/10.18653/v1/2025.acl-long.593.

Zhijing Jin, Abhinav Lalwani, Tejas Vaidhya, Xiaoyu Shen, Yiwen Ding, Zhiheng Lyu, Mrinmaya Sachan, Rada Mihalcea, and Bernhard Schoelkopf. Logical fallacy detection. In Yoav Goldberg, Zornitsa Kozareva, and Yue Zhang, editors, *Findings of the Association for Computational Linguistics: EMNLP 2022*, pages 7180–7198, Abu Dhabi, United Arab Emirates, December 2022. Association for Computational Linguistics. https://doi.org/10.18653/v1/2022.findings-emnlp.532.

Yohan Jo, Shivani Poddar, Byungsoo Jeon, Qinlan Shen, Carolyn Rosé, and Graham Neubig. Attentive interaction model: Modeling changes in view in argumentation. In *Proceedings of the 2018 Conference of the North American Chapter of the Association for Computational Linguistics: Human Language Technologies, Volume 1 (Long Papers)*, pages 103–116, New Orleans, Louisiana, June 2018. Association for Computational Linguistics. https://doi.org/10.18653/v1/N18-1010.

Yohan Jo, Jacky Visser, Chris Reed, and Eduard Hovy. A cascade model for proposition extraction in argumentation. In Benno Stein and Henning Wachsmuth, editors, *Proceedings of the 6th Workshop on Argument Mining*, pages 11–24, Florence, Italy, August 2019. Association for Computational Linguistics. https://doi.org/10.18653/v1/W19-4502.

Yohan Jo, Seojin Bang, Emaad Manzoor, Eduard Hovy, and Chris Reed. Detecting attackable sentences in arguments. In Bonnie Webber, Trevor Cohn, Yulan He, and Yang Liu, editors, *Proceedings of the 2020 Conference on Empirical Methods in Natural Language Processing (EMNLP)*, pages 1–23, Online, November 2020. Association for Computational Linguistics. https://doi.org/10.18653/v1/2020.emnlp-main.1.

Yohan Jo, Seojin Bang, Chris Reed, and Eduard Hovy. Classifying argumentative relations using logical mechanisms and argumentation schemes. *Transactions of the Association for Computational Linguistics*, 9:721–739, 2021a. https://doi.org/10.1162/tacl_a_00394.

Yohan Jo, Haneul Yoo, JinYeong Bak, Alice Oh, Chris Reed, and Eduard Hovy. Knowledge-enhanced evidence retrieval for counterargument generation. In Marie-Francine Moens, Xuanjing Huang, Lucia Specia, and Scott Wen-Tau Yih, editors, *Findings of the Association for Computational Linguistics: EMNLP 2021*, pages 3074–3094, Punta Cana, Dominican Republic, November 2021b. Association for Computational Linguistics. https://doi.org/10.18653/v1/2021.findings-emnlp.264.

Thorsten Joachims. Training linear SVMs in linear time. In *Proceedings of the 12th ACM SIGKDD International Conference on Knowledge Discovery and Data Mining*, KDD '06, pages 217–226, New York, NY, USA, 2006. Association for Computing Machinery. https://doi.org/10.1145/1150402.1150429.

Kristen Johnson and Dan Goldwasser. Classification of moral foundations in microblog political discourse. In Iryna Gurevych and Yusuke Miyao, editors, *Proceedings of the 56th Annual Meeting of the Association for Computational Linguistics (Volume 1: Long Papers)*, pages 720–

730, Melbourne, Australia, July 2018. Association for Computational Linguistics. https://doi.org/10.18653/v1/P18-1067.

Kristen Johnson, Di Jin, and Dan Goldwasser. Leveraging behavioral and social information for weakly supervised collective classification of political discourse on Twitter. In Regina Barzilay and Min-Yen Kan, editors, *Proceedings of the 55th Annual Meeting of the Association for Computational Linguistics (Volume 1: Long Papers)*, pages 741–752, Vancouver, Canada, July 2017. Association for Computational Linguistics. https://doi.org/10.18653/v1/P17-1069.

Ralph H. Johnson and Anthony J. Blair. *Logical Self-Defense*. International Debate Education Association, New York/Amsterdam/Brussels, 2006. ISBN 9781932716184.

Daniel Jurafsky and James H. Martin. *Speech and Language Processing: An Introduction to Natural Language Processing, Computational Linguistics, and Speech Recognition, with Language Models*. 3rd edition, 2026. URL https://web.stanford.edu/~jurafsky/slp3/. Online manuscript released January 6, 2026.

Masayuki Kawarada, Tsutomu Hirao, Wataru Uchida, and Masaaki Nagata. Argument mining as a text-to-text generation task. In Yvette Graham and Matthew Purver, editors, *Proceedings of the 18th Conference of the European Chapter of the Association for Computational Linguistics (Volume 1: Long Papers)*, pages 2002–2014, St. Julian's, Malta, March 2024. Association for Computational Linguistics. https://doi.org/10.18653/v1/2024.eacl-long.121.

Zixuan Ke, Winston Carlile, Nishant Gurrapadi, and Vincent Ng. Learning to give feedback: Modeling attributes affecting argument persuasiveness in student essays. In *Proceedings of the Twenty-Seventh International Joint Conference on Artificial Intelligence, IJCAI-18*, pages 4130–4136. International Joint Conferences on Artificial Intelligence Organization, 7 2018. https://doi.org/10.24963/ijcai.2018/574.

Nitish Shirish Keskar, Bryan McCann, Lav R. Varshney, Caiming Xiong, and Richard Socher. CTRL: A conditional transformer language model for controllable generation, 2019. https://doi.org/10.48550/arXiv.1909.05858.

Daniel Khashabi, Sewon Min, Tushar Khot, Ashish Sabharwal, Oyvind Tafjord, Peter Clark, and Hannaneh Hajishirzi. UNIFIEDQA: Crossing format boundaries with a single QA system. In Trevor Cohn, Yulan He, and Yang Liu, editors, *Findings of the Association for Computational Linguistics: EMNLP 2020*, pages 1896–1907, Online, November 2020. Association for Computational Linguistics. https://doi.org/10.18653/v1/2020.findings-emnlp.171.

Dora Kiesel, Patrick Riehmann, Henning Wachsmuth, Benno Stein, and Bernd Froehlich. Visual analysis of argumentation in essays. *IEEE Transactions on Visualization and Computer Graphics*, 27(2):1139–1148, February 2021a. https://doi.org/10.1109/TVCG.2020.3030425.

Johannes Kiesel, Kevin Lang, Henning Wachsmuth, Eva Hornecker, and Benno Stein. Investigating expectations for voice-based and conversational argument search on the web. In Luanne Freund, Heather O'Brien, Ioannis Arapakis, Orland Hoeber, and Irene Lopatovska, editors, *5th ACM SIGIR Conference on Human Information Interaction & Retrieval (CHIIR 2020)*, pages 53–62. Association for Computing Machinery, March 2020. https://doi.org/10.1145/3343413.3377978.

Johannes Kiesel, Nico Reichenbach, Benno Stein, and Martin Potthast. Image retrieval for arguments using stance-aware query expansion. In Khalid Al-Khatib, Yufang Hou, and Manfred Stede, editors, *Proceedings of the 8th Workshop on Argument Mining*, pages 36–45, Punta Cana, Dominican Republic, November 2021b. Association for Computational Linguistics. https://doi.org/10.18653/v1/2021.argmining-1.4.

Johannes Kiesel, Milad Alshomary, Nicolas Handke, Xiaoni Cai, Henning Wachsmuth, and Benno Stein. Identifying the human values behind arguments. In *Proceedings of the 60th Annual Meeting of the Association for Computational Linguistics (Volume 1: Long Papers)*, pages 4459–4471, Dublin, Ireland, May 2022. Association for Computational Linguistics. https://doi.org/10.18653/v1/2022.acl-long.306.

Johannes Kiesel, Milad Alshomary, Nailia Mirzakhmedova, Maximilian Heinrich, Nicolas Handke, Henning Wachsmuth, and Benno Stein. SemEval-2023 task 4: ValueEval: Identification of human values behind arguments. In Atul Kr. Ojha, A. Seza Doğruöz, Giovanni Da San Martino, Harish Tayyar Madabushi, Ritesh Kumar, and Elisa Sartori, editors, *Proceedings of the 17th International Workshop on Semantic Evaluation (SemEval-2023)*, pages 2287–2303, Toronto, Canada, July 2023. Association for Computational Linguistics. https://doi.org/10.18653/v1/2023.semeval-1.313.

Kaan Kilic, Saskia Weck, Timotheus Kampik, and Helena Lindgren. Argument-based human–AI collaboration for supporting behavior change to improve health. *Frontiers in Artificial Intelligence*, 6, February 2023. https://doi.org/10.3389/frai.2023.1069455.

Jonathan Kobbe, Ines Rehbein, Ioana Hulpus, and Heiner Stuckenschmidt. Exploring morality in argumentation. In Elena Cabrio and Serena Villata, editors, *Proceedings of the 7th Workshop on Argument Mining*, pages 30–40, Online, December 2020. Association for Computational Linguistics. URL https://aclanthology.org/2020.argmining-1.4/.

Christian Kock. Dialectical obligations in political debate. *Informal Logic*, 27(3):233–247, 2007. https://doi.org/10.22329/il.v27i3.483.

Martha Kolln. *Rhetorical Grammar: Grammatical Choices, Rhetorical Effects*. Longman, New York, 2003.

Takahiro Kondo, Koki Washio, Katsuhiko Hayashi, and Yusuke Miyao. Bayesian argumentation-scheme networks: A probabilistic model of argument validity facilitated by argumentation schemes. In Khalid Al-Khatib, Yufang Hou, and Manfred Stede, editors, *Proceedings of the 8th Workshop on Argument Mining*, pages 112–124, Punta Cana, Dominican Republic, November 2021. Association for Computational Linguistics. https://doi.org/10.18653/v1/2021.argmining-1.11.

Kai Konen, Sophie Jentzsch, Diaoulé Diallo, Peer Schütt, Oliver Bensch, Roxanne El Baff, Dominik Opitz, and Tobias Hecking. Style vectors for steering generative large language models. In Yvette Graham and Matthew Purver, editors, *Findings of the Association for Computational Linguistics: EACL 2024*, pages 782–802, St. Julian's, Malta, March 2024. Association for Computational Linguistics. https://doi.org/10.18653/v1/2024.findings-eacl.52.

Robert Koons. Defeasible reasoning. In Edward N. Zalta and Uri Nodelman, editors, *The Stanford Encyclopedia of Philosophy*. Metaphysics Research Lab, Stanford University, summer 2025 edition, 2025. URL https://plato.stanford.edu/entries/reasoning-defeasible/.

Erik Körner, Gerhard Heyer, and Martin Potthast. Same side stance classification using contextualized sentence embeddings. In Yamen Ajjour, Khalid Al-Khatib, Philipp Cimiano, Roxanne El Baff, Basil Ell, Benno Stein, and Henning Wachsmuth, editors, *Same Side Stance Classification Shared Task 2019*, volume 2921 of *CEUR Workshop Proceedings*, pages 21–25. CEUR-WS.org, July 2021a. URL https://ceur-ws.org/Vol-2921/paper3.pdf.

Erik Körner, Gregor Wiedemann, Ahmad Dawar Hakimi, Gerhard Heyer, and Martin Potthast. On classifying whether two texts are on the same side of an argument. In *Proceedings of the 26th Conference on Empirical Methods in Natural Language Processing (EMNLP 2021)*, pages 10130–10138. Association for Computational Linguistics, November 2021b. https://doi.org/10.18653/v1/2021.emnlp-main.795.

Nataliya Kosmyna, Eugene Hauptmann, Ye Tong Yuan, Jessica Situ, Xian-Hao Liao, Ashly Vivian Beresnitzky, Iris Braunstein, and Pattie Maes. Your brain on ChatGPT: Accumulation of cognitive debt when using an AI assistant for essay writing task, June 2025. https://doi.org/10.48550/arXiv.2506.08872.

Marcin Koszowy, Steve Oswald, Katarzyna Budzynska, Barbara Konat, and Pascal Gygax. A pragmatic account of rephrase in argumentation: Linguistic and cognitive evidence. *Informal Logic*, 42(1):49–82, 2022. https://doi.org/10.22329/il.v42i1.7212.

Fajri Koto, Jey Han Lau, and Timothy Baldwin. Top-down discourse parsing via sequence labelling. In Paola Merlo, Jorg Tiedemann, and Reut Tsarfaty, editors, *Proceedings of the 16th Conference of the European Chapter of the Association for Computational Linguistics: Main Volume*, pages 715–726, Online, April 2021. Association for Computational Linguistics. https://doi.org/10.18653/v1/2021.eacl-main.60.

Milen Kouylekov and Matteo Negri. An open-source package for recognizing textual entailment. In Sandra Kübler, editor, *Proceedings of the ACL 2010 System Demonstrations*, pages 42–47, Uppsala, Sweden, July 2010. Association for Computational Linguistics. URL https://aclanthology.org/P10-4008/.

Travis Kriplean, Jonathan Morgan, Deen Freelon, Alan Borning, and Lance Bennett. Supporting reflective public thought with ConsiderIt. In *Proceedings of the ACM 2012 Conference on Computer Supported Cooperative Work*, pages 265–274, Seattle Washington USA, February 2012. Association for Computing Machinery. https://doi.org/10.1145/2145204.2145249.

Katarina Krüger, Anna Lukowiak, Jonathan Sonntag, Saskia Warzecha, and Manfred Stede. Classifying news versus opinions in newspapers: Linguistic features for domain independence. *Natural Language Enginnering*, 23(5):687–707, 2017. https://doi.org/10.1017/S1351324917000043.

Dilek Küçük and Fazli Can. Stance detection: A survey. *ACM Computing Surveys*, 53(1):1–37, February 2020. https://doi.org/10.1145/3369026.

Tobias Kuhn. A survey and classification of controlled natural languages. *Computational Linguistics*, 40(1):121–170, 03 2014. https://doi.org/10.1162/COLI_a_00168.

Shivani Kumar and David Jurgens. Are rules meant to be broken? Understanding multilingual moral reasoning as a computational pipeline with UniMoral, 2025. https://doi.org/10.48550/arXiv.2502.14083.

Werner Kunz and Horst WJ Rittel. Issues as elements of information systems. Technical Report Working Paper No. 131, Institute of Urban and Regional Development, University of California, Berkeley, 1970.

Zhenzhong Lan, Mingda Chen, Sebastian Goodman, Kevin Gimpel, Piyush Sharma, and Radu Soricut. ALBERT: A lite BERT for self-supervised learning of language representations. In *International Conference on Learning Representations*, 2020. URL https://iclr.cc/virtual_2020/poster_H1eA7AEtvS.html.

Anne Lauscher, Goran Glavaš, and Kai Eckert. ArguminSci: A tool for analyzing argumentation and rhetorical aspects in scientific writing. In Noam Slonim and Ranit Aharonov, editors, *Proceedings of the 5th Workshop on Argument Mining*, pages 22–28, Brussels, Belgium, November 2018a. Association for Computational Linguistics. https://doi.org/10.18653/v1/W18-5203.

Anne Lauscher, Goran Glavaš, and Simone Paolo Ponzetto. An argument-annotated corpus of scientific publications. In Noam Slonim and Ranit Aharonov, editors, *Proceedings of the 5th Workshop on Argument Mining*, pages 40–46, Brussels, Belgium, November 2018b. Association for Computational Linguistics. https://doi.org/10.18653/v1/W18-5206.

Anne Lauscher, Lily Ng, Courtney Napoles, and Joel Tetreault. Rhetoric, logic, and dialectic: Advancing theory-based argument quality assessment in natural language processing. In *Proceedings of the 28th International Conference on Computational Linguistics*, pages 4563–4574, Barcelona, Spain (Online), December 2020. International Committee on Computational Linguistics. https://doi.org/10.18653/v1/2020.coling-main.402.

Anne Lauscher, Tobias Lueken, and Goran Glavaš. Sustainable modular debiasing of language models. In Marie-Francine Moens, Xuanjing Huang, Lucia Specia, and Scott Wen-Tau Yih, editors, *Findings of the Association for Computational Linguistics: EMNLP 2021*, pages 4782–4797, Punta Cana, Dominican Republic, November 2021. Association for Computational Linguistics. https://doi.org/10.18653/v1/2021.findings-emnlp.411.

Anne Lauscher, Henning Wachsmuth, Iryna Gurevych, and Goran Glavaš. Scientia potentia est: On the role of knowledge in computational argumentation. *Transactions of the Association for Computational Linguistics*, 10:1392–1422, 2022. https://doi.org/10.1162/tacl_a_00525.

Tamar Lavee, Matan Orbach, Lili Kotlerman, Yoav Kantor, Shai Gretz, Lena Dankin, Michal Jacovi, Yonatan Bilu, Ranit Aharonov, and Noam Slonim. Towards effective rebuttal: Listening comprehension using corpus-wide claim mining. In Benno Stein and Henning Wachsmuth, editors, *Proceedings of the 6th Workshop on Argument Mining*, pages 58–66, Florence, Italy, August 2019. Association for Computational Linguistics. https://doi.org/10.18653/v1/W19-4507.

John Lawrence and Chris Reed. Argument mining using argumentation scheme structures. In *Proceedings of the Conference on Computational Models of Argument*, pages 379–390, 2016. http://doi.org/10.3233/978-1-61499-686-6-379.

John Lawrence and Chris Reed. Using complex argumentative interactions to reconstruct the argumentative structure of large-scale debates. In Ivan Habernal, Iryna Gurevych, Kevin Ashley, Claire Cardie, Nancy Green, Diane Litman, Georgios Petasis, Chris Reed, Noam Slonim, and Vern Walker, editors, *Proceedings of the 4th Workshop on Argument Mining*, pages 108–117, Copenhagen, Denmark, September 2017. Association for Computational Linguistics. https://doi.org/10.18653/v1/W17-5114.

John Lawrence and Chris Reed. Argument mining: A survey. *Computational Linguistics*, 45(4): 765–818, 2019. https://doi.org/10.1162/coli_a_00364.

John Lawrence, Floris Bex, Chris Reed, and Mark Snaith. AIFdb: Infrastructure for the Argument Web. In *Proceedings of the Conference on Computational Models of Argument*, pages 515–516, 2012. http://doi.org/10.3233/978-1-61499-111-3-515.

John Lawrence, Chris Reed, Colin Allen, Simon McAlister, and Andrew Ravenscroft. Mining arguments from 19th century philosophical texts using topic based modelling. In Nancy Green, Kevin Ashley, Diane Litman, Chris Reed, and Vern Walker, editors, *Proceedings of the First Workshop on Argumentation Mining*, pages 79–87, Baltimore, Maryland, June 2014. Association for Computational Linguistics. https://doi.org/10.3115/v1/W14-2111.

John Lawrence, Mark Snaith, Barbara Konat, Katarzyna Budzynska, and Chris Reed. Debating technology for dialogical argument: Sensemaking, engagement, and analytics. *ACM Transactions on Internet Technology*, 17(3):1–23, August 2017a. https://doi.org/10.1145/3007210.

John Lawrence, Jacky Visser, and Chris Reed. Harnessing rhetorical figures for argument mining: A pilot study in relating figures of speech to argument structure. *Argument & Computation*, 8(3): 289–310, 2017b. https://doi.org/10.3233/AAC-170026.

John Lawrence, Jacky Visser, and Chris Reed. BBC Moral Maze: Test your argument. In *Computational Models of Argument*, pages 465–466. IOS Press, 2018. https://doi.org/10.3233/978-1-61499-906-5-465.

John Lawrence, Jacky Visser, and Chris Reed. An online annotation assistant for argument schemes. In Annemarie Friedrich, Deniz Zeyrek, and Jet Hoek, editors, *Proceedings of the 13th Linguistic Annotation Workshop*, pages 100–107, Florence, Italy, August 2019. Association for Computational Linguistics. https://doi.org/10.18653/v1/W19-4012.

Quoc Le and Tomas Mikolov. Distributed representations of sentences and documents. In Eric P. Xing and Tony Jebara, editors, *Proceedings of the 31st International Conference on Machine Learning*, volume 32, pages 1188–1196, Bejing, China, 22–24 Jun 2014. PMLR. URL https://proceedings.mlr.press/v32/le14.html.

Jinhyuk Lee, Wonjin Yoon, Sungdong Kim, Donghyeon Kim, Sunkyu Kim, Chan Ho So, and Jaewoo Kang. BioBERT: A pre-trained biomedical language representation model for biomedical text mining. *Bioinformatics*, 36(4):1234–1240, 09 2019. ISSN 1367-4803. https://doi.org/10.1093/bioinformatics/btz682.

Yuanyuan Lei and Ruihong Huang. Boosting logical fallacy reasoning in LLMs via logical structure tree. In Yaser Al-Onaizan, Mohit Bansal, and Yun-Nung Chen, editors, *Proceedings of the 2024 Conference on Empirical Methods in Natural Language Processing*, pages 13157–13173, Miami, Florida, USA, November 2024. Association for Computational Linguistics. https://doi.org/10.18653/v1/2024.emnlp-main.730.

Ran Levy, Yonatan Bilu, Daniel Hershcovich, Ehud Aharoni, and Noam Slonim. Context dependent claim detection. In Junichi Tsujii and Jan Hajic, editors, *Proceedings of COLING 2014, the 25th International Conference on Computational Linguistics: Technical Papers*, pages 1489–1500, Dublin, Ireland, August 2014. Dublin City University and Association for Computational Linguistics. URL https://aclanthology.org/C14-1141/.

Mike Lewis, Yinhan Liu, Naman Goyal, Marjan Ghazvininejad, Abdelrahman Mohamed, Omer Levy, Veselin Stoyanov, and Luke Zettlemoyer. BART: Denoising sequence-to-sequence pre-training for natural language generation, translation, and comprehension. In Dan Jurafsky, Joyce Chai, Natalie Schluter, and Joel Tetreault, editors, *Proceedings of the 58th Annual Meeting of the Association for Computational Linguistics*, pages 7871–7880, Online, July 2020. Association for Computational Linguistics. https://doi.org/10.18653/v1/2020.acl-main.703.

Chang Li, Aldo Porco, and Dan Goldwasser. Structured representation learning for online debate stance prediction. In Emily M. Bender, Leon Derczynski, and Pierre Isabelle, editors, *Proceedings of the 27th International Conference on Computational Linguistics*, pages 3728–3739, Santa Fe, New Mexico, USA, August 2018. Association for Computational Linguistics. URL https://aclanthology.org/C18-1316/.

Hao Li, Viktor Schlegel, Riza Batista-Navarro, and Goran Nenadic. Do you hear the people sing? Key point analysis via iterative clustering and abstractive summarisation. In Anna Rogers, Jordan Boyd-Graber, and Naoaki Okazaki, editors, *Proceedings of the 61st Annual Meeting of the Association for Computational Linguistics (Volume 1: Long Papers)*, pages 14064–14080, Toronto, Canada, July 2023. Association for Computational Linguistics. https://doi.org/10.18653/v1/2023.acl-long.786.

Hao Li, Yuping Wu, Viktor Schlegel, Riza Batista-Navarro, Tharindu Madusanka, Iqra Zahid, Jiayan Zeng, Xiaochi Wang, Xinran He, Yizhi Li, and Goran Nenadic. Which side are you on? A multi-task dataset for end-to-end argument summarisation and evaluation. In Lun-Wei Ku, Andre Martins, and Vivek Srikumar, editors, *Findings of the Association for Computational Linguistics ACL 2024*, pages 133–150, Bangkok, Thailand and virtual meeting, August 2024a. Association for Computational Linguistics. https://doi.org/10.18653/v1/2024.findings-acl.9.

Hao Li, Viktor Schlegel, Yizheng Sun, Riza Batista-Navarro, and Goran Nenadic. Large language models in argument mining: A survey, 2025. https://doi.org/10.48550/arXiv.2506.16383.

Jialu Li, Esin Durmus, and Claire Cardie. Exploring the role of argument structure in online debate persuasion. In Bonnie Webber, Trevor Cohn, Yulan He, and Yang Liu, editors, *Proceedings of the 2020 Conference on Empirical Methods in Natural Language Processing (EMNLP)*, pages 8905–8912, Online, November 2020. Association for Computational Linguistics. https://doi.org/10.18653/v1/2020.emnlp-main.716.

Ming Li, Jiuhai Chen, Lichang Chen, and Tianyi Zhou. Can LLMs speak for diverse people? Tuning LLMs via debate to generate controllable controversial statements. In Lun-Wei Ku, Andre Martins, and Vivek Srikumar, editors, *Findings of the Association for Computational Linguistics ACL 2024*, pages 16160–16176, Bangkok, Thailand and virtual meeting, August 2024b. Association for Computational Linguistics. https://doi.org/10.18653/v1/2024.findings-acl.956.

Yingjie Li, Tiberiu Sosea, Aditya Sawant, Ajith Jayaraman Nair, Diana Inkpen, and Cornelia Caragea. P-stance: A large dataset for stance detection in political domain. In Chengqing Zong, Fei Xia, Wenjie Li, and Roberto Navigli, editors, *Findings of the Association for Computational*

Linguistics: ACL-IJCNLP 2021, pages 2355–2365, Online, August 2021. Association for Computational Linguistics. https://doi.org/10.18653/v1/2021.findings-acl.208.

Chin-Yew Lin and Eduard Hovy. The automated acquisition of topic signatures for text summarization. In *COLING 2000 Volume 1: The 18th International Conference on Computational Linguistics*, 2000. URL https://aclanthology.org/C00-1072/.

Jiayu Lin, Rong Ye, Meng Han, Qi Zhang, Ruofei Lai, Xinyu Zhang, Zhao Cao, Xuanjing Huang, and Zhongyu Wei. Argue with me tersely: Towards sentence-level counter-argument generation. In Houda Bouamor, Juan Pino, and Kalika Bali, editors, *Proceedings of the 2023 Conference on Empirical Methods in Natural Language Processing*, pages 16705–16720, Singapore, December 2023. Association for Computational Linguistics. https://doi.org/10.18653/v1/2023.emnlp-main.1039.

Zhouhan Lin, Minwei Feng, Cicero Nogueira dos Santos, Mo Yu, Bing Xiang, Bowen Zhou, and Yoshua Bengio. A structured self-attentive sentence embedding. In *International Conference on Learning Representations*, 2017. URL https://openreview.net/forum?id=BJC_jUqxe.

Ziheng Lin, Hwee Tou Ng, and Min-Yen Kan. A PDTB-styled end-to-end discourse parser. *Natural Language Engineering*, 20(2):151–184, 2014. https://doi.org/10.1017/S1351324912000307.

Anna Lindahl and Lars Borin. Annotation for computational argumentation analysis: Issues and perspectives. *Language and Linguistics Compass*, 18(1):e12505, 2024. https://doi.org/10.1111/lnc3.12505.

Anna Lindahl, Lars Borin, and Jacobo Rouces. Towards assessing argumentation annotation - a first step. In *Proceedings of the 6th Workshop on Argument Mining*, pages 177–186, Florence, Italy, August 2019. Association for Computational Linguistics. https://doi.org/10.18653/v1/W19-4520.

Marco Lippi and Paolo Torroni. Context-independent claim detection for argument mining. In *Proceedings of the International Joint Conference on Artificial Intelligence*, pages 185–191, 2015. https://www.ijcai.org/Proceedings/15/Papers/033.pdf.

Marco Lippi and Paolo Torroni. Argumentation mining: State of the art and emerging trends. *ACM Transactions on Internet Technology*, 16(2):10:1–10:25, 2016. Special issue on Argumentation in Social Media. https://doi.org/10.1145/2850417.

Bing Liu. *Sentiment Analysis: Mining Opinions, Sentiments, and Emotions*. Cambridge University Press, Cambridge/UK, 2015. ISBN 9781139084789. https://doi.org/10.1017/CBO9781139084789.

Huadai Liu, Xu Wenqiang, Xuan Lin, Jingjing Huo, Hong Chen, and Zhou Zhao. AntCritic: Argument mining for free-form and visually-rich financial comments. In Nicoletta Calzolari, Min-Yen Kan, Veronique Hoste, Alessandro Lenci, Sakriani Sakti, and Nianwen Xue, editors, *Proceedings of the 2024 Joint International Conference on Computational Linguistics, Language Resources and Evaluation (LREC-COLING 2024)*, pages 1306–1317, Torino, Italia, May 2024a. ELRA and ICCL. URL https://aclanthology.org/2024.lrec-main.117/.

Xiao Liu, Yansong Feng, and Kai-Wei Chang. CASA: Causality-driven argument sufficiency assessment. In Kevin Duh, Helena Gomez, and Steven Bethard, editors, *Proceedings of the 2024 Conference of the North American Chapter of the Association for Computational Linguistics: Human Language Technologies (Volume 1: Long Papers)*, pages 5282–5302, Mexico City, Mexico, June 2024b. Association for Computational Linguistics. https://doi.org/10.18653/v1/2024.naacl-long.296.

Xiaodong Liu, Pengcheng He, Weizhu Chen, and Jianfeng Gao. Multi-task deep neural networks for natural language understanding. In Anna Korhonen, David Traum, and Lluís Màrquez, editors, *Proceedings of the 57th Annual Meeting of the Association for Computational Linguistics*, pages 4487–4496, Florence, Italy, July 2019a. Association for Computational Linguistics. https://doi.org/10.18653/v1/P19-1441.

Yang Liu. Fine-tune BERT for extractive summarization, 2019. https://doi.org/10.48550/arXiv.1903.10318.

Yinhan Liu, Myle Ott, Naman Goyal, Jingfei Du, Mandar Joshi, Danqi Chen, Omer Levy, M. Lewis, Luke Zettlemoyer, and Veselin Stoyanov. RoBERTa: A robustly optimized BERT pretraining approach, 2019b. https://doi.org/10.48550/arXiv.1907.11692.

Zhexiong Liu, Meiqi Guo, Yue Dai, and Diane Litman. ImageArg: A multi-modal tweet dataset for image persuasiveness mining. In Gabriella Lapesa, Jodi Schneider, Yohan Jo, and Sougata Saha, editors, *Proceedings of the 9th Workshop on Argument Mining*, pages 1–18, Online and in Gyeongju, Republic of Korea, October 2022. International Conference on Computational Linguistics. URL https://aclanthology.org/2022.argmining-1.1/.

Zhexiong Liu, Mohamed Elaraby, Yang Zhong, and Diane Litman. Overview of ImageArg-2023: The first shared task in multimodal argument mining. In Milad Alshomary, Chung-Chi Chen, Smaranda Muresan, Joonsuk Park, and Julia Romberg, editors, *Proceedings of the 10th Workshop on Argument Mining*, pages 120–132, Singapore, December 2023a. Association for Computational Linguistics. https://doi.org/10.18653/v1/2023.argmining-1.12.

Zhexiong Liu, Diane Litman, Elaine Wang, Lindsay Matsumura, and Richard Correnti. Predicting the quality of revisions in argumentative writing. In Ekaterina Kochmar, Jill Burstein, Andrea Horbach, Ronja Laarmann-Quante, Nitin Madnani, Anaïs Tack, Victoria Yaneva, Zheng Yuan, and Torsten Zesch, editors, *Proceedings of the 18th Workshop on Innovative Use of NLP for Building Educational Applications (BEA 2023)*, pages 275–287, Toronto, Canada, July 2023b. Association for Computational Linguistics. https://doi.org/10.18653/v1/2023.bea-1.24.

Zhexiong Liu, Diane Litman, Elaine L Wang, Tianwen Li, Mason Gobat, Lindsay Clare Matsumura, and Richard Correnti. eRevise+RF: A writing evaluation system for assessing student essay revisions and providing formative feedback, In *Proceedings of the 2025 Conference of the Nations of the Americas Chapter of the Association for Computational Linguistics: Human Language Technologies (System Demonstrations)*, pages 173–190, April 2025. https://doi.org/10.18653/v1/2025.naacl-demo.18.

Keith Lloyd. Rethinking rhetoric from an Indian perspective: Implications in the "Nyaya Sutra". *Rhetoric Review*, 26(4):365–384, 2007. https://doi.org/10.1080/07350190701577892.

Liane Longpre, Esin Durmus, and Claire Cardie. Persuasion of the undecided: Language vs. the listener. In Benno Stein and Henning Wachsmuth, editors, *Proceedings of the 6th Workshop on Argument Mining*, pages 167–176, Florence, Italy, August 2019. Association for Computational Linguistics. https://doi.org/10.18653/v1/W19-4519.

Luca Lugini and Diane Litman. Argument component classification for classroom discussions. In Noam Slonim and Ranit Aharonov, editors, *Proceedings of the 5th Workshop on Argument Mining*, pages 57–67, Brussels, Belgium, November 2018. Association for Computational Linguistics. https://doi.org/10.18653/v1/W18-5208.

Stephanie Lukin, Pranav Anand, Marilyn Walker, and Steve Whittaker. Argument strength is in the eye of the beholder: Audience effects in persuasion. In *Proceedings of the 15th Conference of the European Chapter of the Association for Computational Linguistics: Volume 1, Long Papers*, pages 742–753. Association for Computational Linguistics, 2017. URL https://aclanthology.org/E17-1070/.

Yiwei Luo, Dallas Card, and Dan Jurafsky. Detecting stance in media on global warming. In Trevor Cohn, Yulan He, and Yang Liu, editors, *Findings of the Association for Computational Linguistics: EMNLP 2020*, pages 3296–3315, Online, November 2020. Association for Computational Linguistics. https://doi.org/10.18653/v1/2020.findings-emnlp.296.

Kelvin Luu, Chenhao Tan, and Noah A. Smith. Measuring online debaters' persuasive skill from text over time. *Transactions of the Association for Computational Linguistics*, 7:537–550, 2019. https://doi.org/10.1162/tacl_a_00281.

Anastasios Lytos, Thomas Lagkas, Panagiotis Sarigiannidis, and Kalina Bontcheva. The evolution of argumentation mining: From models to social media and emerging tools. *Information Processing & Management*, 56(6):102055, November 2019. https://doi.org/10.1016/j.ipm.2019.102055.

Ruotian Ma, Xin Zhou, Tao Gui, Yiding Tan, Linyang Li, Qi Zhang, and Xuanjing Huang. Template-free prompt tuning for few-shot NER. In Marine Carpuat, Marie-Catherine de Marneffe, and Ivan Vladimir Meza Ruiz, editors, *Proceedings of the 2022 Conference of the North American Chapter of the Association for Computational Linguistics: Human Language Technologies*, pages 5721–5732, Seattle, United States, July 2022. Association for Computational Linguistics. https://doi.org/10.18653/v1/2022.naacl-main.420.

Xuezhe Ma and Eduard Hovy. End-to-end sequence labeling via bi-directional LSTM-CNNs-CRF. In Katrin Erk and Noah A. Smith, editors, *Proceedings of the 54th Annual Meeting of the Association for Computational Linguistics (Volume 1: Long Papers)*, pages 1064–1074, Berlin, Germany, August 2016. Association for Computational Linguistics. https://doi.org/10.18653/v1/P16-1101.

Fabrizio Macagno. Argumentation schemes in AI: A literature review. Introduction to the special issue. *Argument & Computation*, 12(3):287–302, January 2021. https://doi.org/10.3233/AAC-210020.

Fabrizio Macagno and Aikaterini Konstantinidou. What students' arguments can tell us: Using argumentation schemes in science education. *Argumentation*, 27:225–243, 2013. https://doi.org/10.1007/s10503-012-9284-5.

Jean-Guy Mailly. Using enthymemes to fill the gap between logical argumentation and revision of abstract argumentation frameworks. In *Proceedings of the 16th International Workshop on Non-monotonic Reasoning*, pages 95–104, 2016. https://nmr.krportal.org/proceedings/NMR2016Proceedings.pdf#page=103.

William Mann and Sandra Thompson. Rhetorical Structure Theory: Towards a functional theory of text organization. *Text - Interdisciplinary Journal for the Study of Discourse*, 8:243–281, 1988.

Santiago Marro, Elena Cabrio, and Serena Villata. Graph embeddings for argumentation quality assessment. In Yoav Goldberg, Zornitsa Kozareva, and Yue Zhang, editors, *Findings of the Association for Computational Linguistics: EMNLP 2022*, pages 4154–4164, Abu Dhabi, United Arab Emirates, December 2022. Association for Computational Linguistics. https://doi.org/10.18653/v1/2022.findings-emnlp.306.

André Martins, Mário Figueiredo, Pedro Aguiar, Noah Smith, and Eric Xing. AD3: Alternating directions dual decomposition for map inference in graphical models. *Journal of Machine Learning Research*, 16:495–545, 2015. https://jmlr.csail.mit.edu/papers/volume16/martins15a/martins15a.pdf.

Tobias Mayer, Elena Cabrio, and Serena Villata. ACTA: A tool for Argumentative Clinical Trial Analysis. In *Twenty-Eighth International Joint Conference on Artificial Intelligence IJCAI-19*, pages 6551–6553. International Joint Conferences on Artificial Intelligence Organization, August 2019. https://doi.org/10.24963/ijcai.2019/953.

Tobias Mayer, Elena Cabrio, and Serena Villata. Transformer-based argument mining for healthcare applications. In *Proceedings of the European Conference on Artificial Intelligence (ECAI)*, pages 2108–2115, 2020. https://doi.org/10.3233/FAIA200334.

James H. McBurney. The place of the enthymeme in rhetorical theory. *Speech Monographs*, 3(1): 49–74, 1936. https://doi.org/10.1080/03637753609374841.

Aline Menin, Franck Michel, Fabien Gandon, Raphaël Gazzotti, Elena Cabrio, Olivier Corby, Alain Giboin, Santiago Marro, Tobias Mayer, Serena Villata, and Marco Winckler. Covid-on-the-Web: Exploring the COVID-19 scientific literature through visualization of linked data from entity and argument mining. *Quantitative Science Studies*, 2(4):1301–1323, December 2021. https://doi.org/10.1162/qss_a_00164.

Stefano Menini and Sara Tonelli. Agreement and disagreement: Comparison of points of view in the political domain. In Yuji Matsumoto and Rashmi Prasad, editors, *Proceedings of COLING 2016, the 26th International Conference on Computational Linguistics: Technical Papers*, pages 2461–2470, Osaka, Japan, December 2016. The COLING 2016 Organizing Committee. URL https://aclanthology.org/C16-1232/.

Stefano Menini, Federico Nanni, Simone Paolo Ponzetto, and Sara Tonelli. Topic-based agreement and disagreement in US electoral manifestos. In Martha Palmer, Rebecca Hwa, and Sebastian Riedel, editors, *Proceedings of the 2017 Conference on Empirical Methods in Natural Language Processing*, pages 2938–2944, Copenhagen, Denmark, September 2017. Association for Computational Linguistics. https://doi.org/10.18653/v1/D17-1318.

Hugo Mercier and Dan Sperber. Why do humans reason? Arguments for an argumentative theory. *The Behavioral and brain sciences*, 34(2):57–74, 2011. https://doi.org/10.1017/S0140525X10000968.

Rafael Mestre, Razvan Milicin, Stuart E. Middleton, Matt Ryan, Jiatong Zhu, and Timothy J. Norman. M-Arg: Multimodal argument mining dataset for political debates with audio and transcripts. In Khalid Al-Khatib, Yufang Hou, and Manfred Stede, editors, *Proceedings of the 8th Workshop on Argument Mining*, pages 78–88, Punta Cana, Dominican Republic, November 2021. Association for Computational Linguistics. https://doi.org/10.18653/v1/2021.argmining-1.8.

Rada Mihalcea and Paul Tarau. TextRank: Bringing order into text. In Dekang Lin and Dekai Wu, editors, *Proceedings of the 2004 Conference on Empirical Methods in Natural Language Processing*, pages 404–411, Barcelona, Spain, July 2004. Association for Computational Linguistics. URL https://aclanthology.org/W04-3252/.

Tomás Mikolov, Kai Chen, Greg Corrado, and Jeffrey Dean. Efficient estimation of word representations in vector space. In Yoshua Bengio and Yann LeCun, editors, *Workshop Track Proceedings of the 1st International Conference on Learning Representations*, 2013. URL https://openreview.net/forum?id=idpCdOWtqXd60.

George A. Miller. WordNet: A lexical database for English. *Communications of the ACM*, 38(11): 39–41, November 1995. https://doi.org/10.1145/219717.219748.

Shachar Mirkin, Guy Moshkowich, Matan Orbach, Lili Kotlerman, Yoav Kantor, Tamar Lavee, Michal Jacovi, Yonatan Bilu, Ranit Aharonov, and Noam Slonim. Listening comprehension over argumentative content. In Ellen Riloff, David Chiang, Julia Hockenmaier, and Jun'ichi Tsujii, editors, *Proceedings of the 2018 Conference on Empirical Methods in Natural Language Processing*, pages 719–724, Brussels, Belgium, October-November 2018. Association for Computational Linguistics. https://doi.org/10.18653/v1/D18-1078.

Nailia Mirzakhmedova, Marcel Gohsen, Chia-Hao Chang, and Benno Stein. Are large language models reliable argument quality annotators? In Philipp Cimiano, Anette Frank, Michael Kohlhase, and Benno Stein, editors, *Proceedings of the First International Conference on Robust Argumentation Machines*, volume 14638 of *Lecture Notes in Computer Science*, pages 129–146. Springer, 2024a. https://doi.org/10.1007/978-3-031-63536-6_8.

Nailia Mirzakhmedova, Johannes Kiesel, Milad Alshomary, Maximilian Heinrich, Nicolas Handke, Xiaoni Cai, Valentin Barriere, Doratossadat Dastgheib, Omid Ghahroodi, MohammadAli SadraeiJavaheri, Ehsaneddin Asgari, Lea Kawaletz, Henning Wachsmuth, and Benno Stein. The Touché23-ValueEval dataset for identifying human values behind arguments. In Nicoletta Calzolari, Min-Yen Kan, Veronique Hoste, Alessandro Lenci, Sakriani Sakti, and Nianwen Xue, editors, *Proceedings of the 2024 Joint International Conference on Computational Linguistics, Language Resources and Evaluation (LREC-COLING 2024)*, pages 16121–16134, Torino, Italia, May 2024b. ELRA and ICCL. URL https://aclanthology.org/2024.lrec-main.1402/.

Amita Misra, Pranav Anand, Jean E. Fox Tree, and Marilyn Walker. Using summarization to discover argument facets in online idealogical dialog. In Rada Mihalcea, Joyce Chai, and Anoop Sarkar, editors, *Proceedings of the 2015 Conference of the North American Chapter of the Association for Computational Linguistics: Human Language Technologies*, pages 430–440, Denver, Colorado, 2015. Association for Computational Linguistics. https://doi.org/10.3115/v1/N15-1046.

Amita Misra, Brian Ecker, and Marilyn Walker. Measuring the similarity of sentential arguments in dialogue. In Raquel Fernandez, Wolfgang Minker, Giuseppe Carenini, Ryuichiro Higashinaka, Ron Artstein, and Alesia Gainer, editors, *Proceedings of the 17th Annual Meeting of the Special Interest Group on Discourse and Dialogue*, pages 276–287, Los Angeles, September 2016. Association for Computational Linguistics. https://doi.org/10.18653/v1/W16-3636.

Raquel Mochales and Aagje Ieven. Creating an argumentation corpus: Do theories apply to real arguments? A case study on the legal argumentation of the ECHR. In *Proceedings of the 12th International Conference on Artificial Intelligence and Law*, ICAIL '09, pages 21–30. Association for Computing Machinery, June 2009. https://doi.org/10.1145/1568234.1568238.

Raquel Mochales Palau and Marie-Francine Moens. Argumentation mining: The detection, classification and structuring of arguments in text. In *Proceedings of the International Conference on AI and Law*, pages 98–107, 2009. https://doi.org/10.1145/1568234.1568246.

Raquel Mochales Palau and Marie-Francine Moens. Argumentation mining. *Artificial Intelligence and Law*, 19(1):1–22, 2011. https://doi.org/10.1007/s10506-010-9104-x.

Sanjay Modgil and Henry Prakken. The $ASPIC^+$ framework for structured argumentation: A tutorial. *Argument & Computation*, 5(1):31–62, January 2014. https://doi.org/10.1080/19462166.2013.869766.

Saif Mohammad, Svetlana Kiritchenko, Parinaz Sobhani, Xiaodan Zhu, and Colin Cherry. SemEval-2016 task 6: Detecting stance in tweets. In *Proceedings of the 10th International Workshop on Semantic Evaluation (SemEval-2016)*, pages 31–41, 2016. https://doi.org/10.18653/v1/S16-1003.

Saif M. Mohammad, Parinaz Sobhani, and Svetlana Kiritchenko. Stance and sentiment in tweets. *ACM Transactions on Internet Technology (TOIT)*, 17(3):1–23, June 2017. https://doi.org/10.1145/3003433.

Benjamin Molinet, Santiago Marro, Elena Cabrio, Serena Villata, and Tobias Mayer. ACTA 2.0: A modular architecture for multi-layer argumentative analysis of clinical trials. In Lud De Raedt, editor, *Proceedings of the Thirty-First International Joint Conference on Artificial Intelligence Demo Track*, pages 5940–5943. International Joint Conferences on Artificial Intelligence Organization, 7 2022. https://doi.org/10.24963/ijcai.2022/859.

Gaku Morio, Hiroaki Ozaki, Terufumi Morishita, Yuta Koreeda, and Kohsuke Yanai. Towards better non-tree argument mining: Proposition-level biaffine parsing with task-specific parameterization. In Dan Jurafsky, Joyce Chai, Natalie Schluter, and Joel Tetreault, editors, *Proceedings of the 58th Annual Meeting of the Association for Computational Linguistics*, pages 3259–3266, Online, July 2020. Association for Computational Linguistics. https://doi.org/10.18653/v1/2020.acl-main.298.

Gaku Morio, Hiroaki Ozaki, Terufumi Morishita, and Kohsuke Yanai. End-to-end argument mining with cross-corpora multi-task learning. *Transactions of the Association for Computational Linguistics*, 10:639–658, 2022. https://doi.org/10.1162/tacl_a_00481.

Luca Mouchel, Debjit Paul, Shaobo Cui, Robert West, Antoine Bosselut, and Boi Faltings. A logical fallacy-informed framework for argument generation. In *Proceedings of the 2025 Conference of the Nations of the Americas Chapter of the Association for Computational Linguistics: Human Language Technologies (Volume 1: Long Papers)*, pages 7296–7314, Albuquerque, New Mexico, 2025. Association for Computational Linguistics. https://doi.org/10.18653/v1/2025.naacl-long.374.

Elena Musi, Myrto Aloumpi, Elinor Carmi, Simeon Yates, and Kay O'Halloran. Developing fake news immunity: Fallacies as misinformation triggers during the pandemic. *Online Journal of Communication and Media Technologies*, 12(3), July 2022. https://doi.org/10.30935/ojcmt/12083.

Elena Musi. Framing to make an argument: The case of the genocide hashtag in the Russia-Ukraine war. *Argumentation*, 38:269–288, 2024. https://doi.org/10.1007/s10503-024-09632-1.

Elena Musi, Debanjan Ghosh, and Smaranda Muresan. Towards feasible guidelines for the annotation of argument schemes. In Chris Reed, editor, *Proceedings of the Third Workshop on Argument Mining (ArgMining2016)*, pages 82–93, Berlin, Germany, August 2016. Association for Computational Linguistics. https://doi.org/10.18653/v1/W16-2810.

Elena Musi, Tariq Alhindi, Manfred Stede, Leonard Kriese, Smaranda Muresan, and Andrea Rocci. A multi-layer annotated corpus of argumentative text: From argument schemes to discourse relations. In Nicoletta Calzolari, Khalid Choukri, Christopher Cieri, Thierry Declerck, Sara Goggi, Koiti Hasida, Hitoshi Isahara, Bente Maegaard, Joseph Mariani, Hélène Mazo, Asuncion Moreno, Jan Odijk, Stelios Piperidis, and Takenobu Tokunaga, editors, *Proceedings of the Eleventh International Conference on Language Resources and Evaluation (LREC 2018)*, pages 1629–1636, Miyazaki, Japan, May 2018. European Language Resources Association (ELRA). URL https://aclanthology.org/L18-1258/.

Elena Musi, Nadin Kökciyan, Khalid Al Khatib, Davide Ceolin, Emmanuelle Dietz, Klara Maximiliane Gutekunst, Annette Hautli-Janisz, Cristián Santibáñez, Jodi Schneider, Jonas Scholz, Cor Steging, Jacky Visser, and Henning Wachsmuth. Toward reasonable parrots: Why large language models should argue with us by design. In Elena Chistova, Philipp Cimiano, Shohreh Haddadan, Gabriella Lapesa, and Ramon Ruiz-Dolz, editors, *Proceedings of the 12th Argument Mining Workshop*, pages 24–31, Vienna, Austria, July 2025. Association for Computational Linguistics. https://doi.org/10.18653/v1/2025.argmining-1.3.

Arianna Muti, Federico Ruggeri, Khalid Al Khatib, Alberto Barrón-Cedeño, and Tommaso Caselli. Language is scary when over-analyzed: Unpacking implied misogynistic reasoning with argumentation theory-driven prompts. In Yaser Al-Onaizan, Mohit Bansal, and Yun-Nung Chen, editors, *Proceedings of the 2024 Conference on Empirical Methods in Natural Language Processing*, pages 21091–21107, Miami, Florida, USA, November 2024. Association for Computational Linguistics. https://doi.org/10.18653/v1/2024.emnlp-main.1174.

Sara Nabhani, Khalid Al Khatib, Federico Pianzola, and Malvina Nissim. Storytelling in argumentative discussions: Exploring the use of narratives in ChangeMyView. In Elena Chistova, Philipp Cimiano, Shohreh Haddadan, Gabriella Lapesa, and Ramon Ruiz-Dolz, editors, *Proceedings of the 12th Argument Mining Workshop*, pages 217–227, Vienna, Austria, July 2025. Association for Computational Linguistics. https://doi.org/10.18653/v1/2025.argmining-1.21.

Nona Naderi and Graeme Hirst. Argumentation mining in parliamentary discourse. In Matteo Baldoni, Cristina Baroglio, Floris Bex, Floriana Grasso, Nancy Green, Mohammad-Reza Namazi-Rad, Masayuki Numao, and Merlin Teodosia Suarez, editors, *Principles and Practice of Multi-Agent Systems*, pages 16–25, Cham, 2016. Springer International Publishing. https://doi.org/10.1007/978-3-319-46218-9_2.

Nona Naderi and Graeme Hirst. Classifying frames at the sentence level in news articles. In Ruslan Mitkov and Galia Angelova, editors, *Proceedings of the International Conference Recent Advances in Natural Language Processing, RANLP 2017*, pages 536–542, Varna, Bulgaria, September 2017. INCOMA Ltd. https://doi.org/10.26615/978-954-452-049-6_070.

Ivan Namor, Pietro Totis, Samuele Garda, and Manfred Stede. Mining Italian short argumentative texts. In *Proceedings of the Italian Conference on Computational Linguistics (CLiC-it)*, volume 2481 of *CEUR Workshop Proceedings*, pages 1–6, Bari, 2019. CEUR-WS.org. URL https://ceur-ws.org/Vol-2481/paper53.pdf.

Ani Nenkova, Lucy Vanderwende, and Kathleen McKeown. A compositional context sensitive multi-document summarizer: Exploring the factors that influence summarization. In *Proceedings of the 29th Annual International ACM SIGIR Conference on Research and Development in Information Retrieval*, SIGIR '06, pages 573–580, New York, NY, USA, 2006. Association for Computing Machinery. https://doi.org/10.1145/1148170.1148269.

Lily Ng, Anne Lauscher, Joel Tetreault, and Courtney Napoles. Creating a domain-diverse corpus for theory-based argument quality assessment. In Elena Cabrio and Serena Villata, editors, *Proceedings of the 7th Workshop on Argument Mining*, pages 117–126, Online, December 2020. Association for Computational Linguistics. URL https://aclanthology.org/2020.argmining-1.13.

Dat Quoc Nguyen, Thanh Vu, and Anh Tuan Nguyen. BERTweet: A pre-trained language model for English tweets. In Qun Liu and David Schlangen, editors, *Proceedings of the 2020 Conference on Empirical Methods in Natural Language Processing: System Demonstrations*, pages 9–14, Online, October 2020. Association for Computational Linguistics. https://doi.org/10.18653/v1/2020.emnlp-demos.2.

Huy Nguyen and Diane Litman. Extracting argument and domain words for identifying argument components in texts. In *Proceedings of the 2nd Workshop on Argumentation Mining*, pages 22–28, 2015. https://doi.org/10.3115/v1/W15-0503.

Huy Nguyen and Diane Litman. Context-aware argumentative relation mining. In Katrin Erk and Noah A. Smith, editors, *Proceedings of the 54th Annual Meeting of the Association for Computational Linguistics (Volume 1: Long Papers)*, pages 1127–1137, Berlin, Germany, August 2016. Association for Computational Linguistics. https://doi.org/10.18653/v1/P16-1107.

Vlad Niculae, Joonsuk Park, and Claire Cardie. Argument mining with structured SVMs and RNNs. In Regina Barzilay and Min-Yen Kan, editors, *Proceedings of the 55th Annual Meeting of the Association for Computational Linguistics (Volume 1: Long Papers)*, pages 985–995, Vancouver, Canada, July 2017. Association for Computational Linguistics. https://doi.org/10.18653/v1/P17-1091.

Timothy Niven and Hung-Yu Kao. NLITrans at SemEval-2018 task 12: Transfer of semantic knowledge for argument comprehension. In Marianna Apidianaki, Saif M. Mohammad, Jonathan May, Ekaterina Shutova, Steven Bethard, and Marine Carpuat, editors, *Proceedings of the 12th International Workshop on Semantic Evaluation*, pages 1099–1103, New Orleans, Louisiana, June 2018. Association for Computational Linguistics. https://doi.org/10.18653/v1/S18-1185.

Timothy Niven and Hung-Yu Kao. Probing neural network comprehension of natural language arguments. In Anna Korhonen, David Traum, and Lluís Màrquez, editors, *Proceedings of the 57th Annual Meeting of the Association for Computational Linguistics*, pages 4658–4664, Florence, Italy, July 2019. Association for Computational Linguistics. https://doi.org/10.18653/v1/P19-1459.

Daphne Odekerken, AnneMarie Borg, and Matti Berthold. Accessible algorithms for applied argumentation. In *First International Workshop on Argumentation and Applications*, volume 3472 of *CEUR Workshop Proceedings*, pages 92–98. CEUR-WS.org, 2023. URL https://www.ceur-ws.org/Vol-3472/short3.pdf.

Daniel J. O'Keefe and Sally Jackson. Argument quality and persuasive effects: A review of current approaches. In *Argumentation and Values: Proceedings of the Ninth Alta Conference on Argumentation*, pages 88–92, 1995.

Stefan Ollinger, Lorik Dumani, Premtim Sahitaj, Ralph Bergmann, and Ralf Schenkel. Same side stance classification using contextualized sentence embeddings. In Yamen Ajjour, Khalid Al-Khatib, Philipp Cimiano, Roxanne El Baff, Basil Ell, Benno Stein, and Henning Wachsmuth, editors, *Same Side Stance Classification Shared Task 2019*, volume 2921 of *CEUR Workshop Proceedings*, pages 26–30. CEUR-WS.org, July 2021. URL https://ceur-ws.org/Vol-2921/paper4.pdf.

OpenAI, Josh Achiam, Steven Adler, Sandhini Agarwal, Lama Ahmad, Ilge Akkaya, Florencia Leoni Aleman, Diogo Almeida, Janko Altenschmidt, Sam Altman, Shyamal Anadkat, Red Avila, Igor Babuschkin, Suchir Balaji, Valerie Balcom, Paul Baltescu, Haiming Bao, Mohammad Bavarian, Jeff Belgum, Irwan Bello, Jake Berdine, Gabriel Bernadett-Shapiro, Christopher Berner, Lenny Bogdonoff, Oleg Boiko, Madelaine Boyd, Anna-Luisa Brakman, Greg Brockman, Tim Brooks, Miles Brundage, Kevin Button, Trevor Cai, Rosie Campbell, Andrew Cann, Brittany Carey, Chelsea Carlson, Rory Carmichael, Brooke Chan, Che Chang, Fotis Chantzis, Derek Chen, Sully Chen, Ruby Chen, Jason Chen, Mark Chen, Ben Chess, Chester Cho, Casey Chu, Hyung Won Chung, Dave Cummings, Jeremiah Currier, Yunxing Dai, Cory Decareaux, Thomas Degry, Noah Deutsch, Damien Deville, Arka Dhar, David Dohan, Steve Dowling, Sheila Dunning, Adrien Ecoffet, Atty Eleti, Tyna Eloundou, David Farhi, Liam Fedus, Niko Felix, Simón Posada Fishman, Juston Forte, Isabella Fulford, Leo Gao, Elie Georges, Christian Gibson, Vik Goel, Tarun Gogineni, Gabriel Goh, Rapha Gontijo-Lopes, Jonathan Gordon, Morgan Grafstein, Scott Gray, Ryan Greene, Joshua Gross, Shixiang Shane Gu, Yufei Guo, Chris Hallacy, Jesse Han, Jeff Harris, Yuchen He, Mike Heaton, Johannes Heidecke, Chris Hesse, Alan Hickey, Wade Hickey, Peter Hoeschele, Brandon Houghton, Kenny Hsu, Shengli Hu, Xin Hu, Joost Huizinga, Shantanu Jain, Shawn Jain, Joanne Jang, Angela Jiang, Roger Jiang, Haozhun Jin, Denny Jin, Shino Jomoto, Billie Jonn, Heewoo Jun, Tomer Kaftan, Lukasz Kaiser, Ali Kamali, Ingmar Kanitscheider, Nitish Shirish Keskar, Tabarak Khan, Logan Kilpatrick, Jong Wook Kim, Christina Kim, Yongjik Kim, Jan Hendrik Kirchner, Jamie Kiros, Matt Knight, Daniel Kokotajlo, Lukasz Kondraciuk, Andrew Kondrich, Aris Konstantinidis, Kyle Kosic, Gretchen Krueger, Vishal Kuo, Michael Lampe, Ikai Lan, Teddy Lee, Jan Leike, Jade Leung, Daniel Levy, Chak Ming Li, Rachel Lim, Molly Lin, Stephanie Lin, Mateusz Litwin, Theresa Lopez, Ryan Lowe, Patricia Lue, Anna Makanju, Kim Malfacini, Sam Manning, Todor Markov, Yaniv Markovski, Bianca Martin, Katie Mayer, Andrew Mayne, Bob McGrew, Scott Mayer McKinney, Christine McLeavey, Paul McMillan, Jake McNeil, David Medina, Aalok Mehta, Jacob Menick, Luke Metz, Andrey Mishchenko, Pamela Mishkin, Vinnie Monaco, Evan Morikawa, Daniel Mossing, Tong Mu, Mira Murati, Oleg Murk, David Mély, Ashvin Nair, Reiichiro Nakano, Rajeev Nayak, Arvind Neelakantan, Richard Ngo, Hyeonwoo Noh, Long Ouyang, Cullen O'Keefe, Jakub Pachocki, Alex Paino, Joe Palermo, Ashley Pantuliano, Giambattista Parascandolo, Joel Parish, Emy Parparita, Alex Passos, Mikhail Pavlov, Andrew Peng, Adam Perelman, Filipe de Avila Belbute Peres, Michael Petrov, Henrique Ponde de Oliveira Pinto, Michael, Pokorny, Michelle Pokrass, Vitchyr H. Pong, Tolly Powell, Alethea Power, Boris Power, Elizabeth Proehl, Raul Puri, Alec Radford, Jack Rae, Aditya Ramesh, Cameron Raymond, Francis Real, Kendra Rimbach, Carl Ross, Bob Rotsted, Henri Roussez, Nick Ryder, Mario Saltarelli, Ted Sanders, Shibani Santurkar, Girish Sastry, Heather Schmidt, David Schnurr, John Schulman, Daniel Selsam, Kyla Sheppard, Toki Sherbakov, Jessica Shieh, Sarah Shoker, Pranav Shyam, Szymon Sidor, Eric Sigler, Maddie Simens, Jordan Sitkin, Katarina Slama, Ian Sohl, Benjamin Sokolowsky, Yang Song, Natalie Staudacher, Felipe Petroski Such, Natalie Summers, Ilya Sutskever, Jie Tang, Nikolas Tezak, Madeleine B. Thompson, Phil Tillet, Amin Tootoonchian, Elizabeth Tseng, Preston Tuggle, Nick Turley, Jerry Tworek, Juan Felipe Cerón Uribe, Andrea Vallone, Arun Vijayvergiya, Chelsea Voss, Carroll Wainwright, Justin Jay Wang, Alvin Wang, Ben Wang, Jonathan Ward, Jason Wei, CJ Weinmann, Akila Welihinda, Peter Welinder, Jiayi Weng, Lilian Weng, Matt Wiethoff, Dave Willner, Clemens Winter, Samuel Wolrich, Hannah Wong, Lauren Workman, Sherwin Wu, Jeff Wu, Michael Wu, Kai Xiao, Tao Xu, Sarah Yoo, Kevin Yu, Qiming Yuan, Wojciech Zaremba, Rowan Zellers, Chong Zhang, Marvin Zhang, Shengjia Zhao, Tianhao Zheng, Juntang Zhuang, William Zhuk, and Barret Zoph. GPT-4 technical report, 2024. https://doi.org/10.48550/arXiv.2303.08774.

Juri Opitz and Anette Frank. Dissecting content and context in argumentative relation analysis. In Benno Stein and Henning Wachsmuth, editors, *Proceedings of the 6th Workshop on Argument Mining*, pages 25–34, Florence, Italy, August 2019. Association for Computational Linguistics. https://doi.org/10.18653/v1/W19-4503.

Juri Opitz, Philipp Heinisch, Philipp Wiesenbach, Philipp Cimiano, and Anette Frank. Explainable unsupervised argument similarity rating with abstract meaning representation and conclusion generation. In Khalid Al-Khatib, Yufang Hou, and Manfred Stede, editors, *Proceedings of the 8th Workshop on Argument Mining*, pages 24–35, Punta Cana, Dominican Republic, November 2021. Association for Computational Linguistics. https://doi.org/10.18653/v1/2021.argmining-1.3.

Lawrence Page, Sergey Brin, Rajeev Motwani, and Terry Winograd. The PageRank citation ranking: Bringing order to the Web. Technical Report SIDL-WP-1999-0120, Stanford InfoLab, 1999.

Fabio Paglieri and John Woods. Enthymemes: From reconstruction to understanding. *Argumentation*, 25:127–139, 2011. https://doi.org/10.1007/s10503-011-9203-1.

Alonso Palomino, Khalid Al Khatib, Martin Potthast, and Benno Stein. Differential bias: On the perceptibility of stance imbalance in argumentation. In Yulan He, Heng Ji, Sujian Li, Yang Liu, and Chua-Hui Chang, editors, *Findings of the Association for Computational Linguistics: AACL-IJCNLP 2022*, pages 411–421, Online only, November 2022. Association for Computational Linguistics. https://doi.org/10.18653/v1/2022.findings-aacl.39.

Giovanni Paolini, Ben Athiwaratkun, Jason Krone, Jie Ma, Alessandro Achille, Rishita Anubhai, Cicero Nogueira dos Santos, Bing Xiang, and Stefano Soatto. Structured prediction as translation between augmented natural languages. In *Proceedings of the 9th International Conference on Learning Representations (ICLR)*, pages 1–26, 2021. https://iclr.cc/virtual/2021/spotlight/3411.

Loreto Parisi, Simone Francia, and Paolo Magnani. UmBERTo: an Italian language model trained with whole word masking. https://github.com/musixmatchresearch/umberto, 2020.

ChaeHun Park, Wonsuk Yang, and Jong Park. Generating sentential arguments from diverse perspectives on controversial topic. In Anna Feldman, Giovanni Da San Martino, Alberto Barrón-Cedeño, Chris Brew, Chris Leberknight, and Preslav Nakov, editors, *Proceedings of the Second Workshop on Natural Language Processing for Internet Freedom: Censorship, Disinformation, and Propaganda*, pages 56–65, Hong Kong, China, November 2019. Association for Computational Linguistics. https://doi.org/10.18653/v1/D19-5007.

Joonsuk Park and Claire Cardie. Identifying appropriate support for propositions in online user comments. In Nancy Green, Kevin Ashley, Diane Litman, Chris Reed, and Vern Walker, editors, *Proceedings of the First Workshop on Argumentation Mining*, pages 29–38, Baltimore, Maryland, June 2014. Association for Computational Linguistics. https://doi.org/10.3115/v1/W14-2105.

Joonsuk Park and Claire Cardie. A corpus of eRulemaking user comments for measuring evaluability of arguments. In *Proceedings of the Eleventh International Conference on Language Resources and Evaluation (LREC 2018)*, pages 1623–1628, Miyazaki, Japan, May 2018. European Language Resources Association (ELRA). URL https://aclanthology.org/L18-1257/.

Joonsuk Park, Cheryl Blake, and Claire Cardie. Toward machine-assisted participation in eRulemaking: An argumentation model of evaluability. In *Proceedings of the 15th International Conference on Artificial Intelligence and Law*, ICAIL '15, pages 206–210, New York, NY, USA, 2015. Association for Computing Machinery. https://doi.org/10.1145/2746090.2746118.

Debjit Paul, Juri Opitz, Maria Becker, Jonathan Kobbe, Graeme Hirst, and Anette Frank. Argumentative relation classification with background knowledge. In *Computational Models of Argument*, Frontiers in Artificial Intelligence and Applications, pages 319–330. IOS Press, 2020. https://doi.org/10.3233/faia200515.

Amirreza Payandeh, Dan Pluth, Jordan Hosier, Xuesu Xiao, and Vijay K. Gurbani. How susceptible are LLMs to logical fallacies? In Nicoletta Calzolari, Min-Yen Kan, Veronique Hoste, Alessandro

Lenci, Sakriani Sakti, and Nianwen Xue, editors, *Proceedings of the 2024 Joint International Conference on Computational Linguistics, Language Resources and Evaluation (LREC-COLING 2024)*, pages 8276–8286, Torino, Italia, May 2024. ELRA and ICCL. URL https://aclanthology.org/2024.lrec-main.726/.

Andreas Peldszus and Manfred Stede. From argument diagrams to argumentation mining in texts: A survey. *International Journal of Cognitive Informatics and Natural Intelligence (IJCINI)*, 7(1): 1–31, 2013. https://doi.org/10.4018/jcini.2013010101.

Andreas Peldszus and Manfred Stede. Joint prediction in MST-style discourse parsing for argumentation mining. In Lluís Màrquez, Chris Callison-Burch, and Jian Su, editors, *Proceedings of the 2015 Conference on Empirical Methods in Natural Language Processing*, pages 938–948, Lisbon, Portugal, September 2015. Association for Computational Linguistics. https://doi.org/10.18653/v1/D15-1110.

Andreas Peldszus and Manfred Stede. Rhetorical structure and argumentation structure in monologue text. In Chris Reed, editor, *Proceedings of the Third Workshop on Argument Mining (ArgMining2016)*, pages 103–112, Berlin, Germany, August 2016a. Association for Computational Linguistics. https://doi.org/10.18653/v1/W16-2812.

Andreas Peldszus and Manfred Stede. An annotated corpus of argumentative microtexts. In *Argumentation and Reasoned Action: Proceedings of the 1st European Conference on Argumentation, Lisbon 2015 / Vol. 2*, pages 801–816. College Publications, London, 2016b.

James W. Pennebaker, Roger J. Booth, Ryan L. Boyd, and Martha E. Francis. Linguistic Inquiry and Word Count: LIWC2015. Pennebaker Conglomerates, Austin, TX, 2015. https://www.liwc.net.

Jeffrey Pennington, Richard Socher, and Christopher Manning. GloVe: Global vectors for word representation. In Alessandro Moschitti, Bo Pang, and Walter Daelemans, editors, *Proceedings of the 2014 Conference on Empirical Methods in Natural Language Processing (EMNLP)*, pages 1532–1543, Doha, Qatar, 2014. Association for Computational Linguistics. https://doi.org/10.3115/v1/D14-1162.

Chaïm Perelman and Lucie Olbrechts-Tyteca. *The New Rhetoric: A Treatise on Argumentation*. University of Notre Dame Press, 1969. https://doi.org/10.2307/j.ctvpj74xx.

Bryan Perozzi, Rami Al-Rfou, and Steven Skiena. DeepWalk: Online learning of social representations. In *Proceedings of the 20th ACM SIGKDD International Conference on Knowledge Discovery and Data Mining*, KDD '14, pages 701–710, New York, NY, USA, 2014. Association for Computing Machinery. https://doi.org/10.1145/2623330.2623732.

Isaac Persing and Vincent Ng. Modeling thesis clarity in student essays. In *Proceedings of the 51st Annual Meeting of the Association for Computational Linguistics (Volume 1: Long Papers)*, pages 260–269. Association for Computational Linguistics, 2013. URL https://aclanthology.org/P13-1026/.

Isaac Persing and Vincent Ng. Modeling prompt adherence in student essays. In *Proceedings of the 52nd Annual Meeting of the Association for Computational Linguistics (Volume 1: Long Papers)*, pages 1534–1543. Association for Computational Linguistics, 2014. https://doi.org/10.3115/v1/P14-1144.

Isaac Persing and Vincent Ng. Modeling argument strength in student essays. In *Proceedings of the 53rd Annual Meeting of the Association for Computational Linguistics and the 7th International Joint Conference on Natural Language Processing (Volume 1: Long Papers)*, pages 543–552. Association for Computational Linguistics, 2015. https://doi.org/10.3115/v1/P15-1053.

Isaac Persing and Vincent Ng. End-to-end argumentation mining in student essays. In Kevin Knight, Ani Nenkova, and Owen Rambow, editors, *Proceedings of the 2016 Conference of the North American Chapter of the Association for Computational Linguistics: Human Language Technologies*, pages 1384–1394, San Diego, California, June 2016. Association for Computational Linguistics. https://doi.org/10.18653/v1/N16-1164.

Isaac Persing and Vincent Ng. Why can't you convince me? Modeling weaknesses in unpersuasive arguments. In *Proceedings of the Twenty-Sixth International Joint Conference on Artificial Intelligence, IJCAI-17*, pages 4082–4088, 2017a. https://doi.org/10.24963/ijcai.2017/570.

Isaac Persing and Vincent Ng. Lightly-supervised modeling of argument persuasiveness. In Greg Kondrak and Taro Watanabe, editors, *Proceedings of the Eighth International Joint Conference on Natural Language Processing (Volume 1: Long Papers)*, pages 594–604, Taipei, Taiwan, November 2017b. Asian Federation of Natural Language Processing. URL https://aclanthology.org/I17-1060.

Isaac Persing and Vincent Ng. Unsupervised argumentation mining in student essays. In Nicoletta Calzolari, Frédéric Béchet, Philippe Blache, Khalid Choukri, Christopher Cieri, Thierry Declerck, Sara Goggi, Hitoshi Isahara, Bente Maegaard, Joseph Mariani, Hélène Mazo, Asuncion Moreno, Jan Odijk, and Stelios Piperidis, editors, *Proceedings of the Twelfth Language Resources and Evaluation Conference*, pages 6795–6803, Marseille, France, May 2020. European Language Resources Association. ISBN 979-10-95546-34-4. URL https://aclanthology.org/2020.lrec-1.839/.

Isaac Persing, Alan Davis, and Vincent Ng. Modeling organization in student essays. In *Proceedings of the 2010 Conference on Empirical Methods in Natural Language Processing*, pages 229–239. Association for Computational Linguistics, 2010. URL https://aclanthology.org/D10-1023/.

Georgios Petasis. Segmentation of argumentative texts with contextualised word representations. In Benno Stein and Henning Wachsmuth, editors, *Proceedings of the 6th Workshop on Argument Mining*, pages 1–10, Florence, Italy, August 2019. Association for Computational Linguistics. https://doi.org/10.18653/v1/W19-4501.

Philipp Petrenz and Bonnie Webber. Stable classification of text genres. *Computational Linguistics*, 37(2):385–393, 2011. https://doi.org/10.1162/COLI_a_00052.

Jonas Pfeiffer, Aishwarya Kamath, Andreas Rücklé, Kyunghyun Cho, and Iryna Gurevych. Adapter-Fusion: Non-destructive task composition for transfer learning. In Paola Merlo, Jorg Tiedemann, and Reut Tsarfaty, editors, *Proceedings of the 16th Conference of the European Chapter of the Association for Computational Linguistics: Main Volume*, pages 487–503, Online, April 2021. Association for Computational Linguistics. https://doi.org/10.18653/v1/2021.eacl-main.39.

Jakub Piskorski, Nicolas Stefanovitch, Nikolaos Nikolaidis, Giovanni Da San Martino, and Preslav Nakov. Multilingual multifaceted understanding of online news in terms of genre, framing, and persuasion techniques. In Anna Rogers, Jordan Boyd-Graber, and Naoaki Okazaki, editors, *Proceedings of the 61st Annual Meeting of the Association for Computational Linguistics (Volume 1: Long Papers)*, pages 3001–3022, Toronto, Canada, July 2023. Association for Computational Linguistics. https://doi.org/10.18653/v1/2023.acl-long.169.

Barbara Plank. The "problem" of human label variation: On ground truth in data, modeling and evaluation. In Yoav Goldberg, Zornitsa Kozareva, and Yue Zhang, editors, *Proceedings of the 2022 Conference on Empirical Methods in Natural Language Processing*, pages 10671–10682, Abu Dhabi, United Arab Emirates, December 2022. Association for Computational Linguistics. https://doi.org/10.18653/v1/2022.emnlp-main.731.

Moritz Plenz, Philipp Heinisch, Anette Frank, and Philipp Cimiano. PAKT: Perspectivized argumentation knowledge graph and tool for deliberation analysis. In Philipp Cimiano, Anette Frank, Michael Kohlhase, and Benno Stein, editors, *Robust Argumentation Machines*, pages 89–107, Cham, 2024. Springer Nature Switzerland. https://doi.org/10.1007/978-3-031-63536-6_6.

Moritz Plenz, Philipp Heinisch, Janosch Gehring, Philipp Cimiano, and Anette Frank. From argumentation to deliberation: Perspectivized stance vectors for fine-grained (dis)agreement analysis. In *Findings of the Association for Computational Linguistics: NAACL 2025*, pages 1525–1553, Albuquerque, New Mexico, 2025. Association for Computational Linguistics. https://doi.org/10.18653/v1/2025.findings-naacl.83.

H. José Plug and Jean H. M. Wagemans. From fact-checking to rhetoric-checking: Extending methods for evaluating populist discourse. In *Vox Populi*, pages 236–252. Edward Elgar Publishing, August 2020. https://doi.org/10.4337/9781789901412.00023.

Maria Poiaganova and Manfred Stede. From debates to diplomacy: Argument mining across political registers. In *Proceedings of the 12th Workshop on Argument Mining*, pages 205–216, Vienna, Austria, July 2025. https://doi.org/10.18653/v1/2025.argmining-1.20.

Marco Polignano, Pierpaolo Basile, Marco de Gemmis, Giovanni Semeraro, and Valerio Basile. Alberto: Italian BERT language understanding model for NLP challenging tasks based on tweets. In Raffaella Bernardi, Roberto Navigli, and Giovanni Semeraro, editors, *Proceedings of the Sixth Italian Conference on Computational Linguistics*, volume 2481 of *CEUR Workshop Proceedings*, pages 1–6. CEUR-WS.org, 2019. URL https://ceur-ws.org/Vol-2481/paper57.pdf.

John L. Pollock. Defeasible reasoning. *Cognitive Science*, 11(4):481–518, 1987. https://doi.org/10.1207/s15516709cog1104_4.

Peter Potash and Anna Rumshisky. Towards debate automation: A recurrent model for predicting debate winners. In Martha Palmer, Rebecca Hwa, and Sebastian Riedel, editors, *Proceedings of the 2017 Conference on Empirical Methods in Natural Language Processing*, pages 2465–2475, Copenhagen, Denmark, September 2017. Association for Computational Linguistics. https://doi.org/10.18653/v1/D17-1261.

Peter Potash, Robin Bhattacharya, and Anna Rumshisky. Length, interchangeability, and external knowledge: Observations from predicting argument convincingness. In *Proceedings of the Eighth International Joint Conference on Natural Language Processing (Volume 1: Long Papers)*, pages 342–351, Taipei, Taiwan, November 2017a. Asian Federation of Natural Language Processing. URL https://aclanthology.org/I17-1035/.

Peter Potash, Alexey Romanov, and Anna Rumshisky. Here's my point: Joint pointer architecture for argument mining. In Martha Palmer, Rebecca Hwa, and Sebastian Riedel, editors, *Proceedings of the 2017 Conference on Empirical Methods in Natural Language Processing*, pages 1364–1373, Copenhagen, Denmark, September 2017b. Association for Computational Linguistics. https://doi.org/10.18653/v1/D17-1143.

Martin Potthast, Lukas Gienapp, Florian Euchner, Nick Heilenkötter, Nico Weidmann, Henning Wachsmuth, Benno Stein, and Matthias Hagen. Argument search: Assessing argument relevance. In *42nd International ACM Conference on Research and Development in Information Retrieval (SIGIR 2019)*, pages 1117–1120. Association for Computing Machinery, July 2019. https://doi.org/10.1145/3331184.3331327.

Prakash Poudyal, Jaromir Savelka, Aagje Ieven, Marie Francine Moens, Teresa Goncalves, and Paulo Quaresma. ECHR: Legal corpus for argument mining. In Elena Cabrio and Serena Villata, editors, *Proceedings of the 7th Workshop on Argument Mining*, pages 67–75, Online, December 2020. Association for Computational Linguistics. URL https://aclanthology.org/2020.argmining-1.8/.

John Pougué-Biyong, Valentina Semenova, Alexandre Matton, Rachel Han, Aerin Kim, Renaud Lambiotte, and Doyne Farmer. DEBAGREEMENT: A comment-reply dataset for (dis)agreement detection in online debates. In Joaquin Vanschoren and Sai-Kit Yeung, editors, *Proceedings of the Neural Information Processing Systems Track on Datasets and Benchmarks 1, NeurIPS Datasets and Benchmarks 2021*, pages 1–12, 2021. URL https://datasets-benchmarks-proceedings.neurips.cc/paper/2021/hash/6f3ef77ac0e3619e98159e9b6febf557-Abstract-round2.html.

Vinodkumar Prabhakaran, Owen Rambow, and Mona Diab. Automatic committed belief tagging. In *Coling 2010: Posters*, pages 1014–1022, Beijing, China. Coling 2010 Organizing Committee, 2010. URL https://aclanthology.org/C10-2117.pdf.

Rashmi Prasad, Nikhil Dinesh, Alan Lee, Eleni Miltsakaki, Livio Robaldo, Aravind Joshi, and Bonnie Webber. The Penn Discourse Treebank 2.0. In *Proceedings of the Sixth International*

Conference on Language Resources and Evaluation (LREC'08), pages 2961–2968, Marrakech, Morocco. European Language Resources Association (ELRA), 2008. URL http://www.lrec-conf.org/proceedings/lrec2008/pdf/754_paper.pdf.

Arthur N. Prior. Logic, Traditional. In Donald M. Borchert, editor, *Encyclopedia of Philosophy*, volume 5, pages 493–506. 1967. 2nd ed. Macmillan Reference, 2006. ISBN: 0-02-865785-3.

Sukannya Purkayastha, Anne Lauscher, and Iryna Gurevych. Exploring Jiu-Jitsu argumentation for writing peer review rebuttals. In Houda Bouamor, Juan Pino, and Kalika Bali, editors, *Proceedings of the 2023 Conference on Empirical Methods in Natural Language Processing*, pages 14479–14495, Singapore, December 2023. Association for Computational Linguistics. https://doi.org/10.18653/v1/2023.emnlp-main.894.

Jan Wira Gotama Putra, Simone Teufel, and Takenobu Tokunaga. Multi-task and multi-corpora training strategies to enhance argumentative sentence linking performance. In Khalid Al-Khatib, Yufang Hou, and Manfred Stede, editors, *Proceedings of the 8th Workshop on Argument Mining*, pages 12–23, Punta Cana, Dominican Republic, November 2021. Association for Computational Linguistics. https://doi.org/10.18653/v1/2021.argmining-1.2.

Sung-Jun Pyon. The recursive argument structure. *Argumentation*, 39:419–449, 2025. https://doi.org/10.1007/s10503-024-09644-x.

Peng Qi, Yuhao Zhang, Yuhui Zhang, Jason Bolton, and Christopher D. Manning. Stanza: A Python natural language processing toolkit for many human languages. In Asli Celikyilmaz and Tsung-Hsien Wen, editors, *Proceedings of the 58th Annual Meeting of the Association for Computational Linguistics: System Demonstrations*, pages 101–108, Online, July 2020. Association for Computational Linguistics. https://doi.org/10.18653/v1/2020.acl-demos.14.

Liang Qiu, Yizhou Zhao, Jinchao Li, Pan Lu, Baolin Peng, Jianfeng Gao, and Song-Chun Zhu. ValueNet: A new dataset for human value driven dialogue system. In *Thirty-Sixth AAAI Conference on Artificial Intelligence, AAAI 2022, Thirty-Fourth Conference on Innovative Applications of Artificial ntelligence, IAAI 2022, The Twelveth Symposium on Educational Advances in Artificial Intelligence*, pages 11183–11191. AAAI Press, 2022. https://doi.org/10.1609/AAAI.V36I10.21368.

Minghui Qiu and Jing Jiang. A latent variable model for viewpoint discovery from threaded forum posts. In Lucy Vanderwende, Hal Daumé III, and Katrin Kirchhoff, editors, *Proceedings of the 2013 Conference of the North American Chapter of the Association for Computational Linguistics: Human Language Technologies*, pages 1031–1040, Atlanta, Georgia, June 2013. Association for Computational Linguistics. URL https://aclanthology.org/N13-1123/.

Carlotta Quensel, Neele Falk, and Gabriella Lapesa. Investigating subjective factors of argument strength: Storytelling, emotions, and hedging. In Elena Chistova, Philipp Cimiano, Shohreh Haddadan, Gabriella Lapesa, and Ramon Ruiz-Dolz, editors, *Proceedings of the 12th Argument Mining Workshop*, pages 126–139, Vienna, Austria, July 2025. Association for Computational Linguistics. https://doi.org/10.18653/v1/2025.argmining-1.12.

Randolph Quirk, Sidney Greenbaum, Geoffrey Leech, and Jan Svartvik. *A Comprehensive Grammar of the English Language*. Longman, New York, 1985.

Alec Radford, Jeffrey Wu, Rewon Child, David Luan, Dario Amodei, and Ilya Sutskever. Language models are unsupervised multitask learners. *OpenAI*. https://cdn.openai.com/better-language-models/language_models_are_unsupervised_multitask_learners.pdf.

Rafael Rafailov, Archit Sharma, Eric Mitchell, Stefano Ermon, Christopher D. Manning, and Chelsea Finn. Direct preference optimization: Your language model is secretly a reward model. In *Proceedings of the 37th International Conference on Neural Information Processing Systems*, NIPS'23, pages 1–14, Red Hook, NY, USA, 2024. Curran Associates Inc. URL https://proceedings.neurips.cc/paper_files/paper/2023/hash/a85b405ed65c6477a4fe8302b5e06ce7-Abstract-Conference.html.

Colin Raffel, Noam Shazeer, Adam Roberts, Katherine Lee, Sharan Narang, Michael Matena, Yanqi Zhou, Wei Li, and Peter J. Liu. Exploring the limits of transfer learning with a unified text-to-text transformer. *Journal of Machine Learning Research*, 21(140):1–67, 2020. URL http://jmlr.org/papers/v21/20-074.html.

Pavithra Rajendran, Danushka Bollegala, and Simon Parsons. Contextual stance classification of opinions: A step towards enthymeme reconstruction in online reviews. In *3rd Workshop on Argumentation Mining*, pages 31–39, 2016. https://doi.org/10.18653/v1/W16-2804.

Alan Ramponi, Agnese Daffara, and Sara Tonelli. Fine-grained fallacy detection with human label variation. In Luis Chiruzzo, Alan Ritter, and Lu Wang, editors, *Proceedings of the 2025 Conference of the Nations of the Americas Chapter of the Association for Computational Linguistics: Human Language Technologies (Volume 1: Long Papers)*, pages 762–784. Association for Computational Linguistics, April 2025. https://doi.org/10.18653/v1/2025.naacl-long.34.

Sarvesh Ranade, Rajeev Sangal, and Radhika Mamidi. Stance classification in online debates by recognizing users' intentions. In Maxine Eskenazi, Michael Strube, Barbara Di Eugenio, and Jason D. Williams, editors, *Proceedings of the SIGDIAL 2013 Conference*, pages 61–69, Metz, France, August 2013. Association for Computational Linguistics. URL https://aclanthology.org/W13-4008/.

Christof Rapp. Aristotle's Rhetoric. In Edward N. Zalta and Uri Nodelman, editors, *The Stanford Encyclopedia of Philosophy*. Metaphysics Research Lab, Stanford University, Winter 2023 edition, 2023. URL https://plato.stanford.edu/entries/aristotle-rhetoric/.

Olesya Razuvayevskaya and Simone Teufel. Finding enthymemes in real-world texts: A feasibility study. *Argument & Computation*, 8(2):113–129, 2017. https://doi.org/10.3233/AAC-170020.

Chris Reed. Implicit speech acts are ubiquitous. Why? They join the dots. In *Proceedings of the Conference of the Ontario Society for the Study of Argumentation*, pages 1–15, 2011.

Chris Reed and Katarzyna Budzyńska. How dialogues create arguments. In *Proceedings of the Conference of the International Society for the Study of Argumentation*, 2011. https://rozenbergquarterly.com/issa-proceedings-2010-how-dialogues-create-arguments/.

Chris Reed and Glenn Rowe. Araucaria: Software for argument analysis, diagramming and representation. *International Journal on Artificial Intelligence Tools*, 13(04):961–979, December 2004. https://doi.org/10.1142/S0218213004001922.

Chris Reed, Raquel Mochales Palau, Glenn Rowe, and Marie-Francine Moens. Language resources for studying argument. In Nicoletta Calzolari, Khalid Choukri, Bente Maegaard, Joseph Mariani, Jan Odijk, Stelios Piperidis, and Daniel Tapias, editors, *Proceedings of the Sixth International Conference on Language Resources and Evaluation (LREC'08)*, Marrakech, Morocco, May 2008. European Language Resources Association (ELRA). URL https://aclanthology.org/L08-1553/.

Chris Reed, Katarzyna Budzynska, Rory Duthie, Mathilde Janier, Barbara Konat, John Lawrence, Alison Pease, and Mark Snaith. The Argument Web: An online ecosystem of tools, systems and services for argumentation. *Philosophy & Technology*, 30(2):137–160, June 2017. https://doi.org/10.1007/s13347-017-0260-8.

Nils Reimers and Iryna Gurevych. Sentence-BERT: Sentence embeddings using Siamese BERT-networks. In *Proceedings of the 2019 Conference on Empirical Methods in Natural Language Processing and the 9th International Joint Conference on Natural Language Processing (EMNLP-IJCNLP)*, pages 3982–3992, Hong Kong, China, November 2019. Association for Computational Linguistics. https://doi.org/10.18653/v1/D19-1410.

Nils Reimers, Benjamin Schiller, Tilman Beck, Johannes Daxenberger, Christian Stab, and Iryna Gurevych. Classification and clustering of arguments with contextualized word embeddings. In Anna Korhonen, David Traum, and Lluís Màrquez, editors, *Proceedings of the 57th Annual*

Meeting of the Association for Computational Linguistics, pages 567–578, Florence, Italy, July 2019. Association for Computational Linguistics. https://doi.org/10.18653/v1/P19-1054.

Ines Reinig, Maria Becker, Ines Rehbein, and Simone Ponzetto. A survey on modelling morality for text analysis. In Lun-Wei Ku, Andre Martins, and Vivek Srikumar, editors, *Findings of the Association for Computational Linguistics: ACL 2024*, pages 4136–4155, Bangkok, Thailand, August 2024a. Association for Computational Linguistics. https://doi.org/10.18653/v1/2024.findings-acl.245.

Ines Reinig, Ines Rehbein, and Simone Paolo Ponzetto. How to do politics with words: Investigating speech acts in parliamentary debates. In Nicoletta Calzolari, Min-Yen Kan, Veronique Hoste, Alessandro Lenci, Sakriani Sakti, and Nianwen Xue, editors, *Proceedings of the 2024 Joint International Conference on Computational Linguistics, Language Resources and Evaluation (LREC-COLING 2024)*, pages 8287–8300, Torino, Italia, May 2024b. ELRA and ICCL. URL https://aclanthology.org/2024.lrec-main.727.

Paul Reisert, Naoya Inoue, Naoaki Okazaki, and Kentaro Inui. A computational approach for generating Toulmin model argumentation. In *Proceedings of the 2nd Workshop on Argumentation Mining*, pages 45–55. Association for Computational Linguistics, 2015. https://doi.org/10.3115/v1/W15-0507.

Paul Reisert, Naoya Inoue, Naoaki Okazaki, and Kentaro Inui. Deep argumentative structure analysis as an explanation to argumentative relations. In *Proceedings of the Conference of the Association for Natural Language Processing*, pages 38–41, 2017. https://anlp.jp/proceedings/annual_meeting/2017/pdf_dir/C1-1.pdf.

Paul Reisert, Naoya Inoue, Tatsuki Kuribayashi, and Kentaro Inui. Feasible annotation scheme for capturing policy argument reasoning using argument templates. In Noam Slonim and Ranit Aharonov, editors, *Proceedings of the 5th Workshop on Argument Mining*, pages 79–89, Brussels, Belgium, November 2018. Association for Computational Linguistics. https://doi.org/10.18653/v1/W18-5210.

Ehud Reiter and Robert Dale. *Building Natural Language Generation Systems*. Studies in Natural Language Processing. Cambridge University Press, 2000. ISBN 9780511519857. https://doi.org/10.1017/CBO9780511519857.

Yupei Ren, Xinyi Zhou, Ning Zhang, Shangqing Zhao, Man Lan, and Xiaopeng Bai. Towards comprehensive argument analysis in education: Dataset, tasks, and method. In Wanxiang Che, Joyce Nabende, Ekaterina Shutova, and Mohammad Taher Pilehvar, editors, *Proceedings of the 63rd Annual Meeting of the Association for Computational Linguistics (Volume 1: Long Papers)*, pages 14215–14231, Vienna, Austria, July 2025. Association for Computational Linguistics. https://doi.org/10.18653/v1/2025.acl-long.696.

Rodney A. Reynolds and J. Lynn Reynolds. Evidence. In James Price Dillard and Michael Pfau, editors, *The Persuasion Handbook: Developments in Theory and Practice*, pages 427–444. Sage, Thousand Oaks, CA, 2002. https://doi.org/10.4135/9781412976046.n22.

Eddo Rigotti and Sara Greco Morasso. Comparing the Argumentum Model of Topics to other contemporary approaches to argument schemes: The procedural and material components. *Argumentation*, 24(4):489–512, 2010. https://doi.org/10.1007/s10503-010-9190-7.

Ruty Rinott, Lena Dankin, Carlos Alzate Perez, Mitesh M. Khapra, Ehud Aharoni, and Noam Slonim. Show me your evidence - an automatic method for context dependent evidence detection. In Lluís Màrquez, Chris Callison-Burch, and Jian Su, editors, *Proceedings of the 2015 Conference on Empirical Methods in Natural Language Processing*, pages 440–450, Lisbon, Portugal, September 2015. Association for Computational Linguistics. https://doi.org/10.18653/v1/D15-1050.

Irfan Robbani, Paul Reisert, Surawat Pothong, Naoya Inoue, Camélia Guerraoui, Wenzhi Wang, Shoichi Naito, Jungmin Choi, and Kentaro Inui. Flee the flaw: Annotating the underlying logic of fallacious arguments through templates and slot-filling. In Yaser Al-Onaizan, Mohit Bansal, and Yun-Nung Chen, editors, *Proceedings of the 2024 Conference on Empirical Methods in Natural Language Processing*, pages 20524–20540, Miami, Florida, USA, November 2024. Association for Computational Linguistics. https://doi.org/10.18653/v1/2024.emnlp-main.1142.

Stephen Robertson and Hugo Zaragoza. The probabilistic relevance framework: BM25 and beyond. *Foundations and Trends in Information Retrieval*, 3(4):333–389, 2009. https://doi.org/10.1561/1500000019.

Stephen E. Robertson, Steve Walker, Susan Jones, Micheline Hancock-Beaulieu, and Mike Gatford. Okapi at TREC-3. In Donna K. Harman, editor, *Proceedings of The Third Text REtrieval Conference, TREC 1994, Gaithersburg, Maryland, USA, November 2-4, 1994*, volume 500-225 of *NIST Special Publication*, pages 109–126. National Institute of Standards and Technology (NIST), 1994. URL https://www.microsoft.com/en-us/research/wp-content/uploads/2016/02/okapi_trec3.pdf.

Julia Romberg, Maximilian Maurer, Henning Wachsmuth, and Gabriella Lapesa. Towards a perspectivist turn in argument quality assessment. In Luis Chiruzzo, Alan Ritter, and Lu Wang, editors, *Proceedings of the 2025 Conference of the Nations of the Americas Chapter of the Association for Computational Linguistics: Human Language Technologies (Volume 1: Long Papers)*, pages 7458–7485, Albuquerque, New Mexico, April 2025. Association for Computational Linguistics. https://doi.org/10.18653/v1/2025.naacl-long.382.

Sara Rosenthal and Kathleen McKeown. Detecting opinionated claims in online discussions. In *Proceedings of the IEEE International Conference on Semantic Computing*, pages 30–37, 2012. https://doi.org/10.1109/ICSC.2012.59.

Sara Rosenthal and Kathy McKeown. I couldn't agree more: The role of conversational structure in agreement and disagreement detection in online discussions. In Alexander Koller, Gabriel Skantze, Filip Jurcicek, Masahiro Araki, and Carolyn Penstein Rose, editors, *Proceedings of the 16th Annual Meeting of the Special Interest Group on Discourse and Dialogue*, pages 168–177, Prague, Czech Republic, September 2015. Association for Computational Linguistics. https://doi.org/10.18653/v1/W15-4625.

Dan Roth and Wen Tau Yih. A linear programming formulation for global inference in natural language tasks. In *Proceedings of the Eighth Conference on Computational Natural Language Learning (CoNLL-2004) at HLT-NAACL 2004*, pages 1–8, Boston, Massachusetts, USA, 2004. Association for Computational Linguistics. URL https://aclanthology.org/W04-2401/.

Allen Roush and Arvind Balaji. DebateSum: A large-scale argument mining and summarization dataset. In Elena Cabrio and Serena Villata, editors, *Proceedings of the 7th Workshop on Argument Mining*, pages 1–7, Online, December 2020. Association for Computational Linguistics. URL https://aclanthology.org/2020.argmining-1.1.

Shamik Roy and Dan Goldwasser. Weakly supervised learning of nuanced frames for analyzing polarization in news media. In *Proceedings of the 2020 Conference on Empirical Methods in Natural Language Processing (EMNLP)*, pages 7698–7716, Online, November 2020. https://doi.org/10.18653/v1/2020.emnlp-main.620.

Benedek Rozemberczki and Rik Sarkar. Characteristic functions on graphs: Birds of a feather, from statistical descriptors to parametric models. In *Proceedings of the 29th ACM International Conference on Information & Knowledge Management*, CIKM '20, pages 1325–1334, New York, NY, USA, 2020. Association for Computing Machinery. https://doi.org/10.1145/3340531.3411866.

Mattes Ruckdeschel, Ringo Baumann, and Gregor Wiedemann. Argument mining of attack and support patterns in dialogical conversations with sequential pattern mining. In Philipp Cimiano, Anette Frank, Michael Kohlhase, and Benno Stein, editors, *Robust Argumentation Machines*, pages 39–56, Cham, 2024. Springer Nature Switzerland. https://doi.org/10.1007/978-3-031-63536-6_3.

Ramon Ruiz-Dolz and John Lawrence. Detecting argumentative fallacies in the wild: Problems and limitations of large language models. In Milad Alshomary, Chung-Chi Chen, Smaranda Muresan, Joonsuk Park, and Julia Romberg, editors, *Proceedings of the 10th Workshop on Argument Mining*, pages 1–10, Singapore, December 2023. Association for Computational Linguistics. https://doi.org/10.18653/v1/2023.argmining-1.1.

Ramon Ruiz-Dolz, Jose Alemany, Stella M. Heras Barberá, and Ana García-Fornes. Transformer-based models for automatic identification of argument relations: A cross-domain evaluation. *IEEE Intelligent Systems*, 36(6):62–70, 2021. https://doi.org/10.1109/MIS.2021.3073993.

Ramon Ruiz-Dolz, Chr-Jr Chiu, Chung-Chi Chen, Noriko Kando, and Hsin-Hsi Chen. Learning strategies for robust argument mining: An analysis of variations in language and domain. In Nicoletta Calzolari, Min-Yen Kan, Veronique Hoste, Alessandro Lenci, Sakriani Sakti, and Nianwen Xue, editors, *Proceedings of the 2024 Joint International Conference on Computational Linguistics, Language Resources and Evaluation (LREC-COLING 2024)*, pages 10286–10292, Torino, Italia, May 2024a. ELRA and ICCL. URL https://aclanthology.org/2024.lrec-main.898/.

Ramon Ruiz-Dolz, John Lawrence, Ella Schad, and Chris Reed. Overview of DialAM-2024: Argument mining in natural language dialogues. In Yamen Ajjour, Roy Bar-Haim, Roxanne El Baff, Zhexiong Liu, and Gabriella Skitalinskaya, editors, *Proceedings of the 11th Workshop on Argument Mining (ArgMining 2024)*, pages 83–92, Bangkok, Thailand, August 2024b. Association for Computational Linguistics. https://doi.org/10.18653/v1/2024.argmining-1.8.

Ramon Ruiz-Dolz, Joaquin Taverner, John Lawrence, and Chris Reed. NLAS-multi: A multilingual corpus of automatically generated Natural Language Argumentation Schemes. *Data in Brief*, 57: 111087, December 2024. https://doi.org/10.1016/j.dib.2024.111087.

Ramon Ruiz-Dolz, Stella Heras, and Ana García-Fornes. An introduction to computational argumentation research from a human argumentation perspective. *Autonomous Agents and Multi-Agent Systems*, 39(1):11, February 2025. https://doi.org/10.1007/s10458-025-09692-x.

Ramon Ruiz-Dolz, Zlata Kikteva, and John Lawrence. Mining complex patterns of argumentative reasoning in natural language dialogue. In Wanxiang Che, Joyce Nabende, Ekaterina Shutova, and Mohammad Taher Pilehvar, editors, *Proceedings of the 63rd Annual Meeting of the Association for Computational Linguistics (Volume 1: Long Papers)*, pages 7421–7435, Vienna, Austria, July 2025. Association for Computational Linguistics. https://doi.org/10.18653/v1/2025.acl-long.368.

Ameer Saadat-Yazdi, Jeff Z. Pan, and Nadin Kokciyan. Uncovering implicit inferences for improved relational argument mining. In Andreas Vlachos and Isabelle Augenstein, editors, *Proceedings of the 17th Conference of the European Chapter of the Association for Computational Linguistics*, pages 2484–2495, Dubrovnik, Croatia, May 2023. Association for Computational Linguistics. https://doi.org/10.18653/v1/2023.eacl-main.182.

Jerrold Sadock. Speech acts. In Laurence Horn and Gregory Ward, editors, *The Handbook of Pragmatics*, pages 53–73, Wiley, New York, 2005. https://doi.org/10.1002/9780470756959.ch3.

Rudra Ranajee Saha, Laks V. S. Lakshmanan, and Raymond T. Ng. Stance detection with explanations. *Computational Linguistics*, 50(1):193–235, March 2024. https://doi.org/10.1162/coli_a_00501.

Sougata Saha and Rohini Srihari. ArgU: A controllable factual argument generator. In Anna Rogers, Jordan Boyd-Graber, and Naoaki Okazaki, editors, *Proceedings of the 61st Annual Meeting of the Association for Computational Linguistics (Volume 1: Long Papers)*, pages 8373–8388, Toronto, Canada, July 2023. Association for Computational Linguistics. https://doi.org/10.18653/v1/2023.acl-long.466.

Swarnadeep Saha, Prateek Yadav, Lisa Bauer, and Mohit Bansal. ExplaGraphs: An explanation graph generation task for structured commonsense reasoning. In Marie-Francine Moens, Xuanjing Huang, Lucia Specia, and Scott Wen-Tau Yih, editors, *Proceedings of the 2021 Conference on Empirical Methods in Natural Language Processing*, pages 7716–7740, Online and Punta Cana, Dominican Republic, November 2021. Association for Computational Linguistics. https://doi.org/10.18653/v1/2021.emnlp-main.609.

Saumya Sahai, Oana Balalau, and Roxana Horincar. Breaking down the invisible wall of informal fallacies in online discussions. In Chengqing Zong, Fei Xia, Wenjie Li, and Roberto Navigli, editors, *Proceedings of the 59th Annual Meeting of the Association for Computational Linguistics and the 11th International Joint Conference on Natural Language Processing (Volume 1: Long Papers)*, pages 644–657, Online, August 2021. Association for Computational Linguistics. https://doi.org/10.18653/v1/2021.acl-long.53.

Ahmed Sahlane. Argumentation and fallacy in the justification of the 2003 war on Iraq. *Argumentation*, 26:459–488, 2012. https://doi.org/10.1007/s10503-012-9265-8.

Patrick Saint-Dizier. Processing natural language arguments with the <TextCoop> platform. *Journal of Argumentation and Computation*, 3(1):49–82, 2012. https://doi.org/10.1080/19462166.2012.663539.

Patrick Saint Dizier. The lexicon of argumentation for argument mining: Methodological considerations. *Anglophonia*, 29:3187, 2020. https://doi.org/10.4000/anglophonia.3187.

Reza Sanayei, Srdjan Vesic, Eduardo Blanco, and Mihai Surdeanu. Can LLMs judge debates? Evaluating non-linear reasoning via argumentation theory semantics. In Christos Christodoulopoulos, Tanmoy Chakraborty, Carolyn Rose, and Violet Peng, editors, *Findings of the Association for Computational Linguistics: EMNLP 2025*, pages 21244–21262, Suzhou, China, November 2025. Association for Computational Linguistics. https://doi.org/10.18653/v1/2025.findings-emnlp.1159.

Victor Sanh, Lysandre Debut, Julien Chaumond, and Thomas Wolf. DistilBERT, a distilled version of BERT: Smaller, faster, cheaper and lighter. In *Energy Efficient Machine Learning and Cognitive Computing 5th Edition. Co-located with NeurIPS 2019*, 2019. URL https://www.emc2-ai.org/assets/docs/neurips-19/emc2-neurips19-paper-33.pdf.

Maarten Sap, Saadia Gabriel, Lianhui Qin, Dan Jurafsky, Noah A. Smith, and Yejin Choi. Social bias frames: Reasoning about social and power implications of language. In Dan Jurafsky, Joyce Chai, Natalie Schluter, and Joel Tetreault, editors, *Proceedings of the 58th Annual Meeting of the Association for Computational Linguistics*, pages 5477–5490, Online, July 2020. Association for Computational Linguistics. https://doi.org/10.18653/v1/2020.acl-main.486.

Akira Sasaki, Kazuaki Hanawa, Naoaki Okazaki, and Kentaro Inui. Other topics you may also agree or disagree: Modeling inter-topic preferences using tweets and matrix factorization. In Regina Barzilay and Min-Yen Kan, editors, *Proceedings of the 55th Annual Meeting of the Association for Computational Linguistics (Volume 1: Long Papers)*, pages 398–408, Vancouver, Canada, July 2017. Association for Computational Linguistics. https://doi.org/10.18653/v1/P17-1037.

Misa Sato, Kohsuke Yanai, Toshinori Miyoshi, Toshihiko Yanase, Makoto Iwayama, Qinghua Sun, and Yoshiki Niwa. End-to-end argument generation system in debating. In *Proceedings of ACL-IJCNLP 2015 System Demonstrations*, pages 109–114. Association for Computational Linguistics and The Asian Federation of Natural Language Processing, 2015. https://doi.org/10.3115/v1/P15-4019.

Ekaterina Saveleva, Volha Petukhova, Marius Mosbach, and Dietrich Klakow. Discourse-based argument segmentation and annotation. In Harry Bunt, editor, *Proceedings of the 17th Joint ACL - ISO Workshop on Interoperable Semantic Annotation*, pages 41–53, Groningen, The Netherlands (online), June 2021a. Association for Computational Linguistics. URL https://aclanthology.org/2021.isa-1.5/.

Ekaterina Saveleva, Volha Petukhova, Marius Mosbach, and Dietrich Klakow. Graph-based argument quality assessment. In Ruslan Mitkov and Galia Angelova, editors, *Proceedings of the International Conference on Recent Advances in Natural Language Processing (RANLP 2021)*, pages 1268–1280, Held Online, September 2021b. INCOMA Ltd. URL https://aclanthology.org/2021.ranlp-1.143.

Ramit Sawhney, Arnav Wadhwa, Shivam Agarwal, and Rajiv Ratn Shah. GPolS: A contextual graph-based language model for analyzing parliamentary debates and political cohesion. In Donia Scott, Nuria Bel, and Chengqing Zong, editors, *Proceedings of the 28th International Conference on Computational Linguistics*, pages 4847–4859, Barcelona, Spain (Online), December 2020. International Committee on Computational Linguistics. https://doi.org/10.18653/v1/2020.coling-main.426.

Ramit Sawhney, Shivam Agarwal, Arnav Wadhwa, and Rajiv Shah. TEC: A time evolving contextual graph model for speaker state analysis in political debates. In Zhi-Hua Zhou, editor, *Proceedings of the Thirtieth International Joint Conference on Artificial Intelligence, IJCAI-21*, pages 3552–3558. International Joint Conferences on Artificial Intelligence Organization, 8 2021. https://doi.org/10.24963/ijcai.2021/489. Main Track.

BigScience Workshop. BLOOM: A 176B-parameter open-access multilingual language model, Journal of Machine Learning Research 25(422):1–74, 2024.

Robin Schaefer and Manfred Stede. Annotation and detection of arguments in tweets. In Elena Cabrio and Serena Villata, editors, *Proceedings of the 7th Workshop on Argument Mining*, pages 53–58, Online, December 2020. Association for Computational Linguistics. URL https://aclanthology.org/2020.argmining-1.6/.

Robin Schaefer and Manfred Stede. Argument mining on Twitter: A survey. *it - Information Technology*, 63(1):45–58, 2021. https://doi.org/10.1515/itit-2020-0053.

Robin Schaefer, René Knaebel, and Manfred Stede. On selecting training corpora for cross-domain claim detection. In Gabriella Lapesa, Jodi Schneider, Yohan Jo, and Sougata Saha, editors, *Proceedings of the 9th Workshop on Argument Mining*, pages 181–186, Online and in Gyeongju, Republic of Korea, October 2022. International Conference on Computational Linguistics. URL https://aclanthology.org/2022.argmining-1.17.

Robin Schaefer, René Knaebel, and Manfred Stede. Towards fine-grained argumentation strategy analysis in persuasive essays. In Milad Alshomary, Chung-Chi Chen, Smaranda Muresan, Joonsuk Park, and Julia Romberg, editors, *Proceedings of the 10th Workshop on Argument Mining*, pages 76–88, Singapore, December 2023. Association for Computational Linguistics. https://doi.org/10.18653/v1/2023.argmining-1.8.

Robin Schaefer, Sophia Rauh, and Manfred Stede. On complex argumentation structures in tweets. *Argumentation et Analyse du Discours*, 34, 2025. https://doi.org/10.4000/13q0j.

Roger C. Schank. *Dynamic Memory: A Theory of Reminding and Learning in Computers and People*. Cambridge University Press, USA, 1983. ISBN 0-521-24858-2.

Oliver Scheuer, Frank Loll, Niels Pinkwart, and Bruce M. McLaren. Computer-supported argumentation: A review of the state of the art. *International Journal of Computer-supported Collaborative Learning*, 5:43–102, 2010. https://doi.org/10.1007/s11412-009-9080-x.

Benjamin Schiller, Johannes Daxenberger, and Iryna Gurevych. Stance detection benchmark: How robust is your stance detection? *KI-KünstlicheIntelligenz*, 35:329–341, 2021a. https://doi.org/10.1007/s13218-021-00714-w.

Benjamin Schiller, Johannes Daxenberger, and Iryna Gurevych. Aspect-controlled neural argument generation. In *Proceedings of the 2021 Conference of the North American Chapter of the Association for Computational Linguistics: Human Language Technologies*, pages 380–396, Online, June 2021b. Association for Computational Linguistics. https://doi.org/10.18653/v1/2021.naacl-main.34.

Michael Schlichtkrull, Thomas N. Kipf, Peter Bloem, Rianne van den Berg, Ivan Titov, and Max Welling. Modeling relational data with graph convolutional networks. In *The Semantic Web: 15th International Conference, ESWC 2018, Heraklion, Crete, Greece, June 3–7, 2018, Proceedings*, pages 593–607, Berlin, Heidelberg, 2018. Springer-Verlag. https://doi.org/10.1007/978-3-319-93417-4_38.

David C. Schneider, Christian Voigt, and Gregor Betz. ArguNet: A software tool for collaborative argumentation analysis and research. In *Proceedings of the Conference on Computational Models of Natural Argument*, pages 57–61, 2007. https://cmna.csc.liv.ac.uk/CMNA7/papers/Schneider.pdf.

Jodi Schneider, Tudor Groza, and Alexandre Passant. A review of argumentation for the Social Semantic Web. *Semantic Web*, 4(2):159–218, 2013a. https://doi.org/10.3233/SW-2012-0073.

Jodi Schneider, Krystian Samp, Alexandre Passant, and Stefan Decker. Arguments about deletion: How experience improves the acceptability of arguments in ad-hoc online task groups. In *Proceedings of the Conference on Computer Supported Cooperative Work*, pages 1069–1080, 2013b. https://doi.org/10.1145/2441776.2441897.

Daniel Schroter, Daryna Dementieva, and Georg Groh. Adam-Smith at SemEval-2023 task 4: Discovering human values in arguments with ensembles of transformer-based models. In Atul Kr. Ojha, A. Seza Doğruöz, Giovanni Da San Martino, Harish Tayyar Madabushi, Ritesh Kumar, and Elisa Sartori, editors, *Proceedings of the 17th International Workshop on Semantic Evaluation (SemEval-2023)*, pages 532–541, Toronto, Canada, July 2023. Association for Computational Linguistics. https://doi.org/10.18653/v1/2023.semeval-1.74.

John Schulman, Filip Wolski, Prafulla Dhariwal, Alec Radford, and Oleg Klimov. Proximal policy optimization algorithms, 2017. https://doi.org/10.48550/arXiv.1707.06347.

Claudia Schulz, Steffen Eger, Johannes Daxenberger, Tobias Kahse, and Iryna Gurevych. Multi-task learning for argumentation mining in low-resource settings. In Marilyn Walker, Heng Ji, and Amanda Stent, editors, *Proceedings of the 2018 Conference of the North American Chapter of the Association for Computational Linguistics: Human Language Technologies, Volume 2 (Short Papers)*, pages 35–41, New Orleans, Louisiana, June 2018. Association for Computational Linguistics. https://doi.org/10.18653/v1/N18-2006.

Shalom H Schwartz. Are there universal aspects in the structure and contents of human values? *Journal of Social Issues*, 50:19–45, 1994. https://doi.org/10.1111/j.1540-4560.1994.tb01196.x.

Shalom H. Schwartz. An overview of the Schwartz theory of basic values. *Online Readings in Psychology and Culture*, 2, 2012. https://doi.org/10.9707/2307-0919.1116.

Shalom H. Schwartz, Jan Cieciuch, Michele Vecchione, Eldad Davidov, Ronald Fischer, Constanze Beierlein, Alice Ramos, Markku Verkasalo, Jan-Erik Lönnqvist, Kursad Demirutku, et al. Refining the theory of basic individual values. *Journal of Personality and Social Psychology*, 103(4):663–688, 2012. https://doi.org/10.1037/a0029393.

John R. Searle. *Speech Acts: An Essay in the Philosophy of Language*. Cambridge University Press, Cambridge, 1969.

John R. Searle. A classification of illocutionary acts. *Language in Society*, 5:1–23, 1976.

John R Searle. *Rationality in action*. MIT Press, 2003. https://doi.org/10.7551/mitpress/5759.001.0001.

Tianxiao Shen, Tao Lei, Regina Barzilay, and Tommi Jaakkola. Style transfer from non-parallel text by cross-alignment. In *Advances in Neural Information Processing Systems*, pages 6833–6844, 2017. ISBN 9780262194631. URL https://proceedings.neurips.cc/paper_files/paper/2017/file/2d2c8394e31101a261abf1784302bf75-Paper.pdf.

Sam Shleifer and Alexander M. Rush. Pre-trained summarization distillation, 2020. https://doi.org/10.48550/arXiv.2010.13002.

Eyal Shnarch, Ran Levy, Vikas Raykar, and Noam Slonim. GRASP: Rich patterns for argumentation mining. In Martha Palmer, Rebecca Hwa, and Sebastian Riedel, editors, *Proceedings of the 2017 Conference on Empirical Methods in Natural Language Processing*, pages 1345–1350, Copenhagen, Denmark, September 2017. Association for Computational Linguistics. https://doi.org/10.18653/v1/D17-1140.

Eyal Shnarch, Carlos Alzate, Lena Dankin, Martin Gleize, Yufang Hou, Leshem Choshen, Ranit Aharonov, and Noam Slonim. Will it blend? Blending weak and strong labeled data in a neural network for argumentation mining. In Iryna Gurevych and Yusuke Miyao, editors, *Proceedings of the 56th Annual Meeting of the Association for Computational Linguistics (Volume 2: Short Papers)*, pages 599–605, Melbourne, Australia, July 2018. Association for Computational Linguistics. https://doi.org/10.18653/v1/P18-2095.

Parshin Shojaee, Iman Mirzadeh, Keivan Alizadeh, Maxwell Horton, Samy Bengio, and Mehrdad Farajtabar. The illusion of thinking: Understanding the strengths and limitations of reasoning models via the lens of problem complexity, 2025. https://doi.org/10.48550/arXiv.2506.06941.

Ruth Shortall, Anatol Itten, Michiel van der Meer, Pradeep Murukannaiah, and Catholijn Jonker. Reason against the machine? Future directions for mass online deliberation. *Frontiers in Political Science*, 4, October 2022. https://doi.org/10.3389/fpos.2022.946589.

Edwin Simpson and Iryna Gurevych. Finding convincing arguments using scalable Bayesian preference learning. *Transactions of the Association for Computational Linguistics*, 6:357–371, 2018. https://doi.org/10.1162/tacl_a_00026.

Laura Sinikallio, Lili Aunimo, and Tomi Männistö. Systematic review on the current state of computer-supported argumentation learning systems. *Information and Software Technology*, 178: 107598, February 2025. https://doi.org/10.1016/j.infsof.2024.107598.

Ruben Sipos, Pannaga Shivaswamy, and Thorsten Joachims. Large-margin learning of submodular summarization models. In Walter Daelemans, editor, *Proceedings of the 13th Conference of the European Chapter of the Association for Computational Linguistics*, pages 224–233, Avignon, France, April 2012. Association for Computational Linguistics. URL https://aclanthology.org/E12-1023/.

Maria Skeppstedt, Andreas Peldszus, and Manfred Stede. More or less controlled elicitation of argumentative text: Enlarging a microtext corpus via crowdsourcing. In Noam Slonim and Ranit Aharonov, editors, *Proceedings of the 5th Workshop on Argument Mining*, pages 155–163, Brussels, Belgium, November 2018. Association for Computational Linguistics. https://doi.org/10.18653/v1/W18-5218.

Bernd Skiera, Shunyao Yan, Johannes Daxenberger, Marcus Dombois, and Iryna Gurevych. Using information-seeking argument mining to improve service. *Journal of Service Research*, 25(4): 537–548, November 2022. https://doi.org/10.1177/10946705221110845.

Gabriella Skitalinskaya and Henning Wachsmuth. To revise or not to revise: Learning to detect improvable claims for argumentative writing support. In *Proceedings of the 61st Annual Meeting of the Association for Computational Linguistics (Volume 1: Long Papers)*, pages 15799–15816, Toronto, Canada, July 2023. Association for Computational Linguistics. https://doi.org/10.18653/v1/2023.acl-long.880.

Gabriella Skitalinskaya, Jonas Klaff, and Henning Wachsmuth. Learning from revisions: Quality assessment of claims in argumentation at scale. In *Proceedings of the 16th Conference of the European Chapter of the Association for Computational Linguistics: Main Volume*, pages 1718–1729, Online, April 2021. Association for Computational Linguistics. https://doi.org/10.18653/v1/2021.eacl-main.147.

Gabriella Skitalinskaya, Maximilian Spliethöver, and Henning Wachsmuth. Claim optimization in computational argumentation. In C. Maria Keet, Hung-Yi Lee, and Sina Zarrieß, editors, *Proceedings of the 16th International Natural Language Generation Conference*, pages 134–

152, Prague, Czechia, September 2023. Association for Computational Linguistics. https://doi.org/10.18653/v1/2023.inlg-main.10.

Noam Slonim, Yonatan Bilu, Carlos Alzate, Roy Bar-Haim, Ben Bogin, Francesca Bonin, Leshem Choshen, Edo Cohen-Karlik, Lena Dankin, Lilach Edelstein, Liat Ein-Dor, Roni Friedman-Melamed, Assaf Gavron, Ariel Gera, Martin Gleize, Shai Gretz, Dan Gutfreund, Alon Halfon, Daniel Hershcovich, Ron Hoory, Yufang Hou, Shay Hummel, Michal Jacovi, Charles Jochim, Yoav Kantor, Yoav Katz, David Konopnicki, Zvi Kons, Lili Kotlerman, Dalia Krieger, Dan Lahav, Tamar Lavee, Ran Levy, Naftali Liberman, Yosi Mass, Amir Menczel, Shachar Mirkin, Guy Moshkowich, Shila Ofek-Koifman, Matan Orbach, Ella Rabinovich, Ruty Rinott, Slava Shechtman, Dafna Sheinwald, Eyal Shnarch, Ilya Shnayderman, Aya Soffer, Artem Spector, Benjamin Sznajder, Assaf Toledo, Orith Toledo-Ronen, Elad Venezian, and Ranit Aharonov. An autonomous debating system. *Nature*, 591(7850):379–384, March 2021. https://doi.org/10.1038/s41586-021-03215-w.

Carlota Smith. *Modes of Discourse: The Local Structure of Texts*. Cambridge University Press, Cambridge, 2003. ISBN 9780511615108. https://doi.org/10.1017/CBO9780511615108.

Mark Snaith and Chris Reed. TOAST: Online ASPIC+ implementation. In Bart Verheij, Stefan Szeider, and Stefan Woltran, editors, *Computational Models of Argument - Proceedings of COMMA 2012, Vienna, Austria, September 10-12, 2012*, volume 245 of *Frontiers in Artificial Intelligence and Applications*, pages 509–510. IOS Press, 2012. https://doi.org/10.3233/978-1-61499-111-3-509.

Mark Snaith, John Lawrence, and Chris Reed. Mixed initiative argument in public deliberation. *From e-Participation to Online Deliberation, Proceedings of the Fourth International Conference on Online Deliberation, OD2010*, pages 2–13, 2010. http://www.od2010.di.unimi.it/docs/proceedings/Proceedings_OD2010.pdf#page=10.

Parinaz Sobhani, Saif Mohammad, and Svetlana Kiritchenko. Detecting stance in tweets and analyzing its interaction with sentiment. In Claire Gardent, Raffaella Bernardi, and Ivan Titov, editors, *Proceedings of the Fifth Joint Conference on Lexical and Computational Semantics*, pages 159–169, Berlin, Germany, August 2016. Association for Computational Linguistics. https://doi.org/10.18653/v1/S16-2021.

Swapna Somasundaran and Janyce Wiebe. Recognizing stances in online debates. In Keh-Yih Su, Jian Su, Janyce Wiebe, and Haizhou Li, editors, *Proceedings of the Joint Conference of the 47th Annual Meeting of the ACL and the 4th International Joint Conference on Natural Language Processing of the AFNLP*, pages 226–234, Suntec, Singapore, August 2009. Association for Computational Linguistics. URL https://aclanthology.org/P09-1026/.

Swapna Somasundaran and Janyce Wiebe. Recognizing stances in ideological on-line debates. In Diana Inkpen and Carlo Strapparava, editors, *Proceedings of the NAACL HLT 2010 Workshop on Computational Approaches to Analysis and Generation of Emotion in Text*, pages 116–124, Los Angeles, CA, June 2010. Association for Computational Linguistics. URL https://aclanthology.org/W10-0214/.

Wei Song, Dong Wang, Ruiji Fu, Lizhen Liu, Ting Liu, and Guoping Hu. Discourse mode identification in essays. In Regina Barzilay and Min-Yen Kan, editors, *Proceedings of the 55th Annual Meeting of the Association for Computational Linguistics (Volume 1: Long Papers)*, pages 112–122, Vancouver, Canada, July 2017. Association for Computational Linguistics. https://doi.org/10.18653/v1/P17-1011.

Yi Song, Michael Heilman, Beata Beigman Klebanov, and Paul Deane. Applying argumentation schemes for essay scoring. In Nancy Green, Kevin Ashley, Diane Litman, Chris Reed, and Vern Walker, editors, *Proceedings of the First Workshop on Argumentation Mining*, pages 69–78. Association for Computational Linguistics, June 2014. https://doi.org/10.3115/v1/W14-2110.

Zhivar Sourati, Filip Ilievski, Hang-An Sandlin, and Alain Mermoud. Case-based reasoning with language models for classification of logical fallacies. In Edith Elkind, editor, *Proceedings of the Thirty-Second International Joint Conference on Artificial Intelligence, IJCAI-23*, pages 5188–5196. International Joint Conferences on Artificial Intelligence Organization, 8 2023. https://doi.org/10.24963/ijcai.2023/576. Main Track.

Maximilian Spliethöver and Henning Wachsmuth. Argument from old man's view: Assessing social bias in argumentation. In *Proceedings of the 7th Workshop on Argument Mining*, pages 76–87, Online, December 2020. Association for Computational Linguistics. URL https://aclanthology.org/2020.argmining-1.9.

Maximilian Spliethöver, Jonas Klaff, and Hendrik Heuer. Is it worth the attention? A comparative evaluation of attention layers for argument unit segmentation. In Benno Stein and Henning Wachsmuth, editors, *Proceedings of the 6th Workshop on Argument Mining*, pages 74–82, Florence, Italy, August 2019. Association for Computational Linguistics. https://doi.org/10.18653/v1/W19-4509.

Dhanya Sridhar, James Foulds, Bert Huang, Lise Getoor, and Marilyn Walker. Joint models of disagreement and stance in online debate. In Chengqing Zong and Michael Strube, editors, *Proceedings of the 53rd Annual Meeting of the Association for Computational Linguistics and the 7th International Joint Conference on Natural Language Processing (Volume 1: Long Papers)*, pages 116–125, Beijing, China, July 2015. Association for Computational Linguistics. https://doi.org/10.3115/v1/P15-1012.

Aarohi Srivastava, Abhinav Rastogi, Abhishek Rao, Abu Awal Md Shoeb, Abubakar Abid, Adam Fisch, Adam R. Brown, Adam Santoro, Aditya Gupta, Adrià Garriga-Alonso, Agnieszka Kluska, Aitor Lewkowycz, Akshat Agarwal, Alethea Power, Alex Ray, Alex Warstadt, Alexander W. Kocurek, Ali Safaya, Ali Tazarv, Alice Xiang, Alicia Parrish, Allen Nie, Aman Hussain, Amanda Askell, Amanda Dsouza, Ambrose Slone, Ameet Rahane, Anantharaman S. Iyer, Anders Johan Andreassen, Andrea Madotto, Andrea Santilli, Andreas Stuhlmüller, Andrew M. Dai, Andrew La, Andrew Kyle Lampinen, Andy Zou, Angela Jiang, Angelica Chen, Anh Vuong, Animesh Gupta, Anna Gottardi, Antonio Norelli, Anu Venkatesh, Arash Gholamidavoodi, Arfa Tabassum, Arul Menezes, Arun Kirubarajan, Asher Mullokandov, Ashish Sabharwal, Austin Herrick, Avia Efrat, Aykut Erdem, Ayla Karakaş, B. Ryan Roberts, Bao Sheng Loe, Barret Zoph, Bartłomiej Bojanowski, Batuhan Özyurt, Behnam Hedayatnia, Behnam Neyshabur, Benjamin Inden, Benno Stein, Berk Ekmekci, Bill Yuchen Lin, Blake Howald, Bryan Orinion, Cameron Diao, Cameron Dour, Catherine Stinson, Cedrick Argueta, Cesar Ferri, Chandan Singh, Charles Rathkopf, Chenlin Meng, Chitta Baral, Chiyu Wu, Chris Callison-Burch, Christopher Waites, Christian Voigt, Christopher D Manning, Christopher Potts, Cindy Ramirez, Clara E. Rivera, Clemencia Siro, Colin Raffel, Courtney Ashcraft, Cristina Garbacea, Damien Sileo, Dan Garrette, Dan Hendrycks, Dan Kilman, Dan Roth, C. Daniel Freeman, Daniel Khashabi, Daniel Levy, Daniel Moseguí González, Danielle Perszyk, Danny Hernandez, Danqi Chen, Daphne Ippolito, Dar Gilboa, David Dohan, David Drakard, David Jurgens, Debajyoti Datta, Deep Ganguli, Denis Emelin, Denis Kleyko, Deniz Yuret, Derek Chen, Derek Tam, Dieuwke Hupkes, Diganta Misra, Dilyar Buzan, Dimitri Coelho Mollo, Diyi Yang, Dong-Ho Lee, Dylan Schrader, Ekaterina Shutova, Ekin Dogus Cubuk, Elad Segal, Eleanor Hagerman, Elizabeth Barnes, Elizabeth Donoway, Ellie Pavlick, Emanuele Rodolà, Emma Lam, Eric Chu, Eric Tang, Erkut Erdem, Ernie Chang, Ethan A Chi, Ethan Dyer, Ethan Jerzak, Ethan Kim, Eunice Engefu Manyasi, Evgenii Zheltonozhskii, Fanyue Xia, Fatemeh Siar, Fernando Martínez-Plumed, Francesca Happé, Francois Chollet, Frieda Rong, Gaurav Mishra, Genta Indra Winata, Gerard de Melo, Germàn Kruszewski, Giambattista Parascandolo, Giorgio Mariani, Gloria Xinyue Wang, Gonzalo Jaimovitch-Lopez, Gregor Betz, Guy Gur-Ari, Hana Galijasevic, Hannah Kim, Hannah Rashkin, Hannaneh Hajishirzi, Harsh Mehta, Hayden Bogar, Henry Francis Anthony Shevlin, Hinrich

Schuetze, Hiromu Yakura, Hongming Zhang, Hugh Mee Wong, Ian Ng, Isaac Noble, Jaap Jumelet, Jack Geissinger, Jackson Kernion, Jacob Hilton, Jaehoon Lee, Jaime Fernández Fisac, James B Simon, James Koppel, James Zheng, James Zou, Jan Kocon, Jana Thompson, Janelle Wingfield, Jared Kaplan, Jarema Radom, Jascha Sohl-Dickstein, Jason Phang, Jason Wei, Jason Yosinski, Jekaterina Novikova, Jelle Bosscher, Jennifer Marsh, Jeremy Kim, Jeroen Taal, Jesse Engel, Jesujoba Alabi, Jiacheng Xu, Jiaming Song, Jillian Tang, Joan Waweru, John Burden, John Miller, John U. Balis, Jonathan Batchelder, Jonathan Berant, Jörg Frohberg, Jos Rozen, Jose Hernandez-Orallo, Joseph Boudeman, Joseph Guerr, Joseph Jones, Joshua B. Tenenbaum, Joshua S. Rule, Joyce Chua, Kamil Kanclerz, Karen Livescu, Karl Krauth, Karthik Gopalakrishnan, Katerina Ignatyeva, Katja Markert, Kaustubh Dhole, Kevin Gimpel, Kevin Omondi, Kory Wallace Mathewson, Kristen Chiafullo, Ksenia Shkaruta, Kumar Shridhar, Kyle McDonell, Kyle Richardson, Laria Reynolds, Leo Gao, Li Zhang, Liam Dugan, Lianhui Qin, Lidia Contreras-Ochando, Louis-Philippe Morency, Luca Moschella, Lucas Lam, Lucy Noble, Ludwig Schmidt, Luheng He, Luis Oliveros-Colón, Luke Metz, Lütfi Kerem Senel, Maarten Bosma, Maarten Sap, Maartje Ter Hoeve, Maheen Farooqi, Manaal Faruqui, Mantas Mazeika, Marco Baturan, Marco Marelli, Marco Maru, Maria Jose Ramirez-Quintana, Marie Tolkiehn, Mario Giulianelli, Martha Lewis, Martin Potthast, Matthew L Leavitt, Matthias Hagen, Mátyás Schubert, Medina Orduna Baitemirova, Melody Arnaud, Melvin McElrath, Michael Andrew Yee, Michael Cohen, Michael Gu, Michael Ivanitskiy, Michael Starritt, Michael Strube, Michał Swedrowski, Michele Bevilacqua, Michihiro Yasunaga, Mihir Kale, Mike Cain, Mimee Xu, Mirac Suzgun, Mitch Walker, Mo Tiwari, Mohit Bansal, Moin Aminnaseri, Mor Geva, Mozhdeh Gheini, Mukund Varma T, Nanyun Peng, Nathan Andrew Chi, Nayeon Lee, Neta Gur-Ari Krakover, Nicholas Cameron, Nicholas Roberts, Nick Doiron, Nicole Martinez, Nikita Nangia, Niklas Deckers, Niklas Muennighoff, Nitish Shirish Keskar, Niveditha S. Iyer, Noah Constant, Noah Fiedel, Nuan Wen, Oliver Zhang, Omar Agha, Omar Elbaghdadi, Omer Levy, Owain Evans, Pablo Antonio Moreno Casares, Parth Doshi, Pascale Fung, Paul Pu Liang, Paul Vicol, Pegah Alipoormolabashi, Peiyuan Liao, Percy Liang, Peter W Chang, Peter Eck. Beyond the imitation game: Quantifying and extrapolating the capabilities of language models. *Transactions on Machine Learning Research*, 2023. ISSN 2835-8856. URL https://openreview.net/forum?id=uyTL5Bvosj.

Christian Stab and Iryna Gurevych. Annotating argument components and relations in persuasive essays. In Junichi Tsujii and Jan Hajic, editors, *Proceedings of COLING 2014, the 25th International Conference on Computational Linguistics: Technical Papers*, pages 1501–1510, Dublin, Ireland, August 2014a. Dublin City University and Association for Computational Linguistics. URL https://aclanthology.org/C14-1142/.

Christian Stab and Iryna Gurevych. Identifying argumentative discourse structures in persuasive essays. In *Proceedings of the 2014 Conference on Empirical Methods in Natural Language Processing (EMNLP)*, pages 46–56. Association for Computational Linguistics, 2014b. https://doi.org/10.3115/v1/D14-1006.

Christian Stab and Iryna Gurevych. Recognizing the absence of opposing arguments in persuasive essays. In *Proceedings of the Third Workshop on Argument Mining (ArgMining2016)*, pages 113–118. Association for Computational Linguistics, 2016. https://doi.org/10.18653/v1/W16-2813.

Christian Stab and Iryna Gurevych. Recognizing insufficiently supported arguments in argumentative essays. In Mirella Lapata, Phil Blunsom, and Alexander Koller, editors, *Proceedings of the 15th Conference of the European Chapter of the Association for Computational Linguistics: Volume 1, Long Papers*, pages 980–990, Valencia, Spain, April 2017a. Association for Computational Linguistics. URL https://aclanthology.org/E17-1092/.

Christian Stab and Iryna Gurevych. Parsing argumentation structures in persuasive essays. *Computational Linguistics*, 43(3):619–659, 2017b. https://doi.org/10.1162/COLI_a_00295.

Christian Stab, Johannes Daxenberger, Chris Stahlhut, Tristan Miller, Benjamin Schiller, Christopher Tauchmann, Steffen Eger, and Iryna Gurevych. ArgumenText: Searching for arguments in heterogeneous sources. In Yang Liu, Tim Paek, and Manasi Patwardhan, editors, *Proceedings of the 2018 Conference of the North American Chapter of the Association for Computational Linguistics: Demonstrations*, pages 21–25, New Orleans, Louisiana, June 2018a. Association for Computational Linguistics. https://doi.org/10.18653/v1/N18-5005.

Christian Stab, Tristan Miller, Benjamin Schiller, Pranav Rai, and Iryna Gurevych. Cross-topic argument mining from heterogeneous sources. In Ellen Riloff, David Chiang, Julia Hockenmaier, and Jun'ichi Tsujii, editors, *Proceedings of the 2018 Conference on Empirical Methods in Natural Language Processing*, pages 3664–3674, Brussels, Belgium, October-November 2018b. Association for Computational Linguistics. https://doi.org/10.18653/v1/D18-1402.

Maja Stahl, Nick Düsterhus, Mei-Hua Chen, and Henning Wachsmuth. Mind the gap: Automated corpus creation for enthymeme detection and reconstruction in learner arguments. In Houda Bouamor, Juan Pino, and Kalika Bali, editors, *Findings of the Association for Computational Linguistics: EMNLP 2023*, pages 4703–4717, Singapore, December 2023. Association for Computational Linguistics. https://doi.org/10.18653/v1/2023.findings-emnlp.312.

Maja Stahl, Timon Ziegenbein, Joonsuk Park, and Henning Wachsmuth. ArgInstruct: Specialized instruction fine-tuning for computational argumentation. In Wanxiang Che, Joyce Nabende, Ekaterina Shutova, and Mohammad Taher Pilehvar, editors, *Findings of the Association for Computational Linguistics: ACL 2025*, pages 11103–11127, Vienna, Austria, July 2025. Association for Computational Linguistics. https://doi.org/10.18653/v1/2025.findings-acl.579.

Chris Stahlhut. Combatting disinformation via interactive evidence detection. In *Proceedings of the First Conference on Truth and Trust Online*, London, UK, October 2019. URL https://truthandtrustonline.com/wp-content/uploads/2019/09/paper_9.pdf.

Chris Stahlhutt, Christian Stabt, and Iryna Gurevycht. Pilot experiments of hypothesis validation through evidence detection for historians. In *Design of Experimental Search & Information Retrieval Systems*, volume 2167 of *CEUR Workshop Proceedings*, pages 83–89. CEUR-WS.org, 2018. https://ceur-ws.org/Vol-2167/paper7.pdf.

Keith E. Stanovich, Richard F. West, and Maggie E. Toplak. Myside bias, rational thinking, and intelligence. *Current Directions in Psychological Science*, 22(4):259–264, 2013. https://doi.org/10.1177/0963721413480174.

Paul Stapleton and Yanming Amy Wu. Assessing the quality of arguments in students' persuasive writing: A case study analyzing the relationship between surface structure and substance. *Journal of English for Academic Purposes*, 17:12–23, 2015. https://doi.org/10.1016/j.jeap.2014.11.006.

Manfred Stede. *Discourse Processing*. Morgan and Claypool, 2011.

Manfred Stede, Stergos Afantenos, Andreas Peldszus, Nicholas Asher, and Jérémy Perret. Parallel discourse annotations on a corpus of short texts. In *Proceedings of the Tenth International Conference on Language Resources and Evaluation (LREC'16)*, pages 1051–1058, Portorož, Slovenia, May 2016. European Language Resources Association (ELRA). URL https://aclanthology.org/L16-1167/.

Marco R. Steenbergen, Andre Bachtiger, Markus Sporndli, and Jürg Steiner. Measuring political deliberation: A discourse quality index. *Comparative European Politics*, 1:21–48, 2003. https://doi.org/10.1057/palgrave.cep.6110002.

Benno Stein, Yamen Ajjour, Roxanne El Baff, Khalid Al-Khatib, Philipp Cimiano, and Henning Wachsmuth. Same side stance classification. In Yamen Ajjour, Khalid Al-Khatib, Philipp Cimiano, Roxanne El Baff, Basil Ell, Benno Stein, and Henning Wachsmuth, editors, *Same Side*

Stance Classification Shared Task 2019, volume 2921 of *CEUR Workshop Proceedings*, pages 1–7, July 2021. URL https://ceur-ws.org/Vol-2921/overview.pdf.

Katharina Stevens. *The Ethics of Argumentation*. Routledge, New York, August 2025. ISBN 978-1-003-64002-8. https://doi.org/10.4324/9781003640028.

Sainbayar Sukhbaatar, Arthur Szlam, Jason Weston, and Rob Fergus. End-to-end memory networks. In *Proceedings of the 29th International Conference on Neural Information Processing Systems - Volume 2*, NIPS'15, pages 2440–2448, Cambridge, MA, USA, 2015. MIT Press. URL https://proceedings.neurips.cc/paper_files/paper/2015/hash/8fb21ee7a2207526da55a679f0332de2-Abstract.html.

Yang Sun, Guanrong Chen, Caihua Yang, Jianzhu Bao, Bin Liang, Xi Zeng, Min Yang, and Ruifeng Xu. Discourse structure-aware prefix for generation-based end-to-end argumentation mining. In Lun-Wei Ku, Andre Martins, and Vivek Srikumar, editors, *Findings of the Association for Computational Linguistics: ACL 2024*, pages 11597–11613, Bangkok, Thailand, August 2024. Association for Computational Linguistics. https://doi.org/10.18653/v1/2024.findings-acl.689.

Ekaterina Sviridova, Elena Cabrio, and Serena Villata. Mining implicit arguments for reasoning: A survey. *Argument & Computation*. 17(1):3–27, 2026. https://doi.org/10.1177/3231.

John M. Swales. *Genre Analysis: English in Academic and Research Settings*. Cambridge University Press, 1990.

Reid Swanson, Brian Ecker, and Marilyn Walker. Argument mining: Extracting arguments from online dialogue. In Alexander Koller, Gabriel Skantze, Filip Jurcicek, Masahiro Araki, and Carolyn Penstein Rose, editors, *Proceedings of the 16th Annual Meeting of the Special Interest Group on Discourse and Dialogue*, pages 217–226, Prague, Czech Republic, September 2015. Association for Computational Linguistics. https://doi.org/10.18653/v1/W15-4631.

Shahbaz Syed, Khalid Al Khatib, Milad Alshomary, Henning Wachsmuth, and Martin Potthast. Generating informative conclusions for argumentative texts. In Chengqing Zong, Fei Xia, Wenjie Li, and Roberto Navigli, editors, *Findings of the Association for Computational Linguistics: ACL-IJCNLP 2021*, pages 3482–3493, Online, August 2021. Association for Computational Linguistics. https://doi.org/10.18653/v1/2021.findings-acl.306.

Shahbaz Syed, Timon Ziegenbein, Philipp Heinisch, Henning Wachsmuth, and Martin Potthast. Frame-oriented summarization of argumentative discussions. In Svetlana Stoyanchev, Shafiq Joty, David Schlangen, Ondrej Dusek, Casey Kennington, and Malihe Alikhani, editors, *Proceedings of the 24th Annual Meeting of the Special Interest Group on Discourse and Dialogue*, pages 114–129, Prague, Czechia, September 2023. Association for Computational Linguistics. https://doi.org/10.18653/v1/2023.sigdial-1.10.

Maite Taboada, Julian Brooke, Milan Tofiloski, Kimberly Voll, and Manfred Stede. Lexicon-based methods for sentiment analysis. *Computational Linguistics*, 37(2):267–307, 2011. https://doi.org/10.1162/COLI_a_00049.

Chenhao Tan, Vlad Niculae, Cristian Danescu-Niculescu-Mizil, and Lillian Lee. Winning arguments: Interaction dynamics and persuasion strategies in good-faith online discussions. In *Proceedings of the 25th International World Wide Web Conference*, pages 613–624, 2016. https://doi.org/10.1145/2872427.2883081.

Rohan Taori, Ishaan Gulrajani, Tianyi Zhang, Yann Dubois, Xuechen Li, Carlos Guestrin, Percy Liang, and Tatsunori B. Hashimoto. Stanford Alpaca: An instruction-following LLaMA model. https://github.com/tatsu-lab/stanford_alpaca, 2023.

Simone Teufel. Scientific argumentation detection as limited-domain intention recognition. In *Proceedings of the Workshop on Frontiers and Connections between Argumentation Theory and Natural Language Processing*, volume 1341 of *CEUR Workshop Proceedings*, pages 1–9, Forlì-Cesena, Italy, 2014. CEUR-WS.org. URL https://ceur-ws.org/Vol-1341/paper14.pdf.

Simone Teufel and Marc Moens. Summarizing scientific articles: Experiments with relevance and rhetorical status. *Computational Linguistics*, 28(4):409–445, 2002. https://doi.org/10.1162/089120102762671936.

Christopher W. Tindale. *Fallacies and Argument Appraisal. Critical Reasoning and Argumentation*. Cambridge University Press, 2007. https://doi.org/10.1017/CBO9780511806544.

Assaf Toledo, Shai Gretz, Edo Cohen-Karlik, Roni Friedman, Elad Venezian, Dan Lahav, Michal Jacovi, Ranit Aharonov, and Noam Slonim. Automatic argument quality assessment - New datasets and methods. In *Proceedings of the 2019 Conference on Empirical Methods in Natural Language Processing and the 9th International Joint Conference on Natural Language Processing (EMNLP-IJCNLP)*, pages 5625–5635. Association for Computational Linguistics, 2019. https://doi.org/10.18653/v1/D19-1564.

Orith Toledo-Ronen, Roy Bar-Haim, and Noam Slonim. Expert stance graphs for computational argumentation. In Chris Reed, editor, *Proceedings of the Third Workshop on Argument Mining (ArgMining2016)*, pages 119–123, Berlin, Germany, August 2016. Association for Computational Linguistics. https://doi.org/10.18653/v1/W16-2814.

Orith Toledo-Ronen, Matan Orbach, Yonatan Bilu, Artem Spector, and Noam Slonim. Multilingual argument mining: Datasets and analysis. In Trevor Cohn, Yulan He, and Yang Liu, editors, *Findings of the Association for Computational Linguistics: EMNLP 2020*, pages 303–317, Online, November 2020. Association for Computational Linguistics. https://doi.org/10.18653/v1/2020.findings-emnlp.29.

Francesca Toni. A tutorial on assumption-based argumentation. *Argument & Computation*, 5(1): 89–117, January 2014. https://doi.org/10.1080/19462166.2013.869878.

Stephen E. Toulmin. *The Uses of Argument*. Cambridge University Press, 1958.

Stephen E. Toulmin. *The Uses of Argument*. Cambridge University Press, 2nd edition, July 2003. https://doi.org/10.1017/CBO9780511840005.

Hugo Touvron, Thibaut Lavril, Gautier Izacard, Xavier Martinet, Marie-Anne Lachaux, Timothée Lacroix, Baptiste Rozière, Naman Goyal, Eric Hambro, Faisal Azhar, Aurelien Rodriguez, Armand Joulin, Edouard Grave, and Guillaume Lample. LLaMA: Open and efficient foundation language models, 2023a. https://doi.org/10.48550/arXiv.2302.13971.

Hugo Touvron, Louis Martin, Kevin Stone, Peter Albert, Amjad Almahairi, Yasmine Babaei, Nikolay Bashlykov, Soumya Batra, Prajjwal Bhargava, Shruti Bhosale, Dan Bikel, Lukas Blecher, Cristian Canton Ferrer, Moya Chen, Guillem Cucurull, David Esiobu, Jude Fernandes, Jeremy Fu, Wenyin Fu, Brian Fuller, Cynthia Gao, Vedanuj Goswami, Naman Goyal, Anthony Hartshorn, Saghar Hosseini, Rui Hou, Hakan Inan, Marcin Kardas, Viktor Kerkez, Madian Khabsa, Isabel Kloumann, Artem Korenev, Punit Singh Koura, Marie-Anne Lachaux, Thibaut Lavril, Jenya Lee, Diana Liskovich, Yinghai Lu, Yuning Mao, Xavier Martinet, Todor Mihaylov, Pushkar Mishra, Igor Molybog, Yixin Nie, Andrew Poulton, Jeremy Reizenstein, Rashi Rungta, Kalyan Saladi, Alan Schelten, Ruan Silva, Eric Michael Smith, Ranjan Subramanian, Xiaoqing Ellen Tan, Binh Tang, Ross Taylor, Adina Williams, Jian Xiang Kuan, Puxin Xu, Zheng Yan, Iliyan Zarov, Yuchen Zhang, Angela Fan, Melanie Kambadur, Sharan Narang, Aurelien Rodriguez, Robert Stojnic, Sergey Edunov, and Thomas Scialom. Llama 2: Open foundation and fine-tuned chat models, 2023b. https://doi.org/10.48550/arXiv.2307.09288.

Dietrich Trautmann. Aspect-based argument mining. In Elena Cabrio and Serena Villata, editors, *Proceedings of the 7th Workshop on Argument Mining*, pages 41–52, Online, December 2020. Association for Computational Linguistics. URL https://aclanthology.org/2020.argmining-1.5/.

Dietrich Trautmann, Johannes Daxenberger, Christian Stab, Hinrich Schütze, and Iryna Gurevych. Fine-grained argument unit recognition and classification. In *Proceedings of the The Thirty-Fourth AAAI Conference on Artificial Intelligence (AAAI-20)*, pages 9048–9056, New York/NY, 2020. AAAI. https://doi.org/10.1609/aaai.v34i05.6438.

Enrica Troiano, Sebastian Padó, and Roman Klinger. Crowdsourcing and validating event-focused emotion corpora for German and English. In Anna Korhonen, David Traum, and Lluís Màrquez, editors, *Proceedings of the 57th Annual Meeting of the Association for Computational Linguistics*, pages 4005–4011, Florence, Italy, July 2019. Association for Computational Linguistics. https://doi.org/10.18653/v1/P19-1391.

Oren Tsur, Dan Calacci, and David Lazer. A frame of mind: Using statistical models for detection of framing and agenda setting campaigns. In Chengqing Zong and Michael Strube, editors, *Proceedings of the 53rd Annual Meeting of the Association for Computational Linguistics and the 7th International Joint Conference on Natural Language Processing (Volume 1: Long Papers)*, pages 1629–1638, Beijing, China, July 2015. Association for Computational Linguistics. https://doi.org/10.3115/v1/P15-1157.

Charles Twardy. Argument maps improve critical thinking. *Teaching Philosophy*, 27(2):95–116, May 2004. https://doi.org/10.5840/teachphil200427213.

Michiel van der Meer, Piek Vossen, Catholijn M. Jonker, and Pradeep K. Murukannaiah. Do differences in values influence disagreements in online discussions? In Houda Bouamor, Juan Pino, and Kalika Bali, editors, *Proceedings of the 2023 Conference on Empirical Methods in Natural Language Processing*, pages 15986–16008, Singapore, December 2023. Association for Computational Linguistics. https://doi.org/10.18653/v1/2023.emnlp-main.992.

Frans H. van Eemeren. *Reasonableness and Effectiveness in Argumentative Discourse: Fifty Contributions to the Development of Pragma-Dialectics*, volume 27 of *Argumentation Library*. Springer International Publishing, 2015. https://doi.org/10.1007/978-3-319-20955-5.

Frans H. van Eemeren and Rob Grootendorst. *A Systematic Theory of Argumentation: The Pragma-Dialectical Approach*. Cambridge University Press, Cambridge, UK, 2004. ISBN 978052183075. https://doi.org/10.1017/CBO9780511616389.

Frans H. van Eemeren and Peter Houtlosser. Strategic maneuvering. In Frans H. van Eemeren and Peter Houtlosser, editors, *Dialectic and Rhetoric: The Warp and Woof of Argumentation Analysis*, pages 131–159. Springer Netherlands, Dordrecht, 2002. https://doi.org/10.1007/978-94-015-9948-1_10.

Frans H. van Eemeren, Rob Grootendorst, Sally Jackson, and Scott Jacobs. *Reconstructing Argumentative Discourse*. University of Alabama Press, 1993.

Frans H. van Eemeren, Peter Houtlosser, and A. F. Snoeck Henkemans. *Argumentative Indicators in Discourse: A Pragma-Dialectical Study*. Springer, 2007. ISBN 978-1-4020-6243-8. https://doi.org/10.1007/978-1-4020-6244-5.

Tim van Gelder. The rationale for Rationale. *Law, Probability and Risk*, 6(1-4):23–42, 2007. https://doi.org/10.1093/lpr/mgm032.

Lev G. Vassiliev. What we reconstruct in enthymeme reconstruction: A linguistic-argumentative approach. In *Proceedings of the Ontario Society for the Study of Argumentation Conference*, volume 4, 2001.

Eva Maria Vecchi, Neele Falk, Iman Jundi, and Gabriella Lapesa. Towards argument mining for social good: A survey. In Chengqing Zong, Fei Xia, Wenjie Li, and Roberto Navigli, editors, *Proceedings of the 59th Annual Meeting of the Association for Computational Linguistics and the 11th International Joint Conference on Natural Language Processing (Volume 1: Long Papers)*, pages 1338–1352, Online, August 2021. Association for Computational Linguistics. https://doi.org/10.18653/v1/2021.acl-long.107.

Eva Maria Vecchi, Neele Falk, Carlotta Quensel, Iman Jundi, and Gabriella Lapesa. PerspectiveMod: A perspectivist resource for deliberative moderation. In Christos Christodoulopoulos, Tanmoy Chakraborty, Carolyn Rose, and Violet Peng, editors, *Proceedings of the 2025 Conference on Empirical Methods in Natural Language Processing*, pages 34163–34186, Suzhou, China,

November 2025. Association for Computational Linguistics. https://doi.org/10.18653/v1/2025.emnlp-main.1733.
Petar Velickovic, Guillem Cucurull, Arantxa Casanova, Adriana Romero, Pietro Liò, and Yoshua Bengio. Graph attention networks. In *Conference Track Proceedings of the 6th International Conference on Learning Representations*, pages 1–12, 2018. URL https://openreview.net/forum?id=rJXMpikCZ.
Preetika Verma, Kokil Jaidka, and Svetlana Churina. "Reasoning" with rhetoric: On the style-evidence tradeoff in LLM-generated counter-arguments. *Proceedings of the International AAAI Conference on Web and Social Media*, 19(1):1966–1989, Jun. 2025. https://doi.org/10.1609/icwsm.v19i1.35913.
David Vilares and Yulan He. Detecting perspectives in political debates. In Martha Palmer, Rebecca Hwa, and Sebastian Riedel, editors, *Proceedings of the 2017 Conference on Empirical Methods in Natural Language Processing*, pages 1573–1582, Copenhagen, Denmark, September 2017. Association for Computational Linguistics. https://doi.org/10.18653/v1/D17-1165.
Maria Garcia Villalba and Patrick Saint-Dizier. Some facets of argument mining for opinion analysis. In *Proceedings of Computational Models of Argument*, pages 23–34, 2012. https://doi.org/10.3233/978-1-61499-111-3-23.
Oriol Vinyals, Meire Fortunato, and Navdeep Jaitly. Pointer networks. In *Proceedings of the Conference on Neural Information Processing Systems*, pages 2692–2700, 2015. URL https://proceedings.neurips.cc/paper_files/paper/2015/file/29921001f2f04bd3baee84a12e98098f-Paper.pdf.
Jacky Visser, John Lawrence, Jean Wagemans, and Chris Reed. An annotated corpus of argument schemes in US election debates. In *Proceedings of the 9th Conference of the International Society for the Study of Argumentation (ISSA) 2018*, pages 1101–1111. AmsterdamSic Sat, 2019. URL https://hdl.handle.net/11245.1/182b00d1-24c4-4a85-b4a7-eba9b72fe1af.
Jacky Visser, Barbara Konat, Rory Duthie, Marcin Koszowy, Katarzyna Budzynska, and Chris Reed. Argumentation in the 2016 US presidential elections: Annotated corpora of television debates and social media reaction. *Language Resources and Evaluation*, 54(1):123–154, 2020. https://doi.org/0.1007/s10579-019-09446-8.
Jacky Visser, John Lawrence, Chris Reed, Jean Wagemans, and Douglas Walton. Annotating argument schemes. *Argumentation*, 35:101–135, 2021. https://doi.org/10.1007/s10503-020-09519-x.
Denny Vrandečić and Markus Krötzsch. Wikidata: A free collaborative knowledgebase. *Communications of the ACM*, 57(10):78–85, September 2014. https://doi.org/10.1145/2629489.
Nina Wacholder, Smaranda Muresan, Debanjan Ghosh, and Mark Aakhus. Annotating multiparty discourse: Challenges for agreement metrics. In Lori Levin and Manfred Stede, editors, *Proceedings of LAW VIII - The 8th Linguistic Annotation Workshop*, pages 120–128, Dublin, Ireland, August 2014. Association for Computational Linguistics and Dublin City University. https://doi.org/10.3115/v1/W14-4918.
Henning Wachsmuth and Till Werner. Intrinsic quality assessment of arguments. In *Proceedings of the 28th International Conference on Computational Linguistics*, pages 6739–6745, Barcelona, Spain (Online), December 2020. International Committee on Computational Linguistics. https://doi.org/10.18653/v1/2020.coling-main.592.
Henning Wachsmuth, Khalid Al Khatib, and Benno Stein. Using argument mining to assess the argumentation quality of essays. In *Proceedings of COLING 2016, the 26th International Conference on Computational Linguistics: Technical Papers*, pages 1680–1691. The COLING 2016 Organizing Committee, 2016. URL https://aclanthology.org/C16-1158/.
Henning Wachsmuth, Giovanni Da San Martino, Dora Kiesel, and Benno Stein. The impact of modeling overall argumentation with tree kernels. In *Proceedings of the 2017 Conference*

on Empirical Methods in Natural Language Processing, pages 2369–2379. Association for Computational Linguistics, 2017a. https://doi.org/10.18653/v1/D17-1252.

Henning Wachsmuth, Nona Naderi, Ivan Habernal, Yufang Hou, Graeme Hirst, Iryna Gurevych, and Benno Stein. Argumentation quality assessment: Theory vs. practice. In *Proceedings of the 55th Annual Meeting of the Association for Computational Linguistics (Volume 2: Short Papers)*, pages 250–255. Association for Computational Linguistics, 2017b. https://doi.org/10.18653/v1/P17-2039.

Henning Wachsmuth, Nona Naderi, Yufang Hou, Yonatan Bilu, Vinodkumar Prabhakaran, Alberdingk Tim Thijm, Graeme Hirst, and Benno Stein. Computational argumentation quality assessment in natural language. In *Proceedings of the 15th Conference of the European Chapter of the Association for Computational Linguistics: Volume 1, Long Papers*, pages 176–187. Association for Computational Linguistics, 2017c. URL https://aclanthology.org/E17-1017/.

Henning Wachsmuth, Martin Potthast, Khalid Al-Khatib, Yamen Ajjour, Jana Puschmann, Jiani Qu, Jonas Dorsch, Viorel Morari, Janek Bevendorff, and Benno Stein. Building an argument search engine for the web. In *Proceedings of the 4th Workshop on Argument Mining*, pages 49–59. Association for Computational Linguistics, 2017d. https://doi.org/10.18653/v1/W17-5106.

Henning Wachsmuth, Benno Stein, and Yamen Ajjour. "PageRank" for argument relevance. In *Proceedings of the 15th Conference of the European Chapter of the Association for Computational Linguistics: Volume 1, Long Papers*, pages 1117–1127. Association for Computational Linguistics, 2017e. URL https://aclanthology.org/E17-1105/.

Henning Wachsmuth, Manfred Stede, Roxanne El Baff, Khalid Al Khatib, Maria Skeppstedt, and Benno Stein. Argumentation synthesis following rhetorical strategies. In *Proceedings of the 27th International Conference on Computational Linguistics*, pages 3753–3765. Association for Computational Linguistics, 2018a. URL https://aclanthology.org/C18-1318/.

Henning Wachsmuth, Shahbaz Syed, and Benno Stein. Retrieval of the best counterargument without prior topic knowledge. In *Proceedings of the 56th Annual Meeting of the Association for Computational Linguistics (Volume 1: Long Papers)*, pages 241–251. Association for Computational Linguistics, 2018b. https://doi.org/10.18653/v1/P18-1023.

Henning Wachsmuth, Gabriella Lapesa, Elena Cabrio, Anne Lauscher, Joonsuk Park, Eva Maria Vecchi, Serena Villata, and Timon Ziegenbein. Argument quality assessment in the age of instruction-following large language models. In Nicoletta Calzolari, Min-Yen Kan, Veronique Hoste, Alessandro Lenci, Sakriani Sakti, and Nianwen Xue, editors, *Proceedings of the 2024 Joint International Conference on Computational Linguistics, Language Resources and Evaluation (LREC-COLING 2024)*, pages 1519–1538, Torino, Italia, May 2024. ELRA and ICCL. URL https://aclanthology.org/2024.lrec-main.135/.

Jean H.M. Wagemans. Constructing a periodic table of arguments. In P. Bondy and L. Benacquista, editors, *Argumentation, Objectivity, and Bias: Proceedings of the 11th International Conference of the Ontario Society for the Study of Argumentation (OSSA), 18-21 May 2016*, pages 1–12, Windsor, Ontario, 2016. URL https://hdl.handle.net/20.500.14776/16592.

Jean H.M. Wagemans. Argument type identification procedure (ATIP)—version 5 (corrected), August 2025. URL https://periodic-table-of-arguments.org/wp-content/uploads/2025/09/wagemans-2025-argument-type-identification-procedure-atip-version-5-corrected.pdf.

Jeffrey Walker. The body of persuasion: A theory of the enthymeme. *College English*, 56:46–65, 1994. https://doi.org/10.2307/378216.

Marilyn Walker, Pranav Anand, Rob Abbott, and Ricky Grant. Stance classification using dialogic properties of persuasion. In Eric Fosler-Lussier, Ellen Riloff, and Srinivas Bangalore, editors, *Proceedings of the 2012 Conference of the North American Chapter of the Association for Computational Linguistics: Human Language Technologies*, pages 592–596, Montréal, Canada, June 2012a. Association for Computational Linguistics. URL https://aclanthology.org/N12-1072/.

Marilyn Walker, Jean Fox Tree, Pranav Anand, Rob Abbott, and Joseph King. A corpus for research on deliberation and debate. In Nicoletta Calzolari, Khalid Choukri, Thierry Declerck, Mehmet Uğur Doğan, Bente Maegaard, Joseph Mariani, Asuncion Moreno, Jan Odijk, and Stelios Piperidis, editors, *Proceedings of the Eighth International Conference on Language Resources and Evaluation (LREC'12)*, pages 812–817, Istanbul, Turkey, May 2012b. European Language Resources Association (ELRA). URL https://aclanthology.org/L12-1643/.

Douglas Ehninger and Wayne Brockriede. *Decision by Debate*. Dodd, Mead, 1963.

Douglas Walton. *Fundamentals of Critical Argumentation*. Cambridge University Press, 2006. ISBN 978-0-521-82319-7. https://doi.org/10.1017/CBO9780511807039.

Douglas Walton. The three bases for the enthymeme: A dialogical theory. *Journal of Applied Logic*, 6(3):361–379, 2008a. https://doi.org/10.1016/j.jal.2007.06.002.

Douglas Walton. Objections, rebuttals and refutations. In *Argument Cultures: Proceedings of the 8th OSSA Conference*, pages 1–10, 2009. URL https://hdl.handle.net/20.500.14776/13880.

Douglas Walton. *Argumentation Schemes for Presumptive Reasoning*. Routledge, New York, November 2013. ISBN 978-0-203-81116-0. https://doi.org/10.4324/9780203811160.

Douglas Walton and Fabrizio Macagno. A classification system for argumentation schemes. *Argument & Computation*, 6(3):219–245, 2015. https://doi.org/10.1080/19462166.2015.1123772.

Douglas Walton and Chris A. Reed. Argumentation schemes and enthymemes. *Synthese*, 145: 339–370, 2005. https://doi.org/10.1007/s11229-005-6198-x.

Douglas Walton, Chris Reed, and Fabrizio Macagno. *Argumentation Schemes*. Cambridge University Press, Cambridge, 2008. ISBN 9780511802034. https://doi.org/10.1017/CBO9780511802034.

Douglas Walton, Chris Reed, and Fabrizio Macagno. Argumentation schemes. In Pietro Baroni, Dov Gabbay, Massimiliano Giacomin, and Leendert van der Torre, editors, *Handbook of Formal Argumentation*, pages 519–576. College Publications, 2018.

Douglas N. Walton. What is reasoning? What is an argument? *The Journal of Philosophy*, 87(8): 399–419, 1990. https://doi.org/10.2307/2026735.

Douglas N. Walton. *Argumentation Methods for Artificial Intelligence and Law*. Springer, Berlin, 2005. ISBN 978-3-540-25187-3. https://doi.org/10.1007/3-540-27881-8.

Douglas N. Walton. The three bases for the enthymeme: A dialogical theory. *Journal of Applied Logic*, 6(3):361–379, 2008b. https://doi.org/10.1016/j.jal.2007.06.002.

Douglas N. Walton and Erik C. W. Krabbe. *Commitment in Dialogue: Basic Concepts of Interpersonal Reasoning*. SUNY Series in Logic and Language. State University of New York Press, Albany, NY, 1995. ISBN 978-0-7914-2586-2.

Ben Wang and Aran Komatsuzaki. GPT-J-6B: A 6 billion parameter autoregressive language model. https://github.com/kingoflolz/mesh-transformer-jax, May 2021.

Fuyu Wang, Jiangtong Li, Kun Zhu, and Changjun Jiang. InspireDebate: Multi-dimensional subjective-objective evaluation-guided reasoning and optimization for debating. In Wanxiang Che, Joyce Nabende, Ekaterina Shutova, and Mohammad Taher Pilehvar, editors, *Proceedings of the 63rd Annual Meeting of the Association for Computational Linguistics (Volume 1: Long Papers)*, pages 27525–27544, Vienna, Austria, July 2025a. Association for Computational Linguistics. https://doi.org/10.18653/v1/2025.acl-long.1335.

Nailia Mirzakhmedova, Manfred Stede, and Benno Stein. Computational approaches to framing in discourse. Springer, Cham 2027.

Lu Wang and Wang Ling. Neural network-based abstract generation for opinions and arguments. In *Proceedings of the 2016 Conference of the North American Chapter of the Association for Computational Linguistics: Human Language Technologies*, pages 47–57. Association for Computational Linguistics, 2016. https://doi.org/10.18653/v1/N16-1007.

Lu Wang, Nick Beauchamp, Sarah Shugars, and Kechen Qin. Winning on the merits: The joint effects of content and style on debate outcomes. *Transactions of the Association for Computational Linguistics*, 5:219–232, 2017. https://doi.org/10.1162/tacl_a_00057.

Lucy Lu Wang, Kyle Lo, Yoganand Chandrasekhar, Russell Reas, Jiangjiang Yang, Doug Burdick, Darrin Eide, Kathryn Funk, Yannis Katsis, Rodney Michael Kinney, Yunyao Li, Ziyang Liu, William Merrill, Paul Mooney, Dewey A. Murdick, Devvret Rishi, Jerry Sheehan, Zhihong Shen, Brandon Stilson, Alex D. Wade, Kuansan Wang, Nancy Xin Ru Wang, Christopher Wilhelm, Boya Xie, Douglas M. Raymond, Daniel S. Weld, Oren Etzioni, and Sebastian Kohlmeier. CORD-19: The COVID-19 open research dataset. In Karin Verspoor, Kevin Bretonnel Cohen, Mark Dredze, Emilio Ferrara, Jonathan May, Robert Munro, Cecile Paris, and Byron Wallace, editors, *Proceedings of the 1st Workshop on NLP for COVID-19 at ACL 2020*, pages 1–12, Online, July 2020. Association for Computational Linguistics. URL https://aclanthology.org/2020.nlpcovid19-acl.1/.

Tong Wang, Abdelrahman Mohamed, and Graeme Hirst. Learning lexical embeddings with syntactic and lexicographic knowledge. In Chengqing Zong and Michael Strube, editors, *Proceedings of the 53rd Annual Meeting of the Association for Computational Linguistics and the 7th International Joint Conference on Natural Language Processing (Volume 2: Short Papers)*, pages 458–463, Beijing, China, July 2015. Association for Computational Linguistics. https://doi.org/10.3115/v1/P15-2075.

Wenzhi Wang, Paul Reisert, Shoichi Naito, Naoya Inoue, Machi Shimmei, Surawat Pothong, Jungmin Choi, and Kentaro Inui. Identification of multiple logical interpretations in counter-arguments. In Christos Christodoulopoulos, Tanmoy Chakraborty, Carolyn Rose, and Violet Peng, editors, *Proceedings of the 2025 Conference on Empirical Methods in Natural Language Processing*, pages 6418–6433, Suzhou, China, November 2025b. Association for Computational Linguistics. https://doi.org/10.18653/v1/2025.emnlp-main.326.

Xiaoou Wang, Elena Cabrio, and Serena Villata. Argument and counter-argument generation: A critical survey. In Elisabeth Métais, Farid Meziane, Vijayan Sugumaran, Warren Manning, and Stephan Reiff-Marganiec, editors, *Natural Language Processing and Information Systems*, pages 500–510, Cham, 2023a. Springer Nature Switzerland. https://doi.org/10.1007/978-3-031-35320-8_37.

Yini Wang, Xian Zhou, Shengan Zheng, Linpeng Huang, Zhunchen Luo, Wei Luo, and Xiaoying Bai. Uncovering argumentative flow: A question-focus discourse structuring framework. In Christos Christodoulopoulos, Tanmoy Chakraborty, Carolyn Rose, and Violet Peng, editors, *Proceedings of the 2025 Conference on Empirical Methods in Natural Language Processing*, pages 8252–8270, Suzhou, China, November 2025c. Association for Computational Linguistics. https://doi.org/10.18653/v1/2025.emnlp-main.416.

Yiran Wang, Ben He, Xuanang Chen, and Le Sun. Can LLMs clarify? Investigation and enhancement of large language models on argument claim optimization. In Owen Rambow, Leo Wanner, Marianna Apidianaki, Hend Al-Khalifa, Barbara Di Eugenio, and Steven Schockaert, editors, *Proceedings of the 31st International Conference on Computational Linguistics*, pages 4066–4077, Abu Dhabi, UAE, January 2025d. Association for Computational Linguistics. URL https://aclanthology.org/2025.coling-main.273/.

Yizhong Wang, Hamish Ivison, Pradeep Dasigi, Jack Hessel, Tushar Khot, Khyathi Raghavi Chandu, David Wadden, Kelsey MacMillan, Noah A. Smith, Iz Beltagy, and Hannaneh Hajishirzi. How far can camels go? Exploring the state of instruction tuning on open resources. In *Proceedings of the 37th International Conference on Neural Information Processing Systems*, NIPS '23, pages 1–23, Red Hook, NY, USA, 2023b. Curran Associates Inc. URL https://papers.neurips.cc/paper_files/paper/2023/hash/ec6413875e4ab08d7bc4d8e225263398-Abstract-Datasets_and_Benchmarks.html.

Bin Wei and Henry Prakken. Defining the structure of arguments with AI models of argumentation. In *Proceedings of the Conference on Computational Models of Natural Argument*, pages 60–64, 2012. URL https://cmna.csc.liv.ac.uk/CMNA12/paper_16.pdf.

Jason Wei and Kai Zou. EDA: Easy data augmentation techniques for boosting performance on text classification tasks. In Kentaro Inui, Jing Jiang, Vincent Ng, and Xiaojun Wan, editors, *Proceedings of the 2019 Conference on Empirical Methods in Natural Language Processing and the 9th International Joint Conference on Natural Language Processing (EMNLP-IJCNLP)*, pages 6382–6388, Hong Kong, China, November 2019. Association for Computational Linguistics. https://doi.org/10.18653/v1/D19-1670.

Jason Wei, Xuezhi Wang, Dale Schuurmans, Maarten Bosma, Brian Ichter, Fei Xia, Ed Chi, Quoc V Le, and Denny Zhou. Chain-of-thought prompting elicits reasoning in large language models. In S. Koyejo, S. Mohamed, A. Agarwal, D. Belgrave, K. Cho, and A. Oh, editors, *Advances in Neural Information Processing Systems*, volume 35, pages 24824–24837. Curran Associates, Inc., 2022. URL https://papers.neurips.cc/paper_files/paper/2022/hash/9d5609613524ecf4f15af0f7b31abca4-Abstract-Conference.html.

Wan Wei, Xiao Zhang, Xuqin Liu, Wei Chen, and Tengjiao Wang. pkudblab at SemEval-2016 task 6: A specific convolutional neural network system for effective stance detection. In Steven Bethard, Marine Carpuat, Daniel Cer, David Jurgens, Preslav Nakov, and Torsten Zesch, editors, *Proceedings of the 10th International Workshop on Semantic Evaluation (SemEval-2016)*, pages 384–388, San Diego, California, June 2016. Association for Computational Linguistics. https://doi.org/10.18653/v1/S16-1062.

Egon Werlich. *Typologie der Texte*. Quelle und Meyer, Heidelberg, 1975.

Sarah Myers West, Meredith Whittaker, and Kate Crawford. Discriminating systems: Gender, race, and power in AI, Apr 2019. URL https://ainowinstitute.org/publications/discriminating-systems-gender-race-and-power-in-ai-2.

Janyce Wiebe, Theresa Wilson, and Claire Cardie. Annotating expressions of opinions and emotions in language. *Language Resources and Evaluation*, 39(2-3):165–210, 2005. https://doi.org/10.1007/s10579-005-7880-9.

Matti Wiegmann, Khalid Al Khatib, Vishal Khanna, and Benno Stein. Analyzing persuasion strategies of debaters on social media. In Nicoletta Calzolari, Chu-Ren Huang, Hansaem Kim, James Pustejovsky, Leo Wanner, Key-Sun Choi, Pum-Mo Ryu, Hsin-Hsi Chen, Lucia Donatelli, Heng Ji, Sadao Kurohashi, Patrizia Paggio, Nianwen Xue, Seokhwan Kim, Younggyun Hahm, Zhong He, Tony Kyungil Lee, Enrico Santus, Francis Bond, and Seung-Hoon Na, editors, *Proceedings of the 29th International Conference on Computational Linguistics*, pages 6897–6905, Gyeongju, Republic of Korea, October 2022. International Committee on Computational Linguistics. URL https://aclanthology.org/2022.coling-1.600/.

Adina Williams, Nikita Nangia, and Samuel Bowman. A broad-coverage challenge corpus for sentence understanding through inference. In Marilyn Walker, Heng Ji, and Amanda Stent, editors, *Proceedings of the 2018 Conference of the North American Chapter of the Association for Computational Linguistics: Human Language Technologies, Volume 1 (Long Papers)*, pages 1112–1122, New Orleans, Louisiana, June 2018. Association for Computational Linguistics. https://doi.org/10.18653/v1/N18-1101.

Yonghui Wu, Mike Schuster, Zhifeng Chen, Quoc V. Le, Mohammad Norouzi, Wolfgang Macherey, Maxim Krikun, Yuan Cao, Qin Gao, Klaus Macherey, Jeff Klingner, Apurva Shah, Melvin Johnson, Xiaobing Liu, Lukasz Kaiser, Stephan Gouws, Yoshikiyo Kato, Taku Kudo, Hideto Kazawa, Keith Stevens, George Kurian, Nishant Patil, Wei Wang, Cliff Young, Jason Smith, Jason Riesa, Alex Rudnick, Oriol Vinyals, Greg Corrado, Macduff Hughes, and Jeffrey Dean. Google's neural machine translation system: Bridging the gap between human and machine translation, 2016. https://doi.org/10.48550/arXiv.1609.08144.

Amelie Wührl and Roman Klinger. Claim detection in biomedical Twitter posts. In Dina Demner-Fushman, Kevin Bretonnel Cohen, Sophia Ananiadou, and Junichi Tsujii, editors, *Proceedings of the 20th Workshop on Biomedical Language Processing*, pages 131–142, Online, jun 2021. Association for Computational Linguistics. https://doi.org/10.18653/v1/2021.bionlp-1.15.

Adam Wyner, Tom van Engers, and Anthony Hunter. Working on the argument pipeline: Through flow issues between natural language argument, instantiated arguments, and argumentation frameworks. In *Proceedings of Computational Models of Natural Argument*, 2010.

Adam Wyner, Tom van Engers, and Anthony Hunter. Working on the argument pipeline: Through flow issues between natural language argument, instantiated arguments, and argumentation frameworks. *Argument & Computation*, 7(1): 69–89, 2016. https://doi.org/10.3233/AAC-160002.

Adam Wyner, Trevor Bench-Capon, Paul Dunne, and Federico Cerutti. Senses of 'argument' in instantiated argumentation frameworks. *Argument & Computation*, 6(1):50–72, 2015. https://doi.org/10.1080/19462166.2014.1002535.

Yilin Xia, Heng Zheng, Shawn Bowers, and Bertram Ludäscher. AF-XRAY: Visual explanation and resolution of ambiguity in legal argumentation frameworks. In *Proceedings of 20th International Conference on AI and Law*, pages 495–497, July 2025. https://doi.org/10.1145/3769126.3769246.

Ruiyu Xiao, Lei Wu, Yuhang Gou, Weinan Zhang, and Ting Liu. Prove your point!: Bringing proof-enhancement principles to argumentative essay generation. In Yaser Al-Onaizan, Mohit Bansal, and Yun-Nung Chen, editors, *Proceedings of the 2024 Conference on Empirical Methods in Natural Language Processing*, pages 18995–19008, Miami, Florida, USA, November 2024. Association for Computational Linguistics. https://doi.org/10.18653/v1/2024.emnlp-main.1058.

Chang Xu, Cecile Paris, Surya Nepal, and Ross Sparks. Recognising agreement and disagreement between stances with reason comparing networks. In Anna Korhonen, David Traum, and Lluís Màrquez, editors, *Proceedings of the 57th Annual Meeting of the Association for Computational Linguistics*, pages 4665–4671, Florence, Italy, July 2019. Association for Computational Linguistics. https://doi.org/10.18653/v1/P19-1460.

Haoran Xu, Amr Sharaf, Yunmo Chen, Weiting Tan, Lingfeng Shen, Benjamin Van Durme, Kenton Murray, and Young Jin Kim. Contrastive preference optimization: pushing the boundaries of LLM performance in machine translation. In *Proceedings of the 41st International Conference on Machine Learning*, volume 235 of *ICML'24*, pages 55204–55224. JMLR.org, 2024. URL https://proceedings.mlr.press/v235/xu24t.html.

Huihui Xu, Jaromir Savelka, and Kevin D. Ashley. Toward summarizing case decisions via extracting argument issues, reasons, and conclusions. In *Proceedings of the Eighteenth International Conference on Artificial Intelligence and Law*, ICAIL '21, pages 250–254, New York, NY, USA, 2021. Association for Computing Machinery. https://doi.org/10.1145/3462757.3466098.

Ruifeng Xu, Yu Zhou, Dongyin Wu, Lin Gui, Jiachen Du, and Yun Xue. Overview of NLPCC shared task 4: Stance detection in Chinese microblogs. In *Natural Language Understanding and Intelligent Applications: 5th CCFN Conference on Natural Language Processing and Chinese Computing, NLPCC 2016, and 24th International Conference on Computer Processing of Oriental Languages, ICCPOL 2016, Kunming, China, December 2-6, 2016, Proceedings*, Lecture Notes in Computer Science, volume 10102, pages 907–916, 2016. https://doi.org/10.1007/978-3-319-50496-4_85.

Andreas Xydis, Christopher Hampson, Sanjay Modgil, and Elizabeth Black. Enthymemes in dialogues. In *Computational Models of Argument*, pages 395–402. IOS Press, 2020. https://doi.org/10.3233/FAIA200523.

Andreas Xydis, Christopher Hampson, Sanjay Modgil, and Elizabeth Black. Towards a sound and complete dialogue system for handling enthymemes. In Pietro Baroni, Christoph Benzmüller, and Yì N. Wáng, editors, *Logic and Argumentation: 4th International Conference, CLAR 2021, Hangzhou, China, October 20-22, 2021, Proceedings*, Lecture Notes in Computer Science, volume 13040, pages 437-456, Cham, 2021. Springer International Publishing. https://doi.org/10.1007/978-3-030-89391-0_24.

Hiroaki Yamada, Simone Teufel, and Takenobu Tokunaga. Annotation of argument structure in Japanese legal documents. In Ivan Habernal, Iryna Gurevych, Kevin Ashley, Claire Cardie, Nancy Green, Diane Litman, Georgios Petasis, Chris Reed, Noam Slonim, and Vern Walker, editors, *Proceedings of the 4th Workshop on Argument Mining*, pages 22–31, Copenhagen, Denmark, September 2017. Association for Computational Linguistics. https://doi.org/10.18653/v1/W17-5103.

Aiyuan Yang, Bin Xiao, Bingning Wang, Borong Zhang, Ce Bian, Chao Yin, Chenxu Lv, Da Pan, Dian Wang, Dong Yan, Fan Yang, Fei Deng, Feng Wang, Feng Liu, Guangwei Ai, Guosheng Dong, Haizhou Zhao, Hang Xu, Haoze Sun, Hongda Zhang, Hui Liu, Jiaming Ji, Jian Xie, JunTao Dai, Kun Fang, Lei Su, Liang Song, Lifeng Liu, Liyun Ru, Luyao Ma, Mang Wang, Mickel Liu, MingAn Lin, Nuolan Nie, Peidong Guo, Ruiyang Sun, Tao Zhang, Tianpeng Li, Tianyu Li, Wei Cheng, Weipeng Chen, Xiangrong Zeng, Xiaochuan Wang, Xiaoxi Chen, Xin Men, Xin Yu, Xuehai Pan, Yanjun Shen, Yiding Wang, Yiyu Li, Youxin Jiang, Yuchen Gao, Yupeng Zhang, Zenan Zhou, and Zhiying Wu. Baichuan 2: Open large-scale language models, 2023. https://doi.org/10.48550/arXiv.2309.10305.

An Yang, Baosong Yang, Binyuan Hui, Bo Zheng, Bowen Yu, Chang Zhou, Chengpeng Li, Chengyuan Li, Dayiheng Liu, Fei Huang, Guanting Dong, Haoran Wei, Huan Lin, Jialong Tang, Jialin Wang, Jian Yang, Jianhong Tu, Jianwei Zhang, Jianxin Ma, Jianxin Yang, Jin Xu, Jingren Zhou, Jinze Bai, Jinzheng He, Junyang Lin, Kai Dang, Keming Lu, Keqin Chen, Kexin Yang, Mei Li, Mingfeng Xue, Na Ni, Pei Zhang, Peng Wang, Ru Peng, Rui Men, Ruize Gao, Runji Lin, Shijie Wang, Shuai Bai, Sinan Tan, Tianhang Zhu, Tianhao Li, Tianyu Liu, Wenbin Ge, Xiaodong Deng, Xiaohuan Zhou, Xingzhang Ren, Xinyu Zhang, Xipin Wei, Xuancheng Ren, Xuejing Liu, Yang Fan, Yang Yao, Yichang Zhang, Yu Wan, Yunfei Chu, Yuqiong Liu, Zeyu Cui, Zhenru Zhang, Zhifang Guo, and Zhihao Fan. Qwen2 technical report, 2024. https://doi.org/10.48550/arXiv.2407.10671.

An Yang, Anfeng Li, Baosong Yang, Beichen Zhang, Binyuan Hui, Bo Zheng, Bowen Yu, Chang Gao, Chengen Huang, Chenxu Lv, Chujie Zheng, Dayiheng Liu, Fan Zhou, Fei Huang, Feng Hu, Hao Ge, Haoran Wei, Huan Lin, Jialong Tang, Jian Yang, Jianhong Tu, Jianwei Zhang, Jianxin Yang, Jiaxi Yang, Jing Zhou, Jingren Zhou, Junyang Lin, Kai Dang, Keqin Bao, Kexin Yang, Le Yu, Lianghao Deng, Mei Li, Mingfeng Xue, Mingze Li, Pei Zhang, Peng Wang, Qin Zhu, Rui Men, Ruize Gao, Shixuan Liu, Shuang Luo, Tianhao Li, Tianyi Tang, Wenbiao Yin, Xingzhang Ren, Xinyu Wang, Xinyu Zhang, Xuancheng Ren, Yang Fan, Yang Su, Yichang Zhang, Yinger Zhang, Yu Wan, Yuqiong Liu, Zekun Wang, Zeyu Cui, Zhenru Zhang, Zhipeng Zhou, and Zihan Qiu. Qwen3 technical report, 2025a. https://doi.org/10.48550/arXiv.2505.09388.

Kaixun Yang, Mladen Raković, Dragan Gašević, and Guanliang Chen. Does the prompt-based large language model recognize students' demographics and introduce bias in essay scoring? In Alexandra I. Cristea, Erin Walker, Yu Lu, Olga C. Santos, and Seiji Isotani, editors, *Artificial Intelligence in Education: 26th International Conference, AIED 2025, Palermo, Italy, July 22-26, 2025, Proceedings, Part II*, Lecture Notes in Computer Science, volume 15878, pages 75–89, Cham, 2025b. Springer Nature Switzerland. https://doi.org/10.1007/978-3-031-98417-4_6.

Wonsuk Yang, Jung-Ho Kim, Seungwon Yoon, Chaehun Park, and Jong C. Park. A corpus of sentence-level annotations of local acceptability with reasons. In *33rd Pacific Asia Conference on Language, Information and Computation*, pages 288–297, 2019a. URL https://jaslli.org/paclic33/wp-content/uploads/2019/12/34_paclic33_postconf.pdf.

Zhilin Yang, Zihang Dai, Yiming Yang, Jaime Carbonell, Russ R. Salakhutdinov, and Quoc V. Le. XLNet: Generalized autoregressive pretraining for language understanding. In H. Wallach, H. Larochelle, A. Beygelzimer, F. d'Alché-Buc, E. Fox, and R. Garnett, editors, *Advances in Neural Information Processing Systems*, volume 32, pages 5753–5763. Curran Associates, Inc., 2019b. URL https://papers.neurips.cc/paper_files/paper/2019/hash/dc6a7e655d7e5840e66733e9ee67cc69-Abstract.html.

Shunyu Yao, Dian Yu, Jeffrey Zhao, Izhak Shafran, Thomas L. Griffiths, Yuan Cao, and Karthik Narasimhan. Tree of thoughts: Deliberate problem solving with large language models. In *Proceedings of the 37th International Conference on Neural Information Processing Systems*, NIPS '23, pages 1–14, Red Hook, NY, USA, 2024. Curran Associates Inc. URL https://papers.neurips.cc/paper_files/paper/2023/hash/271db9922b8d1f4dd7aaef84ed5ac703-Abstract-Conference.html.

Yuxiao Ye and Simone Teufel. End-to-end argument mining as biaffine dependency parsing. In Paola Merlo, Jorg Tiedemann, and Reut Tsarfaty, editors, *Proceedings of the 16th Conference of the European Chapter of the Association for Computational Linguistics: Main Volume*, pages 669–678, Online, April 2021. Association for Computational Linguistics. https://doi.org/10.18653/v1/2021.eacl-main.55.

Yuxiao Ye and Simone Teufel. Computational modelling of undercuts in real-world arguments. In Yamen Ajjour, Roy Bar-Haim, Roxanne El Baff, Zhexiong Liu, and Gabriella Skitalinskaya, editors, *Proceedings of the 11th Workshop on Argument Mining (ArgMining 2024)*, pages 59–68, Bangkok, Thailand, August 2024. Association for Computational Linguistics. https://doi.org/10.18653/v1/2024.argmining-1.6.

Anar Yeginbergen, Maite Oronoz, and Rodrigo Agerri. Argument mining in data scarce settings: Cross-lingual transfer and few-shot techniques. In Lun-Wei Ku, Andre Martins, and Vivek Srikumar, editors, *Proceedings of the 62nd Annual Meeting of the Association for Computational Linguistics (Volume 1: Long Papers)*, pages 11687–11699, Bangkok, Thailand, August 2024. Association for Computational Linguistics. https://doi.org/10.18653/v1/2024.acl-long.628.

Anar Yeginbergen, Maite Oronoz, and Rodrigo Agerri. Dynamic knowledge integration for evidence-driven counter-argument generation with large language models. In Wanxiang Che, Joyce Nabende, Ekaterina Shutova, and Mohammad Taher Pilehvar, editors, *Findings of the Association for Computational Linguistics: ACL 2025*, pages 22568–22584, Vienna, Austria, July 2025. Association for Computational Linguistics. https://doi.org/10.18653/v1/2025.findings-acl.1161.

Guido Zarrella and Amy Marsh. MITRE at SemEval-2016 task 6: Transfer learning for stance detection. In Steven Bethard, Marine Carpuat, Daniel Cer, David Jurgens, Preslav Nakov, and Torsten Zesch, editors, *Proceedings of the 10th International Workshop on Semantic Evaluation (SemEval-2016)*, pages 458–463, San Diego, California, June 2016. Association for Computational Linguistics. https://doi.org/10.18653/v1/S16-1074.

Ines Zelch, Matthias Hagen, Benno Stein, and Johannes Kiesel. Segmentation of argumentative texts by key statements for argument mining from the web. In Elena Chistova, Philipp Cimiano, Shohreh Haddadan, Gabriella Lapesa, and Ramon Ruiz-Dolz, editors, *Proceedings of the 12th Argument Mining Workshop*, pages 228–242, Vienna, Austria, July 2025a. Association for Computational Linguistics. https://doi.org/10.18653/v1/2025.argmining-1.22.

Ines Zelch, Matthias Hagen, Benno Stein, and Johannes Kiesel. Reproducing the argument quality prediction of Project Debater. In Elena Chistova, Philipp Cimiano, Shohreh Haddadan, Gabriella Lapesa, and Ramon Ruiz-Dolz, editors, *Proceedings of the 12th Argument Mining Workshop*, pages 181–188, Vienna, Austria, July 2025b. Association for Computational Linguistics. https://doi.org/10.18653/v1/2025.argmining-1.17.

Bowen Zhang, Daijun Ding, Liwen Jing, Genan Dai, and Nan Yin. How would stance detection techniques evolve after the launch of ChatGPT?, 2024. https://doi.org/10.48550/arXiv.2212.14548.

Fan Zhang, Rebecca Hwa, Diane Litman, and Homa B. Hashemi. ArgRewrite: A web-based revision assistant for argumentative writings. In John DeNero, Mark Finlayson, and Sravana Reddy, editors, *Proceedings of the 2016 Conference of the North American Chapter of the Association for Computational Linguistics: Demonstrations*, pages 37–41, San Diego, California, June 2016a. Association for Computational Linguistics. https://doi.org/10.18653/v1/N16-3008.

Gechuan Zhang, Paul Nulty, and David Lillis. A decade of legal argumentation mining: Datasets and approaches. In Paolo Rosso, Valerio Basile, Raquel Martínez, Elisabeth Métais, and Farid Meziane, editors, *Natural Language Processing and Information Systems*, pages 240–252, Cham, 2022a. Springer International Publishing. https://doi.org/10.1007/978-3-031-08473-7_22.

Jingqing Zhang, Yao Zhao, Mohammad Saleh, and Peter Liu. PEGASUS: Pre-training with extracted gap-sentences for abstractive summarization. In Hal Daumé III and Aarti Singh, editors, *Proceedings of the 37th International Conference on Machine Learning*, volume 119 of *Proceedings of Machine Learning Research*, pages 11328–11339. PMLR, 13–18 Jul 2020a. URL https://proceedings.mlr.press/v119/zhang20ae.html.

Justine Zhang, Ravi Kumar, Sujith Ravi, and Cristian Danescu-Niculescu-Mizil. Conversational flow in Oxford-style debates. In *Proceedings of the 2016 Conference of the North American Chapter of the Association for Computational Linguistics: Human Language Technologies*, pages 136–141. Association for Computational Linguistics, 2016b. https://doi.org/10.18653/v1/N16-1017.

Susan Zhang, Stephen Roller, Naman Goyal, Mikel Artetxe, Moya Chen, Shuohui Chen, Christopher Dewan, Mona Diab, Xian Li, Xi Victoria Lin, Todor Mihaylov, Myle Ott, Sam Shleifer, Kurt Shuster, Daniel Simig, Punit Singh Koura, Anjali Sridhar, Tianlu Wang, and Luke Zettlemoyer. OPT: Open pre-trained transformer language models, 2022b. https://doi.org/10.48550/arXiv.2205.01068.

Tianyi Zhang, Varsha Kishore, Felix Wu, Kilian Q. Weinberger, and Yoav Artzi. BERTScore: Evaluating text generation with BERT. In *International Conference on Learning Representations*, pages 1–43, 2020b. URL https://iclr.cc/virtual_2020/poster_SkeHuCVFDr.html.

Wenxuan Zhang, Xin Li, Yang Deng, Lidong Bing, and Wai Lam. A survey on aspect-based sentiment analysis: Tasks, methods, and challenges. *IEEE Transactions on Knowledge and Data Engineering*, 35(11):11019–11038, 2023a. https://doi.org/10.1109/TKDE.2022.3230975.

Yizhe Zhang, Siqi Sun, Michel Galley, Yen-Chun Chen, Chris Brockett, Xiang Gao, Jianfeng Gao, Jingjing Liu, and Bill Dolan. DIALOGPT : Large-scale generative pre-training for conversational response generation. In Asli Celikyilmaz and Tsung-Hsien Wen, editors, *Proceedings of the 58th Annual Meeting of the Association for Computational Linguistics: System Demonstrations*, pages 270–278, Online, July 2020c. Association for Computational Linguistics. https://doi.org/10.18653/v1/2020.acl-demos.30.

Zheng Zhang, Jie Gao, Ranjodh Singh Dhaliwal, and Toby Jia-Jun Li. VISAR: A human-AI argumentative writing assistant with visual programming and rapid draft prototyping. In *Proceedings of the 36th Annual ACM Symposium on User Interface Software and Technology*, UIST '23, pages 1–30, New York, NY, USA, October 2023b. Association for Computing Machinery. https://doi.org/10.1145/3586183.3606800.

Zhengyan Zhang, Xu Han, Zhiyuan Liu, Xin Jiang, Maosong Sun, and Qun Liu. ERNIE: Enhanced language representation with informative entities. In Anna Korhonen, David Traum, and Lluís Màrquez, editors, *Proceedings of the 57th Annual Meeting of the Association for Computational Linguistics*, pages 1441–1451, Florence, Italy, July 2019. Association for Computational Linguistics. https://doi.org/10.18653/v1/P19-1139.

Chenye Zhao, Yingjie Li, Cornelia Caragea, and Yue Zhang. ZeroStance: Leveraging ChatGPT for open-domain stance detection via dataset generation. In Lun-Wei Ku, Andre Martins, and Vivek Srikumar, editors, *Findings of the Association for Computational Linguistics: ACL 2024*, pages 13390–13405, Bangkok, Thailand, August 2024. Association for Computational Linguistics. https://doi.org/10.18653/v1/2024.findings-acl.794.

Meiqian Zhao, Chunhua Liu, Lu Liu, Yan Zhao, and Dong Yu. BLCU_NLP at SemEval-2018 task 12: An ensemble model for argument reasoning based on hierarchical attention. In Marianna Apidianaki, Saif M. Mohammad, Jonathan May, Ekaterina Shutova, Steven Bethard, and Marine Carpuat, editors, *Proceedings of the 12th International Workshop on Semantic Evaluation*, pages 1104–1108, New Orleans, Louisiana, June 2018. Association for Computational Linguistics. https://doi.org/10.18653/v1/S18-1186.

Xueguan Zhao, Wenpeng Lu, Chaoqun Zheng, Weiyu Zhang, Jiasheng Si, and Deyu Zhou. Plan dynamically, express rhetorically: A debate-driven rhetorical framework for argumentative writing. In Christos Christodoulopoulos, Tanmoy Chakraborty, Carolyn Rose, and Violet Peng, editors, *Proceedings of the 2025 Conference on Empirical Methods in Natural Language Processing*, pages 9562–9584, Suzhou, China, November 2025. Association for Computational Linguistics. https://doi.org/10.18653/v1/2025.emnlp-main.483.

Ce Zhou, Qian Li, Chen Li, Jun Yu, Yixin Liu, Guangjing Wang, Kai Zhang, Cheng Ji, Qiben Yan, Lifang He, Hao Peng, Jianxin Li, Jia Wu, Ziwei Liu, Pengtao Xie, Caiming Xiong, Jian Pei, Philip S. Yu, and Lichao Sun. A comprehensive survey on pretrained foundation models: A history from BERT to ChatGPT. *International Journal of Machine Learning and Cybernetics*, 16:9851–9915, 2025a. https://doi.org/10.1007/s13042-024-02443-6.

Kevin Zhou, Adam Dejl, Gabriel Freedman, Lihu Chen, Antonio Rago, and Francesca Toni. Evaluating uncertainty quantification methods in argumentative large language models. In Christos Christodoulopoulos, Tanmoy Chakraborty, Carolyn Rose, and Violet Peng, editors, *Findings of the Association for Computational Linguistics: EMNLP 2025*, pages 21700–21711, Suzhou, China, November 2025b. Association for Computational Linguistics. https://doi.org/10.18653/v1/2025.findings-emnlp.1184.

Timon Ziegenbein, Shahbaz Syed, Felix Lange, Martin Potthast, and Henning Wachsmuth. Modeling appropriate language in argumentation. In Anna Rogers, Jordan Boyd-Graber, and Naoaki Okazaki, editors, *Proceedings of the 61st Annual Meeting of the Association for Computational Linguistics (Volume 1: Long Papers)*, pages 4344–4363, Toronto, Canada, July 2023. Association for Computational Linguistics. https://doi.org/10.18653/v1/2023.acl-long.238.

Timon Ziegenbein, Gabriella Skitalinskaya, Alireza Bayat Makou, and Henning Wachsmuth. LLM-based rewriting of inappropriate argumentation using reinforcement learning from machine feedback. In Lun-Wei Ku, Andre Martins, and Vivek Srikumar, editors, *Proceedings of the 62nd Annual Meeting of the Association for Computational Linguistics (Volume 1: Long Papers)*, pages 4455–4476, Bangkok, Thailand, August 2024. Association for Computational Linguistics. https://doi.org/10.18653/v1/2024.acl-long.244.

Cäcilia Zirn, Goran Glavaš, Federico Nanni, Jason Eichorts, and Heiner Stuckenschmidt. Classifying topics and detecting topic shifts in political manifestos. In Daniela Širinić, editor, *PolText 2016: The International Conference on the Advances in Computational Analysis of Political Text*, pages 88–93, Zagreb, 2016. University of Zagreb. URL https://takelab.fer.hr/poltext2016/PolText2016-proceedings.pdf.

Ingrid Zukerman, Richard McConachy, and Kevin B. Korb. Using argumentation strategies in automated argument generation. In *First International Conference on Natural Language Generation (INLG 00)*, volume 14, pages 55–62, 2000. https://doi.org/10.3115/1118253.1118262.

Kolibri 360 GmbH
Ferdinand-Jühlke-Straße 7
99095 Erfurt, Deutschland
produktsicherheit@kolibri360.de